Nicholson School Edition

Between One and Many

The Art and Science of Public Speaking

Sixth Edition

Steven R. Brydon
Michael D. Scott
California State University, Chico

with contributions by
Jeff Butler | Jim Katt | Burt Pryor
University of Central Florida

Boston Burr Ridge, IL Dubuque, IA New York San Francisco St. Louis
Bangkok Bogotá Caracas Lisbon London Madrid Mexico City Milan
New Delhi Seoul Singapore Sydney Taipei Toronto

Nicholson School Edition
BETWEEN ONE AND MANY: THE ART AND SCIENCE OF PUBLIC SPEAKING, Sixth Edition

This book is a McGraw-Hill Learning Solutions textbook and contains select material from *Between One and Many: The Art and Science of Public Speaking,* Sixth Edition by Steven R. Brydon and Michael D. Scott. Copyright © 2008, 2006, 2003, 2000, 1997 by The McGraw-Hill Companies, Inc. Reprinted with permission of the publisher. Many custom published texts are modified versions or adaptations of our best-selling textbooks. Some adaptations are printed in black and white to keep prices at a minimum, while others are in color.

1 2 3 4 5 6 7 8 9 0 QPD QPD 0 9 8

ISBN-13: 978-0-07-726329-4
ISBN-10: 0-07-726329-4

Learning Solutions Manager: Eileen McClay
Learning Solutions Representative: Nada Mraovic
Production Editor: Nina Meyer
Printer/Binder: Quebecor World

Contents

Chapter 2 A Communication Theory Sampler 23

Chapter 3 Your First Speech 39

Chapter 9 Supporting Your Message 209

Chapter 10 Organizing Messages 229

Chapter 12 Delivery: Engaging Your Audience 293

Chapter 13 Effective Use of Visual Aids 331

Preface

Public speaking is a dynamic transaction "between one and many"–between the one who is speaking and the many who are listening. The meaning of the message emerges from the relationship between speaker and audience. Speakers cannot succeed without knowing their audience, and no audience member can benefit by just passively receiving a message. Both speaker and audience–and the transaction between them–are essential to the process. As teachers and as authors, we focus on the transactional nature of successful public speaking.

Public speaking is also an art, a science, and a skill–one that can be learned, improved, and polished. We encourage our students to think of public speaking as a learning experience–they don't have to be perfect at the outset! We also encourage them to think of their speech transactions as a refined extension of their everyday conversations, and we offer them the tools to become the speakers they want to be. Public speakers can draw on a vast body of information, ranging from classical rhetorical theories to empirical communication research. In this book we include traditional topics, such as logos, ethos, and pathos and current ones, such as research on cultural diversity, the role of nonverbal communication in delivery, and the *appropriate* uses of technology in public speaking.

Today's students of public speaking will face many different speech situations in their lives, and they will face audiences of increasing cultural, demographic, and individual diversity. Throughout this book, we focus on ways to adapt to audiences to have the best chance of being heard and understood. We stress the responsibilities and ethical issues involved in being a good public speaker. And we discuss how to be a good audience member: one who knows how to listen, behave ethically, and critically evaluate the message being presented. In sum, we attempt to provide students with a broad understanding of the nature of public speaking as well as the specific skills they need to become successful, effective public speakers, both as college students and throughout their lives.

Features of the Book

Bringing Visual Life to the Text This edition of *Between One and Many* continues the tradition we pioneered with our very first edition–bringing visual life to the art and science of public speaking. We have moved with the advance of technology from VHS tapes in the first three editions, to CD-ROMs in the fourth and fifth editions, to a fully developed online presence. With the popularity of YouTube, Facebook, and MySpace, today's students are accustomed to viewing their video content online–so we embrace this trend. We now provide students with the same type of content found on the Speech Coach CD in a new Web-based Online Learning Center Web site. In addition to the usual videos of sample speeches found with most texts, the innovative Web site provides video segments on the role of public speaking in the lives of people with whom students can identify, concrete skills for mastering speech anxiety, examples of delivery techniques, and concrete advice on the proper role of visual aids, including the frequently misused Microsoft PowerPoint™. The text and Online Learning Center Web site are coordinated, and each of the eight sample student speeches outlined or transcribed in the text is *presented in full* on the Web site. Sample speeches range from a speech of introduction and storytelling presentation, to informative and persuasive speeches, to a speech fully supported with PowerPoint slides. Our Web site also provides a wide range of learning tools, such as an Outline Tutor and PowerPoint Tutorial. The Web content is an integral part of the learning package provided by *Between One and Many.* Visit our comprehensive Online Learning Center Web site at www.mhhe.com/brydon6.

Integrated Pedagogy Throughout the text, boxes are used to focus attention on subjects of special interest. Four different types of boxes appear. In Their Own Words boxes provide examples of speeches by students and public figures, including several student speeches in outline form with annotations. Self-Assessment boxes allow students to evaluate their own skills and attributes (such as speech anxiety and overall communication apprehension). Considering Diversity boxes show how the topic of a chapter applies to today's multicultural, multiracial, and multiethnic audiences. More than an afterthought, these boxes not only add to the discussion of diversity throughout the book but also challenge students to think about diversity as it specifically applies to the topics covered in a given chapter. Speaking of . . . boxes contain current, topical information that relates to the text discussion.

Throughout the book, speechmaking skills are highlighted in special lists labeled Tips and Tactics. A popular feature with students, Tips and Tactics make it easy to apply practical suggestions to speeches. Finally, Web icons in the margins call attention to corresponding video segments and other online features.

Help for Speech Anxiety We recognize that many students come to a public speaking class with some trepidation. As we have done in every edition, we devote a full chapter early in the text to speech anxiety. The text offers many specific, concrete techniques students can use to productively manage and channel their anxiety, and several of these are visualized online. In keeping with the most recent research on speech anxiety and communication apprehension, we distinguish between generalized anxiety about communication and fears that are specific to public speaking and thus are responsive to the techniques we offer to students.

Emphasis on Adapting to Audience Diversity We give significant attention to audience diversity, based in part, on Geert Hofstede's work on understanding cultural diversity. Using Hofstede's dimensions of collectivism and individualism, power distance, uncertainty avoidance, masculinity and femininity, and long-term versus short-term orientation, we offer ideas on how to analyze and adapt to audience diversity across cultures. Diversity encompasses more than culture. Therefore we also offer specific Tips and Tactics students can use to analyze and adapt to the demographic and individual diversity in their audience.

Full Chapter on Ethics We feature a full chapter on ethics. Working from classical and contemporary notions about what constitutes ethical behavior, we provide and reinforce ethical guidelines for both public speakers and audience members. We pay particular attention to the growing problem of plagiarism from the Internet and offer concrete advice on how students can ethically use and cite such sources.

Emphasis on Critical Thinking Central to effective and ethical communication are the abilities to critically evaluate evidence, to present sound reasoning in speeches, and to detect fallacious reasoning in the speeches of others. *Between One and Many* continues to provide a strong critical thinking component based on Toulmin's model of argument. Our discussion of critical thinking is also integrated into our discussion of supporting a speech with valid reasoning and reliable evidence.

Using Technology in Speaking Two major technological innovations have had a great impact on public speaking in the last few years. Presentational software, especially Microsoft's PowerPoint, is a regular feature of presentations in corporations, military briefings, classroom presentations, and professional meetings. We wish we could say that this has been a completely positive development in the history of speechmaking, yet we cannot. For every presentation that uses PowerPoint well, we see many more that punish audience members with too much information, superfluous graphics, and overkill. As a result, we have focused in our text and the Online Learning Center Web site not so much on the mechanics of creating slides (although there is a tutorial to guide students unfamiliar with PowerPoint through the process) but on the dangers of overreliance and the potential benefits of the technology when used properly.

The other major technology, which also has a dark side, is the use of electronic resources for researching a speech. We have devoted a full chapter to research and have thoroughly revised our discussion of using Web-based sources in speeches. We know students will turn to electronic sources for their research, so our goal is to teach them the difference between reliable and unreliable information wherever it is found.

Highlights of the Sixth Edition

Based on feedback from many instructors, we have incorporated a number of changes into this edition to strengthen the book.

Strengthening Discussion of Theory and Research A strong foundation in theory and research has been a hallmark of our approach since the first edition. In the sixth edition, we further strengthen this foundation by adding and integrating principles of the rhetorical tradition in the very first chapter, significantly revising our discussion of the research and consequent skills pertaining to listening, and expanding our discussion of the process of persuasion.

Revision of Listening Chapter We have made substantial and significant changes to Chapter 6 on Listening. In particular, we have moved the discussion of the Toulmin model fallacies to later chapters, and put the emphasis in this chapter on the International Listening Association's suggestions for improving listening skills. Given the intent and scope of this book, we also show how students can use their listening skills to construct and provide useful feedback for speakers, and how speakers can best interpret this feedback to improve their transaction with audience members.

Tackling the Internet Chapter 8 on Researching Your Message has been rebuilt almost from the ground up. We recognize that the first instinct of students today is to turn to their computer and the Internet for information, rather than visit a library or bookstore. Thus we begin our discussion of research by helping them understand how to properly use search engines such as Google, avoid traps such as bogus Web sites, and distinguish reliable from unreliable evidence. We also discuss the widely-used and abused Wikipedia–pointing out how easily false information can be posted there. We share useful information about blogs, YouTube, podcasts, and the like, in terms of their strengths and limitations as research sources. Finally, we stress how libraries now use Internet-based proprietary databases that can also provide reliable information to students.

This doesn't mean that we ignore the print sources on which we personally honed our own research skills decades ago. Instead, we have tried to impress on students that the criteria for evaluating information and sources are the same, regardless of whether the information is communicated in hard copy or electronically. Just because an article appears in print doesn't automatically make the information credible, authoritative, and accurate.

Improved Discussion of PowerPoint The majority of today's students come to college already familiar with the mechanics of PowerPoint, the widely-used presentational software. Not all college classrooms today may be equipped with PowerPoint, however, once students enter their careers, they can expect to be required to use this tool. Computer slides should, as with any visual aid, complement and support a speech, not supplant it. Thus, we have revised our discussion of PowerPoint to instruct students on its best use as a support tool. We offer several basic principles of design that will enhance presentations, rather than overpower them. And we continue to discuss traditional visual aids, from blackboards to overheads. At the same time, we recognize and accept the fact that in the professional world, students need to be prepared to use the latest technology to support their messages–whether it is PowerPoint or its eventual replacement.

Improved Discussion of Persuasion We have significantly reorganized and revised the chapter on Persuasive Speaking. We ground our discussion in the rhetorical situation, but continue to include the findings of social science research, including credibility, message sidedness, evidence and persuasion, fear appeals, the Elaboration Likelihood Model, and Cialdini's speaker-friendly six principles of influence. A new student speech is analyzed in detail for the speaker's use of many of the principles we discuss in the chapter.

New Sample Speeches The majority of speeches in this edition are new to this book. We have retained some speeches, but have added a new sample of organization, informative, and persuasive speeches. As with previous editions, the full speech is available in video in the Speech Coach Video Library at www.mhhe.com/brydon6.

Organization of the Text

The basic chapter structure of the sixth edition remains unchanged. However, as with earlier editions, the chapters are designed so that instructors may assign them in any order they find appropriate.

Part One deals with the foundations of the art and science of public speaking. Chapter 1, Practical Speaking, focuses on the personal, professional, and public reasons for becoming a good public speaker, with specific examples of people with whom students can identify, who use public speaking in their daily lives. We also introduce a model of public speaking and preview the remainder of the book. Chapter 3 provides an overview of the skills needed by public speakers and allows instructors to assign speeches early without having to assign chapters out of order. Topic selection and writing purpose statements have been incorporated into this chapter to provide an early foundation for students in preparing their first speeches. Students with the tools they need to cope with the nearly universal experience of speech anxiety. Chapter 5 deals with ethical speaking and listening, with a special emphasis on avoiding plagiarism.

Part Two makes explicit the idea that focusing on the transaction between speaker and audience is key to success in public speaking. Chapter 6 presents a thorough treatment of listening, with a focus on listening to public speeches, and incorporating guidelines for providing constructive feedback. Chapter 7 provides the tools for analyzing the cultural, demographic, and individual diversity of audience members. In addition, we offer practical suggestions for adapting speeches to audiences once the analysis has been completed.

Part Three is about putting theory into practice. Chapter 8 covers researching the speech. In recognition of the fact that most students already use the Internet, but often without applying critical standards to the information they find, we have focused on the skills needed to distinguish reliable from unreliable Internet sources. Chapter 9 is devoted to supporting speeches with reasoning as well as evidence and introduces the Toulmin model of reasoning. Chapter 10 treats organization from an audience-focused perspective. We include a variety of traditional organizational patterns, such as alphabetical, categorical, causal, time, spatial, Monroe's motivated-sequence, extended narrative, problem–solution, comparative advantage, and stock issues. We also discuss organic patterns such as the star, wave, and spiral. Material related to transitional statements is also located in this chapter. Chapter 11 addresses language use, with particular attention to adapting language to diverse audiences. We suggest ways to choose language that is inclusive rather than exclusive, nonsexist rather than sexist, and thoughtful rather than stereotypic. We also offer techniques for enhancing the effective use of language. Chapter 12 deals with delivery skills, again focusing on audience adaptation. This chapter provides both a strong theoretical foundation based in nonverbal communication research and solid, practical advice for the public speaker. A comprehensive discussion of visual, audio, and audiovisual media that can be adapted to the audience and occasion to enhance most public speeches. Our discussion of PowerPoint has been updated for this edition, with an emphasis on using it to enhance, rather than take the place of, public speaking. Speech Coach online has a PowerPoint tutorial that will enable students to learn the best practices in an interactive fashion.

Part Four addresses the most common contexts for public speaking that students are likely to face in the classroom and in their lives after college. Chapter 14 on informative speaking stresses audience adaptation, particularly in terms of diverse learning styles. Practical applications of learning theories are discussed in relation to speeches that explain, instruct, demonstrate, and describe. Chapter 16 provides a detailed treatment of critical thinking, with a special focus on recognizing and responding to fallacies of reasoning. Finally, Chapter 17 provides a discussion of speaking throughout the student's lifetime. It includes guidelines for speeches of acceptance, introduction, recognition, and commemoration; speeches to entertain; and speaking on television.

Supplements

Visit our Online Learning Center Web site at www.mhhe.com/brydon6 for comprehensive teaching and learning resources.

For Students Fully integrated with our text, the student resources include the Speech Coach Video Library, PowerPoint and outlining tutorials, multiple-choice self-quizzes, detailed chapter outlines and overviews, plus key terms within each chapter and their definitions. Each video segment in the Speech Coach Video Library can be viewed independently of the others and is coordinated with a specific chapter in the text. Marginal text icons indicate where a particular video segment would be appropriate. The Speech Coach videos not only reinforce the text but also preview material to be covered later in more depth.

For Instructors The password-protected instructor section of the Web site includes the Instructor's Manual (IM), written by the text authors. This IM includes a variety of excellent resources for new and experienced teachers. These include strategies for managing multi-sectional courses, a primer for graduate assistants and first-time teachers, and quick references to the speechmaking skills highlighted in each chapter. The IM offers a number of in-class activities, sample syllabi for semester- and quarter-length terms, sample evaluation forms, and transparency masters. In addition, approximately 1,800 test items, including multiple-choice, true–false, and essay questions are available in the Instructor's Computerized Test Bank. PowerPoint lecture slides are also available to aid instructors.

Acknowledgments

We gratefully acknowledge the support and help of many people at McGraw-Hill who played a role in this book, including Suzanne Earth, sponsoring editor; Kate Scheinman, developmental editor; Thomas Brierly, media project manager; Paul Wells, project manager; Cassandra Chu, design manager; PoYee Oster, photo researcher; and Tandra Jorgensen, production supervisor. We also thank Lanie Anderson, manuscript editor, for her attention to detail.

We are especially grateful to Dr. George Rogers, Professor Emeritus at Chico State, who supplied many of the photos for the text and produced the video segments that appear in the Speech Coach Video Library, and to the numerous students who consented to be videotaped for this project. Special thanks go to the speakers who shared their talents in providing sample speeches: Jonathan Studebaker, Montana Kellmer, Shelly Lee Spratt, Rosa Guzman, Trevar Morgan, Arin Larson, Arjun Buxi, and Mitch Bacci. We would also like to thank these individuals for generously consenting to contribute to our effort: Enrique

"Rick" Rigsby, Tomoko Mukawa, and Russ Woody. They are friends, colleagues, former students, and role models; they have all enriched our book and our lives. We also thank Dr. Nichola Gutgold of Penn State Berks–Lehigh Valley College, Lehigh Valley Campus, for sharing her research on women candidates for president and Professor Christine Hanlon of University of Central Florida for her box on Orally Citing sources.

We would also like to thank Robert B. Brydon and Gary Peete (Head of Reference Services, Thomas J. Long Business & Economics Library, University of California-Berkeley) for their assistance in updating the treatment of Internet research in Chapter 8.

A grateful thank you for the reviews and counsel of our peers in the classroom who graciously prepared careful critiques of our manuscript and videotape in various stages of development:

Robert A. Arcuri, Daytona Beach Community College

Deanna Dannels, North Carolina State University

Michele Rees Edwards, Robert Morris University

Robert Greenstreet, East Central University

Mayra Holzer, Valencia Community College

Jason Wayne Hough, John Brown University

Patricia Huber, Madison Area Technical College

Jeffery Chaichana Peterson, Washington State University

K. Michelle Scott, Savannah College of Art & Design

Sharon E. Smith, Penn State Altoona

We appreciate the help of all these individuals in preparing this book, but we are, of course, ultimately responsible for its content. Any errors or omissions are solely our own.

And last, but certainly not least, we wish to thank our wives, Pamela and Randi, who not only showed great patience as we worked on this project but often provided assistance in more ways than we can possibly list.

Foundations

Candlelight vigils were held to protest violence against women at "Take Back the Night" rallies across the nation.

Chapter 1

Practical Speaking

Objectives

After reading this chapter and reviewing the online learning resources at www.mhhe.com/brydon6, you should be able to:

- Describe the relationship between personal success and the ability to speak publicly.
- Explain the role speaking plays in the professional promotion of self.
- Describe how speaking skills can make people better citizens.
- Demonstrate an understanding of the transactional and symbolic nature of the process of public speaking.

Key Concepts

In each chapter we will introduce you to some key terms you need to know. We place these at the beginning of each chapter to alert you to important terms you will encounter. In this chapter look for the following terms:

channel
content (of messages)
decoding
encoding
feedback
interdependence
message
perception
relational component (of messages)
rhetorical situation
symbol
system
transaction

" If all my talents and powers were to be taken from me . . . and I had my choice of keeping but one, I would unhesitatingly ask to be allowed to keep the Power of Speaking, for through it, I would quickly recover all the rest. "

–DANIEL WEBSTER

We begin each new semester with an admission to our students. "We are well aware of the fact that many of you seated here are in attendance only because our class is required for your degree." Next, we ask our students: "How many of you believe the time spent with us studying the art and science of public speaking could be more profitably spent in classes more relevant to your major and future success?"

We make the admission because we know many students would excuse themselves from our class if given a choice. We ask the question because we've learned, through decades of teaching, that it's one students often ask themselves.

So why *is* public speaking required of students at most colleges and universities across the United States? Wouldn't it make greater sense for students to take an additional course in their major or one where the connection to their future success is obvious? For example, wouldn't their time be better spent in coursework facilitating their progress toward becoming an engineer, computer scientist, information manager, investment banker, medical practitioner, Web designer, or public school teacher?

Not necessarily, we tell our students. If they are willing to make even a modest investment of their time and effort in our class, they will find that speaking effectively in public can (1) help them make better grades in other classes, (2) make a difference on their resume, and (3) increase their lifetime of success in their chosen profession.

People admire people who can think on their feet and deliver a powerful presentation. This knowledge and skill is so valuable that, in fact, employers consistently rank it as one of the most desirable characteristics in their new and seasoned employees.[1] Knowledge and skill in public speaking is *that* important. Further, this is true whether we're talking about science and medicine, the law and public service, education and the social sciences, and even the fine arts.

Professional speaker Keith Hawkins

School principal Sandi Young

Kashi nutritionist and spokesperson and surfer Jeff Johnson

But don't just take our word for it. Consider the stories of the three people shown in the photos on page 4. Although Keith Hawkins always wanted to work with people and actually enjoyed speaking in public, he was never certain he could use these two interests to carve out a career. Keith learned in his speech class that some of the highest paid people in the United States are professional public speakers. Whether Keith now counts himself in the highest paid group of professional speakers we can't say. But we do know that Keith, who has been featured in articles in *Time* and the *New York Times,* is a paid professional speaker who has even spoken before the General Assembly of the United Nations.

To view a video that shows the role public speaking can play in people's lives, click on the Speech Coach link on our Online Learning Center Web site, and go to Segment 1.1.

Sandi Young's story is different from Keith's. As a then single mom of two small children, Sandi began her professional life as an elementary school teacher, thinking that would always be her heart's desire. Before too long, however, she found herself back in school as a part-time graduate student. She completed a master's degree and credential in special education and took on a new job and title as a resource specialist for children with special needs. Soon thereafter Sandi was being called on to lead training workshops for other teachers, school administrators, and even parents. "I was doing the very thing I dreaded most as a college student," Sandi says, "making presentations in public to audiences ranging from a few teachers to as many as 1,200 parents, teachers, and administrators." Sandi has since moved on and now is the principal of an elementary school with a staff and student body of more than 300, speaking to groups two or three times a week.

Finally, consider Jeff Johnson, part-time surfer and full-time brand manager and nutritionist at the Kashi Company. Jeff's found a way to combine his love of surfing with his work. Because of his demonstrated skill as a speaker at Kashi, they selected Jeff as their spokesperson in a nationally televised ad. It opens with footage of Jeff locked into a tube off the coast of Brazil. The ad closes with Jeff speaking about the importance of sound nutrition to active lifestyles.

Jeff also speaks on behalf of Kashi when he's not surfing. For example, while appearing on the Food Network he demonstrates how Kashi products can punch up a recipe. If you asked Jeff, he would be the first to admit that frequently speaking in public was not what he expected to be doing when he studied nutrition at the University of Hawaii.

"I now know firsthand what I didn't know while enrolled in my public speaking course," Jeff recounts. "Public speaking can take you places in the corporate world that would be otherwise closed. It's not a substitute but a complement to your degree. And it lets you share your expertise with the audiences you hope to reach with your products."

Public speaking is an essential communication skill in today's world. Public speaking also is an extension and refinement of many of the skills you already practice in your one-on-one and group communication encounters. Our goal in this initial chapter is threefold. First, we demonstrate how common it is for people to use their speaking skills to achieve their personal and professional goals, and to help empower others to achieve theirs. Second, we make clear the connection between public speaking and the other forms of communicating you routinely practice, and we discuss public speaking as a specific kind of system of communication. Finally, we preview the chapters that follow this one.

Self-Assessment

How Much Experience Do You Have Speaking?

Most of us recognize that there is a high degree of correspondence between skill and training. Most of us also will admit that any skill suffers from lack of training and practice, whether it is shooting free throws or solving math problems. With this in mind, answer the following questions:

1. On a scale of 1 to 10, with 1 being little and 10 being considerable, what is your *training* in public speaking?
2. On a scale of 1 to 10, with 1 being little and 10 being considerable, what is your *practice and experience* with public speaking?
3. Given your score for numbers 1 and 2, how would you rate your *effectiveness* as a public speaker on a scale of 1 to 10, with 1 representing ineffective and 10 representing highly effective?
4. How well do you think the three scores you gave yourself correspond? We raise this question because students frequently think they are better speakers than their training and experience would predict.

Using your responses to these four questions as a guide, list 10 public speaking skills you could improve on—for example, listening more attentively, feeling more comfortable speaking, and thinking more critically about speeches you hear from others. Write down those skills or record them in a journal. At the end of the academic term, compare your goals with what you believe you have achieved in the class.

Personal Reasons for Developing Speaking Skills

There are many personal reasons for mastering the art and science of public speaking. Two of the most important involve helping yourself and helping others.

Empowering Self

Understanding the speech transaction and becoming a skilled public speaker in the process is one of the surest paths to self-empowerment. As this chapter was written, for example, the individual voices of women in our community were being heard in the effort to "Take Back the Night." In symposia and open public forums, speeches on once taboo topics such as incest and rape were shared with the on- and off-campus community.

Just before the culminating event, an arm-in-arm parade marched down the main street of our city. Over 40 women took the microphone and told their personal stories to the crowded audience during Survivor Speak Out.[2] As they did, many of them also commented that hearing other women speak in a public setting had given them the courage to step up and speak out themselves, often for the first time in their lives.

Empowering Others

As the preceding example illustrates, public speaking also can be a source of empowerment for others. History is full of examples when a speech initially intended to express one person's convictions helped empower others to join in a common cause. Martin Luther King Jr. gave voice to countless others who shared in his dream of equality. U2's lead singer Bono's impassioned pleas to fight poverty and disease in Africa have inspired many others, including world leaders.

One need not be famous to empower others through speech. For example, consider the case of Edna Morales. We first discovered her, while listening to National Public Radio, as she was interviewed as a speaker at the American Translators Association Annual Conference. We learned from the interview and a subsequent visit to the hospital Web site[3] that she became a medical translator because of her son's illness, liver transplant, and brush with death. While she was watching TV in her native Puerto Rico, a public service announcement came on describing the symptoms of Hepatitis C, such as jaundice and fatigue, which often occur in recipients of blood transfusions. She immediately thought of her own son, Alvin, who had received a blood transfusion and suffered from those exact symptoms.

Medical translator Edna Morales speaks frequently to diverse audiences, seeking to empower them should they face a medical crisis.

Mrs. Morales learned that Alvin was infected and the liver transplant he needed meant traveling to the United States and the Cincinnati Children's Hospital. Even though, as a Puerto Rican native, she understood English, it was still the first time she had to speak in English. While her son's life-saving transplant was a success, Mrs. Morales saw an unfilled need for many other Spanish-speaking families.

Thus, after moving to Cincinnati, she tells us, "I realized I needed to stay here because there was a huge need to help the Hispanic families, and that was going to be my goal."[4] She worked hard to improve her English proficiency, and has fulfilled her goal by becoming a medical translator. She now serves as a liaison between Spanish-speaking patients and hospital staff and is a member of the Family Advisory Board of the Cincinnati Children's Hospital. Further, she speaks frequently to diverse audiences about her experience in the effort to empower them should they face a similar medical crisis.

Professional Reasons for Developing Speaking Skills

Besides empowerment, there are many professional reasons for honing your public speaking skills. To reiterate, the ability to present an effective speech is one of the most desirable skills companies look for in a new hire. Ask any successful person in business or the professions and the chances are high that the person will tell you that skilled speakers are much more likely to fast-track up the rungs of their organization's ladder. Simply put, people who speak well in public are the agents of influence in our culture. They are better able to (1) promote their professional self, (2) present their ideas to decision makers, (3) create positive change in the workplace, (4) contribute worthwhile ideas in meetings, and (5) exhibit their ability to critically think as well as effectively listen.

Promoting Your Professional Self

The chance to speak in public frequently presents us with an ideal opportunity to enhance our professional credibility. Some time ago the authors of this text were treated to a presentation by Dr. Bonnie Johnson. She spoke about work she had done for Intel, the world's largest manufacturer of silicon chips. As someone trained in organizational communication, Dr. Johnson was given permission by Intel to study how well personnel were adapting to technological change in the workplace–for example, electronic workstations. When she had concluded her study, Intel offered her a position with the corporation.

Following her presentation, Dr. Johnson welcomed questions from the audience. One undergraduate asked her why she thought Intel had hired her. "Do you want to know candidly?" she asked. "Because initially they were more impressed with the public presentation I made to top management on the results of my study than with the study itself. They hired me because I not only knew my subject but could effectively speak about it and its implications for Intel."

As shown by Dr. Johnson's evaluation of her experience with Intel, communication skills in general and public speaking skills specifically are both desired and rewarded in the workplace. Surveys of personnel managers at top companies consistently demonstrate that they look for college graduates who not only can communicate interpersonally and in writing but also can deliver a speech well.

Presenting Ideas to Decision Makers

Another reason organizations put such high value on speaking skills concerns the effective communication of ideas. Your success depends not only on your ideas but also on how well you can present those ideas to people whose decisions will affect your career. When you think about it, every occupation and profession involves selling ideas to other people. For example, the life insurance salesperson who must persuade a client to increase coverage is unlikely to close the deal simply by dropping a brochure in the mail. On a larger scale, most corporations require managers to present reports or briefings describing their accomplishments and future plans and goals. Those individuals who seek to move beyond entry-level positions need to be able to convince others of the wisdom of their ideas. Thus, being able to speak to decision makers with confidence and authority is an indispensable tool for corporate success.

Creating Change in the Workplace

One of the most important tasks for any supervisor or manager is to be able to convince colleagues that proposed changes are desirable. To remain competitive, companies must implement new technologies and procedures. Yet many employees fear change. Often the best way to introduce change is to sell employees on new ideas rather than to tell them to simply get used to those ideas. A willing and enthusiastic workforce is far more likely to accept change in the workplace than a reluctant and suspicious one.

Fifty-plus years of empirical research demonstrates that opinion leaders are most effective in selling organizational change. This same body of research also demonstrates that opinion leaders can be found across all levels of organizations. You needn't be the CEO to lead opinion–you simply have to exhibit several of the qualities people recognize in opinion leaders. The ability to communicate effectively, especially in public speaking, is chief among these qualities.

You may not know Sir Jackie Stewart. He is a four-time World Champion in Formula One automobile racing. Long retired, he also is one of the most respected people in all of motors sports. This owes not only to his reputation as a driver, but even more to his activism on behalf of driver safety. A tireless advocate and public speaker–he first got other drivers to reject the idea that accidents were unavoidable, next convinced them that crashes could be made more survivable, and finally enlisted them to pressure car owners and sanctioning bodies to listen. While the odds of a Formula One driver dying in a crash were once about five to one, fatal car crashes have since become a rarity in the sport as a result of safety improvements to the cars, the racecourses, driver equipment, and medical response time.

Becoming a Functioning Force in Meetings

Although small-group communication is not the main focus of this book, many of the skills we discuss–ranging from active listening to critical thinking to making impromptu presentations–are directly applicable to functioning in group meetings. As communication professor Ronald Adler reports, the average business executive spends about 45 minutes out of every hour communicating, much of this time in meetings.[5] Further, surveys show that executives spend as many as 700 hours per year in meetings.[6] Your ability to speak effectively in meetings will be indispensable to your success in the workplace.

Developing Critical Thinking and Listening Skills

It is not enough to know how to present your ideas to others. You also need to listen to the needs of others and to what they say in response to your ideas. On average we spend up to 55 percent of our day in situations that involve the potential to listen.[7] Seldom, however, do we take full advantage of this opportunity. Active listening, which we discuss at length in Chapter 6, is essential to your development as a speaker. First, you won't have anything important to say unless you have listened actively to those around you. Second, listening will make you more effective in working with people. Study after study demonstrates that people who actually hear what is being communicated to them are much more responsive to others than those who listen with "only one ear." Responsiveness to one's audience, moreover, is one of the distinguishing characteristics of some of our nation's best public speakers.

Public speaking skills will help your development as a listener in several ways. For example, learning to give an effective speech requires the ability to analyze your audience, including what they think about you as a speaker and about the topic you plan to address. As part of their audience analysis, the best speakers listen to what audience members say well in advance of speaking. These speakers know that what they hear contains clues about what an audience is thinking. These speakers then use these clues in both the preparation and delivery of their speeches.

Learning to speak requires skill in organizing your thoughts and highlighting key points for listeners. As you learn to do this for your speeches, you will also learn how to organize the information you receive from speakers, separating the important ideas from the unimportant. Finally, speakers have to learn how to research and support their ideas. As a listener, you will need to evaluate the research and support other speakers provide to you. In fact, almost every public speaking skill we will discuss has a parallel skill for the listener.

Public Reasons for Developing Speaking Skills

Skilled public speakers serve as agents of change not only in the workplace but in the larger world as well. Were it not for those who spoke out publicly, the voting age would still be 21 and only white male property owners would be able to vote. All the progress of the past century has resulted from people coming up with new and sometimes controversial ideas and speaking out to persuade others of the wisdom of adopting them.

Becoming a Critical Thinker

As we discuss in Chapter 16, the ability to think critically about your own messages and those of others is essential to reaching sound conclusions about the issues of the day. Not only should speakers strive to base their persuasive efforts on sound reasoning, listeners need to take responsibility to detect unsound reasoning. Some arguments that seem valid actually contain flaws that render them invalid. Becoming a critical thinker will make you less susceptible to phony arguments and less prone to engage in them yourself.

Functioning as an Informed Citizen

Our nation is a democratic republic based on the premise that for our country to thrive there must be a free exchange of ideas. Thus, it is no accident that the First Amendment to the Constitution guarantees freedom of speech, as well as freedom of the press, religion, and peaceable assembly. The fundamental premise of our Constitution is that the people must have the information necessary to make informed decisions. Even if you don't have an immediate need to speak out on an issue of public policy, you will be the consumer of countless speeches on every issue imaginable–from atmospheric warming to zero-tolerance policies in college dorms for drug possession. The ability to forcefully and publicly present your thoughts to others–whether as a speaker or as an audience member questioning a speaker–is more than a desirable skill. It is also a responsibility you owe to others and yourself.

Preserving Freedom of Speech

For some people, the way to deal with unpopular ideas is to invoke a quick fix: censorship. One of our goals in this book is to give you an appreciation for the importance of free speech in a democratic society. The empowerment of more and more citizens to express their views publicly should lead to vigorous debate about those ideas. Those who have confidence in the truth of their own views should welcome the opportunity to debate, rather than suppress, opposing views. Yet hardly a day goes by when we are not treated to an account of some person or some organization trying to suppress another's right to speak freely.

Raising the Level of Public Discourse

Regrettably, much of the public discourse of recent years in response to controversial issues has degenerated into name-calling and emotional appeals. Network and cable TV shows abound that purport to be in the "public's interest" but put uncritical thinking and verbal aggressiveness on display. The hosts and guests of these programs confuse the quality of their rhetoric with the decibel level of their emotional appeals. The same can be said for much of talk radio. The art and science of reasoned argumentation and debate have almost been lost.

Politicians are seldom much better. They evade questions with "talking points," spin counterarguments to their messages rather than try and refute them, and give public speeches replete with baseless claims and half-truths. Rather than engaging their opponents in face-to-face debate, moreover, they've been convinced by political consultants to let their TV ads do the talking for them.

Is it possible to agree to disagree without resorting to name-calling and labeling people with terms that have lost their original meaning? We think it is. In fact, we believe almost any topic–from abortion to religious zealotry–can be debated without the debaters personally attacking each other's pedigrees. Learning to focus one's public speaking skills on the substance of a controversy rather than the personality of an opponent is an important step in raising the level of public discourse. As more Americans learn how to make their views known rationally, and learn the critical thinking skills necessary to evaluate public discourse, the overall level of debate about issues in contemporary society is likely to improve.

Promoting Ethics

People have studied and written about public speaking for more than 2,000 years. One of the constants we find in what people have said about the topic, moreover, is the central role of ethics in the development and presentation of public speeches. Although we may live in a time where some people believe that the ends justify any means, all public speakers have an obligation to embody the practice of ethics in both their message and its presentation. In doing so, public speakers have a unique opportunity to encourage the practice of ethics in the audience members with whom they share their message.

The Public Speaking Transaction

Earlier we said that public speaking is an extension and refinement of the communication skills you use every day. This means public speaking is similar but different from conversation and group discussion. The differences are most notable in terms of (1) planning, (2) organization, and (3) delivery.

To speak well, we need to plan well in advance of the actual transaction. We need to think about, analyze, and adapt to our intended audience. What do we know about our audience members and what do we need to find out about them? We need to plan for the physical location where we will be speaking. If it's a room, does it pose constraints on movement or on eye contact? Can we mediate our message? It is crucial to plan for all the contingencies we may face.

Public speaking also requires a much more organized and coherent message than either conversation or group discussion. In conversation and discussion, communicators can interrupt each other, ask questions, give obvious nonverbal feedback, and ask for clarification when needed. This is not so easily done in the case of public speaking. As a result, we need to organize our message so its meaning is clear and its logic easily followed.

Finally, delivery is more formal with a public speech than with conversation and discussion. Please don't get us wrong–this should not be construed to mean that a speech is stilted or stuffy. Many of the best speeches are conversational in tone. But let's face it, there are some differences. We stand up when speaking, perhaps behind a lectern, whereas audience members are seated. We may use notes and visual aids to enhance our speech. We also may move about the room while speaking.

With this in mind, we can now turn to certain principles that reinforce the similarities between public speaking and its counterparts, beginning with the idea that communication is transactional. Whether the focus is an intimate conversation between lovers, an informative speech before your class, or a speech at a political rally, the process of communication is best viewed as a transactional system.

A **transaction** involves an exchange of verbal and nonverbal messages between two or more people. A **system** is a collection of interdependent parts arranged so that a change in one produces corresponding changes in the remaining parts. Consider a mechanical system such as a car. Its parts show varying degrees of interdependence. **Interdependence** exists when things have a reciprocal influence on one another. Changes in some of a car's parts will produce subtle changes in others. For example, even minor tire tread wear will affect a car's handling. The change is so subtle, though, that most drivers don't notice it. In contrast, changes in other parts of the car can produce changes drivers cannot help noticing. Engine failure, for example, produces obvious changes throughout the hydraulic system of the car, including failure of the car's power steering and power brakes.

transaction
An exchange of verbal and nonverbal messages between two or more people.

system
A collection of interdependent parts arranged so that a change in one produces corresponding changes in the remaining parts.

interdependence
A relationship in which things have a reciprocal influence on each other.

Perhaps this is why the public speaking transaction seems such a significant departure from the more familiar contexts of communication in which we engage. Whereas the changes that occur to the communication system when moving from an interpersonal to a small-group exchange are subtle, the changes that occur to the system when moving to an exchange between one and many can seem rather pronounced. Consider something as simple as the number of people

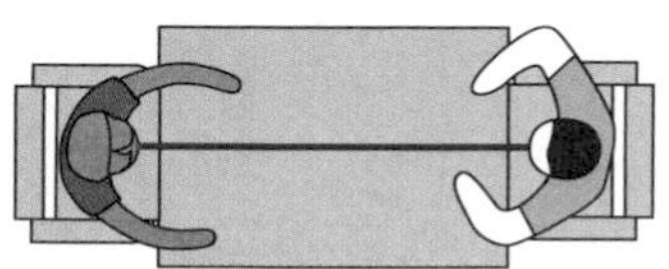

Dyad
(1 line of communication)

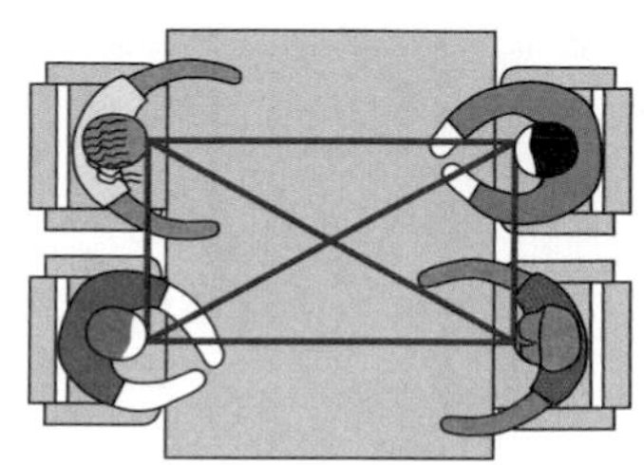

Group of 4
(6 lines of communication)

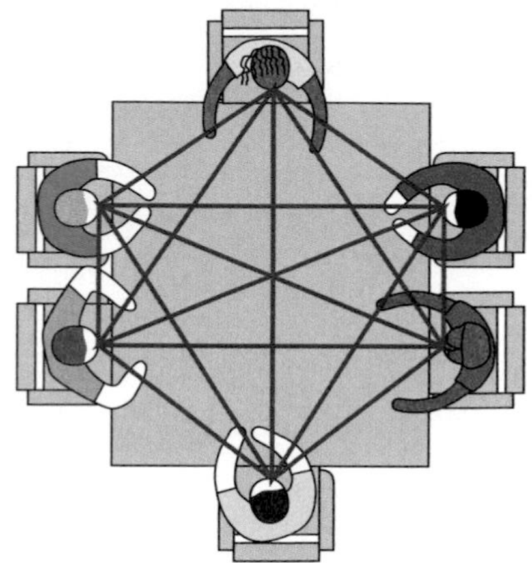

Group of 6
(15 lines of communication)

Exhibit 1.1

Lines of Communication.

The lines of communication increase with the number of people. This may be one reason people are fond of the saying "Too many cooks spoil the broth."

communicating in a system and the number of lines of communication between or among them. As illustrated in Exhibit 1.1, the lines of communication increase geometrically as the number of communicators increases. Whereas this change isn't especially dramatic as you move from two communicators to three or four, the change is staggering by the time you get to a group of even seven.

Exhibit 1.2 models the interdependent parts of the public speaking transaction as a system. Consider (1) the rhetorical situation (context) in which the public speaking transaction takes place, (2) the speaker and the audience, (3) the messages they exchange, (4) the process of constructing and interpreting the symbols they use to convey their messages, (5) the channels through which the messages are sent, and (6) the role perception plays in the process.

The Rhetorical Situation

Scholar and professor Lloyd Bitzer first introduced the concept of the **rhetorical situation.** Bitzer described it as "a natural context of persons, events, objects, relations, and an exigence [goal] which strongly invites utterance."[8] We deal with Bitzer's description of the rhetorical situation in detail in Chapter 7, but we introduce it here as a concept that frames the parts to the whole.

rhetorical situation
A natural context of persons, events, objects, relations, and an exigence [goal] which strongly invites utterance.

Consider first the physical situation that speakers face. It's one thing to speak inside a classroom and quite another to speak at an outdoor graduation ceremony. Whereas we can generally rely on our natural voice to speak inside a classroom, we probably will need a microphone to be heard outside. Changes also may be required in our gestures, movements, and decisions about such things as visual aids.

Next consider what Bitzer calls the "exigence," which is closely related to the goal a speaker seeks to fulfill. What is it about the situation that moves us to

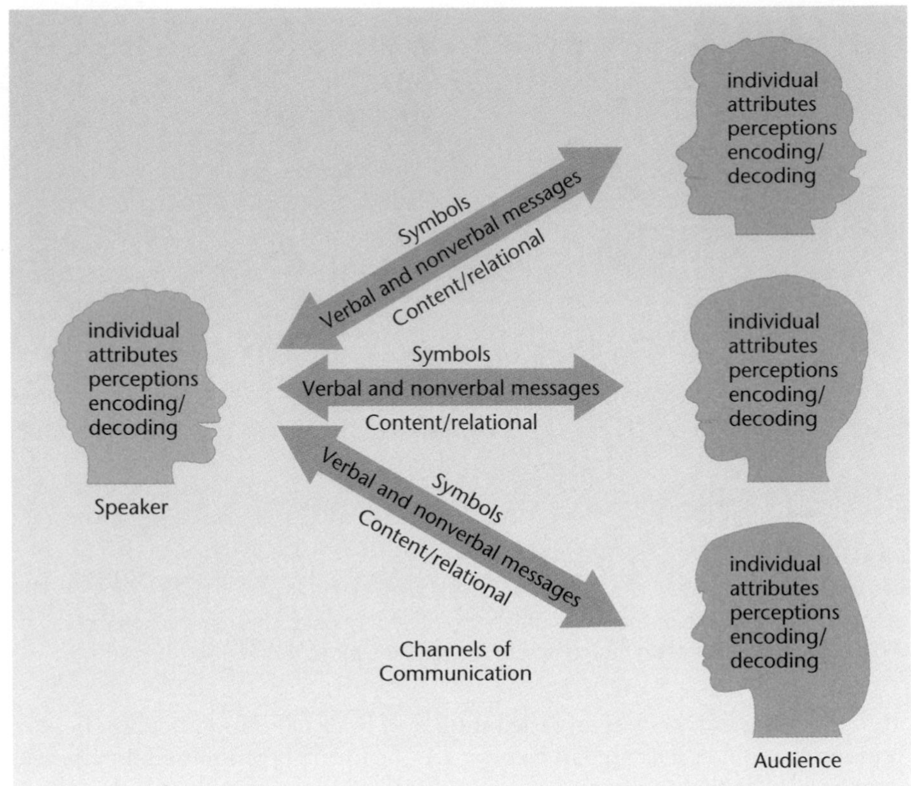

Exhibit 1.2
Public Speaking as a Transaction. In this model of the speech transaction, messages are simultaneously conveyed between speakers and listeners, with both parties functioning simultaneously as sources and receivers of messages. Communication is bound by the situation, and each person's perceptions are significant in interpreting the content and relational components of messages.

speak? Are we speaking to impart important information to our audience, as teachers do on a daily basis? Are we speaking to organize our fellow citizens to fight a perceived wrong? Are we gathered to eulogize a beloved family member or friend? Are we speaking to entertain our audience with amusing stories or jokes?

The physical situation and goals cannot be considered separately. For example, we have listened to a lifetime's worth of graduation speakers in our university's outdoor stadium. Aside from the physical difficulties these speakers have faced, the incompatibility of the speaker's goals and those of the audience has proven to be a minefield for more than a few. Students and parents are not in the mood for an informative lecture, no matter how eloquent. Likewise, the audience typically doesn't want to have their political beliefs changed or be shamed into alumni giving. Yet some speakers we have heard have used each of these as their guiding purpose and alienated their audience in the process.

The Speaker and the Audience Members

In contrast to early models of speaking, which implied the speaker first talks and the audience then responds, the transactional model tells us speaker and audience exchange verbal and nonverbal messages. Even as speakers share their messages with audience members, for example, individual members of the audience are sharing messages right back. Generally this **feedback** is nonverbal in nature and includes such things as eye contact, facial expressions, and body orientation. In some situations, these audience-initiated messages may be verbal, as is the case when members of parliament in the United Kingdom vocalize their approval or disapproval of what the prime minister shares with them. In either case, the audience is not passive during a public speech, and the speaker should note these messages and adapt to them.

feedback
Audience member responses, both verbal and nonverbal, to a speaker.

The sheer number of people in an audience also affects the overall speech transaction. It's one thing to speak with 25 other students in a traditional college classroom. It's quite another to speak to an assembly of the entire graduating class at commencement as people shift restlessly in their seats. Thus, you can no more afford to ignore the size of your audience than you can afford to ignore their feedback, the environment in which the transaction takes place, or the purpose for which you have gathered.

Messages: Content and Relational Components

The **message** is the meaning produced by the speaker and the audience members. In the transactional system modeled here, the message and the medium through which it travels are intentionally blurred. This is because the two are *interdependent*–not independent. What we would like to say to our audience is significantly affected by the manner in which we say it, and the way we convey the message is affected by what we want to say. This reciprocal process has a tremendous impact on how our message is perceived by our audience.

message
The meaning produced by communicators.

All messages are composed of two parts. The first part of the message is its **content,** the essential meaning, the gist or substance, of what a speaker wants to convey. For example, you might wish to convey your affection for another with the three words "I love you." The second part of a message, called its **relational component,** involves the combined impact of the verbal and nonverbal parts of that message as it is conveyed. Consider how you might use your voice, face, and eyes to alter the impact of the words "I love you." You could make these three words an expression of sincere endearment, a plea, or even a statement of wanton desire.

content (of messages)
The essential meaning of what a speaker wants to convey.

relational component (of messages)
The combined impact of the verbal and nonverbal components of a message as it is conveyed.

Meaning is derived from both the content and the relational parts of a message. Moreover, neither part is more important than the other in its contribution to meaning. What you say and how you say it, in other words, are roughly equal in this regard.

Constructing and Interpreting Symbols

When we try to convey our thinking to other people, there is no way to directly communicate our ideas. Our thoughts must be converted into words and gestures whose meaning can be interpreted by those receiving the message. These words and gestures are really **symbols,** things that stand for or suggest other things by reason of relationship or association. This process of converting our thoughts and ideas into meaningful symbols is called **encoding.** These symbols are then interpreted when received by audience members, a process known as **decoding.** This is simpler said than done. Whether an audience decodes a

symbol
Something that stands for or suggests something else by reason of relationship or association.

encoding
The process by which ideas are translated into a code that can be understood by the receiver.

decoding
The process by which a code is translated back into ideas.

speaker's message as encoded depends on many factors, including but not limited to:

- Language
- Culture
- Age
- Gender

Using idioms such as "cool" to describe a car when speaking in front of an audience of non-native English speakers could prove puzzling to them. This problem would also occur with a sentence in which you described the lifestyle of Sean Coombs or Marshall Holmes as "large" or "phat."

Channels

channel
The physical medium through which communication occurs.

A **channel** is the physical medium through which communication occurs. The transmission of the light and sound waves that make up the picture you see on your TV set requires a channel through which they can be signaled and received. Picture and audio are encoded into electronic impulses, which must be decoded by your television receiver. In human communication, we primarily use our senses as channels for the messages we send and receive. We use our voice, eyes, and body, for example, to channel our speeches, conversations, and group discussions. On occasion, we also use our sense of touch, sense of smell, and even our sense of taste as channels of communication.

In the case of public speaking, we can also use supplementary channels of communication to augment the five senses. We can electronically amplify our voice so that it can be better heard or use visual aids such as poster boards, overhead transparencies, and PowerPoint™ slides.

Perceptions

perception
The process by which we give meaning to our experiences.

The transactional system we've been describing demands that we both understand and appreciate the role of perception in public speaking. **Perception** is the process by which we give meaning to our experiences. This process begins when we decide to attend to some stimulus that our senses have picked up on: for example, the driver of the oncoming car whose bright lights are blinding you to the road ahead. Based on your past experiences you instantly organize a message–you flash your bright lights, signaling the other driver to dim his.

Communication unfolds in much the same way. Our senses pick up a smiling face as we walk from one class to the next. When we hear the words, "What's up," also coming from the smiling face, this is what usually happens. First, we organize the facial expression and audible sound into a whole. Second, we give meaning to this whole. Third, we organize a response, smiling back and saying, "Nothing much." Such transactions not only take place in microseconds but also require little to no conscious thought.

On one hand, the instantaneous way we make sense of and respond to the messages we attend to is essential to our survival. On the other, it also can make us overconfident and prone to making mistakes about what we sense, how we perceive what we sense, and how we respond to it.

Take a close look at the lithograph by M. C. Escher on this page. Though it appears at first glance that the water is running downhill, a more careful examination tells you that this is impossible because the water is flowing continuously. Escher was able to create "impossible illusions" by taking advantage of our perceptual predispositions. We assume that the perspective in this print is an accurate representation of reality, when, of course, it cannot be so. When people look at an ambiguous stimulus such as this picture, they automatically look for something familiar . . . something for which they have a preexisting meaning. This helps fool the eye, in this case, into seeing something that cannot exist.

This lithograph, *Waterfall* (1961), by M. C. Escher, creates an "impossible illusion" by taking advantage of our perceptual predispositions.

Again, this tendency to perceive the familiar is both good and bad from the standpoint of public speaking. It is good because it enables us to quickly establish a reference point from which we can plan our own speaking behavior as well as interpret that of others. It's bad because it can blind us to other data that may be even more important to how we behave and interpret the messages of others.

Consider a cross-cultural example. Direct eye contact is perceived as a sign of attention and respect in most of North America. Thus, when we give a speech, we use this knowledge to gauge how our audience is reacting to our message and delivery. This North American norm, however, is not universal. Direct eye contact in some cultures, such as certain Asian societies, is perceived as an aggressive sign of disdain and disrespect.

It's common, then, for unaware North Americans who speak in one of these cultures to walk away from the experience with their confidence severely shaken. They mistakenly perceive their audience's lack of eye contact with them as a sign of disapproval. This mistaken perception, in turn, usually has a negative influence on their entire speaking performance.

As a public speaker, you can never assume that your perceptions of such things as the context, your audience, or the messages your audience feeds back to you are foolproof. Just because some person, some place, or some circumstance strikes you as familiar, that doesn't necessarily make it so.

Words and Things

Finally, public speaking, like other forms of communication, is symbolic.[9] Words are verbal symbols that we use to describe persons, places, and things. Gestures, too, can be symbols, as is the case when we wave our hand to signal good-bye or shake our fist at someone to signal that we are angry. But they are nonverbal.

Although we deal with the symbolic nature of public speaking at length in Chapters 11 and 12, we mention it here because you need to understand that the meaning you attach to the verbal and nonverbal symbols you use to express yourself may not correspond to the meaning others attach to them. What's more, this may be the case even when you think you share a common language. Native speakers of English, for instance, both use and understand what we call idioms, expressions unique to our culture or sometimes to the circle of friends with whom we most identify. Although you may have no trouble making sense of an expression such as "Dude's ride is sweet," imagine how much trouble an international student recently arrived on campus would have in "getting" what the words used in the expression actually mean.

As you prepare for your first speeches, think about the degree to which you and your audience share meaning for symbols you commonly use to express yourself. This means, at a minimum, checking out the degree to which you and your audience share a common language, come from a similar culture, and share a similar socioeconomic background.

Preview

The preceding discussion is a framework for the entire book. In the chapters to follow we flesh out this framework. The concepts just introduced will be refined and expanded to fit the primary topic of a specific chapter.

Because public speaking classes typically are taught in a limited period of time, you can expect to be up on your feet and speaking long before you have learned everything you need to know about the subject. We wrote Chapter 3–which provides an overview of the process of developing, organizing, and delivering your first speech–with this fact clearly in mind.

If you are the least bit anxious about your first speech, then you can look forward. This chapter clears up confusion about the common fear of speaking in public, explains the origins and consequences of this fear on speech performance, and provides you with easily understood and practiced skills to help you manage your fear. What's more, you will learn from reading that these same skills can help to improve your performance even if you are completely confident about your speaking ability.

Chapter 5 zeroes in on a topic of real significance to today's world: ethics. You will learn about varying ethical perspectives and their relationship to the speech transaction. You also will be called on to make a commitment to the ethical practices described there in your own speeches.

To repeat, a major reason for learning about public speaking is the development of listening skills. Much as we need to listen, most of us are not as skilled at it as we need to be. Research shows that most of us would benefit from listening training. Chapter 6 discusses the relationship between good listening habits and effective public speaking. In the process, it details for you the types of listening involved and suggests practices for improving each of these types.

The best prepared and delivered speeches are those that are developed with the audience in mind. Competent public speakers try to learn as much about their audience and the speaking situation as they possibly can. What they learn assists them in predicting what kind of speech will succeed with their audience. Chapter 7 details the process of analyzing your audience and speaking situation, and the necessity of adapting your speech to both.

One of the toughest tasks for many beginning students is getting started. Aristotle called this process of getting started invention. In Chapters 8 and 9 you will learn not only about developing your speech but also about avenues for research you can travel to prepare your speech, including the Internet.

Just as there is more than one way to putt a golf ball, there is more than one way to organize a speech. This is especially true in light of the fact that today's multicultural audience may decode your message using different patterns of organization. You will learn about organizing your message using alternative patterns of speech organization in Chapter 10.

As noted earlier, public speaking is a symbolic transaction. We elaborate on this fact in Chapter 11's treatment of the language of public speaking. You will learn that language is both complex and central to one's cultural heritage. You also will learn how to use this knowledge to your and your audience's advantage in your speeches.

Chapter 12 throws a realistic light on a subject fraught with misinformation: the delivery of your message. How nonverbal communication functions in the delivery of your speech is explained and examples are provided. Common misconceptions about this type of communication also are dispelled.

Using media to enhance your speeches seems such a simple thing. Yet, nothing could be further from the truth. Media such as overheads or media projected from a laptop computer in combination with a projection machine require precise care in both their construction and execution. Public speakers routinely abuse these presentational media in the classroom, in business, and in government.

Informative speaking is far and away the most common type of public speaking you are likely to encounter. Informative speeches are an essential component of most college classes, whether or not they are labeled as such. A lecture essentially is an informative speech. So too is a book report or an oral presentation based on a term paper. Chapter 14 outlines and discusses the types of informative speeches common in everyday life and details the elements that combine to make an effective informative speech.

You will learn about the process of persuasion as well as the process of persuasive speaking. You also will be shown the perceptual characteristics that influence judgments about your credibility and will read about message variables that can enhance the persuasive effect of your speeches.

Chapter 16 extends what you learn about persuasion to thinking and speaking critically. You will be treated to information on deceptive communication practices that are commonly used by unscrupulous communicators, and you'll learn how to recognize the fallacies that frequently characterize their messages. In the process, you also will learn how to avoid using such fallacies in your own reasoning and speaking.

Finally, Chapter 17 introduces life circumstances in which you can expect to be called on to speak. Some of these circumstances, such as a wedding toast, are social. Others, such as being asked without warning at school or at work to make a progress report on a project, are task oriented.

All in all, we think these chapters combine to provide you with the introductory knowledge and skills necessary to see you through not only the speeches you will share in your class but also the lifetime of public speaking all college graduates can expect. Good luck as you proceed.

Summary

To evaluate your understanding of this chapter, visit our Online Learning Center Web site for quizzes and other chapter study aids.

There are many good reasons to study and practice public speaking. Among them are these:

- Public speaking is an essential skill in the professional world.
- Communication in general and public speaking specifically can help empower you and help you empower others.
- Public speaking helps you with your other classes, including those in your major.
- Public speaking skills help to make you a more effective force for change.
- Public speaking helps you become a better listener.
- Public speaking is a key to becoming an informed and active citizen.
- Public speaking helps you think more critically about the issues of the day.

As you move on to the third chapter, remember these important elements:

- Public speaking is a transaction between speaker and audience.
- This transaction is comprised of interdependent rather than independent parts.
- These parts include (1) the rhetorical situation, (2) the speaker and the audience, (3) the message, (4) verbal and nonverbal symbols, (5) the channels used, and (6) perceptions.

Check Your Understanding: Exercises and Activities

1. This chapter suggests that public speaking can empower you. How can public speaking skills empower you to satisfy your most pressing personal and professional needs? Write a short paper or give a brief speech explaining your answer and giving examples.
2. How important are public speaking skills in the profession for which you are preparing? If possible, interview either a practitioner of the profession or a professor in the appropriate department about the ways public speaking might be applicable in your field. Give a brief (1- to 2-minute) presentation to your classmates, or write a short paper about your findings.
3. Attend a meeting of a local government agency, such as a city council, planning commission, or board of supervisors, or attend a student government meeting on your campus. Chances are you will see several speakers present their views in a public forum. Write a short paper about one of the speakers. What impressed you most about the speaker, and what impressed you least? How did the ability to speak help this person achieve his or her goals?

Notes

1. National Association of Colleges and Employers, "Employers Cite Communication Skills as Key, But Say Many Job Seekers Don't Have Them," 26 April 2006. [Retrieved from http://www.naceweb.org/press/display.asp?year=2006&prid=235, 12 November 2006.]
2. Kourtney Jason, "Chico State Takes Back the Night at Annual Event," *The Orion,* 25 October 2006. [Retrieved from http://media.www.theorion.com/media/storage/paper889/news/2006/10/25/News/Chico.State.Takes.Back.The.Night.At.Annual.Event-2407174.shtml, 12 November 2006.]
3. Cincinnati Children's Hospital Medical Center, "Family Advisory Council Members: Edna Morales," [Retrieved from http://www.cincinnatichildrens.org/about/fcc/family/member/edna-morales.htm, 5 November 2006.]
4. Personal communication, 7 May 2007.
5. Ronald B. Adler, *Communicating at Work: Principles and Practices for Business and the Professions,* 3rd ed. (New York: Random House, 1989), 4.
6. Adler, *Communicating at Work,* 216.
7. Anthony P. Carnevale, Leila J. Gainer, and Ann S. Meltzer, *Workplace Basics: The Skills Employers Want* (Washington, D.C.: U.S. Government Printing Office, 1988), 11.
8. Lloyd Bitzer, "The Rhetorical Situation," *Philosophy and Rhetoric* 1 (1968): 5. Bitzer further defines an exigence as "an imperfection marked by urgency; it is a defect, an obstacle, something waiting to be done, a thing which is other than it should be" (6). In this text we prefer to focus on the speaker's goal, which, strictly speaking, is to *overcome the exigence* present in the rhetorical situation.
9. W. Barnett Pearce and Vernon E. Cronen, *Communication, Action and Meaning: The Creation of Social Realities* (New York: Praeger, 1980).

Some knowledge of communication theory can help you be more effective in making oral presentations.

A Communication Theory Sampler

Jim Katt

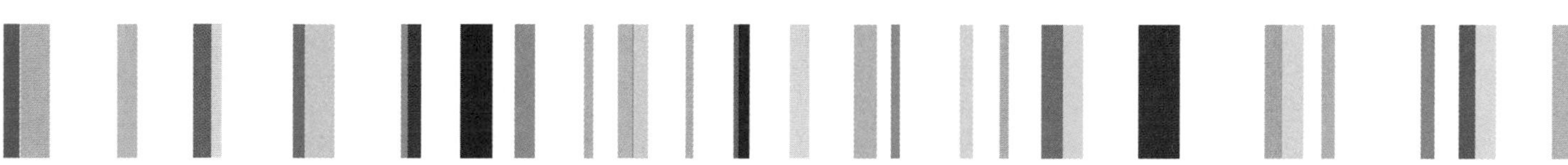

Objectives

After reading and discussing this chapter, you should be able to:

- Explain how the process of communication is pervasive, amoral, and agenda-advancing
- Describe logos, pathos, and ethos, and understand what speakers can do to enhance each of them in their speeches
- Explain the importance of the SMCRE variables
- Demonstrate ways to maximize the likelihood that your audience will be motivated and able to process your message

Key Concepts

amoral
central route
channel
elaboration
environment
ethos
logos
message
motivation
pathos
peripheral route
pervasiveness
source
transactional

> “He who loves practice without theory is like the sailor who boards ship without a rudder and compass and never knows where he may cast.”
>
> –LEONARDO DAVINCI

Although we have been communicating all of our lives, most of us have not put a lot of thought into how the process of communication works. In this course, you will have the opportunity to deliver several speeches. As you prepare for those speeches, knowing about the process of communication will be essential. Fortunately for you, there is a large body of knowledge just waiting to be tapped.

The study of communication has a theoretical basis that draws from contemporary empirical research as well as observations that date back centuries. This chapter makes no attempt to cover the body of knowledge that makes up communication theory, but instead looks at a few selected instances where some knowledge of communication theory can help you be more effective in making oral presentations.

What Is Communication?

Communication is a complex process that, many would argue, is extraordinarily difficult to define. So rather than attempting to define communication, let's examine some of the attributes of this process. Specifically, let's look at how communication is pervasive, amoral, and necessary to advancing our life-agenda.

Communication Is Pervasive

pervasiveness Communication takes place wherever humans are together because people tend to look for meaning, even when a message is not deliberately sent.

Many argue that humans in the presence of other humans cannot *not* communicate. Even when we try not to send any sort of message, it's likely that others will infer meaning from our lack of action. What do you think when someone doesn't call you back, doesn't look at you when you're talking, or doesn't answer your email? If you're like most people, you start making inferences about the other person's motives for not responding–she's doesn't like me; he's just a rude person; she's afraid to talk to me; he's probably really busy; and so on. People tend to look for meaning, even when there is no message. It's human nature. The problem is that, much of the time, the meaning assigned to the lack of an overt message simply isn't correct. Your voicemail is full and all of a sudden people think you don't like them, or you're rude, or you're fearful, or too busy to talk. But what does this inability to turn off the communication process mean for us as communicators and as public speakers? If we cannot *not* communicate, if people are going to assign meaning to our lack of sending messages, then maybe we would be better off trying to send clear messages that have a better chance of being received accurately. If the process of communication is going to continue whether we participate or not, it's better that we become active participants.

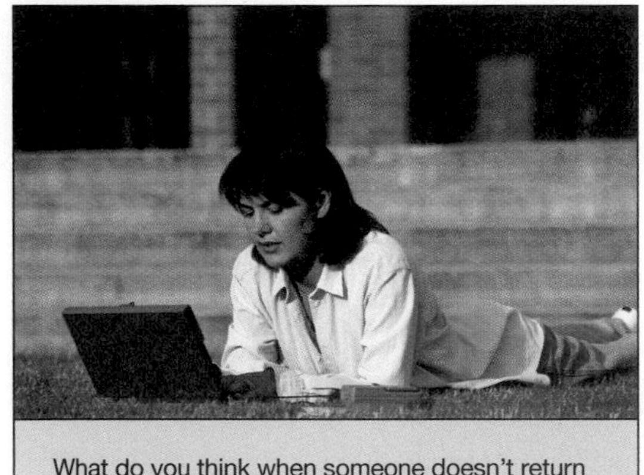

What do you think when someone doesn't return your email or calls?

Communication Is Amoral

amoral The process of communication is ethically neutral.

The word *amoral* is often misused. People use it when they really mean *immoral.* In the context of communication, **amoral** means ethically neutral–neither moral nor immoral. Perhaps a quick analogy will help. Think about those one-celled amoebas you studied in high school biology. You may recall they reproduced *asexually.* Does this mean that the amoebas are sexually deficient or inferior? No, it means they are sexually neutral: neither male nor female. Scholars as far back as Aristotle have argued that the communication process is amoral. The morality, or lack of morality, comes from the people engaged in the process. Perhaps you've tried to persuade a roommate not to go out with a person you know is "bad news." Or, maybe you've tried to talk a friend out of using prescription drugs illegally to stay awake for finals and be more mentally alert. These are examples of moral, ethical communication behavior. In fact, many would argue that *failure* to attempt to influence your friend in these cases would be immoral. Unscrupulous scam artists, who try to sell worthless insurance policies to people who are poor and unknowledgeable, and drug dealers, who try to convince your kids to try their products, use those same methods of persuasion in immoral, unethical ways. The process is neutral–the people engaged in the process provide the morality, or lack of it. This brings us to another aspect of communication: what exactly do we do with it?

Communication Allows Us to Advance Our Life-Agenda

Communication is the means by which each of us advances our life-agenda. As infants, we cried to be fed. Ever since, we have used whatever communication skills we could muster to influence others to think, feel, or act in ways that we believe they should. While such a statement may spark connotations of manipulation or coercion (see the Persuasion chapter to help distinguish "persuasion" from "coercion"), we must remind ourselves that the *process* of communication is ethically neutral and that advancing our life-agenda can be an ethical pursuit, enriching (or, at least, not harming) those around us. Or, it could be an unethical exploitation, advancing our agenda at the expense of others. Which one it is depends on the morality that we, as individuals, bring to the process.

If we acknowledge that communication is a pervasive process that happens with or without our active participation, that it is by this process that we advance our life-agenda, and that it is possible to engage in agenda-advancing behavior in an ethical manner, then communication becomes more than a college course requirement: it's an essential life skill. Becoming a more effective communicator is about more than getting a decent grade in your speech class–it's about becoming more effective at *life.* Most of this book will explore communication in the public speaking context, but much of what you learn about being an effective public speaker can also be applied to becoming a more effective communicator in any context.

What Can We Learn from Aristotle?

Twenty-five hundred years ago, long before anyone dreamed of printing presses, telephones, radio, television, satellite broadcasting, or the Internet, people had lives to live and agendas to advance. Public speaking was the primary mode of communication. Aristotle was a student of Plato, and wrote prolifically on many subjects. He was a keen observer of human behavior and lived in a culture where laws and societal issues were debated and decided orally. It was a society where the most effective orators usually had the most influence, so effective communication was important. Among the many things he wrote about, Aristotle (trans. 1932) identified three types of appeals one might use when speaking. He called them logos, pathos and ethos.

Logos—"*Listen to my message because it makes sense*"

First are logical appeals, or **logos**. Presenting a series of arguments supported by evidence can lead an audience to a "logical" conclusion. Some ways to increase the logical appeal of a message are to be well organized, to be sure that any claims that you might make are based on credible evidence, and that the evidence is clearly presented. On a basic level, if a message does not make logical sense, an audience is unlikely to be moved by it. Consistency is also important. If we compose a mostly logical message that includes a few weak or illogical arguments, there is a danger that the weak arguments will cast doubts on the strong arguments and impugn the entire message. The logos in your presentation says to your audience, "Accept my message because it makes sense."

logos
Logical appeals.

Pathos—"*Listen to my message because of the feelings it evokes*"

Aristotle also recognized the power of emotional appeals, or **pathos**. While sound logos attempts to influence what the audience *thinks*, pathos is concerned with what the audience *feels*. Statistical data and facts help you to appeal logically, but specific examples and stories allow you to appeal emotionally–to make your audience *feel* something about your topic. Some would suggest that while emotional appeals might be effective for some topics, informative or technical speeches should not employ pathos. Although it would be difficult to imagine an effective speech about a technical topic that used only emotional appeals, the absence of pathos would be of equal concern. Why should your audience care about your topic? How should they feel about your topic? Answering these questions provides an emotional component to go along with the logical one. The pathos in your presentation says to your audience, "Accept my message because of the feelings it evokes." Accepting it feels like the right thing to do, or rejecting it feels like the wrong thing to do.

pathos
Emotional appeals.

Ethos—"*Listen to my message because I am a competent and trustworthy person*"

The Greek word for the third type of appeal is **ethos**. Today we call that same concept "credibility." At the most basic level, credibility (ethos) can be defined as an audience's perception of a speaker's competence, trustworthiness, and goodwill (McCroskey & Teven, 1999). That definition seems simple enough, but let's unpack it. Notice that it is the audience's *perceptions*, not reality, that determine ethos. As a presenter, your credibility is based on how competent, trustworthy, and well-intentioned your audience thinks you are, not on how competent, trustworthy, and well-intentioned you actually are. The audience assigns credibility. If you really are competent, but your audience doesn't perceive you to be competent, they will not assign you high credibility. In a like manner, if you really are trustworthy, but your audience doesn't perceive you to be trustworthy, they will not assign you high credibility. Goodwill has to do with your audience's perception of your intentions toward them. Do they feel you have their best interests in mind? Or do they perceive you as self-serving, or someone who just doesn't care one way or the other about them? To be a truly credible speaker your audience must perceive you as competent, trustworthy, and well-intentioned.

ethos
The audience's perception of a speaker's competence, trustworthiness and goodwill; credibility.

How can you maximize your credibility? In the case of competence, if you have expertise, let your audience know about it. Let's assume you are a person who has been involved with computer animation since you were 13 years old. You have already taken several courses in animation and spent one summer interning for an animation company. You are making a presentation about the best type of animation software. If your audience knows about your experience, they will undoubtedly see you as more competent than they would if they had no knowledge of your expertise. But they will not know unless you tell them.

Some presenters are reluctant to mention their qualifications or experience for fear of being perceived as boastful. It is, however, quite possible to present your expertise in a humble manner, thus increasing your audience's perception of your competence without coming across as a braggart. "While some kids were busy conquering Dungeons and Dragons, I was glued to my computer, trying to conquer pixels and polygons. The animation bug caught me when I was 13 years old, and since then I have devoted most of my time to learning animation. Here at the University, I have completed several courses in animation and was lucky enough to have spent last summer interning at Acme Animation."

Sometimes you may be speaking about a subject on which you are not an expert. In these cases you may be able to "borrow" some expertise by citing the qualifications of the sources that you consulted in preparing your speech. For example, you might say, "I've been interested in growing my own herbs, but really didn't know very much about it until I read *The Secret Herb Garden* by Virginia Block, head of Harvard University's Herbal Horticulture department." It's a way of saying to your audience, "I am competent to speak about this topic, because I have consulted expert sources."

In addition to their perceptions of your topical expertise, audiences also have perceptions about your competence as a speaker. A speaker's delivery can affect the audience's perception of that speaker's competence (McCroskey, 2001). Being well-prepared, organized, and appropriately dressed for your speech will also help increase your audience's perception of your competence.

Perceptions of trustworthiness are a little more difficult to influence. Just saying "I'm really trustworthy" tends to have a hollow ring. Fortunately, most audiences will assume you are trustworthy unless you give them evidence to the contrary. Once you give them reason to doubt your honesty or reliability, however, it is difficult to regain their confidence. For this reason, speakers must be careful to present everything in an honest, trustworthy fashion. Many attorneys have won cases by catching opposing witnesses in a lie. Even if the lies had no direct impact on the cases, once it has been established that certain witnesses do not always tell the truth, their trustworthiness is damaged and their testimony becomes unreliable.

Many attorneys have won cases by catching witnesses in a lie.

The perception of goodwill occurs when your audience feels that you care about them, that you have their best interests at heart, and that you are concerned with them. Speeches that are ill-prepared or visual aids that are crudely produced may send a message that the speaker just doesn't care that much about his or her audience. Speakers who value their audiences go to the trouble of being well prepared. Also, a dismissive, flippant, or arrogant attitude may say, "I really don't care about you." Thoughtful speakers show their understanding and concern by adopting a caring attitude toward their audiences.

If you can tell your audience about your competence, avoid giving them any reason to doubt your trustworthiness, and demonstrate that you have their best interests at heart, you maximize the possibility they will perceive you as credible. The ethos in your presentation says to your audience, "Accept my message because I am a competent, trustworthy, and well-intentioned person."

Over the years there has been some disagreement over which type of appeal is most effective in different situations. Since no clear answers have emerged, perhaps the most practical advice is to maximize your logos, pathos, and ethos in every presentation. Keep your logic sound by making a series of clearly stated claims and by avoiding logical fallacies. Include credible statistics and other data to support those claims. Provide specific examples and stories to help your audience feel something about your topic. Be sure your audience knows about your personal expertise, and avoid giving them any reason to doubt your honesty. Appeal to you audience with logic, emotion, and credibility–logos, pathos, *and* ethos.

Tips and Tactics

Increase the Appeal of Your Message

Logos

- be well organized
- use credible evidence
- clearly present your evidence
- maintain consistency by using sound arguments

Pathos

- provide specific examples and stories
- show your audience why they should care about your topic

Ethos

- if you have expertise in your topic, describe it to your audience
- clearly cite the qualifications of your sources
- present your message in an honest and trustworthy fashion
- be well prepared, organized and appropriately dressed
- adopt a caring attitude toward your audience

The SMCRE Factors

In an effort to study the complex process of communication, scholars have found it helpful to categorize or group the many factors involved. One grouping is the SMCRE model, which identifies five groups of communication variables: Source, Message, Channel, Receiver, and Environment. Although these categories can be applied to any communication situation, we will focus on them in the context of public speaking.

In a public speaking situation, the ***source*** is the speaker (including the speaker's perceptions), the ***message*** is the speaker's intended message (as opposed to any other, incidental messages that might become part of the transaction), the ***channels*** are sound and sight (in-person and in real time), the ***receivers*** are the audience (and their perceptions), and the ***environment*** is the situation or context in which the transaction takes place. It may be helpful to remember that these are variables we would see if we could "freeze frame" the communication process and study it in only one direction. In reality, the process of communication is transactional, meaning we "are engaged in sending (encoding) and receiving (decoding) messages simultaneously" (Wenberg & Wilmot, 1974, p. 5). For the purpose of studying and analyzing it, however, we may think of it as happening in one direction. Below are brief descriptions of each category and some examples of variables that fit into each group. Bear in mind that the examples given are just a sampling. If we attempted to present an exhaustive list, there would be scores of variables for each category.

Source
The person initiating the communication.

Message
The message the speaker *intends* to send.

Channel
The means through which the message is sent.

Receivers
The audience to whom the message is delivered.

Environment
The situation or context in which the transaction takes place.

Source Variables

The source is the person who initiates the communication transaction. In the case of speeches, it is the speaker. This model suggests that the overall effectiveness of the communication will be influenced by source factors such as age, gender, intelligence, education, attractiveness, personality, and voice quality as well as perceptual items such as attitudes, prejudices, and values. Furthermore, how these variables affect the process will depend on the situation. Take age, for example. Being a senior citizen may be a positive factor when making a presentation about the impact of the Korean War and a negative factor when making a presentation about which video gaming platform is best. Aristotle believed that arguments should be accepted (or rejected) solely on their own merits, but he recognized that "external matters do count for much, because of the sorry nature of an audience" (Aristotle, trans. 1932, 3, 1, 1404a). Some twenty-three hundred years later, his observation is still accurate–audiences can still be swayed by external matters. Aronson and Mills (1965) presented identical messages attributed to either physically attractive or physically unattractive sources. The audience was more persuaded by the message when it came from an attractive source. Since the topic had nothing to do with grooming, fashion, or fitness, the attractiveness of the source should not have made any difference–but it did.

Message Variables

All of the elements in a message can affect the communication process. Some of these variables would include length of message, organizational scheme, use of humor, types of appeals, types of arguments, or use of evidence. Again, the effects

As businesses increase the use of technology, audiences can be scattered across the world.

Receiver variables will impact how your message is perceived.

would vary with the situation. For example, using humor can often be an effective device, but it might be considered inappropriate and have a negative impact on a speech about world hunger.

Channel Variables

In older versions of this model, the channels were defined by the five senses: sight, sound, touch, taste, and smell. More recently, modalities (live, recorded, computer–mediated, or teleconferenced) within the five senses have also been considered channel variables. Today, we have more choices than ever when it comes to communication channels. Certainly some are preferable to others in a given situation. An email communication might be an effective way to announce an upcoming business meeting, but probably not the ideal channel for a marriage proposal. Most speeches are face-to-face endeavors featuring sounds and sights, but as businesses increase their use of satellite technology, you may find yourself delivering an up-linked speech to an audience that is scattered across the globe.

Receiver Variables

In this model, the receivers are people receiving the message. During a speech, the receivers are the audience. Each member of the audience brings his or her own variables (such as age, gender, cultural background, prior knowledge of topic, listening ability, and mood) and perceptual items (such as attitudes, values, and prejudices). The same topic may require a different approach based on receiver variables. For example, a presentation about the importance of cancer screenings might emphasize screenings for prostate cancer to an audience of men and breast cancer screenings to an audience of women. Effective communicators tailor their messages specifically to the audiences who will be receiving them.

Environment Variables

Communication does not happen in a vacuum: it happens in places. Some places are noisy, some are crowded, some are attractively decorated, some have comfortable chairs, some are too cold, and some are messy. Research has shown that many of these "environmental" factors influence communication. Ask anyone who has tried to make a presentation on a hot, Florida afternoon in a room where the air-conditioning was not working–environmental factors (temperature, in this case) make a difference.

Which Variables Can You Control?

Of the five groups of variables, which, as a speaker, do you have the most control over? Many would answer "source," since we like to think we have control over ourselves. While that may be partially true, there are a lot of source variables, like age, gender, height, ethnicity, and race, over which we have no control. Consider the source variable, attractiveness. Yes, we can spruce ourselves up a little, and even wear clothing highly appropriate to the rhetorical situation, but much of what others find attractive or unattractive in us is out of our control.

In real-world situations we are usually assigned the channel through which we are to communicate. Occasionally your boss may say, "How do you think we can best get the message across?" but, more often, she'll say, "I'm sending you to Toledo to make a speech to the sales force."

Our environments are usually assigned as well. Once we get there, we may be able to adjust the thermostat or the lighting, or re-arrange the chairs, but at best we have only partial control over our environment.

The variables over which we have the least control are the receiver variables. Speakers rarely have the opportunity to choose audience members with certain characteristics. An exception might be during political campaigns, when a candidate may speak to an audience made up entirely of loyal constituents who were handpicked by the politician's staff. This scenario, however, is the exception, not the rule. Most speakers speak to an audience they did not choose.

The variables over which we have the most control are the message variables. Sometimes speakers are assigned a topic, but rarely are the elements of the message prescribed. The message is the invention of the speaker. The speaker generally gets to choose what to include, what to leave out, how to order the information, what evidence to provide, and what words to use.

So, there are many, many variables affecting the process of communication, but, as speakers, we have little control over any except those that make up the message. If communicating effectively is important to us (and it is), can we focus our audience's attention more on our message and less on all of those other things we cannot control? Can we have our audience pay more attention to our arguments and our evidence and less attention to our looks, the temperature of the room, or the fact that they are tired from partying last night? Another communication theory provides a possible answer to these questions.

The Elaboration Likelihood Model (ELM)

The Elaboration Likelihood Model is one of the most thoroughly researched communication theories. First described by Richard Petty and John Cacioppo (1986), the ELM is a comprehensive theory of persuasion. What is described here is a just a portion of the model, but it is a portion that has particular relevance to speakers. The Persuasive Communication chapter will cover the ELM in greater depth and examine how to apply the theory to persuasive presentations. For now, let's examine aspects of the ELM that generalize to any speaking situation.

Central Route or Peripheral Cues?

ELM researchers found that receivers expend a lot of mental energy processing some messages but very little energy processing others. More specifically,

elaboration
The degree to which a receiver scrutinizes a message.

central route
Receivers mentally elaborate on the elements of your message and carefully scrutinize your arguments and evidence.

peripheral route
Receivers give brief attention to the message without elaborated thought.

receivers sometimes mentally elaborate on elements of the message, scrutinizing the arguments and evidence, and at other times receivers give the message only cursory attention, often basing their decision to agree or disagree with the message on peripheral factors such as source attractiveness or the temperature of the room (Anderson & Pryor, 1992). Petty & Cacioppo (1986) termed the effortful scrutinizing of the message **central route** processing, and the casual, more cursory message reception **peripheral route** processing.

Their observation begs the question: "Why do receivers expend the effort to engage in central route processing sometimes, and other times process only peripherally?" Petty and Cacioppo (1986) suggest that people intrinsically want to hold correct attitudes, but don't have the time, inclination, or energy to carefully scrutinize every message they receive. Therefore, they must choose which messages they will process by the more effortful central route. According to their research, when people are *motivated* and *able* to scrutinize a message, they are likely to do so. Alternatively, people who lack either motivation or ability are more likely to be influenced by peripheral cues. The name "Elaboration Likelihood Model" is based on the premise that those who are both motivated and able are more likely to engage in elaborative processing.

ELM research also found that audience attitudes based on central route processing are more persistent, more predictive of behavior, and more resistant to counter-persuasion (Petty & Cacioppo, 1986). So, if you give a speech and your audience changes their attitudes in the direction you advocate based on central route processing, they are more likely to retain those attitudes, more likely to act in accordance with those attitudes, and less likely to be un-persuaded by someone with an opposing view. If we think back to our examination of the SMCRE model, we notice that central route processing is focused primarily on the message variables, and peripheral route processing is focused more on sender, channel, receiver, and environment variables. If our audience is focused primarily on the message, they are basing their attitudes on the variables in the communication process over which we have the most control. If our audience is focused on peripheral cues, they are basing their attitudes on the elements over which we have very little control. All of this suggests that speakers who invent high quality messages have a better chance of being successful communicators if their audiences engage in central route processing.

Motivation and Ability

What can we, as speakers, do to increase the likelihood that our audience will engage in elaborative (central route) processing? Since we know that receivers are more likely to elaborate if they are motivated and able, the question becomes, "What can we do to maximize our audience's motivation and ability?"

Although a number of motivational factors have been studied, the factor most useful to speakers is relevance. If people believe a message is personally important (relevant) to them, they are more motivated to process that message carefully (Petty & Cacioppo, 1979). Anything that we, as speakers, can do to help our audience see how our message is important to them has the potential to increase their motivation. Aristotle observed that "men pay attention to things of importance, to their own interests, to anything wonderful, to anything pleasant; and hence you must give the impression that your speech has to do with the like" (Aristotle, trans. 1932, 3. 14. 1415b). If we can give that impression, and increase our audience's perceptions of relevance, we can increase their motivation, and thus their likelihood to elaborate. So, we should do what we can to make our presentations relevant to our audience. Tell your audience why your speech will be important or useful to them. Moreover, tell them early in your speech, so the likelihood that they will engage in effortful processing of your entire message will be maximized. Sometimes the relevance of a speech is unclear until late in the presentation. In these cases, it is too late for the audience to go back and re-process the message. To maximize your audience's motivation to process your message, make the case for relevance, and make it early.

Ability is the other variable that determines a receiver's likelihood to elaborate. But ability is a receiver variable and there is little we can do to change our audience's ability to process a message. We can, however, avoid doing things that might diminish their ability to process our messages. If, when speaking, we use a lot of jargon that audience members are unfamiliar with, we will lessen their ability to process the message. If a message is spoken in Russian, only those who understand Russian will be able to process the message. Jargon can be a foreign language to the audience who is unfamiliar with it, and its overuse can interfere with their ability to process the message. Another impediment to message processing is the inclusion of too many behaviors that distract from your presentation. Including an occasional "ah" or "um" in your speech will probably not diminish your overall effectiveness. Sometimes, however, speakers include so many "ah's" and "um's" that audience attention is drawn away from the message. When this happens, that audience's ability to process the message in diminished. So, while we cannot increase our audience's innate ability to process our message, we can maximize that ability by *not* doing things that interfere with their ability.

In summary, your audience is more likely to focus on your message (instead of peripheral cues) if they are motivated and able. Perceiving the relevance of your message can increase motivation, and eliminating interfering elements (jargon, technical references, distracting behaviors, etc.) can maximize their ability. Once engaged in the central route, your audience will be more influenced by the message that you invented, and less influenced by peripheral items over which you have no control.

Before leaving the ELM, three items need to be clarified. First, be reminded that this discussion has covered only a portion of the Elaboration Likelihood Model. There is much more to the model, but we have covered only the basics to emphasize the importance of making your messages relevant and accessible to your audience.

Second, although the "route" metaphor suggests a receiver either takes one route or the other–that is, relies on central message processing or peripheral cues–the ELM is *not* an either/or model. Motivation and ability will cause the effect of peripheral cues to be diminished, but not eliminated. Under conditions of high elaboration likelihood, non-message factors will still be a part of the process, but they will be less influential than the message factors.

Third, having your audience focused on your message does not mean they will necessarily accept your message. Increased scrutiny will favor strong messages and expose weak messages (Petty & Cacioppo, 1984). If your audience is following the central route, they may accept *or* reject your message, but they will do so based primarily on the message itself, not on peripheral cues. So, to increase the likelihood for successful communication, make your message relevant, avoid doing anything to impair your audience's ability, and create a strong, logically sound message.

What Have We Learned?

Although this chapter does not pretend to offer a complete overview of communication theory, we have tried to bring together a number of theoretical elements that can be useful in preparing and delivering oral presentations. We have seen the important and pervasive role communication plays in our lives. We have learned from Aristotle that one might appeal to an audience's sense of logic, to their emotions, or to their willingness to accept a competent, trustworthy, and benevolent source. Rather than choosing among these three strategies, look for ways to utilize all three in your speeches. The SMCRE model reminds us that there are many factors that affect our attempts to communicate, but that we have very little control over factors outside of the message itself. The Elaboration Likelihood Model helps explain why audiences sometimes focus on our message and sometimes focus on peripheral factors. Our discussion of the ELM also suggests some ways we might increase the likelihood of keeping our audience message-centered.

It has been said that nothing is more practical than a good theory. As you prepare for speeches in this class and later in your careers, you should find many practical applications for the theories introduced in this chapter.

Speaking of . . .

What Speakers Need to Know about Listening by *Stephan Ihde*

Before an audience can engage in effortful processing of a message, they have to *listen* to the message. As speakers, we can help our listeners make our communication transaction a more profitable experience for them, or we can encourage them *not* to listen to us. Although we will save our in-depth discussion of listening for Chapter 6, let's take time now to consider some strategies that can help persuade your audience to listen to your message.

- *Have a strong message that's relevant to your audience.* Haven't we all heard messages—in class or elsewhere—that we thought were a waste of time? Well, here's an even tougher question: Do others think that about *your* speeches? It's fair to say that, if you don't care about your message, we probably won't either. But having a message that *you* care about with good logos and strong supporting evidence increases the chances that we will care about the message also. Have you made your messages relevant to us? We tend to remember and process things in which we have an interest (Schiefele & Krapp, 1996). Think about how your audience will perceive your message. Also, make sure the arguments in your speech are strong ones (see the Persuasive Communication chapter for more help here).
    - If you're struggling with message delivery, take heart: One added benefit to having a message that's highly relevant to your audience is that, if your delivery still has room for improvement, it's possible that audiences may not be as affected by your poor delivery and may still respond to the highly relevant verbal content of your message (Marsh, Hart-O'Rourke, & Julka, 1997). While this class will give you the opportunity to improve your delivery skills, this research gives all the more reason for you to construct a strong, relevant message.
- *Use confident language.* Holtgraves and Lasky (1999) showed that subjects used both central and peripheral routes to persuasion when the speaker used confident ("strong") language instead of hedging language (e.g., "I suppose that...", "It's kinda true that...", and frequent vocal pauses). As you have confidence in your

topic, that allows us to rest in your confidence and learn from you. Having a clear organizational plan and good practice rehearsal techniques will help you know your material well enough so that hedging language becomes unnecessary. Moreover, action-oriented listeners in your audience will benefit from your preparation.

- *Define any unfamiliar terms and use standard English*. Make sure you clearly explain any terms that your audience doesn't understand. Using vocabulary or concepts that your audience doesn't know is much like speaking a foreign language (Reimann, 2001). When asked how professors could improve speaking to foreign students, Chinese students responded with answers like, "Avoid using colloquial and slang expressions," "Speak clearly and loudly in the classroom," "Use formal English to deliver lectures," and "Try to get rid of strong accent and strange pronunciation" (Huang, 2004). Consider your specific audience's language capacity and vocabulary base and use terms with which they will be familiar.

- *Offer opportunities for clarification*. While your speeches in this class may not have the time or format to do this, remember this when you're giving presentations in the "real world." Take the time to make sure your audience understands your message. If you are visually connecting with your audience, you will know quickly if your audience doesn't understand your message by their reactions and nonverbal expressions to your message. If you build in opportunities for feedback or questions, you can help ensure that misunderstandings get clarified. Asking students to generate their own questions regarding a topic has been shown to improve recall of information (King, 1994).

- *Assume that your audience may not have the same listening style as you*. People utilize different elements from among four primary listening "styles." Those with a *people-oriented* listening style have a high regard for another person's feelings and seek to find common ground with the speaker; they respond keenly to the emotions of others and particularly enjoy harmony and commonality. *Action-oriented* listeners like to receive concise, succinct information that is free from mistakes. These individuals are particularly frustrated by disorganized presentations. *Content-oriented* listeners prefer listening to challenging and complex messages. Someone who is content-oriented is more drawn to evaluate the facts and strengths of arguments. Finally, *time-oriented* listeners are focused on brief listening encounters. A time-oriented person will let others know he or she has only so much time to spend in an interaction and prefers interactions to move along swiftly (Johnston, Weaver, Watson, & Barker, 2000; Watson, Barker, & Weaver, 1995).

Most people tend to create the message that they would like to hear—the message that meets the needs of those with the same listening style as the speaker. But, that message may not meet the needs of those with other listening styles. Since your message is for your audience, construct it so that it meets *their* listening needs. If you know the predominant listening style of your audience, tailor your message to that style. Many times, however, you'll be speaking to an audience that includes a mixture of listening styles. In those cases, try to incorporate some of what each style requires: acknowledge the relational aspects of your topic for the people-oriented listeners, be well-organized and accurate for your action-oriented listeners, give opportunities for further investigation for content-oriented listeners, and be concise for your time-oriented listeners. Finally, as we've said before, provide strong, well-supported arguments. Strong arguments are essential for content-oriented listeners and anyone else engaged in central-route processing of your message. Being sensitive to your audience's needs will help your audience see that you care about them enough to deliver your message in a way they can best receive.

References

Anderson, S., and Pryor, B. (1992). *Speech fundamentals: A contemporary approach.* Needham Heights, MA: Ginn.

Aristotle (trans. 1932). *The rhetoric of Aristotle* (L. Cooper, Trans.). New York: Appleton-Century-Crofts.

Holtgraves, T. & Lasky, B. (1999). Listening power and persuasion. *Journal of Language and Social Psychology, 18(2),* 196–205.

Huang, J. (2004). Voices from Chinese students: Professors' use of English affects academic listening. *College Student Journal,* 38(2), 212–223.

Johnston, M. K., Weaver, III, J. B., Watson, K. W., & Barker, L. B. (2000). Listening styles: Biological or psychological differences? *International Journal of Listening, 14,* 32–46.

King, A. (1994). Autonomy and question asking: The role of personal control in guided student-generated questioning. *Learning and Individual Differences, 6,* 163–185.

Marsh, K. L., Hart-O'Rourke, D. M., & Julka, D. L. (1997). The persuasive effects of verbal and non-verbal information in a context of value relevance. *Personality and Social Psychology Bulletin, 23(6),* 563–579.

McCroskey, J. C. (2001). *An introduction to rhetorical communication* (8th ed.). Boston: Allyn and Bacon.

McCroskey, J. C., & Teven, J. J. (1999). Goodwill: A reexamination of the construct and its measurement. *Communication Monographs, 66,* 90–103.

Mills, J., and Aronson, E. (1965). "Opinion change as a function of the communicator's attractiveness and desire to influence." *Journal of Personality and Social Psychology, 1,* 173–177.

Petty, R., and Cacioppo, J. (1979). Issue involvement can increase or decrease persuasion by enhancing message-relevant cognitive responses. *Journal of Personality and Social Psychology, 37,* 1915–1926.

Petty, R., and Cacioppo, J. (1984). The effects of involvement on responses to argument quantity and quality: Central and peripheral routes to persuasion. *Journal of Personality and Social Psychology, 46,* 69–81.

Petty, R., and Cacioppo, J. (1986). *Communication and persuasion: Central and peripheral routes to persuasion and attitude change.* New York: Springer Verlag.

Reimann, P. (2001). Jargon, abbreviations cloud message being conveyed. *Ophthalmology Times, 26(8),* 76.

Schiefele, U. & Krapp, A. (1996). Topic interest and free recall of expository text. *Learning and Individual Differences, 8,* 141–160.

Watson, K. W., Barker, L. L, & Weaver, III, J. B. (1995). The listening styles profile (LSP-16): Development and validation of an instrument to assess four listening styles. *International Journal of Listening, 9,* 1–13.

Wenberg, J., & Wilmot W. (1973). *The personal communication process.* New York: Wiley.

Your first speeches to your classmates will help you gain experience and confidence, as you can see in the face of our student Satinder Gill.

Your First Speech

Objectives

After reading this chapter and reviewing the online learning resources at www.mhhe.com/brydon6, you should be able to:

- Analyze the basic features of the rhetorical situation as it applies to your first speech.
- Identify the general purposes associated with public speaking.
- Select an appropriate topic for your first speech.
- Construct a specific purpose for your first speech.
- Develop a clear thesis statement for your first speech.
- Prepare your first speech, using appropriate sources for information.
- Organize your speech to (1) open with impact, (2) focus on your thesis statement, (3) connect with your audience, (4) preview your main points, (5) organize your ideas with three to five main points, (6) summarize your main points, and (7) close with impact.
- Present your speech in a conversational, extemporaneous manner.

Key Concepts

audience
brainstorming
canons of rhetoric
credibility
extemporaneous delivery
general purpose
impromptu delivery
invention
main points
manuscript delivery
memorized delivery
preview
signposts
specific purpose
thesis statement

> “Public speaking is not a spectator sport.”
>
> –MILE SQUARE TOASTMASTERS CLUB[1]

Try to imagine how difficult it would be to learn a skill for the first time by only reading about it or only seeing someone else do it; for example, mastering the intricacies of driving a car with a 6-speed manual transmission or modeling the fret work of your favorite band's lead guitarist. Then imagine how much more difficult this would be if you seldom practiced the skill in the course of your everyday life? Wouldn't you agree it would be tough, if not impossible?

Well, imagine you are in a class where the subject and corresponding skill mimic this scenario to a tee. You have read about the subject and skill and seen others practice the skill with varying degrees of success, but have had little opportunity to practice it yourself.

For many beginning public speakers, the preceding scenario is more fact than fiction. The art and science of public speaking are things they have only read about or seen others practice. This is not to say that they have never attempted to speak publicly–only that these attempts have been based on scant knowledge and little or no practice.

We often ask our students how many of them have given at least 100 public speeches in their lives. Rarely is even a single hand raised. What strikes many of them as a lot, however, is very little when compared to the knowledge and repetition necessary to drive a car with a manual transmission, play a lead guitar, or master a new computer game.

The reality is that in order to become a competent public speaker, you will need to get on your feet and speak to your classmates early and often. That's why we assign an early speech in our classes, often the second or third class meeting. These speeches are usually based on personal experience. Not only does this get students speaking early, it also helps classmates learn about each other, which will be important to them later as they match their speech topics to their audience.

This chapter takes a general look at the individual steps you need to master in the process of developing and delivering your first speech. This is not a substitute for the content to follow in later chapters but a detailed preview of it. It's designed to assist you in developing an overall sense of what effective public speaking involves, starting with choosing the right topic and ending with identifying a style of delivery that best suits the situation. The steps we discuss are (1) analyzing the rhetorical situation which you face, including your audience; (2) deciding on a purpose; (3) choosing a topic that is suitable to both the situation and chosen purpose; (4) constructing a specific purpose and developing a clear thesis statement for your speech; (5) preparing the substance of your speech; (6) organizing your speech; and (7) presenting your speech effectively.

First Things First

Analyzing the Rhetorical Situation, Including the Audience

One of your first speech assignments may be to introduce a classmate or yourself, to share a brief story with the class, to prove a controversial point, or to illustrate your pet peeve. Whatever the assignment, you need to understand completely

Today's public speakers need to adapt to multicultural, multiethnic, and multiracial audiences, such as this group of students.

the rhetorical situation in which you find yourself and the expectations that come with the situation. This is essential to effectively develop a speech that fits the situation and addresses those expectations.

For starters, you need to know who is in your audience. **Audience** refers to the individuals who listen to a public speech. Typically, you will be speaking to your classmates, some of whom you may already have come to know in the first few days of class. But even if you have not, you can make certain assumptions about them based on their attendance at your university or college. Do you attend a small, rural, liberal arts college or a large, urban university? What are the common majors emphasized at your institution? Beyond knowing these general facts, you can also observe your classmates in the effort to discover things about them. Are most of them the same age as you, older, or younger? People of the same age tend to share many of the same experiences. For example, the authors of this text grew up in the '50s and '60s. For us, the assassination of President John F. Kennedy was a defining experience. Yet for most of today's younger college students, Kennedy is but a distant historical figure. Although Kennedy's death is still important in a historical sense, the deaths at the World Trade Center, in Pennsylvania, and at the Pentagon on September 11, 2001, probably seem like a defining experience for you and your classmates.

audience
The individuals who listen to a public speech.

Knowing the common experiences you share with your audience allows you to predict what topics are likely to elicit a favorable response. Factors such as the age, sex, and social status of the people with whom you speak may also help you predict audience response. Depending on who they are and what experiences they share, audience members come to any speech situation with a variety of expectations. For example, your classmates probably expect you to speak to them as a peer. If you violate that expectation, taking on an air of superiority, for example, you may not get the response you desire. Only after you thoroughly understand your speech situation, your audience, and their expectations should you begin to consider the purpose for your speech.

Choosing a General Speech Purpose

general purpose
The primary function of a speech. The three commonly agreed upon general purposes are to inform, to persuade, and to entertain.

One of the first decisions a speaker faces is to decide on the **general purpose**–the primary function–of the speech. The three commonly agreed upon general purposes are to inform, to persuade, and to entertain. The most common types of speeches seek to *inform* others about things they do not already know or to *persuade* others to believe or behave in certain ways. Persuasive speeches not only seek change, they also may seek to reinforce social values, as when someone gives a Fourth of July speech or a sermon. Other speeches seek to *entertain* by sharing an enjoyable experience. Obviously, these general purposes are not mutually exclusive. A persuasive speech will also inform the audience, and an informative speech should be interesting enough that it encourages the audience to listen. Nevertheless, the general purpose you either have been assigned or have decided on yourself should tell you something about the topic you ultimately choose. Simply put, some topics may be inappropriate or only marginally appropriate to your purpose. Though controversial topics, for example, lend themselves to a persuasive speech, they are less well suited to an informative speech.

Choosing a Topic

Once you've analyzed your audience, the situation you face, and selected a general purpose, one of the hardest things for many beginning speakers is the selection of a topic. Sometimes your instructor will do this for you, but it's just as likely you'll have to decide on a topic yourself.

In many classes, the first speech you give may not require choosing a complex topic. Many of the suggestions in the pages that follow will not become relevant until later in the class. However, even if you are simply introducing yourself or telling a story, you still need to choose what you will say about yourself or what experience you will relate. Many of the same criteria that govern topic choice for research-based topics also apply to these early speeches. They should be interesting, appropriate, and worthwhile, as should any speech topic.

An obvious place to begin is with your own interests, experiences, and knowledge. Remember to look for topics as you go through your day. For example, you may see a television program, read a blog, or see a video on YouTube that deals with a topic that interests you. A magazine or a newspaper may also suggest a topic.

The Internet, television, newspapers, and magazines are but a few of the places where you might find a topic. They may not even be the best place to start your search. Other sources include campus publications, instructors, and fellow students. The number of places to find a good topic, in fact, is limited only by how aware you are of what's going on around you. The following list summarizes a few good places to look for a topic.

Tips and Tactics

Suggestions for Finding a Topic

- *Make a personal inventory.* What hobbies, interests, jobs, or experiences have you had that would interest others?
- *Talk to friends and classmates.* Perhaps they have ideas to share with you, including topics they would like to know more about.
- *Read.* Newspapers, newsmagazines, and books are filled with ideas. You should commit to reading at least one newspaper a day and one newsmagazine a week while enrolled in this course.
- *Check the Internet.* Many subject areas are discussed on the Internet, and there is a wide range of interest-based chat groups. If you enjoy "surfing the Net," you may well find speech ideas there for the taking.
- *Brainstorm.* **Brainstorming** in a group is a creative process used for generating a large number of ideas. (The activity in the box "Brainstorming for Topics" explains the process in more detail.)

brainstorming
A creative process used for generating a large number of ideas.

In addition to knowing *where* to look for a topic, it is important to know *what* to look for. First, the topic should be interesting to you. If you don't care about the topic, how can you expect your audience to care? Second, select a topic that will be interesting to your audience—or at least one that can be made interesting to them. This is why it is crucial to know as much as possible about your audience. Third, your topic should be appropriate to the situation. If your instructor has asked you to speak on your pet peeve, she or he probably is thinking of topics like dorm food, roommates, or people who blow smoke in your face, not the destruction of the rain forests. Fourth, make sure your topic is appropriate to the time available. One limitation facing all speakers, not just those in a public speaking class, is time. Know what your instructor expects and stick to it. Further, consider the time you have available to prepare. If the speech is due next week, you won't be able to request a book from inter-library loan. Pick a topic that you can research in the time available. Fifth, make sure your topic is manageable. Don't pick a topic that is beyond your abilities or resources. One of your greatest assets in speaking is your own **credibility,** which is the degree to which your audience trusts and believes in you. Nothing will undermine your credibility faster than speaking on a topic with which you are unfamiliar. Know more than your audience. Why else would you speak to them? Finally, it is crucial that your topic be worthwhile. We treat time in our society as a commodity. We bank time, spend time, and buy time. You are angered if someone wastes your time, so don't waste your audience's time. Pick a topic that will inform, persuade, or entertain the audience by presenting them with ideas or information they haven't already heard. Just as we hate to hear an old joke told over again, we don't like to hear for the umpteenth time that we ought to recycle our aluminum cans, unless the speaker tells us something new and insightful about why we should do just that. If you pick a well-worn topic, then you must give it a different "spin" or focus.

credibility
The degree to which an audience trusts and believes in a speaker.

Speaking of . . .

Brainstorming for Topics

In a group of about three to five people, brainstorm different possible speech topics. During brainstorming the following rules apply:

- The goal is quantity of ideas; even silly ideas should be listed.
- No criticism or evaluation is allowed during the brainstorming process.
- One person is designated to write down every idea. Ideally, write ideas on a chalkboard or an easel so that everyone can see them.
- "Hitchhiking" ideas is encouraged. If you can add to or improve on someone else's idea, do it.
- When you think everyone is out of ideas, try to get at least one more from each group member.
- After all the ideas are listed, go through the list and select the best ones. Look for ideas that fit the assignment, are feasible given the time limits, and would be appropriate for this class. Cross off ideas that don't seem to apply.
- Now rank the remaining ideas in order of value. You may want to modify or combine ideas in this process. Which ones are most promising? How well do these possible topics fit the assignment? Will they be interesting and worthwhile for the members of the class?

Tips and Tactics

Six Criteria for an Appropriate Speech Topic

1. The topic should be interesting to you.
2. It should be interesting to your audience—or at least be capable of being made interesting to them.
3. It should be appropriate to the situation.
4. It should be appropriate to the time available.
5. It should be manageable.
6. It should be worthwhile.

specific purpose
The goal or objective a speaker hopes to achieve in speaking to a particular audience.

To view a video of Jonathan Studebaker's Speech of Introduction, click on the Speech Coach link on our Online Learning Center Web site, and go to Segment 2.1.

Writing Your Specific Purpose Statement

You may be assigned a general purpose—to inform, to persuade, or to entertain—for your early speeches. But you will not be assigned a specific purpose. The **specific purpose** is the goal or objective you hope to achieve in speaking to a particular audience. What you want to accomplish specifically with your audience rests with you. For example, assume you are asked to introduce yourself to the rest of the class. What do you want your classmates to think and feel about you? As the speech in the box "Speech of Introduction" on page 46 shows, one of our former students, Jonathan Studebaker, used the opportunity of a speech of self-introduction to inform his audience about his disability. More than that, however, he sought to educate them to understand that persons with a disability are really just like everybody else. Even in early speech assignments, you should try to articulate a specific purpose for your speech.

The specific purpose of a speech is typically expressed in terms of an infinitive phrase that begins with "to." Specific purposes usually fall under one of the general purposes: to inform, to persuade, or to entertain. If you were to give an informative speech on preventing identity theft, for example, you might express your specific purpose as "to inform my audience about the methods of preventing identity theft." This purpose, however, is somewhat vague. More specifically, you might express it as "to have my audience members demonstrate knowledge of the steps they should take to prevent their identity from being stolen." Because this specific purpose includes a way of measuring your results–by having audience members actually demonstrate the knowledge of how to prevent identity theft–it will point you toward a specific goal. The level of audience understanding should be realistic: One speech cannot make them experts at identity protection, but it should give them the basic steps they need to protect themselves from the most common sources of the problem.

On the same topic, you might have a persuasive purpose, for example, "to convince my audience members to sign up for a monthly credit protection service." A successful speech matching this goal would lead to a number of audience members actually enrolling in the recommended credit protection program. Of course, there is a difference in content as well as purpose between these two speeches. The persuasive speech would require you to compare credit protection services, prices, and ease of use. The informative speech would not. Both speeches would have to explain the threat of identity theft; only the persuasive speech would need to motivate audiences to actually sign up for a credit protection service.

Speeches to entertain have the advantage of instantaneous feedback. Speakers know by the audience's laughter or applause whether they have succeeded. So, a speaker might express a specific entertainment purpose as "to entertain my audience with the story of my worst computer nightmares." It is not necessary to state how you will measure whether this goal has been met because success or failure is immediately evident. Often our students use their storytelling speeches as an opportunity to entertain, as did one student who described his driver's license test with "Scary Larry"–his town's most feared examiner.

As you continue to give speeches in your class, work on developing specific purposes that are realistic, that are worthwhile for the audience, and that fulfill your goals as a speaker. Realistic specific purposes are those that can be accomplished in the brief time you have to present your speech considering the views of the audience you are addressing. For example, you might well motivate your audience to drink alcohol responsibly–something that is noncontroversial for most people. But to convince an audience that disagrees with your point of view to change its opinion on a topic like gun control or abortion is unrealistic. On such topics your specific purpose should be more modest–perhaps to have the audience become more open to your point of view.

Thus, examples of realistic specific purposes for persuasive speeches would include:

- To persuade audience members to avoid binge drinking.
- To persuade audience members to consider that a prison sentence is not always the best punishment for first-time drug offenders.
- To persuade the audience that embryonic stem cell research is or isn't a good idea.

In Their Own Words

Speech of Introduction

In the 35 short years of his life, Jonathan Studebaker had an impressive list of accomplishments: honorary football coach for the East-West Shrine game (pictured here), kicking coach for the Chico State Wildcat football team, college graduate, television sports commentator, member of the Chico city planning commission, writer, motivational speaker, and founder of "Project Speak Out." Speaking was Jonathan's passion. When we interviewed him for the first edition of this book, he put it this way: "Speaking isn't broccoli; it's fun!" In the speech transcribed here, Jonathan introduces himself and explains that he is far more than a person with a disability. Compare the experience of reading this speech with that of viewing it on our Online Learning Center Web site (www.mhhe.com/brydon6); click on the Speech Coach link and go to Segment 2.1.

Our former student, Jonathan Studebaker, is pictured here as honorary coach at the Shrine East-West game.

WHO AM I?

by Jonathan Studebaker

Good morning!

Who am I? Why am I here? Seems like I've heard that before. For myself, I've been asked these and other questions. Two of them I'd like to answer for you today.

I've been asked: "Are you a midget?" "What do you have?" "What's your disability?" "Why are you small?" But I'd really like people to ask me: "What do you like to do?" "What's your favorite color?" So what I'll try to do is answer both of these today.

I'm a nice guy. Don't worry, I won't bite. I like to do many things, except water ski. I've gone to school. I've gone to elementary school, high school, and I graduated from Cal State Chico.

A lot of people ask, "So why are you here?" Well, I'm here because I want to educate others. I've coached football at Chico State University. I was the kicking coach for three years. And out of those three years I had two kickers make first team all-conference. So how do you coach football? You do it by simply telling people what to do. Well, how do you do that? You do it by doing a lot of the things that we all do—by studying, by reading, by listening to others. And that's what I've done throughout my life, and that is what made me who I am.

Like I said, I'm a nice person. I'm cheerful, I'm energetic. Okay, so I have a disability. I was born with osteogenesis imperfecta, a disease which causes my bones to be fragile. Have you ever accidentally dropped a glass on the floor? What happens? It breaks. Well, my bones kind of break like glass, which is why I tell people, when you carry me, treat me like your best crystal.

I'm happy about being who I am. I wouldn't change a thing. I've done a lot of things in my life. Like I said, I've coached football, I graduated from college, things that people wouldn't think a person with my condition would do.

So who am I? Well, I'm Jonathan Studebaker, Jonathan Peter Charles Studebaker. Why such a long name? Well, my middle name is Charles, which came later. And Charles is kind of a symbol of a lot of things. My dad used to call me chicken when I was younger. And then it evolved to chicken Charles, and now Charles. Now, some of you might be offended by being called chicken. But, you know what, it doesn't matter to me. I like being who I am. I've been put here to educate others, not by teaching others, but by just being myself.

Thank you.

For informative speeches, examples of specific purposes would include:

- To explain for my audience the basic principles involved in the Heimlich maneuver.
- To illustrate for my audience how to swing dance.
- To share with my audience knowledge about the earliest contributors to hip-hop culture.

Again, your specific purpose must be realistic. It is one thing to explain the basics of the Heimlich maneuver, and quite another to successfully instruct people in using the maneuver in a brief time without any hands-on practice. You can illustrate the basic steps of swing dancing in a few minutes, but teaching someone to really "swing" takes much longer.

In addition to ensuring that your specific purposes are realistic, make sure they are worthwhile. For example, the Heimlich maneuver can save a life. But unless your audience has some interest in swing or hip-hop, why would audience members be motivated to listen to your speech?

Finally, you need to assess your specific purpose carefully in terms of your own goals. What, exactly, do you want to achieve (other than a passing grade on your speech)? For example, what is your reason for teaching the steps of swing? Do you go swing dancing every Saturday night? Do you want to encourage others to join you? Or are you just a fan of the style, but not a participant? Understanding your own goals can help you write a clear and useful specific purpose.

As you develop your specific purpose, keep in mind these factors and the four guidelines listed in Tips and Tactics.

Tips and Tactics

Guidelines for Refining the Specific Purpose of a Speech

- Describe the results you seek.
- Be as specific as possible.
- Express your goal in measurable terms.
- Set a realistic goal.

Whatever speech topic you select, therefore, you need to clarify in your own mind and for your instructor what specific purpose you intend to achieve through the speech. Make sure the specific purpose is realistic, is worthwhile for your audience, and helps you achieve your own goals as a speaker. It will make what comes next much easier.

Writing Your Thesis Statement

Every speech should have a central idea or point. If you want people to save for their retirement at the earliest age possible, your point might be that doing so can make an early retirement possible. You should be able to express this point in a single declarative sentence. We call this a **thesis statement,** a sentence that focuses your audience's attention on the central point of your speech. A thesis statement should make your central point clear; express your point of view on that point; and, if accepted, fulfill your specific purpose.

thesis statement
A single declarative sentence that focuses the audience's attention on the central point of a speech.

Your thesis statement should help the audience understand what response you seek from them. As a case in point, you might be opposed to further restrictions on what you can do in dorm rooms. Assuming you are speaking to a group of student colleagues, you may wish to focus your speech on what they can do to fight the restrictions. Thus, your thesis statement might be, "We need to lobby the board of trustees of the university to stop this unjustified and harmful plan." Notice that the thesis statement here is directly related to the specific purpose of your speech. In this instance, your specific purpose is "to convince other students to lobby the board of trustees to stop the proposed restrictions." The thesis statement, if accepted and acted upon by the audience, will fulfill your specific purpose. While the specific purpose expresses your goal for the audience's response to the speech, the thesis statement expresses the essential message that is designed to fulfill that purpose.

Although the specific purpose is not normally stated explicitly to the audience, the thesis statement should be sufficiently related to that purpose to allow the audience to know what you want to accomplish. As an example, consider a speech on binge drinking. If your specific purpose was to persuade audience members to drink responsibly, your thesis statement might be, "Binge drinking can destroy lives." Or if you wanted to inform your audience of the basic principles of the Heimlich maneuver, your thesis statement might be, "The Heimlich maneuver involves applying pressure to the victim's diaphragm to expel air from the lungs and thus dislodge what is caught in the throat."

The thesis statement is usually stated in the introduction to the speech. There are some exceptions to this guideline, which will be discussed in later chapters. But as a general rule, letting your audience know your central point is important if you are to fulfill your goals as a speaker.

Even a speech to entertain should have a clear thesis. Obviously, there's no easier way to turn off an audience than to say, "Today I'm going to make you laugh." But it would be logical to say, "First dates are often a disaster, and mine was no different." Unlike a Jon Stewart monologue, which is often just a string of jokes, a speech to entertain should have a clear purpose, thesis, and structure.

Preparing Your Speech

Ancient speakers in Greece and Rome knew that public speaking involved several arts, which were sometimes called the **canons of rhetoric.** First, the orator or speaker had to create the substance of a speech, a process known as **invention.** The material used in the speech had to be arranged to have an effective *organization*. The orator had to choose the best words to convey the message, which was known as the *style* of the speech. Once prepared, the speech had to be learned. Ancient speakers did not use notes or other aids and devoted considerable attention to improving their *memory*. Finally, the speech had to be presented orally to an audience. The *delivery* of the speech to an audience involved using both voice and body effectively. Four of these five canons are taught today in virtually every public speaking class or effective speaking seminar. Although speakers today rarely memorize their speeches, they do need to invent them, organize the content, use an appropriate style, and deliver the speech to an audience. These topics are discussed in more detail in Chapters 8 through 12.

canons of rhetoric
The classical arts of invention, organization, style, memory, and delivery.

invention
The creative process by which the substance of a speech is generated.

It may seem odd, at first, to think of a speech as an invention. However, just as it was not enough for the designers at Apple to have the idea for the iPod, it is not enough for you just to have an idea for a speech. You need to invest time and effort in inventing the substance of what you plan to say. Where do you go for the substance of your speech? Here are some general suggestions, which we develop in more detail in Chapter 8.

Personal Experience

As we noted in discussing topic selection, begin with your own experiences. Each of us has had experiences that make us unique. You may be able to rely on hobbies or past job experiences for an early informative speech; for example, one of our students who worked as a beekeeper gave a fascinating speech on honey bees.

Speaking about matters with which you have firsthand experience connects you to your message. What's more, this personal connection may also tell you how to connect your message to the personal and professional needs of your audience. For example, a successful actress, who was enrolled in one of the author's classes at the University of Southern California, gave a speech on how to break into "show biz." Unfortunately, she failed to mention her own experience, which included a role in a Clint Eastwood movie and a recurring role on a television sitcom. Had she done so, her speech would have connected more effectively to the audience, in effect saying, "If I can do this, so can you!"

Even though your personal experience and knowledge are good sources with which to start, don't stop there. No matter how intense your experience or extensive your knowledge, there is always more to learn. In the effort to augment personal experience and knowledge, consult other sources as well.

Outside Sources

When we are given a topic to research, most of us head immediately for our computer and access a free search engine such as Google. For example, when we typed the words "public speaking" into the Google search engine, we received over 78 million "hits" in less than a second–far too many to be useful. That's why you will find numerous "sponsored" links on Google which are actually ads paid for by Web sites to get you to click on their link. Furthermore, there's no easy way to distinguish between reliable and valid sites, and those that are just popular. We won't discourage you from "googling" your topic, but we do want you to go beyond Google in this class.

One of the great benefits of being a college student is that you have resources available to you for research purposes that go beyond those available to the average person. For example, not only do you have access to a physical library, housing thousands–perhaps millions–of books, periodicals, and documents, you may also have access to innumerable proprietary computer resources. For instance, many students have access to databases such as *Academic Search,* which indexes over four thousand periodicals covering everything from the sciences and humanities to popular culture. Those students may also have access to electronic databases, such as *LexisNexis,* which enables them to search newspapers, magazines, and legal articles.

Of course, we cannot give you specific advice for your institution, since every college library is different. However, we can give you some general advice to help you find information for your speeches. In Chapter 8 we will cover this in much more detail. But for now, here are some good sources to consider for researching your speeches.

Consider your library's collection of books and periodicals. Depending on your topic, there may be several published books readily available that will assist you. Keep in mind that books may have a long lead-time before they are published. Thus, on topics that require up-to-date information, you need to rely on more recent sources, such as periodicals, rather than books. A speech on why the United States got involved in the Vietnam War, for example, might well rely on books and encyclopedias, whereas a speech on the current situation in the Middle East would require the most recent sources available. Not only do most libraries have magazines and newspapers to which they subscribe, many also have computerized databases for accessing them. If your library lacks this access, consider using Google News, which has numerous links to newspapers throughout the world. You can also subscribe to the online version of many major newspapers. For example, *The New York Times* and *Los Angeles Times* online are free, although you need to register with them, as with many such publications. Beware, however, that older articles on many news sites require you to pay to access them. Thus a library database, such as *LexisNexis,* may save you money.

Other online sources readily available to students and non-students alike include blogs and wikis. However, as you probably know, anyone can start a blog and wikis rely on their users to add and edit content. The very openness of these sites means that false or misleading information can easily find its way online. When you use such "open Internet" sources, you need to be especially careful that the source of the information is actually credible–something we address in detail in Chapter 8. Conspiracy theories abound on the Internet, from those who claim we never really landed on the moon to others who assert the World Trade Center collapse was an inside job. Be particularly careful about quoting anonymous sources from the Internet.

Another sad fact of life is that the Internet has made cheating easier to do. On the other hand, it has also made cheating easier to detect. Cutting and pasting from the Internet is easy, but if you don't tell your audience the words are quoted and where you found them, you are guilty of plagiarism–a serious academic offense we discuss at length in Chapter 5. Here we want to focus on the fact that if you can find it on the Internet, so can your teacher. We have had the experience of reading a student speech outline and thinking, "this just doesn't sound like it was written by a student." A quick Google search often locates the exact source of the plagiarism. There are two ways to avoid this problem. First, when you copy things from the Internet, be sure to also copy down the source. Second, when you present the material, be clear when the words are quoted, and orally tell the audience where you got the material. So, for example, you might say, "According to the Environmental Protection Agency's Web site, which I accessed on Oct. 29, 2006, 'A warming trend of about 0.7 to 1.5°F occurred during the 20th century. Warming occurred in both the Northern and Southern Hemispheres, and over the oceans.'"[2] Incidentally, this not only will avoid plagiarism, but you make your case stronger because you are citing an authoritative source.

Finally you may be able to interview an expert on the topic of your speech. You may not have to look any further than the other classes you are taking. An interview with an environmental science instructor, for example, could not only give you quotations from an expert about global warming, but also might point you to other sources you would not have found on your own. However, do not expect the person you interview to do your job for you. Be sure to prepare in advance for the interview. Chapter 8 has specific tips to assist you in interviewing sources for your speech.

Tips and Tactics

Resources for Your Speech

1. Begin with your own experiences.
2. Look to outside sources of information:
   a. Search general sources of information, such as books and periodicals.
   b. Conduct computerized searches.
   c. Interview experts.

Regardless of where you find your information, whether from written sources, the Internet, or interviews, remember to carefully record the facts and quotations you discover. Note not only what was said but also who said it, when, and where. Documenting your evidence for an audience will build your credibility, which will enhance the likelihood you will be effective in delivering your speech.

Organizing Your Speech

Someone once said that every speech has three tell 'ems. First you tell 'em what you are going to tell 'em; then you tell 'em; and, finally, you tell 'em what you told 'em. Although a bit simplistic, this captures the basic idea of the three parts of every speech: the introduction, the body, and the conclusion.

Though there are many ways to organize your speech, one of the most helpful patterns we have found for our own students is an adaptation of a system developed by Dr. Loretta Malandro for the business executives she coaches.[3] According to Dr. Malandro, the traditional introduction, body, and conclusion of a speech should include several important steps. Steps 1–4 are the introduction, step 5 is the body of the speech, and steps 6 and 7 are the conclusion.

Tips and Tactics

Seven Steps for Organizing Your Speech

1. *Open with impact.* In this step you capture your audience's attention.
2. *Focus on your thesis statement.* In this step you draw the audience's attention to the central point of your speech.

3. *Connect with your audience.* In this step you let the audience know "what's in it for them."
4. *Preview the body of your speech.* This is where you tell your audience what you are going to tell them in the body of the speech.
5. *Present your main points.* In this step you present the body of your speech. This step constitutes the bulk of your presentation.
6. *Summarize your main points.* In this step you tell the audience what you've told them.
7. *Close with impact.* In this step you leave your audience with a lasting impression.

To help you prepare your speech outline, go to our Online Learning Center Web site and click on the Outline Tutor link.

Let's briefly examine each of these steps and how they relate to the traditional introduction–body–conclusion format of a speech. This relationship is illustrated in Exhibit 3.1.

Introduction

Although you will present the introduction first, in actually writing your speech you normally begin with the body or main points. It is difficult to know how to best introduce a speech before you write it. What follows, therefore, is the order of presentation, not the order of preparation of your speech. To present an effective introduction, you should follow four steps.

Open With Impact

Introduce your presentation dramatically or humorously. There's no surer turn-off than beginning a speech, "Uh, um, well, I guess I'll talk about dorm food today." Begin the speech with something that captures your audience's attention, such as an appropriate joke, a startling statistic, an anecdote, or a reference to current affairs.

Tips and Tactics

Ways to Open Your Speech With Impact

1. Tell a brief story.
2. Use a quotation.
3. Make a startling statement.
4. Refer to the audience, the occasion, or a current event.
5. Use appropriate humor.
6. Relate a personal experience.
7. Ask a thought-provoking question.

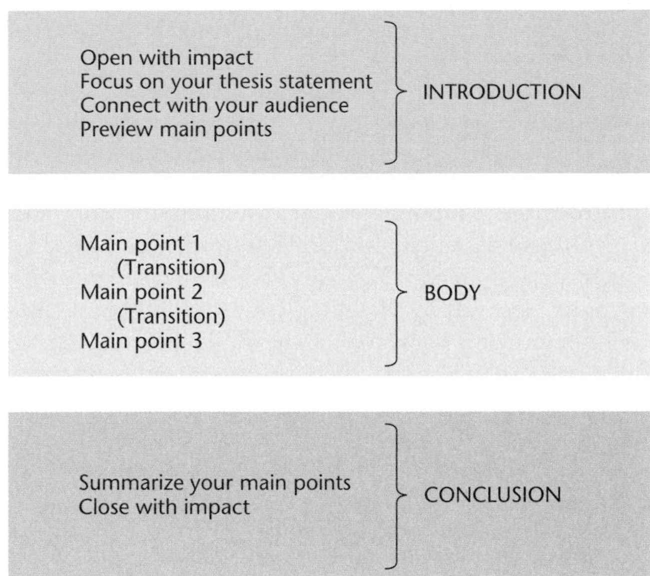

Exhibit 3.1
Organizing Your Speech
This seven-step organizational pattern relates closely to the traditional introduction–body–conclusion pattern.

Focus on Your Thesis Statement

As we noted earlier, the thesis statement captures the central point of your speech. For example, if you are opposed to a planned tuition hike on your campus, you should state clearly, "The students of this campus should not be forced to pay more for less." On the other hand, you might want to inform your audience about the types of financial assistance available to them: "With effort and persistence, you can obtain a student loan or scholarship to help meet your college expenses."

Connect With Your Audience

Answer the questions "What's in this for my audience?" and "Why is it in their personal or professional interest to listen to me?" For example, will the proposed tuition hike keep some in your audience from completing their degrees? Make the connection to your specific audience clear in the introduction to the speech. This is also a good place to build your credibility as a speaker. Let the audience know you understand their concerns and have their best interests at heart. If you have expertise on the topic, let your audience know this now so that they can appreciate what is to come.

Preview

Generally, people like a map of the territory they're entering. The **preview** provides your audience with a map to where you are taking them. It forecasts the **main points** of a speech. Although a preview of points is generally a good idea, there may be exceptions. Had Montana Kellmer previewed the main points of his storytelling speech, for example it would have destroyed the impact of his

preview
A forecast of the main points of a speech.

main points
The key ideas that support the thesis statement of a speech.

surprise ending (see pages 56–57). Depending on the nature of the assignment, therefore, your first speech may not require a preview.

In most of your speeches, however, a preview helps prepare the audience for what follows. You should mention all your main points briefly before treating each one in detail. This is the "tell 'em what you're going to tell 'em" part of the speech. It may be as simple as saying, "I'm going to present three ways to save money on your groceries: clipping coupons, watching for store ads, and buying generic brands." On the other hand, a preview may specifically enumerate the three main points of the speech: "You can save money on your groceries, first, by clipping coupons; second, by watching for store ads; and third, by buying generic brands." The preview helps reduce the audience's uncertainty about what is to follow, and it helps them see the relationship among your various points.

Body

The majority of your speech should develop the thesis you are trying to convey. Usually, the body of the speech is divided into three to five main points that together develop the thesis of your speech.

Organize Your Main Points

A speech that wanders off the topic or whose main points don't follow a logical pattern of development is likely to lose the audience. The same is true of an overly complex speech. Here are some basic patterns for organizing your main points:

To view a video of Montana Kellmer's Storytelling Speech, click on the Speech Coach link on our Online Learning Center Web site, and go to Segment 2.2.

- *Time pattern.* Most stories are arranged chronologically. The use of a narrative or time pattern is one of the most basic forms of speech making. In fact, one of our former professors, Walter R. Fisher, has argued that humans are storytelling animals. In the box "Storytelling Speech," you will see how one of our students, Montana Kellmer, used time in an unusual way to tell his story. Rather than beginning at the beginning, he began part-way through his story, and then used a flashback to tell the audience how he got to that point. He then took us forward from that point to the story's conclusion and its implications for how all of us lead our own lives. You can read his speech on pages 56–57 and view it on our Online Learning Center Web site (www.mhhe.com/brydon6).
- *Spatial pattern.* Some topics are best dealt with spatially. A speech on the solar system might begin with the sun and work out to the most distant planets.
- *Categorical pattern.* Many topics fall into obvious categories. A teacher explaining the federal government to a civics class, for example, is likely to talk about the legislative, judicial, and executive branches. This is sometimes called a topical pattern of organization. If a topic lends itself to natural divisions, this is an excellent way to arrange your speech.

These three ways to organize a speech are summarized in Exhibit 3.2. Other ways to organize a speech are discussed at length in Chapter 10. For now, this will give you a start. The key thing to remember in this regard is to pick a simple pattern and stick with it for the entire speech.

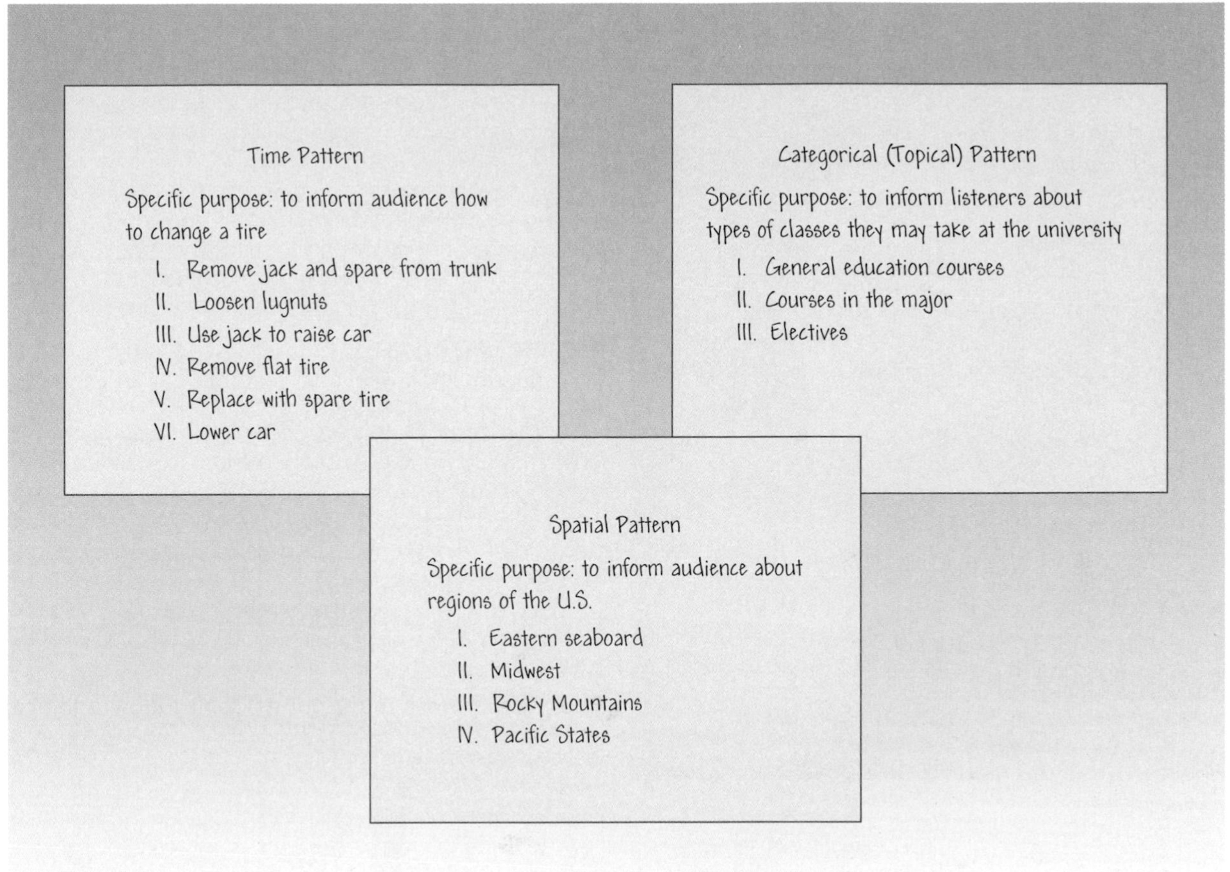

Exhibit 3.2
Common Patterns for Organizing the Main Points of a Speech

Provide Transitions

We also want to emphasize the importance of using transitional statements, such as **signposts,** that bridge your main points. For example, you might say something as simple as, "My second point is . . ." or "Now that you understand the problem, let's examine some possible solutions." The goal in using transitions is to provide your audience with guides along the path of your speech so that they will know where you have been, where you are, and where you are going next.

signposts
Transitional statements that bridge main points.

Conclusion

All too often, speakers invest so much energy in developing the introduction and body of their speeches that they run out of gas at the end. The impact with which you conclude a speech is just as important as the impact with which you began.

In Their Own Words

Storytelling Speech

Montana Kellmer

The best speeches tell a story with a purpose in mind. As you read this speech, ask yourself what the speaker's purposes were. How did his story impact you in terms of your own life experiences? This transcript was prepared from a video of Montana's speech. Compare the experience of reading this speech with that of viewing it on our Online Learning Center Web site (www.mhhe.com/brydon6); click on the Speech Coach link and go to Segment 2.2.

MOVING FORWARD
by Montana Kellmer

"Fourth and goal, six seconds left, let's do this guys, it's our last shot. [Inaudible] 24 crossbow pass, on one, it's coming to you, ready, break!" I walk up to the line, put my hands under the center, check to see if everyone's set, call off the cadence: "Down, six, hut!" I take the snap, drop back to pass; the whole world fades to black.

Let's back up 14 years. "Where you going dad?" "Son, I gotta go." "Where you going dad?" "Son, I have to leave." My parents split up when I was 3 years old. While most kids were worrying about what time Cookie Monster was coming on, when mommy was bringing home cookies, all I wanted to know was when my father was coming back.

My family had three custody battles. Each cost them $30,000 apiece. That's a total of $90,000. Money wasn't the biggest issue, though. It was the head games. I'm 9 years old, my father comes to me and tells me he's not going to talk to me if I live with my mother. My mom comes to me and asks me to pick. I'm 9 years old, how am I supposed to choose which parent I want to live with? I love them both equally.

Summarize Your Main Points

Tell 'em what you've told 'em. That is the first and most important function of a conclusion. Remind the listeners of what they've heard.

Close With Impact

Just as a salesperson doesn't like the customer to walk out the door without buying something, you don't want your audience to leave without at least thinking about doing what you've asked them to do. So, find a way to reinforce your specific purpose. It's also your last chance to leave a favorable impression. Just as listeners are turned off by an introduction that begins "Today I want to tell you about . . . ," you can undermine the effectiveness of an excellent speech with a poor conclusion, such as "Well, I guess that's about it." Finish with a flourish that is as powerful as your opening.

Some time passes and a sad little boy grows into an angry young man. Adolescence comes. I'm hurt, lonely, and confused, and now it has all led to rage. I turn to baseball and football to deal with my anger. I'm doing pretty well. Pretty proud of myself—I'm starting on both teams. It's pretty fun, but there's some problems. I started drinking when I was 13; started drinking pretty heavily; and now I'm 17. Grades have gone down; I'm getting in a lot of fights. I actually recall this one time I was walking down the hall, someone said something about my mother, I didn't let it slip for 2 seconds out of their mouth. I slammed his head into a pole. He began to slide down. Worst thing about it was that I started laughing at him. He was unconscious. I had an apathetic attitude; I didn't care. I was tired of the hurt, tired of the pain, and tired of the confusion. I didn't feel anything anymore.

Back to where we started. What had happened was, junior year, I was playing in a football game and dropped back to pass and I had a heart attack. They're loading me into the ambulance and all I could hear was, "Stay with me kid," slap me in the face, "stay with me kid," slap me in the face. And they brought out those paddles. Clear, boom, nothing. Clear, boom, the whole world was fading to white. What was happening was I was dying. For the first time I felt at home with myself, at peace, this mess was over. I could move on.

This turned my life around. Coming out of the hospital, I looked in the mirror and realized what I was doing to myself. Told myself, Montana, you can no longer hold this against yourself. Get over it, move past it, and move on. And I did.

If one good thing came out of all this, it's my independence. Growing up, I grew up by myself and I learned to be an independent young man. I set goals and I attained them. If I see something I want, I usually get it. I walked through fire twice, once when I was 3 years old and once when I was 17. What hasn't killed me has only made me stronger.

Forgiving is easy, forgetting is harder. But I feel I have. Abe Lincoln once said, "People are just as happy as they want to be." I firmly believe that. Don't let the emotions get the best of you. Just remember when you wake up and you're having a rough day, and you look in that mirror, and you feel like the whole world has let you down, you feel like you can't go on any longer. Just realize it's never too late to turn yourself around. Get back on that horse and keep riding. Thank you.

Tips and Tactics

Ways to Close Your Speech Effectively

- Present a short, memorable *quotation*.
- Use an *anecdote* or a brief *story* that illustrates your point and leaves a lasting impression on your audience.
- Make a *direct appeal* or "call to action."
- *Return to your opening.* This is one of the best ways to end a speech because it brings the listeners full circle.

So, conclude your speech by *summarizing* your main points and *closing with impact.*

Presenting Your Speech

There's a story told about the great speaker of ancient Greece, Demosthenes, who said that the first, second, and third most important things in rhetoric were—delivery, delivery, and delivery.[4] Although the story is probably apocryphal, it does illustrate the importance of effective delivery. No matter how well thought out your speech, or how many hours you put in at the library, or how elegant your outline, unless the speech is effectively presented, your message will not have its desired impact. In Chapter 12 we deal at length with the nature of delivery, including the important functions nonverbal communication serves for a speaker. In the meantime, the following guidelines will help you present your beginning speeches.

Keep in mind that you have three tools as a public speaker: your *voice,* your *face and eyes,* and your *body.* If you manage these effectively, you will be able to get your message across to your audience.

Use Your Voice Effectively

How you use your voice is critical to effective communication. Some basic guidelines will enable you to speak most effectively.

Speak Conversationally

Think of public speaking as heightened conversation. Don't attempt to emulate political orators: Most audiences are put off by their techniques. Speak as you do in conversation, but enlarge your voice sufficiently to be heard by all in the room. Avoid shouting. This not only strains your voice but can alienate your audience. It is certainly appropriate and even advisable to ask those in the back of the room if they can hear you, should there be any doubt.

Vary Your Voice

Nothing is more deadly to a speech than a monotone voice. Vary the rate at which you speak, the pitch (high or low) at which you speak, and the volume (loudness). The goal is to present your speech enthusiastically, sincerely, and energetically. Let the audience know you care about your topic and them.

Use Your Face and Eyes Effectively

The face is one of the most complex and expressive parts of our anatomy, capable of communicating thousands of messages. Use your facial expression to reinforce your verbal message. The eyes, in particular, convey a great deal. Consider a person who gazes at you without pause. This will tend to make you uncomfortable. On the other hand, in our North American culture, a person who refuses to look at us communicates a negative message. (In some other cultures, such as certain Asian societies, no such negative message is communicated by avoiding eye contact.) As a speaker communicating to a North American audience, therefore, maintain eye contact. This does not mean staring at just one portion of the room or shifting your eyes randomly. Rather, look at one member of your audience, then shift your gaze to another member, and so on. Be alert for audience responses to what you are saying. Are they restless, interested, puzzled? Such feedback can help you adapt to the audience as you speak.

Use Your Body Effectively

Your body is the third tool you use to communicate your message. Your body communicates to your audience through *posture, movement, gestures,* and *dress.*

Posture

How do you want to stand during your speech? Some speakers are comfortable behind a lectern, whereas others prefer to move away from it or dispense with it entirely. Choosing not to use a lectern can be an effective way of lessening the physical and psychological distance between yourself and the audience. If your preference is to use a lectern, do not use it as a crutch or bass drum. Avoid leaning on or clutching the stand, as well as beating on it with your open palm. Instead, find a comfortable, erect posture and stand slightly behind the lectern. Keep in mind that to breathe effectively you need to have good body posture.

Movement

Movement should be spontaneous and meaningful. Though good speakers avoid pacing and random movements, it is perfectly appropriate–in fact, desirable–to move to emphasize an important idea or a transition between points. There is no reason a speaker's feet have to be nailed to the floor. Use your body to communicate your message whenever possible.

Gestures

It is common in everyday conversation to gesture with your hands. In fact, try this experiment: Give someone directions from your school to your home *without* moving your hands. You will find it virtually impossible. The key to effective use of gestures in a public speech is that they should be appropriate to the point you are making and clearly visible to your audience. The larger the room, the larger the gesture needs to be for your audience to see it. On the other hand, too many gestures, especially if they appear to be the result of nervousness, such as fidgeting, can be distracting to an audience. Finally, your gestures should be natural extensions of what you do in everyday conversation. They should never be or appear to be forced or rehearsed.

Dress

Your dress as a speaker should be *appropriate* to the situation and the audience. A good rule of thumb is business casual in a classroom. As you can see in the photos on page 60, business casual is a step above what you normally might wear to class, but a step below more formal dress. People make instant judgments about other people and, as one shampoo ad proclaims, "You never get a second chance

A good rule of thumb for classroom speeches is to dress in business casual attire.

to make a first impression." In no case should your dress detract from the message you want to convey.

Methods of Delivery

There are four common ways to deliver a speech:

- Write out a *manuscript* and read it to your audience.
- *Memorize* your speech and recite it from memory.
- Present a spontaneous, unrehearsed *impromptu* presentation.
- Combine preparation and spontaneity in an *extemporaneous* presentation.

Each type of delivery has its advantages and limitations.

Manuscript Delivery

manuscript delivery A mode of presentation that involves writing out a speech completely and reading it to the audience.

When a speaker uses **manuscript delivery,** the speech is written out completely and read to the audience. Few speakers are very good at reading a speech. In fact, except for politicians and other officials who rely on ghostwriters to prepare their speeches, most of us will not have occasion to give a manuscript speech.

Though it might seem easy to write out your speech in advance and read it to the audience, this is easier said than done. One disadvantage of written speeches is that most people don't write as they speak. Speeches delivered from a manuscript can have an artificial quality. Sentences are often too long and complex. The audience loses track of the point being made. "Oral essays" tend not to be an effective way to communicate with an audience.

If the manuscript pages get out of order or some are missing, you may be forced to improvise or stop your speech altogether. Most teachers have had the painful experience of watching a speaker fumble for words as he or she looks frantically for the next page of the speech. Overreliance on a manuscript can lead to such embarrassing moments.

Another disadvantage of manuscript delivery is that you lose eye contact with your audience. Not only does this inhibit feedback, it reduces your contact with the audience, which, as we will see later, is a major factor in establishing your credibility as a speaker.

The principal situation in which you will want to deliver a speech from a manuscript is if it is critical that you be quoted accurately. For example, public officials usually speak from a manuscript to ensure that they are accurately quoted in the media, to which copies are usually provided. For your first speeches, however, you should avoid the manuscript speech.

This speaker loses eye contact with the audience by looking down at note cards.

Memorized Delivery

An alternative to reading a speech is to memorize it. **Memorized delivery** is a mode of presentation in which the speech is written out and committed to memory before being presented to the audience without the use of notes. This method of delivery eliminates the problems associated with maintaining eye contact. And, presumably, an able speaker can quickly drop a section of a memorized speech should time run short. But, on the whole, memorized speeches today are confined to the theater and speech tournaments. The reason is simple: Memorization requires an enormous investment of time for even a brief speech. Further, if you forget the speech, you are faced with either a very noticeable silence or "winging it." Finally, memorized speeches usually sound memorized. They are simply oral essays without the physical manuscript.

memorized delivery
A mode of presentation in which a speech is written out and committed to memory before being presented to the audience without the use of notes.

Impromptu Delivery

A spontaneous, unrehearsed mode of presenting a speech is termed **impromptu delivery.** We are frequently called on to give impromptu speeches, although we usually don't think of them as speeches. For example, when your instructor calls on you to explain the day's reading assignment–or when you explain to your bank why you really aren't overdrawn–you are making an impromptu speech. In fact, most of our everyday conversations are spontaneous.

impromptu delivery
A spontaneous, unrehearsed mode of presenting a speech.

Nevertheless, for most speaking situations, the impromptu method of speaking is of limited usefulness. Even experienced public speakers usually have "canned" or set pieces on which they rely when they are called on to make impromptu presentations. For example, candidates for public office prepare for their debates and press conferences for days beforehand. Every conceivable question is asked in rehearsal, and possible answers are practiced.

For beginning speakers, impromptu speeches should be approached as a learning tool to enhance the principles that apply to other speeches. To rely on impromptu speeches for all of your assignments is not wise.

Impromptu speaking is discussed in more detail in Chapter 12, but here are a few pointers to keep in mind if you are called on to give an impromptu presentation early in the semester.

Tips and Tactics — Making an Impromptu Presentation

- Think about what basic point you want to make about the topic. Are you for or against it? If you don't know, you might list the pros and cons of the issue and let the audience reach its own conclusion. If you are not informed on the topic, try linking it to something on which you do have information.
- Think of one or more points that support your position.
- If you have time, think of an attention-getter as an introduction.
- State your topic in the introduction: It buys you time and then you are sure the audience knows what you are saying.
- As a conclusion, summarize what you've said.

If you do not have time to organize your thoughts, at least take a moment to think of your thesis and two or three main points. Believe it or not, in a few seconds you can organize a fairly decent impromptu speech. We engage in spontaneous conversations all the time. Thinking and speaking are not mutually exclusive.

Extemporaneous Delivery

extemporaneous delivery
A mode of presentation that combines careful preparation with spontaneous speaking. The speaker generally uses brief notes rather than a full manuscript or an outline.

The best mode of presentation for most beginning speakers is **extemporaneous delivery,** which combines careful preparation with spontaneous speaking. The speaker generally uses brief notes rather than a manuscript or an outline. Some instructors require students to first outline their speech in a formal way, in which case the outline should serve as a preparatory tool, not an abbreviated speech manuscript. Other instructors require only that students prepare note cards to help them recall their main and supporting points. (For an example of a speaker's note cards, see Exhibit 3.3.) Practicing the speech in advance allows you to fix the ideas in your head without memorizing the exact wording.

The extemporaneous method allows you to be prepared yet flexible. If you see from the audience feedback that people are disagreeing with you, you can re-explain a point or add another example. If the audience seems bored, you might skip ahead to your most interesting example. Most teachers employ an extemporaneous method when lecturing to their classes. Students are invited to interact with their instructor, ask questions, and perhaps challenge a point. An extemporaneous speech should be a true transaction between speaker and listener.

INTRO #1

I. Football game
   A. Call the play
   B. Drop back to pass
   C. World fades to black

(Transition: Let's back up 14 years)

BODY #2

I. Where are you going, Dad?
   A. Family splits up when I was 3
   B. $90,000 in custody fights
   C. At 9 asked to choose one parent

(Transition: Time passes, I grow into angry young man)

#3

II. Adolescence
   A. Baseball and football
   B. Start drinking at 13
   C. Beat someone unconscious for insult

(Transition: Back to where we started)

#4

III. Football game
   A. I had heart attack
   B. Loaded into ambulance—"stay with us kid"
   C. Paddles
   D. I was dying

(Transition: This changed my life)

CONCLUSION #5

I. Get over it—move on
   A. What doesn't kill me only makes me stronger
   B. Abe Lincoln: "People are just as happy as they want to be."

II. When things seem rough, get back on that horse and keep riding.

Exhibit 3.3

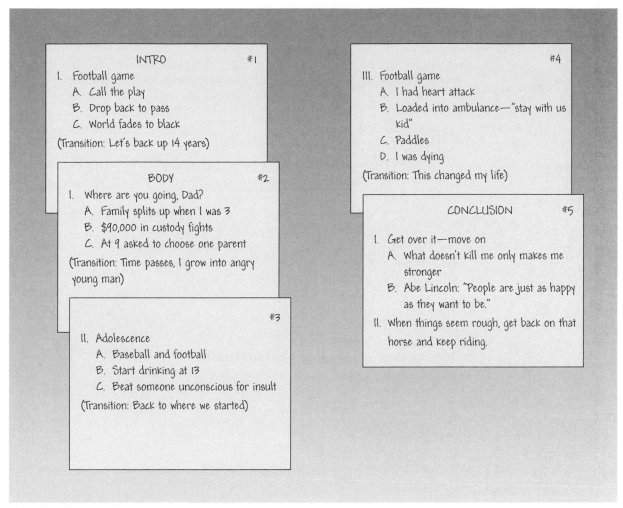

Speaker's Note Cards

These notes correspond to Montana Kellmer's speech found on pages 56–57.

Summary

To evaluate your understanding of this chapter, visit our Online Learning Center Web site for quizzes and other chapter study aids.

Given the preceding framework, commitment, and practice, you should be able to comfortably prepare and present your first speech.

The essential steps in developing an effective speech are to:

- Analyze the situation with which you are faced, including both the nature of your assignment and the audience.
- Decide on a general purpose.
- Choose a topic that is suitable to both the situation and the audience.

- Formulate a specific purpose.
- Write a clear thesis statement.
- Prepare the substance of your speech.
- Organize your speech.
- Present your speech effectively.

There are many ways to come up with an appropriate topic, including:

- Making a personal inventory
- Talking to friends
- Reading widely
- Checking the Internet
- Brainstorming

An appropriate speech topic should be:

- Interesting to you
- Interesting to your audience
- Appropriate to the situation
- Appropriate to the time available
- Manageable
- Worthwhile

The primary function of a speech is expressed as a general purpose:

- To inform
- To persuade
- To entertain

A specific purpose describes your goal or objective in speaking to a particular audience.

The thesis statement focuses your audience's attention on the central point you wish to make in your speech.

Resources for preparing your speech include:

- Your own experiences
- General sources of information
- Computerized searches
- Interviews with experts

A clearly organized speech:

- Opens with impact
- Focuses on your thesis statement
- Connects with your audience

- Previews your main points
- Organizes your ideas with three to five main points
- Summarizes your main points
- Closes with impact

Common organizational patterns include:

- Time
- Spatial
- Categorical

Transitional statements, including signposts, make organization clear.

In presenting your speech use your voice, face, and body.

Of the four methods of speech delivery, we recommend the extemporaneous method.

Check Your Understanding: Exercises and Activities

1. Write a one- or two-page analysis of the audience for your first speech. What characteristics do your classmates seem to have in common? Are they similar to or dissimilar from you in age, social status, and background? What assumptions can you make about them based on their attendance at your university or college? How will what you know about your classmates affect your choice of speech topic and specific purpose?
2. Come up with three possible topics for your first speech. For each topic, consider whether it is (a) interesting to you, (b) interesting to your audience, (c) appropriate to the situation, (d) appropriate to the time available, (e) manageable, and (f) worthwhile. Based on this analysis, which topic do you believe is best for your first speech?
3. Once you have selected the best topic, determine what general purpose it would fulfill and phrase a specific purpose that you would hope to achieve in presenting the speech.
4. Make a list of appropriate sources for information about the topic you have chosen for your first speech.
5. Using the format discussed in this chapter, prepare an outline that organizes your speech so that it (a) opens with impact, (b) focuses on your thesis statement, (c) connects with your audience, (d) previews your main points, (e) organizes your ideas with three to five main points, (f) summarizes your main points, and (g) closes with impact.
6. View a speech on video and then read a transcript of the speech. Both of the speeches transcribed in this chapter are at SpeechCoach online. After both reading and viewing the speech, write a short paper that answers the following questions: (a) What seemed to be the greatest strength of this speech? (b) What seemed to be the greatest weakness of this speech? (c) What differences did you note between reading a transcript of the speech and actually seeing the speech delivered?

Notes

1. Mile Square Toastmasters Club (2006), *www.milesquare.org.* [Retrieved from http://www.milesquare.org/appiesnet/appieskb/kb1/index.cgi?SHOW+11+Top%20Questions, 28 October 2006.]
2. U.S. Environmental Protection Agency, *State of Knowledge,* 19 October 2006 [Retrieved from http://www.epa.gov/climatechange/science/stateofknowledge.html, 29 October 2006.]
3. The formula was originally developed by Dr. Loretta Malandro and is taught in her program "Speak With Impact," offered by Malandro Communication Inc., Scottsdale, Arizona. We have modified it to add a preview to the introduction.
4. George Kennedy, *The Art of Persuasion in Greece* (Princeton, N.J.: Princeton University Press, 1963), 283.

Understanding Communication Apprehension

Jeff Butler

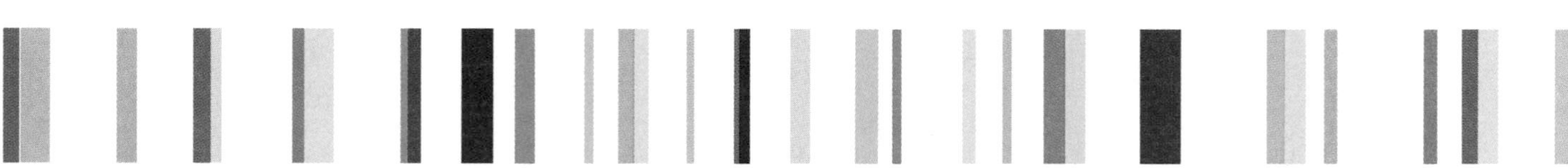

Objectives  

After reading this chapter, you should be able to:

- Understand the differences between normal anxiety and communication apprehension.
- Identify and explain the four potential causes of communication apprehension.
- Understand how culture can affect a person's level of communication apprehension.
- Identify the current research findings regarding high communication apprehension and academics.
- Understand and use the skills that have been shown to reduce the effects of communication apprehension.

Key Concepts  

collectivistic cultures
communication apprehension
communibiology
cultural factors
environmental reinforcers
generalized anxiety
genetic contributors
individualistic cultures
kinesics
learned helplessness
negative self-talk
positive self-talk
proactive imagination
self-talk

"No one can make you feel inferior without your consent."

—ELEANOR ROOSEVELT

Normal Speaker Anxiety

This chapter is about a common phobia called communication apprehension. Before discussing details about this phobia, it's important that we distinguish between normal anxiety and communication apprehension.

Most people, even experienced speakers, feel some anxiety before (or during) a speech. This anxiety often takes the form of "butterflies" in your stomach, a quaver in your voice, or adrenaline-induced symptoms such as trembling hands or increased heart rate. These symptoms are usually comparatively mild and typically diminish during your speech. They're a bit like the chill you feel when you first jump into the water when you go swimming. It's a little uncomfortable at first, but the discomfort fades quickly. Most of the American population experiences some form of this mild anxiety when they give a speech. If you think these symptoms are similar to how you feel before and during a speech, then you probably are experiencing normal levels of anxiety about speaking. If that's the case, then the rest of this chapter is important to you for informative and educational reasons, but it's not discussing something you've actually experienced.

Even if you don't experience communication apprehension yourself, you will encounter people who do. Consequently, the rest of this chapter should prove valuable because it promotes an understanding of communication apprehension. Such an understanding is important for two reasons. First, we often discount other people's phobias. A common reaction to another person's report of extreme nervousness about speaking is the reply, "Oh yeah, I get nervous, too." Non-phobic speakers who make this or a similar response often think they feel the same way as a genuine apprehensive, but they don't. Think of your own worst phobia (for me, it's fear of heights). Perhaps you're afraid of flying, or snakes, or clowns. The stark terror these phobias inspire in affected persons is the same way most high apprehensives feel about giving speeches. It's not mild anxiety; it's gut-wrenching fear, and people who are not apprehensive need to understand how truly traumatic that fear is.

Second, forcing someone who is phobic about speaking to give speeches can actually increase the intensity of their phobia. This is important in light of another common response to persons who experience communication apprehension. Often, victims of apprehension are urged to "just get up there and do it." While this sort of sink-or-swim approach may work for some activities, it usually doesn't work for high apprehensives and can make the apprehension worse. I often wonder how much damage has been caused by well-intentioned instructors who forced apprehensive students to "get up there like everyone else." High apprehension can often be overcome through the use of techniques discussed later in this chapter, but forcing someone to speak when they're afraid is ineffective and often counterproductive.

What Is Communication Apprehension?

communication apprehension
Fear and avoidance of communication with other people.

Communication apprehension (CA) is a type of anxiety that involves the fear and avoidance of communication with other people (McCroskey, 1993). It's widespread, with various surveys identifying components of CA, such as fear of public speaking, as the most common phobia in the United States (Motley, 1997). Millions of Americans experience some form of CA. In fact, about 16% of the American population experiences anxiety based on high levels of communication apprehension (Daly & McCroskey, 1984).

Communication apprehension has many forms. For example, some people don't usually feel nervous about speaking, but may find a specific situation threatening. Such a person might normally feel comfortable talking with a supervisor, but would be anxious about conversing with that supervisor during an annual evaluation. Others might be relaxed during normal conversations but experience anxiety about a forthcoming public speech. In contrast to these situation-specific forms of CA, other people experience **generalized anxiety** about almost all communication in almost all settings with almost all people (Daly & McCroskey, 1984). This generalized anxiety is regarded as the most serious form of CA.

generalized anxiety
Feelings of anxiety associated with communication in nearly all situations with almost all people.

Because your current course requires public speaking, this chapter will focus primarily on anxiety related to oral presentations, but please remember this fear is only one aspect of the phenomenon we label "communication apprehension." In other words, CA is not just a new term for "stage fright." It encompasses more than a fear of public speaking, even though that is what this chapter emphasizes.

What Are the Causes of Communication Apprehension?

The cause of communication apprehension is the subject of considerable debate among communication scholars. Although individual researchers may support certain potential causes and disagree with others, most would agree that the available evidence centers around four potential causes: genetic contributors, environmental reinforcers, personality traits, and cultural factors.

Genetic Contributors

Researchers subscribing to **communibiology** suggest that CA may have a predominantly hereditary basis. Citing studies of identical twins who were raised together and comparing them with identical twins who were separated at birth, they have discovered commonalities in personality and behavior which suggest people may inherit preferences (temperaments) to behave in certain ways. Temperament traits don't mandate specific behaviors (you aren't genetically destined for a certain occupation, for example), but combinations of inherited proclivities may exert powerful influences on our behavioral preferences. A person who inherits a tendency to be high in extraversion and low in self-doubt, for example, is unlikely to experience CA, while someone who has inherited high introversion and high self-doubt has a higher probability of feeling anxiety about speaking (Beatty, McCroskey, & Valenic, 2001). Communibiology is the newest research category and probably the most controversial, but it raises legitimate questions about the role of **genetic contributors** in human behavior.

communibiology
The study of the biological bases of human communication.

genetic contributors
Combinations of inherited tendencies that may exert influences on our behavioral preferences.

Self-Assessment

How Anxious Are You About Public Speaking?

The following scale measures communication anxiety in general, as well as anxiety resulting from communication in four specific contexts: (1) dyads, (2) small groups, (3) meetings, and (4) public settings. Upon completion of the measure, you may find that although your overall score is indicative of mild levels of communication anxiety, you are moderately to highly anxious about communicating in one or more specific contexts. Some research, for example, indicates that communicating in groups, meetings, and public settings is most anxiety arousing for students much like you. In any case, the techniques introduced in this chapter will help you cope with your communication anxieties, regardless of their contextual source.

Personal Report of Communication Apprehension (PRCA-24)

Directions: This instrument is composed of 24 statements concerning your feelings about communication with other people. Please indicate in the space provided the degree to which each statement applies to you by marking whether you (1) Strongly Agree, (2) Agree, (3) Are Undecided, (4) Disagree, or (5) Strongly Disagree with each statement. There are no right or wrong answers. Many of the statements are similar to other statements. Do not be concerned about this. Work quickly; just record your first impression.

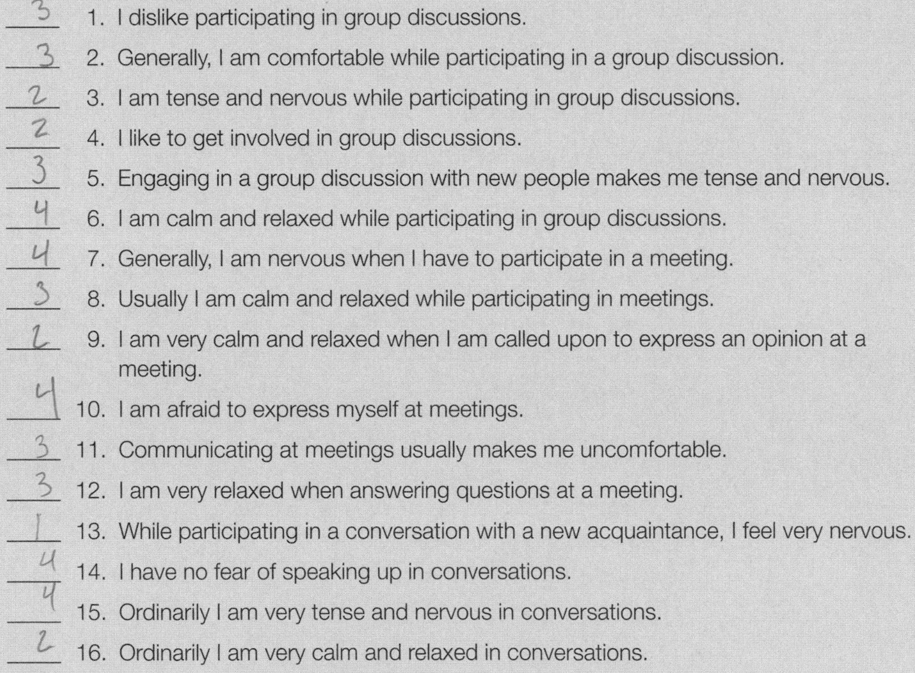

__3__ 1. I dislike participating in group discussions.
__3__ 2. Generally, I am comfortable while participating in a group discussion.
__2__ 3. I am tense and nervous while participating in group discussions.
__2__ 4. I like to get involved in group discussions.
__3__ 5. Engaging in a group discussion with new people makes me tense and nervous.
__4__ 6. I am calm and relaxed while participating in group discussions.
__4__ 7. Generally, I am nervous when I have to participate in a meeting.
__3__ 8. Usually I am calm and relaxed while participating in meetings.
__2__ 9. I am very calm and relaxed when I am called upon to express an opinion at a meeting.
__4__ 10. I am afraid to express myself at meetings.
__3__ 11. Communicating at meetings usually makes me uncomfortable.
__3__ 12. I am very relaxed when answering questions at a meeting.
__1__ 13. While participating in a conversation with a new acquaintance, I feel very nervous.
__4__ 14. I have no fear of speaking up in conversations.
__4__ 15. Ordinarily I am very tense and nervous in conversations.
__2__ 16. Ordinarily I am very calm and relaxed in conversations.

environmental reinforcers
Factors within our environment that contribute to our fear of speaking.

Environmental Reinforcers

Rewards, punishments, and negative **environmental reinforcers** are also likely contributors to communication apprehension. Researchers who believe that environmental factors contribute to the fear of public speaking suggest that behavior that is rewarded is likely to be repeated while behavior that is punished will be decreased or extinguished (Richmond & McCroskey, 1998). Consider two

5 17. While conversing with a new acquaintance, I feel very relaxed.

3 18. I'm afraid to speak up in conversations.

5 19. I have no fear of giving a speech.

2 20. Certain parts of my body feel very tense and rigid while giving a speech.

4 21. I feel relaxed while giving a speech.

4 22. My thoughts become confused and jumbled when I am giving a speech.

4 23. I face the prospect of giving a speech with confidence.

1 24. While giving a speech I get so nervous, I forget facts I really know.

Scoring

To determine your anxiety level, compute the following formulas. The higher your score, the more significant your level of anxiety. (The numbers in parentheses in the formulas refer to the numbered questions above.)

Group = 18 − (1) + (2) − (3) + (4) − (5) + (6)

Meeting = 18 − (7) + (8) + (9) − (10) − (11) + (12)

Dyadic = 18 − (13) + (14) − (15) + (16) + (17) − (18)

Public = 18 + (19) − (20) + (21) − (22) + (23) − (24)

Overall CA = Group + Meeting + Dyadic + Public

Making Sense of Your Score

Your combined score for all 24 items should fall somewhere between 24 and 120. If your score is lower than 24 or higher than 120, you need to recalculate it. A score above 83 indicates high communication apprehension; a score between 55 and 83 indicates normal apprehension, which is the norm for most people. Low apprehension is anything less than 55. Your subscores indicate the degree to which you are anxious when speaking in public, talking in a group, or engaging in conversation with another person. These scores can range between 6 and 30. The higher your score is, the more anxiety you feel. A score above 18 on the public speaking subset suggests you feel a manageable level of speech anxiety. Regardless of your score on this subset, you can significantly benefit from the skills and techniques presented in this chapter. A score of 18 or above on the other two subsets also suggests you feel some anxiety about interpersonal and group communication.

Source: James C. McCroskey, *An Introduction to Rhetorical Communication,* 7th ed. (Needham Heights, Mass.: Allyn & Bacon, 1997).

children raised in different environments. Carol was raised in a home where communication was encouraged and rewarded. Since her communication ability was reinforced, she improved her communication skills. Carol would be an unlikely candidate for high CA. Burt, on the other hand, was raised to believe that "children should be seen, not heard." His early attempts at communication were criticized and ridiculed. Since Burt's communication behavior was punished, he engaged in less of it and did not develop into a competent communicator. Because competence and confidence are often linked together, Burt would be more likely to develop high communication apprehension.

Learned helplessness
A person feels unable to predict whether a behavior will result in a reward or punishment; therefore, he or she avoids the behavior all together if possible.

Another environmental contributor to communication apprehension involves uncertainty about the outcome of communication. **Learned helplessness** occurs if a person's communication behavior is rewarded one time and punished the next, since it makes it difficult for that person to predict the consequences of communication (Richmond & McCroskey, 1998). Poor Rufus never knew what reaction he would receive when he talked to his mother. One day he would be told how smart he was, and the next he would be called "stupid" and told to keep his mouth shut. Since he couldn't predict the outcome of his communication behavior, he withdrew from communication whenever possible. Because he withdrew, he failed to develop skill and confidence in his communication ability. These circumstances placed Rufus at risk for developing high CA.

Researchers who believe environmental factors are primary contributors to communication apprehension probably represent the majority of communication scholars. Still, their findings are sometimes questioned because they offer only a partial explanation for the overall cause of communication apprehension. Critics argue that even their best research accounts for only a comparatively small percentage of the reasons people experience CA (Beatty, et al., 2001).

Personality Traits

Certain personality traits appear to be associated with high CA. When researchers compared mean scores of groups of people with high CA with mean scores of groups of people with low CA, they found high CAs tended to have lower tolerance for uncertainty, less self-control, less adventurousness, lower emotional maturity, higher introversion, lower self-esteem, and lower assertiveness (Richmond & McCroskey, 1998).

These results should be interpreted carefully. First, correlation alone can never imply causality. Sometimes something that is correlated with something else is actually a casual factor (people who smoke are more likely to develop cancer because cigarette smoking is one of the causes of lung cancer), but other times two phenomena can occur together and have nothing to do with each other (every serial killer in history has had a mother, but it does not follow that motherhood causes serial killers). Since all the research cited in this section is correlational, it would be dangerous to imply causality. Consider the research on high communication apprehension and self-esteem, for example. When researchers suggest a correlation between low self-esteem and high CA, we don't really know if low self-esteem causes high CA, high CA causes low self-esteem, some other factor causes both of them, or whether they occurred together but are totally unrelated.

Questions can also be raised about the framework of comparison used for this research. Although most researchers tend to view high CAs as disadvantaged when compared to their low CA counterparts, an equally good argument is that low CAs are uniquely gifted, and high CAs are no different in personality than the normal population. There is credible research in support of this argument (Butler, 1986).

Cultural Factors

Scholars of intercultural communication argue that the culture in which we are raised can affect our level of CA. These researchers suggest that some cultures, such as those found in many Asian, Arab, and South American countries, are comparatively collectivistic. **Collectivistic cultures** tend to discourage individual assertiveness and stress group harmony. Other cultures, such as those found in the United States and other western countries, are comparatively **individualistic cultures**, stressing individual assertiveness over group harmony. A growing body of research suggests a strong correlation between high CA and collectivistic cultures, probably because collectivistic cultures discourage assertiveness and often value silence (Zhang, Butler, & Pryor, 1996; Sarquisse, Butler, & Pryor, 2003).

collectivistic cultures
Cultures that discourage individual assertiveness and stress group harmony.

individualistic cultures
Societies that stress individual assertiveness over group harmony.

Summary: Causes of Communication Apprehension

Most communication researchers would agree that the factors discussed in this section represent significant contributors to high communication apprehension, but many would argue over which factors were most predominant. Controversies such as these are characteristic of scientific progress, since competing claims are tested against each other until research reveals which are most strongly supported by the evidence.

Please also note that the above categories are not necessarily discrete. Culture, for example, can be viewed as a part of one's environment, and personality characteristics may contain a hereditary component. Nevertheless, most researchers would agree that heredity, environment, personality, and culture all contribute to communication apprehension.

What Are the Effects of Communication Apprehension?

The effects of communication apprehension have been widely studied, with research results generally painting a gloomy picture of the effects of high CA. These effects are widespread, affecting people in virtually every aspect of their lives including self-perception, relationships, work satisfaction, occupational choices, and academic success (Daly & McCroskey, 1984).

Since this chapter is designed for college students, academic effects will be primarily emphasized. Persons curious about effects unrelated to the classroom should consult the references cited above for a more comprehensive review. From an academic standpoint, high communication apprehension appears to be detrimental to success. Some of its specific effects are described below.

CA and Standardized Test Scores

Although research has revealed no significant difference in intelligence between high and low CAs, scores on standardized tests such as the ACT tend to be significantly lower for high CAs than for their low CA counterparts (Daly & McCroskey, 1984).

CA and Grades

Some (but not all) studies have found that high CAs have lower mean grade point averages than low CAs. This is particularly true in courses that require oral participation (Daly & McCroskey, 1984).

CA and Class Selection

High and low CAs differ in their choice of classes. Low CAs prefer small classes with lots of participation while high CAs prefer large classes with little participation (Daly & McCroskey, 1984). High CAs also tend to select classes where they can use their seating preferences to avoid communication. While most low CAs choose seats in the front, middle section of a typical classroom, high CAs tend to select seats that are out of the instructor's normal zone of participation, such as seats in the back or on the sides of the room (Daly & McCroskey, 1984).

High CAs try to avoid classes that involve group projects and discussions. When they are required to take such classes, they choose obscure seating positions and minimize participation. Their comments are often irrelevant, and they seldom disagree with other group members. They are also less likely to engage in productive brainstorming (Daly & McCroskey, 1994).

CA and College Graduation

Perhaps as a result of the factors discussed earlier in this section, graduation rates for high CAs are lower than those for low CAs. Research by Ericson and Gardner (1992), for example, found that "high communication apprehensives had tendencies to not complete their degrees" (p.132). In fact, 50% of the high apprehensives they studied failed to graduate, and incoming freshmen with high CA were more likely to drop out of school than those with low CA.

Summary: Effects of Communication Apprehension

Research on the academic effects of high CA paints a bleak picture for those affected by this form of anxiety. Highly apprehensive students have comparatively lower test scores, grades, and graduation rates than their low apprehension counterparts. In spite of these findings, high CA students can take encouragement from three observations.

First, remember the previously cited research was comparative in nature. For example, high CAs have lower grades only when compared with low CAs. Such a comparison *could* demonstrate that low CAs average uniquely high grades–not that high CAs average uniquely low grades. A more telling comparison could have been made by comparing the mean GPAs of high and low CAs with the GPAs of students with normal levels of apprehension, but such comparisons were not examined in the research cited in this section. This lack of data makes it hard to determine whether or not high CAs are truly disadvantaged.

Second, the research cited in this section draws its conclusions by comparing mean group scores and is not designed to be applied to individual students. Pretend, for example, that researchers compare groups of engineering majors and computer science majors and conclude that engineering majors have higher mean

IQ scores than computer science majors. Would this research prove that every engineering major is smarter than every computer science major? Of course not! In spite of the differences in group means, there would still be plenty of engineering majors with low scores, and lots of computer science majors with high scores. Research conducted on groups simply can't be generalized to individuals, and those who make such generalizations are committing a classic research fallacy known as the ecological fallacy. Conclusion? Even though mean group GPA's differ, there are still plenty of high CA students with excellent grades.

Third, the negative effects of high communication apprehension can be mitigated. The next section will discuss ways individual students can reduce their speech-based anxiety. These are methods I have used and found to be effective in nearly two decades of working with highly apprehensive students.

How Do We Reduce the Effects of Communication Apprehension?

There are a number of different strategies for reducing high communication apprehension. We will concentrate on the ones that do not require professional supervision and that have proven effective for most high CA students.

Use Positive Self-Talk

The first strategy focuses on a phenomenon called **self-talk**. We probably talk to ourselves more than we talk to other people, and the nature of our self-talk often influences our perceptions of reality. Researchers have discovered that persons with high communication apprehension often engage in **negative self-talk**, which is critical and negative (Bullard & Carroll, 1993). When thinking about a forthcoming speech, high CAs often bombard themselves with criticism. Typical thoughts include, "My speech will be boring," "People will think I'm stupid," or "I'll lose my place and people will laugh at me." Unfortunately, thoughts like these can easily turn into self-fulfilling prophecies, so many high CAs literally become their own worst enemies.

self-talk
Silent communications with oneself that influence our perceptions of reality.

negative self-talk
Destructive self-criticism.

Most high CAs who engage in negative self-talk learned this self-destructive habit from someone else, usually parents, teachers, or even friends. Unfortunately, many high CAs incorporate these descriptions by others into their self-perception and come to believe that that's just the way they are. Then they perpetuate their negative self-image by engaging in self-criticism and self-doubt. Over time, these people *become* their own negative descriptions. If you call yourself a loser (or a terrible public speaker, for that matter) enough times, chances are you will become what you say you are.

Luckily, self-talk doesn't have to be negative. Furthermore, *you* are in charge of how you talk to yourself! Picture yourself walking across campus. As you walk, you encounter a friend who greets you. Undoubtedly you will respond with a "good morning" or some similar greeting instead of something that makes no sense. "Good morning" is seldom followed with a nonsensical response like "prune juice for dinner." This illustration is silly, but it makes a crucial point, namely that you are in charge of what you say to other people. You have the ability to control your conversational responses. You also have the power to control what you say to yourself! If you are busily talking yourself into being a poor public speaker, there is only one person on the planet who can reverse that trend. You see that person every time you look into the mirror.

This is not to suggest that reversing negative self-talk is easy. Old habits are hard to break–but it can be done. The next time that inner voice tells you you're a loser, tell it to shut up! Replace negative self-descriptions with **positive self-talk**. Think, "My speech will be interesting," or "People will enjoy what I have to say." Better yet, say these things to yourself out loud (your car is a good place for this, even if other drivers think you are crazy). Remember, when you speak, your brain listens, and you–not old habits–are in charge of what you say.

positive self-talk
The use of positive coping statements instead of negative self-talk.

From a physiological standpoint, the thoughts we have about ourselves trigger interesting reactions in our brains. Researchers who study electrical activity in the human brain report that thoughts about ourselves trigger up to 100 times more neuronal firings than random thoughts, and thoughts about ourselves spoken out loud generate up to 1,000 times more neuronal firings than random thoughts (Bullard & Carroll, 1993). In other words, our brains devote considerable energy to processing our self-talk, especially when we say things about ourselves out loud. When we talk, our brains listen.

Tips and Tactics

While You Speak

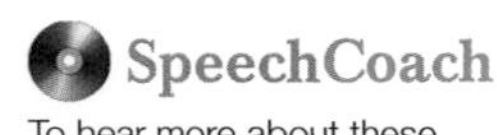

SpeechCoach
To hear more about these Tips and Tactics, go to Audio Tips and Tactics on your CD.

- Take time to get comfortable before you start to speak. Take a couple of deep breaths, make eye contact with a friendly face, and smile.
- Don't obsess on your audience. Important as the audience is to your success, you need to keep their importance in perspective. Remember that your audience wants you to succeed and that the audience is uncomfortable when you are uncomfortable.
- Dress appropriately for the occasion. Not only will it help make you feel more confident, but it will also increase your credibility with your audience.
- Talk to yourself about what's going well. Tell yourself that you are okay and that your audience is with you.
- Avoid reading "too much" into the feedback you receive while speaking. Not every cough or squint or wrinkled-up nose or furrowed brow is meant to "tell you" how you are doing. Also, the whispering between the two discourteous people at the back of the room is not about your appearance or your speech.
- Avoid overreacting to what you *perceive* to be negative feedback. Not only are we predisposed to notice it more than positive feedback, but we also tend to overcompensate by paying more attention than they deserve to the one or two people we *think* are negative.
- Remember, even if you are a little nervous, the research tells us your audience won't notice it as much as you will.

Use Positive Visualization

Positive self-talk mainly affects the verbal areas of the brain. Other parts of the brain are primarily influenced by visual images. Consequently, we can influence our visual perceptions with visualized images. One could label these images **proactive imagination**. Things that we imagine can have a very real impact on how our brain processes information. Remember, your brain receives visual data only in the form of electrical impulses, and these impulses seem real to your brain whether they come from actual or imagined events. That's why movies (or nightmares) can trigger strong emotional and physical responses in us even though nothing "real" is actually happening.

proactive imagination The process of visualizing yourself giving a successful speech.

kinesics The study of body movement and facial expressions.

You can use this property of your brain to help overcome high CA by visualizing yourself successfully giving a speech. Picture yourself speaking confidently to a smiling, interested audience. Visualize yourself giving an articulate, informative presentation–the more detail, the better. Combining visualization with self-talk allows you to positively influence both the visual and verbal areas of your brain.

Visualization is best practiced with your eyes closed while you are lying down. Closing your eyes helps eliminate most competing visual information, so it is easier for you to picture what you are trying to proactively imagine (Bullard & Carroll, 1993). It's also a good idea to prepare a "script" to guide your visualization (Bullard & Carroll, 1993). You might picture yourself standing and walking to the front of the room, then visualize yourself speaking articulately to a smiling, interested audience. Visualization is a powerful technique for reducing high CA, especially when used in conjunction with positive self-talk.

Many athletes use visualization to improve their game.

Utilize Kinesic Inputs

Kinesics is the study of body movement and facial expressions. Researchers who investigate the impact of kinesics on our moods have made an interesting discovery: our facial expressions can influence how we feel. Most of us think that facial expressions are usually the result of our feelings, and we're right. In general, expressions are the result, not the cause, of emotions. But nonverbal reactions also perform a second, more subtle function. In addition to reflecting our feelings, they also influence them. Communication researchers have discovered that changing facial expressions can alter our state of mind (Kleinke, Peterson, & Rutledge, 1998). High CAs can use this discovery to their advantage. Never mind how you feel inside; when it's your turn to give a speech, smile, walk confidently to the front of the room, and then sound and act as if you are interested in your topic. You can literally reduce some of your anxiety by acting confidently.

Change Your Perspective

Remember the last time you watched individual competitive events like diving or figure skating during the Olympics? The contestant would finish and then nervously wait for his or her evaluation. Eventually, the judges would each hold up a card with a number on it and the numbers would be tallied for a final score. That system works fine for Olympic competition, but it can't accurately be applied to many speaking situations. The trouble is that some high CAs don't realize that. Consider the plight of Jim.

Poor Jim regarded his audience as a group of critics. He felt they were keenly focusing on every word he said and every movement he made. Any tiny error he committed would be recorded and deducted from his score. Since he regarded his audience as a group of hostile critics, he anticipated his speech with trepidation.

Jim's classmate, Mike, cultivated a different attitude about his speech. Instead of regarding it as a performance, he saw it as an opportunity to share information about his topic with his audience. He was excited to exchange information about his home state of Arkansas and his favorite football team, the Razorbacks, with his classmates, and pictured them not as critics, but as interested receivers of his message. Mike wanted to do a good job, but he recognized that most human communication contains a few errors and figured that if he made a mistake, his audience would get over it. He wasn't too worried about his upcoming speech.

Changing your facial expressions can alter your state of mind—smile!

As you can see from these examples, your attitude about the purpose of a speech and the role of the audience can play a significant part in how much anxiety you feel. If you carry unrealistic attitudes about your job as a speaker or the perspective of the audience into your speech, you will probably experience increased anxiety.

Let's go back and analyze Jim's position. Jim's first mistake was to regard his speech as a performance. The truth is that most contemporary speeches don't sound much like rehearsed performances; they are more like enlarged conversations. In the early days of our country, speeches were seen as entertainment, and speakers were applauded for their oratorical skills. Renowned speakers like Daniel Webster and William O. Douglas gave flawless, moving performances–some over three hours long. We still have vestiges of that style. You see it in a few evangelists, and in the State of the Union Address. Most speeches though, are comparatively informal. Think of a presidential news conference, a Pentagon briefing, or a college lecture. These speeches just *aren't* performances.

Jim's second mistake involved his misinterpretation of the audience's expectations. As you listen to other students' speeches, monitor your own attentiveness and behavior. Are you listening with critical attention, ready to pounce on the smallest error, or are you listening in a more detached way, trying to understand the main points the speaker is trying to make? In fact, do you really care all that much about what the other speakers are saying at all? How much time do you spend agonizing over other students' speeches out of class? Do you discuss them in detail with your friends or lay awake at night thinking about them? Probably not.

The bottom line is this: most of your small mistakes will hardly be noticed by your classmates, and even if you really blow it, other people won't think about it all that much. Thinking otherwise places you in an imaginary world–a place where speeches are like theater performances and audiences are like predatory tigers ready to pounce.

Jim's classmate, Mike, was considerably closer to the truth. He recognized that if he offered his audience interesting, relevant information, delivered with reasonable articulation and enthusiasm, he would probably be okay. When it comes to your public speaking perspective, you want to "be like Mike."

Be Prepared

This section is last because it is probably the least important component of anxiety reduction for high CAs. Still, it deserves some consideration. Most anxiety doesn't seem to be linked to how well prepared a person is to give his or her speech. You may recall that lack of preparation was not one of things discussed in the *Causes of Communication Apprehension* section of this chapter. There are two ways, however, that lack of preparation can lead to increased apprehension.

First, a person who is already nervous about giving a speech certainly doesn't need any additional negative baggage. In other words, if the poor guy is predisposed to be anxious about speaking, comes from a background that was punishing and critical, has personality characteristics associated with apprehension, and comes from a culture that discourages speaking, he sure doesn't need anything else to contribute to his anxiety. Being unprepared can do just that. I have won state championships for college impromptu and extemporaneous speaking (never mind what year), yet I still feel a little nervousness when I'm unprepared, so pity the poor high CA who is unprepared.

Second, one specific type of nervousness is clearly linked to the lack of preparation. Although it may sound tautological, lack of preparation definitely leads to nervousness about not being prepared. I personally cherish the fine art of procrastination and am an ardent practitioner, but if you experience apprehension about public speaking, it really doesn't pay to put off speech preparation. Perhaps you can get away with procrastinating on assigned papers and studying for exams, but if you're already nervous, procrastinating on speech preparation is a poor move.

Speaking of . . .

From the Author: Some Final Thoughts for Persons Who Experience High Communication Apprehension

Please don't mistake these suggestions about coping with apprehension for a panacea. The solutions offered here are the best answers we currently have, but they aren't miracle cures. There are at least three problems with what I've suggested.

First, the solutions I've proposed usually reduce apprehension, but they seldom eliminate it. If you experience uncommonly high anxiety about public speaking, the methods I've discussed should lower your discomfort to tolerable levels, but you'll still probably experience some nervousness before and during your speech. Ideally, I'd like to offer you a method that would completely eliminate your discomfort about speaking, but it's probably more realistic for you to expect to reduce it enough so that you can complete class assignments that require oral presentations. Even a reduction in anxiety can be important. It can make a significant difference in your college grades and in your career success after you graduate.

Second, reducing anxiety can be a slow process. Don't expect one week of positive self-talk and positive visualization to undo years of habituated anxiety. Your nervousness will decrease gradually, and you may not experience a meaningful decline in it until your second or even third speech. Anxiety reduction is a bit like working out or losing weight. It works, but it's slow.

Third, these methods won't work effectively for everyone. Over the years, I've known a few people (probably fewer than 5% of my high CA students) who diligently used the methods I've recommended without much effect. These students lie at the extreme end of the high CA spectrum. They're the people who can't sleep for days prior to giving a speech, become physically ill before class, pass out while speaking, and repeatedly register for and then drop the basic speech class. I had one student who dropped the course three times before I met him.

If you think you are one of the students who fall into this extreme category, I strongly urge you to consider enrolling in our special "high apprehension" section of the Fundamentals of Oral Communication course. We offer the course both spring and fall terms.

College is so filled with short-term deadlines and obligations that it's hard to think of long-term consequences. When I admitted that we can't always help people with extremely high CA, I was speaking with a degree of candor that you don't often find in college texts or popular self-improvement manuals. I'm speaking with that same blunt honesty now. The consequences of high CA reach far beyond your college education. In this chapter, I restricted my discussion of the results of high communication apprehension to the college environment, partly because a complete discussion would have at least doubled the length of this chapter, but mostly because I didn't want to bury you under an avalanche of bad news. I won't bury you now either, but I want to make it abundantly clear that communication apprehension affects more things—and bigger things—than a few college classes. People with extremely high communication apprehension don't do well in relationships, in employment, in life. High CA is seriously bad stuff, and deciding to "just live with it" should only be a last ditch option. I'm not overstating when I say that if you don't overcome it now, you may pay for it for the rest of your life.

In the end, more than anything else, it comes down to courage. Are you going to give in to the apprehension monkey on your back, or are you going to go to war with it? The war isn't easy, but you'll carry the consequences of your choice for the rest of your life. Both Abraham Lincoln and Winston Churchill suffered from high communication apprehension. If they had lacked the courage to overcome it, I wonder if their names would mean anything to us today.

Make good choices and don't give up.

References

Beatty, M. J., McCroskey, J. C., & Valenic, K. (2001). *The biology of communication: A communibiological perspective.* Cresskill, NJ: Hampton Press.

Bullard, B., and Carnol, K. (1993). *Communicating from the inside out.* Dubuque, Iowa: Kendall/Hunt.

Butler, J. F. (1986). Personality characteristics of subjects high and low in apprehension about communication. *Perceptual and Motor Skills, 62,* 895-898.

Daly, J. A., & McCroskey, J. C. (1984). *Avoiding communication.* Beverly Hills, CA: Sage.

Ericson, P. M., & Gardner, J. W. (1992). Two longitudinal studies of communication apprehension and its effects on college students' success. *Communication Quarterly, 40,* 127-137.

Kleinke, C. L., Peterson, T. R., & Rutledge, T.R. (1998). Effects of self generated facial expressions on mood. *Journal of Personality and Social Psychology, 74,* 272-279.

McCroskey, J. C. (1993). *An introduction to rhetorical communication,* 6th ed. Englewood Cliffs, NJ: Prentice-Hall.

Motley, M. T. (1997). *Overcoming your fear of public speaking: A proven method.* Boston, MA: Houghton Mifflin.

Richmond, V. P., & McCroskey, J. C. (1998). *Communication: Apprehension, avoidance, and effectiveness,* 5th ed. Boston, MA: Allyn and Bacon.

Sarquisse, V., Butler, J., & Pryor, B. (2003). A comparison of communication apprehension scores between Americans and Argentineans. *North American Journal of Psychology, 5,* 223-228.

Zang, Y., Butler, J., & Pryor, B. (1996). A comparison of apprehension about communication in China and the United States. *Perceptual and Motor Skills, 82,* 1168-1170.

Former Enron Executive Lynn Brewer has become a crusader for ethics in business.

Ethical Speaking and Listening

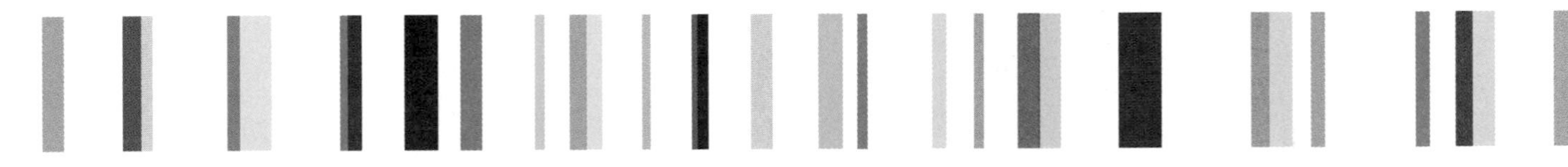

Objectives

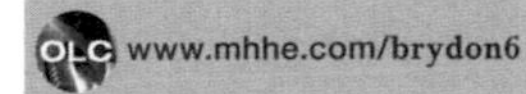

After reading this chapter and reviewing the online learning resources at www.mhhe.com/brydon6, you should be able to:

- Demonstrate an understanding of the differences among ethical relativism, universalism, utilitarianism, and situational ethics.
- Apply ethical principles to a variety of different public speaking situations.
- Explain plagiarism and the role of attribution in avoiding plagiarism.
- Explain and apply the basic ethical obligations of both speakers and listeners.

Key Concepts

categorical imperative
cultural relativism
ethical relativism
ethics
goodwill
good reasons
plagiarism
situational ethics
trustworthiness
universalism
utilitarianism

> "The time is always right to do what is right."
>
> –MARTIN LUTHER KING JR.[1]

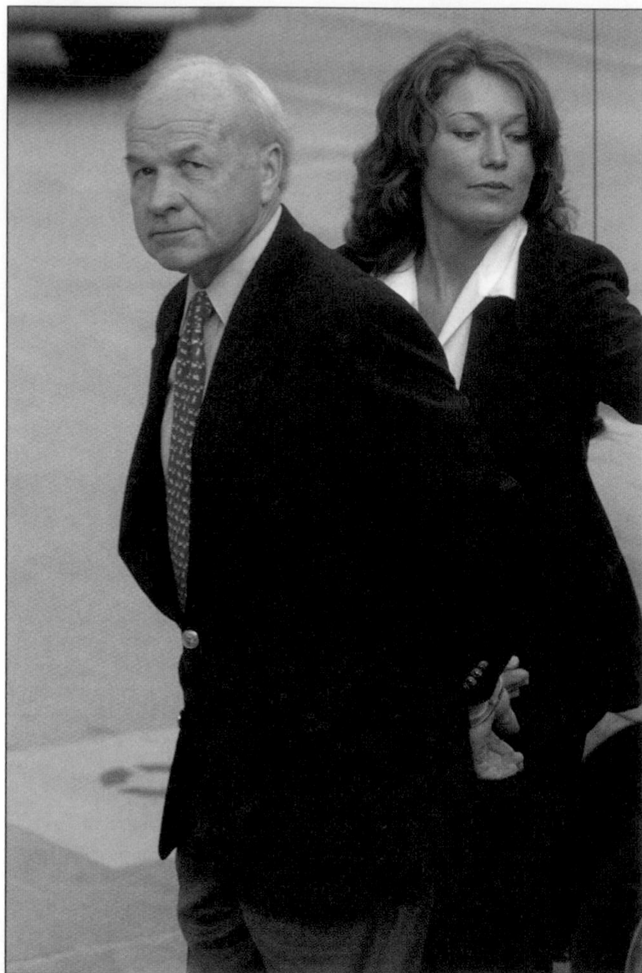
Enron founder Ken Lay was tried and convicted for his unethical and illegal business practices.

Imagine that you are an executive at a Fortune 100 company making as much as $30,000 per day in stock options. You hear rumors about the company's financial stability at the same time you watch your Chief Executive officer on TV tell the audience that the company could not be in better financial health. You hear another rumor that those above you are selling their stock in the company at the same time the CEO is encouraging rank and file employees to buy more. But you say nothing, silenced by the power, prestige, and financial success you currently enjoy as a result of your job.

Fast-forward five years. Hundreds of Indiana University students and faculty are assembled to hear you give a speech on why you finally quit the preceding job in disgust, and became one of the biggest whistleblowers in the history of private industry. Your name is Lynn Brewer, your Chief Executive Officer was Ken Lay, and the corporation was a company named Enron.[2]

Far-fetched as this example may seem, it is the absolute truth. Lynn Brewer's conscience finally got the best of her. She gave up the title, the power, and the money and spilled the goods on a group of people so greedy that they bankrupted their company and destroyed the financial security of the employees who had trusted them. Now she stood before a group of students as a public speaker, her purpose straightforward. As the co-founder and CEO of The Integrity Institute, Lynn Brewer was there to share a cautionary story about ethical lapses and ruined lives; to warn students against being seduced by power and money; to convince her audience that there is no excuse for the kind of unethical behavior in which Enron executives engaged.

Reading this chapter won't make you a famous whistleblower, but it can further your understanding of what it means "to do the right thing" in general, and in the public speaking transaction specifically. Clearly *unethical behavior* is reported daily in our media, and it is easy to become confused about the principles that underscore ethics and the practice of these principles in daily life. We begin with some basic questions that repeatedly come up when discussing ethics. In the process, we introduce some of the thinking that has been advanced on the topic of ethics by history's best minds. We then show how ethics can guide us in the development as well as delivery of our speeches and in our role as consumers of the information shared in the speeches of others.

Basic Ethical Questions

Ethics is a system of principles of right and wrong that govern human conduct. To get a better grip on this latter fact, let's look at a number of important questions philosophers have been pondering for over 2,000 years, beginning with the relevance of such an "old" subject to modern life.

ethics
A system of principles of right and wrong that govern human conduct.

Why Care About Ethics?

We live in a world where many people take to heart mottos such as "win at all costs" or "I'm spending my children's inheritance." So why should we look out for anyone's interests but our own? For example, why should we think or care about the fact that the shoes we wear were constructed by illiterate kids in another country for less than 50 cents a day or the car we drive may be contributing to global warming?

For starters, we should care about ethics because, in the long run, ethical practices are in our own self-interest. We benefit from physicians being trained to "first do no harm," police informing us of our constitutional rights before interrogating us, and laws protecting against discrimination because of our gender or the color of our skin.

On the flip side, we owe those who behave ethically toward us the same in return. This kind of reciprocity, in fact, is a major ingredient in the social glue necessary to build relationships and communities of people bound by a common purpose: for example, your public speaking class. Can you imagine the consequences if everyone in your class lived by a different set of rules for developing and presenting speeches? Do you think you would be comfortable speaking in your class if there were no ethical guidelines for the audience about cell phones, talking during speeches, or blurting out opinions about what you say even as you say it?

Ethical practices, then, are to everyone's benefit. When we are treated ethically it increases the chances that we will treat others in kind. The payoff is a more cohesive, caring, and civil society in which to live and learn.

But there is yet another reason for us to look at the nature of ethical conduct as it relates to public speaking. Ethical behavior gives rise to trust. Perceptions of trustworthiness, moreover, influence the degree to which people actually believe what we have to say to them and vice versa. In a very real sense, then, the chances of our public speeches actually informing or influencing our audience depend on whether we are perceived as ethical *and* trustworthy.

Is Everything Relative?

Ethical relativism is a philosophy based on the belief that there are no universal ethical principles. This theory goes back at least as far as the Sophists, who believed that truth was relative and depended on circumstances.[3]

ethical relativism
A philosophy based on the belief that there are no universal ethical principles.

The most radical version of relativism asserts that any one person's ethical standards are as good as the next person's. Although this philosophy has the advantage of simplicity, it makes a civilized society impossible. Life would be, essentially, a free-for-all. When a group of people holds such a radical view, the

As our society becomes more culturally diverse, different ethical systems are increasingly relevant to speakers.

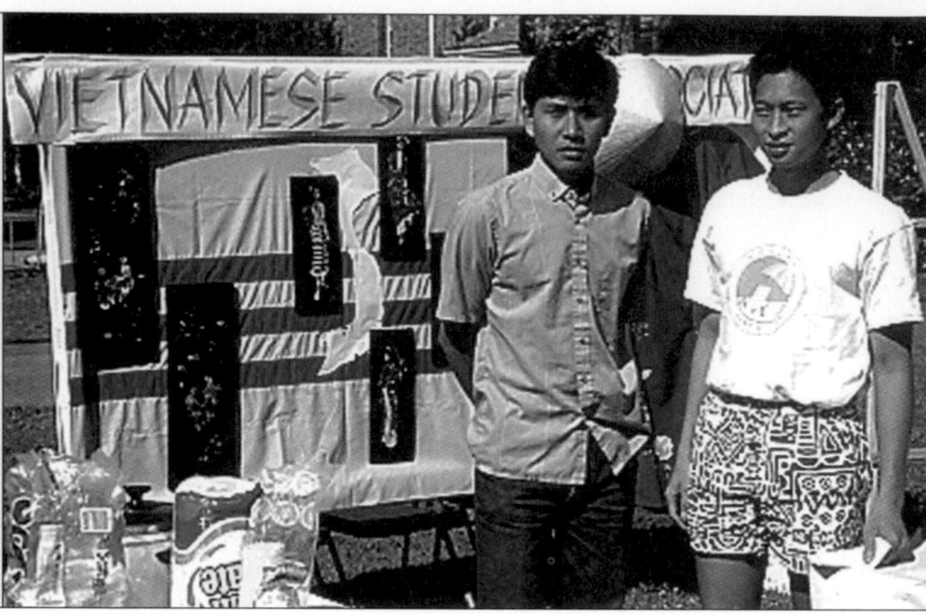

consequences for society are potentially disastrous. After all, the Nazis believed they were entitled to enslave and kill Jews and other "undesirables."

cultural relativism The notion that the criteria for ethical behavior in one culture should not necessarily be applied to other cultures.

Yet, many people endorse, or say they believe in, **cultural relativism,** the notion that the criteria for ethical behavior in one culture should not necessarily be applied to other cultures. This was the position of the Sophist Protagoras, who argued that moral laws are based on the conventions of a given society. Examples of such differences among cultures are easy to find. (See the box "Culture and Credit" for one.) So, too, is controversy. Consider polygamy, which usually involves a man having more than one wife. In the United States, polygamy is not only seen as immoral by most people, it is also against the law. Yet polygamy is practiced openly in parts of Arizona and Utah by a small number of people who believe it is consistent with their religious beliefs.

Similarly, there are cultural differences in ethical standards governing communication. One such difference involves the extent to which people should be "brutally honest" in certain situations. In collectivist cultures, "saving face" is important to the good of all society, so people are often indirect and may stretch the bounds of truthfulness in certain situations. To do either in an individualistic culture such as that of the United States could be regarded as unethical communication. Can either culture claim superiority over the routine communication practices of the other? Not really.

At the same time, there are limits to what most people will accept based on cultural relativism. Customs change over time as people reexamine their ethical values. Human sacrifice was once a routine part of some religions, yet no one today would consider such behavior ethical. Less than a century and a half ago, a significant number of Americans believed that slavery was ethical and gave their lives to defend the institution. Over 60 years ago, during World War II, American citizens of Japanese ancestry were interned in "relocation" camps, while those of German and Italian ancestry remained free.

Considering Diversity

Culture and Credit

It is sometimes surprising to speakers who come from a traditional Euro-American background that practices they take for granted as being acceptable are held to be morally wrong in other cultures. For example, taking out a loan for college expenses, a car, or a new wardrobe is routine for most Americans. However, those who practice the religion of Islam may find such practices morally unacceptable. As reporter Fahizah Alim explains in an article about a Sacramento, California, restaurant owner, Khaled Umbashi, many Muslims view the interest charged today by banks as *riba* (usury), which is forbidden by the Qur'an. Umbashi refuses to borrow money to improve or advertise his restaurant because "his Islamic religion forbids him from borrowing the funds and paying interest on that loan. . . . 'Our Islamic religion prohibits paying or charging compounded interest,' says Umbashi, a native of Libya."

Not all Muslims agree with this interpretation of the Qur'an. For example, Asghar Aboobaker, a Muslim who has written on the topic, holds that "this is a very complicated issue, and there are many, many camps." On the other hand, Irfan Ul Haq, a Muslim businessman, economist, and author, believes, "Much of the world's financial crisis has to do with the interest based system."

Thus, although most of those raised in a Western culture find nothing wrong with borrowing money, some Muslims consider such a practice not just unwise but morally objectionable.

We mention this story because we have heard countless speeches on topics that involve credit or paying interest on a loan. We actually heard a student boast in a speech how he capitalized on the "bull market" by using money from student loans to purchase stock. This student emphasized that with a rate of return of 22 percent on one stock pick, he was making 14 percent on the $5,000 student loan on which he was being charged 8 percent interest.

Clever as our stock-wise student was, his ethics might be questioned by students in general. Certainly the Muslim students in his audience were given pause by his speech.

Knowing and respecting culturally diverse moral principles is often essential to your success in a culturally diverse society.

Source: Fahizah Alim, "No Credit: For Muslims, Asking for a Loan Is a Question of Religion," *Sacramento Bee,* 29 August 1998, Scene, 1, 3.

We need to be careful not to exaggerate cultural differences, however. Philosophy professor James Rachels, for example, points out that different cultures often agree on underlying principles but disagree on how they are to be applied. For example, he notes that even apparently inhumane practices, such as that of the early Inuit, who once left the elderly to die in the snow, are grounded in the need of the family to survive in a harsh environment. Rachels argues that "the Eskimos' values are not all that different from our values. It is only that life forces upon them choices that we do not have to make."[4]

Are There Rules for Every Situation?

In contrast to ethical relativism is **universalism,** the philosophy that there are ethical standards that apply to all situations regardless of the individual, group, or culture. Immanuel Kant, an 18th-century philosopher, developed such a philosophy. He proposed the **categorical imperative:** *"Act only on that maxim through which you can at the same time will that it should become a universal law."*[5] To will the maxim be universally applicable means that you would want everyone to obey the same rule as you are proposing.

Suppose, for example, that you think it's acceptable for anybody to lie at any time, so you propose, as a universal rule, that lying is permissible for any reason. What would the result be? Lies would deceive no one because lying had become the rule. Thus, a universal law that lying is permissible would in fact make lies

universalism
The philosophy that there are ethical standards that apply to all situations regardless of the individual, group, or culture.

categorical imperative
Immanuel Kant's ethical principle that we should act only in a way that we would will to be a universal law.

ineffective. Consider voting as another example. You might think you don't need to vote because your own vote doesn't make a difference. But imagine that as a universal rule: "Since individual votes don't matter, voting is unnecessary." If not voting were a universal rule, democracy would collapse. So Kant gives us a test for specific ethical rules. To be an ethical principle, a rule or maxim must be capable of being applied universally.

One of the most important ethical rules that Kant proposed relates directly to the public speaker. Kant proposed the maxim *"Act in such a way that you always treat humanity whether in your own person or in the person of any other, never simply as a means, but always at the same time as an end."*[6] One practical implication of this maxim is that speakers should treat audience members with respect, not simply as a means of achieving their goals. Conversely, audience members should respect and treat speakers as fellow human beings, not as objects of derision. Obviously, then, tactics that deceive or demean either an audience or a speaker would be unacceptable.

Kant's categorical imperative is not without drawbacks. Consider truth telling. If lying is unacceptable in any circumstance, innocent people may suffer as a consequence. Miep Gies, for example, lied to authorities throughout World War II to protect the Jews she was hiding from the Nazis, including a young girl named Anne Frank. But even us common folk sometimes tell "little white lies," especially when they are intended to protect the feelings of others. Although we may be told as children, "honesty is the best policy," we soon learn not to take the saying *too* literally. Thus, we choose to be less than brutally honest when asked to comment on a friend's appearance or let our true feelings be known about the friend's latest "love interest." In short, even the most highly ethical among us are likely to occasionally tell something less than "the truth, the whole truth, and nothing but the truth."

Of course, one can reformulate Kant's rule and say people shouldn't lie except under certain circumstances, such as when necessary to save lives or prevent hurt feelings. But that creates another problem: How do we know which actions fall under these conditions? Rachels points out a key problem with Kant's universalism: "For any action a person might contemplate, it is possible to specify more than one rule that he or she would be following; some of these rules will be 'universalizable' and some will not. . . . For we can always get around any such rule by describing our action in such a way that it does not fall under that rule but instead comes under a different one."[7]

Does the Good of the Many Outweigh the Good of the Few?

utilitarianism
The philosophy based on the principle that the aim of any action should be to provide the greatest amount of happiness for the greatest number of people.

Another ethical standard, utilitarianism, was proposed by English philosophers Jeremy Bentham, John Stuart Mill, and Henry Sidgwick. **Utilitarianism** is based on the principle that the aim of any action should be to provide the greatest amount of happiness for the greatest number of people. These philosophers sought the greatest good for the greatest number. And they specifically defined the good as that which creates happiness—"not the agent's own greatest happiness, but the greatest amount of happiness altogether."[8]

This certainly is a useful standard for the public speaker. Most topics on which you will speak are about choices and trade-offs. If we trim social spending to fund a tax cut, some people will suffer while others will benefit. If we crack down on crime and build more prisons, there will be less money for schools and colleges. What constitutes the greatest good for the greatest number? As a speaker, you have an obligation to your audience to thoroughly research your subject to determine what position will ensure the greatest good and to put that greatest good ahead of mere personal gain. If you fail to fully inform your audience of the facts, if you lie to or deceive them, how can *they* rationally decide what will promote the general good?

Utilitarianism, of course, has its critics. Many would say it promotes ethical relativism. After all, if the greatest good for the greatest number means that some minority of people are oppressed, would not utilitarianism justify that oppression? Could not a Hitler rationalize his extermination of the Jews in the name of the greater good for all of Germany? Certainly that is not what the utilitarians contemplated. But critics of utilitarianism have a point. Seeking the greatest happiness for all does not guarantee that particular individuals will not suffer unjustly.

If you think these issues are mere philosophical musings, think about the controversy surrounding the use of embryonic stem cells in basic research. A growing body of scientific data suggests that stem cell research could lead to effective treatments for Parkinson's disease, multiple sclerosis, and paralysis resulting from injury to the spinal cord. Because this research involves the use of discarded embryonic cells from fertilized human eggs from fertility clinics, however, many people consider it immoral and therefore unethical. Should the convictions of people who count themselves in this latter group be ignored because they are in a minority? Not only is this a very real dilemma, but it is one that is politically charged as well, as the controversy over ads featuring Michael J. Fox supporting candidates for office in 2006 demonstrates.

How Do Specific Situations Affect Ethical Principles?

Another approach to ethics is known as **situational ethics.** According to this philosophy, there are overriding ethical maxims, but sometimes it is necessary to set them aside in particular situations to fulfill a higher law or principle, such as love. As one writer put it, "What acts are right may depend on circumstances . . . but there is an absolute obligation to will whatever may on each occasion be right."[9]

situational ethics
The philosophy that there are overriding ethical maxims, but that sometimes it is necessary to set them aside in particular situations to fulfill a higher law or principle.

Situational ethics is particularly useful in explaining how what appears to be the same kind of act can be ethical in one case and unethical in another. For example, most people agree that giving a classroom speech written by someone else is unethical. The principle that a student should do his or her own work is embedded in American education. At the same time, no one expects Jon Stewart to write all of his own jokes or the president of the United States to write all of his own speeches. In those situations, everybody knows that Stewart has comedy writers and the president has ghostwriters.

Critics of situational ethics argue that this is just relativism in another guise and thus provides no criteria for ethical judgment.[10] However, situationists do not contend we should abandon all ethical principles. As ethicist Joseph Fletcher writes: "The situationist enters into every decision-making situation fully armed with the ethical maxims of his community and its heritage, and he treats them with respect as illuminators of his problems. Just the same he is prepared in any situation to compromise them or set them aside *in the situation* if love seems better served by doing so."[11]

One problem with situational ethics, however, is that it would allow the use of unethical means to achieve ethical goals.[12] That brings us to our final question.

Do the Ends Justify the Means?

You may have heard the old saying "The ends don't justify the means." In other words, it is not acceptable to do something that is otherwise unethical just because it will produce a desirable result. To do so raises serious ethical concerns. As a speaker you need to concern yourself with ends (goals) as well as the means you use to achieve them.

In terms of ends, many of your topics are likely to be about issues of right and wrong, morality and immorality, the weighing of the good of the many against the good of the few. Understanding how people make ethical decisions is important to your choice of topic and the goals you seek. Obviously, the first and foremost ethical obligation of any speaker is to seek ethical ends: that is, to make sure you are striving to achieve a goal that is ethical and just. So, as you choose your topics, adapt to your audience, and seek to fulfill your goals as a speaker, you should always focus on accomplishing ethical ends.

Not only should your goals be ethically sound, but how you seek to reach those goals should also be ethical. Good ends should never, for example, justify withholding the true purpose of a speech from our audience. Suppose we want to raise money to improve the medical care received by impoverished children in a third world country. Suppose, too, that the missionary arm of a controversial religious group would administer the money we raised. Should we reveal this in our speech, knowing that we have atheists and agnostics in the audience who would be less favorably disposed to donate if made aware of who would administer the money?

Consider our earlier example regarding stem cell research. Would a speaker raising money for the Muscular Dystrophy Society be justified in not telling the audience that some of the money could be used to fund embryonic stem cell research? It's not an easy question to answer, is it? But it is exactly the kind of question we need to ask ourselves when weighing the ends we seek with a public speech.

Ethical Norms for Public Speakers

Developing standards for ethical public speaking is not an easy task. Probably the closest thing to a code of conduct for public speakers is the National Communication Association's Credo for Free and Responsible Communication in a Democratic Society, reprinted in the box "Codes of Conduct for Public Speaking." More than by any specific code of conduct, however, ethical public speakers are guided by the traditional standards of rhetoric that date back more than 2,000 years. Sophists were known for their philosophical relativism. Some Sophists carried this philosophy to its logical extreme, arguing that virtually any rhetorical deception was justified if it furthered their cause.[13]

Speaking of . . .

Codes of Conduct for Public Speaking

Although it is not a full-fledged ethical code, such as those found in law and medicine, the National Communication Association's Credo for Free and Responsible Communication in a Democratic Society forms an important touchstone for the ethical public speaker. Other guidelines that may be of help to the public speaker are found in the American Advertising Association's Code of Ethics, the Code of Ethics of the International Association of Business Communicators, and the Public Relations Society of America's Code of Professional Standards for the Practice of Public Relations.[1]

Credo for Free and Responsible Communication in a Democratic Society[2]

Recognizing the essential place of free and responsible communication in a democratic society, and recognizing the distinction between the freedoms our legal system should respect and the responsibilities our education system should cultivate, we the members of the National Communication Association endorse the following statement of principles:

We believe that freedom of speech and assembly must hold a central position among American constitutional principles, and we express our determined support for the right of peaceful expression by any communicative means available.

We support the proposition that a free society can absorb with equanimity speech which exceeds the boundaries of generally accepted beliefs and mores; that much good and little harm can ensue if we err on the side of freedom, whereas much harm and little good may follow if we err on the side of suppression.

We criticize as misguided those who believe that the justice of their cause confers license to interfere physically and coercively with the speech of others, and we condemn intimidation, whether by powerful majorities or strident minorities, which attempts to restrict free expression.

We accept the responsibility of cultivating by precept and example, in our classrooms and in our communities, enlightened uses of communication; of developing in our students a respect for precision and accuracy in communication, and for reasoning based upon evidence and a judicious discrimination among values.

We encourage our students to accept the role of well-informed and articulate citizens, to defend the communication rights of those with whom they may disagree, and to expose abuses of the communication process.

We dedicate ourselves fully to these principles, confident in the belief that reason will ultimately prevail in a free marketplace of ideas.

[1] Richard L. Johannesen, *Ethics in Human Communication,* 4th ed. (Prospect Heights, Ill.: Waveland Press, 1996), chap. 10.

[2] Used by permission of the National Communication Association.

Such philosophical relativism ran counter to the philosophy of Socrates, who taught that absolute truth was knowable through a question-and-answer technique known as dialectic. Socrates' student Plato wrote two dialogues, the *Gorgias* and the *Phaedrus,* that promoted this Socratic view of rhetoric. To Plato, rhetoric, as practiced by the Sophists, was a sham, with no truth to it, designed to deceive listeners. In the *Phaedrus,* Plato proposes an ideal rhetoric, one based on philosophical truths. The basic function of this rhetoric is to take the truth discovered through dialectic and energize it for the masses.

The best-known response to Plato came from his student Aristotle, whose *Rhetoric* is probably the most influential book on communication to this day. To Aristotle, rhetoric was not the opposite of dialectic but rather its counterpart. Aristotle did not view rhetoric as either moral or immoral. Rather, it was an art that could be put to both good and bad uses. The moral purpose of the speaker was the determining factor. Aristotle believed that "things that are true and things that are just have a natural tendency to prevail over their opposites."[14] Therefore, he stressed the importance of training in rhetoric. Even arguing both sides of a question was not immoral; rather, it was a way of learning how to refute someone who misstates the facts on the other side of an issue. For Aristotle, in sum, rhetoric was an art, not a sham.

Self-Assessment

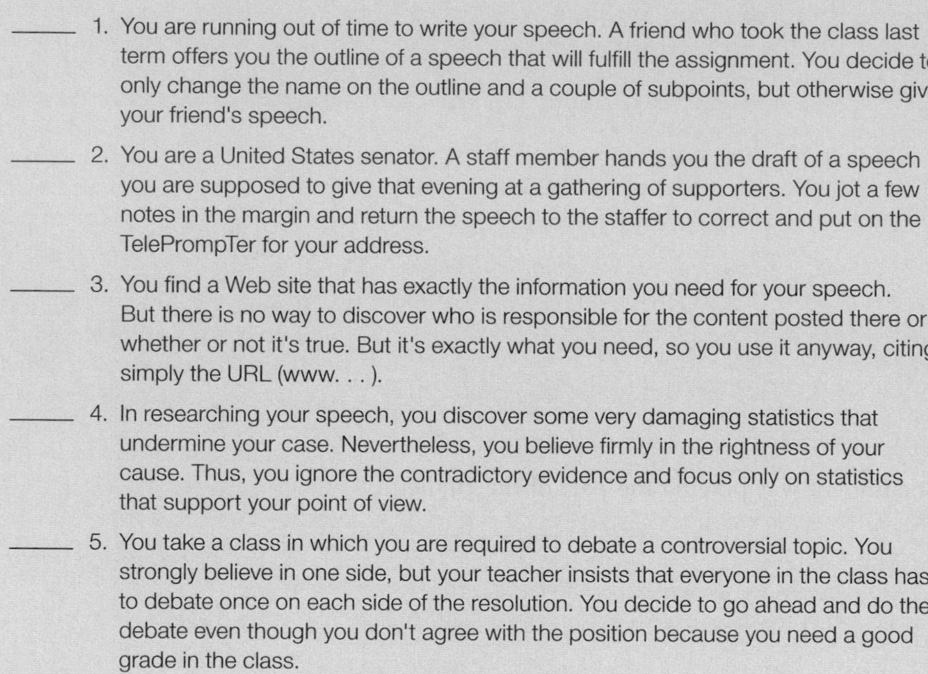

Is it acceptable for a speaker to . . . ?

Read the following scenarios carefully. Put an A next to those that you think are acceptable for a public speaker. Put a question mark next to those that are possibly acceptable in some cases. Mark those that are unacceptable with a U. Be prepared to present your responses in class and to discuss any differences between your responses and those of your classmates.

_____ 1. You are running out of time to write your speech. A friend who took the class last term offers you the outline of a speech that will fulfill the assignment. You decide to only change the name on the outline and a couple of subpoints, but otherwise give your friend's speech.

_____ 2. You are a United States senator. A staff member hands you the draft of a speech you are supposed to give that evening at a gathering of supporters. You jot a few notes in the margin and return the speech to the staffer to correct and put on the TelePrompTer for your address.

_____ 3. You find a Web site that has exactly the information you need for your speech. But there is no way to discover who is responsible for the content posted there or whether or not it's true. But it's exactly what you need, so you use it anyway, citing simply the URL (www. . .).

_____ 4. In researching your speech, you discover some very damaging statistics that undermine your case. Nevertheless, you believe firmly in the rightness of your cause. Thus, you ignore the contradictory evidence and focus only on statistics that support your point of view.

_____ 5. You take a class in which you are required to debate a controversial topic. You strongly believe in one side, but your teacher insists that everyone in the class has to debate once on each side of the resolution. You decide to go ahead and do the debate even though you don't agree with the position because you need a good grade in the class.

In the 1st century AD, the Roman orator and rhetorician Quintilian provided an ethical standard that many emulate to this day. To Quintilian, the ideal citizen-orator is a good person, speaking well. As he put it, "Oratory is the science of speaking well."[15] Further, because no one "can speak well who is not good,"[16] the moral quality of the speaker is not irrelevant. Rather, it is central to the ideal orator.

Today, the issue of ethical standards for public speaking has once again become a central concern for communication educators. What constitutes ethical communication? To assess your own values, see the box "Is it acceptable for a speaker to . . .?" Most of us would agree that speakers should not lie or distort the truth. Beyond that, however, what are the moral obligations of speaker to audience and audience to speaker? Based on the work of the philosophers discussed, as well as several communication scholars, we suggest the following norms or guidelines for the public speaker: (1) Be truthful. (2) Show respect for the power of words. (3) Invoke participatory democracy. (4) Demonstrate mindfulness of cultural diversity. (5) Treat people as ends, not means. (6) Provide good reasons. Let's look at each of these more closely.

Be Truthful

James Jaksa and Michael Pritchard of Western Michigan University have developed a set of ethical norms for speakers. Three of these seem particularly relevant to us. The first is the norm of truthfulness, which is fundamental to all communication.[17] The speaker caught in a lie loses his or her credibility and the goodwill of the audience, which are essential to belief. As domestic diva Martha Stewart learned, sometimes the lie can be worse than the initial offense. Ironically, Martha Stewart was convicted not of insider trading, a crime for which she was never charged, but for lying to investigators about her well-timed sale of ImClone stock. Had she simply told the truth, no matter how painful, she would never have been charged with a crime.[18]

Of course one does not have to tell an outright lie to deceive listeners. As we discuss in more detail in Chapter 16, distortions and omissions can sometimes be as harmful to the truth as outright lies. If you doubt that, we invite you to check out the "facts" in many political ads. A useful Web site for checking the truth of political ads is the University of Pennsylvania's factcheck.org, which provides researched assessment of political ads. Although most are based on a kernel of truth, often what's left out changes the whole meaning of the ad. We recall one political challenger who showed a video clip of the incumbent saying, "I'll do anything to get reelected." What the ad failed to mention was that the incumbent was playing the part of the challenger! The video clip was edited to reflect the exact opposite of the meaning intended by the incumbent. Of course the ad didn't lie outright–the words were actually said–but because the context was omitted, the result was the same as a lie.

A speaker who is unsure of the facts must learn the truth before speaking. Even a speaker who is simply misinformed, not consciously lying, must be held accountable. History is full of examples of people who were given the chance to speak and pass on information they believed to be factual but later was proven wrong. The most recent involved the claim by politicians that Saddam Hussein could launch weapons of mass destruction within 45 minutes and that he was in league with Osama bin Laden and al Qaeda. Both claims turned out to be mistaken, although each was repeatedly stated in public as if it were irrefutable. This is not to say that the removal of Hussein wasn't positive, but not all of the reasons given as justification for his removal turned out to be true.

Show Respect for the Power of Words

Another norm cited by Jaksa and Pritchard is respect for the word.[19] The power of words is undeniable. If you doubt this, just ask radio shock jock Don Imus and Michael Richards, who gained fame as Kramer on *Seinfeld.* Imus lost his radio and television shows when he was heard making racially disparaging remarks about the Rutgers women's basketball team. Even more dramatic was the widely circulated video of Richards at the Laugh Factory in West Hollywood, as he yelled one racial slur after another at two African American audience members who had heckled him during his routine. Many comics are heckled by audience members and many experienced comics have been known to cut hecklers "off at the knees." Richards, however, overstepped the bounds of common decency and was punished for his ethical lapse.

Don Imus lost his radio and television shows for his racially disparaging remarks about the Rutgers women's basketball team

Although freedom of speech is central to our democracy, the courts have recognized that there are limits. As Chief Justice of the Supreme Court Oliver Wendell Holmes Jr. once said, freedom of speech does not give you the right to shout "fire!" in a crowded theater. Although Justice Holmes was speaking metaphorically, the principle he was expressing is as relevant to the current debate about speech codes as it was nearly a century ago. The fact that you can say almost anything that comes to mind in this country doesn't make the content of what you say either ethical or wise. The old saying "Sticks and stones can break my bones, but words can never hurt me" is rubbish. In fact, words are very powerful and can cause great harm as well as great good. The ethical speaker recognizes that words have consequences.

Invoke Participatory Democracy

Jaksa and Pritchard discuss the importance of participatory democracy, which rests on a foundation of choice and respect for people.[20] Citizens must have accurate and ample information to make informed choices. Further, the golden rule of treating others as we would have them treat us applies to public speaking as well as to interpersonal communication. Speakers should put themselves in the shoes of listeners and ask if they are treating them as they would like to be treated. The ethical speaker recognizes the audience as an equal participant in the communication transaction. Similarly, listeners need to show respect and tolerance for speakers, even if the speakers' views are different from their own. Shouting down a speaker, for example, infringes on the speaker's freedom of speech and the public's right to hear a full spectrum of viewpoints.

In other words, ethics in communication is a joint responsibility. For example, there have been many complaints in recent years about negative and deceptive political advertising. Yet political consultants say they are only giving the public what it wants. Although that is no ethical defense for their behavior, we must also realize that deceptive advertising succeeds only because voters fail to protest against it and continue to vote for candidates who engage in such practices.

Demonstrate Mindfulness of Cultural Diversity

In Chapter 7 we discuss adapting to audience members from different cultures. For now, we want you to focus on the importance of being respectful of cultural differences, and mindful of the potential ethical concerns of those who do not share our cultural heritage.

In our earlier discussion of cultural relativism, we mentioned what we consider to be an extreme position: We should neither judge others' cultural practices nor try and impose our own on them. We don't agree with this position.

We think we can be both respectful and mindful of people's culture without accepting their cultural practices as entirely ethical. Likewise, we think one can also try and influence such cultural practices without coercing people to abandon theirs in favor of the ones we practice.

We also believe that there are principles and consequent practices that transcend cultures. Many of these principles are embodied in documents such as the U.N.'s Universal Declaration of Human Rights. Among others, the U.N. General Assembly proclaimed "freedom of speech and belief and freedom from fear and want" as fundamental rights.[21] With freedom of speech enshrined in both the First Amendment to our constitution and the U.N. declaration, public speakers need to be ever mindful of the responsibilities that accompany that right.

For us, then, ethical speakers choose topics and construct their speeches with language that respects the audience diversity typical of today's classroom. Ethical speakers also strive to be mindful of cultural sensitivities that potentially could undermine their speech's effectiveness. This means they adapt to, rather than adopt, every feature of cultural diversity found in their audience.

Treat People as Ends, Not Means

To these principles we wish to add one taken from Kant: namely, that people should never be treated as mere means to an end. Their best interests should be the ends sought by the speaker. Using people as objects, manipulating them even to achieve desirable ends, is never justified. Consider the case of an interview conducted by CNN's Nancy Grace with Melinda Duckett, whose 2-year-old son, Trenton, had disappeared. Grace's questioning inferred that the mother had something to do with the disappearance. "'Why are you not telling us where you were?' Grace demanded, pounding the table. 'Miss Duckett, you are not telling us for a reason. What is the reason?'"[22] Prior to airing the show, Melinda Duckett's body was found at her grandparents' home. She was the victim of an apparent suicide. Despite the tragedy, CNN chose to air the program anyway, which University of Southern California Professor and former Emmy-winning ABC correspondent Judy Muller called "despicable."[23] Of course the program probably garnered high ratings, but it is difficult to imagine a less ethical way to treat the double tragedy of a missing child and dead mother than airing this program. In fact, some, including Melinda Duckett's parents, allege Grace's questioning drove the woman to suicide in the first place.[24] Whatever Ms. Duckett's culpability in the case of the missing child, it is difficult to imagine what purpose, other than ratings, was served by airing the interview after her death.

Provide Good Reasons

Another principle of ethical speaking has been articulated by Karl Wallace, scholar and former president of the Speech Communication Association (now known as the National Communication Association). Wallace believes that the public speaker must offer his or her audience "good reasons" for believing, valuing, and acting.[25] **Good reasons** are statements, based on moral principles, offered in support of propositions concerning what people should believe or how people should act. Wallace believes that ethical and moral values, as well as

good reasons
Statements, based on moral principles, offered in support of propositions concerning what we should believe or how we should act.

relevant information, are the basic materials of rhetoric. Speakers who rely on "good reasons" value all people and the ethical principles to which they adhere. Not only does the use of good reasons help ensure that the speaker uses ethical means, it is also far more likely to be successful in accomplishing the ethical ends sought by the speaker.

Special Issues for Speakers

As a public speaker, you face some special issues that might not be as relevant in other communication situations. A speech is a uniquely personal event. Unlike a written essay, for example, in which the author may be unknown to the reader, a speaker stands as one with his or her words. In fact, Aristotle said that character "may almost be called the most effective means of persuasion" possessed by a speaker.[26] Five important issues need to be addressed, therefore, because of their special significance for public speakers: (1) plagiarism and source attribution, (2) building goodwill and trustworthiness, (3) revealing or concealing true intentions, (4) discussing both sides of a controversial issue, and (5) inducing fear.

Plagiarism and Source Attribution

plagiarism
Using the ideas of others and presenting them as your own.

Plagiarism—using the ideas of others and presenting them as your own—is highly unethical. What makes it a particular sin for speakers is that they are jeopardizing their most important asset—their character. Few students begin their speech assignment intending to plagiarize. But other pressing assignments, poor time management, sloppy note-taking, or just plain laziness often intervene. Students are tempted to use someone else's words or ideas without credit, assuming that no one will be the wiser. The consequences of such behavior can be severe. An example from the authors' own experience illustrates what can happen.

One of our teaching associates (we'll call him Jack) was ill and asked another TA (Jane) to cover his class. It happened that one of the students in Jack's class was the roommate of a student in Jane's. When Jane heard the same speech in Jack's class that she had heard earlier in the week in her own section, bells went off. Of course, it turned out that one roommate had appropriated the other student's speech. The plagiarizer was caught red-handed, but it didn't end there. The original speech writer was guilty of aiding and abetting the roommate. Both students had to face disciplinary action from the university as well as failure in the class.

Although it's true, of course, that this act might have gone undetected had Jack not become ill, this is not the only way plagiarism is discovered. At our university, and we suspect this is true at others as well, professors often talk about speeches they have heard in class. In fact, every speech at our university is recorded on videotape. Over the years, we have discovered several instances of plagiarism. Each time the students have been shocked and repentant. They have come to realize that they have put their college careers at risk for a few extra points on a speech. The negative consequences of plagiarism are not confined to students. Plagiarism can also destroy a reputation or even a career.

How can you avoid plagiarism? First, you need to recognize that there are varying degrees of the offense. Because plagiarism is a form of intellectual theft, we call these variations "the total rip-off," "the partial rip-off," and "the accidental rip-off."

The Total Rip-Off

The case of the roommates who used the same speech is an example of a total rip-off. Here a student simply gives someone else's speech. Usually it is not a speech from a published source, because such speeches don't often fulfill the assignment. Further, if the speech is well known, it is likely to be spotted instantly as a phony. More common is the use of a speech from a classmate who took the class in a previous term or who is in another section. This is clearly academic dishonesty equivalent to cheating on an exam or turning in someone else's term paper. Most universities and colleges suspend or even expel students caught in this sort of dishonesty. If the speech was knowingly given to the plagiarist, the original author can face the same penalties.

Avoiding this type of plagiarism is easy: Don't offer a speech or accept the speech of another person to present as your own. Most students who use other students' speeches do so out of desperation. Our advice is not to put off preparing your speech until the last minute. Give yourself as much time to research and practice as you would to write a paper for an English class. Realize also that giving a speech you don't really know is likely to be a disaster. You will stumble over words and be unable to answer questions. Even if you escape detection, you'll do yourself little good. If you simply cannot get a speech ready to deliver on time, talk to your instructor. Policies will vary, but your own speech, given late, even with a penalty, is far superior to a ripped-off speech given on time.

The Partial Rip-Off

More common than the total rip-off is the partial rip-off. Here a student creates a speech by patching together material from different sources. Rather than quoting the sources, the speaker presents the ideas as if they were original. The irony is that the speaker has done a lot of work. The problem was not that time ran out. Rather, the speaker wanted to be credited with the ideas.

The way to avoid this type of plagiarism is to give credit to your sources orally and to make sure that you use material from these sources only to enhance your own speech. Rather than simply using the words of another, tell the audience who made the statement or where the idea originated. Interestingly, research has shown that under many circumstances, citing sources in your speech enhances your persuasiveness.[27] Audiences are impressed that you have done your homework. It is important to cite sources as you speak, not just in the bibliography of your written outline. Only by citing sources orally can you inform your audience of where the words, phrases, and ideas came from, which is what you need to do to build your credibility as a speaker. When citing sources orally, be sure to do more than just give a vague reference ("I found this quote on the Internet doing a Google search"). To be meaningful to an audience, an oral citation should include the name and qualifications of the author or source, the date, and enough information for listeners to find it themselves. Internet sources pose a particular challenge. Even if there is no person named as author, you should be able to identify the organization responsible for the content. As we discuss in Chapter 8, many seemingly authoritative Web sites are bogus. Be sure your source is credible before using it in the speech. If you cannot identify who is responsible for the content, your problem is bigger than not knowing how to cite the source. At the same time, you don't want to bore your audiences with long Internet URLs that they can't possibly remember. So, for example, rather than saying, "I got this information on fair usage of copyrighted material from www.copyright.gov/title17/92chap1.html#101," you can simply say, "I got this from the U.S. Copyright Office's official Web site, copyright.gov, on November 1, 2007." That is enough information for listeners to check the source themselves. The full URL should be in your written outline, of course, and you should be prepared to provide it to anyone who asks.

Citing sources is important for direct quotations as well as for specific facts, statistics, and ideas derived from the work of others. Thus, you might not quote Martin Luther King Jr. directly, but you would still refer to him as the author of the idea that people should be judged by their character, not their skin color. As you recognize the importance of providing the source of your ideas, keep in mind that your audience doesn't need a quote or source citation for those facts and ideas that are common knowledge for most well-educated people. For example, you wouldn't need a source to declare that "Albert Einstein developed the theory of relativity" or that "*The Daily Show*'s Jon Stewart once hosted the Oscars." The audience also doesn't want to be bored by repeated citations of the same source when it is the basis of multiple subpoints in your speech. It is sufficient to say, "The facts I will be discussing now about global warming come from former Vice President Al Gore's 2006 book and film, *An Inconvenient Truth*."

In sum, our best advice is that if you didn't think of it yourself and it's not part of the common knowledge of your audience, then it's best to cite the source explicitly and orally for the audience. It not only strengthens your credibility, it's also the right thing to do.

The Accidental Rip-Off

Perhaps the most frustrating thing for an instructor who discovers a student's plagiarism is when the student simply doesn't understand what he or she has done wrong. For example, a student may take significant ideas or even quotes from sources listed in a bibliography accompanying the speech, without saying so in the speech. The student sees no problem, responding, "I did cite my sources–they are right there in the bibliography." For the listener, however, there is no way to know which ideas came from outside sources and which are the speaker's own, as mentioned in the previous section. A common variant of this is that the speaker attributes ideas to a source but actually uses a word-for-word quotation without making that clear to the audience. The written version of the speech outline should include quotation marks to distinguish between paraphrased ideas and direct quotations. Further, you should use "oral" quotation marks. Either state that you are quoting someone, or make it clear from your tone of voice that you are in fact quoting someone else's words. Use such phrases as "To quote Martin Luther King Jr. . . ." or "As Martin Luther King Jr. said . . . ."

Try not to let ideas become disassociated from their source. We've all had the experience of remembering an idea or a quote but forgetting where we heard it. Unfortunately, the tendency in a speech is just to use the words. By taking careful notes as you research your speech, you are less likely to accidentally borrow an idea from another source without attribution.

The Internet

Although we deal at length with the use and abuse of the Internet in Chapter 8, we feel duty bound to caution you about the temptations of the Internet. Cyberspace is not only the preferred source of information among students as they prepare their speeches, it also is the source of most of the plagiarism we find in student speeches. Given the sheer amount of information available, it might seem to some that it's nearly impossible for an instructor to find out where a student's ideas and language originated. Think again: It is not only possible, it gets easier by the day. Many universities and colleges are even subscribing to services such as Turnitin.com to discourage plagiarism.

Whether a full-scale rip-off, an incremental theft, or an accidental violation, plagiarism is a serious ethical offense for the public speaker. Furthermore, as the box "Speaking of . . . Copyright" discusses, plagiarism isn't only unethical, in some cases it may even be illegal. Our best advice is to resist the temptation, cite the sources of your ideas for your audience, and take pride in those ideas that are your own. In Chapter 8 we discuss how to record and cite sources in a speech. But the general principle is to let your audience know exactly where your ideas are coming from.

Building Goodwill and Trustworthiness

A speaker's credibility has several components. Two of the most important are goodwill and trustworthiness, which we introduced earlier. **Goodwill** is the perception by audience members that a speaker cares about their needs and concerns. A speaker who truly cares and can communicate that to the audience not only is more likely to be effective but also is much more likely to behave ethically. There is a huge difference, for example, between the speaker who is trying to put one over on listeners and the speaker who really cares about their well-being. If speakers apply the principle developed by Kant of treating people as ends and not means to ends, then that is a mark of goodwill.

goodwill
The perception by the audience that a speaker cares about their needs and concerns.

Trustworthiness is the perception by audience members that they can rely on a speaker's word. A promise made is as good as done. The effect on a speaker's trustworthiness of a broken promise or a revealed lie is devastating. One reason politicians in general are held in such low regard by the public is that so many of them have broken their promises and become untrustworthy in people's eyes.

trustworthiness
The perception by the audience that they can rely on a speaker's word.

As a speaker, you need to realize that you rarely can accomplish your purpose in one speech or even in a short series of speeches. Often your goals will require a long-term commitment. And your relationship to your audience needs to be one of trustworthiness. If you violate their trust, not only have you behaved unethically, you have jeopardized your chances of achieving your goals as well. The solution to this problem is twofold. First, don't make promises you cannot or do not intend to keep. And second, if circumstances might require you to deviate from prior promises, make it clear what limits there are on your promise.

Speaking of . . .

Copyright

In addition to the ethical issues of source attribution, there is a legal issue as well. Most of the materials you find to support your speech, whether in books, periodicals, or on the Internet, are protected by the copyright laws of the United States, even if they do not carry a copyright notice. This is a complex topic. Although we are not lawyers, there are several guidelines that we recommend you follow in your speeches.

First, short quotations or other excerpts are generally considered "fair use" under the law. According to the U.S. Copyright Office's Web site, fair use for "purposes such as criticism, comment, news reporting, teaching (including multiple copies for classroom use), scholarship, or research, is not an infringement of copyright."[1] You should still acknowledge the source, both in your written outline and orally during your speech.

Second, just because something is on the Internet doesn't mean it's not protected by copyright. For example, the popular search engine Google has a feature that allows you to search for images. These can liven up a speech when shown with PowerPoint™. But, beware, because many of the images you find may be protected. Google states on its Web site: "The images identified by the Google Image Search service may be protected by copyrights. Although you can locate and access the images through our service, we cannot grant you any rights to use them for any purpose other than viewing them on the web. Accordingly, if you would like to use any images you have found through our service, we advise you to contact the site owner to obtain the requisite permissions."[2]

Third, be particularly cautious about the use of video from Web sites such as YouTube. As noted on the site "It doesn't matter how long or short the clip is, or exactly how it got to YouTube. If you taped it off cable, videotaped your TV screen, or downloaded it from some other website, it is still copyrighted, and requires the copyright owner's permission to distribute."[3] In fact, many networks have asked YouTube to remove content they believed infringed on their copyright.

So how can you avoid copyright infringement? First, keep quotations brief and to the point. This is good advice for a speech in any event. As long as it's in a classroom situation, you should be fine. Second, with photos, limit your use to public domain sites. For example, photos from government agencies such as NASA are not copyrighted. If you can't find such photos, consider using ones you have taken. For example, one student gave a speech on modern dairy methods and illustrated her speech with photos from our university farm. Third, if you are using PowerPoint and are connected to the Internet, you may be able to put a hyperlink in your presentation, so that the material viewed is directly from the site that created the content. Thus, rather than showing a clip of *The Daily Show* from YouTube, go to the Comedy Central Web site itself.

When you leave the university and enter the workforce, the fair use exemption related to teaching will no longer apply. Learning the importance of respecting copyrights is important, not only ethically, but also to success in your career. In short, the best advice is when in doubt, leave it out. And if you absolutely must use something that is copyrighted in your speech, seek and obtain permission.

[1]United States Copyright Office, *Copyright Law of the United States of America and Related Laws Contained in Title 17 of the United States Code Circular 92* (n.d.) [Retrieved from http://www.copyright.gov/title17/92chap1.html#101, 25 November 2006.]

[2]*Google.com,* "About Image Search: Frequently Asked Questions," 2005. [Retrieved from http://www.google.com/help/faq_images.html, 26 November 2006.]

[3]*YouTube,* "Copyright Tips," 2006. Retrieved from http://www.youtube.com/t/howto_copyright, 26 November 2006.]

Revealing or Concealing Intentions

One of the thorniest issues you face as a speaker is whether or not to reveal your intentions to your audience. Sometimes, to begin your speech by announcing a position that you know your audience drastically opposes is to deny yourself the opportunity to be heard. On the other hand, to conceal your true intentions can be unethical, particularly if those intentions violate what the audience perceives as its best interests. In some ways, this decision may require the application of "situational ethics." Consider a couple of examples.

You are speaking to a potentially hostile audience about a controversial issue. Let's say you want to convince a group like the Moral Majority that we should not have state-sanctioned prayer in school. Should you begin by announcing your position? What is the likelihood that your argument would be heard? On the other hand, suppose you begin by describing a scenario in which the state requires everybody in school to study the Qur'an and pray to Allah. "How would you react?" you ask them. "Well, now reverse the situation," you continue. "What if Muslim students are required to study the Bible and say the Lord's Prayer?" The idea would be to work from a common ground–that Christians should not be forced to pray to a Muslim God–to the logical application of that principle to the issue of state-sanctioned school prayer.

Certainly this approach is no guarantee of persuading the audience of your viewpoint. But it is hard to argue that it is ethically wrong to begin with points of agreement before moving to areas of disagreement. The intentions of your speech are revealed to the audience. When and how those intentions are revealed is a strategic rather than an ethical issue.

On the other hand, consider the case of the person who telephones and asks you if you would be willing to participate in a survey about energy conservation. Sure, you reply, always happy to help out. After going through a series of questions, you realize that the "pollster" is actually a salesperson for a replacement window company. Your time has been wasted, and now you have to figure out how to get off the phone. The clear misrepresentation of intent–pollster as opposed to salesperson–is ethically wrong. And you have been harmed, if for no other reason than the salesperson stole your time. And, as many sellers know, once they get your ear, the likelihood of closing the sale increases.

What makes these two cases different? Both people begin by concealing their intentions, and both eventually do reveal their goals. But in the first case, the speaker does not misrepresent his or her intentions; rather, they are deferred until after some common ground is established. In the second case, a direct misrepresentation is made–there is no poll. While the two cases seem on the surface to be similar, we would argue that the situations are far different and that the difference is ethically relevant.

These types of cases are not always easy or clear-cut. A universal rule–always state your purpose up front–cannot be applied. Speakers must sincerely ask themselves in what ways their interests and those of their audience intersect. They must then decide the best approach to take in any given case, at the same time striving to maintain goodwill and trustworthiness.

Discussing Both Sides of a Controversial Issue

One question with both ethical and practical implications is whether you should provide an audience with only your side of an issue or mention arguments on the other side of the issue as well. For a number of years, speech experts answered this question pragmatically: It depends on the makeup of your audience. If the general level of education in your audience is high school or less, stick to your side only. If the level of education in your audience is beyond high school, introduce the other side as well. Of course this raises some real ethical concerns. It smacks of using the audience as a means rather than treating them as ends. Basically, it says if you can fool enough of the people, no need to worry about fooling all of them.

The authors have never thought much of the recommendation to present only one side of an issue. What's more, we now have research on our side. This research, which combined the findings of more than 25 studies done over the past four decades, suggests that speakers should use a two-sided persuasive message regardless of the audience's level of education. Specifically, the most effective persuasive strategy is to present both sides of a controversial issue along with a refutation of the opposing point of view.[28] If you think about it, this makes good sense. In general, your audience will have heard or will eventually hear the other side of the story. What does it do to the audience's perception of your credibility if they believe they've not been told the whole truth? Two-sided presentations are not only more ethical, they are also more effective. We discuss the issue of "message sidedness".

Inducing Fear

Speakers have used fear as a motivational tool throughout history. When used in moderation by a credible source, contemporary research tells us that fear appeals can influence what people think and how they behave. There is nothing wrong with using reasonable fear to influence people. For example, raising the specter of skin cancer to encourage sun-safe behavior uses fear to save lives. Used ethically, fear appeals are simply another rhetorical device speakers can build into their messages.

The research also shows, however, that when people are excessively fearful they do not always think clearly or reason critically. Thus they are more susceptible to believing false claims and half-truths spoken by speakers who know they are vulnerable in this regard. Such behavior is clearly unethical, but the practice of inducing fear to make people compliant is also quite common.

As Professor Barry Glassner documents in his remarkable book, *The Culture of Fear: Why Americans Are Afraid of the Wrong Things,* we are being made unnecessarily fearful for our personal safety by two primary sources: news media and politicians.[29] Local TV news media devote far more coverage to violent crimes and accidents than to any other topic. This trend gives rise to the impression that our local communities pose a greater threat to our personal safety than they actually do. During election cycles, politicians exploit this false impression by emphasizing the promise to be "tough on crime."

We think speakers should use fear appeals only when there is a genuine risk of harm. What constitutes a genuine risk may be debatable, but speakers should build fear appeals into their messages only after a legitimate, evidence-based debate has been held. To do otherwise is unethical.

Tips and Tactics

Ethical Guidelines for Speakers[30]

- Provide truthful, relevant, and sufficient information to allow audience members to make informed choices.
- Present "good reasons," not just those that may work. Appeal to the best, not the worst, in people.

- Reinforce and be consistent with democratic processes. Recognize the importance of free speech in a democratic society and the right of others to disagree.
- Demonstrate goodwill and trustworthiness toward the audience.
- Put yourself in the position of the listeners and treat them with the same respect you would expect were the roles reversed.
- Recognize that both the means and the ends of a speech should be ethical. Be concerned with the possible consequences of accepting the message as well as with its truthfulness and accuracy.
- Take responsibility for your own work. Plagiarism is the ultimate in intellectual dishonesty.

Ethical Norms for Listeners

People who find themselves in the primary role of listeners also need to think about their ethical obligations. Remember, audience members are very much a party to the public speaking transaction. When you are a listener, you too bear some responsibility for the consequences of the speech. Thus we suggest these norms for ethical listening: (1) Be civil. (2) Take responsibility for the choices you make. (3) Stay informed on the issues of the day. (4) Speak out when you are convinced that a speaker is misinforming or misleading people. (5) Be aware of your own biases.

Be Civil

When we go to the movies at our local Cineplex, we are usually treated to a set of rules that appear on the screen prior to the featured film. These rules basically tell us not to talk to our companions during the film, make sure our cell phones and pagers are turned off, and if in the company of a crying or misbehaving child, to retreat to the lobby out of respect for other audience members. Maybe we need to post a similar set of rules in our classrooms. Every new term it seems as if we have to single out audience members for one or more of the preceding infractions or even walking in or out of the room during a classmate's speech. It is as embarrassing for us as it is embarrassing for them. Moreover, it should never have to happen. The first ethical responsibility of audience members is to be civil to the speaker and other audience members. It is tough enough for people learning to become more effective speakers to manage their presentations without the added distraction of people talking or a cell phone "accidentally" ringing.

Take Responsibility for Choices

The second guideline for listeners is to recognize that unless coerced, they are responsible for the choices they make during and following a communication transaction. This means listeners cannot blame a speaker for the decision to riot following a speech or for violating human rights because they were persuaded to

Advertisers frequently use men and women as sex symbols to promote smoking, even though the practice is both exploitive and unethical.

do so by a charismatic communicator. Just as the judges at the Nuremberg trials following World War II concluded that "following orders" was not an excuse for war crimes, audience members cannot excuse their unethical behavior on the grounds that they were complying with a speaker's request.

Stay Informed

A third guideline, which logically follows from the first two, is that listeners are responsible for keeping themselves informed on issues of the day. People who are uninformed about important topics and vital issues are easy prey for propagandists. History is replete with examples of people who have tried to attribute unethical behavior to ignorance, real or imagined. They range from the people who said they didn't know the Nazis were sending millions of Jews to their death during World War II to the tobacco company executives who claimed tobacco was not addictive. Simply put, ignorance is no excuse for unethical behavior. As a result, we ask our own students to at least think about making a commitment to do the following:

- Read a newspaper daily, preferably one published in a major metropolitan area.
- Read a weekly newsmagazine.
- Read a publication at least once a month that holds a political view contrary to their own.

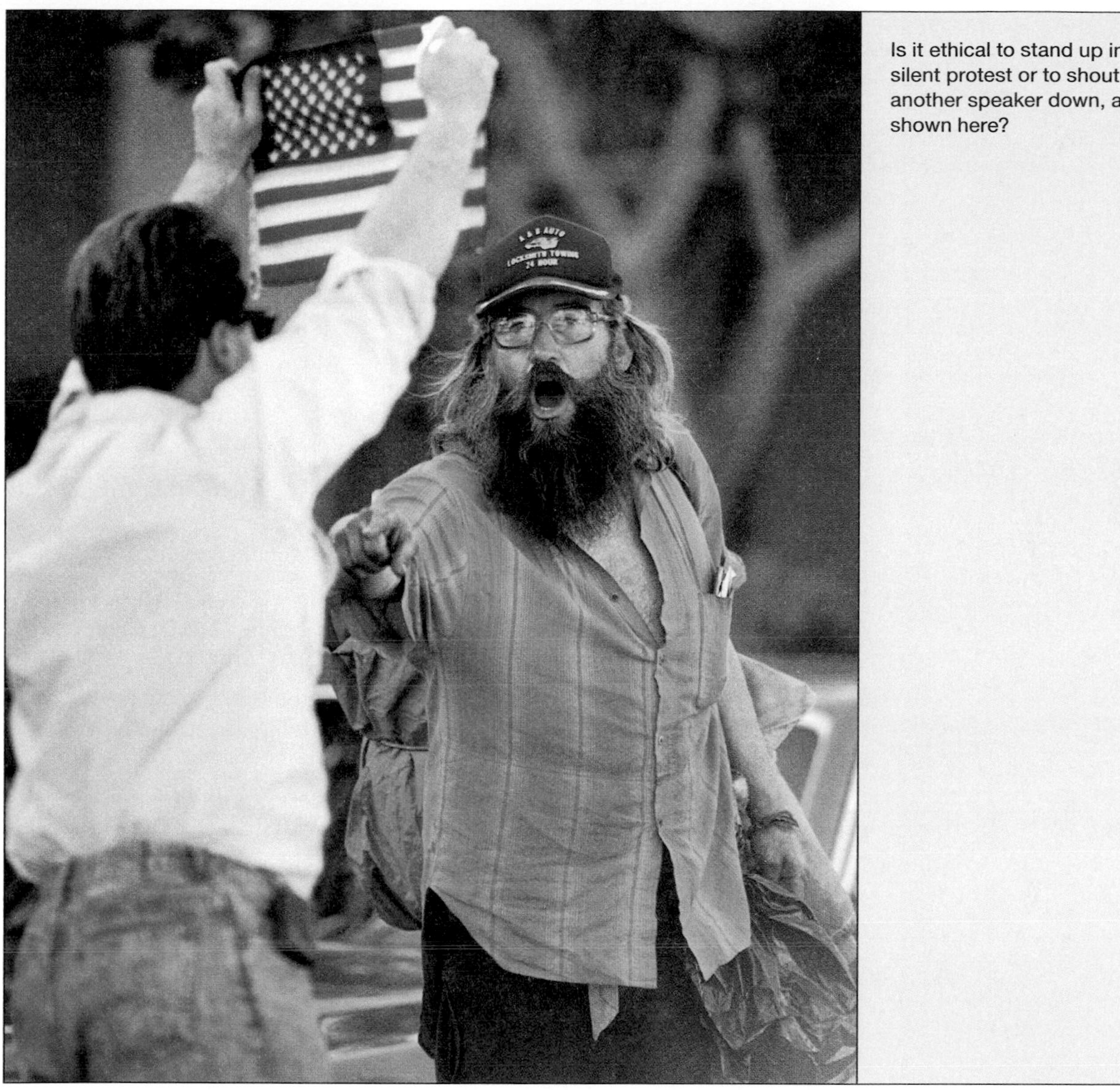

Is it ethical to stand up in silent protest or to shout another speaker down, as shown here?

Speak Out

The fourth guideline for listeners is related to the first three. It involves the audience members' ethical obligation to speak up after a speech when convinced that a speaker is misinforming or misleading people. Most of us have been in situations where we knew someone was bending the truth, leaving out pertinent details, or passing off another's ideas as original. Under some unique set of circumstances, keeping this knowledge to ourselves may be justified. In most circumstances, however, listeners owe it to themselves and others to speak up. Speaking up can take the form of a question for the speaker following a presentation, asking the appropriate agency for equal time to speak, writing a letter to the editor of a newspaper or magazine, or confronting the speaker one on one. Whatever the appropriate medium, constructive objections are generally preferable to silence.

Be Aware of Biases

The final guideline for listeners concerns our subjective view and the manner in which it biases how we receive and process a speaker's message. Perception is colored by our experiences, both real and vicarious. Rather than denying the fact, it's much healthier and realistic for us to admit this to ourselves. Only then can we determine how much of our reaction to a speech is based on its content and relational dynamic and how much is attributable to our individual biases.

Tips and Tactics

Ethical Guidelines for Listeners[31]

- Be civil.
- Be aware that all communication is potentially influential and that there are consequences to accepting any message. Ask what influence the speaker is seeking to exert.
- Stay informed on important topics so that you can judge the accuracy of the communication provided by others. Be willing to independently confirm information that appears questionable.
- Be aware of your personal biases to reduce your susceptibility to appeals to prejudices. Be willing to listen to opposing views with an open mind.
- Be aware of deceptive communication ploys and work to expose those guilty of fallacious reasoning, propaganda ploys, and outright deception. Be willing to speak out in response to deceptive speech.
- Put yourself in the position of the speaker and treat him or her with the same respect you would expect were the roles reversed.
- Provide constructive feedback to the speaker if the opportunity is given.

Summary

OLC www.mhhe.com/brydon6

To evaluate your understanding of this chapter, visit our Online Learning Center Web site for quizzes and other chapter study aids.

Several basic ethical questions are of concern to speakers:

- Why care about ethics? Most people fundamentally want to do what is right.
- Is everything relative? Ethical relativists believe there are no universal ethical principles.
- Are there rules for every situation? Universalists believe there are ethical

standards that apply to all situations regardless of the individual, group, or culture.

- Does the good of the many outweigh the good of the few? Utilitarianism is based on this principle.
- How do specific situations affect ethics? Situational ethicists believe it is sometimes necessary to set aside one ethical principle to fulfill a higher law or principle.
- Do the ends justify the means? Speakers should seek ethical ends utilizing ethical means, such as those found in the National Communication Association's Credo for Free and Responsible Communication in a Democratic Society.

Ethical norms for public speaking are:

- Be truthful.
- Show respect for the power of words.
- Invoke participatory democracy.
- Demonstrate mindfulness of cultural diversity where consistent with ethical principles.
- Treat people as ends, not means.
- Provide good reasons.

Public speakers face special issues:

- Plagiarism–using words or ideas of another without attribution–is considered a serious ethical violation.
- Building goodwill and trustworthiness is essential to successful and ethical public speech.
- Whether to reveal or conceal one's intentions can present an ethical as well as a practical dilemma for speakers.
- Giving a two-sided presentation is both ethically sound and pragmatically more effective.
- Inducing fear can be ethically suspect if done to excess.

Listeners should adhere to the following ethical norms:

- Be civil.
- Take responsibility for the choices they make.
- Stay informed on the issues of the day.
- Speak out when they are convinced that a speaker is misinforming or misleading people.
- Be aware of their own biases.

Check Your Understanding: Exercises and Activities

1. In a brief speech or short paper, explain the reason you believe the best ethical standard for the public speaker is (a) relativism, (b) universalism, (c) utilitarianism, or (d) situational ethics. Define the version of ethics you endorse, and explain why you feel it is the best alternative for public speakers.

2. Read the following cases and answer the questions about each one. Depending on your instructor's directions, either write a short paper responding to one or more of the scenarios or discuss one or more of them in a small group.

   Case A: A student in your public speaking class presents a speech that contains glaring factual errors. As an audience member who is familiar with the topic, you realize that the speaker has not done research and has "made up" certain "facts." What should you do? What do you think the instructor should do?

   Case B: You are preparing a speech arguing against a tuition increase at your college. In your research, you discover strong arguments against your position. Nevertheless, you still believe the tuition increase is a bad idea. Should you share the arguments against your position with your audience, or present only your side of the story?

   Case C: You are required by your instructor to attend a speech outside of class time. You discover on arriving at the lecture hall that the speaker holds views precisely the opposite of your own. What should you do?

   Case D: You are assigned by your teacher to speak for a position you fundamentally oppose on a question about which you hold strong moral beliefs, such as abortion. What should you do?

3. In a short paper, discuss the differences and similarities between the ethical obligations of speakers and listeners. As a speaker, how would you deal with listeners who are unwilling to meet their basic ethical obligations? As a listener, how would you respond to a speaker you felt was unethical?

4. In a short paper, discuss whether you agree with Quintilian that "no one can speak well who is not good." Cite some contemporary or historical examples to support your position.

5. In a short paper, consider the question of whether there can be any situation in which it is ethical to "shock people into action" through the use of especially horrifying or unpleasant images. Give examples to support your position.

6. In your view, what modern politician is most successful at eliciting feelings of goodwill and trustworthiness? Why do you think this person is successful in doing so? Be prepared to discuss your example in class.

7. Administrators, faculty, and students on campuses across the United States are trying to come up with speech codes that strike a balance between First Amendment rights and the right of people in the college community to be protected from hateful and demoralizing language. Working either on your own or in an instructor-assigned group, find out if your school has a speech code that prohibits the use of certain types of words and language. If it does, how would you amend it to fit your or your group's thinking? If it doesn't, what would you include in such a code? Write a short paper on your findings or thoughts, or be prepared to discuss them in class.

Notes

1. "Quotations About Integrity, Ethics, Behavior, Character." [Retrieved from http://www.geocities.com/quotegarden/integrty.html, 2 October 2001.]

2. Whitney Mitchell, "Enron Whistleblower Talks Ethics, Corruption to Business Students," *Idsnews.com,* 6 November 2006. [Retrieved from http://www.idsnews.com/news/story.aspx?id=39019, 24 November 2006.]

3. Samuel Enoch Stumpf, *Socrates to Sartre: A History of Philosophy* (New York: McGraw-Hill, 1966), 35.

4. James Rachels, *The Elements of Moral Philosophy* (New York: Random House, 1986), 21.

5. Immanuel Kant, *Groundwork of the Metaphysics of Morals,* trans. H. J. Paton (New York: Harper & Row, 1964), 88.

6. Kant, *Groundwork of the Metaphysics of Morals,* 96.

7. Rachels, *Elements of Moral Philosophy,* 108–109.

8. John Stuart Mill, *Utilitarianism,* in *Essential Works of John Stuart Mill,* ed. Max Lerner (New York: Bantam Books, 1961), 198–199.

9. William Temple, *Nature, Man and God* (New York: Macmillan, 1934), 405, as cited in Joseph Fletcher, *Situation Ethics: The New Morality* (Philadelphia: Westminster Press, 1966), 27.

10. James A. Jaksa and Michael S. Pritchard, *Communication Ethics: Methods of Analysis,* 2nd ed. (Belmont, Calif.: Wadsworth, 1994), 21.

11. Fletcher, *Situation Ethics,* 26.

12. Fletcher, *Situation Ethics,* 121.

13. Stumpf, *Socrates to Sartre,* 36.

14. Aristotle, *Rhetoric,* trans. W. Rhys Roberts (New York: Modern Library, 1954), 22.

15. Quintilian, *Institutio Oratoria,* trans. H. E. Butler (Cambridge, Mass.: Harvard University Press, 1920), 317.

16. Quintilian, *Institutio Oratoria,* 315.

17. Jaksa and Pritchard, *Communication Ethics,* 65.

18. Greg Farrell, "Martha Stewart Convicted of Four Felonies," *USA Today .com,* 5 March 2004. [Retrieved from http://www.usatoday.com/money/media/2004-03-05-stewart_x.htm, 21 August 2004.]

19. Jaksa and Pritchard, *Communication Ethics,* 64.

20. Jaksa and Pritchard, *Communication Ethics,* 74.

21. United Nations, *General Assembly Resolution 217 A (III) of 10 December 1948.* [Retrieved from http://www.un.org/Overview/rights.html, 25 November 2006.]

22. C. W. Nevius, "CNN Talk Show Reaches a New Depth of Sleaze," 15 September 2006, *San Francisco Chronicle.* [Retrieved from SFGate.com/cgi-bin/article.cgi?file=/c/a/2006/09/15/MNGSAL67FH1.DTL, 25 November 2006.]

23. Nevius.

24. The parents of Melinda Duckett have sued CNN and Nancy Grace, claiming the interview was responsible for their daughter's suicide. See Stephen Hudak, "Parents sue Nancy Grace, say show led to suicide," *Chicago Tribune,* 22 November 2006. [Retrieved from http://pqasb.pqarchiver.com/chicago tribune/access/1166355811.html?dids=1166355811:1166355811&FMT=ABS&FMTS=ABS:FT&type=current&date=Nov+22%2C+2006&author=Stephen+Hudak%2C+Tribune+Newspapers%3A+Orlando+Sentinel&pub=Chicago+Tribune&edition=&startpage=4&desc=Parents+sue+Nancy+Grace%2C+say+show+led+to+suicide, 25 November 2006.]

25. Karl R. Wallace, "The Substance of Rhetoric: Good Reasons," *Quarterly Journal of Speech* 49 (1963): 239–249.

26. Aristotle, *Rhetoric,* 25.

27. James C. McCroskey, "A Summary of Experimental Research on the Effects of Evidence in Persuasive Communication," *Quarterly Journal of Speech* 55 (1969): 169–176.

28. Mike Allen, "Meta-Analysis Comparing the Persuasiveness of One-Sided and Two-Sided Messages," *Western Journal of Communication* 55 (1991): 390–404.

29. Barry Glassner, *The Culture of Fear: Why Americans Are Afraid of the Wrong Things* (New York: Basic Books, 1999).

30. Several of these speaker responsibilities are derived from Sarah Trenholm, *Persuasion and Social Influence* (Englewood Cliffs, N.J.: Prentice Hall, 1989), 18–20.

31. Several of these listener responsibilities are also derived from Sarah Trenholm, *Persuasion and Social Influence.*

2

Between Audience and Speaker

To be a good speaker, you have to be a good listener.

Imagine that it is the 10th week in your term and you have heard approximately 60 speeches from your classroom colleagues. Topics have ranged from how a Vegan diet can save native grasslands to the amount of energy people waste while running the engines of their autos in the fast food drive-through. You've also heard speeches about saving the rain forests, impact-free backpacking, and the joys of using a bicycle to commute. Although you consider yourself a responsible citizen who cares about the environment, you now find yourself listening to another speech on the topic, this time about the evils of SUVs. Having grown up on a farm, you drive a full-size pickup, as does your dad. Because you come from a large family, there's also a Ford Excursion in the family motor pool. And now this student speaking in front of the class is arguing that people who drive these "fossil fueled monstrosities" are partly responsible for the war in Iraq. Having heard enough, you flip open your cell phone and begin sending text messages to your roommate about how bored you are and that you can't wait for the weekend.

Now put yourself in the speaker's shoes. You've waited all semester long for the opportunity to talk about your belief that our country's entanglements in the Middle East are partly a result of our wasteful consumption of fuels such as oil and gas. Your sister is in Iraq right now; her reserve unit was called up six months ago. You feel passionately about the need to reduce America's addiction to foreign oil, you've marshaled your facts, and you've rehearsed your speech for days. Yet you now find yourself losing your focus and fumbling over your words because you can't keep your eyes off this "yahoo" who is more interested in chatting it up on his cell phone than listening to what you have to say. How rude!

Although this example is intentionally over the top, it illustrates a point we make with our own students at the beginning of each semester. With roughly 25 students in a class, for every speech students give they will listen to 24. This means they will spend about 96 percent of their time listening to other speakers and only 4 percent actually giving speeches. Added to the time spent listening to their teachers, we half joke that the class really ought to be called "Public Listening."

We know first hand that it's not always easy to listen to people, especially when we think we have "heard it all before" on their subject. We also know, however, what it's like to try and share a message on a topic we are passionate about, but appears boring or bothersome to some students.

Two points need to be made in this regard. First, listening is both important to audience analysis and to the message you eventually shape for your speech. When you make an effort to listen to your classmates you are not just being courteous; you are learning about their attitudes, beliefs, and values. Second, when you use this knowledge to shape your speech, you demonstrate for audience members the fact that you *respect them and the time they have generously given you.*

This chapter is designed to assist you in becoming a better public speaker and audience member by first becoming a better listener. We begin with the importance of listening and the nature of the process itself. We then focus on the common obstacles we need to overcome to improve listening. Finally, we introduce a framework and set of specific skills that, when put into practice, will help us become effective models of listening.

Listening

Objectives

After reading this chapter and reviewing the online learning resources at www.mhhe.com/brydon6, you should be able to:

- Explain what listening involves.
- Describe the significant role that listening plays for both speakers and audience members.
- Recognize and demonstrate the difference between hearing and listening.
- Identify common misconceptions about listening.
- Demonstrate understanding, appreciative, empathic, and feedback-oriented listening skills.
- Identify and overcome obstacles to listening.
- Provide and accept constructive feedback from classmates and your instructor about public speaking.

Key Concepts

appreciative listening
connotation
context
culture
denotation
empathic listening
listening
mindfulness
pinpoint concentration
selective attention
wide-band concentration

> "To listen is an effort, and just to hear has no merit. A duck hears also."
>
> –IGOR STRAVINSKY

Everyday Importance of Listening

We engage in listening much more than any other communication behavior. As Exhibit 6.1 shows, over the course of our lives listening easily eclipses all other communication activities.[1] Research also reveals that most of us are not very good at listening. The average listener remembers only about half of what was said immediately after hearing a message, and only about half of that–a mere quarter of the original message–48 hours later.[2]

The listening skills you learn and practice in this class will help you both now and in your future. First, as a college student, you are exposed to hundreds of hours of lectures, group discussions, and mediated communication. The ability to process and absorb information is the essence of learning. Not every professor is a brilliant speaker, holding your attention with ease. You need to listen especially well if you are to obtain the maximum benefit from your college career.

Second, listening skills are essential to success in the workforce. One of the key complaints of many employers is that employees do not listen effectively, costing millions of dollars each year in mistakes and inefficiencies. Among the skills employers value in listeners are "listening for content; listening to conversations; listening for long-term contexts; listening for emotional meaning; and listening to follow directions."[3]

Third, listening skills are essential to interpersonal communication, especially in families. How many times have you heard children or parents complain that no one listens to what they say? In interpersonal contexts, listening must go well beyond content, focusing on the emotional and relational components of the communication transaction.

Fourth, listening skills are essential to effectively communicate information to others. You need to adapt your own messages to the feedback you receive from others. Understanding what others need is essential to successfully influencing their beliefs, attitudes, and actions through the speeches you share.

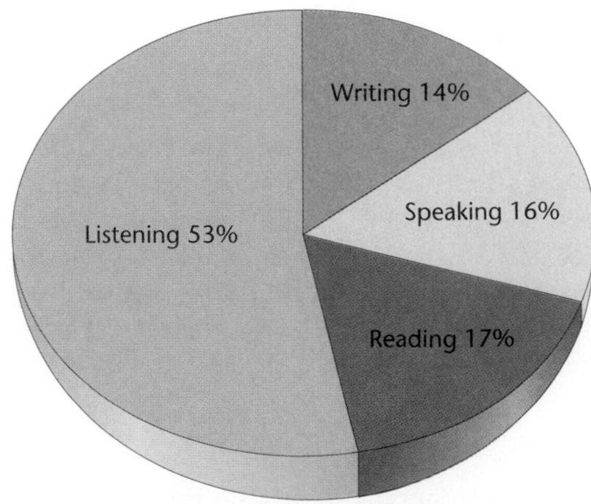

Exhibit 6.1
Listening Relative to Other Types of Communication

The Process of Listening

Listening
The process of receiving, constructing meaning from, and responding to spoken and/or nonverbal messages.

The International Listening Association defines **listening** as "the process of receiving, constructing meaning from, and responding to spoken and/or nonverbalmessages."[4]

Listening is a complex process, part mental and part behavioral. The International Listening Association suggests listening involves: (1) hearing, (2) understanding, (3) remembering, (4) interpreting, (5) evaluating, and (6) responding. These steps are interdependent, meaning that a breakdown in one will lead to problems with the others.

Hearing

Hearing is but a single component of listening. Hearing is all about sound. Hearing requires that we discriminate among the sound waves that enter the inner ear and register with the brain.

Understanding

Comprehending what we hear is more complicated. It depends on the sum total of our experience, including our command of language and knowledge about the context in which we find ourselves. We can hear what we recognize as a word but not necessarily understand it. That requires first the ability to define and apply the word. But even some familiarity with the word we hear doesn't guarantee understanding. We also need to know something about the context in which we hear the word. Prior to Man O' War, a famous racehorse being beaten for the first time, people understood the word "upset" to mean physical and mental stress exclusively. Now, of course, upset may be more frequently used to describe an underdog defeating the odds-on-favorite in a contest.

Remembering

Needless to say, the retention of information we've heard and understood depends on many factors. In situations where we are anxious, it's not uncommon to forget the name of a person we just met. Patients, who are anxious about their health, often remember only half of what their doctors tell them. Remembering, in either the short or long run, what we hear and think we understand requires mastery of techniques we'll introduce later in the chapter.

Interpretation

The accuracy of listening depends greatly on the interpretation of the sounds we hear and think we comprehend. We color what we hear as a result of our attitudes, beliefs, and values. As we suggested in our opening example, it's nearly impossible to listen without filtering what we hear and think we comprehend through the fine mesh of our previous experience.

Evaluation

Whether we like, dislike, or are neutral about something is a natural consequence of our interpretation of what we hear. It is next to impossible to be completely objective. Existing attitudes, beliefs, and values filter the entire process. Becoming a better listener, then, begins with simple recognition of the fact that we are predisposed to use our individual biases to filter what we hear.

Responding

Feedback is an inherent part of the communication transaction. How audience members respond to speakers can be spoken and/or nonverbal. We depend on such responses, moreover, in the effort to determine whether our audience has heard, understood, remembered, interpreted, and evaluated what we've tried to communicate. And this brings us back to something we implied earlier. Listening demands reciprocity between speakers and audiences as they attempt to become better listeners. To know that we've been listened to, we must see and hear a response. To let speakers know we have listened to them, we also must provide them with an audible and/or visual response to their message. Simply put, the process of listening is a two-way street.

Obstacles to Listening

In the effort to become a better, more effective listener, we need to confront some of the main obstacles to listening. Recognition of these obstacles prepares us mentally to embrace the other mental and behavioral skills that make effective listening possible. Of the many obstacles that potentially interfere with listening, we begin with misconceptions about the process itself.

Misconceptions

There are four common misconceptions about listening: (1) it's easy, (2) it's a matter of intelligence, (3) it's no different than reading, and (4) it's not subject to advance planning.[5]

"It's Easy to Listen." Some people think that listening is like breathing—that we are born competent listeners. Of course, that is just as fallacious as assuming that because we breathe, we all breathe well enough to become professional singers. Similarly, just because we've heard others talk to us all of our lives does not mean we are effective listeners. Quite the contrary, our complacency about listening is one of the very things that makes us susceptible to poor listening habits.

"Smart People Are Natural Born Listeners." The fact that we are smart enough to *understand* what a speaker says doesn't mean that we will actually *listen* to what the speaker hopes to share. Smart people are not immune to the psychological filters that bias how they interpret and evaluate other's messages. Smart people may even be quicker to misinterpret a message because they think

they have heard what's being said before or because they dismiss the credibility of the speaker before hearing the speaker out.

"I Can Read, So I Can Listen." Although reading and listening skills might seem to be correlated, that is not the case. In fact, the skills required are quite different. The reader controls the pace of communication, whereas a listener is at the mercy of the person speaking. A reader can reread a confusing passage, whereas a listener may have only one chance to get the point. Reading is typically a solitary activity; listening most often takes place in groups, where it might be hard to hear the speaker or there might be distractions. Listening skills, as you can begin to see, require development in their own right.

"There's No Need to Plan Ahead." A fourth common misconception is that listening just happens–that there's no need to plan for it. Of course, sometimes you will end up listening to an unexpected conversation. But if you know in advance that you will be in a listening situation such as the one you face in your speech class, you should plan ahead. For example, in most introductory speech courses, students provide each other with both oral and written feedback. Who do you think will do a better job: the student who prepares in advance, including a review of criteria for the speech, checklists for speech evaluation, and a clear understanding of the speech assignment, or the one who shows up to class only to be surprised by the fact that he or she will be responsible for providing classmates with feedback about their speeches? Finally, when the tables are turned, whose speeches do you think most likely will benefit from critical evaluation by classmates?

Physical Conditions

The physical environment clearly affects our ability to listen and can be an obstacle too.[6] Among the factors that can inhibit listening are noise, an unpleasant room temperature, poor lighting, physical obstacles, and uncomfortable chairs. A noisy, hot, poorly lit room, with uncomfortable chairs and a post blocking your view, is hardly an ideal listening environment. On the other hand, a quiet, well-lit room

with a clear line of sight, comfortable (but not too comfortable) chairs, and a pleasant temperature allows you to concentrate on the speaker. Although there is usually not much the listener can do about the physical environment, being aware of its impact on listening helps you know how much you need to focus. In addition, you can often choose your location to listen. Students who sit in the back of the classroom, where their view is limited, often are tempted to let their attention drift. Those who move front and center clearly are interested in listening to what is said.

Holding a large audience's attention can be a challenge for a speaker.

The best speakers try to minimize the effects of a troublesome physical environment on audience listening. If the acoustics are bad, they may raise or amplify their voice so that it is more audible. If their line of sight is blocked from some audience members, they may move toward audience members in the back of a room. If some loud activity is occurring within earshot of the audience, they may make light of the situation rather than show that the noise bothers them. No matter what a speaker does to overcome a problem environment, however, audience members also bear some responsibility in this regard.

Cultural Differences

Communication patterns vary from culture to culture. **Culture** is a learned system of beliefs, customs, and values with which specific people identify. The relative importance of the context in which listening takes place differs from one culture to another. Anthropologists Edward T. Hall and Mildred Reed Hall define **context** as the information that surrounds an event and contributes to the meaning of that event.[7] For example, suppose you receive a message on your answering machine from a relative you almost never hear from except in an emergency. The message simply says, "Call me right away." Needless to say, you would be alarmed because you know this person never calls you unless there is a serious problem. On the other hand, if you received the same message from a friend with whom you often get together, you might assume he or she just wants to set up a meeting. The same message has a very different meaning because of the context in which it occurs.

culture
A learned system of beliefs, customs, and values with which specific people identify.

context
information that surrounds an event and contributes to the meaning of that event.

Some cultures rely more than others on unspoken information contained in the context to determine the meaning of a message. In high-context (HC) cultures, such as Japan, the Arab states, and the Mediterranean countries, the context of statements can be extremely important. Much of the meaning in such cultures is carried not only by the words that are spoken but also by the situation in which they are uttered. In low-context (LC) cultures, such as the United States, Germany, and most northern European countries, people rely less on the overall communication situation and more on the words spoken to convey meaning.

When low- and high-context people communicate with each other, the results can be frustrating. Hall and Hall note that HC people are apt to becom e impatient and irritated when LC people insist on giving them information they perceive they don't need. Conversely, low-context people are at a loss when

When high- and low-context cultures meet, listening may become more difficult.

high-context people do not provide *enough* information. Too much information frequently leads people to feel they are being talked down to; too little information can mystify them or make them feel left out.[8] For further discussion of listening in different context cultures, see the box "Considering Diversity: Listening in High- and Low-Context Cultures" on page 115.

Although we cannot give you any simple rule of thumb for dealing with cultural differences in listening, our best advice is to be aware of the culture of the person(s) to whom you are listening or with whom you are speaking. Then, take differences from your own culture into account and try to adjust your behavior accordingly. Finally, if you expect to be listening or speaking to someone from a different culture, which is increasingly likely on a college campus, learn as much as you can in advance about the person's culture.

Personal Problems

Most people have had the experience of being so preoccupied with a personal problem they couldn't pay attention to what someone was saying. Personal problems can easily detract from listening to what is being said. The best advice for overcoming this obstacle is to recognize the situation and to focus on what is being said, as difficult as that may be. For example, if you were plagued by a personal problem prior to an important job interview, chances are you would tell yourself to "get your act together." You need to do exactly the same thing before listening to (or giving) a speech.

Bias

As we have repeatedly said, bias gets in the way of listening. It predisposes us to hear only what we want to hear. All people are biased, though not to an equal degree. Bias reflects an opinion formed without evidence, usually about a person

Considering Diversity

Listening in High- and Low-Context Cultures

As discussed in this chapter, some cultures place greater emphasis on the context in which communication occurs than on what is actually said. In such high-context cultures, as they are called, people realize that what one hears while listening must be deciphered only after thoroughly considering the context in which it is heard. Yes may mean no and vice versa, for example, depending on where and under what circumstances they are uttered. The opposite is true in low-context cultures, where the greatest emphasis is given to the spoken word. People trust what they think they hear without giving undue attention to the context in which it is heard.

One of the major stumbling blocks to the Paris Peace Conference, which laid the foundation for ending the war in Vietnam, was the shape of the conference table. Why? Because the North Vietnamese were concerned about the "message it would send" to those observing the negotiations. Vietnam is a high-context culture.

What kinds of problems do you see occurring when people from high- and low-context cultures listen to each other's speeches? Which of the listening skills discussed in this chapter do you think would most help in overcoming these problems? Be specific!

Source: Edward T. Hall and Mildred R. Hall, *Hidden Differences: Doing Business With the Japanese* (Garden City, N.Y.: Anchor/Doubleday, 1987).

or group of people. Racial, religious, sexual, and other such biases, although forbidden by law, often exist in the reality of people's opinions. Recognizing bias is an important step to overcoming it.

Bias isn't always based exclusively on false generalizations about groups of people. Prior, but incomplete, knowledge can cause people to form hasty judgments. Such was the case with the man who shot and killed a Sikh gas station owner in Arizona shortly after the September 11, 2001, terrorist attacks on the World Trade Center and Pentagon.[9] Not only is it wrong to assume all Arabs and Muslims are terrorists or support terrorists' goals, Sikhs are neither Arab nor Muslim. They actually are a different religious group originating in India.

Regardless of its source, bias is a serious impediment to listening. To overcome bias, listeners need to first recognize its existence, mentally set it aside, and recognize its irrationality. Although this may seem easier said than done, the ability to listen without undue bias is one of the keys to critical thinking and decision making.

Connotative Meanings

Important to this discussion are the related concepts of denotation and connotation. **Denotation** involves the objective, conventional meanings you find in a dictionary for a word. **Connotation** involves meanings you won't always find in a dictionary for a word, or the ideas, images, and emotions people associate with a word. Although denotative meanings can be learned by reading a dictionary, connotations, which are largely determined by cultural usage, are learned over time from seeing and listening to examples. As an illustration of connotation, consider some of the various words used to describe a person who weighs more than average. The word *chubby* is appropriate when describing a baby or toddler, but it would prove hurtful when used to describe a teenager. The word *stocky* doesn't mean the same when used to describe a man as when it is used to describe a woman. And, although it would be okay for a physician to write on a chart that a patient was overweight, it wouldn't be appropriate to write "tubby."

denotation
The generally agreed upon meaning of a word, usually found in the dictionary.

connotation
The secondary meaning of a word, often with a strong emotional, personal, and subjective component.

Anxiety

Anxiety significantly detracts from our ability to process the information to which we are exposed. Anxious speakers often are unable to focus on audience feedback as they speak or actively listen to an instructor's feedback when they finish speaking. Likewise, anxious audience members have difficulty listening actively and remembering what they have heard.

Poor Listening Habits

The final obstacle may be the most common and easily overcome: poor listening habits. Ralph Nichols, one of the seminal researchers on listening, found that poor listeners commonly shared a set of 10 poor listening habits.[10] According to Nichols, poor listeners tend to do the following:

1. Quickly decide that a subject is dull or uninteresting
2. Criticize the speaker's delivery rather than focus on content
3. Jump to conclusions and make a quick evaluation of speakers without hearing them out
4. Listen only for facts, thus missing the speaker's main ideas
5. Try to outline everything the speaker says rather than focusing on the important points
6. Fake attention when they are not really interested
7. Become easily distracted
8. Avoid difficult listening situations
9. Let emotional language interfere with listening to the speaker's message
10. Waste the differential between the rate of speaking (about 125 words a minute) and the rate of thinking (400 to 500 words a minute)

The audience member in the opening example of this chapter exhibited many of these bad habits. Deciding the speech topic was just more of the same old environmentalist rhetoric and becoming distracted to the point of sending a text message were just two of the manifestations of these bad habits. As teachers we've experienced these and many more bad listening practices from our students, who are then often puzzled by their low test scores or missed assignments. Obviously, the cure for these habits is to do just the opposite. You can assess your own listening habits by answering the questions in the box "How Well Do You Listen?" Later in this chapter we discuss a number of ways to improve your listening and overcome these poor listening habits.

The Model Listener

Up to this point we have concentrated on the nature of listening and common obstacles that can interfere with effective listening. We now turn our attention to becoming model listeners. Effective listening begins with the common types of listening in which we engage and what we can expect to gain from each type. Different types of listening are inextricably tied to the goals of listening

Self-Assessment

How Well Do You Listen?

When listening to a speaker, how often do you engage in the following listening behaviors? Circle the number on the scale that best describes your listening behaviors.

		Almost always				Almost never
_____	1. I dismiss the subject as uninteresting.	1	2	3	4	5
_____	2. I criticize the speaker's delivery.	1	2	3	4	5
_____	3. I make a snap judgment about the speech.	1	2	3	4	5
_____	4. I listen for facts rather than the main point of the speech.	1	2	3	4	5
_____	5. I write down virtually everything the speaker says.	1	2	3	4	5
_____	6. I pretend to be paying attention when i'm not interested.	1	2	3	4	5
_____	7. I allow myself to be distracted.	1	2	3	4	5
_____	8. I avoid listening to difficult material.	1	2	3	4	5
_____	9. I let a speaker's words stir up my emotions.	1	2	3	4	5
_____	10. I daydream when a speaker speaks too slowly.	1	2	3	4	5

Add up your the points to see how your listening skills measure up. Total _____

40–50 Excellent listening habits

30–39 Good listening habits, but could improve

20–29 Needs improvement in listening

10–19 Poor listening habits

Source: Based on Ralph G. Nichols, "Do We Know How to Listen? Practical Helps in a Modern Age," *Speech Teacher*, 10 (1961): 118-24.

(Exhibit 6.2). Types and their intended goals include but are not limited to listening to understand, listening to appreciate, listening to empathize, and listening to fulfill the speaker's need for feedback. An additional type, critical listening, which involves assessing a speaker's reasoning, is discussed at length in Chapter 16. Needless to say, these types and goals overlap. Thus, think of them as interdependent rather than independent facets of model listening.

Goals of Listening

Listening to Understand

Understanding, in the truest sense of the word, is a multistep process. Further, there are different levels of understanding, depending on the goal of the listener. The first step in the process of understanding is to discriminate between differing auditory and visual stimuli.[11] As infants we first recognize parental voices, then sounds, words, and eventually the complex structures of language.

Exhibit 6.2 Goals of Listening

Type	Goal	Example
Listening to understand	To recognize meaning based on auditory and visual cues and to comprehend meaning	Listening to a lecture on Einstein's theory of relativity
Appreciative listening	To experience stimulation and enjoyment	Listening to a speech to entertain
Empathic listening	Understand and relate to origins of speaker's thoughts and feelings	Listening to persuasive appeal for stem cell research from a speaker whose health is at risk
Listening to provide feedback	Identifying content and behaviors to facilitate improvement	Listening for clear statement of purpose

Complementary visual stimuli, such as facial expression, gesture, and movement, become part of meaning for us, as does touch. The careful listener is sensitive to both the verbal and the nonverbal nuances of messages. This is especially true for public speaking. Listeners in the audience need to look beyond just the words of a speaker's message. By the same token, speakers need to listen to the entire message received from the audience. This means they should listen not only for aural feedback but for feedback from other sources as well. These sources include the expressions on audience members' faces, their body orientation, and head movements such as nodding in agreement.

Once you have discriminated among various sounds and sights, the next step to understanding is making sense of the aural and visual stimuli received.[12] Successful listening to understand demands that the meaning you assign to a message closely approximates that of the source of the message. How well you understand depends on several factors. Chief among them are vocabulary, concentration, and memory.[13]

Vocabulary

Obviously, you cannot comprehend something for which you don't have meaning. Thus a limited vocabulary has the undesirable effect of limiting your ability to understand messages. In fact, failure to master the necessary vocabulary can be embarrassing or worse. For example, both authors of this text were high school debaters. One of us recalls a particularly embarrassing incident that resulted from not knowing the meaning of the word *superfluous.* Unaware that the other team's plan to remove all "superfluous United States tariffs" meant that they would remove only the unnecessary ones, the author's team produced several examples of tariffs that were essential to American industries. During cross-examination, an opposing team member asked the author, "Do you know what *superfluous* means?" Of course, the author did not know. When the opposition pointed out that every tariff the author's team had cited was, by definition, *not* superfluous, and that only superfluous tariffs would be removed, the debate was, for all practical purposes, lost. Needless to say, a dictionary became standard material for all future debates.

Concentration

A second important factor in listening to understand is concentration. As we know all too well, our minds are easily distracted from the task at hand. If you doubt that, think back to the last time you immediately forgot the name of someone to whom you had just been introduced.

There are two types of concentration: wide-band and pinpoint. **Pinpoint concentration** focuses on specific details. **Wide-band concentration** focuses on patterns rather than details. As a result, wide-band concentration assists you in listening for the tone of the speech or for its larger meaning in a particular context.

pinpoint concentration Listening that focuses on specific details rather than patterns in a message.

wide-band concentration Listening that focuses on patterns rather than details.

Both types of concentration, however, demand that you try to block out stimuli that compete with the message on which you are trying to focus. These competing stimuli range from the obvious, such as a garage band playing in the free-speech area outside your classroom, to the subtle, such as the gastrointestinal growls your stomach makes when you are hungry.

Memory

Closely related to concentration, memory is the third factor that influences listening to understand. Failure to remember often reflects the fact that you also failed to concentrate. Consider again the example of forgetting the name of someone to whom you have just been introduced. Although this very common experience simply may be the result of "mental laziness," most often it is the product of the anxiety accompanying the situation. Both anxiety and preoccupation with feelings of anxiety have a devastating effect on our powers of concentration and memory. As you are being introduced to someone, you may be too busy thinking about how you are being perceived to concentrate on the person's name. It isn't that you forgot the name–it's that you didn't listen for and process the name in the first place.

Much of your day is spent in situations that require comprehensive listening. And nowhere is this more likely to be true than in your speech class. Here are some skills that will help you improve your listening to understand.[14]

Tips and Tactics

Improving Listening to Understand

- *Utilize the time difference between speech and thought effectively.* Most people speak at a rate of about 125 to 150 words per minute, but the human brain can process 400 to 500 spoken words per minute, although that is possible only with a special process known as "compressed speech." By using the time differential to think about what you are hearing, you can better interpret and understand the significance of what is said.
- *Listen for main ideas.* Don't get bogged down in insignificant detail. Rather, focus on understanding the main ideas and principles a speaker is discussing.
- *Listen for significant details.* Though not as important as main ideas, some details are fairly significant. Try to determine which details are illustrative of the main ideas and have significance for understanding what is being said.
- *Learn to draw valid inferences.* What does it all mean? Try to determine what conclusions you can draw from the speech.

Listening to Appreciate and Enjoy

appreciative listening Listening that involves obtaining sensory stimulation or enjoyment from others.

Appreciative listening involves receiving enjoyment from others.[15] This could include listening to music, drama, poetry, or a speech to entertain. Though it might appear that such listening "just comes naturally," the fact is that you can enhance your pleasure by expanding your listening experiences, improving your understanding of what you are listening to, and developing your powers of concentration. Music appreciation classes, for example, help students learn what to listen for in different kinds of music.

This is also true of your speech class. Learning about the various types, styles, and structures of speeches should help you appreciate what a rarity a good speech is. Learning how important it is to construct and share a good speech, moreover, should reinforce your appreciation and give you a more finely tuned ear. Here are some skills that will help you improve your appreciative listening.[16]

Tips and Tactics

Improving Appreciative Listening

- *Use opportunities to gain experience with appreciative listening.* Listening appreciatively, as with all forms of listening, requires experience with different situations.
- *Be willing to listen appreciatively to a variety of writers, speakers, composers, and so on.* Even if you've developed preconceptions about a particular composer or type of music, for example, be willing to listen with an open mind. You may not appreciate Beethoven, and someone else may not appreciate the Deftones. Chances are that with a proper frame of mind you can learn what it is that makes them both appealing to large numbers of people.
- *Develop the ability to concentrate while listening appreciatively.* Many forms of appreciative listening depend on not letting your mind wander. Of course, the greater your experience with a variety of situations that involve listening, the more ability you will have to concentrate on the important aspects of the experience.

Empathic Listening

empathic listening Listening for the purpose of understanding and relating to the origins of a speaker's thoughts and feelings.

Empathy involves: (1) the attempt to understand why others think and feel as they do and (2) using this understanding as a foundation for interpreting their communication behavior. **Empathic listening** involves focusing on both the content and relational components of the speech transaction we introduced in Chapter 1.

The empathic listener tries to use both the content and delivery of a speech to better understand the speaker's reasons for sharing information or attempting to persuade audience members.

Empathic listening requires that listeners overcome the obstacles previously discussed. Genuinely empathic listening also demands more than superficial information about a speaker's background. Thus, either the listener or the speaker must find a way to share appropriate details about the speaker's cultural, demographic, and individual experience. Paying attention and listening to what your classmates say in class and during their speeches is a good start in this respect. Sharing appropriate information about yourself in both your speeches and oral contributions to class discussions will also contribute to their understanding.

Tips and Tactics

Improving Empathic Listening

- Try to focus on people's general comments about topics of discussion and their possible relationship to underlying attitudes, beliefs, and values.
- Take note of information about people's geographic background and group affiliations.
- Listen with your eyes and ears for vocal and facial expressions that may reveal what a speaker is feeling.

Listening to Provide Feedback

One of the unique features about a public speaking class is that audience members are not just listening to speeches for their own benefit. Typically, they are also called on to provide feedback to speakers to assist them in improving their public speaking skills. Although an excessive focus on delivery skills is normally a bad listening habit, in a public speaking class, paying attention to the level of those skills in your classmates is often an integral part of the classroom experience. Not only may you be asked to provide written or oral feedback about other students' delivery, you may find things in your classmates' style that you will want to emulate in your own speeches.

As you provide feedback, keep in mind that your goal should be *constructive criticism.* If a speaker's delivery was ineffective, for example, don't just say the delivery was poor, give specific suggestions for how the delivery could be improved. Rather than saying, "I couldn't hear you," say something like "You should try to increase the volume of your voice so people in the back can hear you clearly." Rather than saying, "Your speech was totally disorganized," try something like "It would be easier to follow the speech if you previewed your main points at the beginning." If comments are to be provided orally, we always recommend that critics begin with a positive and avoid statements that could be embarrassing. Written comments should also be balanced between positive and those that suggest areas in need of improvement. However, one can often be more direct in writing because the comments are only seen by the speaker.

A few guidelines for giving feedback and receiving it as well will help you improve your own performance. Much of what we say here harkens back to the basics of the speech process, which we explained in Chapter 3. Here are some things to look for in evaluating a speech. Your instructor may have specific additional requirements and may provide a standard form for speech evaluation.

Tips and Tactics

Listening to Provide Feedback

- What was the speaker's purpose? Did the speech successfully fulfill that purpose? Was the purpose appropriate to the audience and the situation?
- Did the speaker introduce and conclude the speech with impact?
- Did the speaker have a clear thesis for the speech?

Speaking of . . .

Listening to Feedback from the Audience

Of course, as a speaker, you need to know how to receive the feedback given by your classmates and instructor. Once a speech is over, you become a listener or a reader of written evaluations. The most important suggestion we can make for this role is to avoid the very traps that befall poor listeners. Avoid deciding that the feedback is uninteresting or biased. Hear out your critics, even if you disagree with their judgment. Focus on the main points; don't get distracted by nitpicking. Take notes on what is said. Be genuinely interested—after all, the reason for taking the class is to improve your speaking skills. Don't let yourself get emotional or defensive; it will only make the situation worse. Ultimately, however, you have to be true to yourself. Take the comments as what they are—opinions, albeit educated ones. Use the feedback to improve your speaking, but don't allow yourself to become so obsessed with it that you become overly anxious about speaking. Keep in mind the techniques we dealing with public speaking anxiety. The same principles apply to the anxiety that occurs when we know we are going to be evaluated.

- Did the speaker connect with the audience?
- Did the speaker organize the speech in a manner that was easy to follow?
- Were the main points previewed in the introduction and summarized in the conclusion?
- Did the speaker use good evidence to support claims? Were the sources of evidence disclosed and were they of high quality? Did the evidence justify the claims being made?
- Did the speaker use understandable and appropriate language? Were unfamiliar terms defined?
- Did the speaker deliver the speech effectively? Was it easy to hear the speaker's voice? Were the gestures and movement of the speaker effective or distracting?
- Overall, how effective was the speech in informing, persuading, or entertaining you as an audience member?

Rules of the Road: Improving Specific Listening Skills

Regardless of type and goal, there are some specific rules of the road for listening. These tried and true techniques can help any listener do a better job. Many of these techniques will work in both public speaking and face-to-face interpersonal settings. Keep these rules in mind whatever your listening situation:

mindfulness
The conscious awareness of the speech transaction including the people involved, their purpose for gathering, and the context in which they find themselves.

- *Be mindful.* **Mindfulness** involves conscious awareness of the speech transaction including the people involved, their purpose for gathering, and the context in which they find themselves. Mindful listeners live in the present and are attuned to what is taking place as it happens. Effective listening demands mindfulness.
- *Choose to selectively attend to the speech transaction.* We live in a world where many sources are competing for our attention throughout our day. Because we cannot possibly attend to all of these sources and their messages, we select relatively few, usually because they are potential sources of reward.

One of the best ways to improve as a speaker (reward) is to observe and listen to other speakers. By listening to and observing other speakers we often uncover techniques and tactics we can model in the effort to improve our own speeches.

- *Listen with as many sensory channels as possible.* Communicating in general and speaking specifically involve verbal and nonverbal behaviors. Eye contact, movement and gestures, for example, do not simply complement the content of a speech. They enrich both the meaning and impact of the entire speech transaction. Checking what people say verbally against what their nonverbal behavior communicates also can help you in accurately understanding what is being said.
- *Block out distracting stimuli.* This includes avoiding distracting thoughts as well as external distractions such as looking out the window.
- *Suspend judgment.* Regardless of the type of listening, the same principles that apply to critical listening apply here—don't prejudge a speaker and don't rely on stereotypes. Keep an open mind.

To improve his chances of being understood, our former student and San Francisco radio news reporter Bret Burkhart uses sound to convey visual as well as verbal information to his audience.

- *Focus on the main points.* It's too easy to lose sight of the forest for the trees. Ask yourself what the speaker's main points are and resist the temptation to fixate on minor details.
- *Listen for highlights and transitions.* These verbal cues will help you know what's most important to a speaker's message and when the speaker is moving on to a new main point.
- *Take effective notes.* As Nichols and Lewis point out, there are numerous ways to take notes.[17] Outlining is an obvious method, but there are less obvious ones as well. For example, you can record your notes in two columns, one for facts and the other for principles. Another useful technique is to listen for a while without taking notes and then write a brief paragraph summarizing what has been said. This technique allows you to alternate between intense listening and note-taking in three- or four-minute intervals.

Summary

Listening is necessary to becoming a competent speaker and audience member. Keep the following principles in mind:

- Listening is the process of receiving, constructing meaning from, and responding to spoken and/or nonverbal messages.

To evaluate your understanding of this chapter, visit our Online Learning Center Web site for quizzes and other chapter study aids.

- Listening involves six interdependent steps: hearing, understanding, remembering, interpretation, evaluation, and responding.
- Listening is important to our success in school, work, and our relationships.
- We spend much more time listening than speaking.
- Potential obstacles to listening include misconceptions such as:
    - Listening is easy.
    - Listening is a matter of intelligence.
    - Good readers make good listeners.
    - Listening needn't be planned.
- Other potential obstacles to look out for include:
    - The physical conditions of the speech transaction.
    - Cultural differences.
    - Personal problems.
    - Bias.
    - Confusion about connotative meaning.
    - Anxiety.
    - Poor listening habits.
- The types and goals of listening are tied to each other.
- Listening can be directed at appreciating and enjoying different forms of communication, greater understanding, empathy, and providing speakers with constructive feedback.
- Listening is a skill both mental and behavioral.
- Effective listening skills require practice in:
    - Mindfulness.
    - Choosing to selectively attend to speakers and messages.
    - Listening with as many sensory channels as possible.
    - Recognizing and making an effort to overcome the preceding obstacles.
    - Blocking out distracting stimuli.
    - Suspending judgment.
    - Focusing on a speaker's main points.
    - Listening for highlights and transitions.
    - Taking effective notes.

Audience members should provide constructive feedback to speakers, and speakers should listen with an open mind to audience feedback.

Check Your Understanding: Exercises and Activities

1. In a short paper or speech, describe an incident in which your message was misunderstood or you misunderstood another person's intended message. Were there any tip-offs that the speech transaction was not effective? How could the misunderstanding have been avoided?
2. Planning for upcoming listening situations is important. Consider one of your classes in which the instructor regularly lectures. In what ways can you prepare for listening to the next lecture? Are there any specific listening obstacles you need to overcome? After attending the lecture, see if your understanding was enhanced by your preparation for the class.
3. In a short paper, describe a situation you have experienced in which bias affected the listening process. Choose a situation in which you feel your meaning was distorted due to bias or a situation in which you feel your own biases handicapped you in the listening process.
4. Make a list of 10 words that have varying connotations to different people or in different situations. Be prepared to share your list with classmates in small groups or before the full class, depending on your instructor's directions.
5. Describe three times in a given day during which you engaged in critical listening. Be prepared to share your list with classmates in small groups or before the full class.

Notes

1. Andrew D. Wolvin and Carolyn Gwynn Coakley, *Listening,* 3rd ed. (Dubuque, Iowa: W. C. Brown, 1988), 12–13.
2. Lyman K. Steil, Larry Barker, and Kittie W. Watson, *Effective Listening* (New York: Random House, 1993), 12–13.
3. Anthony P. Carnevale, Leila J. Gainer, and Ann S. Meltzer, *Workplace Basics: The Skills Employers Want* (Washington, D.C.: American Society for Training and Development and U.S. Department of Labor, 1988), 12.
4. International Listening Association, *Home Page,* (n.d.), [Retrieved from http://www.listen.org/Templates/home.htm, 29 December 2006.]
5. Melvin L. DeFleur, Patricia Kearney, and Timothy G. Plax, *Fundamentals of Human Communication* (Mountain View, Calif.: Mayfield, 1993), 112–13.
6. DeFleur, Kearney, and Plax, *Fundamentals of Human Communication,* 113–17. The remaining obstacles to listening are taken from this source.
7. Edward T. Hall and Mildred Reed Hall, *Hidden Differences: Doing Business With the Japanese* (Garden City, N.Y.: Anchor Press/Doubleday, 1987), 7.
8. Hall and Hall, *Hidden Differences,* 10–11.
9. Tamar Lewin, "Sikh Owner of Gas Station Is Fatally Shot in Rampage" [Retrieved from Lexis-Nexis, 24 September 2001] (*New York Times,* 17 September 2001, B16).
10. Ralph G. Nichols, "Do We Know How to Listen? Practical Helps in a Modern Age," *Speech Teacher,* 10 (1961), 118–24.

11. Wolvin and Coakley, *Listening,* 140.
12. Wolvin and Coakley, *Listening,* 188.
13. Wolvin and Coakley, *Listening,* 189–206.
14. Wolvin and Coakley, Listening, 207–25.
15. Wolvin and Coakley, *Listening,* 320.
16. Wolvin and Coakley, *Listening,* 330–33.
17. Ralph G. Nichols and Thomas R. *Lewis, Listening and Speaking: A Guide to Effective Oral Communication* (Dubuque, Iowa: W. C. Brown, 1954), 41–53.

Effective public speakers must adapt to every rhetorical situation they face even if it is less than ideal.

Adapting to Your Audience

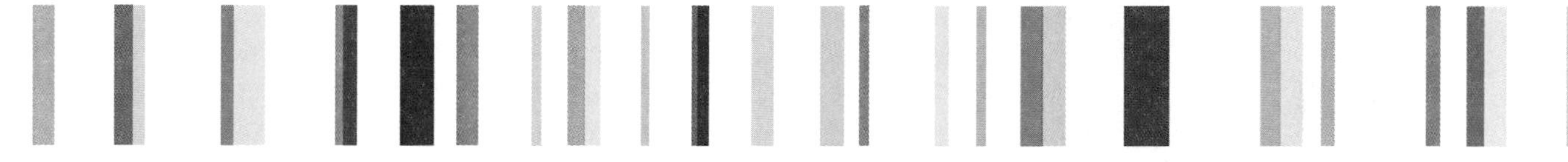

Objectives

After reading this chapter and reviewing the online learning resources at www.mhhe.com/brydon6, you should be able to:

- Define and apply the concept of rhetorical situation.
- Identify short- and long-term goals for speaking to a particular audience.
- Determine whether your audience is voluntary or captive.
- Analyze the cultural, demographic, and individual diversity of your audience.
- Adapt to the cultural, demographic, and individual diversity of your audience.
- Gather information to learn about your audience.
- Confront and adapt to constraints associated with the rhetorical situation.

Key Concepts

attitude
audience diversity
belief
captive audience
central beliefs
constraint
cultural diversity
deficiency needs
demographic diversity
demographics
growth needs
individual diversity
long-term goals
peripheral beliefs
primitive beliefs
rhetorical situation
short-term goals
socioeconomic status
values
voluntary audience

> " I was not planning on speaking here tonight, but this is where my journey has taken me. . . . "
>
> –CAROLYN MCCARTHY
>
> *Wife and mother of victims of the Long Island Railroad massacre, speaking to the 1996 Democratic National Convention.*

In Their Own Words

Mary Fisher Speaks Out on AIDS

The AIDS virus is not a political creature. It does not care whether you are Democratic or Republican; it does not ask whether you are black or white, male or female, gay or straight, young or old. Tonight, I represent an AIDS community whose members have been reluctantly drafted from every segment of American society.

Though I am white and a mother, I am one with a black infant struggling with tubes in a Philadelphia hospital.

Though I am female and contracted this disease in marriage and enjoy the warm support of my family, I am one with the lonely gay man sheltering a flickering candle from the cold wind of his family's rejection.

Source: Official Report of the Proceedings of the Thirty-Fifth Republican National Convention, August 19, 1992.

Mary Fisher, who contracted the HIV virus from her husband, riveted the 1992 Republican Convention with her speech about AIDS.

In previous editions we opened this chapter with the personal stories of people who used their public speaking skills to help them realize a purpose that they neither expected nor wanted in their lives. One was Democratic Congresswoman Carolyn McCarthy, who was driven to seek public office as a result of her husband's senseless murder and her need to do something about the availability of semiautomatic assault rifles. Still another was Mary Fisher, a Republican consultant and mother who became an activist in the campaign against HIV/AIDS as a result of being infected with HIV by an unfaithful husband. We add a new face to the list–that of Patrick Murphy–an Iraq war veteran who was elected in 2006 to Congress from a seat in Pennsylvania that had not voted for his party since 1992. As a soldier, Murphy had patrolled the streets of Baghdad with the 82nd Airborne and was awarded a bronze star. As a citizen, Murphy became disenchanted with the policies of the administration and narrowly defeated an incumbent member of Congress.

McCarthy, Fisher, and Murphy were each presented with a set of circumstances which compelled them to speak out against what they believed were threats to not just their own well-being, but to everyone's life, liberty, and pursuit of happiness.

You can read excerpts of speeches by all three in the boxes labeled "In Their Own Words" in this chapter. The full text of their speeches can be found in Appendix B.

Their success in overcoming these circumstances and realizing their purpose depended mightily on their ability to connect with audiences of tremendous diversity. Their success in connecting with their audience, moreover, depended on their ability to master the main subject of this chapter: The rhetorical situation.

In Their Own Words

Carolyn McCarthy's Journey

December 7th, 1993—that was the day of the Long Island Railroad massacre. My life and the lives of many others changed forever. . . . On that day I started a journey, a journey against gun violence in this nation. Today I am here as a nurse, as a mother, as a person who isn't afraid to speak up on what is going on in this country. . . . The journey I began in 1993 wasn't one that I had planned. Getting involved in politics wasn't anything I ever wanted to do. But this journey will make a difference when our neighborhoods pull together, when government listens to us again. When all of us, Democrats and Republicans, come together to solve our problems, not just fight about them.

Source: Reprinted by permission of the author.

Although we sincerely hope you are never compelled to speak out as a result of the kind of misfortune that visited Carolyn McCarthy and Mary Fisher, as was the case with Congressman Murphy, you may at some point in your life feel compelled to speak out on a topic about which you simply cannot remain silent. Whether you succeed in moving people in your desired direction will depend first on how well you match your public speaking skills to your audience, the context in which you speak, and the inevitable constraints you face.

Carolyn McCarthy, a homemaker and nurse, never expected that one day her personal tragedy would lead her to address the 1996 Democratic National Convention about gun violence.

This chapter is meant to help you prepare not only for unforeseen circumstances in the future, which will motivate you to speak, but also for the one in which you find yourself right now: your speech class. In the pages that follow we focus on a variety of topics, all of which are related to the task of analyzing and adapting to your audience. These topics include the following:

- How public speeches emerge as a response to a rhetorical situation
- The importance of thinking about the purpose and goals of your speech relative to your audience
- How your purpose and goals are mediated by audience diversity
- How best to adapt your speech to diverse audiences
- The importance of identifying and adapting to your potential audience and to the situational constraints you may encounter
- How to gather information about your audience to help you analyze it.

In Their Own Words . . .

Patrick Murphy Speaks on House Floor to Oppose Escalation in Iraq

I take the floor today not as a Democrat or Republican, but as an Iraq war veteran who was a Captain with the 82nd Airborne Division in Baghdad.

I speak with a heavy heart for my fellow paratrooper Specialist Chad Keith, Specialist James Lambert and 17 other brave men who I served with who never made it home.

I rise to give voice to hundreds of thousands of patriotic Pennsylvanians and veterans across the globe who are deeply troubled by the President's call to escalate the number of American troops in Iraq.

I served in Baghdad from June of 2003 to January of 2004. Walking in my own combat boots, I saw first hand this Administration's failed policy in Iraq.

Source: "Press Release: Patrick Murphy Speaks on House Floor on Oppose President Bush's Escalation," February 13, 2007. [Retrieved from http://www.house.gov/apps/list/press/pa08_murphy/021307IrawqSpeech.html, 20 April 2007].

Patrick Murphy, a decorated Iraq war veteran spoke out and was elected to Congress.

The Rhetorical Situation

Understanding the nuts-and-bolts of the rhetorical situation begins with the history behind the art and science of public speaking.

Although the specific term *rhetorical situation* wasn't coined until the late 1960s, its roots can be traced to ancient Greece and the fifth century BC. Then as now there was a need for public speaking skills because democracy requires that people talk about and debate public policy. Further, there were no lawyers, and people had to plead their own case in court. A group of teachers of rhetoric, known as *Sophists,* taught the skills of speaking for a fee. Plato opposed their approach to rhetoric as dishonest and proposed his own philosophy of rhetoric in two dialogues, the *Gorgias* and the *Phaedrus.* Plato believed that one should first discover the truth philosophically and then use rhetoric only in service to truth.

Plato's famous student Aristotle brought order and systematic focus to the study of the rhetorical situation. Aristotle wrote the *Rhetoric,* probably the most influential writing on the subject to this day. Aristotle defined rhetoric as the "faculty of observing in any given case the available means of persuasion."[1] He specified that rhetoric consisted of three modes of proof: *ethos*, the personal credibility of the speaker; *pathos*, putting the audience into a certain frame of mind; and *logos*, the proof or apparent proof provided by the actual words of the speech (*logos* being the Greek word for "word"). In many ways this classification foreshadows much of contemporary communication research with its emphasis on source credibility *(ethos)*, audience analysis and reaction *(pathos)*, and message construction *(logos)*.

The study and practice of rhetoric was further refined by Roman rhetoricians such as Cicero and Quintilian, who developed the canons of rhetoric we discussed in Chapter 3: The classic laws of invention, organization, style, delivery, and memory.

After the Roman period, the study and practice of rhetoric went into a period of decline. As Europe plunged into the Middle Ages, the need for a complete rhetoric was diminished, and human affairs were largely governed by church dogma. Eventually, rhetoric came to be associated almost entirely with matters of style. It is also largely from this period that rhetoric came to be associated with empty words, signifying nothing, as the often heard expression, "that's just rhetoric," suggests.

With the coming of the Enlightenment, rhetoric was rediscovered. There is not sufficient space here to chronicle all the theorists who revived rhetoric. Particularly noteworthy, however, are the trio of Hugh Blair, George Campbell, and Richard Whately, who wrote in the late 18th- and early 19th-centuries. Blair concerned himself largely with style. Campbell was a proponent of a type of psychology emphasizing discrete mental faculties, returning rhetoric to a concern with the audience and pathos. Whately revived the concern with invention. His treatise on the *Elements of Rhetoric* gave a new importance to logic and reasoning in rhetoric.

By the early 20th-century, departments of speech began to emerge as discrete entities on college campuses. Theorists again began writing about rhetoric and rhetorical theory, many of them returning to the subject's fifth-century BC roots in ancient Greece.

Given this rich history, rhetorical scholar Lloyd Bitzer was following well-established tradition when he sought in 1968 to ground rhetoric in situational factors. He defined a **rhetorical situation** as "a natural context of persons, events, objects, relations, and an exigence [goal] which strongly invites utterance."[2] The elements of that situation include an exigence (goal), an audience, and a set of constraints that set the parameters for the rhetorical response.

rhetorical situation
A natural context of persons, events, objects, relations, and an exigence (goal) which strongly invites utterance.

Patrick Murphy, Mary Fisher, and Carolyn McCarthy are examples of people who responded to an exigence (goal) by facing audiences from all backgrounds, cultures, and ideologies. As we discuss your own speech situations, remember that your goals and the audiences you speak to are central to preparing just the right speech. And, as you will discover later in the chapter, there are also factors that will constrain or limit your choices–everything from how much time you have to speak to the legal limits of slander and libel. Let's begin, then, by looking at your goals as a speaker and the specific purpose you seek to fulfill in any given speech situation.

Goals and Specific Purpose

All too often beginning speakers get ahead of themselves in the planning process: for example, they start with the challenges an audience poses without first considering their own purpose in speaking and the goal they hope to achieve. If you have no clear goal to start with, no amount of audience analysis is going to help. We want you to be able to reasonably predict how your audience is likely to respond to your speech. This begins with deciding on your goal and then selecting a specific purpose that will make sense in light of the audience you know awaits you and the goal you hope to achieve.

You can have both **short-term goals** and **long-term goals**. For example, Mary Fisher sought in her speech to have her audience realize that AIDS

short-term goals
Those ends that we can reasonably expect to achieve in the near term.

long-term goals
Those ends that we can hope to achieve only over an extended period of time.

is not a virus that only attacks gays, intravenous drug users, or the sexually promiscuous. She was a married professional, faithful to her spouse, and she contracted the virus from her husband. If audience members recognized that AIDS could infect anyone, not just a few groups, then she would fulfill her short-term goal. In the long term, of course, she desired more–an end to the epidemic and the stigma associated with AIDS. But she first had to choose an attainable goal.

Although we should never lose sight of the "big picture," we should also recognize that the realization of short-term goals makes the realization of long-term goals more probable. Giving up a bad habit for a day, for example, makes giving up the habit for a week or longer much easier for people. It's in the speaker's best interest, then, to focus on what an audience would find palatable in the short run before tackling tougher long-term goals.

Your specific purpose, as discussed in Chapter 3, is the objective you hope to achieve in speaking to a particular audience on a particular occasion. Although your instructor will probably assign you a general purpose for each speech, such as to persuade, to inform, or to entertain, the specific purpose is up to you. The specific purpose should be chosen to fulfill a specific goal.

The Audience

Given the specific purpose and goals you have tentatively established for your speech, you now want to be able to predict whether they make sense in light of your audience. Analyzing your audience is an extension of the process we all go through when meeting and getting to know new people. It begins on a general level and then becomes increasingly specific. When we meet new people, we try to gauge the degree to which they are similar to us; for example, do they share our language and dialect? We then use this information as a basis for predictions about how to introduce ourselves and what topics of conversation and questions would be appropriate. As we get to know people better, we learn more about what makes them unique. We then use this new, more sophisticated knowledge to guide us in broaching more sensitive topics with them.

You do much the same thing with an audience. Instead of focusing on a single person, however, you have the more difficult task of focusing on many. What you discover about them helps you decide what to say and how to say it. You can never know all there is to know about even a small audience. Still, if you are systematic in your analysis, you can learn a tremendous amount about the increasingly diverse people you encounter. You can profitably use what you learn about such people to adapt your purpose, goal, and eventual message so that they welcome rather than reject your speech.

Any hope you have of achieving your speaking goals, however, depends on whether there is an audience "capable of being influenced by discourse and of being mediators of change."[3] Audience analysis begins by knowing who your audience is.

Audience Choice

In looking at your audience, ask yourself two basic questions:

- Do I get to choose my audience?
- Does my audience get to choose whether to listen to me?

In some situations you will be able to choose the audience for your speech. But in many cases, including your public speaking class, you will have no choice. Short of changing class sections, you will not be able to select another audience. Once you leave the classroom, however, you are likely to have some degree of choice about which audiences to address.

When you choose an audience, think about two important questions. First, what do they think of my goals? If an audience is likely to support your goals, then your task is quite different than if they are indifferent or dramatically opposed. Managers of political campaigns nearly always stage audiences by filling them with people who agree with the goals represented by their politicians. The last thing a campaign manager wants is an audience full of unpredictable "wild-cards" who may or may not share the politician's goals.

Second, ask if and how your audience can help you achieve your goals. We've heard speeches in a classroom that urged the approval of an international treaty to reduce global warming. This is a noble goal, but aside from writing a letter to public officials there is very little class members can do to help achieve this goal. On the other hand, college students can personally do their part to fight global warming: take public transportation, ride their bikes, and purchase cars with good gas mileage. The best public speakers not only ask whether their audience supports their goals but also how the audience members can realistically help them achieve those goals.

In addition to your choice of audiences, you need to consider the audience's ability to choose whether to hear you speak. Audiences can be broadly defined as voluntary or captive. A **voluntary audience** is one that chooses to hear a speaker. A **captive audience** is one that has no choice about hearing a speech. Whether audience members are present voluntarily can make a big difference in their response to a speech. For example, when controversial filmmaker Michael Moore came to our campus in the fall of 2003, a standing-room-only audience paid to see him. Although some audience members clearly came to heckle him, the vast majority was there to cheer him on. Compare this to the response of the captive audience who booed him when he used his Academy Award acceptance speech earlier in 2003 to denounce the war in Iraq. Academy members and guests were not there to hear Michael Moore's political views but to celebrate their industry.

voluntary audience
Listeners that choose to hear a speaker.

captive audience
Listeners that have no choice about hearing a speech.

When speaking to your classmates, it is important to remember that they are in the room not as volunteers but because they are required to be there. We regularly discourage students from selecting topics that might be offensive or hurtful to their classmates. Instead, we encourage them to select topics on which their classmates can be influenced and have some power to act.

However you arrive at your audience–whether you choose them or they choose you–it is crucial that you learn as much as you can about them, beginning with an understanding of their diversity–culturally, demographically, and individually.

Audience Diversity

audience diversity
The cultural, demographic, and individual characteristics that vary among audience members.

Audience analysis begins with recognition and acceptance of the fact that today's audience is more diverse than ever. **Audience diversity** represents the cultural, demographic, and individual characteristics that vary among audience members. According to an analysis of the most recent U.S. Census by *USA*

There's a better than even chance that the student seated next to you comes from a different background than you do.

Today, "The nation's diversity increased dramatically over the past decade. . . . There is nearly a 1 in 2 chance that two people selected at random are racially or ethnically different."[4] We see this increasing diversity daily in the classes we teach, and it is in these classes that our students present their speeches.

Recently, for example, one of us taught a public speaking class whose members resembled a small United Nations assembly. There were 15 men and 9 women, although statistically most classes at our university have more women than men. While the median age was about 20, one class member was almost 50, and another was in his 30s. Five students were from Japan. One was from Indonesia, and two others were from Malaysia. Another student was from the former Soviet Republic of Kyrgyzstan. One native-born American student was of Chinese origin, and another traced her ancestry to the Philippines. A number of students were hard-core science majors, while others were pursuing music, public relations, and graphic design. Hobbies ranged from scuba diving and fishing to origami and batik. Although this class's diversity was more dramatic than most, we think it is a preview of a not too distant future.

Once you have recognized and accepted the fact that the people in your audience are not clones of each other, you need to learn about and adapt to their diversity. Three levels of audience diversity are depicted for you in Exhibit 7.1. We begin at the most general level, looking at the cultures to which members of your audience belong. Then we look at some differences in what are termed **demographics**–differences such as age, sex and gender, and ethnicity. Finally, we look at your audience members as individuals. The more you can learn about your audience at each level, the better you can predict their response to your speech.

demographics
Basic and vital data regarding any population.

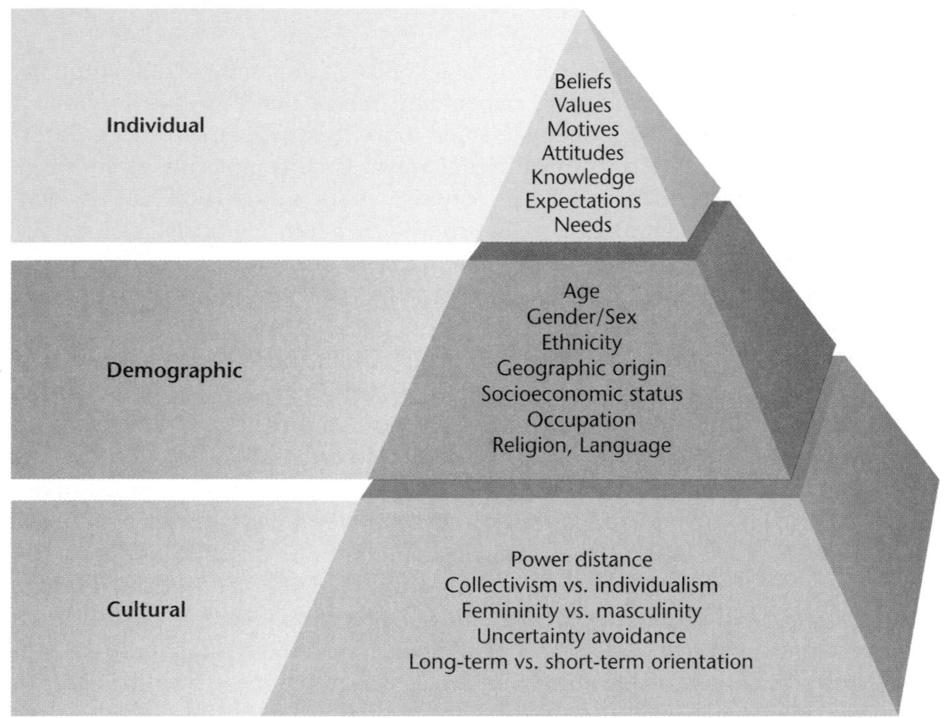

Exhibit 7.1
Levels of Diversity

Discovering Cultural Diversity

Culture is a learned system of beliefs, customs, and values with which people identify. Culture also is more a product of language than of geography. French-speaking Canadians, for example, think of themselves as more French than English, even though Canada has mainly English traditions. Barcelonians think of themselves as Catalonians rather than Spaniards because they speak a dialect that is distinct from the rest of their country. **Cultural diversity** refers mainly to differences among people in terms of beliefs, customs, and values—in a sense, their worldview.

cultural diversity
Differences among people in terms of beliefs, customs, and values—in a sense, their worldview.

Because culture is learned, what is appropriate in one culture may not be perceived as appropriate in another. The list of specific things that make one culture unique from another is inexhaustible. However, recognizing and responding to cultural diversity does not demand that you try to learn everything about a specific culture. To the contrary, discovering what is common but variable among cultures is the key to culturally responsive speaking.

Dutch communication scholar Geert Hofstede says that all cultures vary in terms of at least four dimensions: "power distance (from small to large), collectivism versus individualism, femininity versus masculinity, and uncertainty avoidance (from weak to strong)."[5] In addition, Hofstede notes that a fifth dimension has recently been discovered: long-term versus short-term orientation to life.[6] We think Hofstede's dimensions are a useful guide for analyzing an audience's cultural diversity.

Power Distance

Power distance is "the extent to which the less powerful members of institutions and organizations within a country expect and accept that power is distributed unequally."[7] All societies are unequal, some more than others. However, different societies handle inequality in different ways. For example, there are large power distances in countries in Latin America, Asia, and Africa and in some European countries such as Spain. On the other hand, countries such as the United States and Great Britain and some parts of Europe have smaller power distances. Sweden is an egalitarian country with a small power distance, whereas France has a large power distance.

Power-distance differences have important implications for you as a public speaker. Suppose you are a manager in an international organization announcing company downsizing. You could not assume that an audience from a small-power-distance culture, such as Sweden, would react in the same way to your speech as would one from a large-power-distance culture, such as Japan. Similarly, teachers are treated with deference in large-power-distance cultures, whereas they are treated as near equals in small-power-distance cultures. For example, a professor from a Japanese university teaching in the United States might be surprised to be called by his or her first name, though such a practice is not uncommon at American universities. Conversely, a Japanese student studying in the United States might find it odd that professors expect students to treat them less formally than professors are treated in Japan. Interestingly, this respect is reciprocal. One of us was informed by a Japanese student that not only do students call their professors by last name as a sign of respect, but professors in Japan address students by their last names as well. For an example of how one Japanese student reacts to the culture of an American university, see the box "Between Two Cultures: Tomoko Mukawa."

Collectivism Versus Individualism

The second dimension common to all cultures is collectivism versus individualism. "Collectivism stands for a society in which people from birth onwards are integrated into strong, cohesive ingroups, which throughout people's lifetime continue to protect them in exchange for unquestioning loyalty."[8] In an individualistic society, on the other hand, "everyone is expected to look after himself or herself and his or her immediate family only."[9] Some cultures, notably Asian and Native American, believe the good of the many far outweighs the good of the few. In these collectivist cultures, people shun the individual spotlight. Singling out a member of a collectivist culture while you're giving a speech is likely to embarrass the person.

In cultures where so-called rugged individualism is admired and encouraged, the opposite is true. In the United States, for example, the dominant culture is very individualistic. We champion lone-wolf entrepreneurs who strike it rich, quarterbacks who stand alone in the pocket, and politicians who march to the beat of a different drummer. There is evidence to believe, in fact, that the United States is the most individualistic nation on Earth.[10]

Appealing to enlightened self-interest is key when speakers face audience members from individualistic cultures. Even in the case where these audience members agree about a common goal, they are likely to perceive that the mechanism for achieving the goal is best left to individuals.

Considering Diversity

Between Two Cultures: Tomoko Mukawa

Tomoko Mukawa was born in Japan and lived there until she was 15, when she first came to the United States as a high school exchange student. When she returned to the United States as a college student, Tomoko was struck by the differences in the way students and professors communicate in the two different cultures. Tomoko gives an example of differences between the two cultures:

> I wanted to keep my fluency in Japanese, so I took a class from a Japanese professor. Although the American students were allowed to call the professor by his American nickname, I was required to follow the Japanese tradition of always using his title and surname. He stressed that, as a Japanese student, I needed to preserve my cultural heritage.

Tomoko also noticed that the language in which she spoke made a difference in how she was treated. As an English tutor for Japanese students coming to the United States, Tomoko discovered that when she spoke English she was perceived as more assertive than when she spoke Japanese. "You are like a different person when you speak Japanese," she was told by one of her students.

These experiences illustrate the differences between a large-power-distance culture like Japan and a small-power-distance culture like the United States. In Japan, students would never be familiar with professors, and women are generally not assertive. Simply speaking in her native language changed the way Tomoko was perceived. Language and culture are closely intertwined, as her experience has shown.

In speaking to a more collectivistic audience, one would emphasize the greater good rather than individual benefits. Venezuela's President Hugo Chavez drives people from individualistic cultures crazy with his plans to nationalize private industries. For the collectivist people who voted for Chavez, however, his public speeches reinforce their belief that these industries should benefit the population as a whole, not just the executives and stockholders of individual companies.

The highly individualistic orientation of Americans may be slightly changing given immigration patterns and birth rates. Census data show that more people from collectivist cultures such as Asia reside in the United States today than at any other time in history. American college students today find that people from collectivist cultures are an increasing part of their audience. To find out where you stand as an individual on this dimension, see the box "How Collectivistic or Individualistic Are You?"

Femininity Versus Masculinity

The third dimension of culture in Hofstede's scheme is femininity versus masculinity. Hofstede explains: "Femininity stands for a society in which social gender roles overlap: both men and women are supposed to be modest, tender, and concerned with the quality of life."[11] Masculinity, on the other hand, "stands for

Self-Assessment

How Collectivistic or Individualistic Are You?

The purpose of this questionnaire is to help you assess your individualistic and collectivistic tendencies. Respond by indicating the degree to which the values reflected in each phrase are important to you: Opposed to My Values (answer 1), Not Important to Me (answer 2), Somewhat Important to Me (answer 3), Important to Me (answer 4), or Very Important to Me (answer 5).

___ 1. Obtaining pleasure or sensuous gratification

___ 2. Preserving the welfare of others

___ 3. Being successful by demonstrating my individual competency

___ 4. Restraining my behavior if it is going to harm others

___ 5. Being independent in thought and action

___ 6. Having safety and stability of people with whom I identify

___ 7. Obtaining status and prestige

___ 8. Having harmony in my relations with others

___ 9. Having an exciting and challenging life

___ 10. Accepting cultural and religious traditions

___ 11. Being recognized for my individual work

___ 12. Avoiding the violation of social norms

___ 13. Leading a comfortable life

___ 14. Living in a stable society

___ 15. Being logical in my approach to work

___ 16. Being polite to others

___ 17. Being ambitious

___ 18. Being self-controlled

___ 19. Being able to choose what I do

___ 20. Enhancing the welfare of others

To find your individualism score, add your responses to the *odd-numbered* items. To find your collectivism score, add your responses to the *even-numbered* items. Both scores will range from 10 to 50. The higher your scores, the more individualistic and/or collectivistic you are.

Source: William Gudykunst, *Bridging Differences,* 2nd ed.

a society in which social gender roles are clearly distinct: men are supposed to be assertive, tough, and focused on material success."[12] The United States ranks relatively high on measures of masculinity, ranking 15th out of 53 countries. Despite traditionally being a highly masculine country, this is changing slowly, as evidenced by female CEOs at Xerox and at eBay. Nevertheless, the majority of CEOs in the United States continues to be male. The most feminine cultures are found in Scandinavia and tend not to assign one set of roles to men and another set of roles to women. In these cultures, the professional role a person assumes is a product of ability rather than biological sex. Thus, when imagining a physician or chief executive officer of a company, people don't automatically see a man. In imagining a nurse or secretary, they don't automatically see a woman.

The opposite is true for many other cultures. Some go to extremes in the degree to which one's sex decides one's role. Countries such as Austria, Venezuela, and Japan (which ranks highest on masculinity) have few women in positions of corporate or public authority. Women are assigned roles out of view and out of power. Thus an audience of Japanese men would be polite but predictably unreceptive to a woman speaking on a topic such as reengineering the Japanese corporation. By the same token, a Scandinavian audience would be wary of a male speaker suggesting women belong in the home.

This dimension can be a factor in a number of settings. For example, in masculine cultures, children in school tend to speak out and compete openly. Failure is viewed as a disaster and can even lead to suicide. Boys and girls tend to study different subjects. On the other hand, in feminine cultures, students tend to behave less competitively, failure is not viewed as a catastrophe, and boys and girls tend to study the same subjects. The more you know about which type of culture you are dealing with, the more effective speaker you will be. Even with an American audience, there are likely to be differences in masculinity and femininity based on cultural heritage, age, and progress in gender equity, which may soon reach the highest levels (see box "Speaking of . . . Madam President" on page 150).

Uncertainty Avoidance

The fourth dimension Hofstede discusses is uncertainty avoidance, which is "the extent to which the members of a culture feel threatened by uncertain or unknown situations."[13] As a student you know all about uncertainty and the feelings of discomfort that can accompany it. Instructors who are vague about assignments, tests, due dates, and evaluation not only create uncertainty but also are the ones you probably try to avoid. Just as people vary in terms of the amount of uncertainty they can tolerate, so it is with whole cultures. People who live in "low-uncertainty-avoidance cultures" have considerable tolerance for the kind of ambiguity that can drive some people nuts.

Among societies that *avoid* uncertainty are Greece, Portugal, Guatemala, and Japan. Societies that tend to tolerate uncertainty include Singapore, Jamaica, Denmark, Sweden, Great Britain, India, Philippines, and the United States. If you think about it, if it were not for the tolerance of a certain amount of uncertainty, it is unlikely that new businesses would ever secure the funding of venture capitalists. The United States is by and large a nation of immigrants and their descendants, people who by coming to the "new world" were prepared to accept a very high level of uncertainty.

How is this important to you as a speaker? If you have an audience that can tolerate at least a moderate amount of uncertainty, you do not need to promise certainty. Highly probable outcomes may be sufficient to gain their support. Imagine during the dot-com boom of the late 1990s how entrepreneurs could have obtained funding if they had been forced to guarantee results. On the other hand, total uncertainty is likely to result in rejection of your ideas, particularly in those societies that do not tolerate such ambiguity. You should tailor your appeals to the likely level of uncertainty that your audience is willing to accept.

Long-Term Versus Short-Term Orientation

The final dimension Hofstede discusses is long-term versus short-term orientation to life. "Long-term orientation stands for the fostering of virtues oriented toward future rewards, in particular perseverance and thrift."[14] "Short-term

Speaking of . . .

Madam President

Not only are there more women entering and graduating from college than men, women are playing an increasingly significant role in national and international politics. Professor Nichola D. Gutgold believes we are on the cusp of the first woman president in the U.S. as she explains in her new book, *Paving the Way for Madam President.*

Professor Gutgold discusses the unique challenges women politicians face and the role their public speaking skills play in their success. Read her synopsis of the ever-growing success of women in the political arena, and then discuss with classmates what you would recommend to women candidates about connecting with the diverse audiences they will face on the road to the White House:

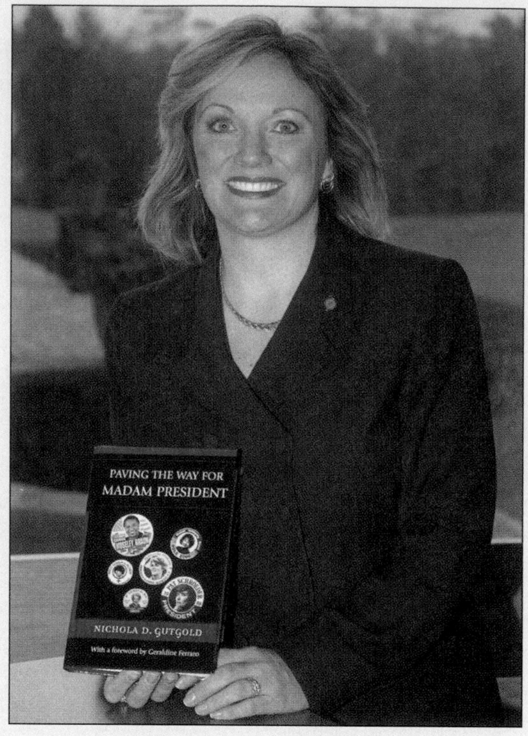

On January 4, 2007, when Representative Nancy Pelosi became the first woman Speaker of the House of Representatives she said, "It is an historic moment for the Congress, and an historic moment for the women of this country. It is a moment for which we have waited over 200 years. . . . For our daughters and granddaughters, today we have broken the marble ceiling. For our daughters and our granddaughters, the sky is the limit, anything is possible for them."[1] *Her optimistic prediction is likely to come true since there are more women serving at every level of government than ever before. Former Secretary of State Madeleine Albright and Secretary of State Condoleezza Rice and several states with women as governors are further proof that women are serving at the highest political levels in the United States.*

Still, Americans have yet to elect a woman President of the United States. In 1984, New York Congresswoman Geraldine Ferraro was on the Democratic ticket, as the vice presidential candidate. The first woman to run for president was Victoria Claflin Woodhull in the fall of 1872. More recently, Republican Senator Margaret Chase Smith, the moral voice of the Senate, brought attention for her 1964 Presidential bid that took her all the way to the convention hall. In 1972, Democratic Congresswoman Shirley Chisholm touted her message of being "unbought and unbossed"[2] *in her groundbreaking presidential campaign. In 1988, outspoken Democratic Congresswoman Pat Schroeder made an exploratory bid that drew headlines in the end, for her tearful reaction during her withdrawal speech more than for her bid. In 1999, Republican Elizabeth Dole, who has since become senator from her home state of North Carolina, discovered that, despite her fame and long political career, it was hard to run against candidates who had unprecedented amounts of money. In 2004 former Illinois Democratic Senator Carol Moseley Braun briefly brought an articulate, and the only female voice to the chorus of Democratic hopefuls. As the 2008 election approaches Hillary Clinton has announced her bid. When Madam President takes office she will owe a debt of gratitude to many women, including Representative Pelosi, Secretary of States Rice and Albright, and all of the women who have run for president, since they have paved the way for her to take her place in the Oval Office.*

Nichola D. Gutgold is associate professor of Communication Arts and Science at Pennsylvania State University, Lehigh Valley Campus. She is author of *Paving the Way for Madam President* (Lexington Press, 2006).

[1] "Text of Nancy Pelosi's Speech" *San Francisco Chronicle,* 4 January 2007. [Retrieved from http://sfgate.com/cgi-bin/article.cgi?f=/c/a/2007/01/04/BAG5ANCTQ27.DTL, 11 January 2007.]

[2] The phrase "unbought and unbossed" had been used by Shirley Chisholm to describe her presidential bid and she summed up her candidacy announcement speech with the phrase. It is also the title of one of her autobiographies: Shirley Chisholm, *Unbought and Unbossed.* (Boston, MA: Houghton-Mifflin, 1970).

orientation stands for the fostering of virtues related to the past and the present, in particular respect for tradition, preservation of 'face,' and fulfilling social obligations."[15]

Asian countries, such as China and Japan, tend to rank very high on the long-term dimension. In fact, this dimension is sometimes called Confucian because many of the values, on both sides of the dimension, are the same as the teachings of Confucius. The United States is in the lower third of countries, and Pakistan is at the bottom of the list, meaning both have a short-term orientation.

Those cultures with a long-term orientation to life tend to adapt long-standing traditions to modern situations, are willing to save and persevere to achieve long-term goals, are willing to subordinate themselves for a purpose, and are thrifty in their use of resources. Short-term-oriented societies respect traditions, are willing to overspend to maintain their lifestyle, and expect quick results. If this scenario sounds familiar it is because we live in a culture that is largely short-term in its orientation. As a group, Americans save less and spend more than any other modern culture in the world.

Thus, knowing whether your audience members share a short- or a long-term culture can significantly affect the content of your speech. Appeals to thrift and patience are likely to be effective in those societies with a long-term orientation, whereas appeals to instant gratification are more effective in societies that have a short-term view of the world. The current debate in the United States over the need to change the Social Security system to protect future generations reflects the results of years of a short-term orientation on the part of American society. That this issue is now being seriously debated suggests that both short- and long-term orientations are competing within the American culture.

Adapting to Cultural Diversity

All five of Hofstede's dimensions are important to analyzing cultural diversity. You shouldn't automatically give one greater credence than another. Rather, tailor your speech to fit with those dimensions that are most relevant to your topic. For example, a speech encouraging students to avoid accumulating credit card debt while in college is going to be better received by those with a long-term orientation than a short-term one.

Further, in a world where cultural diversity is the norm rather than the exception, you can count on audience membership that is not only culturally diverse but also variable with regard to such dimensions as femininity versus masculinity. Thus developing and delivering a speech that appeals to a majority of the cultures represented in your audience is tougher than ever. The wider the range of reasons you present for your position, therefore, the better your chances of success.

Demographic Diversity

After cultural diversity, the second major factor you will want to examine to better understand your audience is how people vary in terms of demographics, which are the basic and vital data regarding any population. Demographic factors include age, gender and sex, ethnicity, geographic origin, socioeconomic status, occupational role, religion, and language usage. **Demographic diversity** refers to the differences among people in terms of such factors. Many of these,

demographic diversity
Variations among people in terms of such attributes as socioeconomic background and level of education.

Speaking of . . .

Connecting with "Generation Me"

Every generation is a little different and possesses a "culture" of its own with unique beliefs, customs, and values. The current generation of young adults between the ages of 18 and 30 recently has been slapped with the label "Generation Me."[1] This label suggests that the beliefs, values, and customs of this group are a manifestation of the attitude that everyone is special, everyone is entitled, and everyone's opinion is of equal value. GenMe'ers are said to have been pampered by overly indulgent and protective parents and told that they can be anything they dream. A survey of 18–25 year olds conducted by the Pew Research Center found that about 80% said that getting rich is a top goal in life for their generation.[2] At the same time GenMe'ers are more accepting of human diversity, non-traditional relationships, gender equality, and willing to volunteer to help out others.

Do you consider yourself a member of "Generation Me"? Do you think the preceding description is accurate? Do you see any unique challenges speakers face in their attempt to connect with an audience dominated by GenMe'ers? If so, what are they and how can they best be met?

[1]Jean M. Twenge, *Generation Me: Why Today's Young Americans Are More Confident, Assertive, Entitled—and More Miserable Than Ever.* (New York: Free Press, 2006).

[2]Martha Irvine, "Young Adults Want Wealth," *The Sacramento Bee,* 23 January 2007, D1.

such as age and ethnicity, are usually readily observable. Others, such as religion, occupation, and socioeconomic status, may be less obvious. We'll start with some of the easier ones to observe and move to the less obvious.

Age

We both began teaching college students in our twenties. As a result, our experience was not that much different than many of our students. Although not identical, our tastes in music, TV, and film were similar enough that we could draw on popular culture for examples that we hoped would make our lectures more relevant to our students. Needless to say, we no longer enjoy this luxury. We need to continually remind ourselves of the fact that the defining experiences in our lives largely occurred before most of our current students were born. Thus, when referring to examples of moving eulogies, we used to cite Ronald Reagan's address to the nation after the explosion of the shuttle *Challenger* in 1986. Today's freshmen were born long after that event. In fact, for most of our students, using Reagan as an example of a speaker is no more a part of their life experience than talking about Franklin Roosevelt or Woodrow Wilson. For a discussion of how today's generation of college age students differs from previous generations, see the box "Speaking of . . . Connecting with Generation Me."

Speakers should know not only the median age of their audience but also the range of ages and how those ages compare to their own. The age demography of the United States is changing at an accelerated rate; so is the demography of the classroom. At one time, college classrooms consisted of a relatively homogeneous group of 18- to 22-year-olds. Today's classroom comprises a much more diverse mix of students. For example, college classes in a state university in the 21st-century are likely to be of mixed ages. It's common for students to be as young as 17 or as old as 75. As a speaker, you need to take into account this demographic diversity in both preparation and delivery of your speech. You have to consider not only how 18- to 22-year-olds are likely to respond to your presentation, but also how continuing and reentry students are likely to respond. Likewise, you will also have to think through the response of students who may or may not be similar to you or other members of your audience. This makes it especially important that you compare your audience with yourself.

Some of the most effective speakers are similar but not too similar to their audience. Reentry students in their 40s can be somewhat intimidated by speaking to classes of 18- to 22-year-old classmates. Similarly, a 20-year-old asked to speak to a group of middle-aged people may feel uneasy. In situations where there is a big difference in age between speaker and audience, points of similarity can be stressed. For example, older students speaking to a younger audience can discuss their children, who might be the same age as the rest of the class. Similarly, younger persons facing an older audience can make reference to parents or grandparents in an effort to find a common thread linking them with the audience.

Gender and Biological Sex

Whether you agree that "men are from Mars and women are from Venus,"[16] you cannot deny that men and women often have difficulty communicating with each other. As our discussion of masculine and feminine cultures illustrates, gender's influence on how people perceive themselves and others is a subject receiving considerable attention. As scholars such as Julia Wood point out, gender is much more than your biological sex.[17] Gender is the blend of social and cultural characteristics associated with maleness or femaleness in a particular culture. Individuals learn gender roles–the expectations their cultures have of them as males or females–in the course of growing up.

As you look out at an audience, you can usually tell who is male and who is female by such outward signs as dress and hairstyle. But unless you have more specific information, you cannot tell who is gay and who is straight, or who is in a committed relationship and who is single. Much gender-related information is probably beyond your knowledge in most public speaking situations.

Some audiences will be predominately one gender or the other, and they may be the opposite of your own. Thus a male speaker facing a largely male audience is in a different situation than one facing a largely female or evenly mixed audience.

One of the first issues you will face is topic selection. For example, one of our students gave a speech about the dangers of breast enhancement surgery. She and the female members of the audience obviously had an interest in the topic. Why should the males care? She made a specific effort to include the men in her audience. She talked in terms of their girlfriends or wives, and made a strong plea to men to accept their mates as they are. Although this topic obviously had a greater direct relevance to the women in her audience, she was careful not to ignore her male audience members.

Ethnicity

Although closely related to culture, ethnicity is not the same thing. For example, in one of our classes recently, we had both a Japanese exchange student and a fifth-generation Japanese American. Both might appear outwardly to share the same ethnic background, but they identified with very different cultures. Anthropologists will tell you that all of us can trace our ethnic roots to other places on the globe. The ethnic origins of many of your classmates may be significant to their self-concept. These same classmates may be actively involved in maintaining and passing on the traditions that define their ethnicity. Thus, if you are ignorant of the ethnic diversity present on your campus, you may inadvertently violate or be insensitive to one or more of these traditions. For example, although born in the United States, one of our students was very proud of her Filipino heritage. Knowing that was important to predicting how she would respond to certain topics, for example, the crisis that was occurring at the time in the Philippines, where hostages had been taken by a rebel group.

It is also important to recognize that many Americans have multiple ethnic backgrounds. Tiger Woods, who is Asian, African American, Native American, and Caucasian, is one of the most prominent examples of this trend. According to the most recent U.S. Census, Woods is not alone. "About 2.4% of Americans, some 6.8 million people, reported themselves as belonging to more than one racial group."[18]

Geographic Origin

The varied makeup of today's audience is also reflected in the geographic origins of the audience members. One of our international students, when asked where she was born, said she was born in the USSR but lived in Kyrgyzstan without ever moving. Of course, when the Soviet Union fell, she became a citizen of a new country. Given that none of her classmates had ever heard of Kyrgyzstan, this student devoted her informative speech to telling us about her homeland.

Look around your campus. The chances are good that the population reflects national and regional demographic diversity. International student attendance at U.S. colleges and universities is at an all-time high. Faculties are becoming more international as well. To deny or ignore how this national diversity influences people's perceptions of each other, including how you are perceived as a public speaker, is foolish. The same can be said for the regional diversity reflected in your student body. Some campuses are near-mirror images of the region in which they exist. Others look more like international cities than like their regional environment.

A speaker can unknowingly offend audience members by using a reference that may be taken as a slight to their geographic home. When the rock group Lynyrd Skynyrd said "I hope Neil Young will remember a southern man don't need him around," they were getting back at Young for lyrics they thought disparaged people in the South. Simply put, some people can be genuinely put off by speakers they perceive to be unfairly stereotyping or making light of their geographic roots. And it's not just southerners, it's also New Yorkers, not-so-laid-back Californians, and a few North Dakotans who were not too happy with the Coen brothers' portrayal of their region in the film *Fargo.* Although you may regard a place as "the armpit of the universe," it's home to someone else who may well be an audience member.

socioeconomic status
Social grouping and economic class to which people belong.

Socioeconomic Status

The social grouping and economic class to which people belong is termed their **socioeconomic status.** Socioeconomic status is not always directly observable. Most universities want diversity in the social and economic backgrounds of their students. Thus your speech class may include students who come from impoverished backgrounds as well as students from affluent families. Although you can sometimes make inferences regarding the social status of your audience, these are not always reliable. For example, one of us once suggested to his class that a proposed tuition increase might lead to fewer minority students attending California universities. One minority student objected, pointing out that one cannot assume that all minority students are necessarily too poor to afford higher tuition.

There is a strong relationship between socioeconomic background and the opinions audience members hold about topics ranging from who should be the next president to tax reform. Knowing the socioeconomic background of an audience, therefore, can inform us of other audience characteristics important to the preparation and delivery of our speeches.

Occupation

Demographic diversity is also reflected by the kind of work people do. On a residential campus, occupational roles are generally expressed in terms of major. At many schools, however, students are already involved in an occupation and pursuing a degree for purposes of advancement or career change. This is especially true of urban and metropolitan schools in or near major cities. One cannot always assume from outward appearances what a person's occupation or former occupation might be. For example, we recall one female student, barely five feet tall, who revealed in one of her speeches that she had been a truck driver for several years. Obviously, her perspective on many issues was affected by that experience. To assume she was uninformed about diesel technology, for example, would have been a clear mistake.

Occupations and coworkers influence how people see the world. Self-employed people, for example, probably see things differently than do people working in the public sector, at a large corporation, or in the home. Just as it is important for speakers to analyze age and social diversity, so it is important to respect the full range of occupations represented in audiences. As you get to know your classmates, you may be able to incorporate references to their majors or jobs when it fits your speech. For example, one student in our classes was a DJ. Other students often mentioned this when it fit with their speech topic, such as how to organize a special event. Audience members appreciate positive references to their occupations, and they can be offended by negative ones. For example, had a student made a derogatory remark about DJs, it could have alienated the audience member who earned his livelihood that way.

Religion

You need to consider religious diversity as a sensitive feature of your audience. At public colleges and universities, you can assume that almost every type of religious belief is represented. Even at universities like Notre Dame, which is affiliated with the Catholic Church, you will find diversity in the religious beliefs of groups of students. In some cases, a person's religion can be identified on the basis of apparel and appearance. Such cases include the Amish, Hasidic Jews, some Muslims, and Hindu Sikhs. Usually, religious affiliations will not be easily visible. You cannot tell a devout Catholic from an atheist by outward appearances.

We want to point out, however, that religious beliefs do not always predict actual attitudes. For example, despite official opposition by many churches to using human embryos for stem cell research, a Harris poll of more than 1,000 Americans revealed that "slightly more than 60% of Catholics and half of born-again Christians surveyed agreed that scientists should be allowed to use stem cells in their medical research."[19]

Perhaps the most important advice we can give about religious beliefs is to be tolerant and respectful of those who do not share your own views. A speech class is a captive audience. A speech that attacks one set of religious beliefs or seeks to proselytize class members is not appropriate for most colleges and universities. Thus you should always assume that there may be audience members who will be deeply offended by religious topics. This doesn't mean that the discussion of religion has no place in a public speaking class. We have heard more than a few good speeches that were successful in explaining common misconceptions about a specific religion or religious sect, describing the similarities between religions, and discussing the origins of certain religious practices. In every instance, however, these speeches were intended to inform audience members–not convince them of the "truth" of a particular religion.

Language

Finally, audience members may differ in terms of how they use language in the reference group with which they most identify. Even people with a common native tongue often create a variation of their language that identifies them as a member of a specific reference group. Every generation of young people, for example, creates a shared vocabulary and syntax that distinguishes it from preceding generations. In the early 1950s college students referred to an object they liked as "real George." Generations that came later replaced *George* with *hip, cool, bitchin'*, and even *hella' bitchin'* in Northern California.

People of Mexican descent in the United States may refer to themselves as Mexican American, Chicano/Chicana, or Latino/Latina, depending on when they were born and where they were raised. And people of African descent may refer to themselves as Blacks or African Americans for similar reasons.

Language groups are not necessarily based on age or ethnicity, however. Special usage and vocabularies also can develop around an activity or interest. Surfers and sailboarders, snowboarders and skiers all have a vocabulary peculiar to their sport, as well as a way of using this vocabulary that is distinctive. The same can be said about computer hackers, photographers, serious backpackers, and white-water enthusiasts. What's more, these groups use their vocabulary not only to identify their own kind but also to differentiate themselves from others.

As the world becomes smaller and linguistic diversity grows even within the borders of the United States, it is important that speakers learn to adapt to their audience's linguistic background. According to the 2000 U.S. Census, 20 years ago only 1 in 10 Americans primarily spoke a language other than English, but today that number has reached 17.6 percent, nearly 1 in 5.[20] You may want to learn a few phrases in another language if you are speaking to an audience that doesn't share your primary language. Taking the time and making the commitment to learn another language signals to members of the language community that you are truly interested in them.

Individual Diversity

For most public speakers, the most difficult aspect of audience diversity is predicting how individual members of the audience will respond to them and their message. What are some of the specific things you should look for in analyzing the individuals who make up your audience? **Individual diversity** is deeply embedded in people's knowledge, beliefs, attitudes, values, motives, expectations, and needs. What makes people truly unique is their individual diversity, which cannot be determined on the basis of their culture or demography alone. When you know people as individuals rather than simply as members of a culture or group, you can make far more precise predictions about how they will respond to your speeches and to you. You can also use this knowledge to plan your speeches and decide whether your purpose and goal are realistic.

individual diversity How individuals in an audience differ in terms of knowledge, beliefs, attitudes, values, motives, expectations, and needs.

One of the great advantages of most public speaking classes is that you will learn to know your audience members as individuals. As we pointed out in Chapter 6, in a class of 25 you will spend about 96 percent of your class time listening to your classmates give their speeches. If you actively listen to them, you will learn a great deal about what they know and think about the world around them. You can use this information as you prepare your own speeches.

Although many of your public speaking situations after college may not allow you to hear all of your audience members speak, you can endeavor to learn as much about them as individuals as possible before you speak. Even in situations where you face an audience "cold," you may be able to make certain assumptions about their interests and belief systems beforehand. For example, if you are asked to speak to the Lion's Club, it is useful to know in advance that they are concerned about raising funds to combat blindness and that they sponsor a public speaking contest for high school students. Any clues you can obtain about the individuals to whom you will be speaking can be valuable in crafting an effective speech.

Knowledge

One of the first things you'll want to know about your audience is what they know–about you and your topic. This is particularly important in selecting a topic for an informative speech. You have probably had the experience of listening to a speaker who simply tells you what you already know. Chances are you were impatient and bored. You have also probably had the experience of listening to a speaker who was almost incomprehensible because he or she used vocabulary you had never heard before, or assumed you had prior knowledge you didn't have about the topic.

Learn as much as you can about your audience's knowledge. Chances are there may be a range of knowledge on the topic you have chosen. If the difference in audience knowledge levels is too varied, preparing your speech may be very difficult. You will find yourself boring some members while losing others. For example, a speech on the federal reserve board may be old hat to economics majors but leave humanities majors mystified. If possible, speak on topics about which audience members are likely to have similar levels of knowledge. If you must rehash certain facts, at least try to put a new spin on them to keep the interest of well-informed audience members. In any event, you want to be sure you are the best-informed person in the room. It's embarrassing, to say the least, to be corrected on the facts by a member of your audience.

Beliefs

belief
An assertion about the properties or characteristics of an object.

We all hold certain beliefs about a wide variety of topics. A **belief** is "an assertion about the properties or characteristics of an object."[21] Some beliefs are relatively obvious and undeniable. For example, we all (presumably) share a belief that the earth is round and revolves around the sun. On the other hand, some beliefs are controversial–for instance, those concerning life after death, abortion, and, as you can see in Exhibit 7.2, evolution. When you are dealing with matters on which people hold beliefs different from yours, you face a serious obstacle. You must either change their relevant beliefs or convince them that such beliefs are not relevant and not necessarily in opposition to your own point of view.

Convincing her congressman, who had strong beliefs on the subject, to change his anti-gun control stand proved impossible for Carolyn McCarthy. So, rather than trying to move his position through speech, she used her newfound public voice to move him out of office. Simply put, all speakers must carefully choose their battles. That requires that you learn as soon as possible whether you have even the slightest chance to engage your audience positively on your topic.

primitive beliefs
Those beliefs learned by direct contact with the object of belief and reinforced by unanimous social consensus (also known as type A beliefs).

central beliefs
Beliefs based directly or indirectly on authority.

Social psychologist Milton Rokeach pointed out that some beliefs are more resistant to change than others.[22] **Primitive beliefs**, also known as type A beliefs, are learned by direct contact with the object of belief and reinforced by unanimous social consensus. A primitive belief would be that "death is inevitable." Type B, or zero consensus, beliefs are based on direct experience but do not require social support. These beliefs are also very resistant to change. For example, "I like myself" is a type B belief; it is not reinforceable by social consensus. Together, type A and B beliefs are core beliefs, which are very resistant to change.

The next two types of beliefs are known as **central beliefs** and are still difficult to change. Type C beliefs are authority beliefs. For example, beliefs in the truth of the Bible or Torah or Qur'an would be a type C belief. Type Ds are derived beliefs, based on authorities' beliefs. For example, Muslims who believe they should abstain from drinking alcohol and eating pork are said to hold derived beliefs. Changing a type D belief requires an understanding of the type C belief from which it is derived. Thus a speaker might point to scripture to try to change a believer's views on a religious matter, but such an argument would have no impact on an atheist or a practitioner of a different religion.

peripheral beliefs
The least central type of beliefs, the easiest to change.

The least central type of beliefs, type E, are called **peripheral beliefs**. For example, someone might like rap music, whereas another detests it. These are the most inconsequential of beliefs. Exhibit 7.3 illustrates the relationship among these levels of belief. Clearly, your chances of changing an audience member's core beliefs are far less than changing central or peripheral beliefs.

How can you learn what people believe? One way is simply to ask. In a speech about cell phone safety, for example, one student asked for a show of hands on how many of her classmates owned cell phones and how many used them while

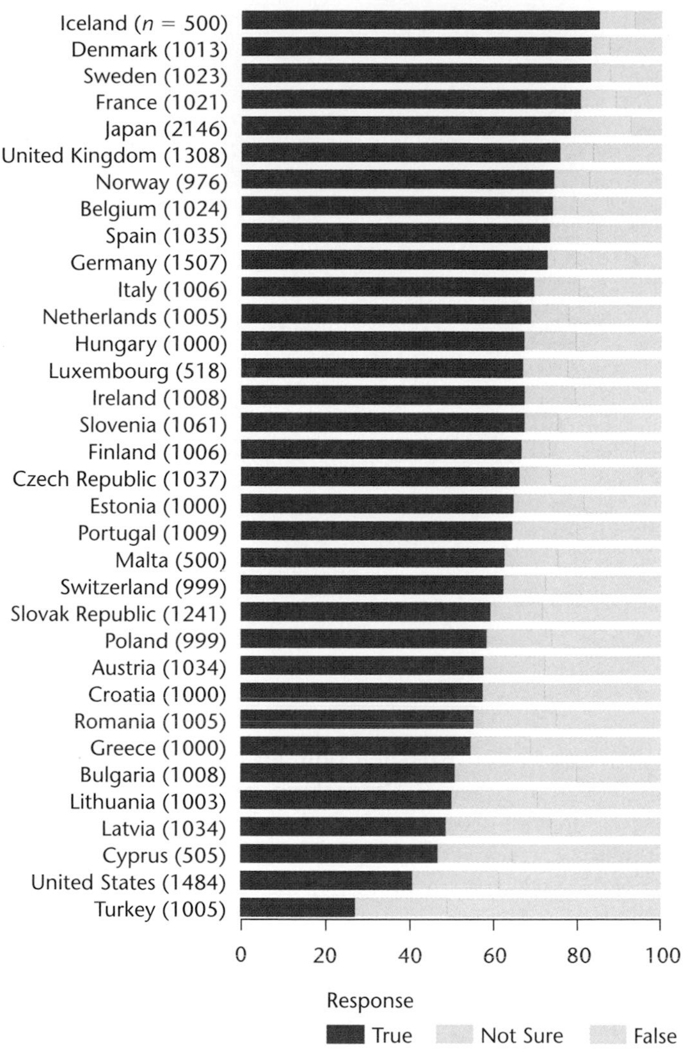

Exhibit 7.2
Public Acceptance of Evolution in 34 Countries, 2005

Source: From Jon D. Miller, Eugenie C. Scott, and Shinji Okamoto, "Public Acceptance of Evolution," *Science* 313 (11 August 2006): 765. Reprinted with permission from AAAS.

driving. Politicians and pollsters are always asking the American public what it believes about a variety of issues. Every year the Cooperative Institutional Research Program at UCLA sponsors a national study of thousands of incoming first-year college students. You may learn from such sources, in a general way at least, what audience members are likely to believe. For example, among entering freshmen in 2006, the national survey showed that 33.8 percent discussed politics frequently in high school (up from 25.5 percent in 2004), 61.2 percent supported legal marital status for same-sex couples, and 66.7 percent believe it is essential or very important to help others who are in difficulty.[23] You might use this information in one of your own speeches, knowing that the survey is representative of most students at colleges throughout the United States.

Exhibit 7.3
A Belief System

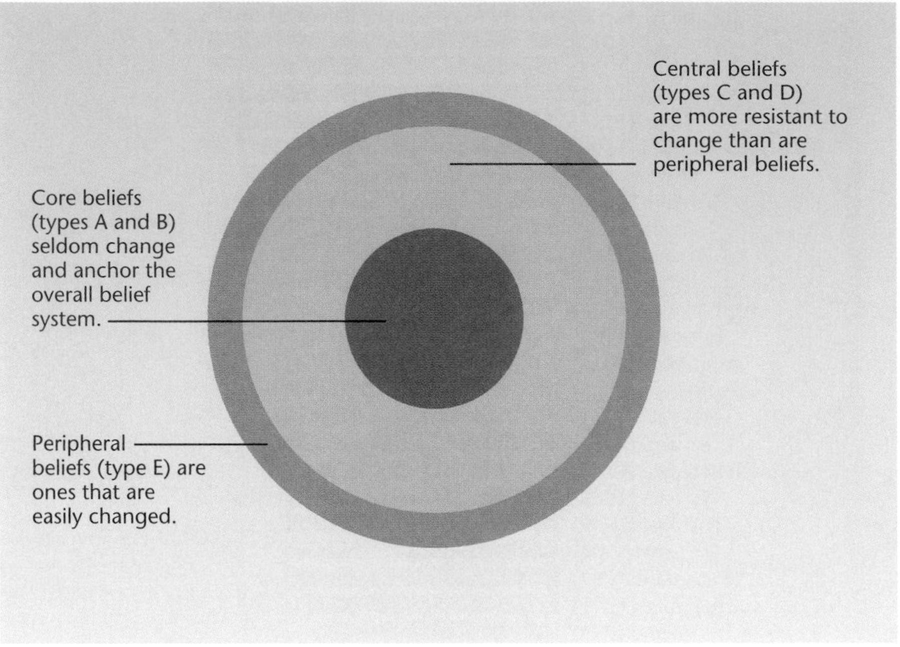
Central beliefs
(types C and D)
are more resistant to
change than are
peripheral beliefs.
Core beliefs
(types A and B)
seldom change
and anchor the
overall belief
system.
Peripheral
beliefs (type E) are
ones that are
easily changed.

Attitudes

attitude
A learned predisposition to respond in a consistently favorable or unfavorable manner with respect to a given object.

An **attitude** is "a learned predisposition to respond in a consistently favorable or unfavorable manner with respect to a given object."[24] Attitudes are not simply beliefs but rather ways of responding, based in part on beliefs. Over the course of our lives, we develop innumerable attitudes on everything from our favorite brand of soft drink to globalization of world business. These attitudes affect how we respond to the messages we hear. Thus knowing your audience's attitudes toward your topic is crucial to your success as a speaker, as one speaker learned when she tried to challenge her classmates' aversion to eating a certain type of food–insects. Eating insects is rare in American culture, and most of her classmates groaned when they heard her topic. She attempted to convince her classmates that eating "bugs" actually could be healthy. Not everyone was convinced, but several of her classmates (and even the professor) ended up sampling her "mealybug chocolate chip cookies." While not dramatically changing her audience's attitudes, the speaker did induce at least some class members to soften their strong attitude against this type of food.

How do you learn your audience's attitudes? Sometimes they are fairly predictable. Most Americans don't eat bugs. On the other hand, without asking, it's not easy to know what your classmates think about the Kyoto Protocol on global warming or how many of them are vegetarians. Never assume that all members of a particular group of people share the same attitudes: Not all Republicans think alike, any more than Democrats do. Nor do all members of a religion–whether Catholics, Protestants, Jews, Baptists, or Muslims–subscribe to exactly the same religious convictions.

It is entirely possible, in fact probable, that in a diverse audience, individuals will have conflicting and even contradictory attitudes. The more you know about the predominant or prevailing attitudes of the group, the better are your chances of a majority of the audience responding positively to what you say in your speech. When an audience is fairly evenly divided, you need to attempt to find some middle ground. Finding areas of common agreement while recognizing and respecting differences of opinion is essential to dealing with an audience of mixed attitudes.

Although California Governor Arnold Schwarzenegger (pictured here with Stan and Roleeda Statham) is a nationally prominent Republican, his views on issues such as abortion and gay rights don't fit the Republican stereotype.

Values

One scholar describes **values** as "more general than attitudes, . . . enduring beliefs that hold that some ways of behaving and some goals are preferable to others."[25] Underlying someone's opposition to animal testing in research, for example, is both a belief about how animals are treated in doing research and a value system that believes all life is important, not just human life.

values
Our most enduring beliefs about right and wrong.

Rokeach classifies values as either terminal (ends in themselves) or instrumental (those that help achieve the ends we seek as humans).[26] Examples of terminal values include a comfortable life, an exciting life, a sense of accomplishment, a world at peace, a world of beauty, equality, family security, freedom, and happiness. Instrumental values are guides to behavior, the means to achieve the ends specified in the terminal values. Examples of instrumental values include ambitiousness, broad-mindedness, capableness, cheerfulness, cleanliness, courage, forgiveness, helpfulness, and honesty.

Although one might not always agree with Rokeach's classification–for example, honesty can certainly be viewed as an end in itself–the basic notion is useful. Some values are desirable in and of themselves, whereas others are instruments for achieving higher, terminal values. For example, forgiveness and courage may be seen as means to achieving a world at peace.

Values, particularly terminal values, are difficult to change because they are learned at an early age and widely shared among people. Values such as fairness, justice, life, patriotism, and so on are not only fundamental but also are taught to us in our most formative years. In fact, our basic value system probably is pretty well determined at a very young age, as Robert Fulghum points out in his best-selling book, *All I Really Need to Know I Learned in Kindergarten.*[27]

Speakers are best advised to appeal to known values shared by their audience rather than try to convince their audience to adopt new values. Some speeches don't just appeal to existing values, they seek to reinforce those values. A Fourth of July speech, a eulogy honoring a great hero, or an inspirational speech can be thought of as fulfilling a value-strengthening function. For the most part, speakers need to treat values as a given and build on them. For example, Martin Luther King Jr.'s "I Have a Dream" speech was not so much a call for new values as for Americans to live up to the values stated in the Declaration of Independence and the Bill of Rights.

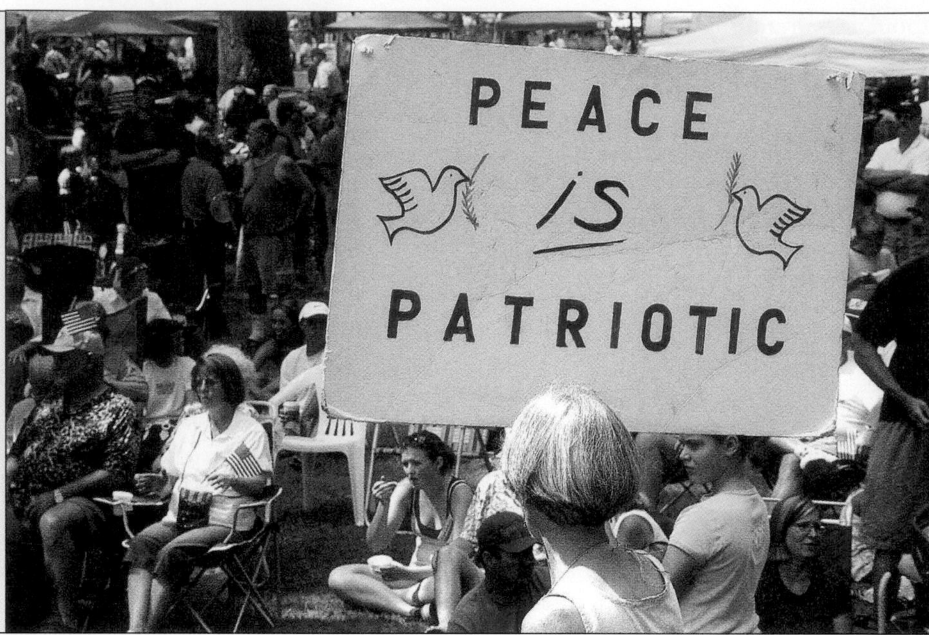

Often those who disagree with government policy invoke patriotic symbols in their protests.

Motives

Humans are motivated by a wide variety of desires, for example, popularity, financial security, love, peace, and so on. You should learn as much as you can about the likely motives of your audience relative to your topic. For example, a speaker at a graduation ceremony can assume that the audience is there to be inspired and to receive their diplomas. A lengthy speech on the War on Terror would be inappropriate for this audience. On the other hand, a graduation speech focusing on the successes of graduates from the same school might be just what the audience wants.

One specific type of motive concerns why your audience members are attending your speech. In most classroom situations, the answer is simple: because they have to. In those situations, you have to work harder at holding the audience's interest and connecting to their needs than if they had come especially to hear you speak. In Chapter 10 we offer some suggestions that will help you connect with an audience and gain their attention. Even audience members who come to hear you need to have their attention held. It is easy to lose an audience and very difficult to recapture their attention, as any experienced speaker can testify.

Expectations

Closely tied to their motives for attending the speech are your audience's specific expectations. If audience members expect to be entertained, and you deliver a serious speech on the dangers of ozone depletion, you are unlikely to receive a favorable reception. Similarly, if most audience members expect a serious lesson on a topic not to be taken lightly, you owe it to them to meet this expectation. It is usually wise to match your speech as much to the audience members' expectations as is possible while still achieving your goals.

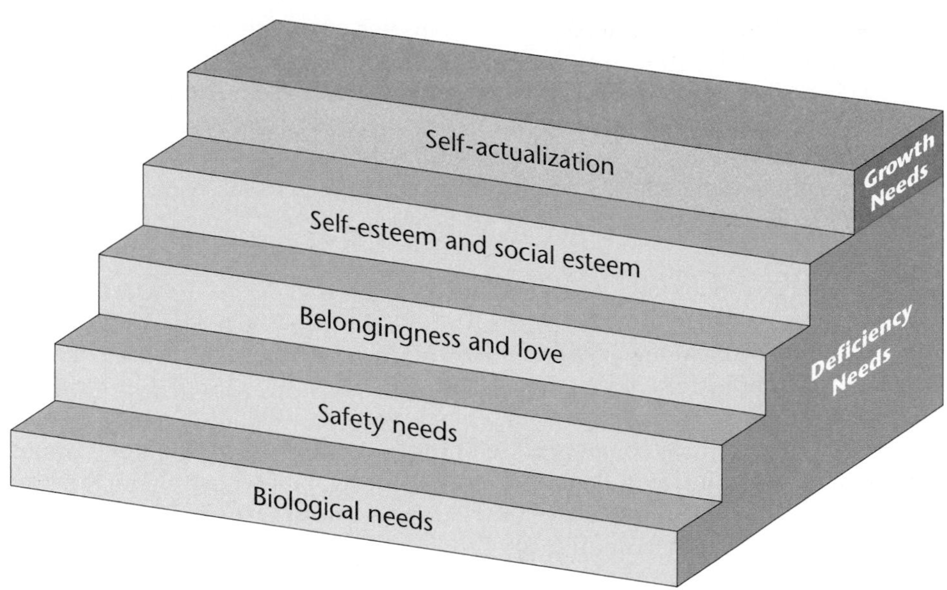

Exhibit 7.4
Maslow's Hierarchy of Needs

Generally, speeches contrary to a majority of audience members' expectations may backfire or, at the very least, be apathetically received. For example, we once attended a graduation ceremony where the speaker used the opportunity to preach his view on "political correctness." Families and friends were there to honor and celebrate the graduates' accomplishments, but they were instead treated to a political statement. Whereas such an address might have been appropriate at a meeting of the faculty senate, it missed the mark for the assembled graduates and their guests. The fact that the audience prematurely applauded and shouted loudly at what they thought was the conclusion of the speech reinforced how inappropriate the speech was.

Needs

Needs are physical and mental states that motivate us to behave in ways that lead to their satisfaction. Abraham Maslow wrote that we experience two sets of personal needs: deficiency needs and growth needs.[28] **Deficiency needs** are basic human needs. **Growth needs** are higher-order human needs. Maslow arranged these two sets of needs in the form of a hierarchy to show that our deficiency needs must be satisfied routinely before our growth needs become important to us.

As Exhibit 7.4 indicates, there are four sets of deficiency needs: (1) *biological needs*, such as food, water, and air; (2) *safety needs*, such as protection from physical harm; (3) *belongingness and love needs,* such as a child's need for the love of a parent; and (4) *self-esteem and social-esteem needs*, which involve believing in our self-worth and finding confirmation of that belief from others. Growth needs are not as straightforward as deficiency needs. They include self-actualization, knowledge and understanding, and aesthetic needs. Self-actualization is the most commonly discussed growth need. According to Maslow, *self-actualization* is the process of fully realizing one's potential. Self-actualized people not only

deficiency needs
Basic human needs, which must be satisfied before higher-order needs can be met. They include needs for food, water, air, physical safety, belongingness and love, and self-esteem and social esteem.

growth needs
Higher-order human needs, which can be satisfied only after deficiency needs have been met. They include self-actualization (the process of fully realizing one's potential), knowledge and understanding, and aesthetic needs.

understand themselves but also accept themselves for who they are and what they have achieved.

As you analyze your audience, consider how your speech can help audience members satisfy their likely needs. For example, many motivational speakers seek to help people satisfy their needs for self-actualization. On the other hand, someone selling home security equipment would appeal to safety needs.

Learning About Your Audience

The preceding discussion of audience diversity may seem overwhelming at first. After all, most of us have only a few friends who we could describe in terms of all of the attributes of cultural, demographic, and individual diversity. Fortunately, as a speaker, you do not need to know everything there is to know about your audience. Rather, focus your efforts on learning about those characteristics most relevant to your speech purpose. There are four basic ways to learn about audience members: observation, asking for information, doing a survey, and visiting online Web pages such as those available though Facebook and MySpace.

Observation

The most direct way to learn about audience members is by careful observation. In your own public speaking class, you will observe your classmates on a daily basis and particularly when they are speaking. You will learn a lot about their cultural background, demographic characteristics, and even their beliefs, attitudes, and values. If you are speaking to an audience outside your classroom, try to observe them in advance of your speech. Many demographic characteristics should be readily observable: age, sex, ethnicity, and so on.

Ask Someone Familiar With the Audience

If you cannot observe the audience for yourself, talk to someone who knows them. In many cases you will be invited to speak by a member of the group. For example, the authors have spoken on numerous occasions to service groups in our community. One of us was recently asked to speak to a group that helps senior citizens deal with Medicare and other health insurance issues. Knowing that helped the speaker to choose examples that would be directly related to their mission. Having had an elderly parent who spent time in a skilled nursing facility helped the speaker to relate to the audience's mission and understand their needs.

Survey Your Audience

In some cases you will have the opportunity to conduct a survey of your audience. This is one of the best ways to determine attitudes, values, beliefs, and knowledge levels, which are typically very hard to determine from mere observation. There is a danger of assuming that based on appearances your audience holds certain attitudes. A speaker may commit a major gaffe if he or she assumes attitudes based solely on culture or demographics.

Speaking of . . .

Surveying Your Audience

1. Do you own a cell phone? Yes _____ No _____ (if no, skip to question 5)
2. About how many hours a month do you use your cell phone? _____
3. Do you ever use your cell phone while driving? Yes _____ No _____
4. If so, do you use a hands-free headset? Yes _____ No _____
5. Do you believe it is safe to use a cell phone while driving?
   _____ Always _____ Never _____ Only with a hands-free headset

6 What is your opinion on laws banning the use of cell phones while driving?
_____ All cell phone use should be banned
_____ Cell phone use should be allowed only with a hands-free headset
_____ There should be no restrictions on cell phone use while driving

Many professional speakers use survey data in designing their speeches. Your instructor may offer you the opportunity to survey your classmates prior to speaking. If so, avail yourself of the opportunity, but be sure to make the survey anonymous and brief. Too many questions will lead to no responses, and requiring respondents to identify themselves may inhibit candor. The box "Surveying Your Audience" provides an example of a survey by a student who plans to speak to the audience about cell phone safety. Notice that the questions focus on the use of cell phones while driving. In particular, this speaker wants to determine if the audience members think that by using hands-free headsets they are driving safely. If so, the speech will need to cite study results that claim that it's the distraction of a conversation more than the use of one hand that is the source of accidents.

Web Pages

Although we encourage you to be cautious to the point of asking for permission, the chances are good that you can learn about your classmates by visiting online social networks such as Facebook.com and MySpace.com. Should a classmate have a blog, you also could turn to it in search of information about his or her cultural, demographic, and individual background. Social networks such as the preceding have blurred the lines that once separated people's personal and public lives. Whereas you once would have had to interview people face-to-face to learn important details about their personal lives, you can now accomplish the same thing with a few clicks of your mouse. In fact, you may learn more about them than you need to know! And that brings us to an important point. Regardless of what you learn about individual audience members online, you should not use the information in a manner that will embarrass them. Further, be careful that you do not include information or photos in your own profile that could embarrass you. We saw one of our students humiliated when the campus newspaper published her picture in an embarrassing pose because one of the young men in the photo was a candidate for student office. Once on the Internet, any expectation of privacy is lost. You also should exercise care and avoid inferring too much about individual audience members on the basis of what you read and see online. This is especially true should you also find what you think is information about specific audience members through Google or Wikipedia.

Needless to say, the Web can be a tremendous source of information about potential audience members, whether or not they are in your class. Most organizations, including service groups such as Lions, Soroptimists, AAUW, and Rotary have Web pages. Many of these Web pages also have links that will enable you to learn information about their individual members. Yet, as we'll discuss in the next chapter dealing with research, Web sites can be corrupted by the unscrupulous. Thus, you will want to exercise every caution when using information from a Web site to analyze audiences.

Confronting Constraints

constraint
A limitation on choices in a rhetorical situation.

We all face certain constraints on action. A **constraint** is a limitation on your choices. Among the common constraints you may face in giving your speech are the facts pertaining to the situation, legal constraints, ethical constraints, nature of the occasion, traditions, time, and resources. Let's examine each of these.

Facts Pertaining to the Situation

President John Adams observed that "facts are stubborn things."[29] Although some people seem oblivious to the facts governing their situation, sooner or later they must face reality. A speaker who hasn't done research is likely to be embarrassed by the lack of knowledge. As we noted earlier, part of preparing for a speech is to find out what it is that your audience knows, and make sure you know more. Furthermore, it is important to cite the sources from which you have learned your facts. Your audience will perceive you as a more knowledgeable speaker if they know you have solid sources for your facts.

Legal Constraints

We all must abide by certain legal constraints in our speaking. Libel and slander laws, for example, forbid certain types of speech. Other laws cover when and where groups may peaceably assemble. Some anti-abortion activists have been successfully prosecuted, for example, for blocking the entrances to abortion clinics. Although the First Amendment guarantees freedom of speech and assembly, these rights are not license to do what you please.

Some speakers, however, have effectively challenged and even broken laws for a purpose. Nelson Mandela was willing to spend much of his life in jail to bring about the end of apartheid in South Africa. Ultimately, this self-sacrifice helped to sway world opinion against the White minority government of South Africa and led to Mandela's election as South Africa's president.

In your case, it is highly unlikely that you will choose to purposefully break the law to further the cause advanced in one of your speeches. Yet unless you check on the legal constraints relevant to your situation, you may accidentally break a law of which you are unaware. In our own experience, we've had students show up to class with everything from exotic beers to poisonous pets, both of which are illegal on our campus. We've learned, consequently, that it is necessary for us to check on the topics and plans of our students well before their time to actually speak. Check with your instructor before you unintentionally pit yourself against the law.

Legal constraints may also affect the range of topics and the positions you take on them. For example, we recently heard a speech on why sharing music files on the Internet through services such as BitTorrent should be totally free of charge. Of course, at the time there had been a great deal of litigation on the issue, and the courts had ruled that such unfettered distribution of music on the Internet, without paying royalties to the artists, violated U.S. copyright laws. Thus the speech was about a topic on which the audience had no power to effect change.

Ethical Constraints

We discussed ethical considerations for public speaking in detail in Chapter 5. At this point, we simply want to remind you of the fact that as a speaker and as a listener you will face ethical constraints. Although something may technically be legal, that doesn't make it ethical.

Nature of the Occasion

What is the nature of the occasion prompting you to speak? You may recall that after the death of former President Ronald Reagan, his son Ron Reagan used the opportunity of his eulogy for his father to issue a thinly veiled attack against politicians who inject their religious preferences into political campaigns. The younger Reagan acknowledged that his father was a deeply religious man, but one who "never made the fatal mistake of so many politicians wearing his faith on his sleeve to gain political advantage. True, after he was shot and nearly killed early in his presidency, he came to believe that God had spared him in order that he might do well. But he accepted that as a responsibility, not a mandate. And there is a profound difference."[30] Some criticized the use of a solemn occasion such as this to raise a political issue; others applauded young Reagan's forthrightness at a time when the nation was watching.

You will most likely give speeches to classes during normal class times. Your audience is a captive one. Given that unavoidable fact, you must always decide whether your topic and presentation are appropriate to this context and occasion. One of our students made his classmates extremely uncomfortable by discussing his own first sexual experience. Such personal disclosure is inappropriate in a classroom setting. Similarly, vulgarity, profanity, and the like are obviously not suitable for the class. Even excessively casual slang is probably not appropriate for an academic environment. When you have a doubt as to the appropriateness of your speech for your class, it is always wise to check with your instructor.

Traditions

Many speeches are governed by tradition. Whereas this is not a major factor in most classroom speeches, it could be when you are called on to speak in situations outside the classroom. For example, many service clubs, such as Rotary or

Lions, have a whole set of traditions that may seem puzzling to the outsider. For instance, there is a good deal of good-natured poking fun at certain members, "fines" are levied for infractions such as getting your name in the paper, and so forth. Major corporations, such as IBM and Apple, each have their own set of traditions. IBM is formal; Apple is much less so. In speaking to either group, therefore, you would want to reflect the degree of formality each expected in terms of dress, demeanor, and style of presentation.

Time

How much time do you have to give your speech? If you have been asked to speak for 5 minutes and you ramble on for an hour, the response will be predictably negative. On the other hand, imagine paying to hear an hour lecture by a major public figure and having the speech end in 10 minutes. You need to know and respect time limits, as well as match how much information you cover in your speech to your allotted time. For instance, it is generally better to cover a narrow topic thoroughly than to try to cover a wide range of points superficially.

Time is also a factor to consider in your preparation. If you have a week to prepare a speech, you probably don't have time to send for information from outside sources. If you have a month, you probably do. You also will need time for practice. Public speaking deserves the same degree of practice as shooting free throws, swinging a golf club, or learning a new trick in gymnastics. Simply put, it cannot possibly be mastered without some degree of repetition. And this means committing time to practice as far in advance of the speech as possible. Relaxation techniques and other approaches to managing anxiety also require time to master.

Resources

Two questions are involved here. First, what resources do you have available to you? Resources include money, information sources, other people who might assist you, and the like. Second, what resources do you need to accomplish your speaking goal? If your resources match or exceed what you need, you are fine. If you lack the necessary resources, however, you must either redefine your goal or obtain more resources.

Suppose you are assigned to give a speech with at least three visual aids. How do you go about getting these? If you have enough money, you may be able to pay to have pictures enlarged to poster size or to have overhead transparencies prepared. If your classroom is equipped with a computer and projector, you may be able to use special software to present part of your speech. If not, what alternative resources do you have? If you have a friend who is an art major, perhaps he or she can help you make posters. Whatever your situation, you need to give careful consideration to the resources you have or will need to obtain to achieve your goal.

Summary

In this chapter, we have provided the tools to analyze your audience and adapt your speech goals, both long- and short-term, to the audience and the situation. Here, we recap the four major areas to consider.

Analyze your audience in terms of cultural variables:

- Power distance
- Collectivism versus individualism
- Femininity versus masculinity
- Uncertainty avoidance
- Long-term orientation versus short-term orientation

Analyze your audience in terms of demographic characteristics:

- Age
- Gender and biological sex
- Ethnicity
- Geographic origin
- Socioeconomic status
- Occupation
- Religion
- Language usage

Analyze your audience in terms of individual diversity, including their:

- Knowledge
- Beliefs
- Attitudes
- Values
- Motives
- Expectations
- Needs

Adapt your goals to the audience and the total rhetorical situation. Consider the following constraints:

- Facts
- Legal constraints
- Ethical constraints
- Nature of the occasion

OLC www.mhhe.com/brydon6

To evaluate your understanding of this chapter, visit our Online Learning Center Web site for quizzes and other chapter study aids.

- Traditions
- Time
- Resources

Check Your Understanding: Exercises and Activities

1. Given the topic of alcohol abuse, how might you develop your speech presentation differently if your audience were made up of (a) high school students, (b) students your own age, (c) bar and tavern owners in your community, or (d) recovering alcoholics? In a short paper, explain how your approach and purpose would differ in each case.
2. Create a model of your belief system, including your core beliefs, authority beliefs, and representative derived beliefs, on one of the following topics: gun control, the importance of voting, abortion, civil unions. What does your belief system say about how susceptible you are to being influenced on the topic selected?
3. Interview a student from another country who is studying at your university. What most surprised him or her about American culture? What would Americans be most surprised to know about his or her culture? Write a short paper or give a short talk about what you have discovered.
4. Learn as much as you can about the cultural, demographic, and individual diversity of your classmates. Construct a short questionnaire that will guide you in preparing for an upcoming speech. After obtaining your instructor's approval, write a survey about your chosen topic. You might ask questions about what your audience already knows about the topic, their attitudes for or against your position, and their level of interest in the topic. Distribute the questionnaire to your classmates and collect their responses (anonymously, of course). Tabulate the results. For example, if your topic is banning the sale of handguns known as Saturday night specials, you might report that 60 percent of your classmates were familiar with the term, while 40 percent were not; that 50 percent agreed with a ban, 20 percent opposed one, and the remainder had no opinion; and that 30 percent felt gun violence was a major issue, while 70 percent did not. Based on these results, write a short paper on how you used this information to shape your speech. Also indicate how your plans for your speech may have changed based on the information from your survey.

Notes

1. Aristotle, *Rhetoric,* trans. W. Rhys Roberts (New York: Modern Library, 1954), 24.
2. Lloyd Bitzer, "The Rhetorical Situation," *Philosophy and Rhetoric* 1 (1968): 5. Bitzer further defines an exigence as "an imperfection marked by urgency; it is a defect, an obstacle, something waiting to be done, a thing which is other than it should be" (6). In this text we prefer to focus on the speaker's goal, which, strictly speaking, is to *overcome the exigence* present in the rhetorical situation.
3. Bitzer, "Rhetorical Situation," 8.

4. Haya El Nasser and Paul Overberg, "Index Charts Growth in Diversity Despite 23% Jump, Segregation Is Still Going on, Researchers Say" [Lexis-Nexis, 5 August 2001] (*USA Today,* 15 March 2001, 3A).

5. Geert Hofstede, *Cultures and Organizations: Software of the Mind* (London: McGraw-Hill, 1991), 14.

6. Hofstede, *Cultures and Organizations,* 14.

7. Hofstede, *Cultures and Organizations,* 262.

8. Hofstede, *Cultures and Organizations,* 260.

9. Hofstede, *Cultures and Organizations,* 261.

10. Hofstede, *Cultures and Organizations,* 53.

11. Hofstede, *Cultures and Organizations,* 261.

12. Hofstede, *Cultures and Organizations,* 262.

13. Hofstede, *Cultures and Organizations,* 263.

14. Hofstede, *Cultures and Organizations,* 261.

15. Hofstede, *Cultures and Organizations,* 262–63.

16. John Gray, *Men Are From Mars, Women Are From Venus: A Practical Guide for Improving Communication and Getting What You Want in Your Relationships* (New York: HarperCollins, 1992).

17. Julia T. Wood, *Gendered Lives* (Belmont, Calif.: Thomson Wadsworth, 2005).

18. Robert A. Rosenblatt, "Census Illustrates Diversity From Sea to Shining Sea; Population: Massive Surge of Immigration in '90s Makes Nearly One in Every Three U.S. Residents a Minority, Report Says. Trend Is Nationwide" [Lexis-Nexis, 5 August 2001] (*Los Angeles Times,* 13 March 2001, Part A; Part 1; Page 16).

19. Reuters News Service, "Six in Ten Americans Favor Stem Cell Research." [Yahoo News, http://dailynews.yahoo.com/h/nm/20010726/hl/stemcell_3.html, 26 July 2001.]

20. David Westphal, "More Speak Spanish in U.S.," *Sacramento Bee,* 6 August 2001, A12.

21. Sarah Trenholm, *Persuasion and Social Influence* (Englewood Cliffs, N.J.: Prentice-Hall, 1989), 6.

22. Milton Rokeach, *Beliefs, Attitudes and Values* (San Francisco: Jossey-Bass, 1968), 6–21.

23. Sylvia Hurtado and John H. Pryor, *The American Freshman: National Norms for Fall 2006,* PowerPoint Slides (Summary), 19 January 2007 [Retrieved from http://www.gseis.ucla.edu/heri/norms06.php, 20 May 2007] Los Angeles: The Cooperative Institutional Research Program, Higher Education Research Institute, University of California at Los Angeles.

24. Martin Fishbein and Icek Ajzen, *Belief, Attitude, Intention, and Behavior: An Introduction to Theory and Research* (Reading, Mass.: Addison-Wesley, 1975), 6.

25. Trenholm, *Persuasion and Social Influence,* 11, based on Rokeach, *Beliefs, Attitudes and Values.*

26. Milton Rokeach, "Change and Stability in American Value Systems, 1968–1971," in *Understanding Human Values: Individual and Societal*, ed. Milton Rokeach (New York: Free Press, 1979), 129–53.

27. Robert Fulghum, *All I Really Need to Know I Learned in Kindergarten* (New York: Ivy Books, 1988).

28. Abraham H. Maslow, *Motivation and Personality*, 2nd ed. (New York: Harper & Row, 1970).

29. John Adams used this phrase in a summation to a jury. You can read a more complete text at http://www.law.umkc.edu/faculty/projects/ftrials/trialheroes/HEROSEARCH5.htm.

30. Ronald Prescott Reagan, "Remarks by [Ronald] Prescott Reagan," 10 June 2004. [Retrieved from http://www.ronaldreaganmemorial.com/remarks_by_Prescott_Reagan.asp, 10 June 2004.]

Putting Theory Into Practice

Going beyond Google can enhance your research.

Researching Your Message

Objectives 

After reading this chapter and reviewing the online learning resources at www.mhhe.com/brydon6, you should be able to:

- Conduct a search of the Internet to find support for a speech.
- Conduct systematic library research to find support for a speech.
- Conduct a meaningful interview with an expert on the topic of a speech.
- Record information in a usable form for your speech.
- Cite sources orally for your audience.

Key Concepts

abstract
blog
Boolean operators
Deep Web
fact
index
key word
online catalog
opinion
podcast
primary sources
research
RSS
secondary sources
subject heading
Surface Web
URL
wiki

“ Genius is one percent inspiration and ninety-nine percent perspiration. ”

–THOMAS EDISON

We have all had the experience of hearing speeches by well-respected speakers who never cite a single source. For example, the authors have heard speeches by Nobel Peace Prize–winners Elie Wiesel and Mikhail Gorbachev. These speakers didn't need to say "according to an article in . . ." to show that they knew what they were talking about. We have also attended many lectures by less well-known speakers who, because of their expertise in a particular area, have not relied on other sources to document their claims.

For most of us, however, and certainly for students beginning their public speaking careers, it is important to use credible evidence from reliable sources to support what is said in our speeches. To do so requires **research**: the process of finding and evaluating supporting materials.

research
The process of finding and evaluating supporting materials.

Why Do Research?

There are several reasons why research is important. First, unless we are simply relating first-hand experience, speeches that neither reflect nor cite research can convey false (or at least questionable) information to an audience. Second, keep in mind our ethical responsibility to provide good reasons to our audience for believing what we say. Without evidence, what assurance do our listeners have that our claims aren't simply made up? Third, unless our audience perceives us as knowledgeable, we are unlikely to convince them of our claims without documentation. Aristotle called such believability *ethos,* and contemporary researchers call it *source credibility.* Both agree that it is key to the art and science of public speaking. Our believability as speakers is enhanced by citing evidence from multiple sources in the body of our speeches.[1] Doing so requires research to uncover evidence from multiple sources. But there's a catch: We need to make sure that we research and orally cite sources that have weight with audience members and that can be readily checked on should audience members so desire. Telling an audience we pulled the evidence from some generic Web site and citing the URL just doesn't cut it.

We know that this is easier said than done. Hence, the remaining sections of this chapter will give you the tools not only to find information for your speeches but also to evaluate that information in a way that will enable you to convey it credibly to an audience.

Developing a Research Plan

Purposeful research begins with a research plan. And a research plan must begin with a thorough analysis of your rhetorical situation, the topic we emphasized in Chapter 7. Who will be your audience? What topics are of interest to them and you? What are your purposes–both general and specific?

For students in a basic speech class, some of these matters are predetermined. For example, your classmates constitute your audience. Depending on how far the term has progressed, you may have a clear idea of what topics interest them. But if it's early in the term then you may want to test-drive some ideas with classmates (we often have brainstorming sessions in class where different topics are discussed).

The general purpose of a speech may also be predetermined by your instructor. You will typically be asked to give a speech to inform or persuade and will face some specific constraints, such as a time limit and requirements for visual aids. Within those limitations, you will make a number of decisions that guide your research plan.

Given that your audience and general purpose are usually predetermined, you will need to decide on a topic for your speech. In Chapter 3 we discussed the standards for a good topic: it should be interesting to audience and speaker, appropriate to the situation and to the available time, manageable, and worthwhile. Once you have a topic, you need to decide what you want the audience to take away from your speech. Will they be able to do something they couldn't do before your speech? One of our students, for example, taught us the art of folding a fitted sheet (no, you don't just roll it up in a ball). Will they be asked to change their attitudes about an issue? Another of our students gave a speech aimed at convincing her classmates to ditch their expensive bottled water and instead attach a simple water filter to their faucet and get pure water for pennies a glass. Whatever topic you pick, you need to be sure that information is readily available for your speech. Sometimes a promising topic will turn out to be too obscure or difficult to research in the time available. You will need to begin research early enough to allow yourself the time to shift topics if necessary.

Often it is not until after you have begun your research that you discover there is not enough information to meet the needs of your proposed presentation—or there is so much information that an entire lecture series would be required to adequately cover your original topic. Be flexible and willing to enlarge or shrink the presentation topic based on your research. One method for getting "the correct topic size" is by enlarging or contracting the time period covered. For instance, you may originally have wanted to speak about the history of U.S. immigration policy but found far too much information. Changing your topic to U.S. immigration policy since the 9/11 attacks would help reduce your presentation to a more manageable size. Another method of adjusting your topic is to modify the geographic area covered. You might find that a speech on Nike's use of child labor in Vietnam does not produce much information, but broadening the topic to include the Nike's operations throughout the entire world gives you enough research material to effectively address the subject.

The Goal: Reliable and Credible Evidence

At this point it is tempting to simply provide a laundry list of places to look for information: the Internet, the library, the daily newspaper, and so forth. We think this is actually backwards. Before you start looking for evidence for your speech, we think you need to know what to look for. More specifically, you need to know what constitutes reliable and credible evidence.

Reference librarians at our university developed a useful tool, which they nicknamed the CRAAP test, for assessing online information. The letters stand for *Currency, Relevance, Authority, Accuracy, and Purpose.*[2] We feel that it is useful for more than just Web sites. In fact, these are the hallmarks of credible evidence, whatever the source.

Currency In today's world, things change at such a rapid pace that often yesterday's news is both stale and downright wrong. Whatever your topic, you want the most current, up-to-date information possible. One advantage of published sources is that the dates are usually apparent. With Web sites, you may not know when the information was posted. (By clicking on the File menu option and then on Properties in Internet Explorer, you may be able to determine the creation and modification date of a Web page.) If you cannot determine the currency of information, it probably should not be used in your speech.

Relevance Sometimes information is interesting but not really helpful in achieving your specific speech purpose. What the Berlin Wall was made of may be interesting, but it may not be relevant to a speech on the economic policies that most contributed to the collapse of East Germany. As we discuss how to conduct searches for information, we will give you some tools for narrowing things down to what is directly relevant to your purpose.

Authority This is probably one of the most important things to look for in doing your research. Ultimately, you need to convince your audience that they should trust the source of information. One of the most common complaints we get from students is that they don't know how to cite sources with an unknown author. In many cases, our response is: "Why should we believe anything from an unknown author?" Instead, find out who said it or at least what group or organization is represented. Only then can you decide if it's worth including in the speech.

Accuracy Even authoritative sources sometimes get it wrong. There's no surefire way to guarantee that information is accurate. Still, using sources that have a reputation for being reliable and truthful helps. Also helpful are different authoritative sources that offer different evidence in support of the same conclusion; for example, a biochemist and a psychologist saying that there is chemical and behavioral evidence supporting the diagnosis of depression. If you can cite evidence from two sources (e.g., Rush Limbaugh and Al Franken) who customarily are authorities for diametrically opposed audiences but agree on what you claim, then you may convince your greatest skeptic in your audience of the accuracy of your message.

Purpose Finally, a good researcher keeps in mind the stated and implied purpose of the source of information. Particularly on controversial topics, a source who has an axe to grind may be suspect. Since we've recently learned that the heads of governmental agencies have paid supposedly "objective" media sources to tout certain policies, we must be doubly on guard in this respect.

For a more detailed discussion of these tests of research, see Tips and Tactics, Evaluating Sources Using the CRAAP Test.

Tips and Tactics

Evaluating Sources Using the CRAAP Test

Currency

- When was the information published or posted? Has the information been revised or updated? Newspapers, books, periodicals, and many Web sites will provide this information. If it's not readily available, look for internal clues. For example, a Web site that speculates about whether Saddam Hussein will be captured, tried, and executed is clearly out of date.
- Is the information current or out of date for your topic? If you are speaking

about the Vietnam War, information from several years ago is probably fine. But if you want to discuss the current war on terror, information even a few days old may be out of date.
- Are the Web site links functional? One of the hints that a Web site is out of date is that it contains dead links.

Relevance

- Does the information answer your question or need?
- Is this information at an appropriate level for your audience?
- Have you looked at a variety of sources before determining that this is one you will use? Is this the best source you can find to make your point?

Authority

- Who is the author/publisher/source/sponsor, and what are their credentials or organizational affiliations? Most books and periodicals will tell you something about the author. Also, a Google search (which we will discuss later) can often help you learn about a source. Clicking "about us" or "contact us" on the Web page may help.
- What are the author's qualifications to write on the topic?
- Is there contact information, such as a publisher or e-mail address?
- Does the **URL** reveal anything about the author or source? For example, is the site a .com, .edu, .gov, .org, or .net? We will discuss these in more detail later in this chapter.

URL
Uniform Resource Locator: the address for Web sites, such as www.mhhe.com.

Accuracy

- Can you tell where the information comes from?
- Is the information supported by evidence such as footnotes or links to other verifiable sources?
- Has the information been reviewed or refereed by experts? A newspaper, for example, normally edits and checks sources before publishing a story; many Web sites do not.
- Can you verify any of the information using another source or from personal knowledge?
- Are there spelling, grammar, or other typographical errors?

Purpose

- What is the purpose of the information? A Web site touting a nutritional supplement is suspect if it invites you to click on a link to buy the product.
- Do the authors/sponsors make their intentions or purpose clear?
- Does the information seem unbiased, or is it merely opinion or propaganda? Does the language or tone seem unbiased and free of emotion?
- Are there obvious political, ideological, cultural, religious, institutional, or personal biases?

The Internet

Lest you think otherwise, we use the Internet daily. Besides e-mail, we use it to post lecture notes and slides on our course homepages, visit chat rooms external to the physical class, and research topics about which we are interested. However, we differ from many of our students in how we go about using Internet technology to find information that will help us with our research and writing.

Simply put, our research skills were honed while wandering through brick and mortar libraries that featured drawers of card catalogs arranged by the Dewey Decimal System, stacks of bound books, printed journals, and even microforms we viewed with the aid of projection machines. Thus our "search" for information relevant to a paper we were writing or to a study we planned was largely limited to what could be housed physically within the confines of the library building.

One benefit of this fact was selectivity. Because space was limited, librarians and other scholars served as gatekeepers who determined what information should be let in and what information should be kept out. Although this system was far from democratic, its purpose was to make sure that the information we found was current, relevant, authoritative, accurate, and explicit in its purpose.

By the late 1980s and early 1990s, chinks in the brick and mortar of this system of warehousing and distributing information were becoming increasingly apparent. The sheer amount of scholarly information was increasing exponentially, and it could neither be evaluated as quickly as needed nor constrained by the physical space that had been built to contain it.

Needless to say, this is no longer a problem. Breakthroughs in information storage and retrieval have largely solved the physical limitations of the traditional library. And personal computers in combination with the World Wide Web have made virtual libraries a reality for most college students and professors. If that were all there was to the story, our task in this chapter would be much simpler.

But as we know, there's more. The same breakthroughs that made virtual libraries possible also have made possible the Open Internet. Yet the Open Internet hasn't simply made the development and dissemination of information more democratic; it has also eliminated many of the filtering processes that let valid information in and kept erroneous information out of every conceivable channel of communication, including speeches. In addition, the huge increase in the volume of resources has buried the researcher with information that needs to be evaluated.

surface web
(Open Internet) Web sites freely accessible to all users over the Internet.

deep web
(Proprietary Internet) Web sites accessible over the Internet only to authorized users and often at a cost.

The Internet is actually made up of several sections. The **Surface Web,** sometimes called the Open Internet, is searchable by Web search engines such as Google, MSN Search, and Yahoo. This part of the Internet often allows you free access to information. The other part of the Internet is the **Deep Web,** which is sometimes referred to as the Proprietary Internet. The Deep Web contains information in private databases that are accessible over the Internet but are not intended to be located (crawled) by search engines. For example, some universities, government agencies, and other organizations maintain databases of information that were not created for general public access and do not allow search engines to index them. Other material on the Deep Web is from commercial publishers who require that you access it through a paid subscription or pay to view certain pages. Many traditional, hardcopy materials such as newspapers, journals, magazines, dictionaries, and encyclopedias have been converted to electronic format and are sold via the Deep Web.

Why should you care about the Deep Web and the Surface Web? If you are using only the Surface Web for your research, then you may be locating only information of limited value. The premium information that will add credibility to your presentation may only be available online through Deep Web databases. Information aggregators such as LexisNexis, Proquest, Factiva, and EBSCO package and resell commercially produced information via the Deep Web. Often your college or local public library has subscriptions with such vendors, allowing you to search, view, and save expensive information for free.

How do you know if you have access to such Deep Web sources? Most library Web pages have guides that explain which premium online resources they provide. If you have a particular title in mind, such as *The New York Times* or *The Economist,* you can often check your library's online catalog to determine if a resource is available either in hardcopy or electronically. These guides and catalogs may have "clickable" links that take you directly to the database containing your title.

With that in mind, consider our most recent experience with Wikipedia, a popular Surface Web site some of our students have cited as the source of information conveyed in their speeches.

Wiki comes from the Hawaiian word for quick.[3] The idea is that anyone can quickly make a change in an entry they find in Wikipedia and it will be instantly available to all users. No one demands that the user document or substantiate the edit. Recently one of us was checking out the entry for our university on Wikipedia to learn what it said about our Speech and Debate team. He found no mention of the team or its role. As the former debate coach, he was bothered by the omission; so, with a few keystrokes, he anonymously added to the history of the school that in 1948 "the speech and debate team was founded by Herbert Rae, Speech & Drama Department Chair."

wiki
The Hawaiian word for quick. A Web site that allows users to edit content easily and quickly—for example, Wikipedia.

Was this entry accurate? Given that the author was in diapers in 1948, it wasn't based on his personal knowledge. Rather, it was based on what he had been told by a retired colleague. No one from Wikipedia could contact the author. Wikipedia only knows the IP address of the computer used to post the information.

Unfortunately, not everyone who visits Wikipedia has such good intentions, as the case of journalist John Seigenthaler Sr. (father of NBC's current anchor John Seigenthaler Jr.) illustrates. For 132 days in 2005, Wikipedia falsely reported that John Seigenthaler Sr.

> was the assistant to Attorney General Robert Kennedy in the early 1960's [sic]. For a brief time, he was thought to have been directly involved in the Kennedy assassinations of both John, and his brother, Bobby. Nothing was ever proven.[4]

As Seigenthaler senior recounts in an article for *USA Today,* no one knew who had posted the false accusations. Even a call to Wikipedia's founder, Jimmy Wales, failed to turn up the name of the perpetrator, since Wikipedia doesn't require contributors to reveal their identity. Further, because of the way the Internet is interconnected, Reference.com and Answers.com posted the same false accusation. Although the false information was eventually removed, this example illustrates that a claim isn't true just because it's found on the Internet.

Don't get us wrong; the Internet can be a marvelous source of information for speakers and even textbook writers. In fact, the example of the false Wikipedia article was found by using the search engine Google, and Seigenthaler's rebuttal to the article was found on the *USA Today* Web site. Thus, our purpose in this chapter is not to insist that only those facts appearing on the printed page are suitable for speeches. Quite the contrary, Surface Web-based information can be as reliable as that appearing in printed sources—even those as reputable as the *New Republic,* which is so prestigious that it is often called the in-flight magazine of Air Force One. In 1998, the *New Republic* was forced to fire its rising star, Stephen Glass, when an online version of *Forbes* revealed that Glass had fabricated a story about a 15-year-old who had hacked the Web site of Jukt Micronics. It turned out that the story was entirely fictitious, right down to the name of the company. *The New Republic*'s investigation revealed that Glass had fabricated at least 27 of 41 articles. The case became the basis of a 2003 motion picture entitled *Shattered Glass.*[5]

It is easy to use the Internet to find information on a speech topic, but it is not as easy to find information that is reliable and valid. Thus, as consumers of information, we must exercise our own critical faculties in assessing the information we receive from the Internet and even traditional sources, particularly when others rely on the information we use in a speech.

We recognize that most students begin their research with the Open Internet—so that is where we'll begin. In the process, let's see if we can improve the process of seeking evidence for your speeches. In the following sections, we provide specific advice on using a wide variety of Open Internet sources, including popular search engines (such as Google, Yahoo, or MSN Live Search), wikis (such as Wikipedia), podcasts, RSS feeds, user-powered news sites, YouTube, and blogs.

Googling

As they say on their Web site, "Google's mission is to organize the world's information and make it universally accessible and useful."[6] Well, they certainly have mastered the goal of accessing a lot of information. Take a popular topic for student speeches, "global warming." We typed those words into the general Google search box and got about 30 million "hits." What can you do with over 30 million sources? And how would you know which ones are reliable and which are bogus? After all, global warming is a controversial topic for some. Thus, Google's very power is also its greatest limitation.

Thankfully, Google has some advanced searching tools. By clicking on the link to "advanced" search, you can limit your search in a variety of ways. Suppose we are interested in the accuracy of the movie *An Inconvenient Truth,* featuring former Vice President Al Gore. We might narrow our search in a number of ways. We could limit our search for sources that contained the name of the film and the word "accurate" or "inaccurate." We could limit our search further by also specifying we were interested in only those sources that did not use the inflammatory word "lie." Although our results were still extensive when we did exactly this, they were reduced from 30 million to a little under 70,000.

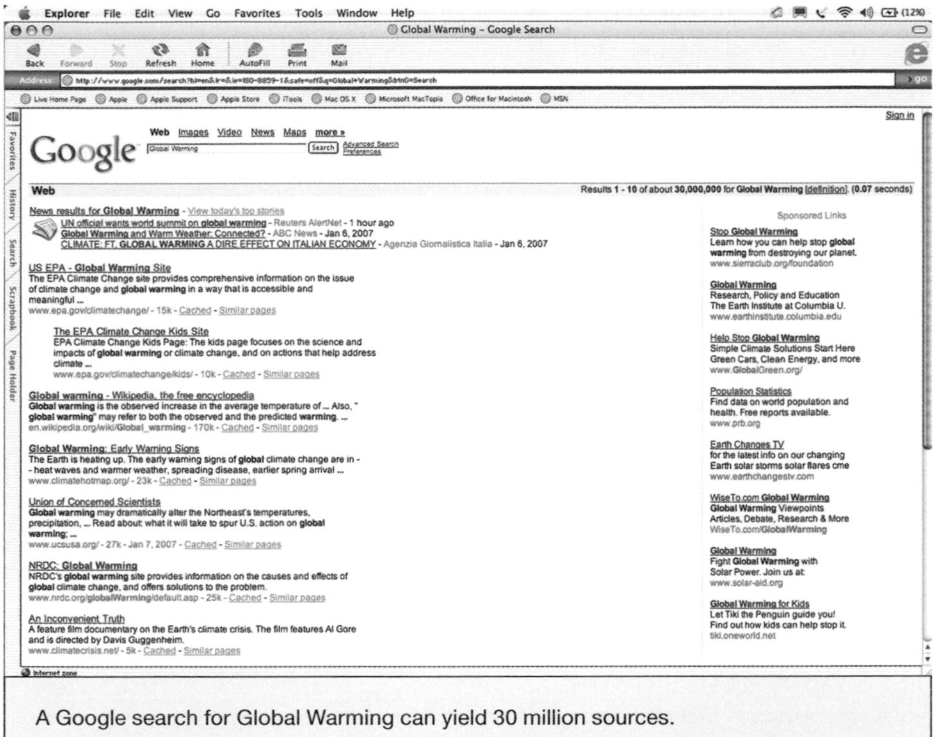

A Google search for Global Warming can yield 30 million sources.

In addition to advanced search tools, Google provides another resource, "Google Scholar," that searches various scholarly sources (peer-reviewed papers, theses, books, articles, etc.). Although many of these sources are readily available on the Web, others may require subscriptions or membership. If that is the case, don't automatically give up; you may be able to find them in your university library or through interlibrary loan. The advantage of using the Google scholar tool is that the authority and accuracy of your research can be much more easily established for your audience. And your search is far more manageable. We found just 51 sources on the Gore film using this search feature.

But Beware . . .

As should be clear from the preceding discussions, we are big fans of Google. However, users need to understand something about how Google arranges results. Google refuses to disclose, for obvious reasons, the exact methods by which it ranks results. This can lead to some startling results. To see how Google searches can go awry, see the box: "Speaking of . . . When Google Misfires" on page 178. Users should also know that, in addition to the regular search results, Google also displays a number of sponsored links that are paid for by various Web sites—a source of revenue for Google. But their presence is no measure of their validity or reliability as a source; it merely indicates that they were willing to pay for advertising through Google.

Google Advanced Search allows users to narrow down their search.

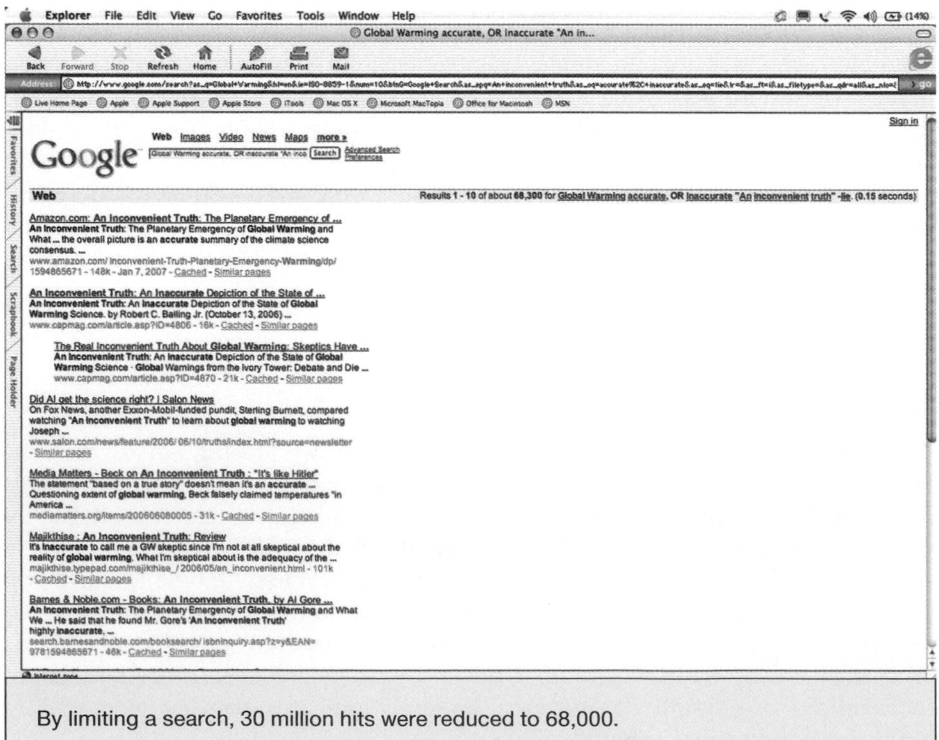

By limiting a search, 30 million hits were reduced to 68,000.

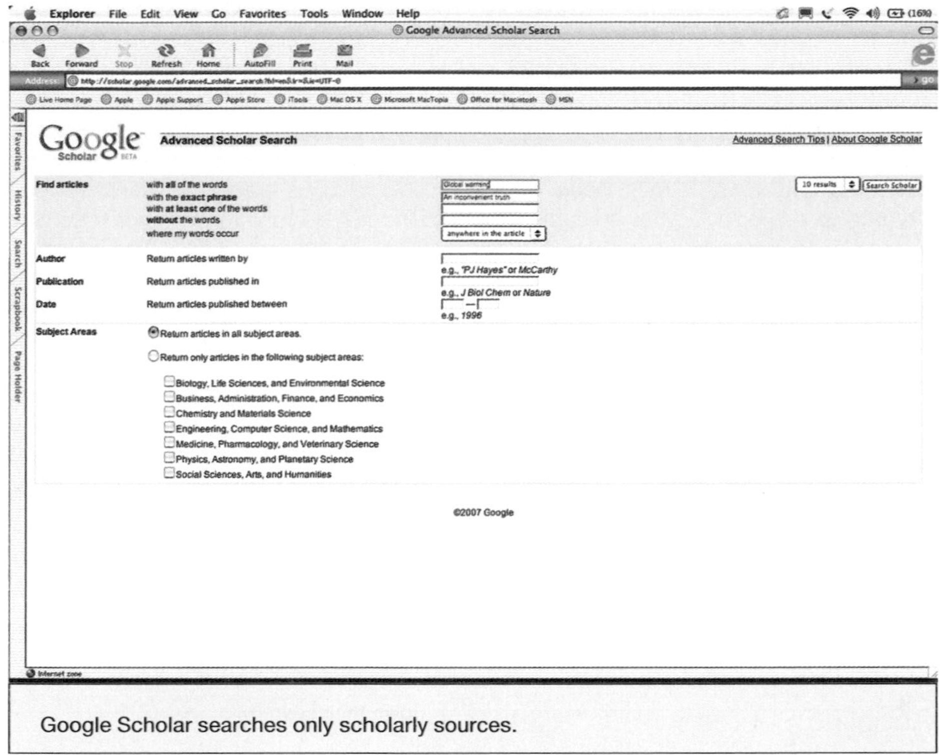

Google Scholar searches only scholarly sources.

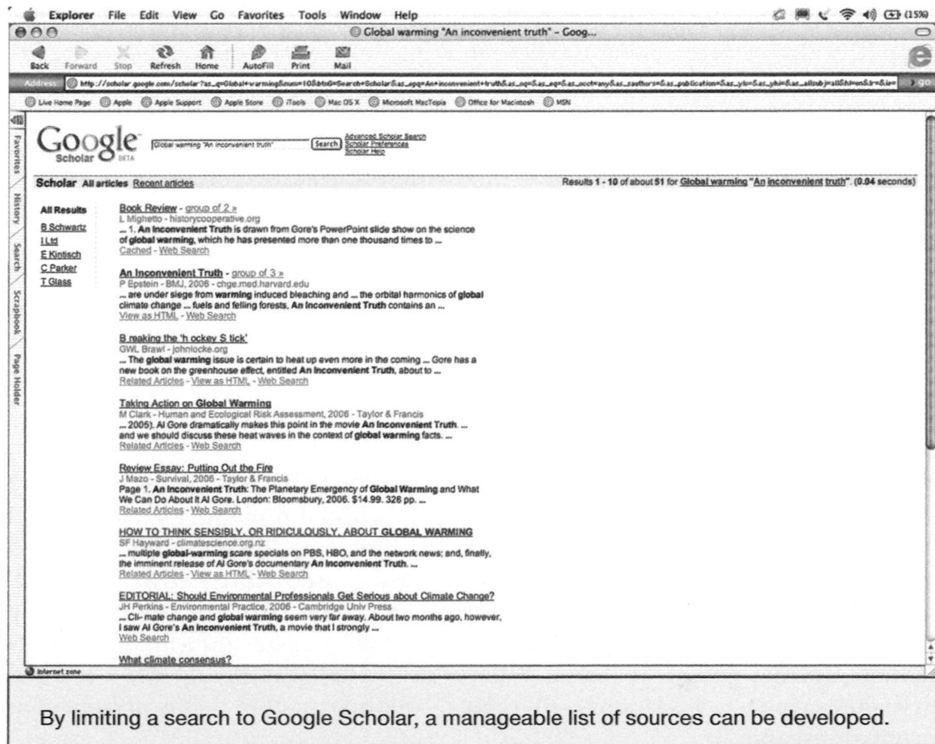

By limiting a search to Google Scholar, a manageable list of sources can be developed.

Speaking of . . .

When Google Misfires

An example of how a Google search can reveal misleading sources occurs when Web sites are ranked by Google based on factors that have nothing to do with credibility. For example, we typed *martinlutherking* into the Google search engine on January 8, 2007. The number one hit was a Web site (http://www.martinlutherking.org/) sponsored by a white supremacist organization. Among the recommended readings on Dr. King was a book by former Ku Klux Klan leader David Duke—hardly a friend of the late civil rights leader. One likely reason it is the number one result on Google is that many librarians put this link on their own Web sites as an example of a bogus site, thus causing it to rank very high in Google's results list. When we typed *martin luther king* as separate words, rather than as a single string of characters, the number one hit was the Nobel Prize organization (http://nobelprize.org/nobel_prizes/peace/laureates/1964/king-bio.html)—but the racist site was still the second ranked hit.

It's also important to be familiar with "Google bombs." By manipulating various characteristics of a Web site, pranksters have been able to move the search results for particular phrases to the number one result in some comical ways. In January 2007, for instance, if you typed *miserable failure* in the search box, the first site that comes up is the official biography of the president, obviously the result of pranksters who dislike him. Not to be outdone by those on the left, the next hit was the biography of filmmaker Michael Moore, probably a result of pranksters on the right. Probably the most famous Google bomb was in 1999 when typing *more evil than satan* in Google's search box took you to Microsoft's home page. Today that phrase will lead you to several articles about Google bombing.

Googling Sources

Before we leave the topic of Google, we want to suggest one additional way it can be a valuable research tool. Suppose you find an interesting article or Web site but there are no qualifications listed for the author. Sometimes a Google search of the author's name (or the name of the organization sponsoring the Web site) will help out. For example, in the When Google Misfires box, we mentioned the Martin Luther King Web site that was linked to a racist group that specifically recommended a book by David Duke. What if you had never heard of Duke? Well, Googling his name–in addition to leading you to his own Web site–takes you to articles about his role in the Ku Klux Klan and his visit to Iran for a conference on Holocaust deniers. If a person's credentials are not known to you, consider Googling the name. You may need to conduct an advanced search (especially if it's a common name), but being able to tell your audience your source's credentials is an important part of building your own credibility.

Wikis

secondary sources
Information sources that rely on other (primary) sources rather than gathering information firsthand.

primary sources
Original sources of information.

Early on in this chapter we introduced the potential abuses of wikis: Web sites that allow users to add, delete, or edit content without providing verification of their contribution. One of the limitations of wikis, in addition to the ease with which they can be edited, is that they are at best a **secondary source**. Whenever possible, speakers should try to locate **primary sources** of information (i.e., the original source) rather than a source that presents information that its authors did not gather firsthand. Wikipedia insists upon being *only* a secondary source; in fact, moderators will remove any information that is presented as original research.

At the same time, we think that wikis do have a role to play in your research. Rather than treating wiki articles as ends in themselves, use the external links and references in the articles to see if there are reliable sources that you can easily access. Wikipedia can be a good quick stop for statistics and factoids, and having the information may make it quicker to find the detail in question. For example, if we need to know the Nobel Prize winner in physics for 1973, we can just go to Wikipedia, search for Nobel Prize Physics, find the name, and then search for a credible primary source on the name. If the wiki was wrong, we'll quickly find that out, but most likely it will help us find good primary sources on the person in question. It is also good for checking the reliability of other sources. It represents an influx consensus of many people. Thus, we suggest using sources such as Wikipedia as a way of locating other sources that can meet the tests of currency, relevance, authority, accuracy, and purpose.

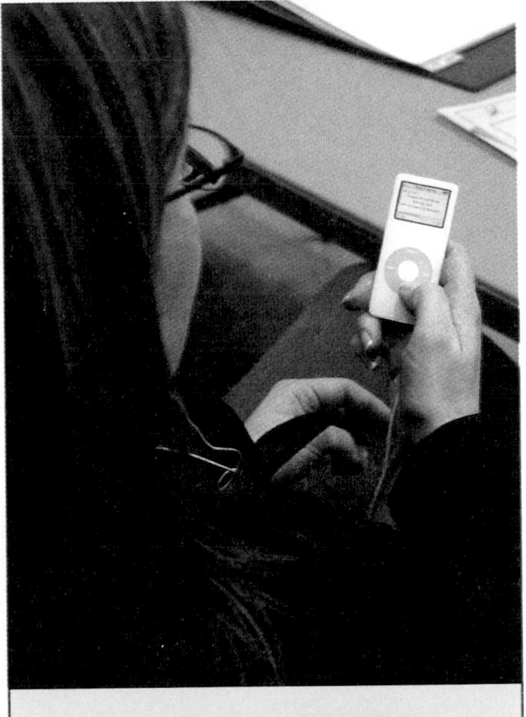

Podcasts can be a good resource if the source is credible.

Podcasts and RSS Feeds

With the widespread use of MP3 players, such as Apple's popular iPod, audio and even video files can be transmitted over the Internet to anyone who is interested in accessing them. A **podcast** is an audio broadcast that has been converted to a digital format (such as MP3) for playback by a digital music player or computer.[7] Some universities make many professors' lectures available in podcast format. For example, in December 2006 one could download a lecture titled "Is Global Warming Real? Climate Change and Our Energy Future" by Professor Robert Dunbar, Professor of Geological and Environmental Sciences at Stanford University. In fact, there were 79 lectures available to the general public on iTunes from Stanford experts, with topics ranging from global warming to electronic voting. Ten lectures were even available in video format. And that's just one university.

podcast
An audio broadcast that has been converted to a digital format, such as MP3, for playback by a digital music player or computer.

It's not only universities that have podcasts available. National Public Radio, the White House, TV networks, and major news sources like the *New York Times* all have podcasts readily available. The key, as with any other source of information, is how well it meets the CRAAP tests we've outlined. Certainly a lecture by a respected professor at a major research institution such as Stanford is as good if not a better source on global warming as a movie by a former vice president.

RSS (Really Simple Syndication)
A syndication format that aggregates updates to various news sites or blogs and transmits them to users.

RSS (Really Simple Syndication) is a format that aggregates updates to various news sites or blogs and transmits them to users.[8] For example, you can sign up for feeds from various news sources, even the White House. RSS is a form of "push technology": it pushes information directly to your desktop. This will send you news headlines that link back to various press releases and Web content without you having to visit the site every time. If you are doing ongoing research on a topic, then signing up for RSS feeds from reputable sources is a way to be sure you have current and relevant information from authoritative and accurate sources. *The New York Times*, for example, offers both podcasts and RSS feeds.

User-Powered News Sites

An interesting variation on search engines like Google and wikis are user-powered news sites. For example, Digg.com allows a user to post content that is then rated by other users. As their Web site explains: "Digg is a user driven social content website. . . . Well, everything on Digg is submitted by our community (that would be you). After you submit content, other people read your submission and Digg what they like best. If your story rocks and receives enough Diggs, it is promoted to the front page for the millions of visitors to see."[9] So rather than relying on some editor to rank stories (as a newspaper would) or on a computer algorithm (as does Google), Digg relies on its users to post news stories and then relies on other users to give their evaluation. You can search the news by topic and then arrange the results by most Diggs to find the articles that were found most useful by the community of users. You can link back to the stories that are most relevant to your topic and also give your own opinion as to whether or not you "Digg" it. For example, in January 2007 we found that the most "Digged" article on global warming was an AP report on an allegation that a major oil company had given millions to groups in an effort to discredit global warming.[10] Digg.com is useful as a different way to search for information on topics, but you still have to assess whether or not the articles that it points to are from credible sources. A similar Web site primarily useful for science and technical news is slashdot.org.

YouTube

One of the most popular and now copied Web sites is YouTube. It allows users to post videos (often of themselves) on the site for anyone to view. Most of the material on the site is entertaining or just odd, but some important videos have found their way onto this site. For example, Senator George Allen of Virginia, who was widely seen as a shoe-in for reelection in 2006 and a likely presidential candidate for 2008, was videotaped (by a campaign worker for his opponent) making what were interpreted as racially insensitive remarks. The story was soon picked up by major news organizations. Not only were Allen's hopes for a presidential campaign destroyed, he was narrowly defeated for reelection in a race that tipped the balance of the U.S. Senate from Republican to Democratic control.

YouTube has become a popular site for viewing video clips submitted by users.

YouTube is a great source for finding video material for use in speeches or as background material. For example, a search for videos on global warming located everything from the trailer to *An Inconvenient Truth* to a spoof making fun of Al Gore. Just as with Wikipedia and other sources where the content is not screened for accuracy, the videos you find on YouTube are only as valid as their original source.

Blogs

Most of us are familiar with **blogs** (short for Web logs). They contain dated entries in reverse chronological order and can range from serious commentary by experts to mere "ranting and raving" by just about anyone with an opinion.[11] Many blogs have a strong persuasive component, especially those related to politics. However, they also tend to contain many links to more reputable mainstream media sources. Even blogs whose authors disagree with your point of view can be a valuable source of links.

blog (short for Web log)
A Web site that contains dated entries in reverse chronological order. They can range from serious commentary by experts to "ranting and raving" by people with no particular qualifications.

fact
Something that is verifiable as true.

opinion
A judgment by someone that is subject to dispute.

The idea of using blogs in a speech brings us to an important distinction: fact versus opinion. A **fact** is something that is verifiable as true. An **opinion** is a judgment by someone that is subject to dispute.

For example, an Associated Press article reported that, according to the National Climatic Data Center, 2006 was the warmest year on record for the United States. At the same time, the article stated, "The center said it is not clear how much of the warming is a result of climate changes induced by greenhouse gases and how much resulted from the current El Niño warming of the tropical Pacific Ocean."[12] That the temperature in 2006 was the highest on record is verifiable, since scientific instruments were used to collect the data. The cause of the high temperature, on the other hand, is a matter of opinion. Even the experts disagree. Thus, if speaking on this topic you would need to cite the qualifications of those offering opinions–whether they come from a blog or a published source. There are numerous blogs dealing with global warming and climate change. Deciding whose opinions we should value is important in meeting the tests of authority dictated by the CRAAP test. The problem with blogs is that anyone can have one. We do not recommend citing blogs unless the source is clearly authoritative on the topic of your speech. Blogs often will have links to the biography or credentials of the blogger. A speaker must do more than cite the name of the blogger; the audience needs to hear why the blogger is a credible source on the topic.

One other aspect of blogs is that they are often the source for reports in traditional news outlets. If that is the case, they are really no more reliable than any other rumor. The danger is that, if the news outlet relies on the blogosphere rather than developing its own sources, misinformation may be spread. A recent example of this occurred when a blog devoted to "outing" closet gay politicians posted an item claiming that a well-known male politician had had sexual relations with at least three men (none of whom was named). A newspaper published the allegations along with the politician's denial. Nobody checked to see which version was true.[13]

A Final Word about Evaluating Internet Information

The trickiest part of doing Internet research is knowing how to tell reliable from unreliable sources. You can tell a lot from a Web site's URL. Once you've used a search engine such as Google or Digg to locate possible Web sites, look at the URL for clues as to whether it is a legitimate source.[14]

- Is it a personal Web page? You can usually tell from the URL because it will often include a person's name following a tilde (~) or percent sign (%).

If the server is a commercial Internet service provider, such as geocities .com, aol.com, or angelfire.com, this is another sign of a questionable source. For most speeches, personal Web pages should be avoided.

- What is the type of domain? Government sites are usually .gov, .mil, or .us. Educational sites are .edu. Nonprofit organizations are .org. The domains .com and .net are generally commercial. Look for the types of sites that are most appropriate for your speech topic. Government and educational sites are often the best place to begin for speeches on current events and issues.
- Who is the Web page's sponsor? For example, the Web site for this text (www.mhhe.com/brydon6) is published by McGraw-Hill Higher Education. One can safely assume that this is a reliable source of information about our text and its supporting materials. Look for pages sponsored by reputable organizations that have a direct bearing on your speech topic.

You should be aware that a .org domain is no guarantee that a site is noncommercial, and .edu is *not* a guarantee of scholarly content–for example, bju.edu (Bob Jones University). Also, be alert to the fact that most university students can put a personal Web page up under their university's domain. Don't rely entirely upon the domain suffix, but consider it a minor tool in your CRAAP toolbox.

There are various sites that can evaluate Web resources. For instance, the Urban Legends Web site (http://snopes.com) is a terrific resource for determining the validity of commonly held ideas or theories. If you type in "miserable failure" in the search box at Urban Legends, you will get a detailed account of how this term became associated with the president. The Librarians' Internet Index (http://lii.org/) is also an excellent resource for locating reliable information on the free Web. The LII performs a similar filtering function for the Internet that librarians have traditionally provided for the patrons of "brick and mortar" libraries. Their mission statement declares: "The mission of Librarians' Internet Index is to provide a well-organized point of access for reliable, trustworthy, librarian-selected websites, serving California, the nation, and the world."[15]

Today's libraries use computer databases to enhance the research process.

The Library

It's common for us to meet students who have never set foot in the library on campus–but this doesn't mean that they haven't used the university's library resources. Today there are really two types of libraries available to students: the brick and mortar building; and the virtual library, available 24/7 from the convenience of a computer at home, on campus, or in an Internet café.

Even so, we require our own students to take a guided tour of the physical library. Some valuable resources for speeches reside only on the shelves of the library or in its special collections departments.

Research for a public speaking class will often involve a trip to the campus library. The library is the intellectual center of most universities and colleges–the repository of the history of ideas and thought. Although campus libraries vary in their extensiveness and degree of sophistication, the basic principles of a library search are the same whether in a physical or virtual library.

The first step in using a library is familiarization. Most campus libraries feature in-person and online guided tours, handouts, and special seminars for groups interested in a particular area of research. Your instructor may have your class take a library tour or send you on a library scavenger hunt to familiarize you with the library. Whatever you do, though, don't wait until you are facing a speech deadline before familiarizing yourself with your library. If you didn't do it during your first few weeks on campus, make it a priority now.

We recommend the following four steps for library research.

Tips and Tactics

Four Steps of Library Research

1. Select key words.
2. Search the library catalog.
3. Search relevant indexes, abstracts, and other databases.
4. Consult reference sources.

Although each step isn't required every time for library research, it's useful to know about each step and how the steps are connected. Let's look at each in detail.

Select Key Words

Key words are significant ones taken from the abstract, title, subject heading, or text of an entry and used to search an electronic database.[16] They are like the combination to a safe: If we have the right combination, we can easily open the door; without it, our chances of opening the door are slim. Thus, the most effective library search begins with searching key words on the topic of interest.

In addition to key words, **subject headings**, developed by the Library of Congress, are standardized throughout libraries across the country. These headings often lead to sources we might otherwise miss. For example, suppose we are interested in the topic of the "three strikes law." We searched our university library's catalog for books on the topic and found three. However, the detailed record for the books revealed that the Library of Congress uses the subject heading *mandatory sentence.* Searching for that term yielded 21 books–a sevenfold increase. Although we normally begin our search using key words and phrases that seem logical, we check the official subject headings and try them as well. These can multiply our results several times over.

Another hint for key word or subject searching is to use truncation and wildcard symbols. For example, at our university a star (*) is used for these purposes. Thus, to search for *sentence, sentences,* and *sentencing,* we would type *sentenc** in the search box. The search engine will find all records with any string of characters following *sentenc.* Similarly, to search for both *woman* and *women,* the key word *wom*n* would do the job. Be sure to ask what characters your library uses as wildcards, as it varies from library to library and database to database.

key word
A word in the abstract, title, subject heading, or text of an entry that can be used to search an electronic database.

subject heading
A standard word or phrase used by libraries to catalog books or other publications.

Search the Library Catalog

online catalog
A computerized database of library holdings.

Boolean operators
Terms, such as *and, or,* and *not,* used to narrow or broaden a computerized search of two or more related terms.

Most libraries today use computerized online catalogs accessible from off campus as well as in the library building. An **online catalog** is a computerized listing of library holdings. Library catalogs are searchable by key words for subject, author, and title. When beginning a search on a topic, it is unlikely that we will know specific authors or titles. Thus, the key words search is the most likely basis for a search.

When using an online catalog or similar database for a key word search, we use **Boolean operators**. These are terms, such as *and, or,* and *not,* used to narrow or broaden a computerized search of two or more related terms. Some databases and library catalogs will *assume* the Boolean operator *and* unless we supply another, while others will require us to type in *and* or +. For example, if we enter search words *human cloning* and the database assumes the *and,* it will locate all sources that use both the word *human* and the word *cloning* even if they are not used together. On the other hand, if the *and* is not assumed, the database may only locate sources where the phrase *human cloning* appears. Depending on our search needs, we need to determine which method is used in the library catalog. Check with a librarian at your school to learn whether you need to use Boolean operators, or experiment with different search combinations until you discover which way your library catalog operates. How Boolean operators can be used to broaden or narrow a search is shown in Exhibit 8.1.

Tips and Tactics

Expanding Your Search

- When we locate a book or other source that is interesting, we check to see what subject headings are used by the library to index the book in addition to the one used to find it. These subject headings can then provide new search terms to expand our search and locate additional sources on our topic.
- When we visit the stacks, we do a little browsing as we find the specific books we have noted. Because books are shelved by subject, it is not unusual to find a book closely related to our topic that we overlooked. This serendipitous search for information often turns up better sources than those we originally found.
- Follow the leads suggested by general books. The authors of books have done much of our work for us. A book's bibliography or footnotes lead to other sources. We read the more recent books first. In many ways, a researcher is like a detective looking for clues. A good general book on a topic is like a room full of clues. The author will have left fingerprints all over the place.

Exhibit 8.1
Boolean Operators Help Narrow or Broaden a Search

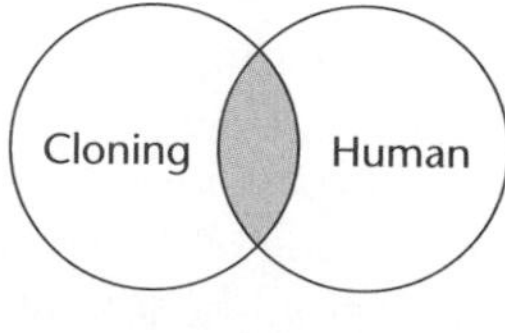

Cloning *AND* Human

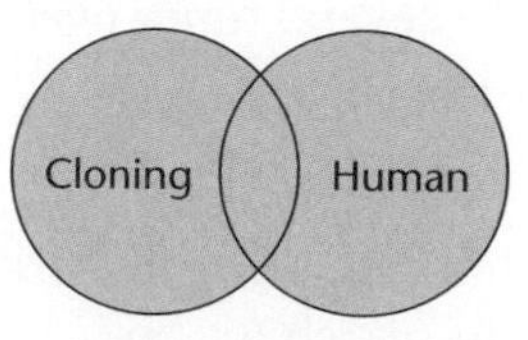

Cloning *OR* Human

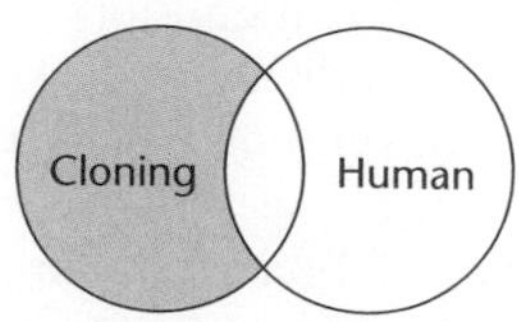

Cloning *NOT* Human

Search Relevant Indexes, Abstracts, and Databases

An **index** is an alphabetical listing of sources by topic of information–usually in newspapers, journals, and magazines that are not freely available via the open Internet. An **abstract** is a summary of an article or a report. Every topic you can imagine is classified in one or more specialized indexes. A good library has hundreds or even thousands of indexes related to specialized fields. Some indexes list and abstract articles in journals. Today, more and more indexes are available in the form of online databases. For example, a partial list of databases available through our university library is provided in Exhibit 8.2.

index
A listing of sources of information—usually in newspapers, journals, and magazines—alphabetically by topic.

abstract
A summary of an article or a report.

Whether your topic is art, science, religion, philosophy, or health and medicine, computerized databases can assist you in finding reliable information. Your library will undoubtedly differ from ours in the available indexes. However, the basic search principles will be the same regardless of the index used.

Let's look at a sample search using a popular database. Academic Search is an excellent source for searching scholarly and professional journals in the social sciences, humanities, and physical sciences. This database contains information on everything from astronomy to religion, law, psychology, and current events. Not only are citations and abstracts of articles available, but Academic Search also allows us to access the full texts of many articles. To search, we simply follow easy on-screen directions to enter appropriate search terms. The same Boolean operators we would use in an online catalog search can be used with most computerized databases. When we enter our search, a list of citations will be produced, and we mark the ones that interest us for viewing. Depending on the library's facilities, we may be able to print, copy to a disk, or even e-mail the results of our search.

To illustrate the power of Academic Search, in May 2007 we did a search for articles on global warming. We typed the words "global warming" into the search box and got 11,414 hits, far too many to be useful. By adding the Boolean operator "and" along with the words "greenhouse gas" we were able to reduce

Exhibit 8.2
Examples of Databases at CSU, Chico, with Description of Coverage

Database	Description of Coverage
Academic Search	More than 4,650 periodicals covering the social sciences, humanities, general science, multicultural studies, education, etc.
Biological Abstracts (BIOSIS)	Nearly 6,000 journals covered, representing agriculture, biochemistry, biotechnology, ecology, immunology, microbiology, etc.
Communication & Mass Media Complete	Scholarly and trade publications in communications, communication disorders, and journalism/mass media; abstracts for several hundred titles, with full text available for more than 200 titles.
CQ Researcher	Full-text issues written in accessible language, including pros/cons, background info, the current situation, and references to other information sources on current affairs controversies.
LexisNexis Academic	Full text news and legal information; includes newspapers, magazines, court opinions, laws, and law review articles.

the number of hits to 909. To make sure our results were from scholarly journals and readily available to us, we further limited our search to peer-reviewed articles that were available in full text (by checking the appropriate boxes on our search screen). That left us with 163 sources. Academic Search also offered options to further narrow the search. We limited it to the United States, which left us with 20 hits—a manageable list. And because all of the articles were available in full text through the computer database, we were able to download them directly to our computer (or we could have e-mailed them to ourselves).

Unlike Open Internet sources, these are all from reputable journals (for example, one article was from the *Bulletin of Atomic Scientists*). A speaker who utilizes articles from sources such as these will have no trouble defending the credibility of the sources cited in the speech.

Although databases such as Academic Search may initially seem to produce far too many results to be usable, a careful narrowing of the parameters of our search can lead to productive and easily accessible results. Although your library may not have this exact database, chances are it has a similar database that can access reliable published information on a wide variety of topics.

Of course, not every library has a physical or electronic copy of every journal listed in any given index or database. Thus you must compare the most promising articles from your search with your library's holding of journals. Some libraries provide listings of the journals they have. The online catalog may also list journals. You would look under the journal title, for example, to see if your library had a particular journal. Even if your library does not have it, you may be able to use interlibrary loan services to obtain a copy, if time permits. Also, some libraries subscribe to special services that enable them to have copies of journals not held in their collections faxed to the library for a nominal charge.

Consult Reference Sources

Frequently we need to find a very specific fact—for example, how much plastic was produced in the United States in a certain year. We could search a dozen articles and never find that number. But a good reference book, such as the *Statistical Abstract of the United States,* puts that kind of information at our fingertips. For an online source of reliable government statistics, try the Web site http://www.fedstats.gov/, which bills itself as "the gateway to statistics from over 100 U.S. Federal agencies."[17] This site includes topics from A to Z, map statistics, links to various federal agencies, and even the ability to access the online version of the *Statistical Abstract of the United States.*

Perhaps we need a good quotation to begin or end our speech. Numerous books of quotations are available. Your library probably has books such as *Bartlett's Quotations* on its shelves. However, an easier way to find quotations is to go to Bartleby.com's Great Books Online at http://www.bartleby.com/, which includes more than 87,000 quotations. You can combine your search to include several sources at once, including the venerable *Bartlett's.* For the first edition of this book, we were interested in a quotation frequently used by the late Robert Kennedy that went something like, "Some men see things as they are and say, why; I dream things that never were and say, why not." We expended several hours of library research tracking down the original source. For this edition we used Bartleby.com, and in less than a minute we had found the original quotation. It is actually, "You see things; and you say 'Why?' But I dream things that never were; and I say 'Why not?'" The original source is George Bernard Shaw's play, *Back to Methuselah.* Ironically, although Kennedy used the quotation as a theme in his 1968 campaign for the presidency, the actual speaker of these words in Shaw's play is the serpent enticing Eve in the Garden of Eden.[18]

Numerous other reference books can be found in libraries, including encyclopedias, some of which are available online. Although the information in general encyclopedias is rather basic, a number of specialized encyclopedias are also available. Here's a representative list of encyclopedias provided by Kristin Johnson, an Instructional Librarian at our university:

- *Encyclopedia of Advertising*
- *Encyclopedia of Global Change*
- *Encyclopedia of the Human Brain*
- *Encyclopedia of Skin and Skin Disorders*
- *Encyclopedia of Death and Dying*
- *Encyclopedia of Criminology and Deviant Behavior*
- *Encyclopedia of Drugs, Alcohol & Addictive Behavior*
- *Encyclopedia of Interior Design*
- *Encyclopedia of North American Sports History*
- *Encyclopedia of Popular Culture*
- *Encyclopedia of Movie Special Effects*
- *Encyclopedia of Creativity*
- *Encyclopedia of Sleep and Dreaming*
- *Encyclopedia of Homosexuality*
- *Encyclopedia of Television*
- *Encyclopedia of World Terrorism*
- *The Film Encyclopedia*
- *International Encyclopedia of Sexuality*
- *Violence in America: An Encyclopedia*

There are countless other reference books to which you can turn in the effort to track down information. For example, almanacs and yearbooks, such as *The World Almanac and Book of Facts* and *Information Please Almanac,* are useful sources of statistics and facts. Digests of information, such as *Facts on File* and *Editorial Research Reports,* are useful sources for information on current issues. Biographies, such as the *Who's Who* series, help you find out about the qualifications of various sources. Atlases are valuable in learning about the world. By consulting a current atlas, you can learn not only where a country is geographically but also important facts about it.

Interviews

We put off discussing interviews until now for a reason. It is tempting to go into an interview before researching the topic. In a sense, we expect the expert to write the speech. Although interviews with experts can offer useful information and may lead to other sources, they cannot substitute for doing our own research. Thus, an interview should be conducted only after going in person or online to the library and searching the Internet.

Finding potential interviewees on most topics is not difficult. On the topic of global warming, try to arrange an interview with a professor of meteorology. At a university, most departments have experts on various topics. Often a call to the department asking if there is anyone familiar with your specific topic will elicit a name. In other cases, simply consult a department's course offerings. Someone who teaches a class on Middle Eastern studies, for example, most likely is an expert in that subject.

Another strategy is to contact organizations related to the topic and ask if someone there would be available to interview. For example, if we were researching the effects of secondhand smoke, the American Lung Association is a likely source of potential interviewees.

Sometimes we already know people who can help. We recall the case of one student who was speaking about a "miracle" weight-loss product. After calling the company's home office and getting the runaround, she contacted her local pharmacist. He informed her that the ingredients in the product were in no way capable of helping a person lose weight–in fact, they were potentially harmful. A brief interview with the pharmacist gave her information she would have had great difficulty finding on her own.

Once we have decided on a person to interview, we recommend the following basic guidelines for before, during, and after the interview.

Before the Interview

- Contact the potential interviewee well in advance. Explain the reason for the meeting and how much time it will take. If the person agrees to be interviewed, ask for a convenient time and place for a meeting (usually at the interviewee's place of business). If possible, confirm the appointment in writing.
- Do some general reading on the topic. Read at least a book or two and some recent articles, or visit relevant Web sites. This will provide a basis for framing questions and focusing on those things that cannot easily be found elsewhere.
- Prepare specific questions in advance. Ask open-ended questions, which will allow the interviewee an opportunity to talk at some length. Of course, be prepared to deviate from the planned questions as answers suggest other avenues to follow.

During the Interview

- Show up on time, dressed professionally, and ready to begin. Thank the person and explain how the interview will be used. Be sure to ask for permission to record the interview if this is desired. If an interview is by phone, there is a legal obligation to inform and gain consent from the other party to record the conversation.
- Using previous research as a guide, begin with general questions and then move to specific ones. Be sure to let the interviewee talk. Don't monopolize the conversation; doing so defeats the purpose of the interview.

- Ask the interviewee if he or she can suggest other sources of information—books, pamphlets, periodicals, or other experts. Often an expert will know of sources we never would have thought of ourselves. Sometimes the interviewee may even loan some relevant journals or other publications.
- Use the listening skills discussed in Chapter 6, especially being mindful, blocking out distracting stimuli, suspending judgment, using multiple channels, and taking effective notes.
- Either record (with permission) or take complete notes during the interview. Ask follow-up questions to make sure to get the essential points on paper. Quotations from the interview used in a speech must be accurate.
- When time is about up, ask the interviewee if there is anything he or she can add to what has been said. Perhaps there is some area that has been completely overlooked.
- Thank the interviewee again for his or her time and exit graciously.

After the Interview

- A follow-up thank-you letter is common courtesy.
- Transcribe the recording or notes while the interview is fresh in your mind. Notes that may have been clear at the moment will quickly fade from memory unless we flesh them out soon after the interview.
- Follow up on leads or other interviews suggested by the interviewee.

Interviews provide a rich source of information and add credibility to our speaking. The fact that a speaker takes the time to speak directly to an expert shows concern for the audience. Further, the audience's perception of a speaker's expertise is enhanced by virtue of the interview. Be sure to let the audience know why the interviewee is a credible source on the topic.

Using Your Research

Preparing References or Works Cited

Before beginning in-depth reading on a topic, we prepare a preliminary list of the sources we have found. For example, 20 sources on global warming might look like they will be relevant. Using either a computer word processor or small note cards (4 by 6 inches is a good size), list the following information about each source.

For all sources: author(s), preferably by full name, if an author is listed; also include the author's qualifications on the subject matter

For books: exact title and the following facts of publication: location, publisher, and date

For periodicals: article title, periodical title, volume number, date, and pages

For government documents: the agency issuing the document as well as the document's full title, date, and publication information

For electronic resources: author, title, and publication information, as well as the e-mail address, Web site, or path by which the material was located and the date we found it, which is very important as Web sites are constantly changing

We always leave space to add information to each citation as we read the source.

All of this information is needed for the formal speech outline. It is easier to prepare the outline if this information is handy rather than having to go back to find it later. In Appendix A we provide samples of how to correctly cite sources according to the systems developed by the American Psychological Association (APA) and the Modern Language Association (MLA).

Recording Information and Avoiding Plagiarism

As we gather materials, we find it is essential to carefully record the supporting materials for our speeches. In Chapter 9 we discuss the types of evidence you will want to record–facts, statistics, quotations from experts, and the like. Whether we write our information on 4 by 6 inch note cards, sheets of notebook paper, or on our computers, accuracy is essential. At the same time, it is important to record information in a way that ensures it will be honestly cited and represented in our speeches. It is especially important that our sources are apparent to our audiences, as discussed in the box, "Speaking of . . . Orally Citing Sources."

With the Internet, the temptation is to simply cut and paste material from the Web pages that we find. This is simple and accurate, but there is one big downside. As discussed in Chapter 5, There is an increasing problem in society with the use of material written by others without proper attribution. *USA Today* recently dismissed a five-time Pulitzer Prize nominee, newspaper reporter Jack Kelley, when it was learned that he had plagiarized and fabricated numerous stories. As Blake Morrison of *USA Today* reports, there was "strong evidence Kelley fabricated substantial portions of at least eight major stories, lifted nearly two dozen quotes or other material from competing publications, lied in speeches he gave for the newspaper and conspired to mislead those investigating his work."[19] Numerous other highly publicized cases of plagiarism have damaged the careers not only of reporters but of many noted academics as well.

As professors, we've regrettably discovered numerous instances of plagiarism. In many cases, the culprit was a downloaded bit of text that the student failed to properly cite in a speech or paper. For example, when asked to write a personal brief essay about her chosen major, one student simply downloaded the description of Communication Studies from another university's Web site. Presumably she knew we would recognize the language from our own Web site, so she found a department elsewhere from which to crib her paper. The language didn't seem natural, so we did a simple Google search for some of the unusual phrases. The result was a clear case of plagiarism, which was reported to the university's authorities. Other students have cited the source in the References or Works Cited of their papers but not indicated which words were direct quotes and which were their own words. In this situation, it's often sloppy recording during the research phase that is at fault.

How can students avoid this type of accidental yet potentially serious plagiarism? Here are some specific recommendations.

Speaking of . . .

Orally Citing Sources by Christine Hanlon (from Nicholson Custom Edition)

Why Cite Sources?

There are several reasons why we should cite sources. According to Carol Bledsoe (former Coordinator of public speaking at University of Central Florida), there are three main reasons why we should cite sources:

- To establish credentials of the source and the data
- To enable the audience to retrieve the material
- To give credit to others

Establishing the Credentials of the Source and the Data

The first reason we should cite sources is to establish the credentials of the source and the data. If we, the audience, do not know why the source is credible, why should we believe that the information is valid? Let's take the following excerpt from a speech as an example:

> According to the CDC, there weren't any monkey pox cases in the United States until the 2003 outbreak.

The speaker has identified the CDC as the source of the data. Although many of us in the United States know that "CDC" is the acronym for Centers for Disease Control, you cannot assume that everyone is familiar with it. If you want to use the acronym for an organization, be sure to first identify what that acronym stands for. For example, state "the Centers for Disease Control, also known as the CDC . . ." Analyzing your audience will help you to determine if there is a time when you can break this rule. There will be times in the workplace when you will use acronyms. However, if you are ever in doubt, explain the acronym so your audience understands it.

Furthermore, there may be audience members who don't know what the CDC is. Be sure to briefly explain the purpose of the organization so your audience understands why the source is credible. Using this example, an appropriate explanation of the CDC could be, "The CDC is the United States' lead federal agency that investigates health problems and conducts research to prevent infectious diseases." Again, you want to analyze your audience to determine if an explanation is necessary.

Enabling the Audience to Retrieve the Material

By indicating where you found the information, you can enable the audience to retrieve the material. In the previous example, the speaker did not clarify where the information about the CDC was located. Was the information located on the CDC's official Web site or in a pamphlet distributed by the CDC, or did it come directly from a researcher who works for the CDC? To enable the audience to retrieve the material, speakers need to be clear about where the information can be found. Let's take some of these examples individually.

Where the information was found	Oral citation that enables the audience to retrieve the material
CDC's official Web site	"According to the CDC's Monkey pox factsheet posted online . . ."
CDC pamphlet	"The CDC's pamphlet entitled 'Tuberculosis: What you need to know' states that . . ."
Researcher who works for the CDC	"In a recent study, CDC researcher Jane Smith found that. . ."

Giving Credit to Others

It is important to give credit to others for their ideas. Many academics and scientists consider their ideas, their intellectual property, as their greatest contribution. There is even an international organization that works to uphold worldwide standards for intellectual property. According to the World Intellectual Property Organization (2004), "these works—intellectual property—are expanding the bounds of science and technology and enriching the world of the arts. "If you use others' ideas during your presentation and fail to cite them, you are essentially *stealing* the ideas of others. There are two important reasons why you should orally cite your sources while presenting speeches, and they are both directly tied to credibility. Failing to cite a source can decrease your credibility, whereas orally citing a source can add to your credibility as a speaker.

There can be serious consequences for speakers who fail to orally cite their sources properly. First, they can be charged with plagiarism. Whenever students fail to orally cite a source in a speech, they are guilty of plagiarism. The reality is that there are consequences to plagiarism, whether or not it was intentional. The bottom line is always to orally cite your sources so you can avoid the situation altogether.

Christine Hanlon (M.A., University of Central Florida) is a public speaking instructor at the University of Central Florida's Nicholson School of Communication. She is also a past president of the Florida Communication Association. Her research interests include family violence and popular culture. She has presented scholarly papers at regional and national conferences for communication, sociology, women's studies, and popular culture associations. Additionally, she has published in past volumes of *Teaching Ideas for the Basic Communication Course*.

Tips and Tactics

How to Avoid Plagiarism

- Don't just automatically cut and paste from sources. Make notes in your own words about the main ideas.
- Keep printouts or photocopies. When doing the final draft of a speech or paper, be sure that any direct quotes are indicated by quotation marks and cited in the body of the speech or paper, not just in the References or Works Cited.
- If a direct quotation is cut and pasted, use a different font to indicate that it is a direct quote. For example, once we have cut and pasted the quotation, we change the font color to red or put it in italics.
- Err on the side of full disclosure. A close paraphrase that is not cited is considered plagiarism, even if it's not a direct quote. If there's any doubt, it doesn't hurt to cite the source, both in the speech outline or manuscript and orally. For example, we discussed Robert Kennedy's paraphrase of the George Bernard Shaw quotation earlier in this chapter. Even though he didn't use the exact words, he would always say something like, "As George Bernard Shaw was fond of saying . . ." Citing sources is not a sign of weakness; rather, research has shown it enhances a speaker's credibility.

Summary

To evaluate your understanding of this chapter, visit our Online Learning Center Web site for quizzes and other chapter study aids.

The process of researching to support your speech is like the process of inventing a new product: You need both a source of inspiration and the willingness to engage in hard work.

- Begin by developing a research plan
- Analyze your rhetorical situation
- Choose an appropriate topic
- Formulate a specific purpose you want to accomplish
- Sources of information for your speech should meet tests of currency, relevance, authority, accuracy, and purpose

Possible sources include:

- The Internet, but with particular attention to distinguishing authentic and reliable Web sites from questionable ones
- Library resources, such as books, periodicals, and databases
- Interviews

Develop a recording system for both sources and data that avoids the danger of plagiarism and ensures accuracy. Be sure to cite sources orally for your audience.

Check Your Understanding: Exercises and Activities

1. Check your understanding of the American Psychological Association and Modern Language Association guidelines for source citations in Appendix A. Provide a correct source citation for each of the following hypothetical sources, using both APA and MLA guidelines:

   A book with one author named Jack Smith, titled College Life, published in New York by University Press in 2005. How would your citation change if Smith were the editor of the book? How would you list a second author, John Q. Doe? How would you list a third author, Mary A. Smith?

   An article titled Dorm Life in American Universities, by Peter Chu, published in the scholarly journal Universities and Colleges, volume 31, December 2005, pages 24–56.

   A chapter by Jose Sanchez titled The Nine Lives Myth, appearing on pages 99–109 in the book Cat Stories, edited by Morris T. Katt, published by Feline Press in San Francisco, California, in 2005.

   An article in Canine Magazine titled Snoopy and Me, by Charlie Brown, pages 56–57, on December 14, 2005, in volume 42. How would you list the article if no author were named?

2. *Worksheet for speech topic choice.* One way to select an appropriate speech topic is to begin with an inventory of your own interests and those of your listeners as revealed by their self-introductions in class. Under each of the following headings, list at least three things that are important to you and to your audience.

	My interests	Audience interests
Hobbies	____________	____________
	____________	____________
	____________	____________
School	____________	____________
	____________	____________
Work	____________	____________
	____________	____________
Goals	____________	____________
	____________	____________

Situational factors ____________________________

Nature of assignment ____________________________

Time available ____________________________

List of three possible topics ____________________________

____

____

3. How would you go about determining on what subject Arthur L. Schawlow and Charles H. Townes are experts? (Hint: They won Nobel Prizes for their discovery.)

4. Although the Internet is an invaluable source of information on almost any topic, it is also a notorious source of misinformation. As an exercise, try to locate the Web site of the Central Intelligence Agency (CIA). How many different Web sites did you find before locating the official page? How did you know when you were at the official site?

Notes

1. James C. McCrosky, "A Summary of Experimental Research on the Effects of Evidence in Persuasive Communication," *Quarterly Journal of Speech* 55 (1969): 169–176.
2. Adapted from Meriam Library, California State University, Chico, "Chico Oasis, Evaluating Information." [Retrieved from http://www.csuchico.edu/lins/Oasis/Ch3/index.html, 14 May 2007.]
3. Chelsea Phua, "Web Site Has Scoop on Davis Community," *The Sacramento Bee,* 10 December 2006, B4.
4. John Seigenthaler, "A False Wikipedia 'Biography,'" 29 November 2005, *USA Today.* [Retrieved from http://www.usatoday.com/news/opinion/editorials/2005-11-29-wikipedia-edit_x.htm, 5 January 2007.]
5. Billy Ray (director), *Shattered Glass,* Lions Gate Entertainment, 2003.
6. "Company Overview," 2005. [Retrieved from http://www.google.com/intl/en/corporate/index.html, 7 January 2007.]
7. "Definition of Podcast," *PCMag.com Encyclopedia* (undated). [Retrieved from http://www.pcmag.com/encyclopedia_term/0,2542,t=podcast&i=49433,00.asp, 9 January 2007.]
8. "Definition of RSS," *PCMag.com Encyclopedia* (undated). [Retrieved from http://www.pcmag.com/encyclopedia_term/0,2542,t=RSS&i=50680,00.asp, 9 January 2007.]
9. "What is Digg?" 2006. [Retrieved from http://digg.com/about, 9 January 2007.]
10. Associated Press, "Group: ExxonMobil Paid to Mislead Public," 3 January 2007. [Retrieved from http://news.yahoo.com/s/ap/20070103/ap_on_bi_ge/exxonmobil_global_warming, 9 January 2007.]
11. "Definition of Blog" *PCMag.Com Encyclopedia* (undated). [Retrieved from http://www.pcmag.com/encyclopedia_term/0,2542,t=blog&i=38771,00.asp, 9 January 2007.]
12. Associated Press, "U.S. Had Warmest Year Yet in 2006," *The Sacramento Bee,* 10 January 2007, A7.
13. Edward Wasserman, "When Do Rumors in Blogosphere Rate Coverage?" *The Sacramento Bee,* 19 November 2006, E3.
14. Based on UC Berkeley–Teaching Library Internet Workshops, "Evaluating Web Pages: Techniques to Apply & Questions to Ask," 27 July 2004. [Retrieved from http://www.lib.berkeley.edu/TeachingLib/Guides/Internet/Evaluate.html, 29 December 2004.]
15. "LII Selection Criteria," 2006. [Retrieved from http://lii.org/pub/htdocs/selectioncriteria.htm, 20 January 2007.]

16. Adapted from Meriam Library, California State University, Chico, "Chico RIO: Research Instruction Online." [Retrieved from www.csuchico.edu/lins/chicorio/glossary.html, 12 November 2004.]

17. See Fed Stats [http://www.fedstats.gov/.]

18. Bartleby.com Great Books Online [Retrieved from http://www.bartleby.com/73/465.html, 27 July 2004.]

19. Blake Morrison, "Ex-USA Today Reporter Accused of Plagiarism," *Sacramento Bee*, 20 March 2004, A8.

Speaking of . . .

Orally Citing Sources by *Christine Hanlon*

Why cite sources?

There are several reasons why we should cite sources. According to Carol Bledsoe (former SPC1600 Coordinator at University of Central Flordia), there are three main reasons why we should cite sources:

- To establish credentials of the source and the data
- To enable the audience to retrieve the material
- To give credit to others

Establishing the credentials of the source and the data

The first reason we should cite sources is to establish the credentials of the source and the data. If we, the audience, do not know why the source is credible, why should we believe that the information is valid? Let's take the following excerpt from a speech as an example:

> "According to the CDC, there weren't any monkey pox cases in the United States until the 2003 outbreak."

The speaker has identified the CDC as the source of the data. Although many of us in the United States know that "CDC" is the acronym for Centers for Disease Control, you cannot assume that everyone is familiar with it. If you want to use the acronym for an organization, be sure to first identify what that acronym stands for. For example, state "the Centers for Disease Control, also known as the CDC ..." Analyzing your audience will help you to determine if there is a time when you can break this rule. For example, if you refer to the University of Central Florida as "UCF" in a speech to an audience of UCF students, they should be able to understand what you are talking about. Similarly, there will be times in the workplace when you will use acronyms. However, if you are ever in doubt, explain the acronym so your audience understands it.

Furthermore, there may be audience members who don't know what the CDC is. Be sure to briefly explain the purpose of the organization so your audience understands why the source is credible. Using this example, an appropriate explanation of the CDC could be, "The CDC is the United States' lead federal agency that investigates health problems and conducts research to prevent infectious diseases." Again, you want to analyze your audience to determine if an explanation is necessary.

Enabling the audience to retrieve the material

By indicating where you found the information, you can enable the audience to retrieve the material. In the previous example above, the speaker did not clarify where the information about the CDC was located. Was the information located on the CDC's official Web site, or in a pamphlet distributed by the CDC, or did it come directly from a researcher who works for the CDC? To enable the audience to retrieve the material, speakers need to be clear about where the information can be found. Let's take some of these examples individually.

Where the information was found	Oral citation that enables the audience to retrieve the material
CDC's official website	"According to the CDC's monkey pox factsheet posted online..."
CDC pamphlet	"The CDC's pamphlet entitled 'Tuberculosis: What you need to know' states that..."
Researcher who works for the CDC	"A recent study by CDC researcher Jane Smith found that..."

Giving credit to others

It is important to give credit to others for their ideas. Many academics and scientists consider their ideas—their intellectual property – as their greatest contribution. There is even an international organization that works to uphold worldwide standards for intellectual property. According to the World Intellectual Property Organization (2004), "these works—intellectual property—are expanding the bounds of science and technology and enriching the world of the arts." If you use others' ideas during your presentation and fail to cite them, you are essentially stealing the ideas of others. There are two important reasons why you should orally cite your sources while presenting speeches, and they are both directly tied to credibility. Failing to cite a source can decrease your credibility, whereas orally citing a source can add to your credibility as a speaker.

There can be serious consequences for speakers who fail to orally cite their sources properly. First, they can be charged with plagiarism. The University of Central Florida's Golden Rule (2004-2005) defines plagiarism as when "another's work is used or appropriated without any indication of the source, thereby attempting to convey the impression that such work is the student's own." Therefore, whenever students fail to orally cite a source in a speech, they are guilty of plagiarism. The reality is that there are consequences to plagiarism, whether or not it was intentional. The bottom line is to always orally cite your sources so you can avoid the situation altogether.

According to Professor John Slater of the Cranberry Middle School in New York, there is "a trend in which students equate cyberspace with 'free'" (O'Hair, Stewart & Rubenstein, 2001, p. 51). This can be dangerous because academic institutions and the business world view these works as intellectual property. "Failure to give proper credit to information found in an online source is not less an instance of plagiarism than failing to cite a print source" (O'Hair, et al, 2001, p. 51). Thus, it is important to avoid plagiarism by orally citing ALL sources, including information found online.

As a speaker, you benefit each time you orally cite a source; you increase your credibility as a speaker. By orally citing your sources, you let your audience know that you have researched your topic and are basing your information on more than just your experiences. More specifically, orally citing your sources can increase your credibility in three ways. First, audiences perceive speakers who orally cite sources as more *trustworthy*. Next, "listeners are more likely to judge a speaker as credible if they perceive him or her as *competent* (knowledgeable, experienced, expert) on the topic" (Hamilton, 2004, p. 372). This competency is gained by "proving" to your audience that your presentation is based on research and not just your personal experience. The final element of credibility that is increased by orally citing a source is *objectivity*. "An objective speaker is one who is open-minded and fair and who appears to view evidence and arguments in an unbiased manner" (Hamilton, 2004, p. 373). Therefore, by orally citing your sources, you cannot only be perceived as more trustworthy, but you can also appear more competent and objective. All of these elements increase your credibility as a speaker.

How do I orally cite a source?

Carol Bledsoe, former SPC1600 Coordinator at UCF, developed a helpful acronym to help you remember how to orally cite a source.

- **C redit** the source of all material which comes from outside sources.
- **I ntegrate** the source citation throughout the speech.
- **T ake** your time citing sources.
- **E stablish** the credentials of sources.

Credit the source

First, speakers should credit the source of all material that comes from an outside source. One of the most frequent mistakes speakers make is simply forgetting to mention the source. The source is the person who initiates the communication. Therefore, the source is the individual or organization (which is a group of individuals) who *created* the information you are using. Web pages do not exist in a vacuum. An individual or organization created those materials and should be cited appropriately.

One frequent problem speakers have with citing online sources is mistaking the Web address with the source. The Web address is simply *where* the information can be found online. For example, the University of Central Florida's Web address is www.ucf.edu; however, the Web address doesn't tell us the source (unless we know what UCF stands for). Isn't it easier to state "the University of Central Florida?" Additionally, the Web address doesn't tell us much about the source and is more difficult for listeners to easily comprehend. Think about the last time you heard someone say something similar to "dubya-dubya-dubya-dot-r-e-d-c-r-o-s-s-dot-org." Did

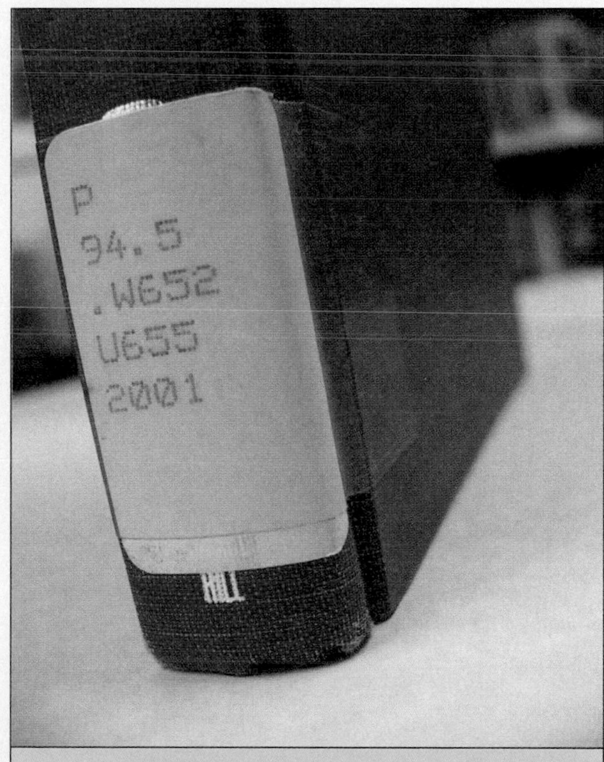

The call number is how we locate a book in the library, but it does not tell us much about the book itself

you write it down? Did you remember the Web address? It simply makes more sense to say "the American Red Cross." To clarify how an online source should be cited, think about how you would cite a book. Let's take the following book as an example:

> Kitch, Carolyn L. (2001). *The Girl on the Magazine Cover: the origins of visual stereotypes in American mass media.* Chapel Hill: University of North Carolina Press.

How would you cite this source? Would you cite the library call number? The library call number is the way that we locate the book in the library (whether organized using the Library of Congress or the Dewey Decimal system).

For this particular book, the label indicating P94.5.W652 U655 2001 is the way that we locate this book in the library. All this number tells us about this source is where to find it. Similarly, when speakers cite a Web address, all they are doing is telling the audience where the source is found online. It seems strange that someone would cite the book as "P 94.5.W652 U655 2001," so why would someone cite a Web source as "dubya dubya dubya dot...?" It simply makes sense to cite the source, not the address of the information.

Integrate the source citation

When citing the source, it is important to use the information to support your points throughout the speech. Many beginning speakers forget to integrate the source citations throughout their presentations and become guilty of citation clumping. Citation clumping is when a speaker tells the audience all of their sources at once (i.e., at the beginning or end of the speech). At times it seems as if the speaker has an additional main point for oral citations. The worst citation clumping offense is evident when speakers provide a citation slide in their PowerPoint presentations. This form of citation abuse is usually evident at the end of the presentation. Even though a speaker orally cites the sources, they don't seem to make any sense because they are not used to support the context of the speech. Balancing the oral citations to support each main point equally is one of the most effective ways to integrate your verbal citations.

Take your time

Although it seems like common sense that speakers should take their time citing sources, this is a common mistake. If you rush through the citation because you want to get it over with, you can lose the effectiveness of having a verbal citation altogether. Quite simply, if your audience cannot clearly hear your information because you rushed through it, they cannot understand the importance of the verbal citation and how it supports your ideas. Therefore, it is important to take your time when citing sources.

Establish the credentials

Establishing the credentials of the source is equally important. If you tell your audience that "Murray Straus stated that over 90% of American families use violence as a form of physical punishment," it doesn't make an impact on your audience unless they know who Murray Strauss is and why he is credible in regards to the idea you are presenting. They don't know if Murray Straus is your roommate, an engineer, or a teacher. In actuality, he is one of the leading researchers in the area of family violence in the United States; however, you cannot expect your audience to know this. As the speaker, it is your responsibility to clarify who your source is and state their credentials with regard to your topic.

References

Bledsoe, C. (2002). SPC1600 Lecture. University of Central Florida.

Hamilton, C. (2004). *The Essentials of Public Speaking for Technical Presentations, second edition.* Belmont, CA: Wadsworth.

Lorenzen, M. (2004). *Avoiding Plagiarism: A Librarian's View.* Accessed online on 6 October 2004 at http://personal.cmich.edu/~loren1mg/plagiarism.html

O'Hair, D., Stewart, R., & Rubenstein, H. (2001). *A Speaker's Guidebook: Text and reference.* Bedford/St. Martin's: New York.

University of Central Florida's Office of Student Conduct. (2004-2005). *Golden Rule.* Accessed online on 5 October 2004 at http://www.goldenrule.sdes.ucf.edu/3_a_Rules%20of%20Conduct.html

World Intellectual Property Organization (2004). *About WIPO.* Accessed online on 5 October 2004 at http://www.wipo.int/about-wipo/en/

This speaker brings examples of food items to support her speech on healthy food choices.

Supporting Your Message

Objectives

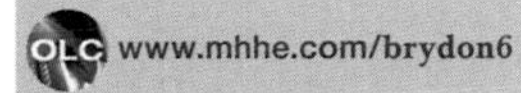

After reading this chapter and reviewing the online learning resources at www.mhhe.com/brydon6, you should be able to:

- Recognize the three basic types of claims: fact, value, and policy.
- Explain the role of evidence in grounding a speech.
- Support a speech with examples that are relevant, sufficient, typical, and without counterexamples.
- Support a speech with verifiable facts from reliable and unbiased sources that are consistent with other known facts.
- Support a speech with numerical data from reliable, unbiased sources.
- Identify reliable polls based on fair questions, an adequate and representative sample, and a meaningful difference compared to the margin of error.
- Support a speech with reliable numerical data, including percentages and averages.
- Support a speech with expert opinion, which is reliable and unbiased.
- Support a speech with clear and accurate explanations.
- Support a speech with vivid and accurate descriptions.
- Support a speech with narratives that have both probability and fidelity for your audience.
- Utilize valid warrants based on authority, generalization, comparison, cause, and sign to connect grounds to claims.

Key Concepts

authority warrant
backing
causal warrant
claim
comparison (analogy) warrant
expert opinion
fact
generalization warrant
grounds
narrative
narrative fidelity
narrative probability
qualifier
rebuttal
sign warrant
warrant

“Everyone is entitled to their own opinion, but not their own facts.”

–SEN. DANIEL PATRICK MOYNIHAN[1]

Have you ever purchased a product that warns, "Requires some assembly?" If you have, then you also know what it's like to learn that the process described on the box is seldom as easy as described. Assembling the parts of your speech can also prove more difficult than initially envisioned. After spending time in the actual or virtual library and systematically searching the Web, for example, it's not uncommon to look at the the notes we've compiled and wonder how we will ever make sense of them in a speech. This chapter is designed to help you translate your research into a meaningful speech. To that end, we first introduce you to a model of reasoning that can guide you in using the materials you've gathered to support your overall message, whether its purpose is to inform or persuade.

Toulmin's Model of Reasoning

claim
A conclusion that speakers want their audience to reach as a result of their speech.

grounds
The evidence a speaker offers in support of a claim.

warrant
The connection between grounds and claim.

A three-part model we have found useful was proposed by philosopher Stephen Toulmin.[2] First, a reasoner has a **claim,** or conclusion, that he or she wishes to establish. Second, there must be **grounds** or evidence to support the claim. Finally, there needs to be linkage between the grounds and the claim, which is provided by a **warrant.**

For example, let's assume a speaker wants to discourage the audience from buying an SUV. The speaker is making the *claim* that you should not buy an SUV. A claim alone, however, does not make an argument; there must be some evidence, or *grounds,* to support the claim. The speaker might point out that SUVs get lousy gas mileage. On the surface this might seem to be reason enough, but keep in mind that gas mileage per se is not the only thing a buyer evaluates. The buyer may be more concerned about performance, vehicle size, or safety than gas mileage. Thus there must be a *warrant,* or a reason, to value gas mileage over other considerations. In this case the *warrant* would be that gas mileage is an important factor in choosing a vehicle.

Exhibit 9.1
The Toulmin Model of Reasoning

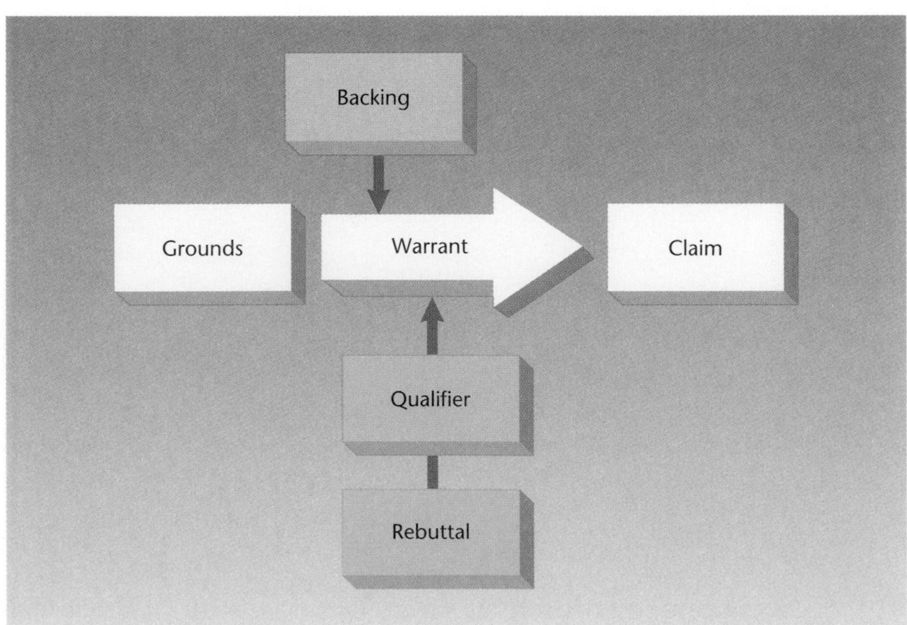

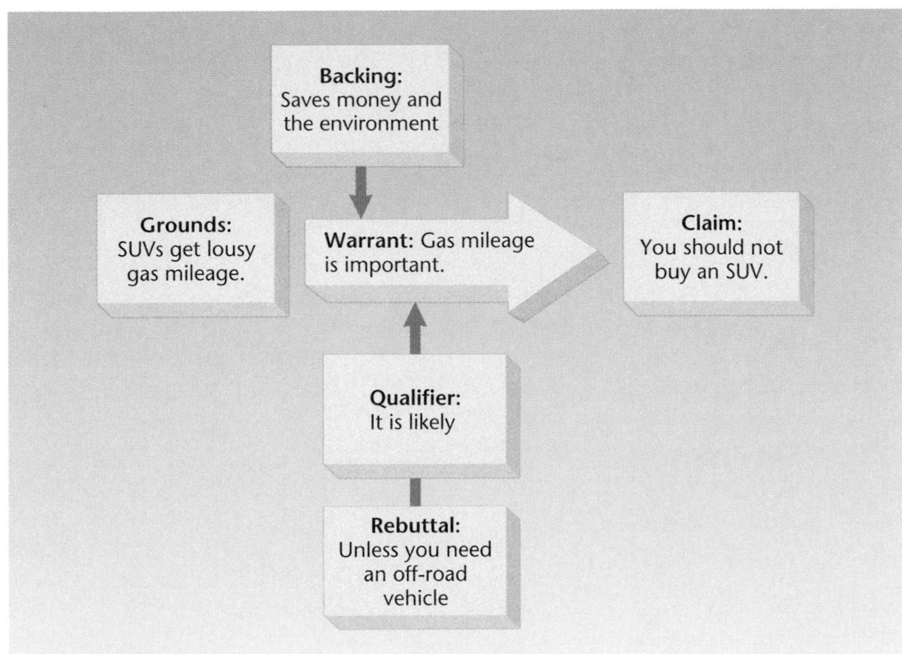

Exhibit 9.2
Analysis of an Argument Using Toulmin's Model

Three additional features *may* be present in an argument. The speaker may provide **backing** to further support the warrant. Thus the speaker might point out that good gas mileage not only saves the consumer money but is also easier on the environment. There may also be an exception, or **rebuttal,** to the argument. For example, what if someone lives where it is necessary to drive off road or where four-wheel-drive is needed to cope with winter snows? The argument is not really so much that *no one* should buy an SUV but that *most* people don't really need one. Thus the argument needs to have a **qualifier** to indicate the level of certitude of the claim. For example, "it is likely" that you should not buy an SUV would qualify the speaker's claim. Visually, the Toulmin model can be depicted as in Exhibit 9.1. Exhibit 9.2 shows you how this analysis would look using our example of why one should not buy an SUV.

backing
Support for a warrant.

rebuttal
An exception to or a refutation of an argument.

qualifier
An indication of the level of probability of a claim.

Claims

We make three basic types of claims when speaking: factual, value, and policy. A *factual claim* states that something is true or false. Some facts are clear-cut: 2 plus 2 equals 4. Others aren't so easy to prove: Is Social Security in danger of bankruptcy or not? The hallmark of factual claims is that they are theoretically verifiable. *Claims of value* make judgments about what is good or bad, right or wrong, moral or immoral. Much of the debate over so-called wedge issues such as gay marriage, stem cell research, and abortion concern value judgments. Finally, *claims of policy* are statements about what a person should do. Most persuasive speeches deal with either claims of value or policy or both. Most informative speeches are primarily about claims of fact. As we look for grounds to support our speeches, we need to carefully assess the types of claims we plan to make. We also need to consider our audience. What facts do audience members already know or believe? What additional facts do they need to know? Will they accept the values implicit in our message? If we advocate policies, we need to base them on facts and values that are established in our speech. Thus research and audience analysis go hand in hand.

Grounds

To succeed as public speakers, we need to ground our claims in facts and opinions. For example, whether we are teaching someone how to swing a golf club or persuading them to share our views on stem cell research, we need to do more than just offer our own opinions. Audiences want us to provide evidence to support our claims. If a speaker says stem cell research could lead to a cure for diabetes, audience members are going to expect the speaker to tell them why and how. We can support a speech and answer the audience's desire for grounding in facts and reliable opinions using these methods:

- Examples
- Facts
- Numerical data
- Opinion
- Explanations
- Descriptions
- Narratives

Examples

An example is a specific instance that represents some larger class. We might cite a recycling program in our hometown as an example of how curbside recycling can work. The test of an example is whether it is actually representative of the larger category. To test whether an example is representative, we need to ask the following questions:

- *What is the relevance of the example to the larger category?* If we are talking about products made from recycled material, then a cardboard box made from new materials, although it could be recycled by the consumer, is not relevant.
- *Are there enough instances to support the generalization?* A few years ago, a disposable-diaper manufacturer ran an ad campaign claiming that its diapers could be turned into compost. However, according to a *Consumer Reports* article, only about a dozen cities had the capability to compost disposable diapers.[3] Thus disposable diapers wouldn't be a good example of a recyclable product.
- *Is the example typical of the larger category?* We should avoid isolated and atypical examples. Just because some types of plastic can be recycled doesn't mean that *all* plastic is recyclable.
- *Are there counterexamples that disprove the generalization?* A counterexample is one example that contradicts the generalization. Whereas several examples

can only suggest the truth of a generalization, even one example to the contrary can disprove it. If a speaker claims all American cars are unreliable, then pointing to just one car line–for example, the Ford Fusion–as having been shown to be reliable disproves that generalization. If counterexamples exist, either the generalization is false or it needs to be reformulated to be less inclusive. Thus we might say, "Many American cars are unreliable," a generalization that one counterexample would not disprove.

Facts

A **fact** is something that is verifiable as true. It is a fact that there are 50 states in the United States. As former baseball great Yogi Berra might say, "You can look it up." On the other hand, the statement that Texas is the best state in which to live is not a fact, though it may be widely believed by Texans.

fact
Something that is verifiable as true.

A fact, of course, is only as good as the source of that fact. To evaluate a fact, ask the following questions:

- *Does the fact come from a reliable source?* Encyclopedias, almanacs, authoritative books, and scholarly articles are usually reliable. On the other hand, if the "fact" comes from someone who has a clear bias about the topic, we should be suspicious. For example, many Internet sites claim to contain facts, such as the existence of extraterrestrials or that there are "black choppers" constantly spying on us. Just because something is on the Internet, we shouldn't assume that it is true, as we illustrated in Chapter 8.
- *Is the fact verifiable?* We should be suspicious of facts that are difficult to verify. For example, there are widely varying estimates of certain types of crime, such as rape. Part of the discrepancy is that many rapes go unreported. Thus the number of reported rapes is multiplied by some factor assumed to represent the number of unreported rapes for every reported one. However, these numbers are impossible to verify for the very reason that the unreported rapes are, by definition, unverifiable. Although these estimates may be useful, they are not facts in the sense of being verifiable.
- *Is the fact the most recent available?* Until 2001, statistics about the federal budget projected a large annual surplus. Yet as this book is being written, these projected surpluses have been replaced by record deficits. A speech built around the existence of budget surpluses would clearly be out of date.
- *Is the fact consistent with other known facts?* Facts do not stand alone. We should be suspicious of alleged "facts" that seem to be inconsistent with other known facts. For example, many tobacco manufacturers once claimed that nicotine was not addictive. However, not only the surgeon general but anyone who has tried to give up smoking can tell you that such a "fact" is suspect. We should double-check sources for possible error and be particularly careful with *secondary sources,* which rely on another source rather than gathering the information firsthand. As we noted in Chapter 8, it is always better to look at *primary sources,* which are the original sources of information, because there may be honest mistakes in transferring information from one source to another. Finally, we should keep in mind what facts the audience already knows. If our facts are inconsistent with what the

audience believes to be true, we first have to convince them that ours are more reliable if we are to have any success.

Numerical Data

Numerical summaries of data, such as percentages, ratios, and averages, are valuable when used judiciously in our speeches. These can be a rich source of information; yet they can also be confusing and misleading. For example, an American automobile manufacturer announced a survey showing that its cars were preferred overwhelmingly to foreign cars. However, it turns out that the company included only 200 people in its survey, none of whom even owned a foreign car.[4]

We are constantly bombarded by numbers that seem authoritative but are of dubious value. Some questions to ask about numerical data are the following:

- *Is the source reliable and unbiased?* The tip-off to the problem with the survey on foreign versus American cars is that it was sponsored by an American car company. Numbers found through general searches of commercial, individual, or organizational Internet sites are often suspect. On the other hand, those found in official sources, such as www.fedstats.gov, are less likely to be biased, because this site collects official government data.
- *Are the numbers based on a poll?* A meaningful poll calls participants, not the other way around. Based on sophisticated sampling techniques and random selection, a national poll can predict a presidential election with about a four-percentage-point margin of error. But when our Internet provider, local television station, or newspaper conducts an "unscientific poll," in which people record their views, the results are meaningless. Only people who are interested in the topic will respond, and there is nothing to prevent someone from responding a hundred times. In short, such polls are worse than worthless because they undermine confidence in legitimate polls.
- *Were unbiased questions asked?* A poll asking whether disposable diapers should be banned was preceded by a statement that disposable diapers account for only 2 percent of trash in landfills. Not surprisingly, 84 percent of those polled felt disposable diapers should not be banned.[5]
- *Was the sample representative?* A representative sample is absolutely necessary for a poll to be reliable and valid. A representative sample is one made up of people who possess the same attributes as the people in the population from which the sample is drawn. A speech class, for example, could be representative of the student body at a college. But unless the class was drawn randomly from the entire student body, we do not know for certain.

  There are many ways to obtain a representative sample, but the most common way is to randomly select people from the population in which we are interested: for example, college students between the ages of 18 and 25; all single mothers in the state; or members of a state bar association. Generally speaking, the larger the sample randomly drawn from a population, the more representative the sample.

  The complexities of sampling theory are beyond the scope of this book. Even so, we want to emphasize that the value of any poll depends on sampling. Thus, at a minimum, we should never accept a poll at face value. We need to find information about the sample on which the results are based.

- *Are the differences in the poll greater than the margin of error?* Good polling results state the margin of error. Keep in mind that the margin of error increases as the sample gets smaller. Whereas the margin of error for a sample of 1,067 people is about plus or minus 3 percent, for 150 people the margin of error is about plus or minus 8 percent.[6] Suppose a poll has a margin of error of plus or minus 4 percent. This means if the poll shows a political candidate ahead of her opponent by 51 to 49 percent, she could be ahead by as much as 55 to 45 percent, or behind by 47 to 53 percent–or any number in between. When only subgroups of a larger sample are considered, there are even more chances for error. For example, on the morning of November 2, 2004, supporters of Senator Kerry were ecstatic when early exit polls from key states such as Ohio and Florida indicated he was defeating President Bush. What they failed to realize was that voters who cast their votes early in the day were not representative of voters at large. In fact, the subgroup sampled in these early exit polls was 59 percent female, a group more likely to support Kerry than were men. When all the results were in, of course, Kerry was defeated in both states and Bush was reelected.[7]
- *What are the percentages based on?* "There's been a 10 percent increase in the rate of inflation!" Sounds pretty alarming, doesn't it? However, unless you know what the underlying rate of inflation is, this is a meaningless figure. Inflation rates are themselves a percentage. Say that inflation is running at 4 percent. That means what cost $100 last year now costs $104. A 10 percent increase in the rate of inflation means that it would cost $104.40–not too bad. On the other hand, a 10 percent rate of inflation means that what cost $100 a year ago now costs $110. Sound confusing? It is. The point is that we need to be sure we understand what percentages are based on before relying on them to prove a point.
- *What is meant by average?* One of the most frequently reported numbers is the average, or mean. Although easily computed, the average is often misleading because it is commonly distorted by numerical extremes. Consider a newspaper report that states the average salary for new college graduates is $40,000 a year. That doesn't mean a majority of college graduates are paid $40,000 a year. It simply means that when we add the salaries paid to all college graduates surveyed and divide that sum by the number of graduates in the sample, that's the mean (the arithmetic average). The number likely has been distorted by graduates in engineering, computer science, and information systems management, who, though few in number, start at salaries two to three times as much as their more numerous counterparts in the liberal arts and social sciences. The most telling number is always the *median,* which is the midpoint in a distribution of numbers. Knowing the median tells us that half of the numbers in the distribution are larger, and half are smaller. In Chapter 16, we discuss the mean and median in more details.

This list of questions is not meant to discourage you from using numerical data. They can be a powerful form of support. The key is to know what your numbers mean and how they were collected, and to avoid biased sources and

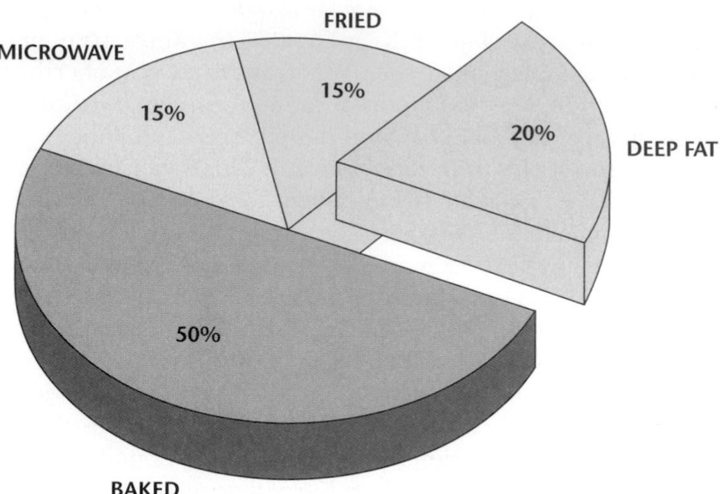

Exhibit 9.3
Visual aids such as pie charts help audiences visualize numerical data.

questionable sampling techniques. Most important, you need to explain enough about the numbers you use to your audience so that they will have confidence in the claims you are making. Useful tests for numerical data can be found in the box "Speaking of . . . Numerical Data."

We must be careful, however, not to overwhelm our audience with numbers. To make numerical data meaningful, we suggest rounding off information presented orally. For example, rather than saying "the Dow closed at 12,997.7," we could simply say "the Dow closed today just below 13,000." Comparisons are also useful. For example, let's say a speaker wants the audience to visualize how much land would be needed to produce corn for ethanol in order to significantly reduce our dependence on foreign oil. The speaker could say it will take 90 million acres to produce the corn. That sounds like a lot, but few of us can really visualize an acre, let alone 90 million. On the other hand, it turns out that that is an area roughly the size of the state of Montana. For an audience, such a comparison would be much more meaningful than raw numbers. Finally, consider using charts, graphs, and other visual aids to express numerical data, as shown in Exhibit 9.3.

Opinion

We all have opinions on all sorts of topics. One of the authors loved *Sicko* and the other hated it. Some people love hip-hop, others can't stand it. The list of topics on which we all have opinions is endless. As speakers, we may want to share our opinions with our audience. However, unless we are recognized experts on a topic, our opinion is unlikely to carry any weight with audience members. After all, why should they give any more weight to our opinion than to their own?

Sometimes speakers have special qualifications that enable them to use their own opinions as support for their speech. For example, a student whose mother

Speaking of . . .

Numerical Data

Tests for using numerical data

- Know the source—is it unbiased and reliable?
- Know what questions were asked—were they fair and unbiased?
- Know how the sample was chosen—is it representative?
- Consider the margin of error—do the differences exceed it?
- Know what percentages are based on—are they percentages of percentages?
- Know the kind of average used—was it the mean (average) or the median (midpoint)?

had terrible complications from breast implant surgery spoke in one of our classes. Her speech was short on quotes from experts but was still very powerful because she told the story of her mother's suffering in a convincing way. If we intend to use our own opinions as support in a speech, we need to be sure to explain to the audience why our opinions are worth considering.

More common than personal opinion in supporting a speech is **expert opinion**–a quotation from someone with special credentials in the subject matter. Quotations from experts, whether gathered from a personal interview or from written sources, can be a persuasive way of supporting your points. However, you need to ask three basic questions about expert opinion:

expert opinion
A quotation from someone with special credentials in the subject matter.

- *What is the source's expertise?* How do you know this person is an expert? Try a Google search or look at biographical sources (such as *Who's Who*) if you do not know who the person is. Look for marks of expertise, such as academic credentials, official positions, or references from other authorities. Finally, make sure your source is an expert in the subject matter of your speech. It is important to explain to your audience why the person you are quoting is an expert they should believe.
- *Does the expert have a reputation for reliability?* How accurate have the expert's previous statements been? If someone has a record of either false or mistaken statements in the past, it is misguided to rely on that person's statements today.
- *Is the source unbiased?* If a source has a vested interest in one side of a topic, his or her opinions are automatically suspect. Your audience needs to be assured that you are not relying on sources who have an axe to grind.

Explanations

An explanation is an account, an interpretation, or a meaning given to something. Detailed explanations may prove useful in a speech. But to be effective, explanations must meet three tests:

- *Is the explanation clear?* A complex or unclear explanation may only confuse your audience. One way to clarify an explanation is to use comparisons and contrasts. Thus someone might explain a nuclear power plant by comparing it to a teakettle whose source of heat is a nuclear reaction.

- *Is the explanation accurate?* An explanation that is clear is not necessarily complete or correct. Make sure the explanations provided are as complete and accurate as possible, given the limitations of the speech situation.
- *Is the explanation interesting?* Unfortunately, explanations can be boring to an audience, particularly if they are highly technical. One way to overcome this problem is to make sure there are specific, vivid examples that make the explanations come to life. For example, Al Gore's film, *An Inconvenient Truth*, shows ice melting in a glass to illustrate the way melting glaciers might change sea level.

Descriptions

A description is a word picture of something. For example, you might describe a place you have visited or researched. Consider the following statement from a speech by one of our students, Chalsey Phariss: "Imagine a place where the rivers are flowing, the sun is shining, and the fun is unlimited, where there is never a dull moment, and the freedom of the outdoors will captivate your mind." This description leads into a speech about the "Lake of the Sky," Lake Tahoe.[8]

Descriptions should meet the following tests:

- *Is the description accurate?* Descriptions can be tested for accuracy by comparing them with the thing being described. Thus, for the Tahoe example, looking at pictures of the lake or actually visiting it would help to verify the description.
- *Is the description vivid?* To hold an audience's attention, we need to paint a word picture. Calling Lake Tahoe by its Native American name, "Lake of the Sky," is much more vivid than simply describing the blueness of the water. Photographs and other visual materials, can sometimes supplement descriptions in a speech.

Narratives

narrative
An extended story that is fully developed, with characters, scene, action, and plot.

A **narrative** is an extended story that is fully developed, with characters, scene, action, and plot. Narratives sometimes provide an effective way of driving home a point to an audience. An effective narrative builds gradually from the beginning, through conflict, to a climax. The conflict is then resolved, and the ending of the story often ties back into the beginning.

Narratives can be more than a useful supporting tool for a speech; in some cultures narrative is an organizing principle of speaking. The storyteller in North and Central American cultures, for example, is revered. We were in the audience when actor-activist Edward James Olmos spoke at our university. His speech was largely a series of stories–about his career, his family, how people of different cultures can come to understand one another. Award-winning rhetorical scholar Walter Fisher has argued, in fact, that human beings are fundamentally storytellers. Fisher believes that reasoning is done in the form of narrative. Even if you don't accept Fisher's narrative paradigm, it is undoubtedly the case that a well-told story, real or fictional, can captivate an audience. Fisher claims that two basic tests apply to narrative reasoning:[9]

These skiers share a story—one of the most common ways in which people communicate.

- *Does the narrative have probability?* **Narrative probability** is the internal coherence or believability of a narrative. Does a story make sense in and of itself? If you've seen the *Back to the Future* trilogy, you may have wondered how there could be two Doc Browns and two Marty McFlys and even two DeLorean time machines at the same time and place. Setting aside Doc's explanations of the space-time continuum, trying to sort out the paradoxes and inconsistencies of time travel is one sure way to a gigantic headache. When using a narrative to support a speech, it needs to be clearly plausible to the audience for it to be believed.

narrative probability The internal coherence or believability of a narrative.

- *Does the narrative have fidelity?* **Narrative fidelity** is the degree to which a narrative rings true to real-life experience. Even if a story makes sense internally, it may not make sense in terms of the real world. For example, in Chapter 8, we mentioned the case of Stephen Glass, a writer for the *New Republic* who was caught making up stories out of whole cloth. In fact, the story that exposed his fabrications was uncovered by an online publication, *Forbes Digital Tool,* because the details of Glass's account of a youthful hacker outsmarting a powerful Silicon Valley company did not ring true for those familiar with technology. For example, the alleged Web site of this multi-million dollar cutting edge technology company was an amateurish looking AOL site and the "hacker's convention" he described seemed implausible. In fact, the location turned out to have been closed on the very day Glass claimed the convention occurred. Because the details of his story lacked fidelity, Glass's lies were exposed. Once one story unraveled, it soon turned out that most of what he had written for the *New Republic* was fabricated.

narrative fidelity The degree to which a narrative rings true to real-life experience.

When we tell a story to an audience, we should let them know if it is true or hypothetical. But either type of story needs to ring true to the audience's own

Stephen Glass was caught fabricating stories for the *New Republic* when his story on hackers didn't ring true.

experience if it is to have impact. For a speech to have impact, the narratives need to have probability and fidelity.

Warrants

Once we have provided grounds for a claim, we need to connect the grounds and the claim. As previously stated, Toulmin calls this the warrant. A simple example will illustrate this point. I look out the window in the morning. It's an overcast, windy, gray day. I grab my umbrella before I head out the door. I've reasoned from *grounds* (clouds and wind) to the *claim* (I need my umbrella). What links the two? Clearly, my experience has taught me to believe the *warrant* that clouds and wind are a sign of impending rain (see Exhibit 9.4). We do not always have to state the obvious if we know our audience will mentally fill in the warrant. But on more complex issues, or where we don't know what warrants the audience might accept, it may be necessary to spell out this linkage.

In this section we describe five commonly used types of warrants. These are ways we can explicitly connect our grounds with the claims we make. To the extent that we are able to link our evidence with our claims, we are likely to be successful in convincing our audiences to accept what we say. The five most common types of warrants are these:

- Authority
- Generalization
- Comparison
- Causal
- Sign

Authority Warrants

authority warrant
Reasoning in which the claim is believed because of the authority of the source.

When we rely on the opinions of experts to support our claims, we are using an authority warrant. An **authority warrant** asserts that the claim is to be believed because of the authority of the source. This is the reason it is important that we tell our audience why the people we quote are experts whose opinions matter. If a doctor tells us to lose weight, we are likely to trust her judgment and at least *try* to shed the unwanted pounds. If Oprah Winfry endorses a particular

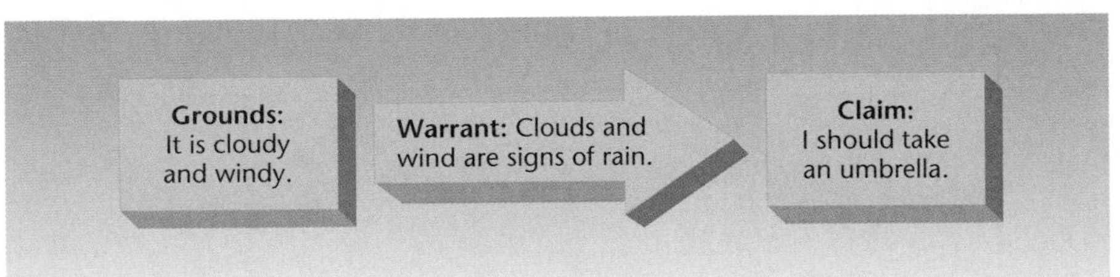

Exhibit 9.4
Supporting a Claim
The claim "I should take an umbrella" is supported by appropriate grounds and a warrant.

diet, however, that doesn't prove it will work for us. Unfortunately, celebrities often persuade people even though they don't have expertise in the area. In our speeches, we try to make sure the authorities we cite not only are credible to the audience but also are knowledgeable about the topic. When we cite our own opinion, we need to be particularly careful to explain to the audience why we have the authority to speak on the topic. Authority warrants are subject to tests of whether the authority is truly an expert, has accurate information, and is unbiased.

Tips and Tactics

Using Authority Warrants

- Make sure the authority is an expert in the area being discussed.
- Make sure the authority is acting on reliable information.
- Use only unbiased authorities.

An example of reasoning from an authority warrant is shown in Exhibit 9.5. Based on the grounds (the doctor tells you that the best way to lose weight is to go on the NutriSystem diet) and the warrant (the doctor is an expert in treating obesity), you decide to accept the *claim* (and go on the NutriSystem diet).

To test the validity of this reasoning, we must know whether the doctor is an expert in the area of treating obesity, whether she has reliable information about the state of your health and the effectiveness of the NutriSystem diet, and whether she is biased. If the doctor is a dermatologist, for example, there is no reason to believe she is competent to advise patients on what diet is best. Further, suppose the only information she has about the NutriSystem diet is what she's read in the popular press rather than in medical journals. And finally, suppose it turns out she gets a referral fee from the sponsors of the diet for sending them a customer. In such a case, that expert opinion would be unreliable on all three counts.

As speakers, we are wise to tell our audiences specifically why the experts we quote are reliable and that they have no axe to grind. Otherwise, a skeptical audience may reject our claims.

Generalization Warrants

generalization warrant
A statement that either establishes a general rule or principle or applies an established rule or principle to a specific case.

A **generalization warrant** is a statement that either establishes a general rule or principle or applies an established rule or principle to a specific case. Warrants involving generalizations are used in two ways. Some warrants take

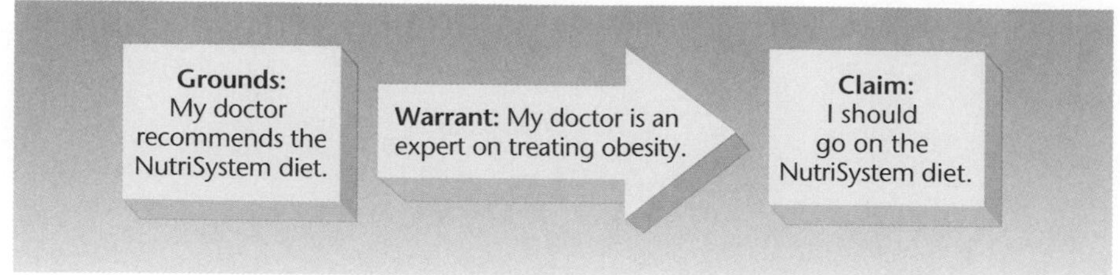

Exhibit 9.5
An Example of the Use of Authority to Support a Claim

specific examples and use them to establish generalizations. Others take previously established generalizations and apply them to specific cases. Exhibit 9.6 illustrates the relationship between a generalization-establishing warrant and a generalization-applying warrant.

Establishing Generalizations

A warrant that establishes a generalization uses specific examples, statistics, narratives, and the like to reach general conclusions. Warrants establishing generalizations are subject to tests of relevance, quantity, typicality, precision, and negative example.

Tips and Tactics

Establishing a Generalization

- Are the specific instances relevant to the generalization?
- Are there enough specific instances to establish the claim?
- Are the specific instances typical of the larger population?
- Has overgeneralization from only a few instances been avoided?
- Are there no significant known negative examples?

Examples, numerical data, and narratives are all good ways to establish a generalization. However, relying on isolated examples and narratives is risky. A blend of numbers and examples is more effective in establishing a generalization than use of only a few examples or narratives. The story of Subway's spokesperson, Jared, who lost more than a hundred pounds on his all-sub sandwich diet, although compelling, hardly proves that eating at Subway will guarantee weight loss. Using his story along with other types of evidence—numerical data, expert opinion, and descriptions of the low-fat, low-carb alternatives at Subway—would be a stronger way to establish the claim that eating at Subway is a good way to lose weight (assuming it really is).

Applying Generalizations

Once we know a generalization is true, we can apply it to a specific instance and reach some valid conclusions about that specific instance. For example, we know that anyone born in the United States or its territories is, by definition, a U.S. citizen. Thus, if Jane shows us her birth certificate and it says she was born

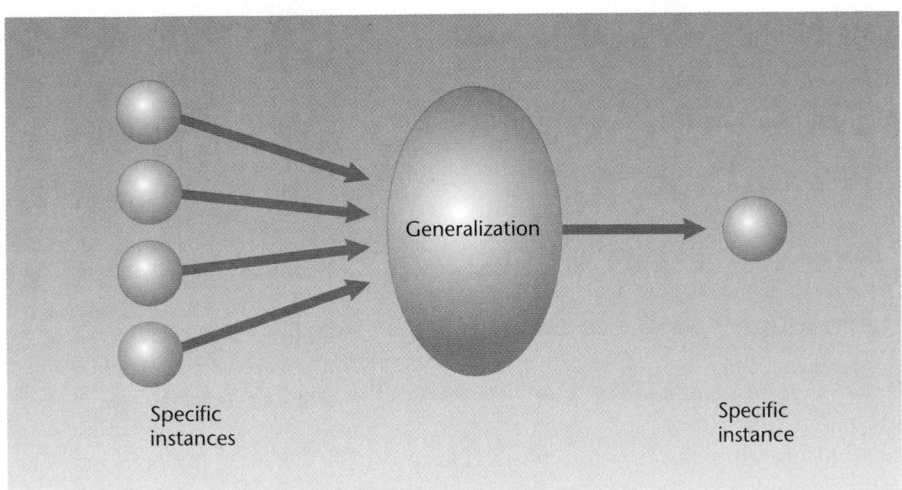

Exhibit 9.6

Relationship Between Generalization-Establishing and Generalization-Applying Warrants

Generalizations are established based on a number of specific instances. Once accepted, generalizations are then applied to further specific instances.

in Alaska, we know she is a U.S. citizen. Warrants applying generalizations are subject to tests of support, applicability, and exceptions.

Tips and Tactics

Applying a Generalization to a Specific Instance

- The generalization needs to be well-supported and accepted by the audience.
- The generalization should apply to the case at hand.
- If there are exceptions to the generalization, make sure the specific case isn't one of the exceptions.

Even though all persons born in the United States and its territories are native-born citizens, there are exceptions–for example, someone who has renounced his or her citizenship. And, of course, just because a person isn't born in the United States doesn't mean that person is not a U.S. citizen. Children born of citizen parents are citizens even if they are born outside the United States. When applying generalizations in a speech, it is important to make sure the audience accepts the general rule being used and knows the instance being discussed clearly falls within that category.

Comparison (Analogy) Warrants

Reasoning based on a **comparison (analogy) warrant** claims that two cases that are similar in some known respects are also similar in some unknown respects. We often use examples or narratives as points of comparison. In informative speaking, analogies are particularly useful for explaining complex subjects in simple terms. For example, one student drew an analogy between stripping the insulation off a wire and the effect multiple sclerosis has on the central nervous system. Analogies are subject to tests of familiarity, literalness versus figurativeness, similarity, and relevance.

comparison (analogy) warrant
A statement that two cases that are similar in some known respects are also similar in some unknown aspects.

Tips and Tactics

Using Comparisons or Analogies

- Make sure your audience is familiar with at least one part of the analogy.
- Use literal analogies for proof and figurative analogies for clarity and emphasis.
- Show that similarities outweigh the differences.
- The similarities, not the differences, should be most relevant.

Let's begin with whether or not the audience is familiar with one of the parts of the analogy. Suppose a speaker told you that a *euphonium* was like an *enthymeme.* What? Neither term is likely to be familiar, so the analogy is worthless (it is also wrong–but that's another story). We have to be sure our audience understands the point of comparison being made. There is a difference between literal and figurative analogies. A *literal analogy* claims that two different instances are really similar. For example, a lot of people compared September 11, 2001, to December 7, 1941 (the date on which Pearl Harbor was bombed). This is certainly a literal comparison–both were attacks on U.S. soil by foreign enemies (Hawaii was not yet a state, but it was a U.S. territory at the time of the attack). A *figurative analogy*, on the other hand, is a device of language used to enhance the effectiveness of a speech. A figurative analogy clearly seeks to establish some similarity between the two items being compared, but no one could reasonably argue that they are really alike. Saying September 11 was like being sucker-punched is not literally comparing two things that are the same. In the first instance, thousands died and the nation was plunged into war. In the second instance, about all that is hurt is the victim's pride. There's nothing wrong with figurative analogies–they can add a lot to a speech–but they don't constitute proof in the same way that literal ones can. There is no logical force to such arguments.

Next, in a good analogy or comparison, the similarities should outweigh the differences. If they do not, the analogy will not be very powerful. For example, when comparing September 11 and Pearl Harbor, there are clearly many similarities. However, unlike Pearl Harbor, our attackers did not identify themselves. Rather than being a state, we ultimately learned that our enemies were a shadowy network of terrorists scattered in many places. The tactics that worked to win World War II would not necessarily be the same as those needed in the War on Terror.

Finally, the similarities, rather than the differences, should be most relevant to the claim being made. In the comparison of 9/11 to Pearl Harbor, the difference in fighting terrorists as compared to a conventional army has made the War on Terror a long-term effort that will not end in a dramatic surrender ceremony as did World War II.

Causal Warrants

causal warrant
A statement that a cause will produce or has produced an effect.

Reasoning based on a **causal warrant** claims that a cause will produce or has produced an effect. Reasoning from *cause to effect* involves predicting what will happen if some action is taken. For example, it is the claim of Al Gore's film, *An Inconvenient Truth,* that unless the world reduces its use of so-called greenhouse glasses, global warming will cause ocean levels to rise–flooding low lying areas such as Florida and even Manhattan. On the other hand, we sometimes reason from *effect to cause,* looking at why something has occurred. Gore also claims that the once feared hole in the ozone layer has been reduced because of the nations that banned the use of CFCs, once found in everything from hairspray to air conditioners. Causal warrants are subject to tests of relatedness, other causes, and side effects.

For example, we recall a student who wanted to convince her classmates to avoid getting a tattoo. One of the effects she claimed that could be caused by improper tattooing (with dirty needles) was hepatitis, a serious disease. She cited experts who cautioned against tattooing and pointed out that among the unintended side effects was the pain and expense of removing tattoos later in life. She even offered another way to cause the desired effect of a tattoo–namely, a technique called Mehndi, which creates body art that lasts only a few weeks.

Tips and Tactics

Using Causal Warrants

- Show how the cause is related to the alleged effect.
- Rule out other causes of the effect.
- Consider "side effects" in addition to the desired effect.

Sign Warrants

Perhaps you've heard someone say, "It's going to rain. I can feel it in my bones." Or you've read a newspaper article stating that the economy is in a recovery because the latest "leading economic indicators" are pointing upward. These are examples of reasoning from sign. A **sign warrant** is reasoning in which the presence of an observed phenomenon is used to indicate the presence of an unobserved phenomenon. In sign reasoning, the warrant asserts that the grounds provide a reliable sign that the claim is true. Some signs are infallible; most are merely probable. The absence of brain waves is considered legally as an infallible sign of death. On the other hand, no one would claim that the rise or fall of stock prices is even close to an infallible sign of the state of the economy. Sign warrants are subject to tests of reliability and conflicting signs.

sign warrant
Reasoning in which the presence of an observed phenomenon is used to indicate the presence of an unobserved phenomenon.

Tips and Tactics

Using Sign Warrants

- Show that the signs are reliable indicators of the claim.
- Rule out conflicting signs.

A detective examines a crime scene for signs of forced entry, struggle, and the like. Anyone who is a fan of Sherlock Holmes will recall that he often made a case based on the most obscure signs. One small sign would point him to the guilty suspect every time. Unfortunately, in real life such reliable signs are more difficult to find. In using sign reasoning, show how reliable such signs have been in the past. For example, in persuading students of the value of a college degree, we can point to evidence from countless surveys showing that having a college degree is associated with a higher lifetime income. It is important, however, to rule out conflicting signs for an audience. Some people question the correlation between college degrees and income by pointing out that those from affluent families are more likely to go to college in the first place. Thus the higher income later in life might be more a matter of greater family resources, not simply getting a college degree. Unless a sign is infallible, most sign reasoning at best indicates the probability that a claim is true.

Summary

To evaluate your understanding of this chapter, visit our Online Learning Center Web site for quizzes and other chapter study aids.

There are three basic types of claims:

- Claims of fact deal with statements that are verifiable.
- Claims of value deal with statements about right or wrong, good or bad, moral or immoral.
- Claims of policy state that something should be done.

Many types of grounds are effective in supporting speeches:

- Examples should be relevant, of sufficient quantity, and typical, and without counterexamples.
- Facts should be from a reliable source, verifiable, recent, and consistent with other known facts.
- Numerical data should be from a reliable and unbiased source, based on fair questions, from a representative sample. Polls should report the sample size and margin of error. Know what percentages are based on and whether the mean or median is being cited.
- Expert opinion should come from a subject matter expert who is reliable and unbiased.
- Explanations should be clear and accurate.
- Descriptions should be accurate and vivid.
- Narratives should have probability (coherence) and fidelity for the audience.

Five basic types of warrants link grounds and claims:

- Authority warrants assert that the opinions of the experts quoted are reliable and valid to support the claim being made.
- Generalization warrants either establish a general rule based on specific instances or apply an accepted generalization to a specific instance.
- Comparison (analogy) warrants assert that two things are similar to each other and that what is true of the well known is also true of the less known.

- Causal warrants assert that either a cause will lead to an effect or a known effect was due to a cause.
- Sign warrants assert that a sign (such as clouds) is a reliable indicator of some other condition (such as impending rain).

Check Your Understanding: Exercises and Activities

1. A speaker arguing that we should buy American products presents the following example: "I purchased a Japanese car last year. Since I purchased it, I have had nothing but trouble. I think this proves that you should buy American!" Compare this example with the tests of examples discussed in this chapter. Which of the tests does it fail to meet?
2. How would you go about verifying the "fact" that the leading causes of death in the United States are heart disease, cancer, and infectious diseases? What sources would you consult? Are these in fact the three leading causes of death?
3. Obtain a recent poll (one that appears in an article in, for example, *USA Today* or *Newsweek*). Does the poll meet the tests of numerical data outlined in this chapter? How large was the sample, and what was the margin of error? Did differences in the poll exceed the margin of error? What, if anything, does the article on the poll not tell you that you need to know to properly interpret the poll?

Notes

1. FactCheck.org, 2004. [Retrieved from http://www.factcheck.org, 5 August 2004.]
2. This was first developed by Stephen Toulmin, *The Uses of Argument* (London: Cambridge University Press, 1958). It has been revised by Stephen Toulmin, Richard Rieke, and Allan Janik, *An Introduction to Reasoning,* 2nd ed. (New York: Macmillan, 1984).
3. "Selling Green," *Consumer Reports*, October 1991, 687–92.
4. Cynthia Crossen, "Lies, Damned Lies–and 'Scientific' Studies," *Sacramento Bee*, Forum, 24 November 1991, 1–2. (Reprinted from the *Wall Street Journal.*)
5. Crossen, "Lies, Damned Lies–and 'Scientific' Studies."
6. Robert S. Erikson and Kent L. Tedin, *American Public Opinion*, 6th ed. (New York: Longman, 2001), 29.
7. "Down to the Wire," *Newsweek*, 15 November 2004, 127.
8. Chalsey Phariss, "Lake Tahoe," speech delivered at California State University, Chico, 18 April 1998.
9. Walter R. Fisher, *Human Communication as Narration* (Columbia: University of South Carolina Press, 1987).

Computer projection can help a speaker's organization become clear to the audience.

Organizing Messages

Objectives

After reading this chapter and reviewing the online learning resources at http://www.mhhe.com/brydon6, you should be able to:

- Develop an organizational strategy geared to your audience and purpose.
- Refine the specific purpose of your speech.
- Develop a clear thesis statement for your speech.
- Organize the body of your speech.
- Recognize organizational patterns used across diverse cultures.
- Utilize appropriate transitions from one point to the next in your speech.
- Construct an effective introduction and conclusion for your speech.
- Prepare a formal outline for a speech to your class.
- Prepare and utilize speaker's notes for a speech to your class.
- Handle audience questions after a speech.

Key Concepts

alphabetical pattern
categorical pattern
causal pattern
comparative advantage
extended narrative
formal outline
Monroe's motivated-sequence
problem–solution pattern
refutational pattern
rhetorical question
spatial pattern
speaker's notes
spiral pattern
star pattern
stock issues pattern
subpoint
supporting point
time pattern
wave pattern

> "Every discourse, like a living creature, should be so put together that it has its own body and lacks neither head nor feet, middle nor extremities, all composed in such a way that they suit both each other and the whole."
>
> –PLATO

This speaker's gesture accompanies the first main point of her speech.

In everyday conversation, we often speak in a random and seemingly disorganized fashion. We freely jump around topics, modify opinions, and offer clarifications on an "as needed" basis. Normally we have no reason to formally structure our messages, which are by nature spontaneous and unpredictable, verbal as well as nonverbal.

As we move from informal conversation to speeches in public, however, the "rules" for effective communication change significantly. Listeners want structure from speakers. They want to know where speakers are taking them, including a verbal map that alerts them to important points along the way. They also don't want to have to guess about when they have reached the destination the speaker promised.

Thus, as speakers, we must develop an organizational strategy geared towards our audience. This strategy will reflect our analysis of the rhetorical situation, and may lead to necessary changes to our specific purpose. We will develop a thesis statement, outline the body of the speech, and construct an introduction as well as conclusion. We'll also plan on communicating these through previews and transitional statements–sometimes called signposts. Finally, when our speech is fully prepared, we'll reduce the preceding to speaker's notes, which allow us maximum flexibility in delivering the speech to the audience.

Focusing on the Audience

In Chapter 7, we discussed how important it is to ground your speech in an analysis of the rhetorical situation. This is particularly important for organization. For example, what is the audience's attitude toward our topic? Suppose we have an audience that is either disinterested or hostile. If we save our best for last, no one may be listening. On the other hand, if our audience is highly interested and supportive, saving our most powerful material for the end may be best.

Refining the Specific Purpose

In Chapter 3 we defined specific purpose as a speaker's goal or objective in speaking to a particular audience. Although we will have a tentative specific purpose when we begin researching the speech, we may want to refine it in light of our research and audience analysis. Let's suppose for example, we begin developing our speech wanting our audience to completely stop using cell phones while driving. Further along in our research and analysis, however, we begin to suspect that most audience members believe they can drive and talk at the same time. We might amend our purpose, then, to convincing them to use hands-free devices while driving.

Focusing on the Thesis Statement

Recall from Chapter 3 that a thesis statement focuses our audience's attention on the central point of the speech. Our analysis of the audience may determine when and how to present our thesis statement. Normally, the thesis statement comes in the introduction. However, in a persuasive speech, a hostile audience may tune us out as soon as they hear a position with which they disagree. In that case, it's advisable to hold off stating our position until the end of the speech, beginning with common ground and working up to controversy.

Once we refine the specific purpose and formulate the thesis statement, it is time to organize the body of the speech. Although you might think that the introduction should be written first, this is rarely the case. Until we have constructed the body of the speech, it is difficult to find an appropriate introduction. Also, in sifting through our ideas and research, we might find something that makes a perfect introduction.

Organizing the Body of the Speech

As Plato suggested, every speech needs parts that are "composed in such a way that they suit both each other and the whole." Thus, our speech needs a well-organized body to support the thesis statement and achieve our purpose. Carefully thought-out main points, subpoints, and supporting points will provide that organization.

Main Points

As we discussed in Chapter 3, the key ideas that support the thesis statement of a speech are the *main points.* They should fully develop the thesis statement. As a result of understanding these points, our audience should be informed, persuaded, or entertained in accordance with our specific purpose. In developing our main points, we should keep the following five guidelines in mind.

Tips and Tactics

Guidelines for Developing Main Points

- Limit the number of main points.
- Focus each main point on one main idea.
- Construct main points so that they are parallel in structure.
- State main points as simply as the subject will allow.
- Give all main points equal treatment.

Number

Every speech needs to be anchored around two or more main points. (If there is only one main point, then that is, in effect, the same as the thesis statement, and the subpoints are in fact the main points.) In our experience, more than five main points is too much for an audience to absorb. Three main points seems to be ideal. The audience (not to mention the speaker) usually can easily grasp three key ideas, especially if they are organized in a memorable way. As the number of points increases, each main idea tends to be devalued, and the chances of forgetting one or more ideas increases. Obviously, some topics do not fit into three neat pigeonholes. But if we end up with six, seven, or eight main points, our speech is likely to suffer. Either we are trying to cover too much, or we really have six to eight subpoints, which could be organized into fewer main points, each with two or three subpoints.

Focus

The main points should fully develop the thesis statement without going beyond the focus of the speech. For example, if we are speaking about trends in contemporary music, our thesis statement might be "Pop music is more diverse than ever." This statement then could be divided into three main points:

I. Pop music is international.
II. Pop music is multicultural.
III. Pop music is multitongued.

Think of the thesis statement as limiting the territory covered by the speech. As we construct the body, we include only those items that directly support our thesis statement. At the same time, we do not allow our thesis statement to be incompletely supported. By the end of the speech, we should have fulfilled the promise of the thesis statement–no more, no less.

Each main point should focus on one main idea. For example, this main point is confusing:

I. Today's pop music is international; the heart of the recording industry is in Los Angeles.

These ideas should be expressed in two separate main points.

I. Today's pop music is international.
II. Even so, the heart of the recording industry remains in Los Angeles.

Using two separate points does not mean they are unrelated. However, the two ideas are clearly different.

Parallel Structure

Main points form the essence of a speech, so they should be clear, concise, and memorable. One technique to help achieve this is to construct main points in parallel fashion. For example, which of the following versions of main points would work best for our pop music speech? Here is one version:

I. Today's pop music comes from all over the world.
II. Many cultures are represented in today's pop music.
III. The language of pop music is no longer simply English.

Or consider this version:

I. Pop music transcends national boundaries.
II. Pop music transcends culture.
III. Pop music transcends language.

Obviously, the second example is easier to remember. The repetition of the phrase "pop music transcends" in all three main points stresses the focus of this speech.

We want to be clear that mere repetition is not the same as parallel structure. What is important is that in constructing the main points, a key phrase or concept begins each point. Repeating words randomly throughout the speech is not the same thing as having a parallel structure for your main points.

Simplicity Versus Complexity

A reader can reread anything that is complex or confusing. An audience has only one chance to process information. Main points phrased as complex sentences may lose an audience. Concise and simple language makes the structure of a speech clear. Compare the following two examples:

I. AIDS is transmitted through unprotected sexual relations, including homosexual and heterosexual encounters.
II. AIDS is transmitted when drug users, often desperate for their next fix, share dirty needles.
III. AIDS is transmitted by the exchange of blood, such as in a transfusion or between a mother and her unborn child.

I. AIDS is transmitted by unprotected sex.
II. AIDS is transmitted by sharing needles.
III. AIDS is transmitted by blood.

Which of the two do you think the audience will remember? Main points should be as simple as the subject will allow.

Balance

The main points of the speech should be in balance. For example, if one main point composes two-thirds of the speech, audience members may become confused and wonder what they missed.

Subpoints

Subpoints are to main points what main points are to the thesis statement. A **subpoint** is an idea that supports a main point. Each main point should have between two and five subpoints. Consider, for example, our speech on diversity in pop music.

subpoint
An idea that supports a main point.

I. Pop music transcends national boundaries. *[main point]*
   A. The pop music charts feature artists from not only the U.S. but Brazil, Canada, and France, to name a few. *[sub point]*
   B. The most popular recording artist in the world is from Spain. *[sub point]*

II. Pop music transcends cultures.
   A. African American and Caribbean cultures are well represented in today's pop music.
   B. Many Anglo musicians have adapted the music of their ancestral culture to the contemporary pop scene.

III. Pop music transcends language.
  A. Ricky Martin sings in Spanish about La Vida Loca.
  B. Lil' Kim, Pink, and Christina Aguilera sing in French about Lady Marmalade.

It makes no sense to have only one subpoint under a main point. For example:

I. Pop music transcends national boundaries.
  A. The pop music charts feature artists from not only the U.S. but Brazil, Canada, and France, to name a few.

If a main point is not divisible into at least two subpoints, it probably isn't really a main point. Rather, it should be a subpoint under another main point. Like main points, subpoints should be parallel in structure, simply stated, and given equal treatment.

Supporting Points

supporting point
An idea that supports a subpoint.

Sometimes the subpoints within a speech require further support and subdivision. Thus, we might have supporting points for each subpoint. A **supporting point** is an idea that supports a subpoint. Returning to our example of pop music, the body of a speech might be organized as follows:

[main point] II. Pop music transcends cultures.
[subpoint] A. African American and Caribbean cultures are well represented in today's pop music.
[supporting point] 1. Hip-hop music has obvious ties to African American culture.
[supporting point] 2. Reggae and SKA have obvious ties to Caribbean culture.
B. Many Anglo musicians have adapted the music of their ancestral culture to the contemporary pop scene.
1. Groups such as U2 and the Corrs have been influenced by their Celtic roots.
2. The lyrics of Sting are suggestive of traditional English ballads.

Each supporting point could be further subdivided, but such a detailed substructure probably would lose the audience. For a normal classroom speech, it is unlikely there will be time to develop points beyond this level.

If we must further subdivide a supporting point, we use lowercase letters in the outline as follows:

[main point] II. Pop music transcends cultures.
[subpoint] A. African American and Caribbean cultures are well represented in today's pop music.
[supporting point] 1. Hip-hop music has obvious ties to African American culture.
[further support] a. The rhythms are African American.
[further support] b. The music fuses elements of rhythm and blues, soul, and rap.
2. Reggae and SKA have obvious ties to Caribbean culture.
a. Bob Marley continues to be popular.
b. As does his son Ziggy.

Exhibit 10.1 illustrates the relationship among various levels of support in a speech.

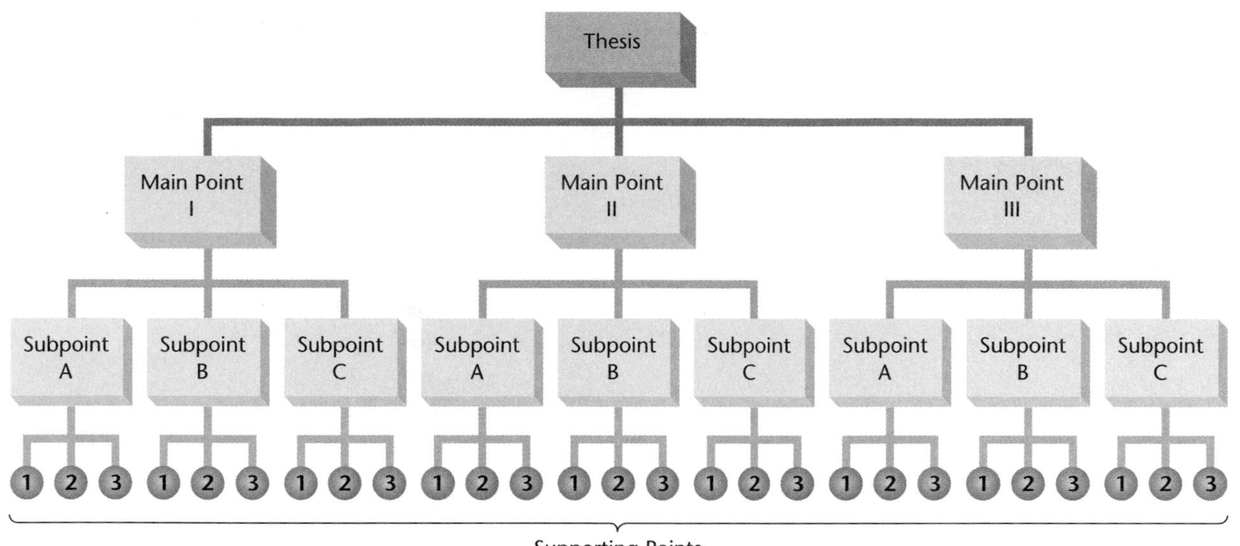

Exhibit 10.1
Relationship of Points in a Traditional Speech

Traditional Patterns of Organization

A number of different patterns can be used to organize the body of a speech. In Chapter 3, we introduced three of those patterns: time, spatial, and categorical. We now add eight traditional patterns of organization: extended narrative, alphabetical, problem-solution, stock issues, comparative advantage, refutational, causal, and Monroe's motivated-sequence. We begin by briefly reviewing the three patterns introduced in Chapter 3: time, spatial, and categorical, which can be seen in Exhibit 3.2. We will then introduce the additional organizational patterns in more detail.

Time

Many speech topics are best organized in a simple **time pattern**. Speeches on historical events or that deal with a process are well suited to this pattern. Viewers of The History Channel are familiar with this pattern

time pattern
A pattern of organization based on chronology or a sequence of events.

Spatial

A **spatial pattern** is an organization based on physical space or geography. Some topics, usually informative, lend themselves to a spatial or geographic order. Every time you turn to the weather channel, you will see the weather described using this pattern.

spatial pattern
A pattern of organization based on physical space or geography.

Categorical

A **categorical pattern** is an organization based on natural divisions in the subject matter. Animals can be divided into mammals, reptiles, birds, and so forth. When using this pattern, however, we need to be careful that we don't create false categories. Much social and ethnic prejudice is rooted in stereotyping people into arbitrary categories.

categorical pattern
A pattern of organization based on natural divisions in the subject matter.

TV meteorologists often use a spatial pattern to explain the weather.

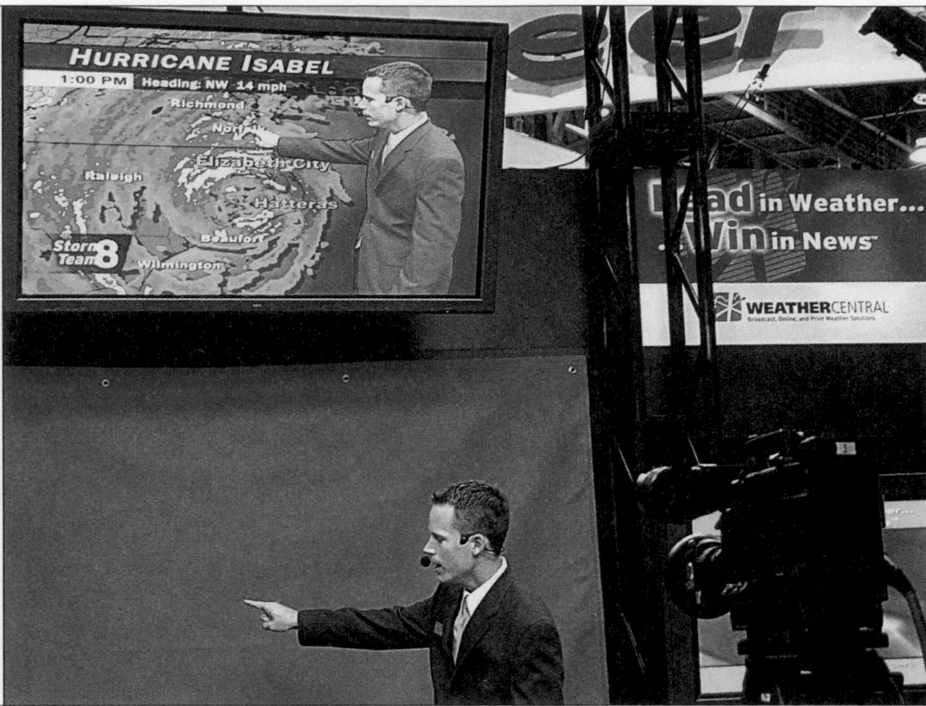

Extended Narrative

extended narrative A pattern of organization in which the entire body of the speech is the telling of a story.

An **extended narrative** is a pattern of organization in which the entire body of the speech is the telling of a story. In Chapter 9, we introduced narrative as a form of support for a speech. As support, one main point of a speech might be a narrative, but the other main points might be in the form of statistics, expert opinions, facts, and the like. However, an extended narrative means the whole speech is one story. In this case we tell a story in sequence, with a climactic point near the end of the speech. This organizational pattern is often very useful in speeches to entertain. Thus, if we were to tell the story of a blind date, we might pattern our speech as follows:

I. I am asked to go out on a blind date.
II. I meet the date.
III. Disaster follows.

Sometimes a persuasive speech can also be built around an extended narrative of some incident that dramatizes the problem being addressed in the speech. An example of an extended narrative in a persuasive speech might be the following:

I. Jim had too much to drink at a fraternity party.
II. His frat brothers dared him to hop a moving freight train.
III. Jim attempted to jump onto the moving train.
IV. He lost his balance and fell under the train; both of his legs were severed.
V. Jim lived and has dedicated his life to fighting alcohol abuse.

Notice that a story needs not only a plot line but also characters, including a central character with whom the audience can identify. In this particular story, the speaker would seek to create a sympathetic portrayal of Jim, who becomes the protagonist. Of course, each point would be developed in detail, and the audience should be held in suspense as the story unfolds. The moral of the story should not have to be stated explicitly but should be apparent to the audience. This is one of those speeches in which stating the thesis at the beginning would actually undermine the effectiveness of the speech. By the end of the speech, however, no one would doubt the speaker's central idea.

Alphabetical

Another useful way to organize a speech is so that the main points are in an **alphabetical pattern** or so they spell out a common word. For example, dermatologists have developed what they call the A-B-C-D method of detecting skin cancer through self-examination.[1] These steps form a useful way of organizing a speech and help the audience remember what to look for. This pattern is particularly suited for informative speeches where the goal is for the audience to remember what they've learned. For example, here are the things we should look for in examining moles for skin cancer:

alphabetical pattern
Main points are in alphabetical order or spell out a common word.

I. Asymmetry–one half unlike the other half.
II. Border irregularity–scalloped or poorly circumscribed border.
III. Color varies from one area to another.
IV. Diameter–larger than 6 mm (diameter of a pencil eraser).

Problem–Solution

problem–solution pattern
A pattern of organization that analyzes a problem in terms of (1) harm, (2) significance, and (3) cause, and proposes a solution that is (1) described, (2) feasible, and (3) advantageous.

Sometimes we speak to propose a solution to an ongoing problem. This is frequently the case when we speak persuasively. One way to approach this type of speech is to use the **problem–solution pattern,** a pattern of organization that analyzes a problem in terms of (1) harm, (2) significance, and (3) cause, and proposes a solution that is (1) described, (2) feasible, and (3) advantageous. A specific example of this pattern might be a speech about the need for better health care. In this case, we might organize the speech in the following way:

I. Millions of Americans are denied access to adequate health care. *[problem]*
   A. People suffer and die without this care. *[harm]*
   B. More than 46 million Americans lack basic health insurance. *[significance]*
   C. There is a gap between government-sponsored health care (Medicaid and Medicare) and private insurance. *[cause]*
II. We need a program of national health insurance to fill the gap. *[solution]*
   A. All businesses will be taxed to provide national health insurance. *[description]*
   B. Similar programs exist in almost every other industrialized country in the world. *[feasibility]*
   C. No longer will people be denied access to medical care simply because they cannot pay. *[advantages]*

The relationship between harm and significance is important. Harm has to do with the bad consequences of the problem–in this case, potential suffering and death. Significance has to do with the extent of the problem. If 100 people in a nation of 300 million were at risk of suffering or death because of an inadequate health care system, this would be unfortunate. If millions were at risk, however, then the problem would be significant.

We also need to recognize that there can be numerous different solutions to the same problem. Thus it is important to stress both the feasibility and the advantages of the solution we propose if we hope to have it adopted by our audience.

Stock Issues

stock issues pattern
A four-point pattern of organization that is based on (1) ill, (2) blame, (3) cure, and (4) cost.

Closely related to the problem–solution pattern is what is often called the **stock issues pattern**, which is well suited to persuasive speeches. This pattern is based on the model of deliberative debate, and it addresses four key questions: first, how serious is the problem; second, who is to blame; third, how should it be solved; and finally, is the solution worth the cost. These four stock issues are referred to as (1) ill, (2) blame, (3) cure, and (4) cost. For example, a speech about campus parking problems could have the following four main points:

[ill] I. The lack of parking is causing a serious problem on our campus.
[blame] II. The problem exists because parking rules are not enforced, which allows many nonstudents to take up our parking spots.
[cure] III. The problem can be cured by raising fines and increasing patrols.
[cost] IV. The costs of the increased patrols will be paid for by higher fines.

As with the problem–solution pattern, we need specific subpoints to show that the facts support the serious nature of the problem and that we have correctly identified its cause. The solution needs to be well thought out and explained. And we must be sure that the costs of our solution do not outweigh the benefits of solving the problem.

Comparative Advantage

The stock issues and problem solution approaches rely on the presumption that "if it ain't broke, don't fix it." Although an inviting slogan, imagine how many modern miracles would never have been invented if everyone had followed that maxim. For example, CD-ROMs and even old vinyl 45s were perfectly adequate ways to enjoy music. But the ascendancy of MP3 players, such as Apple's iPod, show that if one can develop a better product, people will buy it. The comparative advantage approach to speech organization is based on this logic. First one describes the current state of affairs, second a plan of action is proposed, and finally, the speaker points out that life will be better if the plan of action is adopted. So, one might imagine a few years ago a speaker encouraging the audience to get an iPod instead of buying more CDs.

I. CDs let the music producer decide what you will hear.
  A. Often albums have only one or two good tracks.
  B. You are paying for music you may not like, just to get what you want.
II. There's a new way to get your music.
  A. MP3 players allow you to buy just the tunes you want.
  B. Specific tracks can be ripped from CDs or downloaded from the Internet for a nominal cost.
III. MP3 players have advantages over CDs.
  A. They are more portable.
  B. You only buy the music you want to listen to.
  C. In the long run they cost less than buying your music on CDs.

comparative advantage
A pattern of organization based on the idea that things can be better even if they are not currently harmful.

Thus, the **comparative advantage** organizational pattern is built on the assumption that things can be better even when neither harmful nor undesirable now.

Refutational

Sometimes we are in a position to answer the arguments of another speaker, for example, in a debate. Alternatively, we may read or hear something with which we disagree. These types of persuasive speeches often call for the **refutational pattern** of organization, which involves the following steps:

refutational pattern
A pattern of organization that involves (1) stating the argument to be refuted, (2) stating the objection to the argument, (3) proving the objection to the argument, and (4) presenting the impact of the refutation.

I. State the argument we seek to refute.
II. State our objection to the argument.
III. Prove our objection to the argument.
IV. Present the impact of our refutation.

For example, if we wanted to refute a proposed national health insurance plan, we might argue the following points:

I. The proponents of national health care say the government should control health care. *[States the argument you seek to refute.]*
II. Government bureaucrats, not physicians or patients, will then control medical choices. *[States your objection to the argument.]*
III. People from Canada, which has national health insurance, often have to come to the United States for medical care they are denied by their government-run program. *[Presents proof for your objection.]*
IV. The quality of American health care will decline in a program run by government bureaucrats. *[Presents the impact of your objection.]*

Causal

The **causal pattern** of organization moves from cause to effect or from effect to cause. It is often useful in persuasive presentations and also can be used in some informative speeches. In cause-to-effect speeches, we are dealing with some known activity and showing our audience that it will produce certain effects. If these are desirable effects, we would be endorsing the activity. If they are undesirable, we would be suggesting that the audience avoid it. To illustrate this organizational pattern, suppose we wanted to convince our audience to quit smoking:

causal pattern
A pattern of organization that moves from cause to effect or from effect to cause.

I. Cigarette smoke contains a number of harmful chemicals. *[Cause]*
  A. Carbon monoxide reduces the body's ability to absorb oxygen.
  B. Nicotine is an addictive substance.
  C. Tar is made up of thousands of cancer-causing chemicals.
II. Cigarette smoking leads to significant health problems. *[Effect]*
  A. Carbon monoxide has been linked to low-birth-weight babies.
  B. Nicotine makes quitting smoking difficult.
  C. Tar is a principal source of lung cancer in smokers.

On the other hand, if we wanted to convince our audience of the need to reduce the power of special interests in Washington, we might argue from various effects back to the cause:

I. The country is in economic trouble. *[Effect]*
  A. Real wages are declining.

B. Many industries are moving overseas.
C. Our trade deficit is growing.

[Cause]

II. We have a system of government that is too tied to special interests.
A. Lobbyists influence Congress to make bad economic decisions.
B. Politicians are more interested in getting reelected than in solving problems.
C. Only by breaking the power of special interests can we get our economy back on track.

Whether we move from cause to effect or from effect to cause, we need to provide proof of the causal links asserted in the speech. Simply because two things occur one after the other does not prove one caused the other. For example, just because a car breaks down doesn't mean the last person to drive it is responsible for the breakdown.

Monroe's motivated-sequence A five-step organizational scheme, developed by speech professor Alan Monroe, including (1) attention, (2) need, (3) satisfaction, (4) visualization, and (5) action.

Monroe's Motivated-Sequence

A five-step organizational scheme developed by speech professor Alan Monroe, and thus termed **Monroe's motivated-sequence**, is another useful pattern.[2] These five steps overlap somewhat with the introduction and conclusion of a speech, as well as the body. They are as follows:

[Introduction] I. *Attention*: Gain your audience's attention.
[Body] II. *Need*: Show the audience that a need exists that affects them.
[Body] III. *Satisfaction*: Present the solution to the need.
[Body] IV. *Visualization*: Help the audience imagine how their need will be met in the future.
[Conclusion] V. *Action*: State what actions must be taken to fulfill the need.

To see how this motivated sequence might work, consider a speech on national health insurance:

I. *Attention*: A child dies when her parents can't afford to take her to the doctor.
II. *Need*: You could become one of millions of uninsured Americans who face financial ruin if they become seriously ill.
III. *Satisfaction*: National health insurance would guarantee all Americans the right to health care, regardless of their income.
IV. *Visualization*: The United States would join nations like Canada, where no one fears seeing a doctor because of the cost.
V. *Action*: Write your senator and representative today, urging the passage of national health insurance.

Obviously, the motivated-sequence pattern is most directly suited to persuasive presentations. However, an informative presentation could use at least some of these steps, because informative speaking typically is the first step in a persuasive campaign. In an informative presentation, it is important to show the audience why they need to learn the information being presented and, of course, to satisfy that need. Helping an audience visualize how they will use the information is also valuable. And often the speaker will then want the audience to put what they have learned into action.

Organic Patterns of Organization

These 10 patterns of organization are primarily linear in nature and are well suited to audiences rooted in a Western European tradition. For example, scholar Cheryl Jorgensen-Earp has suggested that women and some ethnic speakers use less linear, more organic patterns, such as the wave, the spiral, and the star.[3]

Wave

Many women and African Americans use the **wave pattern**. Much like a wave cresting, receding, and then cresting again, a speech following this pattern continually returns to the basic theme, repeating a phrase again and again throughout the speech. Perhaps the most familiar example is the "I Have a Dream" speech, by Dr. Martin Luther King Jr., which gets its title from the constant repetition of that phrase. In addition, King uses the theme "Let freedom ring" repeatedly as he brings the speech to its dramatic conclusion. Exhibit 10.2 illustrates the wave pattern of speaking.

wave pattern
A pattern of organization in which the basic theme, often represented by a phrase, is repeated again and again, much like a wave cresting, receding, and then cresting again.

Spiral

Another pattern suggested by Jorgensen-Earp is a **spiral pattern**. It too repeats points, but each point grows in intensity as the speech builds to its pinnacle at the conclusion. For example, we recall a motivational speech by one of our former students, Rick Rigsby. He was speaking of how he learned about life from the death of his wife, Trina, from breast cancer when she was in her 30s. At one point she told him that it wasn't how long you lived but how you lived that mattered. As the speech progressed, Rick returned to this theme again and again, each time with more emotional intensity. At the end of his speech he asked the audience this question: "How are you living?" Thus he spiraled to a climax that had been foreshadowed throughout the speech. Exhibit 10.3 illustrates the spiral pattern of organization.

spiral pattern
A pattern of organization that employs repetition of points, with the points growing in intensity as the speech builds to its conclusion.

Star

A third organic pattern identified by Jorgensen-Earp is the **star pattern**, in which various points all grow from a central idea. Because all of the points of the star are of equal importance, a speaker can present the points in any order in support of the common theme that encircles the star and holds the speech

star pattern
A pattern of organization in which all of the points are of equal importance and can be presented in any order to support the common theme.

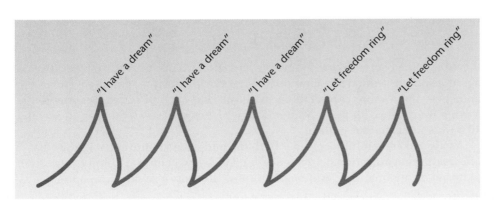

Exhibit 10.2
Wave Pattern
Martin Luther King Jr. used a wave pattern in his speech.

Exhibit 10.3

Spiral Pattern

Each point in a spiral pattern repeats the theme with greater intensity.

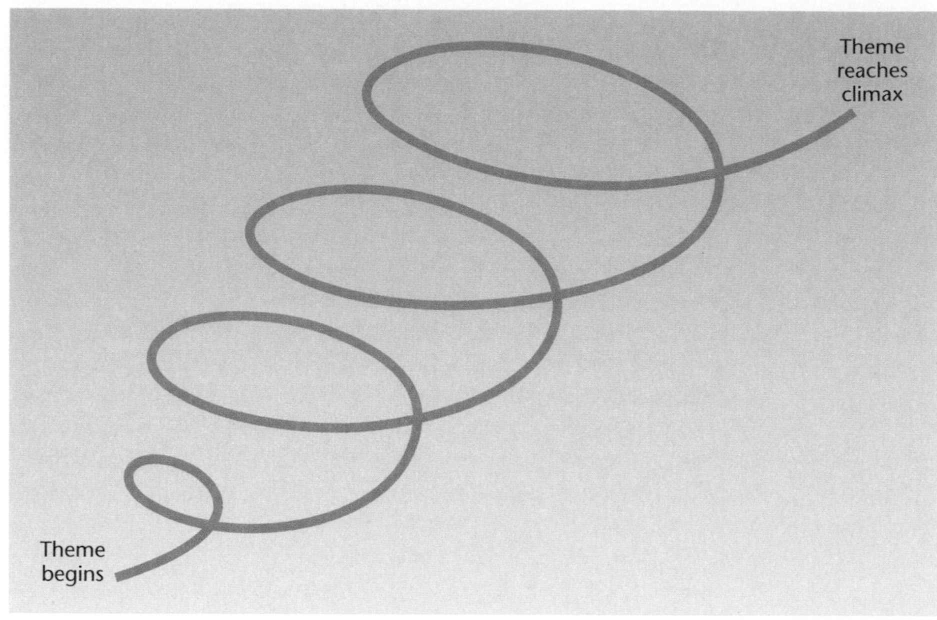

Exhibit 10.4

Star Pattern

In a star pattern all points grow from a central idea.

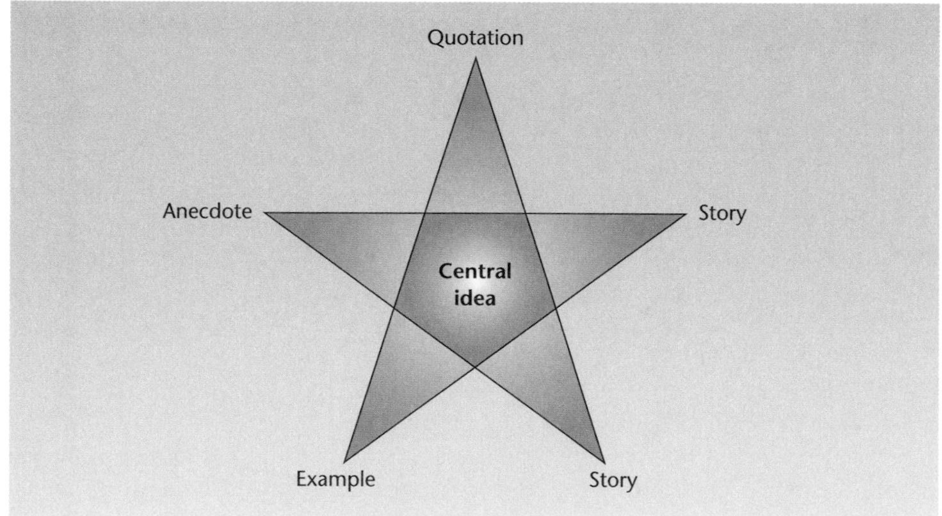

together. When actor Edward James Olmos spoke at our university several years ago the speech seemed like a random list of stories and anecdotes to some in the audience. But a more careful analysis shows that each of his stories was really a point on a star, with the central message being "we are all one gang." Exhibit 10.4 illustrates the star pattern.

As a speaker, carefully consider both the audience's cultural background as it affects their organizational preferences and your own cultural affinity for certain patterns of organization. Although cultural diversity provides the opportunity

Speaking of . . .

Organizational Patterns

Any of the patterns we've discussed could be used to fulfill any speech purpose. However, certain patterns seem more suitable for one or two purposes than do others. This table highlights the patterns most likely to be useful for each speech purpose.

Pattern	Informative	Persuasive	Entertaining
Time	X		X
Spatial	X		
Categorical	X	X	X
Extended Narrative	X	X	X
Alphabetical	X	X	X
Problem–Solution		X	
Stock Issues		X	
Comparative Advantage		X	
Refutational		X	
Causal	X	X	
Motivated-Sequence		X	
Wave	X	X	X
Spiral	X	X	X
Star	X	X	X

to expand the ways in which speeches may be organized, it should be used only when you are certain of your skill in this respect.

The box titled "Speaking of . . . Organizational Patterns" summarizes the patterns we have discussed and suggests which patterns work best for various speech purposes. Whatever pattern we choose, we want to be sure it is appropriate for our audience, topic, and purpose. Sticking with one pattern for all the main points of the speech also helps to avoid audience confusion.

Transitions

In addition to constructing the actual body of the speech, it is important to help our audience follow our organization. As Chapter 3 explained, *signposts* are one type of transitional statement that bridges main points. They tell the audience where we have been and where we are going. Transitions help those who have become lost or inattentive to pick up the thread of a speech.

Transitions serve to verbally link our thoughts as we speak. It's always a good idea to let our audience know that there is a sequence to our message–"Let's consider three important issues"–and then to remind them where we are in that sequence–"Having covered the first issue, let's now look at the second."

For example, to add a point, we use words or phrases such as *furthermore*, *in addition to*, and *besides*. To emphasize something, phrases such as *above all*, *indeed*, and *most important* are useful. To emphasize time, we use words such as *then, afterward, eventually, next, immediately, meanwhile, previously, often, usually,* and *later.* Cause and effect can be suggested by the words *consequently, therefore,* and *thus.* To stress that we are using an example, we say, "for example" or "for instance." The progress from one point to another in our speech can be highlighted by terms such as *first, second, third,* or *furthermore.* Contrast can be indicated by use of *but, however, instead, nevertheless* and phrases such as *to the contrary, on the other hand,* and *in contrast.* The conclusion of a speech can be indicated by phrases such as *to sum up, for these reasons, in retrospect,* and *in conclusion.*[4]

Tips and Tactics

Techniques for Transitional Statements

- *Refer to preceding and upcoming ideas.* "Now that you know what computer viruses are, I'll discuss how to prevent their spread to your computer."
- *Enumerate key points.* "First, never assume that a program from a friend or computer bulletin board is virus free."
- *Give nonverbal reinforcement.* Changes in vocal inflection signal a change is coming. Movement can signal a transition. Some speakers physically move from one place to another while speaking in order to emphasize that they are moving from one point to the next. Others hold up fingers to indicate the number of points.
- *Use visual aids to reinforce transitions.* Moving to the next PowerPoint™ slide or putting up a new transparency clearly signals to the audience that we are moving on. It's also a way to help us remember the sequence of our speech.
- *Words can cue the audience that we are changing points*: Next, another, number, moving on, finally, therefore, and in summary.

Introducing the Speech

After organizing the body of the speech, it is time to construct the introduction and conclusion. Recall from Chapter 3 that an introduction should do four things: open with impact, focus on the thesis statement, connect with the audience, and preview the rest of the speech. Let's look at each of these functions in turn.

Open With Impact

A speech should immediately grab the audience's attention. First impressions count. One way to control this impression is to open the speech with impact. The most common ways are with a story; a quotation; a startling statement; a reference to the audience, the occasion, or a current event; appropriate humor; a personal experience; or a thought-provoking question.

Story

A brief story, real or hypothetical, is often a good way to begin. For example, one of our students began her speech by describing the strange behavior of a person who was staggering and incoherent, and finally collapsed. The quick conclusion of most of her audience was that the person was drunk. Not only was this conclusion wrong, the truth startled the class. The person was diabetic and suffering from insulin shock. Needless to say, the class became far more interested in hearing the speech about diabetes than if the speaker had simply begun, "Today I'm going to tell you about diabetes."

Quotation

As we pointed out in Chapter 8, there are numerous sources of quotations, including those online. If we are having trouble deciding how to begin a speech, we often can find a quotation that will captivate the audience and reinforce our main ideas.

Sometimes a quotation can provide a vivid description of the very topic we are speaking about. Mary Schoenthaler, one of our former students, began her speech with this quotation: "Don't mind the burning smell. It reminds most people of chicken left in the oven too long."[5] The significance of the quotation is that it was from Bill Hatfield, a salesman for laser equipment used to remove tattoos. This quotation helped make Mary's point that one should not make the decision to get a tattoo lightly, since removal is both expensive and unpleasant.

Startling Statement

Humans are attracted naturally to surprising, startling, and unusual events. A surprising or startling statement will provoke the audience's undivided attention. For example, a student in our class began her speech by announcing that her sister had died of toxic shock syndrome. As you'd expect, her audience was startled and paid rapt attention to the speech that followed.

Reference to the Audience, Occasion, or Current Events

Professional speakers often tailor their speeches to a specific audience and situation, saying such things as "I'm so happy to be here at [fill in the blank] college" or "I join with you in praising your football team's come-from-behind victory last night."

Some speakers also refer to a previous speaker. Consider an instance where two students chose to speak on gun control, each taking the opposite side of the topic. The second speaker wisely incorporated a reference to the prior speech in her introduction. To ignore a speech on the same topic, particularly one at odds with your own speech, is likely to turn off an audience. Without attempting to refute the other speaker, she acknowledged those opposing views but also stated that she would present the other side of the issue.

Finally, current events may spark interest and controversy with an audience. We recall a student who spoke on binge drinking who began the speech by referring to the recent tragic death of a student on our campus.

Appropriate Humor

A classic *Far Side* cartoon shows Abraham Lincoln delivering the Gettysburg Address. His speech, however, begins with a joke, "And so the bartender says, 'Hey! That's not a duck!'" After a pause for laughter, Lincoln continues, "Four-score and seven years ago. . . ."

Obviously, one would not begin a serious speech such as the Gettysburg Address with a joke. Humor, if not used properly, can backfire. It is best used on occasions when the audience will find it appropriate. An after-dinner speech or a commencement address, for example, is frequently an opportunity to use humor.

Emmy and Golden Globe-winning comedy writer Russ Woody, began his commencement address to the 1998 graduating class from his alma mater with these words: "Look . . . I write sitcoms for a living, so don't expect much. Which means . . . basically, I'm gonna tell a few jokes, hit a few well-worn platitudes, and try to sell you a Dodge minivan."[6] Of course Russ's speech did far more than just present a string of jokes. But his opening humor not only was self-deprecating, it also helped establish common ground with his audience as he went on to describe his own graduation experience: "The man who gave the commencement speech talked for close to 15 hours. He said we were all sailing ships out on the ocean of life, and we were the beating hearts of an upwardly mobile nation, and we had a bunch of mountaintops to climb . . . And the only thing I *really* came away with, besides hathair, was something about a new technology in ventilation systems that was greatly improving the output of poultry in tested areas of Missouri." Russ captured his audience's attention and let them know he appreciated how they would react to a long, boring speech, heavy on clichés and irrelevant to their lives.

However we use it, though, humor should be tied to the substance of our speech. Telling an irrelevant joke can detract from the main idea rather than enhance it. It can also make the speaker look foolish.

Finally, we need to be sensitive with regard to humor. Ethnic, sexist, and off-color jokes, for example, can get a speaker into justifiable trouble.

Personal Experience

Often there is no other more compelling testimony on a topic than personal experience. Not only can a personal experience draw in the audience and get their attention, it also can serve to build speaker credibility. For example, the speaker on diabetes referred to earlier had a brother who was diabetic. However, she did not mention this fact until she had finished her speech. Had she begun with her own experiences with a diabetic brother, she would have enhanced her credibility for the remainder of the speech.

One last example from a former student illustrates how one can use personal experience to his or her advantage. Karen Shirk began her speech on the importance of wearing seatbelts by holding up a piece of a brake light and a CD player faceplate, which she informed us, were the only remaining parts of a car that was totaled in an accident from which she walked away unscathed because she was wearing her seatbelt. It's one thing to cite boring statistics about the number of lives saved by wearing seatbelts and quite another to show dramatically how you survived a very serious accident because you were wearing one.

Thought-Provoking Question

Sometimes a good question can effectively open a speech. A **rhetorical question** is one that the audience isn't expected to answer out loud. For example, one student began a speech on secondhand smoke this way: "How many of you have ever returned home smelling as though you were a stand-in for the Marlboro Man?"[7] The attention-getting language worked well. However, beginning with a question can be ineffective if the question is not thought provoking. For example, beginning a speech with "How many of you would like to learn to snow ski?" isn't likely to have much impact on an audience. Also, with rhetorical questions, audiences are sometimes unsure whether the question is meant to be answered out loud. On the other hand, we have seen speakers who effectively begin their speeches by asking audience members to respond to a series of questions with a show of hands. Questions, rhetorical or real, should be used only if they add impact to the opening of the speech.

rhetorical question
A question that the audience isn't expected to answer out loud.

Focus on the Thesis Statement

The central idea we want to convey to an audience should be captured by our thesis statement. Although we have developed a thesis statement before writing the body of the speech, now is a good time to reflect on its phrasing. Have we really focused on the essential theme of the speech? The thesis statement must be broad enough to incorporate all of our main points. At the same time, the thesis statement cannot be so broad that our speech seems to leave something out.

As noted earlier, there may be situations, such as with a hostile audience, when we should not explicitly state our thesis early in the speech. In the introduction in these situations, we indicate the general topic area of the speech, focusing on an area of common agreement, rather than the thesis. The thesis would then emerge toward the end of the speech, after the arguments in support have been explained.

Connect With the Audience

No speech should be constructed without asking, "What's in it for the audience? What needs or desires will be fulfilled by listening to my speech?" The introduction is an opportunity to make the link between the speech topic and audience members. If we make this link in the introduction, we are much more likely to gain the audience's collective ear.

The introduction is an opportunity to build our credibility. We can stress our similarity to the audience. The student who spoke on toxic shock syndrome used her family's tragedy to stress that the same thing could happen to any woman. She not only made a connection with her classmates, she established her personal credibility by virtue of her experience and her subsequent research on the topic.

We can also use it to stress our expertise. For example, consider a student who was speaking about how to succeed in television and film. She failed to connect with her audience by mentioning her own résumé, which included numerous television and film roles, including a film with Clint Eastwood and a recurring role on a popular sitcom. Finally, we can use this as an opportunity to stress our goodwill for the audience. By connecting with their needs and aspirations, we can let them know we are speaking for them, rather then merely to them. We have heard (or some might say endured) scores of commencement addresses over our long careers in higher education. The one common feature of those that were successful is that they focused on the students in the graduating class, rather than providing an opportunity for the speaker to brag about his or her accomplishments. Even those who had gone on to prestigious careers (and to be invited as a commencement speaker that's pretty much a requirement) usually put the focus on their audience, not themselves. Ed Rollins, who managed President Reagan's re-election campaign, began his commencement speech at his alma mater by announcing that he had graduated "summa cum lucky." His advice to students stressed how much they could accomplish if they put their education to good use.

Although connecting with the audience is an important part of the introduction to a speech, the connection should not be made only once. In fact, throughout the speech we should draw a connection between our message and our audience whenever possible.

Preview the Speech

Although no one knows who first said, "Tell 'em what you're going to tell 'em; tell 'em; and then tell 'em what you told 'em," it is a saying with more than a grain of truth. As we noted in Chapter 3, a *preview* is a forecast of the main points of a speech. It simply tells audience members what they are going to hear. In many ways, it is a summary before the fact. By telling audience members what will follow, a preview helps them put our statements into a coherent frame of reference.

The way to preview a speech is rather simple: Cue the audience to the fact that we are previewing the main points of our speech, and then state the points in the same sequence they will be presented. A brief preview might be "In today's speech, I would like to share the definition, transmission, and prevention of computer viruses." Or we may want to enumerate our main points, saying, "Today, I want to first define computer viruses; second, explain how they are transmitted; and third, offer a way to prevent them from infecting your own computer."

By permission of Johnny Hart and Creator's Syndicate, Inc.

It is not always necessary, however, to be so explicit. There are often subtler ways of previewing a speech. For example, "All computer owners need to know what computer viruses are, how they are transmitted, and how to detect and prevent them."

Tips and Tactics

Ways to Open With Impact

Effective ways to open a speech with impact include:

- Story
- Quotation
- Startling statement
- Reference to the audience, occasion, or current events
- Appropriate humor
- Personal experience
- Thought-provoking question

Concluding the Speech

The conclusion of a speech should be brief and memorable. The last thing an audience wants to hear after "In conclusion . . ." is a 10-minute dissertation on some new aspect of the topic. When we say those magic words "in conclusion" or "to wrap up," we should be prepared to conclude. Avoid introducing points that were not covered in the body of the speech. If we have another main point to cover, then it belongs in the body of the speech, not the conclusion. There are, consequently, only two basic things to do in concluding a speech: summarize and close with impact.

Summarize

The summary tells the audience, very briefly, what we have told them in the speech. This is where clear, concisely developed main points pay off. Sometimes we may wish to explicitly number the main points in the summary. For example, "Remember, there are three types of bikes you'll see on campus. First, there are cruisers; second, there are mountain bikes; and third, there are touring bikes."

Close With Impact

The final words of a speech should be memorable. The close is our last chance to make a lasting impression on the audience. As with the opening, it should be relevant to the main thesis of the speech. A few of the common techniques for closing are a short, memorable quotation, an anecdote or a brief story, a direct

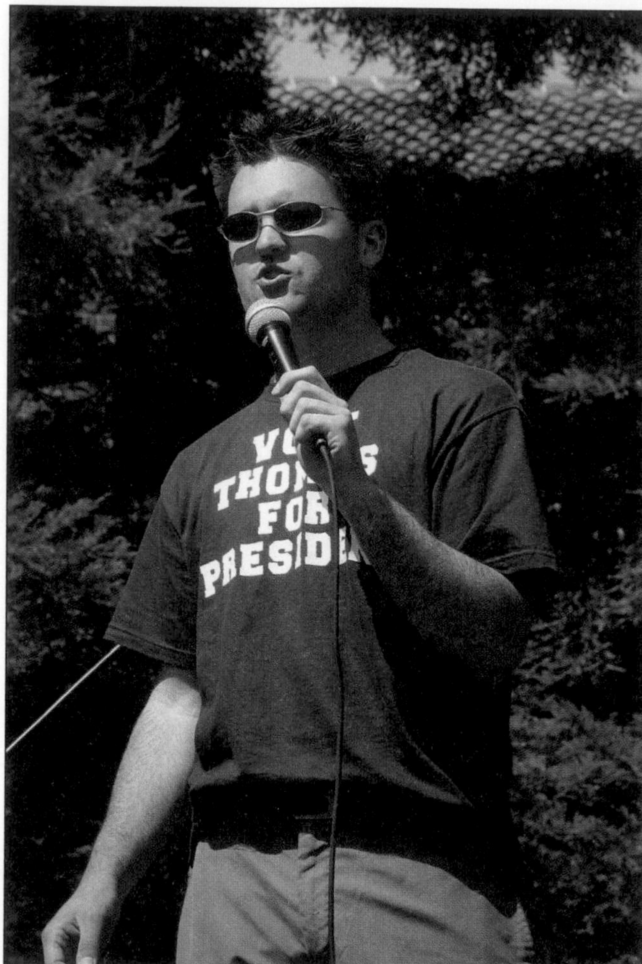

This speaker's t-shirt makes a direct appeal for action—to earn students' votes in an election.

appeal to action, and a return to the opening theme. If we have delayed presenting our thesis statement for strategic reasons, it should be incorporated just prior to this point (right after the summary). If we stated the thesis earlier, it should be reiterated here.

Quotation

The same principles apply to a closing quotation as to an opening one. We want to capture the essence of our talk in a few words. If someone has said it better, then it is perfectly appropriate to quote that person. In the conclusion, first state the person quoted and then state the quotation. For example, it is less effective to say, "'I have a dream,' said Martin Luther King Jr.," than to say, "As Martin Luther King Jr. once stated, 'I have a dream.'"

Anecdote

The key in the closing is to be brief and to the point. A long, drawn-out story will undermine the effectiveness of the rest of the speech. A concluding anecdote should highlight our main focus, not detract from it. As with opening stories, such anecdotes can be real or hypothetical but should be clearly identified as such.

Direct Appeal to Action

Concluding with an appeal to action is typical of a persuasive speech and is an explicit part of the motivated sequence. It involves telling audience members specifically what they can do to fulfill their needs or solve a problem–for example, sign a petition, write to Congress, or change their own behavior. A direct appeal to the audience is often the most appropriate way to conclude a persuasive presentation.

Return to Opening

One of the most effective ways to close a speech is to return to where we began. Not only does this remind the audience of our introduction, it also gives our speech a sense of closure. It takes us and our audience full circle. For example, the speech that began by describing a person suffering from insulin shock ended by telling the audience that they would now know how to recognize when someone was in insulin shock and would be able to get help. If we can find a way to tie our opening and closing together, we can intensify the impact of both.

Tips and Tactics

Ways to Close With Impact

Effective ways to close a speech with impact include:

- Quotation
- Anecdote
- Direct appeal to action
- Return to opening

Handling Audience Questions

Depending on the situation and time available, many speakers take questions from the audience after they finish their formal presentation. For some helpful guidelines, we invite you to read the box, "Speaking of . . . Handling the Q&A" on page 241. The question and answer period is often one of the most important parts of a speech. It is one last chance to demonstrate mastery of the subject matter, enhance credibility, and clear up anything the audience may have missed in the speech.

To help you prepare your speech outline, go to our Online Learning Center Web site and click on the Outline Tutor link.

Preparing the Formal Outline

Once you have a rough structure of your speech, including the body, introduction, and conclusion, your instructor may recommend that you prepare a formal outline of the speech. A **formal outline** is a detailed outline used in speech preparation but not, in most cases, in the actual presentation. Usually, such an outline should be prepared on a computer, depending on your instructor's requirements. Such outlines help you put your ideas down in a clear and organized fashion. If submitted in advance of a speech, it also allows instructors to give you feedback and make suggestions.

formal outline
A detailed outline used in speech preparation, but not, in most cases, in the actual presentation.

There are two basic types of outlines. *Phrase* or *key word outlines* are meaningful to the speaker but probably would not make a lot of sense to anyone else. For example, a speaker might prepare the following outline for her own use:

Intro: Tell story
I. Rock music
II. Volume
III. Deafness
Conclusion: Same story 10 years later

Because this outline probably would make sense only to the speaker, beginning speakers are frequently expected to prepare a *full-sentence outline.* In this type of outline, you include a full statement indicating what each main point and subpoint cover. All the parts of the speech are included, even transitions. Generally, a formal outline should include the following:

- The specific purpose, stated as an infinitive phrase (to . . .), describing exactly what the speaker wants the speech to accomplish.

Speaking of . . .

Handling the Q&A

Frequently after a speech, you will be expected to take questions from the audience. You should not be fearful of this situation, as it is actually an opportunity to gain important feedback from your audience as well as to clarify points that may not have been completely understood. Successfully answering questions, even hostile ones, can add to your credibility as a speaker. The key is to regulate that feedback in a constructive manner. Some basic guidelines for handling the question-and-answer period following a speech are given below.[1]

Controversial filmmaker Michael Moore takes audience questions.

- *Announce at the outset that you will take questions at the end of your speech.* Under no circumstances take questions during the speech, as it will cause you to lose control of the situation. When audience members know they will have the opportunity to ask questions at the end of the speech, they will be able to think about them as you speak.
- *Overprepare for your speech.* You need to know more than you cover in the speech if you are to take questions. If you expect a hostile audience, it is a good idea to anticipate their toughest questions and prepare answers in advance.
- *Restate questions if they cannot be heard by all.* If you are speaking with a microphone, someone asking a question from the audience probably cannot be heard. Restating the question not only allows everyone to hear what was asked, it also allows you time to think of an answer. If a question is wordy, hostile, or imprecise, try to rephrase it in a way that neutralizes some of the problems with the question.
- *Answer questions directly with facts to back up your answers.* This requires you to be fully prepared. However, if you don't know the answer, just say so. You can always promise to obtain the facts and get back to the questioner at a later date. It is better to admit you don't know an answer than to be proved wrong because you tried to bluff your way through an answer.
- *Take questions from different audience members.* Don't let yourself get into a debate or an argument with one audience member. Insist that everyone who has a question gets a chance to ask it before you return to a previous questioner. Choose questioners from different parts of the room as well so that everyone feels he or she will get a chance.
- *Be brief.* Answer questions as succinctly as possible and move on to the next question. Overly long answers bore the audience and frustrate others who want to ask questions.
- *Announce when you are near the end of the Q&A.* When you sense the audience growing restless, the questions have become repetitive, or you are near the end of your allotted time, simply announce that you can take only one or two more questions.
- *At the end of the Q&A, restate the focus of your speech and summarize its essential points.* This is your chance to get in the last word and remind the audience of the basic theme of your speech. Depending on the situation, you may want to make yourself available for informal discussion after the speech.

[1]Some of these guidelines are based on a pamphlet by Robert Haakensan, *How to Handle the Q&A* (Philadelphia: Smith Kline & French Laboratories, Department of Public Relations, n.d.).

- Three sections–labeled introduction, body, and conclusion–each separately outlined and beginning with the Roman numeral "I."
- The introduction, including opening, thesis statement, connection with the audience, and preview.
- The body, including main points, subpoints, supporting points, and further support, and, if your instructor requires them, transitions (in parentheses) between the main points.
- The conclusion, including a summary and a close.
- "References" or "Works Cited" (depending on whether you use APA or MLA style). Specific quotations or facts drawn from a source should also be cited in the main outline. Of course, you should check with your instructor about the specific outlining requirements, if any, for your class. Some instructors prefer a different source citation system, for example, than the ones discussed in this text. Appendix A provides a Guide for Source Citation using APA and MLA formats.

Outlines typically use a standard outline notation, which indicates the levels of subordination of points:

I. Main point
  A. Subpoint
    1. Supporting point
      a. Further support

Any subdivision should include at least two matching points. Thus an "A" subpoint implies there should also be at least a "B." Supporting point "1" should be matched by at least a "2," and further support "a" should be followed by at least a "b."

Many instructors prefer that outlines be written in complete sentences, at least through the level of subpoints. This provides a clearer idea to your instructor of what you are going to say. Divide separate ideas into different sentences. If you outline using paragraph form, what you really have is an essay with outline notation scattered throughout. Thus, the following is not really in outline form:

I. The first men on the moon were Americans. Neil Armstrong stepped out first. He was followed by Buzz Aldrin. At the same time, Michael Collins orbited the moon.

This paragraph could be turned into the following outline:

I. The first men on the moon were Americans.
  A. Neil Armstrong stepped out first.
  B. He was followed by Buzz Aldrin.
  C. At the same time, Michael Collins orbited the moon.

Notice how each sentence is placed in a separate point. The more general statement is the main point, and the specific instances are subpoints.

Some aspects of an outline do not need to be in complete-sentence form. For example, a speaker who wants to list the components of a larger whole, such as ingredients or tools, could use an outline like this:

1. Cigarette smoke has three components:
  a. Carbon monoxide
  b. Nicotine
  c. Tar

In Their Own Words

Sample Speech Outline

Title of speech.

FLY INFESTATION
by Rosa Guzman

Rosa Guzman

Specific purpose is to provide the audience with information that can help them deal with a common problem.

Specific Purpose: To engage and provide the audience with knowledge and information on fly infestation.

Introduction

Speaker begins with a common occurrence all her audience members can relate to.

I. **Open with Impact:** Envision having lunch, when all of a sudden you notice a fly has landed on your food.
   A. Wouldn't you want to know where this fly came from?
   B. Flies, like any other type of species, have a biological history.
   C. If flies have a biological record, wouldn't you be interested in knowing if they've left a trace of it on your food?

Thesis statement is labeled, but may not fully convey the scope of the speech.

II. **Thesis:** Awareness of fly infestation is crucial when operating a business.

The speaker provides three reasons this topic is important to audience members.

III. **Connect:** Familiarizing yourself with the biology of flies may encourage you to help prevent fly infestation.
   A. It will enable you to manage a successful business
   B. If will facilitate satisfying your workers and customers.
   C. As a customer, it will enable you to enjoy an afternoon meal at a business.

Preview of speech is provided.

IV. **Preview:** Today I will inform you about flies as well as fly infestation and the prevention of it at a business or even your own home.

Body of speech is labeled.

Body

Main points begin with Roman numeral I.

I. **Main Point:** There are three basic ways of knowing there's a fly infestation.
   A. More than eight flies in a given area could be considered a potential fly infestation.
   B. The detection of nearby larva (AKA... maggots) could serve as evidence of a fly infestation.
   C. Live insects with dead insects and fly spots or droppings.

Note transitional statements between main points.

(**Transition:** Now that you know the three basic ways of knowing there's a fly infestation, let's learn about the biological evolution of flies.)

II. **Main Point:** The biology of a fly includes its life stages, physical characteristics, and traits.

References cited in the speech are listed by author name and date in parentheses.

   A. A house fly has four life stages (Yeats, 2005).
      1. The first stage is the egg.
      2. The second stage is the larva.

3. The third stage is the pupa.
4. The fourth stage is the adult.

B. There are several physical characteristics of a fly.
1. A fly smells through a pair of stick-like feelers between the eyes.
a. The feelers make it possible for the files to catch odors humans can't smell.
b. The short hairs on a fly's feet help it keep from falling off a wall or ceiling.
2. All sorts of germs are attached to a fly's stick-padded feet.
a. The diseases include Amoebic dysentery, leprosy, and tuberculosis.
b. The average number of germs found on a fly's body is 1,250,000 and can go as high as 6,600,000.
3. A fly only consumes liquid.

C. There is a specific trait a fly has to have in order to survive.
1. Flies must convert their food into liquid.
2. It regurgitates liquids already swallowed, waits until the surface is softened and liquefied, and then re-swallows.

(**Transition:** Knowing about the biology of a fly is important; this brings me to my final point.)

III. **Main Point:** There are ways of eliminating flies from a fly infested business. (Illinois Department of Public Health, 2005)
A. Insect proofing.
B. Removal of breeding environment.
C. Professional help; contact your nearest pest control business.
D. Proper sanitation.

Conclusion

Conclusion is labeled and begins with a new Roman numeral I.
Main points summarized.

I. **Summarize:** In conclusion, the biology of a fly may help you prevent a future fly infestation.
A. Know the signs of a fly infestation.
B. Know the physical traits and characteristics of a fly.
C. Know how to eliminate a fly infestation.

II. **Close with impact:** Let's hope a fly doesn't land on your food today!

Speech closes by returning to opening scenario.

Speaker lists references at end of speech with full bibliographic citation. We discuss American Psychological Association (APA) and Modern Language Association (MLA) methods of source citation in Appendix A. Your instructor may prefer a different method of citing sources. Whatever method is used, accurate source citation is important. Specific facts taken from sources should be noted in the outline where they are used.

References

Beat fly infestations with regular monitoring. (2005, May). *Poultry World,* 159 (6), 21

Illinois Department of Public Health. (2005). *The house fly and other filth flies.* Retrieved September 25, 2006, from www.idph.state.il.us/envhealth/pcfilthflies.htm

Rentokil Pest Control United Kingdom. (2006). *Flies pest control.* Retrieved September 25, 2006, from www.uk.rentokil.com

Yeats, D., & Wiegmann, B. (2005). *The evolutionary biology of flies.* New York: Columbia University Press.

To view a video of Rosa Guzman's speech, click on the Speech Coach link on our Online Learning Center Web site, and go to Segment 9.1.

You need to use judgment, therefore, when you are asked to write a complete-sentence outline. Use complete sentences for your main points and subpoints and anywhere the meaning would not be clear if not expressed in complete-sentence form. The box "Sample Speech Outline: Fly Infestation" by Rosa Guzman follows the suggested format. Remember, however, to check with your instructor for specific requirements in your class.

Preparing Speaker's Notes

speaker's notes Brief notes with key words, usually written on cards, used by a speaker when presenting a speech.

The outline is a preparation tool. How you use this tool exactly depends on the preferences of your instructor. For our own students, however, one option is to use **speaker's notes**, which are brief notes with key words, usually written on cards. Final notes should be meaningful to the speaker, but not necessarily to anyone else. Whatever notes are used, it is important to rehearse until it is unnecessary to look at the note cards frequently. It is especially important to know the introduction and conclusion very well. The best open or close to a speech can be undone by a speaker who reads it from cards rather than making direct eye contact with the audience.

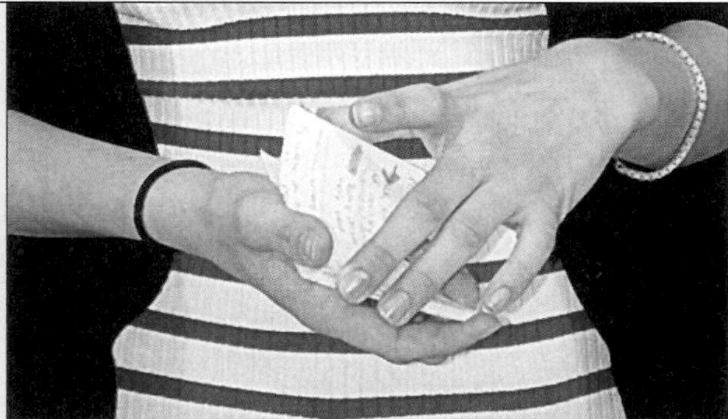

This student uses note cards that she has highlighted for quick reference.

Cards about 4 by 6 inches in size seem to work best. Larger cards are too obtrusive; smaller cards require us to strain to see our notes and to constantly be shuffling them. The following are some helpful hints for preparing note cards should you choose to do so.

Tips and Tactics

Tips for Preparing Speaker's Notes

- *Use bright colors and large, bold lettering.* This will make the notes easier to see.
- *Use no more than five or six lines per note card if cards are used.* If too much is crammed on one card, it will be confusing.
- *Put each part of a speech on a separate card or page.* For example, the introduction might go on one, the body on another, and the conclusion on a third.
- *Number the cards or pages.* It is easy to lose track of your place while speaking. One way to help prevent this from happening is to number each card or page.
- *Write on only one side of a card or page.* Writing on both sides compounds the chances of losing your place.
- *Highlight main ideas.* Just like highlighting key passages in books, highlight the points you wish to emphasize.
- *Use notes to make comments to yourself.* It is perfectly appropriate, for example, to write prompts on notes. For example, write "O.H." to remind yourself to show an overhead at that point in the speech.
- *Don't try to write out the speech word for word.* This only encourages reading the speech rather than presenting it in a conversational manner. The only exception to this rule would be exact quotations, facts, or statistics, which obviously need to be written out.

Speaker's notes contain all the same ideas as the complete outline, but the words are designed to cue us to what comes next. Practice is needed to speak from these notes and still be assured of covering all the ideas in the original outline. And this is the final point we wish to make: Successful speakers practice prior to an actual presentation. No matter how good the organization seems, it is only as good as the speaker's ability to deliver it. That takes practice. And practice doesn't mean running through the speech the night before or, even worse, the morning of the presentation. It means devoting significant amounts of time to practicing the speech until we have internalized its basic organization.

Summary

To effectively organize a speech:

- Focus on the audience when organizing the speech.
- Refine the specific purpose.
- Create a clear thesis statement.

To evaluate your understanding of this chapter, visit our Online Learning Center Web site for quizzes and other chapter study aids.

Organize the body of the speech before tackling the introduction or conclusion. Remember that:

- Two to five focused main points should fully develop the thesis statement.
- Use parallel structure, simplicity, and balance.
- Develop main points by using subpoints, supporting points, and further support.

Organize the speech body in one of several patterns:

- Time
- Spatial
- Categorical
- Extended Narrative
- Alphabetical
- Problem–Solution
- Stock Issues
- Refutational
- Comparative Advantage
- Causal
- Motivated-Sequence
- Wave
- Spiral
- Star

Use transitional statements to help the audience follow the organization of the speech.

The introduction to a speech should:

- Open with impact
- Focus on the thesis statement
- Connect with the audience
- Preview the body of the speech

Effective openings may include:

- A brief story
- A quotation
- A startling statement
- Reference to the audience
- The occasion, or a current event

- Appropriate humor
- A personal experience
- A thought-provoking question

The conclusion to a speech should:

- Summarize the main points of the speech
- Close with impact

Ways to close include:

- Quotation
- Brief anecdote
- Direct appeal to action
- Return to the opening theme

A formal outline is sometimes required of beginning speakers. Many instructors prefer students to use standard outline notation and write a complete-sentence outline.

Speaker's notes, usually placed on small cards or pages, can be used when presenting the speech.

Check Your Understanding: Exercises and Activities

1. Consider the following speech introductions. Rewrite them to fit the "open, focus, connect, and preview" model suggested in this chapter.

   Today, I'm going to talk to you about pit bulls. I got attacked last week by a pit bull, and I think they are really dangerous. Something's got to be done!

   Have any of you ever thought about going snowboarding? I really like to snowboard, and that's what my speech is going to be about.

   I think capital punishment is wrong. What if somebody who was innocent got killed? I'm going to persuade all of you that life without parole is a better way to go.

2. View a speech on our Online Learning Center Web site at www.mhhe.com/brydon6. Using the format described in this chapter, construct a complete-sentence outline of the speech. How closely did the speech seem to follow the steps indicated in the chapter? Was the speech easy to outline? If not, how could the speaker have made the organization clearer?

3. Analyze a print ad in a magazine or newspaper to see whether it uses a problem–solution, causal, or motivated-sequence. If so, explain how each step is fulfilled. If not, discuss how the ad might be modified to fit one of these organizational patterns.

4. On the following pages is an outline of a speech, followed by a list of points in scrambled order. Your task is to match the appropriate sentence from the scrambled list with the points in the outline. This may be done as an individual or a group exercise, depending on your instructor's preference.

Specific purpose: ______________________________

Introduction

I. Open with impact: ______________________________

II. Focus on the thesis statement: ______________________________

III. Connect with your audience: ______________________________

IV. Preview: ______________________________

Body

I. Main point: ______________________________

A. ______________________________

B. ______________________________

C. ______________________________

(*Transition:* ______________________________)

II. Main point: ______________________________

A. ______________________________

B. ______________________________

C. ______________________________

(*Transition:* ______________________________)

III. Main point: ______________________________

A. ______________________________

B. ______________________________

C. ______________________________

Conclusion

I. Summarize: ______________________________

A. ______________________________

B. ______________________________

C. ______________________________

II. Close with impact: ______________________________

Scrambled list:

1. Use fresh bread, preferably whole grain.
2. Use a quality jelly or jam, made without artificial additives.
3. Use either plain or chunky peanut butter.
4. You must have the necessary ingredients.
5. Fold the wax paper neatly around the sandwich.
6. Place the sandwich in a paper bag.
7. Use a biodegradable wrapper, such as wax paper, rather than plastic wrap.
8. You need to package the sandwich to take to school.
9. Put the two slices together.
10. Spread the first slice with peanut butter.
11. Spread the other slice with jelly or jam.
12. You need to assemble the sandwich.
13. To inform the class how to make a peanut butter and jelly sandwich.
14. First make sure you have the necessary ingredients.
15. Finally, wrap the sandwich.
16. Second, assemble the sandwich.
17. Enjoy your lunch and go to a movie with the money you've saved.
18. You can save money and eat better.
19. Today you will learn how to make the perfect peanut butter and jelly sandwich.
20. Are you tired of spending $5 for a greasy hamburger and fries?
21. Making a peanut butter and jelly sandwich involves three basic steps: having the ingredients, assembling the sandwich, and packaging the sandwich.
22. After you have the ingredients, you need to make the sandwich.
23. Unless you are eating it immediately, the sandwich must be wrapped to stay fresh.
24. To review, there are three steps:

Notes

1. American Cancer Society, "Check and Protect Your Skin," 30 April 2007. [Retrieved from http://www.cancer.org/docroot/SPC/content/SPC_1_Skin_Cancer_Protection_and Detection_Feature.asp, 25 May 2007.]
2. Alan Monroe, *Principles and Types of Speech* (New York: Scott, Foresman, 1935). See also the most recent edition: Bruce E. Gronbeck, Raymie E. McKerrow, Douglas Ehninger, and Alan H. Monroe, *Principles and Types of Speech Communication*, 12th ed. (New York: HarperCollins, 1994).

3. Cited in Clella Jaffe, *Public Speaking:* A *Cultural Perspective* (Belmont, Calif.: Wadsworth, 1995), 187–92. Based on a telephone interview by Jaffe with Jorgensen-Earp, as well as the latter's unpublished works.
4. Jay Silverman, Elaine Hughes, and Diana Roberts Wienbroer, *Rules of Thumb*: *A Guide for Writers* (New York: McGraw-Hill, 1990), 99.
5. Mary Schoenthaler, "Tattoos v. Mehndi," speech delivered at California State University, Chico, 24 April 1999.
6. Russ Woody, "Commencement Address," speech delivered at California State University, Chico, 23 May 1998.
7. Deidra Dukes, "The Right to Breathe," speech delivered at California State University, Chico, 1992.

Stephen Colbert treats his audience to a segment titled "The Word" on his popular show *The Colbert Report*.

Language: Making Verbal Sense of the Message

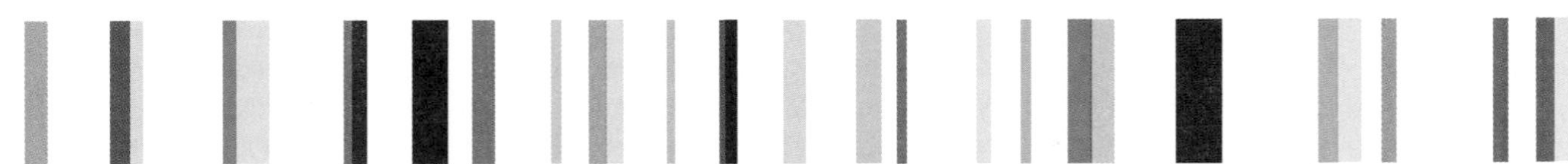

Objectives

After reading this chapter and reviewing the online learning resources at http://www.mhhe.com/brydon6, you should be able to:

- Construct examples that illustrate the relationship between language and thought.
- Describe the role language plays in relating to cultural, demographic, and individual diversity.
- Use rhetorical devices such as metaphor and simile to vary language intensity in your speeches.
- Use concrete language, as well as contrast and action, to reduce uncertainty on the part of your audience.
- Use verbal immediacy and transitional devices in your speeches.
- Avoid marginalizing and totalizing language, using inclusive language instead.
- Avoid sexist and stereotypic language.

Key Concepts

analogy
antithesis
credibility-enhancing language
immediate language
inclusive language
language
language intensity
linguistic relativity hypothesis
marginalizing language
metaphor
receiver-centric
sexist language
simile
totalizing language
verbal qualifiers

" How can I tell what I think until I see what I say? "

–EDWARD MORGAN FORSTER[1]

Whether or not satirist extraordinaire Stephen Colbert took a course in general semantics while attending Northwestern University, we cannot say. But it's clear that he understands the importance of words and language and skillfully uses them to skewer those naive enough to believe that, "Sticks and stones may break their bones but words will never hurt them." With tongue firmly in cheek, for example, Colbert treats viewers of his hit show on Comedy Central to a nightly feature he calls, "The Word." During the inaugural show of the *Colbert Report*, he even introduced his audience to a word of his own invention: "Truthiness."

According to Colbert, truthiness is a condition that describes people who base their opinions on gut reaction rather than the reasoning and evidence demanded by models of argument. Truthiness is a product of what people feel intuitively, rather than reason logically. Thus, a person in a state of truthiness might say, "I don't know . . . I just *feel* like I can trust the guy," rather than, "I trust him because he's given me example after example of the fact that I can."

Although truthiness was named word of the year by the dictionary folks at Merriam-Webster in 2006, it remains to be seen whether it becomes a part of people's accepted vocabulary. Even so, its example illustrates a point we will make repeatedly in this chapter. Language is a living and dynamic feature of the communication landscape. The words we choose to string together to express ourselves change. They change because the evolving world in which we live requires it.

This chapter links words and language to the art and science of public speaking. Our goal is twofold. First, we want to demonstrate how people use words and language to shape the world we see and think about. Second, we want to show how you can use words and language to breathe life into your speeches so that audiences can share the world you see and think about. Topics we will cover include:

- How words and language relate to what we see and think
- How understanding words and language assist us in audience analysis
- And how we can actually use language to make our speeches instruments of understanding and influence.

Word Power

language
The rule-governed word system we use to verbally commmunicate.

Language is the rule-governed word system we use to verbally communicate. Stripped to the barest of essentials, words are symbolic substitutes for the things they represent. The word *chair* is not the actual thing, for example, but a symbolic representation of it. And the word *love* is not the emotion that prompts us to use it in conjunction with someone about whom we care deeply. Yet the power these "symbolic substitutes" have in shaping what we think or feel about persons, places, and things can be mind-boggling.

There is considerable evidence, for example, that words "frame" how we see the world and how we interpret our experience. Knowing this, people who hope to influence us choose specific words and phrases to maximize the chances that we will interpret their messages as *they* intend them to be interpreted. When

Self-Assessment

Language Sensitivity

Read each response and record whether you Strongly Agree (SA), Agree (A), Neither Agree nor Disagree (N), Disagree (D), or Strongly Disagree (SD) with the statement.

1. I am always mindful of the words and phrases I use to express myself.	SA	A	N	D	SD
2. I try to avoid using offensive words and phrases.	SA	A	N	D	SD
3. I try to avoid speaking in clichés.	SA	A	N	D	SD
4. I can express myself without using slang.	SA	A	N	D	SD
5. I try not to use colloquial expressions excessively.	SA	A	N	D	SD
6. I can easily switch from informal to formal speech.	SA	A	N	D	SD
7. I try to adapt my language to different people and situations.	SA	A	N	D	SD
8. I can be clear and eloquent.	SA	A	N	D	SD
9. I am not turned off by people who use words I don't know.	SA	A	N	D	SD
10. I am not easily put-off by words I judge offensive.	SA	A	N	D	SD

SA=5 A=4 N=3 D=2 SD=1

Add your score using the preceding scale.

successful, such people shape both the meaning we give to words and phrases and how we react to their referents.

As a case in point, the words and phrases politicians repeatedly use to describe themselves and define issues are no accident. They are the result of consultants, focus groups, and surveys of people just like us. Think about two "hot button" issues that have characterized recent political campaigns: taxes and abortion.

One of the best examples of how the meaning of words can be manipulated is the federal tax levied on a family's inheritance. Even though less than one percent of all families are touched by this tax, many politicians rail against this "death tax" as if 99 percent of all families will have to pay it.

Another example involves how politicians have distorted the abortion debate by framing it with the terms pro-choice and pro-life. Survey after survey shows that abortion is not a black and white issue. Most people believe that while abortion should be a last resort, it should still be an option in a majority of cases. The term pro-choice lets politicians avoid the more evocative term, pro-abortion. It also helps them avoid being specific about where they do or do not draw the line in terms of a "woman's right to choose." Of course, the term pro-life accomplishes the same thing for politicians who want to avoid saying that, in most cases, they believe a woman's only choice is to give birth.

We are not suggesting that you should model your use of words and phrases after that of people who put politics above principles. However, we do want you to critically examine the relationship between words, phrases, and thought. We also want you to examine how you can use your knowledge of audience analysis to choose words and phrases for your speeches that will help share

Speaking of . . .

Linguistic Relativity

linguistic relativity hypothesis
The idea that what prople perceive is influenced by the language in which they think and speak.

What is true of individual words is even more true of the language you speak. Whether you speak English, French, Spanish, or Russian makes a difference in how you experience and interpret the world. According to the **linguistic relativity hypothesis,** introduced more than 40 years ago by cultural anthropologist Benjamin Whorf, what we perceive is influenced by the language in which we think and speak. Different languages lead to different patterns of thought.[2]

Whorf formulated this hypothesis while studying the Native American language of the Hopi. He discovered there are no words in their language for the concept of incremental time: no seconds, no minutes, and no hours. Thus it would never occur to the Hopi that someone could be half an hour early or late for a visit, because they have no words for the concept.

Each language has certain concepts that cannot be easily expressed in other languages. The expression "something was lost in the translation" doesn't mean part of a statement was literally lost as it was translated from one language to another. It means an identical idea couldn't be found in the second language, so part of the statement's original meaning was diminished.

[2]Benjamin Lee Whorf, *Language, Thought, and Reality* (New York: Wiley, 1956).

your vision with individual audience members. This process begins with the difficult task of assessing the role language plays in your general life, and the role it can potentially play in the preparation and delivery of your speeches. For example, before reading any further, respond to the self-assessment box, which concerns: (1) how you use a language and (2) how you respond to others' use of language.

If you carefully read and truthfully responded to the statements in the self-assessment box, your summed scored should reveal the degree to which you are aware of how your language can affect others, and how others' language can affect you. While clichés, slang, and colloquialisms are usually okay in a conversation with friends, they are inappropriate in a job interview. They also should be avoided or only used with a specific purpose in mind in your speeches. When you adapt your language to people and situations or switch from informal to formal language, it shows that you are mindful of this fact.

receiver-centric
A person's assumption that the meaning he or she gives to a word or a phrase is its exclusive meaning.

Your reaction to others' language also is an indication of how flexible or inflexible you are in giving meaning to words and phrases. Some people are **receiver-centric**–easily turned off to a speaker's language. Receiver-centric audience members apply a very narrow range of meaning to words. Without consulting either the speaker, other audience members, or considering how the context comes into play, receiver-centric audience members force their meaning on the message. Words can, and very often do, have diverse meanings depending on the context in which they are used and the life experiences of those using them; you can read about this in the box "Speaking of . . . Linguistic Relativity." What's more, the speech transaction is not a one-way street where the speaker or the audience member controls meaning. Simply said, the more we know about the nuances of words and language, the better equipped we are to make good use of them in conversation and speeches. Similarly, the more we know about

This ad uses words to describe snow conditions rich in imagery for skiers and snowboarders but meaningless for those not involved in these sports.

words and language, the better equipped we will be as audience members in formulating a thoughtful impression of what a speaker is trying to say.

Last year, people skied on champagne powder, windblown pack, groomed, corn snow, cold smoke, frozen granular, firm, good crud, bottomless powder, sugar, machine tilled, crust, hero powder, buffed snow, man made, corduroy, ball bearings, velvet, cut up powder, spring snow, ballroom, and acre after acre of virgin powder.
[*Eskimos may have more words for snow, but we have more lifts.*]
THE ASPENS
SNOWMASS • BUTTERMILK
ASPEN MOUNTAIN
Aspen Central Reservations 1-800-262-7736 Snowmass Central Reservations 1-800-332-3245.
The Aspen Skiing Company Hotels: The Little Nell, The Snowmass Club 1-800-525-6200.

Language and Audience Analysis

Having seen that words and language color people's perception and experience, we can now examine the relationship between language and the three types of diversity (cultural, demographic, and individual) introduced in Chapter 7. Understanding the connections between language and diversity is crucial to effective speaking because today's audience is more diverse than ever.

Language and Cultural Diversity

The United States is a multiracial, multiethnic, multicultural nation. With the exception of Native Americans, 98 percent of the population can trace its ancestry to another country.

Recall from Chapter 7 that *cultural diversity* is multidimensional, including audience characteristics such as individualism/collectivism and masculinity/femininity. Knowing something about the dimensions of culture reflected in the audience is essential to choosing appropriate language for a speech.

One of the authors, for example, had the opportunity to attend an IBM recognition event where former NFL quarterback and Monday Night football announcer Joe Theismann was one of the keynote speakers. Theismann's audience included many people from IBM operations in the Far East and Latin America, both of which are largely collectivistic in outlook. Although most North Americans in the audience responded positively to Theismann's speech, not everyone did. His remarks were perceived as egotistical and self-aggrandizing by people from such places as Japan, Taiwan, Singapore, Argentina, and Venezuela. As one person from Buenos Aires remarked, "You would have thought American football was an individual sport listening to him [Theismann]–that he won the Super Bowl single-handedly. Does he know a word other than I?"

All too often speakers choose language appropriate to their culture, but not necessarily to the cultures of their audience members. Like Theismann, they naively assume that what is good enough for their culture is good enough for everyone's. Of course, this kind of thinking is not only inaccurate, it is arrogant.

Even commonplace language choices, such as what name to call a person, can be influenced by culture. In many, such as those that use the Spanish language, strangers are not addressed informally, and certainly not by their first names. A salesperson, for example, who addresses a potential client by his or her first name may, unintentionally, offend that person. Yet this is commonplace in the U.S. The best advice is to ask people how they prefer to be addressed rather than automatically assuming that they want to be on a first-name basis.

Language and Demographic Diversity

Recall from Chapter 7 that *demographic diversity* is reflected in the groups to which people belong and with which they identify. This includes such characteristics as nationality, race and ethnicity, gender, and religion. Demographic diversity also includes social and economic class, the region of the country that people call home, and the generation to which people belong.

Demographic diversity, although always an important consideration of a speaker's audience analysis, has become even more so. Today's college classroom is likely to be populated by people with a variety of different demographic backgrounds. Race and ethnicity, as cases in point, are often an important part of today's audience diversity.

How we refer to a specific racial or ethnic group can have a strong impact on the individual members of that group in our audience. For example, when Anglos speak to a gathering of English-speaking people of Mexican descent, they need to choose the appropriate language in referring to the audience. Scholars Mario Garcia and Rodolfo Alvarez suggest that people of Mexican descent in

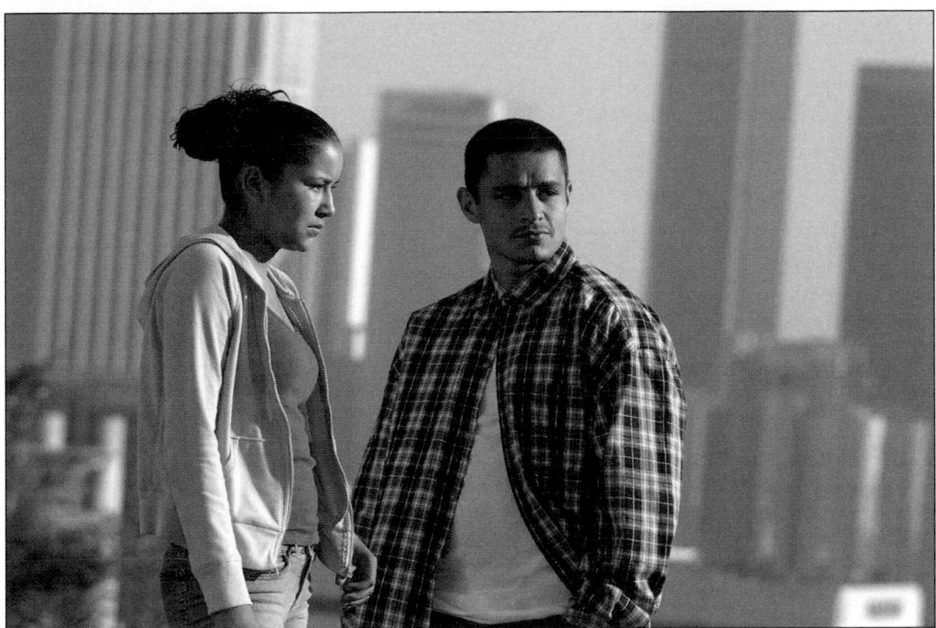

The 2006 Sundance Film Festival award winner, *Quinceañera,* tells the story of a young Latina girl, Magdalena, who becomes pregnant on the brink of her 15 birthday and is cast out by her parents, forcing her to live in a very different culture than that of her middle class upbringing.

the United States constitute several rather than a single demographic group.[2] Two such reference groups are Mexican Americans and Chicanos/Chicanas. The Mexican American group comprises people who immigrated from Mexico to border states, such as California and Texas, following World War II. According to Garcia and Alvarez, people who consider themselves Mexican Americans are generally older and more conservative than those who identify themselves as Chicanos or Chicanas, who are generally younger and more militant.

Chicanos and Chicanas came of age in the 1960s and gained some attention in the 1970s. They perceived Mexican immigrants who wanted to assimilate with the predominant Anglo culture as sellouts. To distinguish themselves from the Mexican American group, Chicanos and Chicanas adopted specific patterns of behaving, including their own code words. The list of code words included *vendido* (sellout) and *socios* (the old boy network). Today, members of this demographic group sometimes refer to each other as *veteranos* (veterans). Thus, referring to Chicanos/Chicanas as Mexican Americans in a speech could prove inappropriate even though you were trying to be responsive to ethnicity. As speakers, we need to learn as much as possible about the language preferences of our audiences. Otherwise, we may inadvertently lose at least some of them.

The varied preferences of Spanish-speaking people apply to many other demographic groups as well. Some African Americans prefer being referred to as Black. And though they may be too polite to tell you so, the Chinese, Hmong, Japanese, Korean, Laotian, and Vietnamese prefer being referred to by their nationality rather than being categorized as Asian.

As speakers, we cannot afford to overlook the demography of our audience in choosing language. How we refer to people who identify themselves with specific demographic groups and the words we use in talking about the demographic groups themselves will influence not only how the content of our speech is received but audience perceptions of our credibility as well.

Language and Individual Diversity

Choosing appropriate language for a speech doesn't stop with a consideration of cultural and demographic diversity. We also must consider and evaluate *individual diversity*, which reflects such factors as personal views on the meaning of gender, sexual orientation, and religious beliefs. The fact that someone is Catholic, Jewish, Muslim, Hindu, or Protestant, for example, doesn't tell us much about the diversity of beliefs held by people who consider themselves members of one of these religious groups. Moreover, religious beliefs are only one element of the individual diversity of our audience. Consequently, before choosing the language with which to construct a speech, we will also have to explore other individual beliefs, attitudes, and values of the people in our audience.

As a case in point, think about an audience of people who describe themselves as Christians. Such people are extraordinarily diverse in what they believe individually. Some think the Bible is to be taken literally as the word of God; others believe the Bible should be interpreted metaphorically. Knowing this kind of information in advance is essential for speakers who want the language of their speech to be effective.

Remember, the words and sentences with which we construct the speech will influence the meaning of our speech in the minds of the audience members. We want to control this process as much as possible. Thus, doing our homework about the relationship between language and diversity as it reflects our speech transaction is a matter of common sense, not political correctness.

Tips and Tactics — Language and Audience Diversity

- Be mindful of how words and phrases can shape meaning.
- Consider how you use words to "frame" debates and discussions.
- Actively search for information about the role of language in cultures other than the one with which you most identify.
- Exercise caution when labeling demographic groups . . . don't assume that there is a one-size-fits-all word for people in ethnic or religious groups.
- When possible, use words and language that reflect the individual diversity in your audience.

Using Language Effectively

Let's assume that we have thoroughly analyzed how audience diversity should be reflected in our choice of words to construct our speech. We are now ready to begin writing the outline of our speech with language that will enhance our credibility with the audience and create a high degree of mutual understanding. There are a number of guidelines to follow in this process. The first rule is to choose language appropriate to the rhetorical situation. The second rule concerns choosing language that makes every member of our audience feel included in our message. This is known as inclusive language, as opposed to marginalizing or totalizing language, concepts we will explain shortly. The third rule concerns choosing language that will enhance rather than undermine audience perceptions of our competence and trustworthiness as a speaker.[3] The fourth rule concerns using language to its fullest potential to involve our audience in the speech. The fifth rule focuses on using language that will help us manage our speech, and help our audience understand what we want to communicate.

Use Language Appropriate to the Rhetorical Situation

The language of a speech needs to reflect the overall rhetorical situation we face, not just audience members. In addition to being appropriate to audience diversity, language also should be appropriate to the context in which we find ourselves. We've learned that we can face the same or similar audience in very different contexts. For example, we have given speeches honoring a retiring colleague to an audience that also has listened to us argue in a speech that a policy proposed by the university administration should be rejected. Although the audience was the same, our rhetoric, in style and in substance, was different.

Along the same lines, language should reflect the purpose of a speech and the goal we hope to achieve. An informative speech demonstrating how to read a company's annual report requires language very different from a persuasive speech advocating the replacement of the company's Board of Directors.

Use Inclusive Language

The next rule in choosing the words of a speech is to use language that is inclusive. **Inclusive language** helps people believe that they not only have a stake in matters of societal importance but also have power in this regard. Inclusive language doesn't leave people out of the picture because of their gender, race, ethnicity, age, religion, sexual orientation, or ability. Put another way, inclusive language doesn't marginalize people.

Marginalizing language diminishes people's importance and makes them appear to be less powerful, less significant, and less worthwhile than they are. Marginalizing language also appeals to biases audience members may hold consciously or subconsciously.

At the same time, inclusive language doesn't totalize people.

Totalizing language defines people on the basis of a single attribute, such as race, ethnicity, biological sex, or disability. In a speech, the following statements would exemplify totalizing:

"The dyslexics in this audience . . ."

"As a woman, you've got to learn to assert yourself."

"As a victim of racism . . ."

inclusive language
Language that helps people believe that they not only have a stake in matters of societal importance but also have power in this regard.

marginalizing language
Language that diminishes people's importance and makes them appear to be less powerful, less significant, and less worthwhile than they are.

totalizing language
Language that defines people exclusively on the basis of a single attribute, such as race, ethnicity, biological sex, or ability.

"Because you are Latino . . ."

"This is really a guy book."

Each of these statements could be well-meaning and intended to demonstrate the speaker's sensitivity to people with disabilities, women, Latinos, and men. Yet what each statement does in reality is call attention to a single attribute among audience members and treat the attribute as if it were the only thing about audience members that truly counts. People are more than their disability, women and men are more than their biological sex, and people discriminated against by racists are more than simply victims. Speakers need to use language that acknowledges that people are complex individuals.

immediate language Language that reduces the psychological distance that separates speakers and audience members and stresses that speech is a transaction.

Finally, inclusive language is **immediate language**; it reduces the perception that people are psychologically distant from each other–with little or nothing in common. Remember the example of Joe Theismann? His use of the personal pronoun "I" actually made him seem more distant from members of the audience. Inclusive language emphasizes the fact that a speaker and audience are a collective rather than two separate entities. For example, the late Barbara Jordan not only used immediate language in her distinguished political career, she also spoke eloquently about inclusive speech. Both facts are featured in her speech, "We, the People," printed in the box on page 263.

Lest you think otherwise, inclusive language is not the same as the politically correct language talk show hosts justifiably satirize. Inclusive language is firmly rooted in the ethical principles we introduced in Chapter 5. Consider inclusive language in terms of Immanuel Kant's categorical imperative. Have you ever had someone use language to purposely hurt you? Did you think the language was justified or mean-spirited?

We need to think through what motivates us to use certain words and phrases before we use them. We also need to weigh the possible consequences of these words and phrases before speaking them. And we need to ask ourselves ahead of time, how would we interpret and respond to words and phrases if they or their equivalents were directed at us?

We are not saying that you must avoid critical words and phrases in your verbal characterizations of people. We are simply asking you to put the shoe on the other foot to first measure how you think you would respond in similar circumstances.

Tips and Tactics

Inclusive Language

1. Inclusive language avoids defining people on the basis of their gender, sexual orientation, disability, racial, ethnic, or religious identity. Inclusive language uses terms such as *humankind* rather than *mankind, athlete* rather than *woman athlete,* and *friend* rather than *Islamic friend.*
2. Inclusive language reflects the self-referents used by the members of a minority group; for example, *gay* or *lesbian* rather than *homosexuals* and *person with a disability* rather than *disabled person.*
3. Inclusive language is immediate. As you can read in Exhibit 11.1, it's about *we* rather than *me* and *us* rather than *you and I.*

In Their Own Words

"We, the People" *by Barbara Jordan*

We are dedicated to keeping the memory of Barbara Jordan alive. Recipient of the Presidential Medal of Freedom, Congresswoman and State Senator from Texas, she was arguably one of the most gifted speakers of the 20th-century. Many experts regard her keynote address to the Democratic Convention in 1976 as the top political speech in modern history. Here is a brief excerpt of her statements during the debate on the impeachment of President Nixon in 1974:

We, the people. It is a very eloquent beginning. But when that document was completed on the 17th of September in 1787, I was not included in that "We, the people." I felt somehow for many years that George Washington and Alexander Hamilton just left me out by mistake. But through the process of amendment, interpretation and court decision I have finally been included in "We, the people."[1]

Two decades later, Jordan was asked to head the United States Commission on Immigration Reform. Testifying before the very congressional committee of which she was once a member, Jordan echoed her words from long ago:

I would be the last person to claim that our nation is perfect. But we have a kind of perfection in us because our founding principle is universal—that we are all created equal regardless of race, religion or national ancestry. When the Declaration of Independence was written, when the Constitution was adopted, when the Bill of Rights was added to it, they all applied almost exclusively to white men of Anglo-Saxon descent who owned property on the East Coast. They did not apply to me. I am female. I am black. But these self-evident principles apply to me now as they apply to everyone in this room.[2]

[1] "Barbara Jordan: A Passionate Voice," *Sacramento Bee,* 18 January 1996, A16.

[2] Jerelyn Eddings, "The Voice of Eloquent Thunder," *U.S. News and World Report,* 29 January 1996, 16.

Exhibit 11.1

How to Say It More Immediately

Less Immediate	More Immediate
I Me You Them	We Us
I think It's my opinion I know	Wouldn't you agree? How many of us believe . . . ?
Tell Show Explain	Share Look at
Talk to	Talk with

Use Credibility-Enhancing Language

In Chapter 5 we discussed credibility in terms of the relationship between ethical conduct and perceptions of the speaker's trustworthiness. Here we want to emphasize that credibility also depends on whether audience members perceive that a speaker is a competent source of information. Does the speaker appear to know what he or she is talking about?

How speakers use language influences perceptions of competence in the eyes of audience members. For example, a number of researchers have documented that there is a difference between "powerful" and "powerless" speech.[4] Powerless speech is characterized by the use of language such as hedges (I *kind of* agree with you), qualifiers (I *could* be wrong), hesitations (uhs and ums), and tag questions (That's right, *isn't it?*). On the other hand, powerful speech is fluent and direct and avoids these types of phrases. Messages containing a significant amount of powerless language produce lower ratings of a speaker's competence and attractiveness, whereas powerful speech produces higher ratings on these dimensions.

credibility-enhancing language
Words that emphasize rather than undermine audience perceptions of a speaker's competence.

verbal qualifiers
Words and phrases that erode the impact of what a speaker says in a speech.

Therefore, the third rule to follow in constructing the text of our speech is to use powerful, **credibility-enhancing language**, words that emphasize rather than undermine audience perceptions of our competence. Language that enhances perceptions of competence avoids verbal qualifiers.[5] **Verbal qualifiers** erode the impact of what we say in a speech.

Beginning speakers often use verbal qualifiers without thinking of them as such. They say, for example:

"It's just my opinion, but . . ."

"You'll probably disagree, but . . ."

"This is my belief, but you may think otherwise."

"I'm pretty sure, though I could be wrong in stating . . ."

"Of course, your opinion counts at least as much as mine."

Credibility-enhancing language emphasizes the significance of what we say in a speech. Whether giving an informative, persuasive, or testimonial speech, we should be the expert on the subject or person. Not only does this require that we do our homework, it also requires that we choose language that illustrates the fact. Using language such as the following is one way of accomplishing this without appearing to be a "know-it-all" to the audience.

"Ten years of research demonstrates that . . ."

"For the past four summers, I've been involved with . . ."

"I recently was certified to . . ."

"Scholars tell us . . ."

Each of these statements begins with a phrase that emphasizes the speaker's credibility. They imply that through either research or experience, the speaker knows his or her subject well. We should not exaggerate claims beyond what we know to be true, but we should take full credit for the facts as we know them. This is not to say that we should never qualify what we say. In persuasive speeches, especially, the evidence may demand that we temper the claims we make. It is unethical to make an absolute claim in a persuasive speech when the evidence only partly supports the claim. This is another reason for conducting research on the topic prior to constructing a speech.

There are other ways to use language to increase the audience's perception of our competence. Some of the best are also the most obvious. They include using correct grammar, correct pronunciation, and correct usage of a word. Although we can get away with grammatically incorrect language in conversation, it usually sticks out like a sore thumb when speaking in public.

Grammar

In an otherwise effective speech on educational reform, for example, President Bush asked his audience, "Is your children learning?" He meant to say, "Are your children learning?" Although this was but a single grammatical mistake, it became the most memorable part of the speech in terms of what was written and said about it afterwards.

Some of the most common grammatical mistakes we hear in our own students' speech are double negatives, incorrect subject-verb agreement, and inappropriate slang.

A double negative occurs when someone uses a negative to modify another negative. As in mathematics, a negative times a negative is actually a positive. Thus, "No one never works around here" really means that there is no person who "never works." That suggests people really do work–the opposite of what the speaker intended.

Incorrect subject-verb agreement occurs when a plural subject is matched with a singular verb or vice versa. Avoid such sentences as "We is going to the movies."

Finally, unless they are essential to the speech, certain expressions common in everyday conversation are inappropriate in a speech. Many speech teachers object in particular to the overuse of "you know," "you guys," and "like." It is irritating to hear, "You know, like, I really mean it, you guys."

This is far from a complete list of grammatical pitfalls for the speaker. And a speech is not as formal as written English. Although you are not supposed to end a sentence with a preposition, it is not uncommon to hear someone say, "I know what it's all about." The best advice we can give is that if you are in doubt about any grammatical issues, consult someone who is knowledgeable and ask his or her advice, or check a grammar handbook, such as Diana Hacker's *A Pocket Style Manual*, which you can order from Amazon.com.

Pronunciation

It is easy to mispronounce a word, especially when it is a word we do not routinely use or have heard others use incorrectly. For example, how do you pronounce the word *nuclear*? Many people, including those in positions of authority, pronounce it "nuk-u-lar."The correct pronunciation is "nuk-le-ur." How do you pronounce the word *vehicle*? Many people pronounce it "ve-hick-ul." The correct pronunciation is "ve-ik-ul." Mispronunciation of words may seem a picky point to you. Yet when speaking before an educated audience, mispronunciation is one of the surest ways to risk their perceiving you as incompetent.

Mispronunciation of words can lead to problems other than your competence being undermined. One of the most significant involves meaning. Frequently, for example, people say "assure" when they mean "ensure." Assuring your child that she is safe is not the same as ensuring the safety of your child. *Assure* and *ensure* mean two different things.

Usage

Incorrect usage of a word is the final credibility-detracting issue we want to caution you about. We hear many students who confuse the words *except* and *accept.* We also hear students use the terms *irregardless* and *orientated* when what they really mean is *regardless* and *oriented.* Again, this may strike you as picky on our part. But it's not. When we hear people use words inaccurately, it opens the door for us to question their credibility in areas other than language as well.

Truthfulness

Perceptions of a speaker's credibility are not just based on audience perceptions of the speaker's competence. Audiences also must believe that the speaker is trustworthy. As a result, speakers, need to make sure that the words they use to make a point are borne out by their actions. Saying one thing and doing another has a way of catching up with people. This is especially true in an age of YouTube, MySpace, and *The Daily Show.* More than a few college students have had the words on their résumés contradicted by their actions on either MySpace or YouTube. And more than a few politicians have been caught by Jon Stewart and his staff saying one thing and doing something completely opposite.

Tips and Tactics

Credibility-Enhancing Language

1. Avoid qualifiers such as *I'm pretty sure* or *I'm kind of certain.* Instead, assert yourself with statements such as *I'm convinced, I strongly believe,* or *I am of the firm belief.*
2. Avoid tag questions that make it seem as if you are uncertain. For example, instead of saying, "I think this is a problem but you may not," say, "This is a problem for all of us." Avoid saying, "I believe we have no other choice, what do you think?" Instead, say, "Wouldn't you agree that we have no other choice?"
3. Don't be afraid to interject experience or training that gives you expertise or insight to your topic. Personal experience is a powerful form of evidence in the eyes of the audience. Share with your audience the fact that "I've now been rock climbing for over three years"; or "Proper nutrition is not only something I try to practice, it's a subject in which I've taken two courses"; or "This past year marked my tenth year of being smoke free."
4. Use familiar words. When we are not familiar with a word, we are more prone to mispronounce or misuse it. If the audience is unfamiliar with the word, they will fail to understand our meaning even when the word is used correctly. Our best advice is to stick to words that are familiar to both the audience and speaker.
5. Buy a dictionary so that when you do incorporate a word you do not routinely use in your speech, you can consult the dictionary to find out the

word's denotative meaning and phonetically correct pronunciation. Watch out for words that sound alike but mean different things, such as *except* and *accept*, *access* and *assess*, or *ask* and *axe*. Also watch out for words that are spelled and pronounced alike but may have different meanings depending on usage (homonyms). For example, the word *quail* can be used in reference to a type of bird or in reference to cowering in terror.

6. Don't use language that plays fast and loose with the truth.

Use Language to Its Fullest Potential

Language, as the surprise-hit documentary *Wordplay* shows, is food for the mind. In fact, there is increasing evidence that using language to its fullest potential can help thwart degenerative diseases such as Alzheimer's. Thus the fourth rule, using language to its fullest potential in your speeches, will feed your brain at the same time it makes you a better speaker.

Of the many ways you can use language, we encourage you to first take advantage of:

- Language appropriate to the diverse ways audience members process information.
- Language that shows and tells what you hope to share in your speech.
- Language that is rhythmic.
- Language that varies the intensity of your speech.

Visual, Auditory, and Kinesthetic Speech

In the 1980s Professor Howard Gardiner introduced the idea that not all people process information the same way. He also pointed out that whether people process what they are being taught depends on whether it is conveyed to them through a channel appropriate to their "preferred" style of information processing.[6]

Research shows that some people need to see a lesson, others need only to hear it, and still others need to become immersed in the subject matter. These three styles of learning are technically called visual, auditory, and kinesthetic. The obvious way for a speaker to deal with these three is to augment a speech with visual aids, speak audibly and clearly, or involve the audience in demonstrations or other hands-on experiences. Yet sometimes options one and three are impossible for a speaker.

To get around this fact, author and corporate trainer Loretta Malandro encourages her clients to connect metaphorically with the varied learning styles present in most audiences. Exhibit 11.2 suggests a number of specific visual, auditory, and kinesthetic words that help the audience better process a speech.

Although we may not be able to literally show our audience members prejudice, we can connect with visual learners by

- asking them to envision a world free of hate,
- drawing a picture of racism or sketching out an example for them, or
- making a hazy concept such as affirmative action crystal clear so that they can see the problem.

Exhibit 11.2
Words Linked to Vision, Hearing, and Touch

VISUAL WORDS			
Focus	Graphic	Watch	Colorful
Bright	Illustrate	Vision	Glimpse
Show	Color	Brilliant	Look
Pretty	See	Evident	Sight
Envision	Picture	Sketch	Shining
Draw	Hazy	Oversight	Hidden
View	Peek	Clearly	Notice
Clear	Imagine	Perspective	
AUDITORY WORDS			
Listen	Ringing	Compliment	Pardon
Hear	Resonate	Loud	Sound
Discuss	Yell	Silent	Request
Declare	Told	Shout	Whispering
Implore	Call	Talk	Quiet
Acclaim	Assert	Noisy	Ask
Harmony	Profess	Orchestrate	
Petition	Noise	Address	
KINESTHETIC WORDS			
Feel	Terrified	Hunger	Contact
Pressure	Burdensome	Doubt	Nurture
Hurt	Firm	Shocking	Emotion
Get the point	Tense	Heavy	Graceful
Experience	Touchy	Touch	Sensual
Longing	Pushy	Concrete	Weighty problem
Wait	Shatter	Irritated	

Source: Excerpted from: *Twenty-First Century Selling.* © Dr. Loretta Malandro. Taught in her program "Speak With Impact," offered by Malandro Communication Inc., Scottsdale, Arizona.

Although we may not be able to let them literally feel our thoughts, we can connect with audience members who need to experience some things by asking them to imagine

- what racism feels like,
- that a problem is a giant weight pressing down on them, or
- how oppressed people hunger for freedom.

And though we may not be able to literally produce the sound of abused children for our audience members, we can connect to auditory learners by asking them

- whether they hear what we are trying to say,
- to imagine what it's like to live in a world where they cannot speak out for themselves, or
- to imagine the mournful sound of children crying.

The point is simple. Not everyone in the audience will respond in a like manner to the words we speak. Thus, to maximize audience members'receptivity to what we say, we must make every effort to use expressive words that reflect their different styles of information processing.

Words That Show and Tell

One of the best ways to respond to the diverse styles of information processing in your audience, is to combine the preceding suggestions with language that helps you show *and* tell your audience what's on your mind. For example, metaphors, similes, and analogies help audiences see and listen to your speech.

Metaphor is one of the most powerful sources of expressive language. A metaphor is a figure of speech in which a word or phrase literally denoting one kind of object or idea is used in place of another to suggest a likeness or an analogy between them. It's one thing, for example, to say that a corporation is "polluting the environment." It's quite another to say that the same corporation is "raping virgin timberland." To say that "freedom is an open window" or that "music unshackles the mind and spirit" would be metaphorical. Metaphors provide an audience with a kind of linguistic break from the expected. Thus, just when audience members may be losing interest in a speech, a phrase or word can grab them by the lapels and help them "see" what we are trying to say.

metaphor
A figure of speech in which words and phrases that are primarily understood to mean one thing are used in place of another to suggest likeness or an analogy between them. Race car drivers, for example, may have to "wrestle with" a car that is difficult to control.

Metaphors should fit the topic. For example, sports metaphors are often used in the popular media to describe political contests. Thus, a political candidate who does well in a debate "hits a home run," whereas a less successful candidate "strikes out." Sometimes a desperate politician is said to "throw a Hail Mary pass," while the favored candidate is said to "sit on a lead." Be careful, however, not to mix metaphors. It sounds odd to say, "He scored a touchdown while steering the ship of state through troubled waters." Metaphors can add spice and interest to a speech, but they must be used appropriately.

Simile is a form of figurative language that invites a direct comparison between two things that are quite different. A simile usually contains the word *like* or *as*. "Sharp as a tack," "tight as a snare drum," and "pointed as an ice pick" are examples of simile. Similes can also be used effectively to "show" the audience what we are attempting to communicate.

simile
Invites the listener to make a direct comparison between two things or objects that are quite different, such as "my roommate lives like a pig in slop" or is "dumb as a rock."

analogy
An extended metaphor or simile. Suggesting that the rebuilding of Iraq is much like rebuilding Germany and Japan after WWII is an analogy.

Similes differ from metaphors in that they explicitly state the comparison, whereas metaphors imply it. Similes are useful, therefore, in making a comparison very clear to the audience. For example, a speech on preventing sexually transmitted diseases might use a simile such as "Having unprotected sexual relations is like playing Russian roulette with a 357 Magnum." On a topic such as drunk driving, you might say, "Drunken drivers are like unguided missiles."

Analogies are extended metaphors or similes. Analogies can be effective in helping an audience imagine something you are trying to describe. In an informative speech on writing a basic software program, for example, one of our students used a cooking recipe to help students follow along. In another informative speech, we had a student describe fly-fishing for wild trout as analogous to chasing butterflies with a net.

Our use of metaphor, simile, and analogy in speeches is limited only by our imagination. What's more, we can get ideas for their effective use from listening to other speakers and from reading both fiction and nonfiction works.

Rhythmic Speech

Rhythm is part of the natural order. We often hear people speak about the "rhythm of life" or the "rhythm of the season." Perhaps this is the reason we are so easily drawn to beating drums and chanting people. In any case, the best speakers know that a speech needs rhythm every bit as much as does the DJ at a dance club. To create rhythm, speakers commonly use alliteration, parallel structure, repetition, and antithesis.

Alliteration is the repetition of the same initial sound in a series of words. Jesse Jackson is famous for using alliteration to make his speeches more expressive and memorable. Instead of saying, "People need to be given a purpose," for example, Jackson might say, "Empower people with pride, and purpose is sure to follow."

One of the most famous alliterations of American political history came from former Vice President Spiro Agnew, who called his opponents in the media "nattering nabobs of negativism." The power of alliteration comes from the way it sticks in audience members' minds. The danger is that if the alliteration seems forced, it may be memorable, but ineffective.

Parallel structure is the use of the same structure for each main point of the speech. It provides a way to help the audience remember key points, and at the same time it serves as a verbal cue that we are presenting a main point. For example, when John F. Kennedy ran for president, he used the phrases "I am not satisfied . . . we can do better" to highlight each of his major criticisms of the Republican administration.

In developing a speech outline, look for a consistent refrain or phrase that can serve as the touchstone for the structure of the speech. For example, a speech on gang violence might be built around several main points that each begin, "We can only stop gang violence if we all . . . ." The use of parallel structure helps audiences anticipate the points to come and remember them when the speech is over. However, be careful to use parallel structure that fits the speech. If not, it will seem forced and artificial.

Repetition is the use of the same words repeatedly in a speech to drive home a point. Unlike parallel structure, in which the same phrase is used only to build each main point, repetition uses a word or phrase repeatedly throughout the speech to emphasize the essential point that the speaker seeks to convey. If you recall the speech by Barbara Jordan in the box on page 263, you will note that the phrase "We, the people" is repeated three times in one short excerpt. The theme of that speech is clearly conveyed by that one phrase, taken from the U.S. Constitution.

antithesis
The use of opposites, e.g., light–dark.

Antithesis involves the use of opposites. In addition to adding another rhythmic element to a speech, language that links opposites can add intensity and even urgency to a speech. History is replete with speeches that feature antithesis and range from Jesus' declaration that the "least will be first" to President Theodore Roosevelt's promise to "speak softly and carry a big stick."

Another example of antithesis is the contemporary use of the term "Chicken Hawk." It has commonly been applied to describe militaristic politicians who advocate the use of the armed forces, even though these politicians have never served in the armed forces in peacetime much less during war.

Language Intensity

The degree to which words and phrases deviate from neutral affects **language intensity**. The intensity of words varies along a continuum ranging from relatively neutral to highly intense. For example, *savory* and *delicious* are more intense than *tastes good.* By the same token, the phrase *I find you attractive* is not nearly as intense as *you rock my world.* Intense language is much more likely to enlist the attention of the audience than neutral language. We can increase language intensity by using action words and humorous language. We can also increase intensity with metaphor and simile, which we have already discussed.

language intensity
The degree to which words and phrases deviate from neutral.

Action Words Try to use words that are exciting and action oriented. For example, which do you find more involving, "The speech was well received" or "The speech was a knockout"? What about "He got mad" versus "He went ballistic"? How about "dunk" versus "monster slam" or "excited" versus "out-of-control." Action words and action-loaded metaphors help listeners picture what you say.

Humor In Chapter 10 we talked about using humor to open a speech. The guidelines for using humor we discussed there apply to this discussion as well. Humor should be appropriate and relevant to our topic or the occasion and mindful of the diversity in our audience. Having said that, we also want to emphasize what feminist Gertrude Stein is alleged to have said on her deathbed. When asked if it was hard to die, Stein said, "No . . . dying is easy. Comedy is hard."

Although humorous language can increase the intensity of a speech, not all speakers are well suited to using it. Some people really can't tell a joke. If you count yourself in this latter group, don't try being something you are not. On the other hand, if humor is customary to your communication style, use it to your advantage. Poke fun at yourself but not at your audience. Tell a joke you have successfully told before, if appropriate. And share humorous anecdotes you have shared before, assuming that they suit your speech purpose.

Contrast and Action A final way to intensify language is to incorporate contrasting phrases and words that suggest action. In discussing the irrationality that often grips the minds of people when going to war, German philosopher Friedrich Nietzsche wrote, "How good . . . bad music and bad reasons sound when we march against the enemy."[8] Nietzsche's simple contrast between good and bad is much more effective in making war seem illogical than any extended discussion would have been. And this would have been especially true had Nietzsche delivered the line in a speech.

Managing Language

The final rule for using language effectively involves using language that (1) assists us in managing our speech, (2) helps audience members understand the intended meaning of our message, and (3) avoids unneccessarily alienating audience members.

Define Terms

As discussed in Chapter 6, words have denotative and connotative meanings. If we look in the dictionary for the definition of a word, the first entry we will find is the most agreed-upon meaning for the word when the dictionary was published. This is also the denotative meaning of the word.

Connotative meanings for a word evolve over time. Usually, connotative meanings are given birth by groups of people bound by some collective purpose or activity. The word *nose* means the tip of the board to surfers, for example, but also may refer to the fragrance of a newly opened bottle of wine to the connoisseur.

Because words have both denotative and connotative meanings, we must be careful in our assumptions about shared meaning with an audience. We should never assume that the meaning we most commonly assign to a word will always be the same for our audience. When in doubt, then, it is in everyone's interest to define our terms in the course of our speeches.

Be Careful With Colloquial Words and Idioms

Our everyday conversations are liberally peppered with colloquial words and idioms. The temptation to generalize them in formal speech and writing is understandable. Even so, they should be avoided. Conversational colloquialisms such as "gonna," "gotta," or "wanna" undermine audience perceptions of credibility. For the non-native speakers in your audience, they are also likely to be meaningless.

This happens even more so with idioms. These figures of speech have highly idiosyncratic use and meaning. While we may know what it means when someone gets "antsy" or is "all ears," non-native speakers probably would be baffled by the term and expression. Because idioms also can be regional, native speakers also can be confused in this regard. For example, whereas Southern Californians are likely to think of the word "ramp" as an entrance or exit from the freeway, a Southern West Virginian, upon hearing the word, is more likely to think of a pungent plant that is the focus of festivals in the spring.

Use Concrete Words and Phrases

Speakers do not always use language to enlighten an audience. Sometimes speakers intentionally use language to keep their audience in the dark. Political consultants will tell reporters that a candidate misspoke rather than said something stupid. Military spokespeople will tell an audience that collateral damage occurred rather than candidly admit innocent civilians were injured or killed. And the spokesperson for a company will announce to the general public that it is "right sizing" the workforce, when it would be more accurate to say 1,000 employees were losing their jobs.

We do ourselves and our audience a favor when we speak in concrete language. Concrete language consists of words and phrases that increase the chance of our audience interpreting the meaning of our message as intended. Put another way, concrete language is void of words and phrases so abstract that each person in our audience can walk away from the speech with a different interpretation of what was said.

The easiest way to make language concrete is to use words our audience recognizes and routinely uses; for example, *cat* instead of *feline*, *sneaky* rather than *surreptitious*, *book* rather than *tome*, and *abusive* rather than *vituperative language.* We can also make our language more concrete by providing our audience with details that will clarify our intended meaning. For example, instead of saying a person is tall or short, give the person's actual height. Rather than describing someone as a criminal, detail the nature of his or her crime or criminal record as well. And rather than arguing that someone is either conservative or liberal, provide the audience with detailed evidence that supports the claim.

Use Oral Language

The language in our speeches should look and sound more like the language of conversation than the language of written discourse. However, the language in our speeches needs to be a refined version of that used when conversing. We should strive to use language in our speeches that is grammatically sound and clearly enunciated. By the same token, we should feel free to use contractions more liberally in a speech, split all the infinitives we want, and end a thought with a preposition. Spoken thought and written sentences are similar but not identical. It's a good idea to read aloud and even record a speech. We can then listen critically to what we have said, and check to make sure that it sounds like we are conversing with rather than formally talking to our audience.

Keep It Simple

Less is often more in a speech. By that we mean simple words and simple sentences are usually better than polysyllabic words and compound, complex sentences. "Ask not what your country can do for you . . . but what you can do for your country," is much easier to hear and understand than the following:

> It's important that each of you gives some thought to the kinds of demands that you make on your government, and at the same time begin to think about the meaning of sacrifice, and what you possibly could do to help out your government and elected leaders.

When possible, it also is important to avoid jargon our audience may not fully understand. While the term "cognitive dissonance" is fine when speaking to a group of psychologists, the term "post-buyer's remorse," which is a form of cognitive dissonance, is better suited to a general audience. If we find that there is no substitute for jargon, we must define the jargon in concrete terms for our audience.

Use Transitional Words and Phrases

Still another technique to manage a speech is to make effective use of transitions, which we explained in Chapter 10. We've repeatedly emphasized how important it is to let our audience know where we are going with our speech. You know from your own experience in taking lecture notes that it's much easier to follow an instructor who uses verbal transitions that alert you to changes in direction or clearly link one thought to another. You need to do the same for the members of your audience.

Transitional words and phrases tell our audience we are about to make or already have made a shift in direction. They also serve to verbally link our thoughts as we speak. It's always a good idea to let the audience know that there is a sequence to our message–"Let's consider three important issues"–and then to remind the audience where we are in that sequence–"Having covered the first issue, let's now look at the second."

It's also a good idea to let the audience know that the speech is about to end by using transitional words and phrases such as *lastly, to summarize, to conclude*, and *in closing*. Audiences are likely to grow impatient if they think a speech will never end.

Be Consistent

Because we are more accustomed to using informal language, making the switch to the oral language required in a speech can be difficult. One behavior we have observed with our own students when they speak is a form of *code switching*. This simply means that they sometimes switch back and forth between the language of public speaking and the language of informal conversation. For example, in the beginning of their speech they avoid colloquialisms and carefully enunciate their words. As they move further into their speech and feel more relaxed, though, they sometimes fall back into an informal style full of clipped words, idioms, and slang. Simply put, the language we use should be consistent throughout our speech. It's okay to be conversational in tone; it's not okay to treat our audience to language more appropriate to the street.

Slang Words and Perceived Obscenities

We subscribe to the adage, "when in doubt . . . leave it out." Slang words such as "dude" or "dawg" have their place. Normally, that place is not the classroom where you are learning and mastering the art and science of public speaking. If you are unsure about a word and whether it qualifies as slang, ask your instructor!

Also try and avoid words that may be perceived as obscene. We are not prudes in this respect. But we have learned personally over the years that obscenities are truly in the eye of the beholder. Words we regard as mild at worse have proven highly offensive to some of our students. How do we know? Because these students have felt offended enough to tell us outside of class.

Avoid Stereotypes

This tennis player defies the stereotyping language so often used to describe persons with disabilities.

Do you see anything wrong with the following references?

"John's a victim of cystic fibrosis."

"Don't forget that Susan's wheelchair bound!"

"It's okay, Lupe, there's plenty of disabled seating in the new auditorium."

"The Howards' baby is physically challenged."

According to the Disabled Student Services on our campus, each of these statements is constructed with inappropriate language. If you're surprised, then please know that so were we. We've heard terms like *victim of* and *physically challenged* used by people in all walks of life, including student speakers.

The fact that we think we know what constitutes appropriate language doesn't excuse us from researching the subject. Language is dynamic and in a continuous process of change. What's more, words such as *victim* or terms such as *wheelchair bound* once were acceptable. Today, however, people with disabilities are defining their own terms on their own grounds. Further, in doing so, those with disabilities have said they prefer the following descriptors to the first set we listed for you:

"John has cystic fibrosis."

"Don't forget that Susan's in a wheelchair."

"It's okay, Lupe; there's plenty of accessible seating in the new auditorium."

"The Howards' baby has a disability."

Thus, we want to remind you of the adage "It's better to remain silent and be thought a fool than to open your mouth and prove it." When in doubt about words and their consequences, consult an authority.

Of course, it is not just people with disabilities who are stereotyped. People in different professions, of different ethnicities, and with different sexual orientations, to name just a few categories, are frequently the subject of stereotypic language. The competent speaker avoids such stereotypes. One particular type of stereotype deserves discussion in its own right, sexist language.

Avoid Sexist Language

sexist language
Language, such as *housewife* and *fireman,* that stereotypes gender roles.

Sexist language is language that stereotypes gender roles, for example, *housewife* and *fireman.* Why is sexist language a problem? It conveys, intentionally or not, a stereotype of certain roles and functions, based on biological sex. When the head of an academic department is referred to as a chair*man*, a member of the U.S. House of Representatives is called a Congress*man*, and a flight attendant on an airplane is known as a steward*ess*, it is clear which roles are held to be "male" and which ones "female." An effective public speaker avoids sexist language.

One of the easiest ways to unintentionally convey sexism is to use singular pronouns in the masculine form. For years, speakers and writers excluded women from their examples involving a single person, saying such things as

> "If a person is strong, he will stand up for himself."
>
> "When someone believes something, he shouldn't be afraid to say so."
>
> "An individual should keep his promise."

If we have no other choice in constructing examples to illustrate our speech, we can do one of two things with regard to singular pronouns. First, we can say "he or she" in conjunction with a singular verb. Second, we can use "she" in some cases and "he" in others. Yet both of these alternatives are awkward, and neither is likely to please everyone in our audience. Thus, we suggest a third alternative: Use plural nouns and pronouns when constructing examples to make the speech more vivid, involving, and inclusive. Instead of saying, "If a person is strong, he will stand up for himself," say, "Strong people stand up for themselves." Instead of saying, "When someone believes something, he shouldn't be afraid to say so," try, "When people believe something, they shouldn't be afraid to say so." And instead of saying, "An individual should keep his promise," simply say, "People should keep their promises."

Summary

To evaluate your understanding of this chapter, visit our Online Learning Center Web site for quizzes and other chapter study aids.

Although words alone can't break our bones, words are powerful symbols and should be treated as such. In recognition of this fact, keep the following in mind as you construct your speeches:

- Language is symbolic and influences the process of perception.
- Language reflects the multiracial, multiethnic, multicultural audience of today.
- Effective language is inclusive rather than marginalizing or totalizing.
- Effective language enhances your audience's perception of your credibility.
- Effective language connects with the visual, auditory, and kinesthetic styles of processing information present in your audience.
- Effective language takes advantage of devices such as metaphor, simile, alliteration, parallel structure, and repetition.
- Effective language avoids unfair stereotypes and the use of words that perpetuate sexism.

Check Your Understanding: Exercises and Activities

1. Rewrite the following paragraph using inclusive language:

   When a speaker begins his speech, the first thing he must do is thank the chairman of the group for the opportunity to speak to his group. As we know, the quality that separates man from the animals is the ability to speak. Regardless of his job, a man must know how to speak clearly. Similarly, a woman must know how to impart language skills to her children. Thus, every speaker is urged to use language to the best of his ability.

2. Write five transitional statements without using the following words:

   first (second, third, etc.)

   therefore

   next

   finally

   in conclusion

3. Company X has an internal policies manual that is written in marginalizing language. As an employee of the company, you find the language disturbing and believe the language in the manual should be changed. Write a letter to the head of the documents division explaining why you believe such changes are necessary and why you believe the changes will enhance the image of the company. (Thanks to Dr. Madeline Keaveney for suggesting this exercise.)

4. Exclusive language is marginalizing and biased. Provide an inclusive-language alternative for each of the following, or state under what conditions the term might be appropriately used in a speech. [Adapted from Rosalie Maggio, *The Bias-Free Word Finder: A Dictionary of Nondiscriminatory Language* (Boston: Beacon Press, 1991).]

   actress

   airline stewardess

   businessman

   craftsmanship

   doorman

   executrix

   goddess

   meter maid

   mother

   majorette

   Mrs. John Doe

   old wives' tale

   waitress

Notes

1. W. H. Auden and L. Kronenberger, *The Viking Book of Aphorisms* (New York: Dorsett Press, 1981), 238.
2. Earl Shorris, Latinos: *A Biography of the People* (New York: Norton, 1992), 95–100.
3. Julia T. Wood, ed., *Gendered Relationships* (Mountain View, Calif.: Mayfield, 1996), 39–56.
4. See, for example: W. M. O'Barr, *Linguistic Evidence: Language, Power, and Strategy in the Courtroom* (New York: Academic Press, 1982); James J. Bradac

and Anthony Mulac, “A Molecular View of Powerful and Powerless Speech Styles: Attributional Consequences of Specific Language Features and Communication Intentions,” *Communication Monographs* 51 (1984): 307–319.

5. H. Giles and J. Wiemann, “Language, Social Comparison, and Power,” in *Handbook of Communication Science*, ed. C. R. Berger and S. H. Chaffee (Newbury Park, Calif.: Sage, 1987).

6. Howard Gardner, *Intelligence Reframed: Multiple Intelligences for the 21st Century* (New York: Basic Books, 1999).

7. Auden and Kronenberger, *The Viking Book of Aphorisms,* 359.

How you say something can be as important as what you say.

Delivery: Engaging Your Audience

Objectives

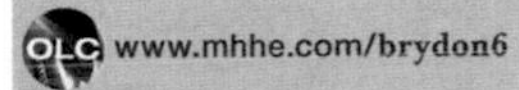

After reading this chapter and reviewing the online learning resources at www.mhhe.com/brydon6, you should be able to:

- Describe how to adapt your style of delivery to the audience and rhetorical situation.
- Describe when manuscript, memorized, impromptu or extemporaneous methods of delivery are most appropriate to a speech.
- Define nonverbal behavior and distinguish between verbal and nonverbal behavior.
- Describe the relationship between delivery and the eight basic dimensions of the nonverbal system.
- Display nonverbal behaviors characteristic of effective delivery, including control of the speaking environment; proper attire; eye contact and expressive facial cues; vocal variation in pitch, range, rhythm, and tempo; clear and distinct vocal articulation; and gestures and movements that serve as emblems, illustrators, and regulators.
- Control distracting self-adaptive behaviors.
- Use time to enhance your credibility and communicate urgency, drama, humor, and the like during your speech.
- Explain the guidelines for developing a proactive, rather than reactive, delivery.
- Display nonverbal examples of complementing, contradicting, and repeating the message; substituting for a verbal cue; increasing the perception of immediacy; exciting the audience; and delivering a powerful speech.

Key Concepts

emblem

environment

illustrators

nonverbal behavior

proactive delivery

regulators

self-adapting behaviors

zone of interaction

“ What people do is frequently more important than what they say. ”

–EDWARD T. HALL
anthropologist[1]

President Bush was often criticized for his speaking delivery as this photo from 2001 depicts.

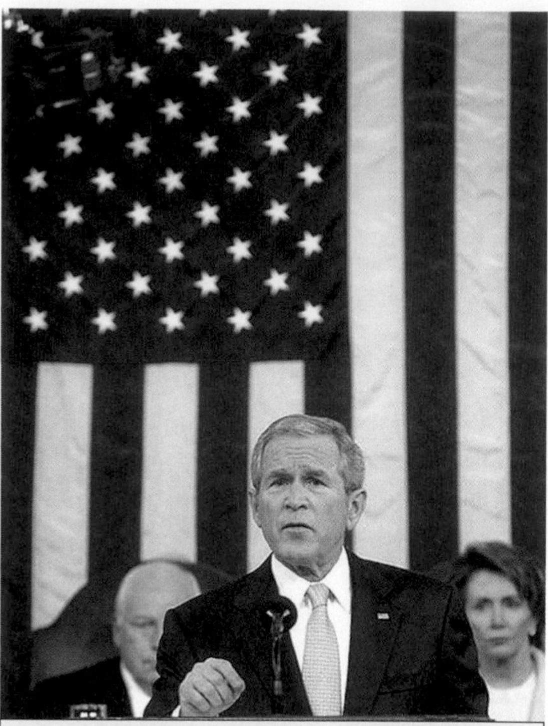

In his 2007 State of the Union address President Bush displayed confident delivery.

Justified or not, few politicians in recent history have had the delivery of their public speeches scrutinized as much as those of President George W. Bush. Pundits and comedians alike have criticized his posture and facial expression when speaking, as well as his tone and pronunciation. Thus it was with professional interest that we read several critiques of President Bush's 2007 State of the Union address in which experts in communication and linguistics noted that his nonverbal communication, especially, had changed for the better.

The comments of University of Nevada, Las Vegas, professor Joseph Valenzano typified the responses of the experts. Valenzano claims that the arrogance and cockiness noted by critics in previous Bush speeches was absent in his 2007 State of the Union speech.

> He used to have the forward lean, (this) half-cocked little smile, like I've got you. But he didn't do it once. He stood there straight, never once leaning over. Very professional, probably the most professional speech he's ever delivered. There was the perception of him being more humble.[2]

The change in President Bush's style of delivery is not surprising. In this age of high stake politics, it's not uncommon for visible public figures to get help with the delivery of their speeches. Besides politicians, many CEOs of Fortune 500 companies are coached on their style of delivery; the goal is to communicate an image that isn't simply professional but also warm and engaging. Their coaches know what teachers of public speaking have taught for at least 2,000 years: Effective speeches are the product of the complementary verbal and nonverbal elements that characterize all communication transactions.

To view a video for an example of different delivery styles, click on the Speech Coach link on our Online Learning Center Web site, and go to Segment 11.1.

This chapter focuses on the delivery of your speech. Please recognize from the beginning that there is no single method of effectively delivering your speeches. It depends on you and the style with which you are most comfortable, the occasion, and the context in which you find yourself. Given this framework, we first look at adapting your delivery to your audience and rhetorical situation, including the four most common methods of delivery. Next we discuss how you can use your voice to enhance your delivery. Finally, we examine the functional role of nonverbal communication in the process of effectively delivering a speech.

Focusing Your Delivery on Your Audience

Never forget that public speaking is a transaction between the speaker and the audience. Just as the language we choose for our message should reflect the nature of our audience, so too should our delivery. As a result, let's look first at the role audience diversity and the speech occasion play in deciding which method of delivery is your best choice.

Choosing an Appropriate Method of Delivery

In Chapter 3 we introduced four methods of delivery: manuscript, memorized, impromptu, and extemporaneous. As we analyze our audience and rhetorical situation, one of our most important decisions will be choosing an appropriate method of speech delivery. Your choice should complement your overall communication skills and reinforce your strengths as a public speaker. Realize that none of these methods is foolproof–be sure to choose wisely.

Manuscript Delivery

Manuscript delivery involves writing out the speech completely and reading it to the audience. This method may be the best choice when an audience requires precise information or our words will be quoted by others. Any time we use a manuscript, eye contact, movement, and gestures are restricted. If a manuscript must be used, therefore, learn it well. Practice repeatedly so that you do not have to look down often. Mark up the manuscript with notes to yourself, and underline or highlight main ideas. Also, be sure pages are numbered so that they will not get out of order. Use a large typeface and double or even triple spacing. Manuscript speaking is more difficult than most people realize. Success depends on practice and skill in converting words on a page into a living speech.

Texas Governor Rick Perry uses a TelePrompTer as he gives his State of the State address.

An electronic version of manuscript speaking involves the use of a TelePrompTer. To avoid the appearance of reading verbatim from a written speech, for instance, public figures, newscasters, and actors frequently use a TelePrompTer instead of a written manuscript. As you can see in the photograph on page 283 the text is not visible to the audience. Thus, nonverbal contact with the audience is better than with a manuscript. Nevertheless, to effectively use a TelePrompTer requires direction and practice. As with any manuscript speech, the goal is to sound natural.

Memorized Delivery

A speaker using memorized delivery writes out the speech and commits it to memory before presenting it without notes. Most audiences don't expect a memorized speech unless they are watching a professional speaker, an actor delivering lines in a play, or a student competing in a speech tournament. Although memorization allows the speaker to concentrate on eye contact, movement, and gesture, it does so at a price. You may forget parts of your speech, and it requires a greater investment of time than any other method.

If you must write a speech to be memorized, keep the organization simple and memorable. A good rule of thumb is to memorize the speech in small chunks. Practice reciting your speech from the beginning through as far as you have it memorized. The repetition of earlier parts will help fix them in your mind. Don't panic if you forget a part of the speech. Try to ad-lib for a bit, and often the next section will come to mind. Finally, try to make your delivery of the speech sound as spontaneous and unrehearsed as possible.

Impromptu Delivery

There will inevitably be times when you will be expected to give an impromptu speech–a spontaneous, unrehearsed method of speaking. Usually, these short speeches are given in response to someone who asks you to say a few words, make a toast, or respond to an inquiry in class or at work. No one knows better than you the chances that you'll be asked to say a few words at a social occasion or in a professional setting. With this in mind, we offer the following suggestions:

Forewarned is Forearmed. If there is even the slightest chance you'll be asked to speak, you should prepare in advance. Does this mean that you should write out a speech? Not really. What we are talking about here is anticipating what you might be asked to say based on the context in which you'll find yourself. This will, at the very least, enable you to mentally rehearse your response. Should you not be asked to speak, you'll only be better prepared for the next time one of these occasions to speak pops up.

Get Organized. The thing that impresses people the most about people who speak effectively off-the-cuff is organization. One of the most effective patterns for organizing au impromptu speech is to (1) introduce the points we want to make, (2) expand on the points, and (3) conclude with a summary of those points. This harks back to the "tell 'em what you're going to tell 'em, tell 'em, and then tell 'em what you told 'em" sequence introduced in Chapter 10. Consider a classroom example, in which the instructor asks, "What's your take on the effects of rap lyrics on violence?" One student responds: "I have two points to make about the effects of rap. First, the effects are exaggerated. Second, most people who think rap affects violence are clueless about modern music. So what I'm saying is they're making a mountain out of another molehill." Notice in this example that the first sentence not only previews the points being made but also restates in modified form the question asked. The two points are made and then summarized in the final sentence. Compare this response with another hypothetical but not atypical one from a student: "I don't know . . . I guess I disagree. It's just a bunch of people who are out of it coming down on alternative music. Get a life, you know?" This response is both disorganized and equivocal, bringing us to our next tip.

Take a Position. Few of us are impressed with people who are wishy-washy. When someone asks a speaker, "What's your opinion?" we think the speaker is obligated to give it. On the other hand, if a speaker has not yet formulated a clear-cut opinion, an audience would much rather hear the person say, "I'll get more information and I'll get back to you" than hem and haw in response to such a query.

Use Powerful Language. Powerful language goes hand in hand with the preceding guidelines. Recall that powerful language avoids the use of unnecessary qualifiers and vague questions. Powerful people say such things as "My opinion is firm" or "My experience leads me to the unequivocal belief. . . ." Powerful people do not say, "I could be wrong, but I think . . ." or "I believe it's okay, do you?" Impromptu speaking is tough enough without undermining your authority with powerless language.

Hitchhike. It's sometimes effective to begin an impromptu message with what others have already said on the matter. This hitchhiking technique shows that you have been actively listening. It also acknowledges the contributions of others, even when we disagree with what they've said. For example. "Bill's point that this situation demands caution is well taken, but I must respectfully disagree for a couple of reasons." We also might say, "Let me summarize what's been said thus far, and then I'll add my two cents worth." Again, this kind of bridge tells our audience we are tuned in *and* organized.

Use Stories and Anecdotes. If you know a story or an anecdote that contains a lesson that is both relevant and straightforward, by all means use it as a basis for your impromptu speech. Organizational culture often gives rise to stories about people and events that can be used in an impromptu speech. Some stories and anecdotes are generally known and can be applied to almost any point you choose to make. The real power of Aesop's fables, for instance, is that each contains multiple lessons you can apply to life. The same is true of many well-known children's stories such as *Goldilocks and the Three Bears* and *The Boy Who Cried Wolf.*

Invest in Reference Works. Impromptu speaking is a matter of when, not if. Thus, we recommend purchasing for your personal library at least two kinds of reference books, First, look for a book composed of famous quotations from well-known and widely recognized people. At the same time, invest in a book of anecdotes compiled from the lives of the famous and notorious. Then find and commit to memory quotes and anecdotes that can be applied generally to topics and issues you may be asked to speak about.

Informal situations such as this one invite a conversational delivery style.

Extemporaneous Delivery

For most students who are still learning to give a speech, extemporaneous speaking remains their best choice. Extemporaneous delivery combines careful preparation with spontaneity. Brief notes, rather than a manuscript or outline, are used. This enables the speaker to maintain eye contact, move freely, gesture, and adapt to audience feedback. Some speakers dispense with using a lectern altogether and simply hold their notes in one hand. (Avoid holding them in both hands, as this restricts the ability to gesture.)

Today's audiences are more likely to expect and appreciate the extemporaneously delivered speech than other methods of delivery. Just as it allows the speaker to remain in contact with the audience, so does it allow the audience to remain connected to the speaker. Audience members not only can give feedback to someone speaking extemporaneously but also can assess the degree to which their feedback registers with the speaker.

This doesn't mean that extemporaneous speaking is without drawbacks. Notes can restrict the speaker's range of gestures and can be distracting when waved about while speaking. Finally, speakers can get carried away with notes, writing down so many words that the notes almost become a manuscript. (See Exhibit 12.1 for a summary of the modes of delivery.)

Delivering Speeches to Diverse Audiences

Both the method and style of delivery should reflect the diversity of the audience. Throughout this chapter we offer numerous specific examples of cases in which a particular nonverbal behavior means one thing to one culture

Exhibit 12.1
Advantages and Disadvantages of Delivery Mode

Mode of Delivery	Advantages	Disadvantages
Manuscript	Accuracy Precision May be quoted	Loss of eye contact Written rather than oral style Easy to lose place
Memorized	Keeps eye contact with audience Freedom of movement	Easy to forget Appears "canned" Extensive preparation required Lack of spontaneity
Impromptu	Spontaneous Maintains eye contact with audience Adaptable to situation	Lack of time to prepare Can be anxiety arousing Can be embarrassing if speaker fails to anticipate possible questions
Extemporaneous	Combines preparation and spontaneity Can maintain eye contact Adaptable Allows for accuracy in wording where necessary	Excessive use of note cards can inhibit spontaneity Poor use of note cards can limit ability to gesture

and something entirely different to another. For example, consider how three different audiences might respond to the same speech. As we speak, a North American audience returns our eye contact and nods in agreement with us. A British audience also returns our eye contact, but heads remain motionless. And a West African audience avoids making direct eye contact with us altogether. What should we make of their feedback in each situation? Before you decide, perhaps it would help to know this: When the British agree with a speaker, they sometimes blink rather than nod their head. Further, the more direct the eye contact of West Africans, the less they respect the person to whom it is directed. Knowing the typical patterns of nonverbal behavior in a given culture is essential if we are to accurately interpret the nonverbal behaviors of our audience members.

Another example of differences among culturally diverse audiences concerns voice. Almost from birth, the norm for the North American culture is "to speak up and let yourself be heard." What is normative here, however, may be loud in Japan or among the upper class in Great Britain. And much as we may want to be heard, we don't want to be perceived as loudmouths in these cultures.

In contrast to the norm in these two cultures, African American audiences sometimes are verbal participants in the speech transaction. When audience members agree with the speaker, they may let the speaker know with audible feedback. When they disagree, they may also let the speaker know. Rather than being a sign of disrespect to the speaker, this kind of audience participation is an outgrowth of a rich "call-and-response" tradition with roots in the African American church.

Adapting Delivery to the Speech Occasion

How we present our speech depends on the specific rhetorical situation we face and the kind of delivery our audience is likely to expect. A speech commemorating or honoring a person calls for a formal and dignified delivery. Other speech situations call for an energetic, dynamic delivery. A motivational speaker, for example, usually dispenses with the lectern and moves about the stage, perhaps even into the audience. A lively style is expected and rewarded. Then there are situations that call for a lighthearted, comic style of delivery. For example, "roasts" honoring someone are often punctuated with good-natured joking at the honoree's expense. Unlike a commemorative speech, a delivery at a roast should be informal and lively. The key is to understand what the audience expects in a given situation and match your delivery style to those expectations.

Discovering Your Personal Style

A class in public speaking shouldn't be looked on as an episode of *Extreme Make-Over.* All of us have a personal "style" of communicating that has been evolving over the course of our lives. Our goal is to assist you in developing and adapting your personal style to the demands of the public speaking transaction both now and in the future. This involves teasing out the elements of your personal style that can work for you when you speak, and modifying elements of your personal style that may be undermining your ability to truly shine.

Many styles of speaking can work to the advantage of a speaker. Some speakers are dramatic and have a flair for telling stories, revealing things about themselves with which the audience can identify. They have a high level of energy as is evidenced by their gestures and facial expressions. Other speakers are nearly deadpan but still highly effective. As we recommend in the Self-Assessment box "Assessing Your Personal Style" on page 289, build on the style of delivery that comes most naturally to you rather than trying to mimic a style unsuitable to you.

Your Voice

Before we talk about what makes voices as unique as fingerprints, we want to re-emphasize the fact that what you say and how you say it are not the same thing. The spoken word has two dimensions. One dimension is content–the words themselves and the way they are configured to form sentences. The other dimension is vocalic–the sound that shapes the meaning the spoken word conveys to the audience. Consider the sentence "I love you." By changing the pitch, volume, and inflection of your voice as you utter the sentence, you can actually alter the meaning the sentence conveys to another person. It can be sensuous or sincere, for example, depending on the tone of voice with which it is spoken.

In a sense, words are like musical notes, and the voice is like an instrument. In the hands of a skilled musician, notes are not simply played but are shaped by the musician. Skilled guitarists playing the same notes can produce quite different sounds, depending on how they bend or agitate the strings with their fingertips. Skilled speakers do much the same thing with the pitch, tempo, and rhythm of their voices.

Self-Assessment

Assessing Your Personal Style

Most of us have a personal style of communicating. Some of us are perceived as open, some dramatic, and others are attentive. Perceptions of our style are largely based on nonverbal behaviors such as eye contact and facial expressions, the sound of our voice and body language. The following is designed to assist you in assessing your personal style of communicating. We believe most beginning public speakers are best served by building on nonverbal behaviors that come naturally rather than trying to make wholesale changes in them. As a result, think about what each of the following statements and your responses to them say about your customary style of expressing yourself nonverbally.

Read each response and record whether you Strongly Agree (SA), Agree (A), Neither Agree or Disagree (N), Disagree (D), or Strongly Disagree (SD) with the statement.

1. I think people see me as bland.	SA	A	N	D	SD
2. I think people find me entertaining.	SA	A	N	D	SD
3. I think I'm a little introverted.	SA	A	N	D	SD
4. I show what I'm thinking and I'm feeling in my facial expressions.	SA	A	N	D	SD
5. I try and conceal my true feelings from others.	SA	A	N	D	SD
6. I gesture a lot.	SA	A	N	D	SD
7. I think I make a memorable impression.	SA	A	N	D	SD
8. I dislike conflict.	SA	A	N	D	SD
9. I'd like to be a performer.	SA	A	N	D	SD
10. I prefer that others take the lead in conversations.	SA	A	N	D	SD

Statements 1, 3, 5, 8, and 10 are associated with people who are cautious about communicating and avoid arguing. People who tend to agree with these items generally would be less demonstrative in their nonverbal behavior than people who tend to agree with items 2, 4, 6, 7, and 9. These items reflect people who are fairly dramatic in their nonverbal behavior.

The best speakers are ultimately those who are flexible enough to adapt their personal style to the rhetorical situation. That kind of flexibility typically evolves with time and practice. Thus, we repeat what we said previously: First get comfortable with what comes to you naturally. People who force facial expressions and gestures, for example, are less effective because such a forced style is usually perceived as "canned" and phony.

In the effort to help you gain better control of your voice, you need to know how sound is produced and how it can be manipulated. You also need to appreciate the role articulation plays in the process of shaping this sound so that it is meaningful to your audience. Finally, you need to accept the fact that you are better off speaking in your own voice than trying to imitate the voice of someone else.

Vocal Production

The production of sound in the voice is fairly straightforward. You take in air and expel the air through the trachea across your vocal cords, which are contained in the larynx (voice box), and then across your teeth, tongue, and lips. Variations in the amount of air expelled, the positioning of the vocal cords, or

Chris Cornell of Audioslave is known for his powerful voice.

the placement of the teeth and tongue and position of the lips will result in variations in the sounds produced. Shallow breathing and the rapid expulsion of air across the vocal cords, for example, will produce a much different sound than breathing deeply and then slowly expelling the air. In the first case, your voice is likely to be described as feminine and in the second masculine, even though neither is necessarily true. The basic mechanical operation of the voice, however, is not as important to the topic at hand as are the characteristics of the voice. These include volume, pitch, range, rhythm, and tempo.

Volume

How loudly you project your voice is a consequence of both the amount of air you expel when speaking and the force with which you expel it. For example, try to speak loudly without first taking a fairly deep breath. Surprising, isn't it? Some examples of people capable of speaking with great volume are actor/talk show host Oprah Winfrey, broadcaster Rush Limbaugh, actor James Earl Jones (the person you hear saying "CNN"), and Audioslave singer Chris Cornell. On the other hand, some examples of more soft-spoken voices include actor George Clooney, TV host Diane Sawyer and singer Norah Jones.

You need not be loud to be heard. What's more, speaking in a consistently loud voice is likely to grate on the ears of your audience. You want to *project* your voice, not break eardrums with it. The key is to vary the volume of your voice depending on the impact you hope to have with your audience. Sometimes lowering the volume of your voice will draw your audience in, whereas a sudden increase in volume may startle your audience. As a public speaker, you need to have enough volume to be heard by your audience. But that can vary tremendously depending on the size of your audience, the room in which you are speaking, and the availability of a microphone. Seasoned speakers prepare differently depending on these factors. That is to say, they vary the volume with which they practice depending on where and with whom they will be speaking. You should do the same thing. Practice your speech as if you were delivering it in the classroom where you will speak, to an audience equivalent in size to your actual class. When you actually do speak to your class, moreover, look for feedback about volume in the faces and posture of audience members. If those in the back of the room are leaning forward or look puzzled, you may need to raise your volume. On the other hand, if people seated in the first row are leaning back in their seats, you may be speaking too loudly.

Pitch

The degree to which your voice is high or low is its pitch. A person who sings bass has a low pitch, whereas a person who sings soprano has a high pitch. The bass knob on your stereo lowers pitch, the treble knob raises it. Pitch is a key to vocal inflection, and effective speakers vary their pitch to shape the impact of their words. They may lower pitch to sound more serious or raise it to convey a sense of urgency. Control of pitch depends not only on their skill as a speaker but on the natural range of their voice as well.

Range

The extent of the pitch, from low to high, that lies within your vocal capacity is known as range. Just as a piano has a tremendous range in pitch, some speakers have a great vocal range. On the other hand, some speakers are like an electric bass guitar, which no matter how well played, does not have much range. As a speaker, you need to make the fullest use of your normal conversational vocal range. That means you first need to discover the bottom and top of your own vocal scale.

To get a sense of how pitch and range control the inflection in your voice, audio-record yourself. Recite the alphabet beginning in your normal voice. Then raise your pitch with each new letter until your voice cracks. Next do the same thing, but lower your voice as you recite. Play back the recording and note where your voice begins to break as you go up and then breaks as you go down. This will give you an audible idea about the limits of your vocal range, as well as at what pitches your voice sounds relaxed and natural. Then practice varying your pitch within this relaxed and natural range, using the audio recorder to further get in touch with your natural pitch and range.

Rhythm

Think of rhythm as the characteristic pattern of your volume, pitch, and range. Perhaps you have heard someone describe a speaker's voice as "singsong." This means the speaker's voice goes consistently up and then down in pitch, almost as if the person were talking to a small child.

Some speakers use predictable rhythm to great effect. Many evangelical preachers have a decided rhythm in their sermons. The Reverend Jesse Jackson is an easy target for comedic impersonators because of the predictable rhythm with which he takes his audience up, and then pauses before taking them down. Jackson heightens this effect with his inflection and frequent use of alliteration, which we discussed in Chapter 11.

Tempo

The rate at which you produce sounds, or how quickly or slowly you speak, will influence how you are perceived. Tempo also tends to vary across and even within cultures. In the United States, for example, speech in the South is relatively slow in tempo, whereas in the East, tempo is accelerated. This is readily apparent if you compare the voices of actress Holly Hunter, who is from the South, and Marisa Tomei, from the East.

Because tempo varies, you have to use good judgment in terms of how quickly or slowly you speak. Doing either to the extreme can turn off your audience. An excessively rapid pace can be perceived as a sign of nervousness. An excessively slow pace may suggest a speaker is not well prepared. Researchers have found that moderate to fast rates of speaking tend to be associated with increased perceptions of a speaker's competence on the part of the audience.[3] Other researchers have noted a ceiling to that effect, however, meaning that too fast a rate of speaking can backfire.[4] In addition, when audiences perceive speech rates as similar to their own, they are more likely to find speakers socially attractive and to comply with their requests.[5] The best advice is to moderately vary your tempo. Not only will this accommodate the different preferences of individuals in your audience, it will also enhance the overall effect of your message.

Your tempo is also affected by pauses. Sometimes a brief moment of silence can convey much to an audience. Pausing just before delivering a crucial word or phrase helps grab the audience's attention. Pausing after you've made an important point gives it time to sink in. Used judiciously, pauses can be an effective rhetorical device. It is also better to pause a moment than to fill the air with "ums," "uhs," and "you knows," which are really vocalized pauses. The best way to control disfluencies such as these is to practice your speech until it is second nature.

Articulation

If you expect an audience to understand what you are saying, you need clear articulation, which refers to the distinctness with which you make individual sounds. You may have experienced the frustration of listening to someone who sounds mushy, failing to distinctly vocalize sounds. A common articulation problem comes from either running together differing sounds or dropping parts of a word: *goin'* instead of going, *wanna* instead of *want to,* or *whatcha doin'?* in place of *what are you doing?* A good way to test your articulation is to audio-record your speech and listen critically to yourself. If you find a consistent articulation problem or set of problems, you may want to find out if your college or university offers a course in voice and articulation. Sometimes drama or theatre department courses in voice for performers can be of assistance. Severe articulation problems are often best treated by a speech pathologist. But for most students in public speaking classes, exercising care, practicing, and slowing down are the keys to being understood by the audience.

In Chapter 11 we emphasized the importance of using words correctly. This is a good place to reemphasize the fact. As you practice articulating words, make sure that you are also pronouncing them correctly. "Nu-ku-lar" is still wrong, no matter how well you articulate it.

As we said in Chapter 11, mispronounced words tend to undermine audience perceptions of a speaker's credibility. This is true whether the mispronunciation involves a term unique to a profession or the name of a person or place. Medical terms such as hemangioma can tie up the tongue of even the most articulate speaker. So, too, can place names such as Mexico's Cacaxtla or the last name of recognized football star Troy Polamalu.

For some words, the correct pronunciation is as close as a dictionary. In addition, some online dictionaries (e.g., http://www.howjsay.com) let you type in a word and actually hear it pronounced. For terms and names like those in our example, however, a dictionary may be no help at all, and the advice of an expert is required: a physician, an authority on Central America, or the actual person whose surname we will otherwise murder. The time for such consultation is well in advance of the day you are scheduled to speak. Until the correct pronunciation becomes a habit, you cannot be sure that you will be able to speak terms as they are intended to be spoken. That requires repetition and lots of practice using the terms in the body of your speech.

In the final analysis, judgments about the relationship between the qualities of your voice and the quality of your delivery will depend on the preceding characteristics operating in concert. Important as pitch or tempo may be on their own, it is their collective impact with range and rhythm that most counts.

Speaking in Your Own Voice

With these qualities of voice in mind, let's now turn to your voice specifically. Are you pleased with the way it sounds and complements your overall delivery? No matter how you answer this question, it is just as important for you to find your own voice as a speaker as it is for authors to find their own voice when they write. We mention this need to find your own voice with good reason. When public speaking students are advised to make better use of their voice in their delivery, all too often they take this to mean they must change their voice to some ideal. The ideal, moreover, is usually thought to be the voice of a television or radio personality.

We don't encourage you to imitate the vocal delivery of someone who hosts a game show, reads the news, or introduces music videos. Instead, we encourage you to experiment with your voice; for example, record your attempts to convey varying emotions in your voice, listen to yourself, and then repeat the process. This kind of exercise will let you hear what your vocal strengths and weaknesses are. In the process, be realistic but not unfairly harsh about how you think you sound. Chances are, what you think you hear is much different from what others hear.

Finally, recognize that important as it is, your voice is but a single component of your overall delivery. Not all good speakers have tremendous "pipes." For example, the *Today Show's* Matt Lauer and *Good Morning America's* Robin Roberts are both engaging, but their voices would hardly be described as rich in timbre. Further, if you were to listen to a number of paid speakers, you would see that this is the case with them as well. All of us tend to underutilize the full potential of our voices. What ultimately counts, then, is whether we're willing to do the hard work necessary to rectify this fact.

Tips and Tactics

Improving Your Voice

Like it or not, people will make judgments about you based on the way you sound. Although we want you to be comfortable with your voice, the following tips may help you if you think something about your voice needs to be changed.

- *Relaxation:* More than one problem with voice can be solved by monitoring tension in your vocal apparatus. Nasality, shrillness, or screeching, and excessive rate of speech are often a consequence of tension/stress. The same relaxation techniques can be used to alleviate the impact of tension/stress on your voice.
- *Vocal variation:* Audio-record yourself or have someone record you when you speak. If you find as a result of monitoring your audiotape that greater vocal variation is needed, pick out someone whose vocal characteristics you admire

and repeatedly listen to the person. Then try to model the vocal variation in which the person engages. Repeat this process while using an audio recorder.

- *Being heard:* Have a friend monitor your speaking volume. When you speak too softly, tell your friend to raise an index finger within your view. Use this signal to increase the volume of your voice. The goal is to be easily heard, even in the back of the room.

Nonverbal Characteristics of Delivery

nonverbal behavior A wordless system of communication.

Nonverbal behavior is a wordless system of communicating. What makes a behavior nonverbal as opposed to verbal? Is it the absence of sound? That cannot be the case, because sign language is considered a form of verbal communication, with signs merely substituting for written or spoken language. Although scholars argue about the exact definition of nonverbal behavior, most agree that it is distinct from verbal behavior in at least three ways: It is continuous, uses multiple channels simultaneously, and is spontaneous. Among adults, nonverbal behavior also is considered to be more revealing about a person than it may actually be.

The Continuous Nature of Nonverbal Behavior

Verbal behavior, composed of words, is discrete. This means verbal behavior can be divided into distinct elements, as was the case when you first began to learn about nouns, verbs, and adjectives. These elements of composition are governed by complex rules, dictating how they should be combined in your speech to form phrases, clauses, and sentences. Each word has a denotative meaning that can be found in the dictionary. Words must be arranged in a precise manner to convey the intended meaning. For example, the words *I am happy* must be arranged in that order to convey the intended meaning. To say, "Am I happy" changes the statement to a question. To say, "Happy am I" seems odd to English speakers. When words with agreed-on meanings are used in a specified order, the meaning of the verbal behavior is apparent as in this example. This is not so with nonverbal behavior, which is continuous rather than divisible.[6]

Consider the expression of happiness as you speak. What the audience sees is a complex message that involves the entire face. The muscles of the face contract, affecting the eyebrows, the corners of the mouth, and the corners of the eyes. Unlike verbal behavior, these involuntary movements cannot be broken down into compositional elements. The eyes, for example, do not convey "I," while the eyebrows say "am" and the mouth represents "happy." You cannot rearrange the components to convey a different meaning, as you can with "I," "am," and "happy." There are no highly defined rules of grammar to explain the meaning conveyed by these facial expressions. Only the total, continuous combination of these elements can constitute the nonverbal expression of happiness.

The Simultaneous Use of Multiple Channels

Returning to the example of expressing happiness, nonverbal behavior also involves the simultaneous use of multiple channels.[7] For example, try conveying an emotional expression, such as happiness, anger, sorrow, or bewilderment, through a single channel of communication, such as your mouth or eyes or hands. You'll soon see that it is difficult if not impossible. At the same time, you'll recognize that we use these multiple channels simultaneously rather than sequentially. When happy, we express the emotion all over our face, not with our eyes first, mouth second, eyebrows and forehead third and fourth.

The Spontaneous Nature of Nonverbal Behavior

As the preceding characteristics might lead you to believe, another distinguishing characteristic is that nonverbal behavior is spontaneous. With the possible exception of so-called Freudian slips, when people unintentionally say what they really mean, verbal behavior is planned behavior.[8] We consciously think about the words we speak and write, though we do so with such speed it may not occur to us.

Smiles, gestures, and body language occur at a subconscious level. This doesn't mean that people never plan or orchestrate gestures when they speak. Sometimes they do, and their nonverbal behavior is likely to look phony. Most of us learn to distinguish between authentic and phony nonverbal behaviors by the time we reach our teens. Unless nonverbal behavior is rehearsed to the point it becomes habit, planned gestures especially will be recognized as insincere. This is a major reason for people putting so much stock in the meaning they infer from nonverbal behavior.

What Nonverbal Behavior Reveals

Finally, adults tend to believe what they think nonverbal behavior reveals about people in general and speakers specifically. This is especially true when people perceive that a speaker's nonverbal behavior contradicts what the person says. In North American culture, for example, adults associate the truth with eye contact. In other cultures, however, direct eye contact is associated with disrespect if the speaker and listener have different levels of status.

A couple of points need to be made in this regard. Nonverbal behavior can be revealing about a person, but research tells us that we are far more confident in our conclusions about what it reveals than we should be. As an audience member, be cautious about inferring too much about a speaker on the basis of nonverbal behavior alone. As a speaker in this culture, though, you cannot afford to ignore the importance an audience will attach to your eye contact, posture, and manner of gesturing. This is particularly so with respect to audience perceptions of your credibility. Avoid innocent but consequential mistakes such as failing to look directly at audience members when you make claims you want them to believe.

A Few Words of Caution

Before moving on, we want to reinforce the complementary relationship between verbal and nonverbal behavior. Many people mistakenly claim that meaning is 90 percent the result of nonverbal behavior. While it is true that we infer much of what a person "feels" on the basis of such behaviors as eye contact and facial expressions, we need to balance these inferences with what the person actually says. We also need to evaluate these inferences on the basis of the cultural context in which we observe them. Some cultures are simply more nonverbally expressive than others, like France and Italy. Some cultures, such as Indonesia, frown on people revealing too much nonverbally. As audience members, we need to be careful about reading too much into the nonverbal elements of delivery when listening to a speaker.

Delivery and the Nonverbal Communication System

Recall that a system is a collection of interdependent and interrelated components. A change in one component will produce changes in them all. The nonverbal system has as its components several interdependent dimensions of behavior that profoundly affect the delivery of a speech. The specific dimensions we discuss in this section are the environment, appearance, the face and eyes, gestures and movement, posture, touch, and time. As a speaker intent on delivering a message effectively, you need to approach these dimensions systematically. Further, the verbal language with which you construct your speech should take into account what you've learned from your systematic assessment of the nonverbal dimensions.

The Environment

environment
The physical surroundings as you speak and the physical distance separating you from your audience.

For our purposes, **environment** refers to the physical surroundings as we speak and the physical distance separating us from our audience. Both surroundings and physical space have an undeniable impact not only on our delivery but also on how the speech is perceived by our audience.

The physical characteristics of the room in which we speak–for example, lighting, temperature, comfort, and aesthetics–will influence both us and the audience physically and psychologically.[9] A bright, aesthetically neutral room, which is neither sterile nor plushly decorated, and in which the temperature is 68 degrees, will have a much different overall impact on the speech transaction than a room that is dimly lit, richly furnished, and 75 degrees. Whereas in the first, both speaker and audience are likely to be alert and attentive, the second might prove so comfortable that neither the speaker nor the audience is sufficiently aroused for the transaction. Thus we would have to plan our delivery accordingly. Whereas a "normal" pattern of delivery probably would be appropriate in the first environment, we likely would need to put extra energy and enthusiasm into the delivery to succeed in the second.

A second environmental consideration is the physical layout of the room. We have been in situations where student presentations were hindered by pillars supporting the roof, by the width and length of the room, and by immovable objects such as tables. Sometimes we have no alternative but to do the best we can in such situations. As a result, we move more than we had planned as we speak, abandon visual aids that would prove impossible for our entire audience to see, or make gestures larger and more exaggerated than is customary.

At other times, however, we will have the opportunity to physically arrange the room in which we will speak. This may include the position of a lectern, elevation of a stage, and configuration of an audience. Given this opportunity, experienced speakers will arrange the environment in concert with their style of delivery. Speakers who have a traditional style of delivery may prefer a lectern,

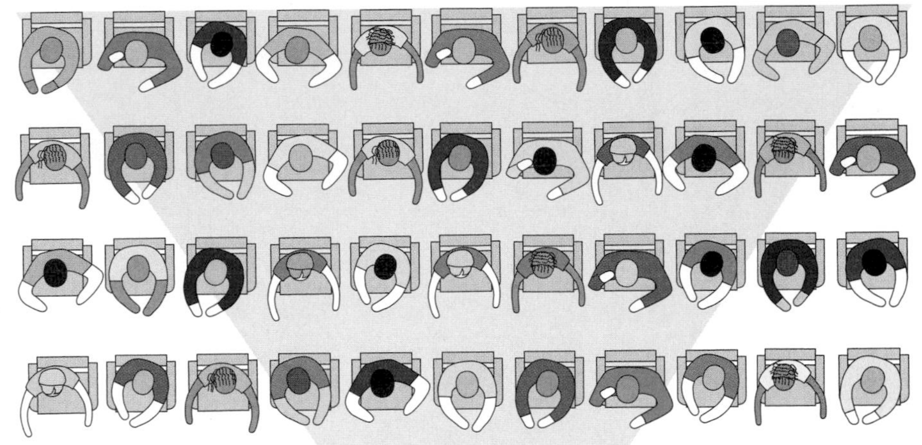

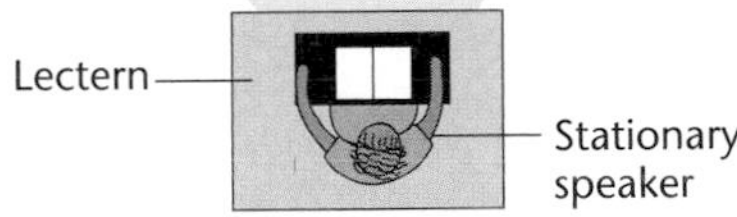

Exhibit 12.2

Zone of Interaction in the Traditional Room Setting

Where people are seated in rows and the speaker is stationary, eye contact between speaker and audience is limited to the shaded area. The speaker must turn to make eye contact with those outside the shaded area.

perhaps an overhead projector or keyboard immediately to their side, and an elevated stage from which to speak. Speakers who are much less formal in their style of delivery may want the room to be arranged so that they can move from side to side or even up and down its length.

Both the traditional and informal styles of delivery can be equally effective. However, the room layout consistent with the traditional style is more restrictive than its counterpart in two ways. The first way concerns the **zone of interaction,** the area in which speakers can easily make eye contact with audience members (Exhibit 12.2). The second way concerns the amount of space physically separating speakers from their audience.

zone of interaction
Area of an audience in which speaker and audience members can make eye contact.

The zone of interaction is limited to the range of your peripheral vision. The immediate zone of interaction between speakers and their audience diminishes as a room gets larger. To compensate for this fact, speakers have two choices. Either they can shift the zone of interaction by looking from side to side, or they can physically move from one point to another when they deliver their speeches. This latter choice is illustrated in Exhibit 12.3. Obviously, in a very large room the traditional style of delivery limits us to looking from side to side in the attempt to shift the zone of interaction. This means that we cannot help but ignore part of our audience part of the time.

The traditional style of delivery also allows less flexibility in manipulating the physical distance separating speakers from their audiences. Whereas a speaker who moves about the room can reduce or increase distance physically as well as psychologically, a relatively stationary speaker is restricted to the latter. Thus, for those who prefer this style of delivery, eye contact becomes their primary agent for managing how immediate they are perceived to be by their audience, a point which we discuss shortly.

To summarize, the relationship of the speaking environment to delivery is a significant one. Not only does it influence our style of delivery, it also influences

Exhibit 12.3
Shifting the Zone of Interaction With Movement
Changing positions can increase the perception of inclusiveness as well as add energy to your speech.

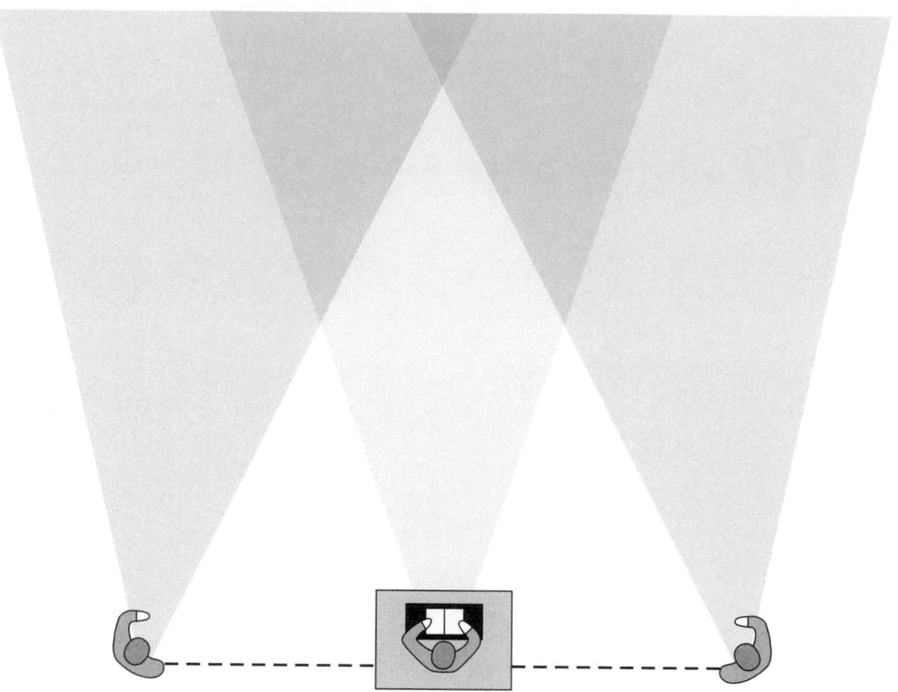

how we are perceived by our audience. Experienced public speakers try to plan the delivery of their speeches accordingly. When faced with a "tough room," for example, they know that the arousal level of their delivery will need to increase if they are to reach their audience. Inexperienced speakers, on the other hand, all too often play "victim" to their speaking environment. Instead of surveying and planning for the environment, they simply deliver their speech as if the environment were of no consequence to them. As a student of public speaking, you know what's good and bad about the layout of the classroom in which you must speak. Thus you, too, should plan your delivery accordingly. The box "Speaking of . . . Seating Arrangements" discusses another factor you should consider when planning your delivery.

Tips and Tactics

The Speaking Environment

- Check out the room in which you'll speak well in advance. Take note of the seating arrangement, availability of lectern, and availability of equipment necessary to any media you will be using.
- If permissible, consider changing the environment to better reflect your speech purpose and style of delivery.
- Rehearse planned movement, including how you will use any equipment necessary for your presentational media.
- If possible, try to set the room temperature to between 68 and 70 degrees. Check lighting at the same time.

Speaking of . . .

Seating Arrangements

Can the physical seating arrangement have an impact on both your speech and the manner in which it is perceived? A very dramatic one. As a result, you should think about your goals as a speaker and the physical layout of the room in which you speak. Traditional rows will focus attention exclusively on you. A horseshoe arrangement, however, allows audience members to make eye contact with each other. And speaking at the head of a conference table not only narrows the zone of interaction but also puts a physical barrier between you and your audience. Which of these arrangements do you think would most likely encourage audience feedback and participation? Why?

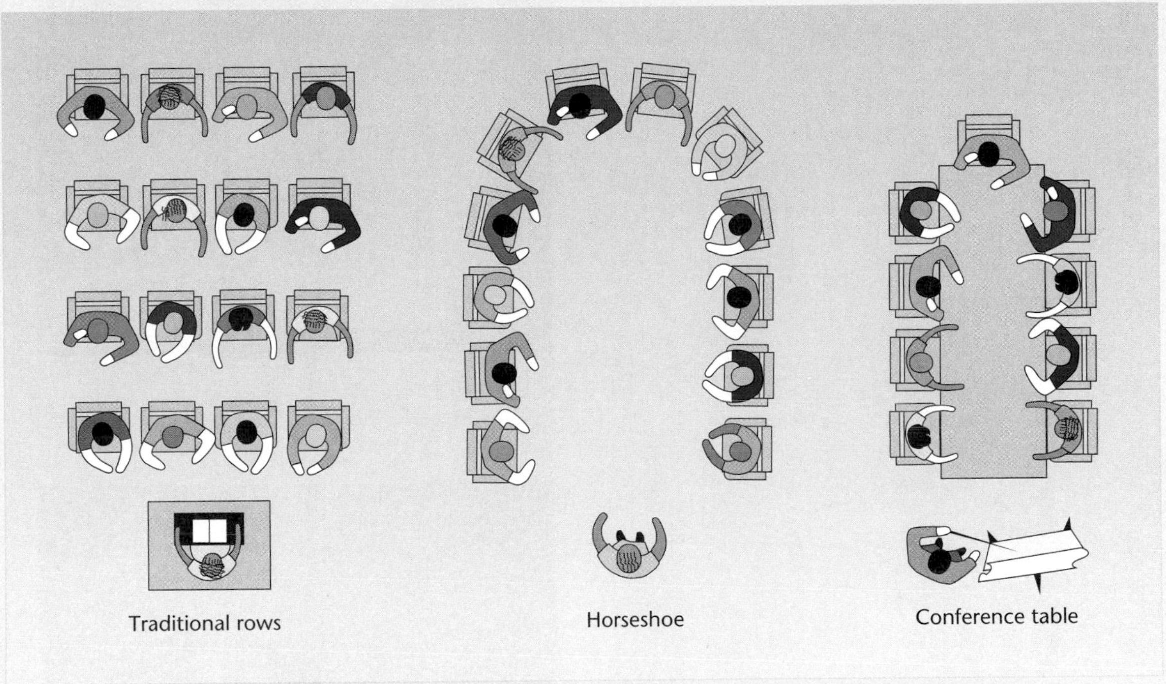

Appearance

Appearance often has a disproportionately significant effect on audience perceptions of a speaker's message and delivery.[10] Speakers never get a second chance to make a first impression with an audience. First impressions are based largely on appearance, including body type and height, skin and hair color, and clothing and accessories.

The significance of appearance to public speaking can be measured in at least two ways. The first involves audience members' first impressions. The second involves how people perceive themselves as a result of their appearance and the impact this perception has on their self-confidence and delivery.

According to communication expert Dale Leathers, "Our visible self functions to communicate a constellation of meanings which define who we are and what we are apt to become in the eyes of others."[11] These "others" are the people with whom we come into contact, including the members of our audiences.

Audience members use appearance initially to make judgments about a speaker's level of attractiveness and degree of similarity. The consequences

Business casual

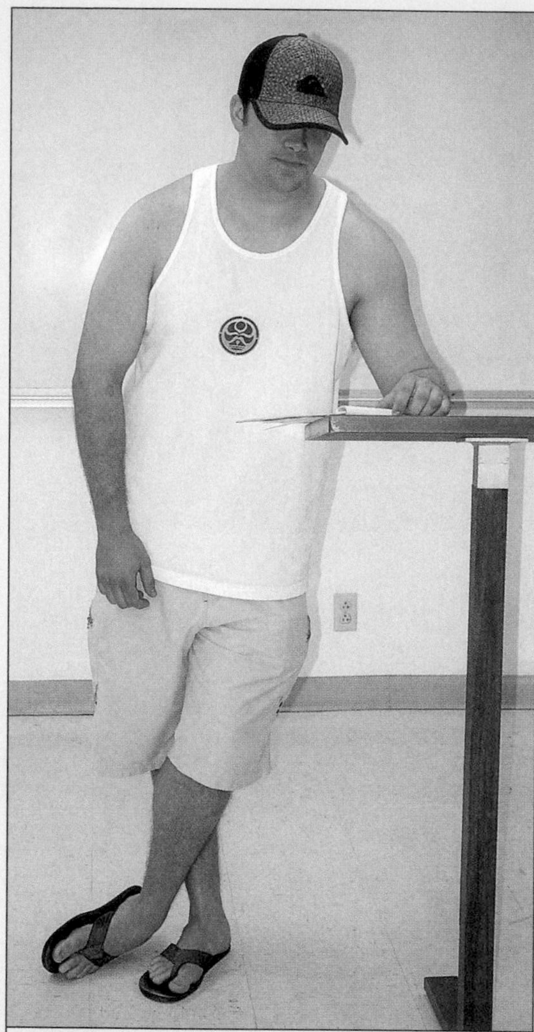

What does this speaker's dress and posture communicate about his attitude toward the assignment and the audience?

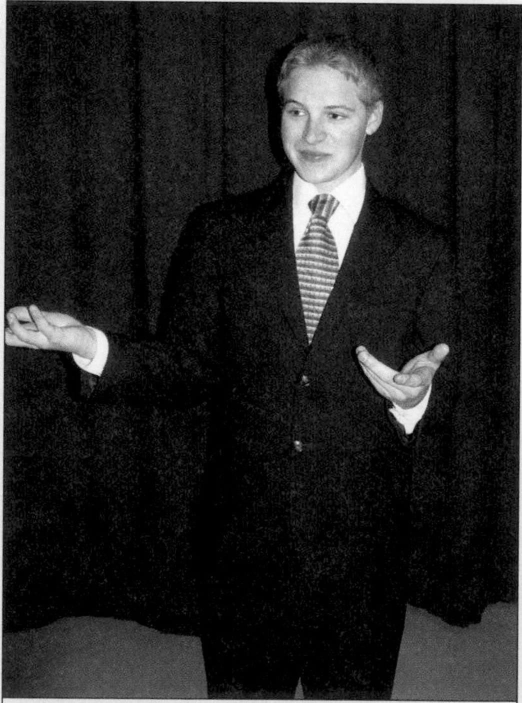

Business formal

of this judgment are far-reaching for speakers. Research tells us that speakers perceived as attractive by audience members also are perceived as smart, successful, sociable, and self-confident. As a result, speakers who fall into this category enjoy an audience whose initial impression of them is favorable.

Yet appearance influences more than an audience's initial impression of a speaker. Appearance also can have a very real effect on a speaker's self-confidence. Research tells us that speakers who feel they appear attractive report greater self-confidence than those reporting otherwise.[12]

Although some facets of your appearance and their impact on audience perception are outside your control–for example, body type and height–you can easily control one facet: your dress. Simply said, your dress should be appropriate to the situation. Obvious as this advice may seem, it is frequently ignored by students in public speaking classes. All too often they show up to speak dressed as if they had thought little about the appropriateness of their attire. Their attitude, as reflected in their dress, seems to be saying, "It's just a speech class."

Consider an analogy. Good students know what the research suggests about the relationship between the appearance of a term paper and the mark it receives. Frequently, it's the difference between a minus or a plus in their grade. Good students, therefore, go to some length to make sure that their papers not only conform to the requirements but "look" impressive as well.

The same relationship may exist between appearance and the marks students receive on their speeches. Although an Armani suit may not turn a mediocre speech into an outstanding one, it certainly won't cause the speaker to lose points. Inappropriate attire or careless grooming will never add points to a speech; moreover, there is a chance they will unnecessarily detract from such things as the speaker's perceived competence. Although we do not recommend formal business attire for most classroom speeches, we urge you to consider a form of attire often called "business casual." For both men and women, business casual could include a polo shirt or sweater, slacks, and shoes you would normally wear in an office. Appropriate dress confers status on you and shows respect for your audience.

The Eyes

Although today's technology makes it possible to actually see our online communication partner using a Web cam, many e-mail and Internet chat room users still use emoticons (or symbols) such as a smiley face to add emotion to their messages. Such symbols are designed to approximate what would be communicated through the eyes and face in normal conversation.

The eyes have been called the windows to the soul. Perhaps, then, it is only fitting that many people also believe eye contact is the single most important variable in delivering a speech. The eyes connect speaker and audience. The eyes also tell the speaker and the audience much about each other.

To repeat, in the North American culture, people use eye contact to make judgments about:

- Whether a person is competent
- Whether a person can be trusted
- Whether a person is approachable

Can you identify the meaning of these different facial expressions?

Competence and trustworthiness are two key components of a speaker's credibility; that is, the degree to which a speaker is perceived as believable. Generally, the more a speaker makes eye contact with audience members, the more credible the speaker will be perceived. Because credible speakers are also likely to have more influence with an audience, it only makes good sense for the speaker to maintain as much eye contact as possible with an audience.

Eye contact also has the power to reduce physical distances psychologically. When we make and sustain friendly eye contact with people at a distance, it makes us feel "closer" to each other. It also helps to make people appear attractive and open to dialogue. As was the case with competence and trustworthiness, this is clearly to a speaker's benefit.

But there is yet another reason for maintaining eye contact with an audience. Eye contact is an important source of audience feedback. In North America, for example, an audience will use eye contact to let the speaker know the degree to which it is engaged. Speakers can then use this feedback to make decisions about whether they need to modify their speech to gain the audience's attention.

Having established its importance to delivery, let's talk about how you can optimize the positive effects of eye contact. First, recognize that you cannot fake eye contact! People know you are looking directly at them or looking only at the tops of their heads. Second, some eye contact is better than no eye contact at all. Ideally, however, eye contact works best when you look at individual members of the audience as you speak. This type of eye contact personalizes a public message. All too often, people think eye contact means looking at the audience members as a group, beginning with those in the center seats, and then turning to those seated to our right or left. To the contrary, effective eye contact means making every person in the room feel as if we were speaking only to him or her.

The Face

Eye contact works best when it is complemented with appropriate facial expressions. The face and eyes, for example, can communicate happiness, surprise, fear, anger, disgust, contempt, sadness, or interest. The face and eyes can also modify the intensity of any of these nonverbal expressions of emotion.[13]

Just as you can use metaphor to manipulate language intensity, you can use your face and eyes to intensify your delivery. In most cases, you intensify what you say in this manner with little or no conscious thought. As you grow angry, for example, the muscles in your face tense and your eyes narrow spontaneously. The purveyor of bad news can make things even worse by accentuating it with the face and eyes.

You can also use your face and eyes to neutralize the message you deliver. Based on an analysis of your situation, you may know that at least some members of the audience will disagree with your views. Suppose you are in a class situation that requires you to deliver a persuasive speech. If your topic is a truly controversial one, you can reasonably predict that not everyone in your audience will agree with everything you say. Although you may not be able to win them over, you also don't want to alienate them. As a result, you may want to use your face and eyes to neutralize some of the more contentious and evocative points you wish to make.

In a sense, what you give an audience in your face and eyes will determine what you can expect to get back from that audience. An intensely worded argument accompanied by the delivery of an equally intense message in the face and eyes invites the same from those who differ with you. On the other hand, using the face and eyes to neutralize the message improves your chance of a more favorable response from your audience. The city of Palo Alto, California, took this to an extreme when it considered a guideline that would have discouraged city council members from using facial expressions to show their disagreement, frustration, or disgust at meetings. The idea behind the guideline was that it would promote civility and defuse conflict among council members and between council members and constituents during public meetings. Good intentions, however, do not always make for good policy. The guideline was unworkable because it is nearly impossible to suppress nonverbal expressions of underlying feelings. In addition, the guideline violated council members' First Amendment rights.[14]

To close, keep in mind that what we have suggested here is based on North American norms. Remember that many cultures frown upon the sustained and focused eye contact that North Americans value. Members of many Asian cultures, for example, view such eye contact as rude and even hostile. Both speakers and audience members should keep this in mind. As a speaker, recognize that when international students appear uncomfortable or don't return your attempts to make eye contact, it may be the result of their culture. As an audience member, realize that your expectancies about eye contact may be at odds with the norms of the international student who is speaking.[15]

Tips and Tactics

Using Your Eyes and Face

- Always face your audience when speaking; avoid turning your back to the audience unless absolutely necessary.
- Make eye contact with people before you begin. Maintain eye contact by meeting the gaze of individual audience members in all parts of the room.
- Avoid excessive eye contact with one person; for example, your instructor.
- Don't be afraid to be expressive with your face.

This speaker illustrates her point with gesture.

Gestures and Movement

You've heard the expression "different strokes for different folks." Nowhere is it more applicable than to the subject of gestures and movement relative to delivery. Although Ronald Reagan neither moved nor gestured very much when he spoke, he was a consummate public speaker. And though you practically have to nail Elizabeth Dole's feet to the floor to keep her from moving, she too is a public speaker of notable achievement. Thus, before we say a single word about how much or how little you should gesture or move as you speak, we want to say this: Your gestures and your movements as you grow as a public speaker should be a refined reflection of what you do naturally.

As is the case with the eyes and face, gestures and movements also can be used to intensify or lessen the emotional impact of verbal messages. Many gestures, for instance, serve as *affect displays;* that is, they visibly communicate feelings. Placing both hands near the heart at the same time you explain how important a subject is to you is an example. So, too, are clenched fists, open palms held face up, or lightly slapping the side of the face.

Gestures such as pointing can regulate the flow of interaction.

Given the preceding caveat, gesturing and moving can complement your delivery in several ways.[16] These include making your delivery more emblematic, making your delivery more illustrative, and regulating the speech transaction.

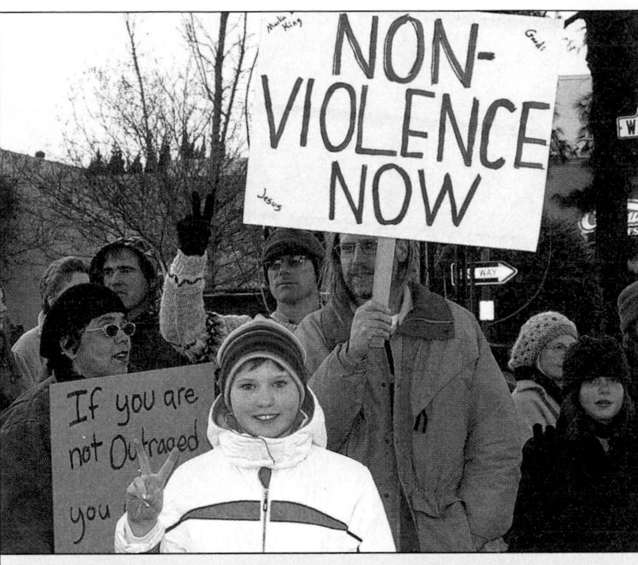

This photo shows people with fingers in a "V"—which is an emblem know as a peace sign.

Emblems

The speeches of the best public speakers are usually rich in emblems. An **emblem** is a nonverbal behavior that can be directly translated into words and phrases and may replace them.[17] For example, it's now widely understood that when a person holds up his or her hand to an ear with the thumb and little finger extended and the other fingers curled under, it means "call me." Emblems must meet the following criteria:

1. The emblem means something specific to the audience members.
2. The emblem is used intentionally by the speaker to stimulate meaning.
3. The emblem can be easily translated into a few words.

emblem
A nonverbal symbol that can be substituted for a word.

As a case in point, U.S. service personnel in Iraq are advised that the okay sign made by Americans with the thumb and forefinger actually is considered an "evil eye" by Iraqis. Further, they are warned, "To signal a vehicle to stop, place arm in front of you, palm down, and then move entire arm up and down. If you simply face the palm toward a person, it means hello, not stop, as in America."[18]

Illustrators

Nonverbal behaviors that accompany speech and "show" what is being talked about are called **illustrators.** Although a lot like emblems, they are more general and seldom translate into a few words. The most common way we nonverbally illustrate is with our hands. Verbal directions or descriptions beg for the use of our hands. Try giving someone directions or describing an object–say, a spiral staircase–without using your hands.

illustrators
Nonverbal symbols used to visualize what is being spoken.

Regulators

Gestures called **regulators** can influence the amount and type of feedback received from the audience. If you hold up your hand when asking audience members whether they've ever felt frustrated waiting in line, for example, you are much more likely to prompt them to raise their hands as well. If you are stationary throughout a speech, your audience will give you much different feedback than if you were to move and periodically change the zone of interaction. Using gestures and movement to regulate feedback requires planning and rehearsal. An unnatural or inappropriate gesture or specific movement may elicit a response from the audience that you don't expect.

regulators
Nonverbal behaviors that influence the speech transaction.

This speaker demonstrates good posture.

This speaker's posture undermines his message.

Regulating audience feedback is particularly important when a speaker answers audience questions. Without regulation, such question-and-answer sessions can turn ugly.

Posture

This dimension is obviously related to movement, gestures, and your overall appearance. Posture is vital to your delivery and the manner in which it is received. People make all kinds of attributions about speakers on the basis of their posture, ranging from how confident a speaker is to how seriously the speaker takes the topic and the situation. At the least, consequently, you will want to guard against an audience making an incorrect attribution about you because you slouched, folded your arms across your chest, stood with one hand on your hip, or put your hands in your pockets.

Because the norms governing appropriate posture vary across cultures, there are no hard-and-fast rules for speakers to follow. Still, given what we know generally about the culture of the beginning public speaking class, there are some steps you can follow to achieve a good posture for delivering your speeches. Remember that the more you slouch and shrink posturally, the less powerful you are likely to be perceived. Remember as well that posture influences the mechanics of your voice. Standing with shoulders back stretches the diaphragm and opens the air passages. That's one reason opera singers invariably have good posture. It helps them use their voice to full effect.

Tips and Tactics

Guidelines for Posture While Delivering a Speech

- Find your center of balance. Usually this means standing with your feet apart at about shoulder width.
- Pull your shoulders back, sticking your chest out and holding your stomach in.
- Keep your chin up and off your chest.
- Initially let your arms rest at your sides with palms open, which will allow you to gesture easily as you speak.

Touch

Touch, which is by far the most intimate and reinforcing of the nonverbal dimensions, can affect your delivery in at least two ways.[19] The first involves **self-adapting behaviors,** which are distracting touching behaviors that speakers engage in unconsciously.

self-adapting behaviors
Nonverbal behaviors used to cope with nervousness; for example, self-touching or grasping the sides of a lectern with hands.

In arousing situations, people frequently touch their face, hair, or clothes without realizing it. Just as frequently they touch some convenient object. They may squeeze the arm of a chair, roll their fingers on a tabletop, trace the outside edge of a glass with a fingertip, or mistake the top of a lectern for a conga drum. They do these things unconsciously.

Because public speaking is arousing, it too can provoke these self-adaptive forms of touch. Further, they can needlessly detract from your delivery. Tugging at an earlobe, rubbing the outside of your upper arm, or jingling the change in your pocket won't help your delivery. Neither will pounding on the lectern with the palms of your hands or rocking it from side to side.

The second way touch can affect your delivery concerns other people. At some point it's likely that your presentations will involve other people. Corporate trainers spend much of their lives giving informative presentations that involve audience participation. The same can be said for sales managers, teachers, attorneys, and practitioners of public relations. Touch very often comes into play in these scenarios. Sometimes it's as simple but as important as shaking a person's hand. At other times it may involve guiding someone by the hand, patting someone on the back, or even giving a more demonstrative tactile sign of approval. At the same time, you must avoid touch that can be interpreted as inappropriate. For example, there have been several widely reported cases of schoolteachers accused of inappropriately touching students. Unwelcome touching can, in fact, be grounds for accusations of sexual harassment.

Touching oneself can be a great distraction when speaking.

Time

The final nonverbal dimension to think about relative to delivery is time. As journalist Michael Ventura writes,

> Time is the medium in which we live. There is inner time—our personal sense of the rhythms of time experienced differently by each of us; and there is imposed time—the regimented time by which society organizes itself, the time of schedules and dead-lines, time structured largely by work and commerce.[20]

First, time varies from one individual to the next. Research confirms what you no doubt long ago suspected. The internal body clock each of us has regulates not only when we sleep but also peak performance when we're awake. Some people perform best from early to midmorning, some during the middle of the day, and others late at night. What is true of performance in general, moreover, is true of public speaking specifically. During our time awake, there are periods when our speaking abilities peak, depending on our individual body clock. Most of us know from our own experience that we either are or are not very alert in the early morning or late afternoon. To the extent possible, attempt to schedule a speaking time when you know your mind and body will be alert.

Time affects your delivery in other ways as well. For example, the time limits you face as a speaker can have an impact on your delivery. As a result of attempting to cover too much material, for example, time limits may cause you to hurry your delivery. Conversely, if you find that you're about to finish your speech under the minimum time requirement of an assignment, you may slow down your delivery in an attempt to meet the time requirement.

The audience's perception of your delivery will also be affected by your "timing," a term frequently used in reference to actors and comics. Just as their timing of a joke or dramatic monologue can spell the difference between success and failure, so too can your timing. Rushing a punch line or dramatic anecdote, for instance, may negate its intended effect. Telling a story too slowly may do likewise.

Because the norms that govern the use of time vary across cultures, how quickly or how slowly you deliver your speech may be a consideration. Whereas a relatively speedy style of delivery may be well received in New York City, it may be received as evidence of the "little time" you have for an audience in parts of the South and Southwest. Conversely, a slow rate of speech, which some mistakenly confuse with the speed at which a person thinks, may prove irritating to audience members whose culture is fast paced.

Finally, whether you are "on time" or late, not only for a speech but just in general, affects your credibility in our North American culture. People who are on time are perceived as efficient and courteous, both of which affect perceptions of competence and trustworthiness. People who are routinely late give the impression they are disorganized and not especially considerate of the time needs of an audience. This is very true of both your classmates and your instructor.

Making the Most of Nonverbal Behavior in Delivery

The eight dimensions of nonverbal behavior we've been talking about perform a number of important functions in speech delivery.[21] As we've discussed, these dimensions interact to make speeches more emblematic and illustrative. They can also help regulate audience feedback and intensify or lessen the emotional impact of what you say during a speech. Other ways that nonverbal dimensions such as the face, eyes, and voice function to facilitate the delivery of your messages include complementing, contradicting, and repeating the message; substituting for a verbal cue; increasing the perception of immediacy;

exciting the audience; and delivering a powerful speech. Consider how you might use these dimensions to maximize your nonverbal behavior in delivering your speech.

This speaker's smile contradicts the force of his gestured fist.

Complementing Your Message

A complementary nonverbal cue serves to reinforce what you verbally share with your audience. A genuine smile on your face as you thank your audience for the opportunity to speak, for example, carries more weight than either message standing on its own. There are many ways to complement the delivery of your message nonverbally. Changing the expression on your face, raising the pitch of your voice, or even breaking off eye contact are just a few of them.

Contradicting Your Message

Often, people contradict themselves nonverbally while communicating interpersonally. Forcing a smile and saying, "I had a great time" is a classic example. Although the smile may have covered up how they really felt, chances are it only served to contradict what they said but didn't mean. Usually people try to keep this from happening.

In the case of public speaking, however, you can use contradiction to enhance your delivery, for example, by rolling your eyes, shrugging your shoulders, or having a sarcastic expression. Certainly Shakespeare knew that contradiction could enhance delivery. He frequently wrote speeches for his characters that invited actors to contradict their verbal statements with nonverbal cues. For example, in Marc Antony's eulogy of Julius Caesar, the line "But Brutus was an honorable man" is usually delivered by an actor in a sarcastic voice that says exactly the opposite. Because it is an attention-getting device, this kind of antithesis in a speech can enhance the impact with which the verbal message is delivered.

This speaker's head in hand repeats his frustration nonverbally.

Repeating Your Message

Repetition is one of the most common ways speakers manipulate their message nonverbally. It's also one of the easiest ways to do this. Raising three fingers as you say you have three points to make doesn't require the oratorical skill of a Colin Powell.

Repetition differs from complementing in a significant way. Whereas a complementary nonverbal cue reinforces the message, a repetitious one serves to make it redundant. The classic example of repeating a message is when *Star*

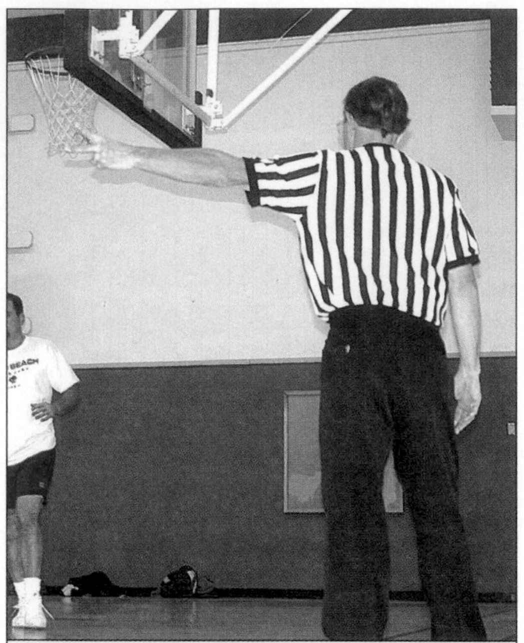

This referee holds out two fingers to repeat his message that the shooter gets two free throws.

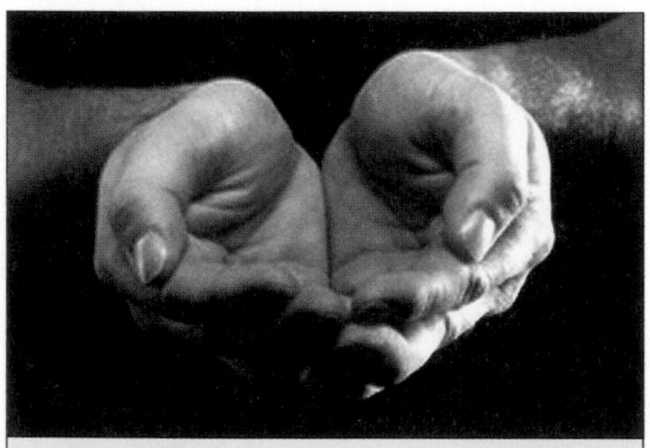

Reaching out with open palms can substitute for a verbal message.

Trek's Mr. Spock makes the Vulcan V sign while saying, "Live long and prosper." Other examples include nodding your head up and down while communicating agreement and shaking your head from side to side when communicating disagreement.

Substituting for a Verbal Cue

Have you ever seen entertainers and politicians raise their hands and motion in the attempt to stop an audience's continued applause? They are using a nonverbal cue as a substitute for a verbal one. In many circumstances, such a nonverbal cue is both more appropriate and more effective than a verbal one. An icy stare shot in the direction of someone talking as you speak is likely to be less disruptive, for example, than politely asking the person to be quiet. Shrugging your shoulders, reaching out with open palms, and raising your eyebrows, moreover, may more clearly communicate your bewilderment than actually saying you're puzzled by something.

Increasing the Perception of Immediacy

Nonverbal behavior can also increase the perception of immediacy between you and your audience. Immediacy concerns how psychologically close or distant people perceive each other, as well as the degree to which they perceive each other as approachable.[22]

Generally, the perception of immediacy between people is desirable because people who are perceived as immediate are also perceived as friendly and approachable, stimulating, open to dialogue, and interpersonally warm.

Because public speaking normally takes place in a setting that arbitrarily puts physical distance between speakers and their audiences, speakers usually have to reduce this physical distance psychologically. You can do this in at least two ways. The first, which we discussed at length in Chapter 11, involves the use of immediate language. The second is to make your delivery more nonverbally immediate.

The easiest and most effective way to make the delivery more immediate is through nonverbal channels. Eye contact is the perfect medium. Even when people are separated by substantial physical distance, eye contact enables them to bridge this distance in a psychological sense. The best public speakers, for example, are often the ones who make you feel as if they are speaking to you, and only you, with their eyes as well as their voices.

Eye contact is not the only medium, however, through which you can achieve greater immediacy with your audience. Immediacy can also be achieved with facial expressions such as a smile, with a conversational rather than condescending tone of voice, and by standing beside the lectern instead of appearing to hide behind it.

Exciting the Audience

One way to gauge the effectiveness of a speech is by the degree to which it stimulates the audience. The best speakers make listeners think, provoke them to laugh, or motivate them to act. Generally, an audience's degree of excitement can be traced to the degree of excitement the audience senses in the speaker.

The level of excitement of public speakers is most noticeable in their delivery. This includes rate of speech, volume of speech, and vocal as well as facial expressions. Excited speakers, the research tells us, speak faster and louder than speakers unaroused by their topic or by the transaction between them and their audience. Excited speakers, the research also tells us, reveal more of themselves as they speak, through changes in facial expressions as well as changes in the pitch of their voice.

Does this mean that someone who simply is excited also is a good speaker? Of course not. Too much excitement can be as distracting as too little excitement can be boring. The idea, then, is to moderate your excitement for your topic or audience rather than to inappropriately exaggerate it with your delivery.

Delivering a Powerful Speech

When it comes to public speaking, the power of words depends mightily on the manner in which they are delivered. No doubt many speech writers have suffered as the power of the words they so carefully crafted was wiped out by the person delivering them. This shouldn't and needn't be the case. With care and practice, you can capitalize on the varying dimensions of nonverbal behavior to make the delivery of your speech powerful. Some of the ways you can do this are obvious; others are more subtle.

Posture is an obvious way you can control the power of delivery. Standing tall and self-assured, in and of itself, communicates power. When combined with movement away from the lectern, this is even more the case.

You can also enhance the power of your delivery with your eyes, with your voice, and through movement and gestures. In North America, at least, powerful speakers make eye contact, speak in a controlled and confident tone of voice, reduce the distance between themselves and their audience by moving closer to them, and gesture as a natural extension of their spoken message. In stark contrast, speakers whose delivery lacks power avoid eye contact, fail to speak up, and usually try to tie up their hands by sticking them in their pockets, gripping the side of the lectern, or hiding them behind their back.

Taking a Proactive Approach

proactive delivery
Taking the initiative, anticipating, and controlling variables that will affect speech delivery.

Knowing something about the nature and functions of nonverbal behavior should assist you in making your speech delivery proactive rather than reactive. To engage in **proactive delivery** means that the speaker takes the initiative and anticipates and controls for as many variables as possible rather than merely reacting to them. Reactive delivery is like the boxer who only counterpunches. This wait-and-see attitude is rarely the mark of a championship boxer, and it can be disastrous for even the most seasoned public speaker. The guidelines that follow should assist you in making sure that your nonverbal behavior enhances, rather than detracts from, the delivery of your speech.

Tips and Tactics

Guidelines for Proactive Speech Delivery

1. *Take control of your environment.* Regardless of when or where you are speaking, you are responsible for making sure the environment suits your purpose and delivery style. This means checking out and modifying the environment well ahead of the time you are scheduled to speak. Check on the configuration of seats and whether or not they need to be re-arranged. Check on the lighting, including its operation if you need to darken the room. Check on the equipment available, including projectors, screens, video monitors, and computers. During your check make sure you know how to operate them if you plan on using them. If you are using a microphone, make sure you have rehearsed with it and have done a thorough sound check.
2. *Rehearse.* You will never be comfortable with your delivery until you are first comfortable with the content of your speech. If you have to "overly think" about content as you actually speak, then it will impede your ability to complement your message nonverbally. On the other hand, when you are comfortable to the point that your speech becomes second nature, your facial expressions, gestures, and movements will become natural extensions of your message. Rehearsing content, therefore, paves the way for proactive delivery.
3. *Take control of your appearance.* Dressing appropriately is one of the easiest ways to enhance initial impressions of you as the medium of your message. Think about the possible effects of apparel, such as the baseball cap that seems to be attached to your scalp, the baggy shorts you prefer, or the saying on your favorite T-shirt.
4. *Use natural gestures.* Make a video of your practice. Check on your gestures. Do they appear natural and complement your delivery, or do they appear forced and detract from your spoken message?
5. *Time your speech.* Do this more than once and on video if you can. Note your timing and the degree to which the rate at which you speak facilitates the mood you want to communicate to your audience. Also, remind yourself that your practice time probably will be longer than when you actually speak before your audience.
6. *Avoid self-adapting behaviors.* During practice, watch out for self-adapting behaviors such as playing with your hair, tugging on a finger, cracking knuckles, licking your lips, and hiding your hands. Self-adapters such as these will call attention to themselves and undermine perceptions of your power and self-confidence. Before you speak, empty pants pockets of loose change and keys and leave pencils and pens at your desk.

Summary

You have choices when making decisions about how to best deliver your speech. The bottom line, however, is that the method you decide on should reflect your preferred style of speaking, the environment in which you will speak, and the speech occasion.

- Effective delivery involves both what you say and how you say it.
- Speakers may choose from four methods of delivery: manuscript, memorized, impromptu, and extemporaneous.
- Effective delivery demands skill not only in articulating the words you use to express yourself but also in using your voice to shape the meaning of what you articulate.
- Nonverbal communication complements the verbal and vocal delivery of your speech. Unlike language, nonverbal communication is continuous, makes use of channels of communication simultaneously, and is spontaneous.
- Specific facets of the nonverbal communication system that influence delivery include the environment, physical appearance, the eyes, face, gestures and movement, posture, time, and touch.
- Gestures frequently take the form of emblems and illustrators, which regulate the speech transaction.
- Important functions of nonverbal communication in the delivery of speeches include complementing the verbal message, contradicting the verbal message, repeating/reinforcing the verbal message, substituting for a verbal cue, increasing immediacy, and increasing excitement and power in the verbal message.

To evaluate your understanding of this chapter, visit our Online Learning Center Web site for quizzes and other chapter study aids.

Check Your Understanding: Exercises and Activities

1. Observe a speaker outside of your class. Keep track of the number of times the speaker (a) changes the zone of interaction, (b) moves away from the lectern, and (c) gestures. On a scale of 1 to 10, with 10 being the high end, rate the speaker in each of these areas. Compare and discuss your observation and ratings with those of other students. See if a pattern emerges.
2. Make two blank copies of the personal style scale you filled out in the Self-Assessment box on page 289. Next time you speak, ask two class members to fill out these scales in terms of how they perceive your communication style. Compare their assessments with yours. Do they agree? If they do not agree, discuss the differences they see in your style relative to how you see yourself. Also see if you cannot isolate specific nonverbal behaviors that may help you explain any perceived differences.
3. On a scale of 1–10, how confident are you as an audience member in your interpretations of a speaker's nonverbal behavior? Using the same scale, how confident are you as a speaker in your audience's interpretation of

your nonverbal behavior? If you responded as most people do to these two questions, you'll notice a discrepancy. We are more confident in our own interpretative abilities than those of our audience. Nonverbal communication research indicates that all of us are more confident in our ability to decode nonverbal behavior than we should be. This research also shows that this is especially true in terms of decoding nonverbal behaviors we associate with truthful rather than deceptive public speakers. Most of us, in fact, are lousy at deception detection. Discuss with other people in class the implications of this research for the transaction between speakers and audiences.

4. Have someone loosely tie your hands behind your back or try and keep your hands clasped behind your back. Now, standing in front of the class, try to give audience members directions from where you are standing to your exact residence. What lessons about the relationship between nonverbal communication and delivery can be learned from this frustrating exercise? Be specific. Write down at least three and share them with your class.

5. Differences in nonverbal norms, as well as differences in communication styles and patterns, are common across cultures. Choose two or three North American norms for nonverbal behavior–for example, eye contact, gesturing, and time. Interview a student or faculty member from a culture other than North American about how these communication behaviors differ in his or her culture. Write a short paper summarizing your findings.

6. Explain why sign language is a *verbal* behavior, whereas vocal variation in pitch, rate, tempo, and the like are *nonverbal* behaviors, even though sign language is not vocalized and vocal variation is.

7. Explain why nonverbal behavior is continuous, uses multiple channels simultaneously, and is spontaneous and how these characteristics distinguish it from the language of your speech.

8. Review the four guidelines for proactive delivery. Before your next speech, develop a plan to use at least three of these guidelines to improve your delivery skills in that speech.

9. Ask a classmate to apply Exercise 1 to your next speech. Talk with the classmate afterward about the relationship between his or her observations and the overall effectiveness of your delivery.

10. How would you describe your public speaking style? Is it a dramatic or understated style? Is it formal or informal? Ask some of your classmates to choose five adjectives they would use to describe your style of speaking. Compare their adjectives with five of your own. If you take advantage of this exercise, there is a good chance it will at least suggest a visual image of the style you communicate to others as you speak. You can then use this image to refine your style of speaking.

Notes

1. Edward T. Hall, *The Silent Language* (Greenwich, Conn.: Fawcett Publications, 1959), 15.

2. Dan Vierra, "Straight Talk: Bush Praised for Posture if not Words," *The Sacramento Bee,* 25 January 2007, E1.

3. George B. Ray, "Vocally Cued Personality Prototypes: An Implicit Personality Theory Approach," *Communication Monographs* 53 (1986): 266–76.

4. Richard L. Street and Robert M. Brady, "Evaluative Responses to Communicators as a Function of Evaluative Domain, Listener Speech Rate, and Communication Context," *Communication Monographs* 49 (1982): 290–308.

5. David B. Buller and R. Kelly Aune, "The Effects of Speech Rate Similarity on Compliance: An Application of Communication Accommodation Theory," *Western Journal of Speech Communication* 56 (1992): 37–53.

6. J. Burgoon, D. W. Buller, and W. G. Woodhall, *Nonverbal Communication: The Unspoken Dialogue,* 2nd ed. (New York: Harper & Row, 1989). See also M. Knapp and J. A. Hall, *Nonverbal Communication in Human Interaction,* 3rd ed. (Fort Worth, Tex.: Harcourt, Brace, and Jovanovich, 1992).

7. L. A. Malandro, L. Barker, and D. A. Barker, *Nonverbal Communication,* 2nd ed. (New York: Random House, 1989).

8. V. P. Richmond and J. C. McCroskey, *Nonverbal Behavior in Interpersonal Relationships* (Englewood Cliffs, N.J.: Prentice-Hall, 1991).

9. R. Sommer, "Man's Proximate Environment," *Journal of Social Issues* 22 (1966): 60.

10. Ellen Berscheid and Elaine Walster, "Beauty and the Best," *Psychology Today* 5, no. 10 (1972): 42–46.

11. D. Leathers, *Successful Nonverbal Communication: Principles and Practices* (New York: Macmillan, 1986).

12. Malandro, Barker, and Barker, *Nonverbal Communication.*

13. P. Ekman and W. V. Friesen, *Unmasking the Face: A Guide to Recognizing Emotions from Facial Expression* (Englewood Cliffs, N.J.: Prentice-Hall, 1975). See also P. Ekman, W. V. Friesen, and S. Ancoli, "Facial Signs of Emotional Expression," *Journal of Personality and Social Psychology* 39 (1980): 1125–34.

14. Nicole C. Wong, "Palo Alto May Relent–It's OK to Frown." *The Sacramento Bee,* 18 April 2003, A6.

15. P. Ekman, *Telling Lies* (New York: Norton, 1985). See also Bella M. DePaulo, Miron Zuckerman, and Robert Rosenthal, "Humans as Lie Detectors," *Journal of Communication* 30 (1980): 129–39; R. E. Kraut, "Verbal and Nonverbal Cues in the Perception of Lying," *Journal of Personality and Social Psychology* 36 (1978): 380–91.

16. Judee Burgoon, "Nonverbal Communication Research in the 1970s: An Overview," in *Communication Yearbook* 4, ed. D. Nimmo (New Brunswick, N.J.: Transaction Books, 1980), 179–97.

17. Joseph A. Devito, *The Communication Handbook: A Dictionary* (New York: Harper & Row, 1986), 105.

18. Rolf Potts, "A Marine Corps Primer on Cultural Sensitivity in Arab Lands," *Rolf Potts' Vagabonding,* 23 July 2004. [Retrieved from

http://www.vagablogging.net/04-07/a-marine-corps-primer-on-cultural-sensitivity-in-arab-lands.html, 28 May 2007.]

19. Stephen Thayer, "Close Encounters," *Psychology Today* 22, no. 3 (1988): 31–36. See also A. Montague, *Touching: The Significance of the Skin* (New York: Harper & Row, 1971).

20. Michael Ventura, "Trapped in a Time Machine With No Exits," *The Sacramento Bee,* 26 February 1995, C1.

21. Burgoon, Buller, and Woodhall, *Nonverbal Communication: The Unspoken Dialogue;* E. T. Hall, "System for the Notation of Proxemic Behavior," *American Anthropologist* 65 (1963): 1003–26.

22. Malandro, Barker, and Barker, *Nonverbal Communication.*

"The visual aid is not the message, it is your helper, but if used correctly it can have a strong impact on your audience."

Effective Use of Visual Aids

Jim Katt

Objectives

After reading and discussing this chapter, you should be able to:

- Define the term *visual aid* from a functional perspective.
- Describe the ways that visual aids can help you communicate more clearly with your audience.
- Describe the characteristics of effective visual aids.
- Understand the advantages and disadvantages of the various types of visual aids.
- Demonstrate the use of PowerPoint™ in a way that establishes the proper relationship between you and your visuals.
- Be able to incorporate underused techniques when using PowerPoint™.

Key Concepts

What are visual aids?

How visual aids can help us communicate

Characteristics of effective visual aids

Types of visual aids

Using PowerPoint™

“ The ability to simplify means to eliminate the unnecessary so that the necessary may speak. ”

–HANS HOFFMAN

Effective Use of Visual Aids

When you are making a presentation to an audience, your audience has five senses with which to receive your message. Of the five, three have limited use in public speaking: touch, taste, and smell. Yes, there have been presentations where the audience was able to feel the texture of the fabric sample that was passed around, or was treated to some tasty samples of Greek pastry, or got a whiff of freshly baked bread, but most of the time, speakers use the channels of sound and sight. Much of this textbook deals with how to make the sounds of your speech effective. This chapter takes a look at the sights.

One of the best visual aids you can use is yourself. The sight of you–a living, human creature–is important. Your presence shows your audience who is speaking to them and provides something absent in so many of the newer forms of communication. Over twenty years ago, *Megatrends* author Michael Nesmith (1984) accurately predicted that the growth of "high tech" communication would leave people with an increased need for "high touch." Today, we have many ways of sending messages from one person to another. We can bridge the barriers of time and distance. Yet in spite of all the technology that we have invented, and all that we will soon invent, the senders and receivers in the process of communication are still people, not machines or software. There is still a powerful phenomenon that takes place when people speak to other people who are with them in the same place, at the same time. Your presence provides a personal touch in an increasingly impersonal world.

Since Chapter 12 talks about how to effectively present your visual self, this chapter will focus on the use of other visual elements in your speeches. But it is appropriate to be reminded of the importance of ourselves as visuals, because we want to be sure the other visuals you present don't take too much attention away from the most important element of your speech–you.

Defining Visual Aids

visual aids
Visual elements that help your audience receive your message.

Visual aids are visual elements that help (aid) your audience receive your message. It is important to remember that the visual aid, whether it takes the form of an object, a poster, or some sort of projected image, is not the message, and not the messenger; it is just your helper. If, when speaking, you treat the visual aid like it is more important than you are, your audience is likely to begin to feel that it *is* more important than you. It is unfortunate when that happens, because ultimately they would have been able to relate more to you, the person, than they will ever relate to your object, your poster, or your projected image.

Ways Visual Aids Help Us Communicate More Effectively

If used appropriately, visual aids can assist you in getting your message across in several ways. Let's discuss some of those ways.

Attract Audience Attention

Visuals attract the audience's attention. Hold up an object or project a slide and all eyes will be on it. For a speaker, this is a two-edged sword. Drawing your audience's attention away from their daydreaming or looking around the room is a good thing, but drawing your audience's attention away from you, the presenter, is only worthwhile if the visual they're drawn to conveys (or helps convey) your message. This is one reason you don't want to be displaying visual aids throughout the entire speech. When you need to draw attention to something visual, use a visual aid. The rest of the time, put the visual aids away and let the audience pay attention to the presenter.

Emphasize Key Points

Because visuals draw attention, they can be used to emphasize key concepts. When your audience can see as well as hear certain key points, they are likely to remember them (Vogel, Dickson, & Lehman, 1986). A well-constructed bullet list can help your audience see your main points and how they relate to one another. A compelling photograph may stay in your audience's memories far longer than your words. But it's important to realize that this effect can backfire if overused. We have all fallen victim to presenters who have almost the entire text of their speeches written out on PowerPoint™ slides or overhead transparencies, and then proceed to read to us what we are seeing on the screen. This technique fails for several reasons. First, everything in the speech can't be a key point. Someone once noted that there cannot be peaks without valleys. The same logic goes for messages. If you were composing a written message you might bold a key word, for emphasis. But if you bold *all* the words, you end up emphasizing nothing. Secondly, the audience can read for themselves, so it's patronizing to read to them. Finally, when everything is on the screen, the audience gets the idea that *you* aren't very important, since you don't seem to add any value to the transaction. When that happens, you throw away the high-touch impact of your presence. And if you don't add anything to the presentation, you're wasting your audience's time. You could have emailed your slides to them, if that's all you had. Judicious use of visuals for emphasis can be effective in helping your audience know and remember those key concepts.

Show the Relationship Between Points

When you read a book, there are sentences and paragraphs and sections and chapters to help you know how the information goes together. When you listen to someone speak, it can be difficult to know what goes with what. There are some aural things (like clear transitions and signposts) that you can do to make the organization of your speech clearer to your audience. Visuals can also be used for this purpose. A concise bullet list, for example, provides a visual indication of how one point relates to the next, and if you reveal the bullet points one at a time, it helps your audience realize when you are moving from one point to the next.

Wild Animals	Wild Animals	Wild Animals
Wolves	Wolves	Wolves
	Tigers	Tigers
		Bears

Revealing one bullet at a time lets your audience know you are moving from one point to the next.

Simplify Numeric Information

Most people learned numbers visually. We learned to recognize them visually, and we learned to add, subtract, multiply, and divide them visually. So it's little wonder that when we receive a barrage of numeric information orally, it is difficult to follow. When hearing numeric data, many people resort to mentally visualizing the numerals to make sense of them. Properly designed visual aids can make things easier on our audiences. Either by showing them the numbers, or by providing a graphic representation of the values the numbers represent, speakers can make life easier for their audiences, and be more effective presenters.

Graphic representation of numeric data helps your audience make sense of the information.

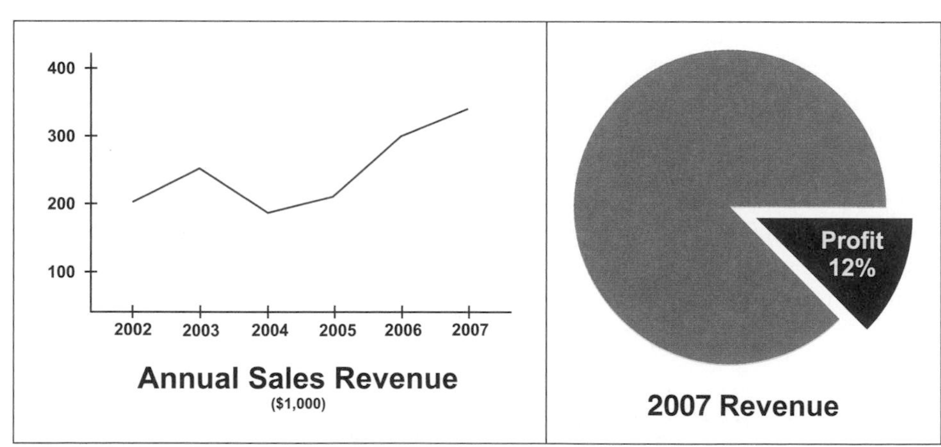

Make Examples More Specific

Perhaps your speech is about your camp counselor who first got you interested in astronomy and inspired you to work hard, get good grades, and go to college to become a rocket-scientist. There would be stories to tell and touching anecdotes to include in your speech, but a photograph of that counselor (maybe even one with you in the shot), would go a long way in helping your audience feel like they *knew* that person, instead of just knowing some things about her. Perhaps it is not a technique that works for every speech, but sometimes a

A picture can take a general idea and quickly make it specific.

well-placed picture can take an example from general to specific in a hurry. I once heard a young woman give a speech about her job driving a huge, off-road dump truck at a coal mining site. She mentioned several times that the truck was very large, but it wasn't until she showed the picture of her standing next to the truck (the top of her head came only to the middle of the wheel) that the audience really got a sense of how large the truck really was. Saying "large" provided a general idea; showing the truck, with her as a reference, made it specific.

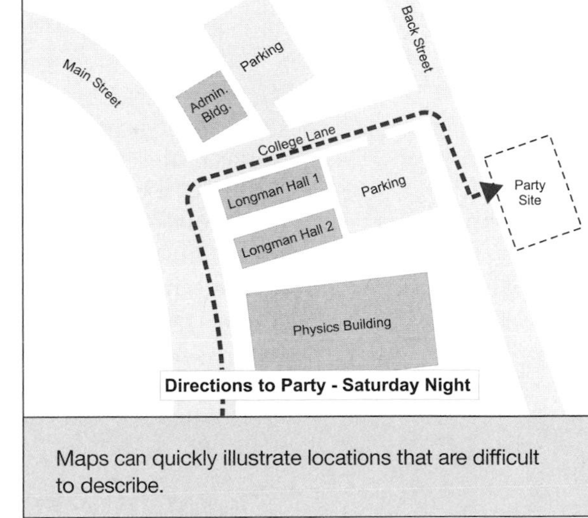

Maps can quickly illustrate locations that are difficult to describe.

Illustrate Difficult-to-Describe Objects or Scenes

Some things are just difficult to put into words. If you wanted to describe a location on the other side of the campus, you could talk about how to get there, or what it was near, or where it was relative to some central feature of the campus–or you could show them a campus map with the location highlighted. Some things are just easier to show than to tell; that's where a good visual aid can be a real helper.

Illustrate Symbolic Relationships

A drawing or diagram is often symbolic rather than literal. Suppose, for a speech about interpersonal communication, you needed to describe the importance of each person's experiences as they relate to the shared experiences between two people in a relationship. You could talk it through, but it is a fairly abstract concept that might become clearer if you introduced a diagram that helped your audience visualize the concept.

Drawings can simplify complex concepts.

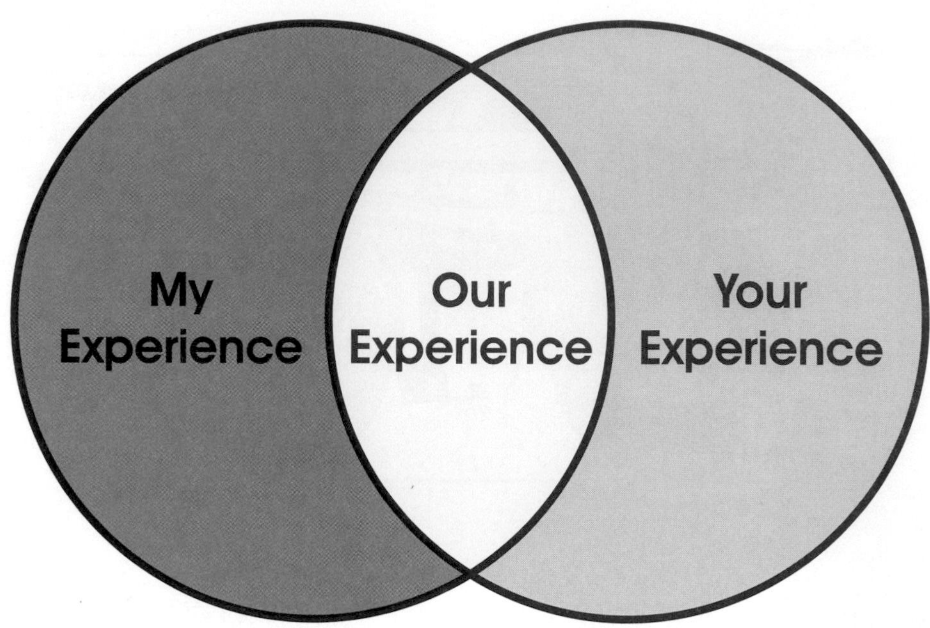

Of course people don't literally walk around with big circles of experience that intersect other people's circles, but the circles provide a symbolic way of representing the experiential relationship.

So visual aids can help speakers attract an audience's attention, emphasize key points, show relationships between points, simplify numeric information, make examples more specific, illustrate things that are difficult to describe, or create symbolic relationships. But this isn't always the case. Frequently, speakers employ visual elements that fail to accomplish any of these functions. In an attempt to avoid having that happen to us, let's examine some of the characteristics of effective visual aids.

Characteristics of Effective Visual Aids

Effective Visual Aids Are Visible

Of course it wouldn't make any sense to have an invisible visual aid, but some speakers create visual aids that might as well be invisible because they are not large enough, or not legible. Ideally, visual aids are not just visible; they are *easy* for the audience to see. If the visuals involve text, the letters must be large enough for everyone to see easily. We'll discuss this more in the PowerPoint™ portion of this chapter, but I recommend that projected visuals (either PowerPoint™ or overhead transparencies) be set in no less than 24-point type. That means that *all* text, even captions, labels, and citations, should be at least 24-point. If you are creating a poster or flip chart, the "correct" size will depend on how large the room is. For small rooms (seating 30 people or fewer) a minimum text size of 1½ inches is suggested, with titles at least twice as large (Hamilton, 1996).

A PowerPoint™ slide of a small object can help your audience see it in detail.

If your visual aid is an object, it needs to be large enough for all to see. One sure way to annoy your audience is to hold up a small object and then say "Well, you probably can't see this, but…." Besides the obvious dysfunction of a visual aid the audience can't really see, the act of showing them the "too small" object can send the unintended message that you really don't care that much about whether or not the audience receives your message clearly. And if they get the idea you don't care, there really isn't any reason for them to care either. If the thing you are talking about is too small, figure out a way to enlarge it for your audience. Often, the easiest method is to find (or take) a digital picture of the object and make the image into a PowerPoint™ slide. In that case, you might still show the actual object, so they can see how small it is, but use the PowerPoint™ slide to allow them to visually examine the object.

Today, most college students have grown up with computers and graphic programs like PowerPoint™. It wasn't that long ago when the most common student visual aid was created with poster board and markers. That put a lot of pressure on the creator to write legibly, so the audience could actually read what was written on the poster. One would think computers would solve the legibility problem, but presenters have found new, computerized ways to make even computer-generated visuals illegible. The PowerPoint™ section of this chapter will cover this issue at some length, but at this point, let's remind ourselves that *legible*, like *large*, is not about making text *possible* to read; it's about making it *easy* to read. Avoid decorative fonts and choose font colors that contrast with the background colors. Old English or script fonts are the modern version of illegible, along with green text over a blue background.

Effective Visual Aids Are Non-Distracting

A good visual aid can draw the audience's attention to key points, but a poor visual aid can draw their attention away from the speaker's message. Some speakers allow their visual aids to be more disruptive than instructive. This unfortunate situation can be avoided by following two guidelines.

First, keep the visual aid out of sight when not in use. Suppose your speech included a reference to the art of M.C. Escher. What if, at the beginning of your speech, you set up an easel with a poster-sized reproduction of one of Escher's optical illusions and then started with your introduction? Do you think the audience would be paying attention to what you were saying? Most of them would be engrossed in the picture, trying to figure out how the illusion works. In this case, your visual serves as a distraction rather than an aid. The solution is to keep it out of sight until you are ready to use it. In the case of a poster on an easel, just bring a sheet of white poster board to cover the visual until you're ready for it. If you are using an overhead transparency, leave the projector turned off until its time comes. If you are using PowerPoint™, display a black slide or use the "B" key (as explained later in this chapter). When you are finished referring to your visual, put it back out of sight, using the same method.

Second, keep the visual aid in your possession if at all possible. There may be occasions where a pass-around visual aid is necessary, but try to avoid those situations. The pass-around visual aid inevitably draws attention away from the presentation as it snakes its way through the audience. And from the perspective of the individuals in the audience, the pass-around is received too early or too late for everyone except the lucky one or two who happen to have it exactly when it's being referred to.

Effective Visual Aids Are Simple and Clear

Because visuals naturally draw attention, it is important that the attention is focused on something that helps communicate your message. Sometimes speakers include too much visual information and leave their audience confused instead of enlightened. As the story goes, someone viewed one of Michelangelo's sculptures, a stunning lion, just after the artist had completed it. The observer asked Michelangelo how he was able to create such a beautiful lion from a block of stone. The artist thought a moment, then said he studied the blank stone until he could "see" the lion inside it. Then, he continued, it was simply a matter of removing all the stone that wasn't the lion. Of course! That explains why everyone who is skillful with a chisel can't create timeless art. It only works for those who can "see the lion." A student gave a speech on jet engines. He explained that there were really only five major components of a jet engine: the air intake, compressor, combustion chamber, turbine, and the exhaust nozzle. That seemed simple enough to his audience. Then he projected an overhead slide that must have been copied from an aircraft repair manual. The illustration showed every nut, bolt, and washer in a commercial airliner's jet engine, along with part numbers and arrows to connect the part number to the parts. It was an incredibly complex visual. As the speaker frantically pointed to various areas in the mass of parts that he claimed corresponded to the five basic components, the audience became confused, quickly gave up trying to understand, and soon tuned out the speaker and his message. Metaphorically speaking, this speaker was guilty of displaying the block of stone and expecting his audience to see the lion within. Good visual aids have nothing extraneous that needs to be chipped away. Good illustrations show

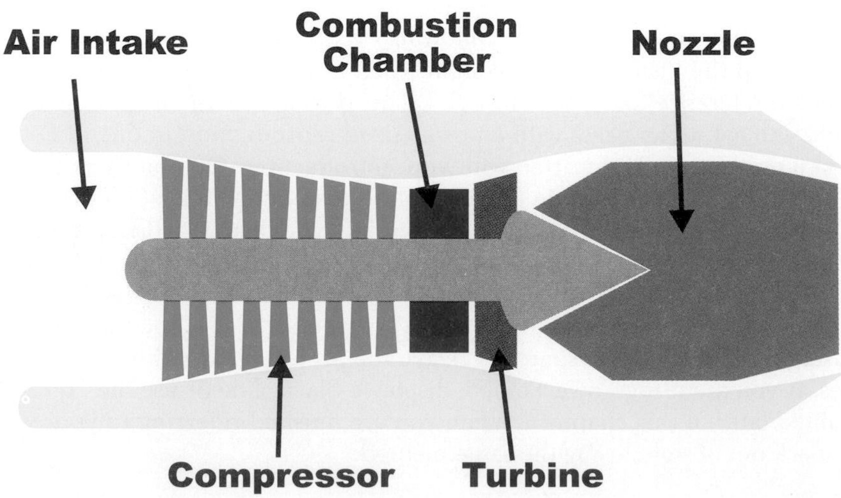

Good illustrations only include the elements you want to discuss.

the elements that are being explained and nothing else. Showing the audience more than you are prepared to explain is, at the least, an annoyance, and, at the most, reason for them to give up on your message altogether.

Effective Visual Aids Are Functional

Some students include visual aids in their presentations because their professor has required them to do so. While adherence to the requirements of the assignment is a good thing, a visual aid that has no communicative purpose is not. Remember the definition at the beginning of the chapter: visual aids are visual elements that help your audience receive your message. If your visual aid doesn't help get your message across, it's not really a visual aid. A student who presented a speech about his job building and selling computers held up a computer mouse at the end of his speech. He said, "By the way, here's a mouse. Most of the computers I sold came with a mouse." What communicative purpose did that visual serve? Was there nothing else in his message that could have been communicated more effectively with the help of a visual aid? During the course of his speech he mentioned that the systems he built offered more features for less money than the brand-name computers. He might have created a visual that pictured one of his computer systems next to a brand-name system. He could have listed the pertinent specifications of each along with the prices, reinforcing his claim that the computers he built were a better value than the brand-name computers. That sort of visual aid would have served a communicative purpose. The mouse did not. In this case, it didn't even fulfill the requirement to have a visual aid–his professor refused to count something that non-functional as a visual aid.

Types of Visual Aids

Objects or Models

Often showing your audience "the thing" that you are talking about goes a long way toward making your speech more effective. Of course, some things are too large or too small, but many objects are portable enough to bring with you and still large enough to see. Often, objects can be used effectively with other visuals. For example, if you were giving a speech that included describing the parts located on the motherboard of a computer, you might bring in an actual motherboard, so your audience gets sense of its overall size, and also have a series of projected pictures that show the individual parts, which would be too small for them to see on the motherboard. Objects can be helpful in a *literal* sense–showing the audience how big the motherboard is–or in a *symbolic* sense.

A student speaking about his job as a server in a restaurant used a waiter's wallet (the leather or plastic folder containing the bill that servers bring to the table) as symbol of ongoing feedback from customers that is reflected by the size of the tips. "Some employees are evaluated once a year," he said. "Servers are evaluated

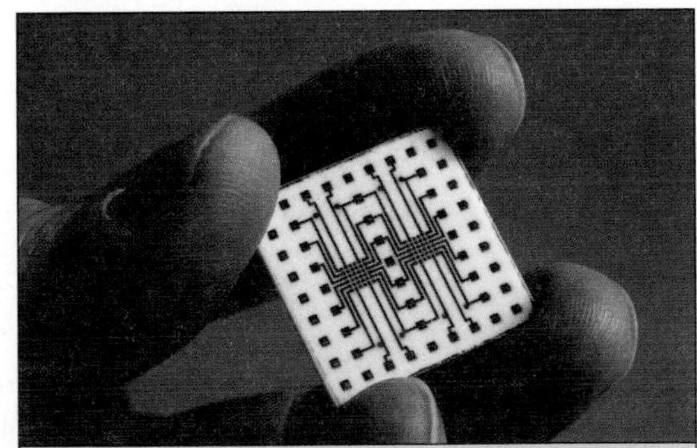

It is better to have pictures of objects that are too small to be seen by your audience.

every day, and the results show up here, in this wallet." The audience members already knew what the wallet looked like, so it wasn't informative in the usual sense, but the speaker made it into a symbol of the evaluative nature of tips. Each time he referred to one of the customer service aspects of his job, he held up the wallet, reminding the audience that being a waiter (and earning tips) is all about customer service. It was an effective–and symbolic–visual.

Some objects would be helpful visual aids, but they are too large, too expensive, or too dangerous to bring with you. In these cases, models or facsimiles may be the answer. The space shuttle is too large, too expensive, and too dangerous to bring with you, but a model might provide a more compelling visual than a drawing or a picture. Speaking of dangerous, remember that college campuses have rules about bringing anything into a classroom that might be dangerous. The campus police at most colleges and universities take such things seriously. For example, a gas can might be the perfect visual object to go with your speech about alternative fuels, but there is probably a rule against bringing combustibles into a classroom. And when you give that speech about bow hunting, you'll probably want to bring in a *picture* of your cross bow and leave the real thing at home.

Posters or Flip Charts

Posters and flip charts are only useful for relatively small audiences, but they have some advantages. They are inexpensive, they do not require special lighting, and they are completely low-tech, so they aren't subject to the technical problems that often plague PowerPoint™ presentations. They do have problems of their own, however. First, if the posters or flip charts are hand drawn, care must be taken to make them legible–not just decipherable, but *easy* to read. As we mentioned previously, text should be no smaller than 1½ inches high and titles should be at least twice as large. Second, some thought needs to go into how they are going to be supported (literally, what's going to hold them up). Poster boards balanced on the chalk tray of a chalkboard will almost always fall down in the middle of your speech. In the same manner, masking tape doesn't really stick to a chalkboard–at least not for long. Some tapes can also damage paint or wall coverings, which leaves you making a bad impression with whoever is hosting the event. Pushpins are effective, providing you bring them and there is a "pinable" surface available. Easels also work well, if the visual is stiff enough not to bend over during your speech. The biggest reason speakers have poster support problems is that they fail to carefully think through the issue *before* their speeches. This isn't rocket science, just one of those cases where an ounce of prevention really *is* better than a pound of cure. Finally, posters should look *professional.* If it looks like an elementary school student scribbled it together moments before your speech, your credibility may be negatively affected.

Overhead Transparencies

The venerable overhead transparency projector is often scornfully viewed by speakers who increasingly prefer to use projected computer images like PowerPoint™. While it is true that presentation software has many advantages over its low-tech predecessor, there are still some merits in using overhead transparencies. First is that overheads can be projected effectively in rooms that are too bright for computer video projectors to work properly. The most important advantage, however, is dependability. About the only thing that can go wrong with the overhead projector is the bulb burning out. Many projectors have spare lamps built into them, making them extremely dependable. Even though projecting PowerPoint™ is hardly cutting-edge technology, there is a lot that can go wrong. Murphy's Law suggests than anything that *can* go wrong *will* go wrong, so overhead transparencies provide fewer opportunities for Murphy to interfere with your speech. Many professional speakers who use PowerPoint™ as their primary presentational aid carry overhead transparencies of key slides just in case disaster strikes. It's a good idea for you to consider doing this as well.

Overhead projectors are generally dependable and can be used when PowerPoint™ cannot or does not work.

There are a few things to bear in mind when using overhead transparencies. First, when creating the transparencies, follow the same rules for text visuals that you would for designing PowerPoint™ slides (discussed later in this chapter). This includes trying to keep the text size at least 24 point. Speakers will sometimes photocopy a page of a book onto a transparency. This almost always makes a poor visual, with text so small that the audience either cannot read it or will not be willing to put forth the effort to read it. Projecting a bad visual doesn't make it a good visual–it just increases the number of people who can see that it's bad.

The overhead projector will project either a landscape or portrait slide, but nearly all screens are oriented for landscape, so compose your slide in the landscape format. Also, be careful with colors. Many of the inks used in inkjet printers are opaque rather than translucent. Since light must shine through the transparency for a color to be projected, opaque colors end up looking black when projected. The best practice is to test your slides prior to your presentation.

Getting the projector positioned and focused is a fairly simple matter, but should be taken care of prior to your speech. There are "Tips for Projecting Overhead Transparencies" listed at the end of this chapter. If you plan to use overhead transparencies, you would do well to read the tips carefully.

PowerPoint™

Presentation software, such as Microsoft's PowerPoint™, has become a standard tool of the workplace, something everyone is expected to know how to use–like word processing or email. In many ways, this is a good thing. Visual information that was once displayed on poster boards, flip charts, or overhead transparencies now can be easily and clearly presented with the help of PowerPoint™ or one of the competing presentation software packages. A well-designed set of PowerPoint™ slides can provide visual support to a spoken message and allow the speaker to devote only a minimal amount of his or her attention to displaying the visuals.

PowerPoint™ is a tool, and like any tool, it can be misused. The experienced carpenter can use saws and chisels to create fine furniture. However, those same tools, badly used, can turn good lumber into worthless scraps of wood. In the realm of carpentry, even the less-than-skillful carpenter generally realizes his or her mistakes and doesn't try to assemble the mis-crafted pieces into furniture. Unfortunately, in the realm of presentations, ill-fashioned PowerPoint™ slides often fail to go into the trash and instead become part of the presentation–to the detriment of both presenter and audience. Are there any among us who have not been the victims of some of the following varieties of PowerPoint™ abuse?

- Speakers who include nearly everything they say on the slides, and spend most of their "presentation" reading the slides to the audience
- Speakers who turn their backs to their audiences, face the screen, and read the slides
- Presentations where every new bullet point or graphic object flies into view in a distracting, annoying manner
- Presentations where the annoying fly-ins are accompanied by even more annoying sound effects
- Speakers who turn the lights out on themselves, their voices becoming disembodied, mystery narrators for their slides
- Text slides that are difficult to read because the text is too small, they are too wordy, poorly laid out, or the color of the lettering blends into the background
- Illustrations, charts, or graphs contain so much information that it is difficult to find the point of the message

Using PowerPoint™ Effectively

There are many books and Web sites that explain how to create slides and operate PowerPoint™ software, but very few resources offer guidance on how to effectively integrate PowerPoint™ visuals into a presentation. The remainder of this chapter concerns using PowerPoint™ effectively and avoiding PowerPoint™ abuse.

Who's the Presenter and Who's the Helper?

One way to avoid PowerPoint™ abuse is to be clear about your role and PowerPoint™'s role in your presentation. It is easy, and sometimes more comfortable, to think of PowerPoint™ as the presenter and you as the helper/technician/projectionist, but to do so relinquishes the power of face-to-face communication. You are the human being–the living, breathing, thinking, feeling person who can relate to and communicate with other humans in a much more powerful way than any arrangement of ones and zeros and pixels. You are the speaker–the communicator, the person in charge of the presentation. PowerPoint™ can be a great helper, but be careful not to let it take over your role as presenter. Here are some things you can do to help keep you and PowerPoint™ in a proper relationship.

Maintain Eye Contact with Your Audience

During your presentation, maintain eye contact with your audience, not with your PowerPoint™ slides. It's okay to sneak a quick peak at the screen every so often, just to make sure it's working, but when you find yourself looking at the screen most of the time and at your audience only occasionally, you are (non-verbally) telling your audience that PowerPoint™ is the presenter and you are just the narrator.

Show Visuals Only When They Add Something to Your Speech

Realize that you do not have to display an image on the screen at all times. It's okay to turn the screen off when you don't need it. In fact, building in some PowerPoint™ down time during your speech is desirable. After all, the PowerPoint™ images are usually larger and more colorful than you are. It is easy for your audience to become immersed in what's on the screen behind you and forget about *you.* Actors refer to this process as being "upstaged." In a theater, the part of the stage closest to the audience is referred to as downstage, while the area farthest away from the audience is upstage. If, while an actor is delivering lines downstage, actors behind him capture the audience's attention by making distracting movements, the distracters are guilty of "upstaging" the actor. A good director will not allow that to happen. When you are making a presentation, you are your own director, and you need to be careful not to allow yourself to be upstaged by your own PowerPoint™.

Building in some time where PowerPoint™ is dark allows your audience to re-connect with you, the presenter. Because it is so easy to create PowerPoint™ slides, presenters often include slides that are not really necessary. Did you ever use poster board and markers to create a visual aid for some high school or middle school presentation? In those cases, would you ever go to the trouble of preparing a poster that said "Introduction" to hold up during the first part of your presentation? Most of us would not, yet speakers using PowerPoint™ do it all the time. In doing so, they not only miss an opportunity to connect with their audience, they demonstrate to their audience that the images shown on the screen may not be all that important. If the audience gets the idea that *you* aren't very important (because you are constantly being upstaged by PowerPoint™), and that your PowerPoint™ isn't very important either (because information like "Introduction" isn't really useful), they will likely tune you *and* your PowerPoint ™ out, and let their minds wander elsewhere.

The solution is to display PowerPoint™ images only when they add something to your speech. The rest of the time, when a visual aid is not essential to your message, turn PowerPoint™ off and take advantage of having your audience's undivided attention. Techniques for making PowerPoint™ "fade to black" are discussed later in this chapter.

Draw Attention to the Content, Not the Package

Your audience only has a limited amount of attention. The more they divide their attention, the less of it is focused on any one thing. While you are making a presentation, you want your audience to be attending to your *message.* What you say and do is an important part of your message, so, naturally, you want your audience to be paying attention to *you.* But it's actually a little more complicated than that. What if you were giving a presentation on wireless widgets and decided to wear an orange and purple striped jump suit? That would certainly get your audience's attention, but would they be paying attention to your wireless widgets or your wardrobe? In fact, all of the attention they gave to your outfit would be attention that did *not* go to your message. So you want your audience to pay attention to the parts of "you" that are your message, and not be distracted by other aspects of "you."

The words and images on your PowerPoint™ slides are also part of your message, but presenters often make the mistake of dressing their messages up in ways that draw attention to the package instead of the content. When text or images fly onto the screen from all directions, the movement is at best distracting and at worst distracting *and* annoying. Either way, the audience is paying attention to the animation effect instead of the content. I find it troubling that the newer versions of PowerPoint™ have included a category of animation effects labeled "exciting." Do we really want the method by which our content appears on the screen to be exciting? Wouldn't it be more effective if our *content* was the exciting part? Art curators know how to frame paintings and photographs in ways that draw the viewers' attention to the picture, not the frame. Speakers using visuals must strive to accomplish the same result.

Use animation effects with extreme caution. For most situations, choose "appear" as the desired effect. If you simply must have things fly in, choose one of the subtle moves and use that same move throughout your presentation. Mixing up animation effects encourages your audience to pay attention to the effects–attention that would be better directed to the message.

PowerPoint™ also allows you to have sound effects accompany slide changes or animation effects. Although many presenters become infatuated with sound effects, the inclusion of sound rarely helps communicate the message and often distracts and annoys the audience. Sound effects should only be used on those rare occasions when they help convey the message. Using sounds as attention-getters only draws attention away from you and your message.

Make Your Visuals Easy for Your Audience to Receive

Some experts suggest that effective visuals should be designed so the viewer can absorb the information in no more than six seconds (Hamilton, 1996). This means text slides must be easy to read. Many authors have written lists of guidelines for creating text visuals, most of which come down to limiting the amount of text and presenting it in the most easy-to-read manner. To that end, I suggest the following:

- maximum six lines of text per slide
- maximum six words per line
- minimum 24 point text
- use phrases, not sentences
- use upper- and lowercase type
- use simple typefaces (fonts)

Paying attention to these simple rules will result in slides that are easier to read. If, when a slide appears on the screen, it looks like it will require some mental energy to decode the information, audience members are likely to either fall into a reading mode (which necessitates ignoring the aural message), or simply tune out the visual altogether. Either way, the visual aid is not aiding the communication process. On easy-to-read text slides, the information jumps off the screen, and the audience does not feel they have to exert significant mental effort.

Slides with graphics should also be comprehensible in six seconds. One common mistake that results in difficult-to-comprehend graphics is the inclusion of too much information. Charts and graphs are efficient ways of displaying a lot of information, but we must be careful not to display more than the audience can reasonably comprehend. A single chart that makes several points can be difficult for audiences to follow. One chart that illustrates one point is usually a better way to go. Also, most presentations do not require a lot of charts and graphs (although that doesn't stop some speakers from including them anyway). Pick just one or two that clearly illustrate the points being made.

Illustrations and diagrams can also suffer from information overload. Illustrations downloaded from the Internet often include more detail than the presenter intends to cover. While it is tempting to use the overloaded illustration and just ignore the extraneous information, there is a good chance that your audience will be distracted by the unexplained items. A good rule of thumb is never to show something you are not going to talk about. This might mean a little extra work. You may have to apply some electronic "White-Out" to the unwanted items, or you may have to create a new, simplified diagram or illustration. Expending the extra effort, however, is a good habit to acquire. Presenters are rarely accused of being too clear, and displaying unsuitable images may convey to your audience that you do not value them sufficiently to create graphics that might actually help them understand and remember your message.

Effective graphic slides are also well identified. This includes **titles**, which tell the audience what they are looking at in general, and **labels**, which identify and call attention to specific items within the slide. PowerPoint™ makes it easy to highlight elements electronically, eliminating the need for presenters to use fingers, sticks, or laser pens to point out items while presenting. Highlighting and labeling are excellent examples of how PowerPoint™'s drawing and animation features can be used to focus the audience's attention on the message rather than distract from it. When using complex graphics, it is also possible to have PowerPoint™ reveal portions of the graphic one at a time, so that the audience does not have to try to comprehend the entire graphic all at once. Some tips for labeling and highlighting are provided later in this chapter.

titles
Describe the general focus of a graphic slide.

labels
Identify specific elements of a graphic slide.

The bottom line is that when your visuals are unclear or difficult to comprehend, your audience is faced with the decision of either devoting a lot of attention to your visuals (at the expense of attending to your oral message), or tuning out your visuals (which usually involves tuning you out as well). In either case, the PowerPoint™ has taken over your presentation.

Underused PowerPoint™ Techniques

Making PowerPoint™ "Fade to Black" during a Presentation

It's difficult to make PowerPoint™ actually "fade," but it is easy to have the screen go dark. As we discussed earlier, there are often times when visuals aren't required, and it would be better to give PowerPoint™ a rest. Having the screen go black accomplishes just that, and there are two techniques for achieving a black screen.

Create a Black Slide

A black slide is a slide with a black background and no text or graphics. When you project it, there is nothing to project, so the effect is the same as if you have turned the projector off. At the end of this chapter there are instructions for creating a black slide–it's not difficult. Many presenters begin their presentations with a black slide. This allows them to connect with their audience during the introduction of the presentation. Later, when a visual image is required, a simple slide advance will display the first image. Black slides work best when you have places in the presentation where you *know* you want to give PowerPoint™ a rest. Inserting the black slide will make it impossible for you to forget to give the graphics a break.

Use the "B" key

Sometimes, in the course of making a presentation, you might want to go to black in a place where you had not planned to do so. The more spontaneous way to achieve a black screen is simply to touch the "B" key (the letter "B" on the keyboard, just above the middle of the space bar). It's easy to remember–"B" for black or "B" for blank. When you touch the key, the screen goes black. When you touch it again, your slides come back on, just where you left off. Be aware that this feature only works when you are in the presentation (slide show) mode.

Whether you do so by using black slides or the "B" key, giving PowerPoint™ some time off during your presentation is a good idea. The slides you show will be more effective if you show only the slides that add something to your presentation.

Using Custom Animation for Your Bullet Lists

One useful feature of PowerPoint™ is the ability to have your bullet points revealed one at a time. This keeps your audience from reading ahead and pondering the points you have not yet covered. Sometimes you may have a list that has main points and sub points.

- Main Point 1
- Main Point 2
    - Sub Point 2.1
    - Sub Point 2.2
    - Sub Point 2.3
- Main Point 3

You may have the sub points revealed along with the main point, or have each sub point revealed separately. Choose the way that helps you present your message most clearly. At the end of this chapter are instructions for adjusting PowerPoint™'s animation settings. What's most important is that you have PowerPoint™ animate your slides the way that is most helpful for *your* presentation. If the default settings are not helpful for your presentation, change them. You're in charge.

Highlighting a slide is a simple technique to clarify your message.

Original Slide

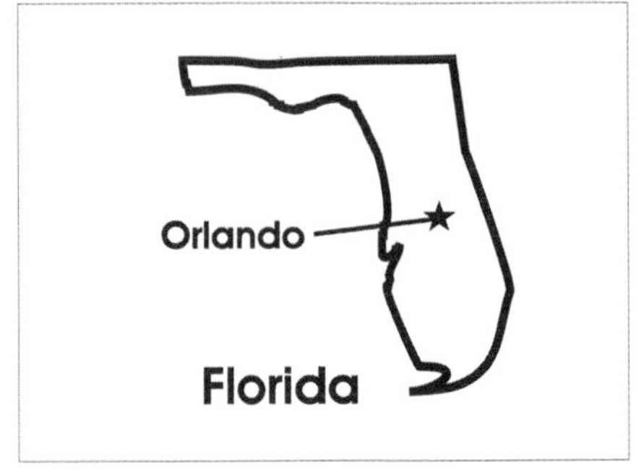

Highlighted Slide

Highlighting Portions of a Slide

Earlier we talked about the need to highlight or point out specific elements on a picture or diagram. There are a number of ways of accomplishing this, but the instructions at the end of this chapter offer one of the more foolproof methods that does not require a lot of advanced PowerPoint™ knowledge. You can use this highlighting technique on charts, graphs, pictures, or diagrams. You can also add labels to go along with your highlights.

For example, if you are talking about the State of Florida, you might display a simple map (as shown above). When you want your audience to know where Orlando is located, you might add a star to highlight the location and a label to make it clear what you are highlighting. This simple technique uses the power of PowerPoint™ to help make your message clearer.

PowerPoint™ Recap

The use of PowerPoint™ can either help or hinder your presentation. It is a wonderful tool that can help you create and present effective visuals, but it can also be used to produce distracting images that overload and annoy your audience. How you use it is your decision, but bear in mind that *you* are the presenter and PowerPoint is your helper. This means *you* (not PowerPoint™) are the most important element in your presentation. This means PowerPoint™ can (and should) go away when it's not needed. This means your slides must be designed in ways that emphasize the content, not the package. This means your audience should never feel like they are the victims of PowerPoint™ abuse.

Final Thoughts on Effective Use of Visual Aids

Whatever type of visual aids you use, it is important to practice your speech with the visual aids–preferably in the location where you will be speaking. Whether your plan is to hold up an object, use a poster on an easel, project overhead

Speaking of . . .

Multimedia Copyright Issues for Speakers by *John T. Morrison*

Most images, sounds, songs, movies or other media found on the Web, on software CDs, scanned from books or magazines, copied from DVDs and VHS movies, or gathered through a variety of other means are *copyright protected*. A copyright legally limits the free use of protected content without express permission from the content owner. Common misconceptions are that media are free when they are unpublished, available without protection, or when the source does not display an explicit copyright notice. Another misconception is that because one has paid for Internet service, a movie, movie rental, or magazine, the content therein is free to use for any purpose. However, media authored by others are rarely free to use indiscriminately, regardless of whether the use is personal, academic or professional. Even media listed as "copyright free" or "royalty free" usually do not allow most forms of commercial use, or even some forms of personal use.

These issues are important in the design and delivery of presentations, particularly as you move from an academic arena to a professional one. The intentional or unintentional use of media you do not own can present a substantial legal peril to both you and your organization. All types of media are property; the fact that they are freely available on the Web or elsewhere does not change ownership rights or privileges.

You may have heard that schools and nonprofit organizations are exempt from copyright issues. This is only partially true, and only within limited parameters. The use of protected content in academic environments is sometimes allowed under what is referred to as "fair use" guidelines (see www.copyright.com), but those guidelines are complex, ambiguous, poorly understood, and often ignored. Even experts disagree on a precise definition of what constitutes "fair use." School environments, therefore, are not automatically exempt from all copyright restrictions. Incorporating Web media into a PowerPoint presentation for a class assignment is generally considered "fair use," but when in doubt, get expert advice. Most colleges, universities, and nonprofit organizations maintain a legal department, which is good place to start. However, it is important to remember that when you leave school and are charged with creating professional presentations, "fair use" no longer applies. You should always be sure you have the right to use the media you present, publish, and sell.

One way to acquire legal authorization to use the media you find is simply to ask for it. Sometimes you'll receive an approval, usually with conditions; other times you may be denied. If you have received an approval, get it in writing, and save copies of all communications. However, approval you receive via email for Web-based content presents some additional complications. Identifying the owner of media found on Web sites may be quite difficult. One place to start is with the sponsoring organization or site owner, if identifying information is available on the Web site. Be careful, however, because there is no guarantee that the owner of the site (or the unseen individual who responds to your request) will supply accurate information. Nor is there any guarantee that the author of the Web site owns the copyright to the media. Even if the person that grants you authority is the creator of the work, there is no guarantee that he or she legally holds the copyright. In the business world, authorship usually belongs to the employer, not the employee who creates the work. Many employees are not aware of this, and they may offer content they create at work as their own.

To further complicate the issue, you often cannot identify copyright-protected images, sound files, videos, etc. by looking at or listening to them. Copyright-protected images and logos, for example, do not have to display a copyright symbol (©). So be careful, since you may be held responsible for

transparencies, or utilize PowerPoint™, practice can make the difference between success and failure. We have all witnessed presentations where problems with visuals not only distracted the audience, but distracted the speaker. Objects that prove to be unexpectedly difficult to hold, posters that slide off their easels, overhead transparencies that are projected upside-down (or backwards), or PowerPoint™ files that the computer refuses to read are the sorts of occurrences that every speaker dreads. But, in most cases, these potential disasters can be avoided with a little preparation. Lack of preparedness can add unnecessary stress to your speaking situation. Visual elements that you have practiced, and that you feel confident using, can help *reduce* anxiety. Do yourself and your audience the favor of practicing your presentation with your visual aids.

Visual aids can make your speeches more interesting, more memorable, and more effective–or not. The key is making the visual elements help you using protected media without permission. Ignorance of ownership is not a viable excuse. Unless you're sure, it is best to avoid using content from a questionable source.

Two certain and safe ways to obtain media for inclusion in professional presentations is to either create your own or license media from organizations dedicated to providing that type of service. Both options can be costly, but licensing is best when time is short, or when your media needs overwhelm the available expertise and equipment. How, where, and how long you intend to use the media will usually affect the cost of licensing. Obviously, media licensed for personal use are generally less expensive than those licensed for professional use. However, even if you obtain a license for media intended for professional use, you should carefully read the agreement; most licenses have many restrictions. Usually, a professional use license allows the holder to incorporate media into Web sites, print materials and presentations, but does not allow incorporating them into products intended for sale. Many other limitations are common. For example, with digital images, the license may limit the display or print resolution, limit the number of copies you may produce that include the image, limit the number of computers or display devices to which you may copy the image, or limit the time of use. Limitations on media use can often be extended, but usually at a higher licensing cost. Personal use licenses, while less expensive, are obviously even more restrictive. You should review the specific licensing agreement you obtain for a thorough explanation of rights and limitations. Finally, remember that personal and professional licenses rarely transfer ownership of media, so you may not resell or sublease media you license.

It may seem that violations of digital media copyrights would be very difficult to detect, particularly given the enormity of the Web, but new technologies make it quite easy. For example, many protected media files have hidden, undetectable digital watermarks. Digital watermarking, also known as steganography, makes imperceptible, encrypted changes to digital media files, allowing media content developers to imbed text, audio, video or images into almost any digital multimedia file. These embedded files definitively identify the author of the media. For instance, a digital picture might contain a text document or an audio recording; an audio file may have a picture, video, text file, or even another audio file inside it. These watermarks are extremely secure and quite undetectable. The organization that produces the watermarked files will typically initiate a regularly scheduled, automated Web search that hunts for copies of the media and reports locations to the source organization. Digimarc (www.digimarc.com) is a leader in these technologies, and offers a variety of services and products.

Finally, when considering the use of media owned by others, be sure to distinguish between copyright infringement and plagiarism; they are not the same. The former involves the illegal use of another's intellectual property without permission or authority; the latter involves the use of another's intellectual property without accurately identifying authorship. Plagiarized content tacitly implies that the plagiarizer is the author. While both copyright infringement and plagiarism are highly unethical, only copyright infringement is an issue of law.

The Golden Rule applies here. If you treat the intellectual property of others the way you wish others to treat yours, you'll usually make the right decision. Legal issues, however, can be very complex, and often seem to function outside the domain of common sense. The bottom line, of course, is to be careful, especially in professional contexts. Your good reputation and that of your organization are far more valuable than any media.

communicate your message more clearly. Don't fall into the trap of including visual elements just because everyone else has visuals, or because they're fun, or because you hope they will make your speech seem more professional. Let form follow function. Use visuals when they help your audience receive your message clearly, and put them away when they do not.

References

Hamilton, C. (1996). *Successful Public Speaking.* Belmont, CA: Wadsworth.

Nesmith, M. (1984). *Megatrends.* New York: Warner.

Vogel, D., Dickson, G., & Lehman, J. (1986). *Persuasion and the role of visual presentation support: The UM/3M study* (MISRC-WP-86-11), Minneapolis, MN: University of Minnesota, Management Information Systems Research Center.

Chapter Addendum

Creating a Black Slide in PowerPoint™

These instructions will vary slightly depending on which version of PowerPoint™ you are using, but the basic technique remains the same.

1. Create a new, blank slide (Insert > New Slide > if you have a choice of layouts, choose "blank").
2. Go into the slide editing, or "normal" view, if you are not already in it (View > Normal).
3. Right click anywhere on the slide. A menu will appear.
4. From the menu, choose "Background." A dialog window will appear.
5. Activate the pull-down menu located in the lower part of the "Background fill" box. Color boxes will appear.
6. Click the black box. You will be returned to the "Background" window.
7. Check the "Omit background graphics from master" box.
8. Click "Apply." Caution: Do not click "Apply to All."

You have created a black slide. To create additional black slides, go into the "Slide Sorter" view, and select (single click) your black slide. While holding down the "Control" key, drag your existing black slide to wherever you need an additional black slide. PowerPoint™ will place a copy of your black slide in the new location, and leave the original where it was.

Adjusting the Animation of Bullet Lists in PowerPoint™

PowerPoint™ makes it fairly easy to set up the animations, although the exact instructions differ from version to version. The instructions below should give you the basic idea.

Customizing Bullet List Animations (Office97™ version)

1. Create a bullet list with sub-points by pressing the *Tab* key before typing the first word of the sub point. PowerPoint™ will automatically indent and add a "sub" bullet. (To return to another main point, press *Shift* + *Tab*.)
2. From the "Slide Show" menu, choose "Custom Animation." A window should appear.
3. In the box labeled "Slide objects without animation" will be a list of the various objects in the slide. The bullet text is probably labeled "text1" or "text2." Select the bullet text. It will become highlighted in the box and on the reduced picture of your slide.
4. Click the "Animate" button. The name of the object should appear in the "Animation Order" box.
5. Click on the "Effects" tab. Under "Entry Animation and Sound" the top selection will probably be set to "Fly In From Left." Change the top selection to "Appear."
6. If you want the each point and its sub points to appear at the same time, skip to step nine.

7. If you want each point and each sub point to appear separately, set the "Introduce Text" settings to "All at once, 2nd level paragraphs," and be sure the box to the left of "Grouped by" is checked.

8. Click "OK."

9. From the "Slide Show" menu, choose "View Show" to test the animation.

Customizing Bullet List Animations (OfficeXP™ version)

1. Create a bullet list with sub points by pressing the *Tab* key before typing the first word of the sub point. PowerPoint™ will automatically indent and add a "sub" bullet. (To return to another main point, press *Shift* + *Tab*.)

2. From the "Slide Show" menu, choose "Custom Animation." A "Custom Animation" pane should appear on the right side of the PowerPoint™ desktop.

3. Click anywhere on your bullet list to select the bullet list text as the element you wish to animate. A box should appear around your bullet list, indicating it has been selected.

4. Click the "Add Effect" button in the "Custom Animation" pane. A sub menu will appear.

5. Select "Entrance" from the sub menu.

6. A list of effects should appear. Locate and click on "Appear."

7. You'll notice that numbers appear in gray boxes to the left of each of your bullet points. These indicate which items will appear on each successive click. (All of the items labeled one will appear on the first click, all of the items labeled two on the second click, etc.) If you want each point and its sub points to appear at the same time, skip to step 10.

8. If you want each point and each sub point to appear separately, activate the drop-down menu in the "Custom Animation" pane labeled "Start" and select "On Click."

9. Notice that the gray boxes have been re-numbered, indicating that each sub-bullet now requires a separate click.

10. Note: If the numbers in the gray boxes do not reflect the order of appearance you desire, click on the double down arrow in the large box in the "Custom Animation" pane. This will allow you to view the controls for each of your bullet points and change them to suit your needs.

11. From the "Slide Show" menu, choose "View Show" to test the animation.

Highlighting Portions of a PowerPoint™ Slide

The exercise below will highlight some text, but the same technique can be used for any visual.

1. Launch the PowerPoint™ program

2. If a "create new presentation using" window comes up, choose "Blank Presentation." If not, drop down the "file" menu and choose "new."

3. A “Choose Auto Layout” window will appear, select the “title slide” layout and click “OK.”

4. Click where it says “Click to add title.” Type your first name, middle initial, and last name.

For the sake of practice, let’s assume that you wanted to call attention to your middle initial in a presentation. The following steps show how to highlight the initial.

5. Enter the “Slide Sorter” view of PowerPoint™ (view > slide sorter).

6. Click on the thumbnail of the slide you just created. A box should appear around the slide, indicating you have selected it.

7. While holding down the “Control Key” click on the slide, drag to the right, and release. You should now have two copies of your slide.

8. Double-click the second slide. This should take you to the “slide editing” (or “Normal”) view.

9. Drop down the “View” menu, select “Toolbars,” and be sure the “Drawing” toolbar is checked.

10. On the “Drawing” toolbar (usually near the bottom of your desktop) there are several drawing tools. One is called the “line tool.” Its icon is a diagonal line. Click on the “line tool” icon.

11. Position your cursor just under the left side of your middle initial.

12. Click and drag to the right, underlining your initial, and release. A line should appear. (Don’t be concerned that it is not very attention-getting. We’ll work on that.)

13. Your line should have little circles on each end, indicating that it is “selected.” If it is not selected, select it by single-clicking on the line.

14. Locate the “Line Style” tool on the “Drawing” toolbar. Its icon is four horizontal lines of increasing thickness. Clicking on the icon opens a window of line style choices. Choose a thick line, like “6 pt.” Your line should become thicker.

15. Locate the “Line Color” tool on the “Drawing” toolbar. Its icon is a brush painting a thick line. Just to the right of the icon is a down arrowhead. Click on the arrowhead. A window with several color boxes should appear. You may choose one of those boxes or click “More Line Colors” to reveal more choices. Choose a bright color, like red, and click “OK.” You should now have a thick, red line below your middle initial.

16. Return to the “Slide Sorter” view (View > Slide Sorter). Notice that you have identical two slides, except that the second one has your middle initial underlined.

17. Click on the first slide.

18. Drop down the "Slide Show" menu and select "View Show." Your first slide should appear in full-screen, presentation mode.

19. Press the spacebar once to advance the slide and notice what happens. You are advancing to the next slide, but because everything except the underline is the same, it appears that the underline has been added to the original slide.

This is a very basic example of highlighting. There are other drawing tools besides the line tool. For example, you could use the rectangle tool or the oval tool to highlight something. *Tip: When you create closed shapes like ovals and rectangles, PowerPoint™ defaults to drawing a filled (colored-in) object. To remove the fill, click the down arrowhead next to the "Fill Color" (paint bucket) icon, and choose "No Fill."*

Alternatively, it is possible to make highlights and labels "appear" by using animations, but often it is easier and quicker to simply copy the slides and add the highlights to the copies. The copy technique is also more likely to work correctly on all versions of PowerPoint™, while animations sometimes work differently from one version to another.

Tips for Projecting Overhead Transparencies

- **Image size** Is determined by the distance of the projector from the screen (the farther away, the larger your image will be). Be sure the projector is far enough away to produce an image that is big enough to be seen by everyone.
- **Focus** Is adjusted by the knob near the lens-head. Check focus prior to your presentation.
- **Vertical position of image** The lens-head tilts to allow you to move the image up or down on the screen. Adjust tilt prior to your presentation.
- **Orientation of slide** If you are standing behind the projector (your back to the screen), place the slide on the glass with the same orientation as if you were reading it (upper left at the upper left, etc.).
- **Position slide with the projector OFF** Whenever possible, turn the projector off to position or change slides. Spare your audience the distraction of watching you set up the next slide.
- **Avoid "giant hand"** Using your finger to point to things on the transparency can have a King Kong effect. If it is necessary to point to items on the slide, use a pencil, pen or other small pointer.
- **Eye contact** Avoid turning toward, or talking to, the screen. Maintain eye contact with your audience.
- **Find a good place to stand** You'll want to avoid standing in the projector beam (and thus casting a distracting shadow on the screen), or blocking part of your audience's view. This is one of the biggest disadvantages of overhead projector use. It is often difficult to find a place that doesn't obstruct someone's view. Stepping back to a position next to the screen is often the only solution–if you are using speaker's notes, be sure to take them with you when you step back.
- **Turn the projector off** when not in use.

In Their Own Words

Sample Speech Outline

GO SUN SMART
by Shelly Lee Spratt

Shelly Lee Spratt

General purpose: To inform
Specific purpose: To inform the audience how to protect themselves from deadly skin cancer.

Introduction

I. **Open with impact:** How many of you can remember a sunburn so bad you could barely put your clothes on? How many of you have simply been burned while spending the day at the beach, tubing on the river, water skiing at the lake, or even skiing or riding your board on a fresh powder day at your favorite mountain?
   A. Did you know that there are over 1 million new cases of skin cancer each year in the United States, including over 51,000 cases of melanoma (Kalb, 2001)?
   B. Did you know that many of these cases can be directly linked to the cumulative effects of the sun?
   C. Did you know that there is no such thing as a safe tan, despite what the indoor tanning industry would like you to believe (Young and Walker, 1998)?

II. **Connect with audience:** Every one of you who raised your hand needs to know that those sunburns you got put you at increased risk for skin cancer. Further, even if you've never burned or you are dark skinned, the information I'll share in a moment is important to you as well.

III. **Thesis:** Skin cancer is not only the fastest growing form of cancer in the United States, it also is one of the easiest forms of cancer to prevent (American Cancer Society, 1996).

IV. **Preview:** As a result, I'd like to look at three important things we all need to know to reduce our risk for skin cancer. First, there are three basic forms of skin cancer. Second, skin cancer is all too often a by-product of too much fun in the sun. And third, you can reduce your risk for developing skin cancer by following some easy steps.

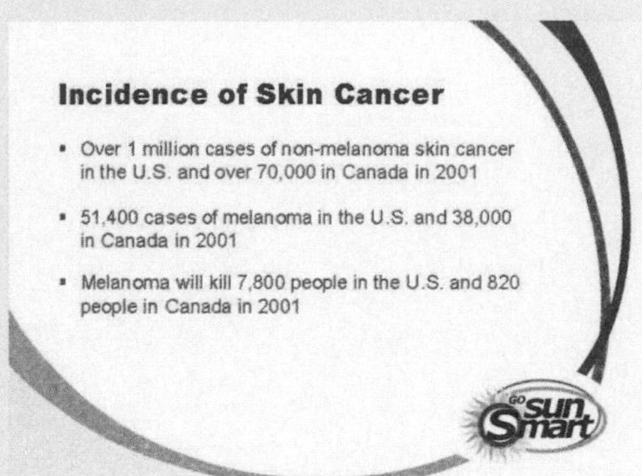

Incidence of Skin Cancer
Over 1 million cases of non-melanoma skin cancer in the U.S. and over 70,000 in Canada in 2001
51,400 cases of melanoma in the U.S. and 38,000 in Canada in 2001
Melanoma will kill 7,800 people in the U.S. and 820 people in Canada in 2001
Go sun Smart

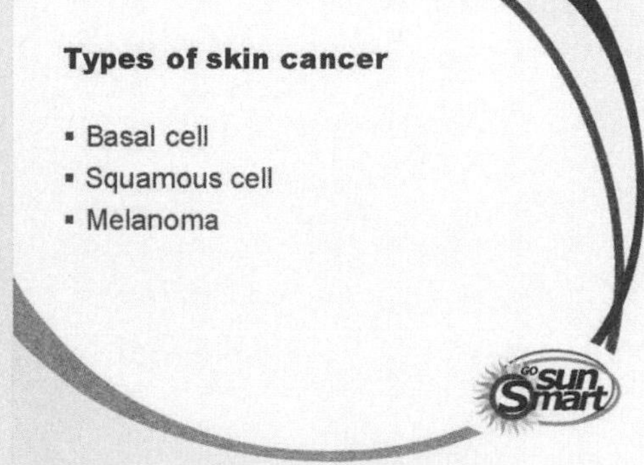

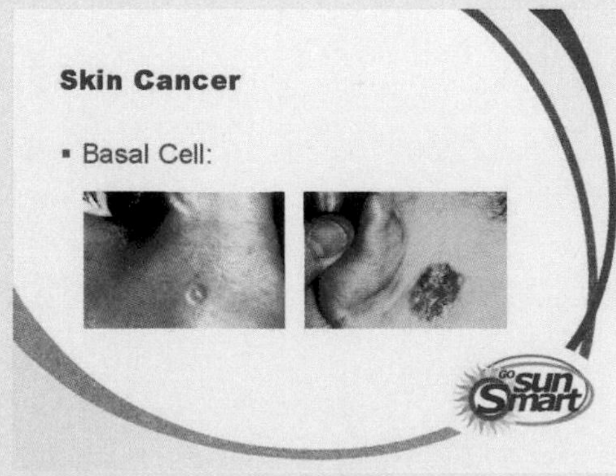

Body

I. There are three types of skin cancer: basal cell, squamous, and melanoma (Kalb, 2001).
   A. Basal cell is the most common and easily treated and is rarely life threatening.
   B. Squamous cell cancer is the next most common, and it too is easily treated and seldom fatal unless completely unattended.
   C. Melanoma, which is the form of skin cancer Maureen Reagan died from, is increasing at an alarming rate in the United States. It is deadly if not treated early in its growth.

(**Transition:** So what causes skin cancer?)

II. Much as we may like the sun, too much of this good thing is bad for us.
   A. The sun's rays contain ultraviolet radiation.
   B. Science has linked ultraviolet radiation from the sun with basal cell and squamous cell skin cancer (Kalb, 2001).
      1. Scientists at the National Cancer Institute also believe that ultraviolet radiation is linked to melanoma, although the relationship is not as clear (Kalb, 2001).
      2. Melanoma can show up anywhere on the skin and can develop in even dark-skinned people.
      3. For example, did you know that Bob Marley died from melanoma skin cancer?
   C. As few as three severe sunburns in childhood put you at increased risk for skin cancer.

(**Transition:** Even though the incidence of skin cancer is increasing, you have considerable control over this risk.)

III. The American Cancer Society and the American Dermatological Association have developed some simple guidelines to follow: (American Cancer Society, 1996)
   A. Avoid the sun between 10 a.m. and 4 p.m. when possible.
   B. Always wear a sunscreen with sun protection factor of 15 or better, and wear sun-protective clothing such as a wide-brimmed hat, long-sleeved shirt, and long pants.
   C. Know the early warning signs of skin cancer, which are A for asymmetry, B for irregular borders, and C for irregular color on moles and freckles especially.
   D. Finally, give yourself a full body check every six months or have someone do it for you.

(**Transition:** In conclusion)

Conclusion

I. **Summarize:** Remember these important facts:
   A. Skin cancer comes in three types: basal, squamous, and melanoma.
   B. Also, keep in mind that while we need the sun, a little sunning is actually a lot.
   C. Finally, be sun smart by practicing sun-safe behaviors such as those suggested by the ADA.

II. **Close with impact:** Skin cancer can kill. With a little common sense, however, it is easily prevented. Please be sun smart.

References

American Cancer Society (1996). *Cancer facts and figures*. Atlanta, GA: The American Cancer Society.

Kalb, C. (2001, August 20). Overexposed. *Newsweek*, 35–38.

Young, J. C. and Walker, R. (1998). Understanding students' indoor tanning beliefs and practices, *American Journal of Health Studies*, 14, 120–128.

Skin Cancer

- Squamous Cell:

Go sun Smart

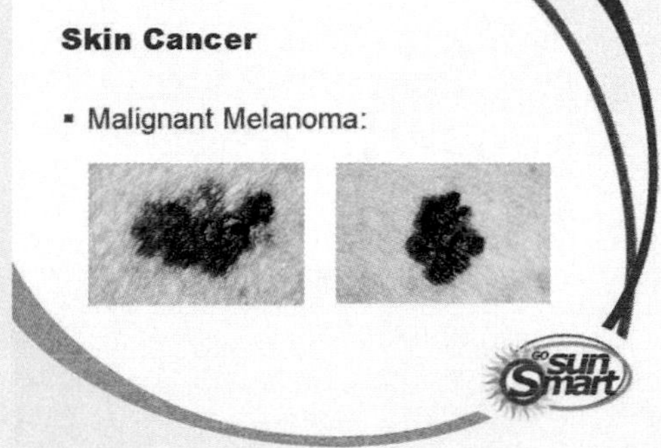

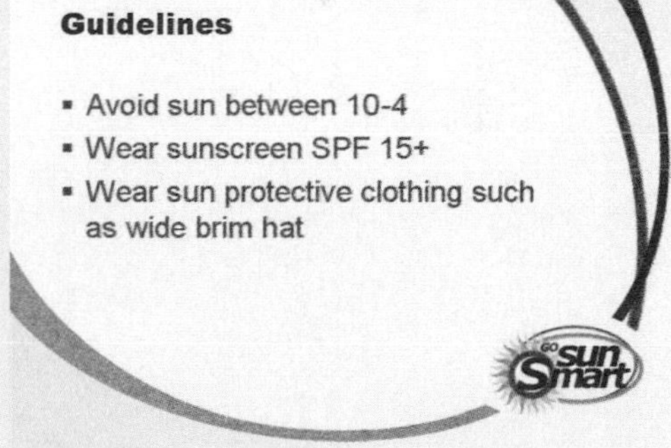

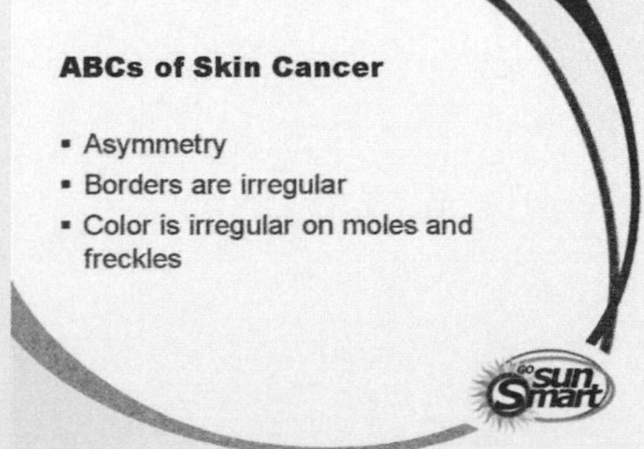

Speaking of . . .

Murphy's Law Revisited

There is no way to be completely prepared for the unexpected. The best defense is to anticipate problems and prepare alternatives. Here are a few of the things that you need to prepare for. (At one time or another, they have all happened to the authors of this book.)

Problem: The battery in your equipment (audio recorder, microphone, or whatever) is dead.

What to do: Test the equipment the morning of your speech and carry a spare battery.

Problem: There is no overhead projector or computer, even though you reserved one.

What to do: Call to confirm your reservation on the morning of your speech. Physically check out the equipment if possible.

Problem: The overhead projector's lightbulb is burned out.

What to do: Most overheads have a spare lightbulb. Make sure you know where it is beforehand.

Problem: The slide projector (film projector, DVD player, etc.) does not work.

What to do: Again, check it out in advance if possible. If it unexpectedly fails, you will need to verbally describe what is on your slides. We recall one case where a person simply stood in front of a blank screen, pretended to show slides, and described them in elaborate detail as he went along ("As you can clearly see from this slide . . ."). It turned a frustrating situation into a humorous one.

Problem: Your visuals are out of order or upside down, or some are missing.

What to do: An ounce of prevention is worth a pound of cure. Check and double-check them before the speech. If you run into this problem, try not to get flustered. Make a joke while you look for the missing visual; if you can't find it, verbally describe the visual or skip a part of the speech.

Problem: The computer you are using for your PowerPoint™ presentation fails, or the projector does not work.

What to do: Be sure to prepare backup visuals. For example, we normally have overhead transpar-encies prepared that duplicate our PowerPoint™ presentations.

Problem: It takes a lot longer than you thought to demonstrate a process using your visuals.

What to do: First, always practice with your visuals so that you know how long it will take. Second, if you are demonstrating a multistep process, have various steps along the way already prepared.

Remember, nothing can happen to you that hasn't already happened to someone else. Most audiences are sympathetic to speakers who are obviously prepared and yet encounter technical difficulties beyond their control. At the same time, audiences have little sympathy when Murphy's Law strikes someone who is just winging it. And keep in mind, "Murphy was an optimist."

Contexts for Public Speaking

Jaime Escalante motivated his students to achieve through the power of *ganas,* the desire to succeed, as he taught them the skills necessary to succeed in mathematics.

Chapter 14 Informative Speaking

Objectives

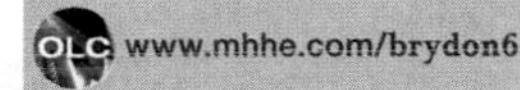

After reading this chapter and reviewing the online learning resources at www.mhhe.com/brydon6, you should be able to:

- Explain how to adapt your informative speech to audiences with diverse learning styles.
- Explain the relationship between informative speaking and persuasion.
- Illustrate how informative speaking can be used in your other classes, at work, and in your community.
- Prepare an informative speech that is audience involving, audience appropriate, audience accessible, and potentially life enriching.
- Prepare informative speeches that explain, instruct, demonstrate, or describe processes, concepts, and skills.

Key Concepts

audience accessible

audience appropriate

audience involving

ganas

informative speaking

learning styles

> “Determination plus hard work plus concentration equals success, which equals *ganas*.”
>
> -JAIME ESCALANTE[1]

Jaime Escalante, whose picture you see in the opening photograph, is not simply a gifted teacher. He is a remarkable person. He immigrated to the United States from Bolivia in 1969, where he had taught mathematics and physics. He spoke not a single word of English. But Escalante had what he called ***ganas***–that is, a desire to succeed regardless of the odds against it. Thus at age 30 he reentered school to work toward his teaching credential, even though it meant subjecting his out-of-shape body to a required course in P.E.

ganas
Spanish term that loosely translates as the desire to succeed.

Escalante's life became the subject of the critically acclaimed film *Stand and Deliver.* In the movie, actor Edward James Olmos portrays Escalante, who took East Los Angeles barrio students who could barely do simple math and, in two years of intensive work, prepared them for the Advanced Placement Test in Calculus. His students were so successful that all 18 who attempted the test in 1982 passed, the most from any high school in Southern California. Each year more students passed; by 1987, 87 of his students passed the exam. Remember, these were students who were not expected to attend college, let alone receive college credit for calculus while still in high school. But as Escalante says, "Students will rise to the level of expectations." When students wanted to quit, Escalante would challenge them by saying, "Do you have the *ganas?* Do you have the desire?"[2]

Although there are many reasons Escalante was able to overcome odds others would have perceived as insurmountable, we think his success in life as well as in the classroom can be found in that word of his: *ganas.* Not only did Escalante have it when he needed it, but also his life is testimony to the fact that he has instilled it in many of his students. As a result, they too have succeeded.

In a sense, this chapter is about *ganas.* Like Jaime Escalante, the best informative speakers do more than simply pass on information to an audience. With their words and actions, they create a desire in their audience to put the information to constructive use. In the case of Escalante, the desire involved a subject that many students prefer to avoid: mathematics. In yours, it may involve anything from how we treat our environment to the kind of foods we eat.

Ryan Neil is an American who speaks fluent Japanese. He is an apprentice and translator for famous Bonsai artist Masahiko Kimura. As Kimura demonstrates his techniques Ryan must accurately translate what he says into English to make the presentation accessible to non-Japanese speaking audiences.

Informative speaking is the process by which an audience gains new information or a new perspective on old information from a speaker. Put another way, the goal of informative speaking is audience learning. An effective informative speaker needs to master several skills, which we will look at in this chapter. These skills include:

informative speaking
The process by which an audience gains new information or a new perspective on old information.

- Focusing on the audience and appealing to their various styles of learning.
- Understanding the relationship between informative speaking and persuasion.
- Understanding the relationship between informative speaking and audience analysis.
- Understanding how you are likely to give informative presentations throughout your life: in the classroom, the workplace, and the community.
- Making informative speeches audience involving, audience appropriate, audience accessible, and potentially life enriching.
- Putting theory into practice in speeches that explain, instruct, demonstrate, or describe.

Focusing on the Audience: Adapting to Different Styles of Learning

Consider the following scenarios. In the first, a high school principal goes before the student body to explain the school board's decision to install metal detectors and surveillance cameras on campus. In the second, a nurse practitioner demonstrates to a group of student nurses how to use a new skin test for food allergies. In the third, an offensive line coach teaches linemen a new offensive scheme they will use in their next football game. In the fourth, a driving instructor at a high-performance racing school explains the concept of heel-and-toe braking and shifting on a road course. And in the fifth, a tennis pro explains how to improve your serve.

Each of these scenarios can be viewed as a speaking situation. Further, each involves a speaker publicly *informing* an audience. In each case, the speaker must focus on relating the information to the needs and goals of the audience members. Jaime Escalante had to first reach out to and connect with his students before he could really begin to teach them calculus. So, too, must every informative speaker reach out to and connect with his or her audience before presenting them with information.

One important consideration in focusing on the audience is recognizing that not everyone has the same style of learning. Not everybody thinks in a linear or "logical" fashion. Some people can simply read a book and absorb the information, whereas others need to hear and see to learn. Still others learn best by doing. Good public speakers recognize these differences and appeal to as many styles as possible.

There are, of course, many useful ways of categorizing how people learn information, such as this listing of diverse **learning styles:** [3]

learning styles
Differences in the way people think about and learn new information and skills.

- *Auditory linguistic:* Learning by hearing the spoken word.
- *Visual linguistic:* Learning by seeing the printed word.

- *Auditory numerical:* Learning by hearing numbers.
- *Visual numerical:* Learning by seeing numbers.
- *Audio-visual-kinesthetic combination:* Learning by hearing, seeing, and doing in combination.
- *Individual:* Learning when by oneself.
- *Group:* Learning in collaboration with other people.
- *Oral expressive:* Learning by telling others orally.
- *Written expressive:* Learning by writing.

At first, such a long list of diverse learning styles may be intimidating. How can one speech or even a series of speeches adapt to all of these different ways of learning? Of course, you cannot be all things to all people. But teachers confront this variety of learning styles every day. Many teachers use a combination of methods–individual and group work, written and oral assignments, print and visual materials–in an effort to adapt to the variety of learning styles in their classrooms.

Rather than trying to guess which learning style is best understood by an audience, it is better to use multiple channels and modes of learning, much as we discussed in the preceding chapter. With this method, you are likely to reach most of your audience members with something that suits their style of learning. In any given audience, there are likely to be individual learners as well as group learners, those who respond best to oral instruction and those who need to read it, and so on. Using posters, overheads transparencies, or PowerPoint™ slides are excellent ways to reinforce visually what we say orally. Distributing a handout after, **and only after,** a speech can help visual learners retain what was said. It helps to provide the audience with an opportunity to use as many senses as possible to process the message. If parts of the presentation can be seen, heard, and even touched, odds increase that the message will sink in.

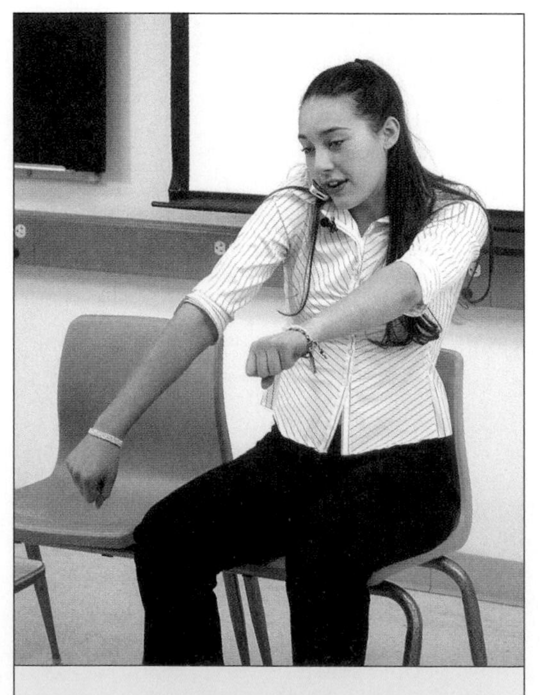

Notice how this student demonstrates the difficulty of driving while talking on a cell phone.

One speech we heard, for example, was about using acupressure to relieve stress. By instructing the class to press on certain points on their bodies, the speaker allowed the audience to use their sense of touch to understand what was being said. Other speakers appeal to the sense of taste. We frequently have international students speak about a food unique to their culture and bring samples for the audience to try. We have also seen student speakers involve their audiences in a group exercise to better appreciate the subject on which they are speaking. Specific examples include a speaker asking fellow students to model the simple yoga poses he first demonstrated and a blind student talking in the dark for part of her speech, so that sighted students might better appreciate what she experienced when listening to a lecture.

Informative Speaking and Persuasion

When you were assigned to read this chapter, it is likely that your instructor also required you to prepare and deliver an informative speech. When is a speech primarily informative, as opposed to being persuasive? Depending on whom you ask, you are likely to get a different answer to this question. Some people would argue that a speech can be exclusively informative–with no purpose other than one person passing information along to an audience. Still others argue that while the line between what is informative and what is persuasive is blurred, it is nevertheless there.

Our position is based on a simple premise. An informative speech is not worth giving unless it is designed to reasonably ensure that it won't go in one ear and then right out the other. What good, for example, is an informative speech on the proper equipment to safely roller blade if it doesn't increase the probability of the audience seriously considering the information? Similarly, what good is to be gained by an informative speech on preventive health practices such as using sunscreen regularly if it has no motivational value for an audience?

Instead of looking at the relationship between informative and persuasive speeches as a dichotomous one, we want you to think about the two in terms of a continuum (Exhibit 14.1). On one end of the continuum is knowledge; on the other end is behavior. Given the poles of this continuum, persuasion is seldom the result of one powerful speech delivered by a singularly credible and charismatic speaker. More typically, persuasion is a process comprised of a series of interdependent messages over time. In the so-called real world, this process–this campaign–begins with someone or some agency providing people with information designed to stimulate them. This information, then, is used as a base from which a more explicitly persuasive campaign can be built to influence people's behavior.

At the same time, we recognize that messages primarily intended to persuade are often couched in the language of information. For example, during World War II, both sides presented their propaganda in the guise of information. In

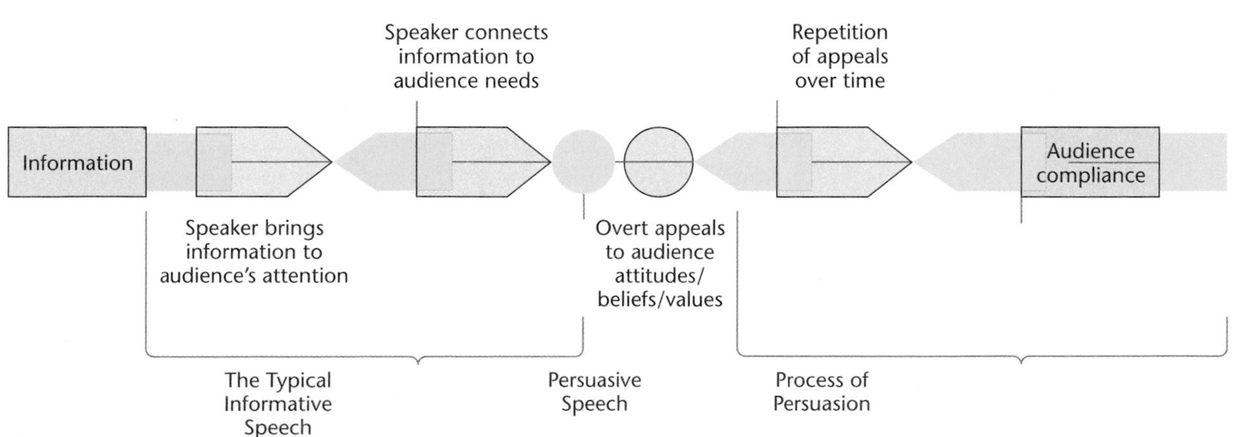

Exhibit 14.1
Continuum of Informative to Persuasive Speaking

fact, the series of films developed by famed director Frank Capra to motivate our troops by telling them *Why We Fight,* was explicitly labeled as "information."

As you select your speech topics, you need to be aware that simply calling something an informative presentation is no guarantee that it will be received by your audience as free of any persuasive intent. For instance, we have heard students speak on such "informative" topics as "10 reasons why Rudy Giuliani should be president." Of course, the speaker gave information in the speech. However, clearly the goal was not to just convey the facts but to motivate the audience to vote a certain way. Thus, before you choose a topic for an informative speech, be sure to ask yourself whether your ultimate goal is really to just provide the facts and information or rather to affect people's attitudes and behaviors. Speeches that focus primarily on the latter goals are more appropriately delivered as persuasive speeches. When in doubt about the appropriateness of a topic, our advice is always to ask for feedback from your instructor.

Informative Speaking and Audience Analysis

In Chapter 7 we discussed how to analyze an audience in terms of cultural, demographic, and individual diversity. As we prepare our informative speeches, it is important to pay special attention to the results of such an analysis. For example, because the purpose of informative speaking is to increase audience knowledge, we need to know what our audience already knows about our topic. If they already know most of what we plan to say, then the speech will bore them. On the other hand, if they are clueless about the topic and we launch into a jargon-filled technical presentation, they will be lost.

Audience culture is equally important for informative speakers. For example, in the movie *Stand and Deliver,* one of the biggest challenges Jaime Escalante faced was the perception by Latino and Latina students that learning math would have no impact on their lives. Because he shared their culture, he makes a point in one scene of talking about how their ancestors, the Mayans, were more mathematically advanced than the Greeks or Romans, who lacked the concept of zero. Escalante says to his students, "you . . . have math in your blood."

Age is another important factor to consider, particularly if it differs greatly from our own. Many older students have taken our classes, and sometimes they need reassurance that they can master the material. Similarly, as we continue to get older while our students for the most part remain 18–22 years old, we find that we must constantly remind ourselves that experiences we remember vividly may be only historical footnotes to our students. For example, the space shuttle *Challenger* exploded shortly after launch in 1986. Although that event is as vivid in our minds as if it had occurred yesterday, we have to remember that the students who read this book were unlikely to have even been born in 1986. On the other hand, they are likely to vividly remember the space shuttle *Columbia,* which disintegrated on reentry in 2003. One example would be effective with an older audience, the other with a younger one.

We also need to carefully analyze our audience's beliefs, attitudes, and values for informative speeches as well as for persuasive speeches. For example, imagine a student in 1998 speaking about why President Bill Clinton was being impeached–his affair with an intern and his alleged perjury about the relationship. When the impeachment was dominating the news, to talk only about the reasons offered in support of Clinton's removal from office would undoubtedly have been controversial. Further, the audience would probably not learn anything new, since one could hardly turn on the TV or glance at a newspaper without seeing a story about the topic. Such a speech would have been seen as a persuasive message designed to move the audience to support the impeachment. By 2008, few college students would have much detailed knowledge or strong attitudes about the topic, having been in about third grade in 1998. With the outcome no longer in doubt, the controversy would now be irrelevant to most students. Thus, essentially the same speech would likely be seen as simply an informative presentation of historical data. This example illustrates that knowing the audience's prior level of knowledge and attitudes about the topic help us adapt a speech to fulfill either persuasive or informative purposes.

Informative Speaking Throughout the Life Span

Informative speaking is probably the form of public speaking you're most likely to be called on to do throughout your life. One of the chief reasons is that informative speaking is used in so many settings, including the classroom, the workplace, and the community.

Informative Speaking in the Classroom

Two time-honored traditions in the college classroom are the term paper and the oral report. Although most students have at least passing familiarity with the elements of a good term paper, many students don't make the connection between the elements of a good oral report and the process of informative speaking.

An oral report basically is an informative speech. Thus, by putting to use what you know about informative speaking, you will be able to give oral reports that are both substantively and stylistically more effective than those of your classmates.

Viewing the oral report as an opportunity to speak informatively has several advantages. First, it provides you with an organizational framework for constructing your report. Second, it reminds you that you have an audience for your report whose background and perceptual reality must be taken into account. Finally, it forces you to think about how relevant the information in your report is to both your instructor and student colleagues.

Informative Speaking in the Workplace

No matter what you plan on doing to make a living, the odds are great that you will need to make informative presentations. Although you won't necessarily have to speak to large numbers of people, you can reasonably expect to speak to your immediate coworkers, department, or supervisors. It is common in the workplace to make informative presentations before groups. For some presentations you will have to stand and speak; other presentations may be delivered from your seat.

Although the different situations require adjustments in your style of delivery, the substantive elements of your informative presentation are the same. You will still need to follow a cohesive organizational sequence and analyze your audience carefully.

Informative Speaking in the Community

You can reasonably expect to speak informatively with members of your community in at least one of two capacities: as a representative of your employer or as a concerned citizen. Private, as well as public, enterprises are justifiably concerned about their image within their local community. Many opinion polls show that the public is increasingly suspicious of the motives of private enterprise and increasingly dissatisfied with the performance of public agencies. It's not uncommon, therefore, for these organizations to make themselves available to service groups, such as Rotary International, the general public, or a citizens' group organized around a specific cause.

Some businesses have a person whose job is company spokesperson; large corporations may even have whole departments dedicated to public relations. Many organizations, however, have come to expect anyone in management to serve as an informative speaker to the community. In fact, private corporations, such as IBM, and public agencies, such as the police or fire department, may actually write such community service into their managers' job descriptions. Thus, just because you currently perceive your intended career as low profile, that doesn't necessarily make it so.

Finally, you may one day want or need to speak informatively as a private citizen. If you live in a community where cable television is available, your city council meetings probably are televised on your community access channel. If you tune in, you will see ordinary citizens making informative presentations at these meetings. Topics can range from the environmental impact of a new housing development to excessive noise from student housing. If you watch several of these presentations, you will probably conclude that very few of the speakers have much training in public speaking; people who do have training are easy to spot.

Your days as a public speaker will not be over once you've completed this class. Given what we've said here, in fact, you should now realize they are just beginning.

Message Keys of Effective Informative Speaking

What makes one speaker's presentation so informative and stimulating that we want to learn more about what we initially thought was a boring topic? And why does another speaker's presentation leave us cold from beginning to end? Is the reason (a) the speaker, (b) the topic, (c) the message, (d) our perceptions, or (e) all of the above? Because the public speaking transaction is an interdependent system, the answer, of course, is (e) all of the above.

Research over the past two decades suggests that the likelihood of an audience's perceiving information as relevant and conducive to learning depends significantly on the degree to which they find it involving, appropriate, accessible, and potentially life enriching.[4]

Audience Involvement

Information is worthless unless people pay attention to it. As with any speech, informative speeches need to be **audience involving.** The history of the world is full of examples of great ideas, practices, and products that failed because no one paid much attention to them. One of the first things we'll want to ensure, then, is that our topic and speech get the audience involved.

audience involving
Informative topic and speech that succeeds in gaining the audience's attention.

Novelty is the quality of being new and stimulating. It can be useful in gaining an audience's interest. Just as plants are heliotropic, we human beings are stimulatropic. Whereas plants continuously orient themselves toward the Sun to activate the process of photosynthesis, we continually orient ourselves toward new sources of stimulation.

Although novelty alone is not enough to sustain an informative speech, it certainly can make a speech more effective. Time and again, research has documented the fact that the perception of novelty heightens selective exposure, selective attention, and selective retention of information. In other words, people are likely to seek out, pay attention to, and remember novel information. The most obvious way to get the benefit of novelty in an informative speech is to choose a topic that is new for the audience. We are much more likely to captivate the audience members with the unfamiliar than with the mundane. Novelty, however, shouldn't be confused with the obscure. For example, whereas computer software for accountancy probably would be an obscure topic for most audiences, the fact that the software could save us money on our income taxes might be a novel topic.

Another way to use novelty to our advantage is in the construction of the message. Even though the rule of thumb is to structure a speech so that the audience can predict what comes next, this is not an unbending rule. Sometimes it is to our advantage to violate the expectancies of an audience. Writers, for example, sometimes begin with a story's end and then backtrack. Similarly, a skilled speaker could start a speech with what normally would be considered its conclusion and build backward. You may recall this is exactly what the storytelling speech by Montana Kellmer did in Chapter 3.

Novelty in our delivery can work to our advantage when speaking informatively. Audiences, for instance, generally are accustomed to speakers who are relatively stationary. Movement may add needed novelty to our presentation. In addition, some of our suggestions about the nonverbal dynamics of delivery in Chapter 12 will help introduce novelty to a presentation.

Finally, for an audience to become fully involved with an informative speech, they need to find it enjoyable. One of the most involving experiences of a visit to a national park, for example, is to go on a guided tour with a knowledgeable guide who can inform us with facts and anecdotes we might not otherwise learn, as Yosemite Tour Guide Jack Peters points out in the box, "Speaking of . . . Learning and Enjoyment."

Speaking of . . .

Learning and Enjoyment

Jack Peters, Yosemite Tour Guide

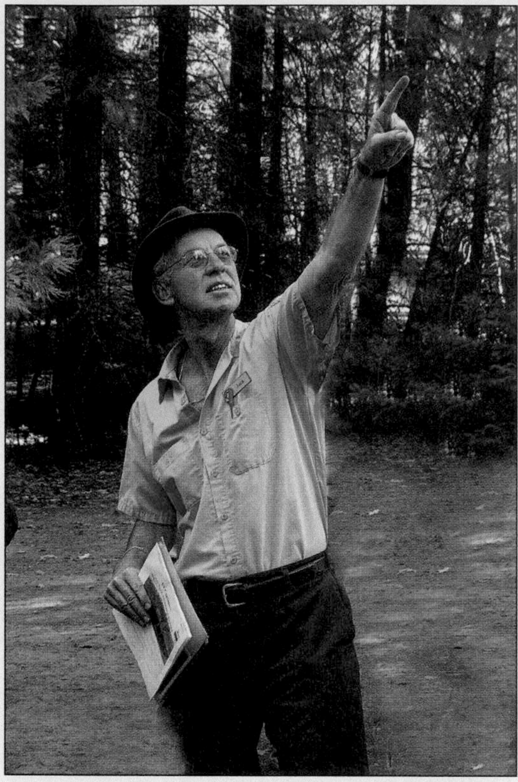

Yosemite tour guide Jack Peters

Consider what Jack Peters, a Yosemite National Park tour guide has to say about his experience as an informative presenter:

Like many people before me I wandered into Yosemite National Park for a visit and ended up living and working there. My degree in economics didn't really prepare me to be a tour guide, so I started from the bottom up in my training. First I listened to, and sometimes copied, other people's tours until I developed my own narrative style and informational content. In my line of work, style and substance often share equal importance as communication tools. If the guests relate to you personally, that is how you present the material; they will be more receptive to and retain more of the information you put forward. The inevitable question at day's end is "did you enjoy the tour?" rather than "what did you learn?" Learning and enjoying do not have to be mutually exclusive, as we all know.

The importance of communication should be self-evident. The better we communicate, the more we understand about our world, and ultimately, ourselves. So I just go up to that microphone and let 'er rip!

Audience Appropriateness

Although novelty can increase the chances of an audience initially paying attention, the information we share also needs to be compatible with what audience members believe is appropriate to the occasion. If our topic immediately turns the audience off, the audience also will tune us out.

Early in this book we said that communication is perceptual and that the process of perception is selective. Basically, people perceive what they choose to perceive. **Audience appropriateness** is the audience's perception that a message is consistent with their belief systems–their attitudes, beliefs, values, and lifestyle. All too often, speakers fail to take appropriateness into account when choosing a topic and then constructing their informative speech.

audience appropriate
Informative topic and speech that takes into account the occasion and audience members' belief systems.

For example, we've heard several informative speeches on sexually transmitted illnesses (STIs) and their prevention. We've also had students approach us after class and tell us they were offended or made to feel uncomfortable as a consequence of (1) the information in some of these speeches, (2) their perception that these speeches promoted a lifestyle with which they disagreed, and (3) the use of visual aids they didn't perceive to be in good taste. To a large degree, we were surprised by these reactions to a topic we believe needs to be openly discussed. We don't feel that student speakers should altogether avoid sensitive topics such as this one. However, they do need to consider the question of compatibility with audience belief systems so that they can soften or qualify the information to make it appropriate for everyone in the audience.

Consider how we might approach an informative speech on stem cell research for two different audiences. The first audience is composed of family members of people with diseases such as Alzheimer's, Parkinson's, and diabetes. The second is a religious group whose members believe that life begins at the moment of conception. The first group is likely to be hopeful that embryonic stem cell research can provide a cure for their loved ones. The second is likely to oppose any research that could lead to the destruction of what they believe is human life. A speech virtually the same would engender quite different reactions from these two groups. In approaching the second group, we need to make it clear that our intent is not to attack their deeply held religious beliefs. We might qualify the information in the speech with statements such as these:

> "I realize that for many people the whole issue of stem cell research raises ethical concerns, and I am mindful of these concerns."
>
> "Putting aside our religious views for the moment, let me describe what we know about the potential benefits of stem cell research."
>
> "Regardless of how you feel about this issue, I'd like you to put yourself in the shoes of someone who has just learned his or her young daughter has been diagnosed with juvenile diabetes and faces a lifetime of insulin shots, with potentially fatal complications."

The point is that information that is potentially incompatible with audience members' worldviews can be made appropriate if it is presented in a way that acknowledges the audience's point of view.

Audience Accessibility

Simply put, audience members cannot benefit from information that they cannot grasp. An **audience accessible** informative speech is one that the audience readily understands. Suppose, for example, that you are a biology major and you want to inform an audience about mapping the human genome. Should you use words peculiar to your major? Should you use the same approach with an audience of beginning speech students as you would with a group of seniors in a biochemistry class? Of course not.

audience accessible
Content the audience is able to understand, regardless of its complexity.

Research tells us that one of the quickest ways to turn off an audience is to unnecessarily complicate a topic. We don't have to avoid complex topics for our informative speeches. In fact, they are likely to be both novel for the audience and interesting for us to research. The goal is to make complex topics accessible and compelling.

Jaime Escalante's calculus classes in *Stand and Deliver* are models of the presentation of complex information. He broke the lessons into easy-to-digest bits, what he called "step by step." In fact, he would say to his students, "This is easy." It's not so much the complexity of the topic as the complexity of a speaker's explanation that makes a topic difficult for an audience to understand.

An excellent way to reduce the complexity of a speech is through analogies or comparisons. Explain a complex process, for example, by comparing it with a common process based on the same principle. In his speech on stem cell research to the 2004 Democratic National Convention, for example, Ron Reagan talked about such research providing us with a "personal biological repair kit."[5]

Visual aids can also be helpful in reducing complexity. For example, we recall a speech about a complex carbon molecule in which the speaker used a Tinkertoy model to show what the molecule looked like. The speaker also used an analogy, calling the molecule a "soot ball," to help the audience visualize what it would be like.

One final way to make a speech accessible to audience members is to clearly define any terms that may be unfamiliar to some or all of them. For example, suppose you heard a speech on bovine spongiform ecephalopathy. Unless the speaker explained that this was commonly known as mad cow disease, you would likely be lost and probably disinterested. Even more obscure are speeches that only use acronyms, or letters representing key words. For example, a speech on BSE would be confusing at best if the audience did not know that it was the official acronym for mad cow disease. Furthermore, whatever term is used for the disease, it needs a fuller definition, explaining that it is a chronic, degenerative disorder of a bovine's central nervous system.

Life Enrichment

When we introduced the tools you need to get started on your first speech, we talked about the importance of connecting with your audience. If they are to learn, audience members need to know explicitly why it is in their interest to listen to what you have to say.

When we connect with our audience, we are in effect saying, "My topic and message are potentially life enriching." Life enrichment can take the form of a more informed view on some topic or an improved way of behaving. Don't think that just because you have a good idea, people will necessarily see what you see. History is replete with good ideas, the proverbial better mousetrap, that are collecting dust for want of the public's attention. Consider two examples from Everett M. Rogers's classic work, *The Diffusion of Innovations.*[6]

If you have studied the history of science, you may recall that the disease scurvy, caused by a deficiency of vitamin C, was a serious problem for sailors on long voyages. As early as 1601, it was found that sources of vitamin C effectively inhibited scurvy. Yet it took almost 200 years for the British Navy to put this finding to use on its ships and almost 75 years more for sources of vitamin C to be made available on commercial ships.

The second example concerns the arrangement of the keyboard on typewriters and personal computers. If you have ever thought the keys were illogically arranged, you are not alone. A far better method of arrangement of keys has been available since 1932. The Dvorak method is more efficient than the system almost everybody uses and is more easily mastered. So why weren't you taught the Dvorak method in the beginning? Because the one you use was invented in 1873 and has been designed into almost all keyboards ever since. One of the reasons for staying with the less logical keyboard was that the metal keys of early typewriters stuck when the typist worked too quickly. Thus, the keyboard we use today on computers was originally invented to *slow down* typists on mechanical typewriters.

All too often speakers assume that audience members will recognize they have something to gain personally or professionally from a speech. What may be perfectly obvious to the speaker, however, may be just the opposite for the audience. Consider a case with which you already have some experience—college classes. Regardless of the subject matter of their classes, most college professors believe that the information they have to share is absolutely essential to every student's intellectual well-being. So secure are they in this belief, in fact, some seldom spend any time convincing students that there are "good reasons" for their being in the professor's class.

Occasionally, this oversight doesn't much matter—for example, when students are taking a course in their major. Students listen because they know they "have to learn" what is being taught, regardless of how well it's being taught. This is seldom the case, though, when they find themselves in a required course outside their major. "Why do I need a course in art history?" complains the computer science major, while the chemistry major asks, "Why do I need a class in public speaking?"

Just as teachers have an obligation to connect their course to the professional aspirations of students, speakers have the same kind of obligation to their audiences. It's not enough that their information is perceived as involving or appropriate by their audience. Their information—their speech—must also be readily perceived as enriching audience members' lives.

The two speeches outlined in this chapter are by students who make a special effort explain the life-enriching aspects of their topics. The first speech on bees and beekeeping by Trevor Morgan, explains that bees are essential to the production of about one-third of all the food we eat. Rather than treating bees as pesky insects, he hopes his listeners will learn to appreciate their value to our lives. The second speaker, Arin Larson, speaks about a topic that probably doesn't immediately affect most of her college-age audience—preselecting the sex of a child. But she points out that this knowledge can enrich one's life later on, especially in helping couples avoid sex-linked diseases. You may wonder why she even mentions color blindness in her speech. In fact, she spoke shortly after another speaker who had discussed the causes of color blindness, including how it is a sex-linked trait. Thus, she took advantage of the audience having been primed to be concerned about such sex-linked disorders.

Putting Theory Into Practice

Now that we have covered some of the principles related to conveying information to an audience, it's time to plan your own informative speech. This section offers some practical suggestions for how to give an informative speech. We discuss four ways to inform an audience: explanation, instruction, demonstration, and description. Informative speeches may employ more than one of these modes of informing. And the list is not exhaustive. Nevertheless, these four categories should be a useful way of thinking about how to translate the principles of informative speaking into an actual speech.

Speeches That Explain a Process

One of the primary functions you may wish to accomplish in an informative speech is to explain a process. Technically, a *process* is a continuous phenomenon without an obvious beginning or end. Examples of processes are plentiful

To better understand an informative speech explaining a process, click on the Speech Coach link on our Online Learning Center Web site, and go to Segment 13.1 to view Trevor Morgan's speech on bees.

in science and include photosynthesis, erosion, and osmosis. Because true processes are complex and often hidden from our ordinary senses, their explanation requires genuine creativity from a speaker. At a minimum, we must break down the process into increments that the audience can readily comprehend. If the process involves a specialized vocabulary, we also need to define terms for the audience. Because the process also may be invisible, we may have to create visuals that approximate the process.

The key to explaining a process is to find the right complement of language and visual media for your audience. This involves finding the best analogies, metaphors, and similes to start. You can then complement these elements of language with static visual media such as overheads or dynamic visual media such as a DVD or CD-ROM, or even the actual objects themselves. You can review an outline of a speech explaining a process in the box, "Sample Informative Speech Outline: Bees and Beekeeping" by Trevor Morgan on pages 374–375.

Speeches That Explain a Concept

Although not as difficult to explain as a process, a concept demands care on the part of the speaker who chooses to explain it. A *concept* is a symbolic abstraction that pulls together a class of objects that share common attributes. The word *ball,* for example, is also a concept that can be applied to baseballs, basketballs, soccer balls, golf balls, racketballs, squash balls, and volleyballs. Although different in size and purpose, these types of balls share at least one common attribute: They are round.

The key to explaining a concept is to describe the essential attributes that distinguish it from other concepts. How is a democracy different from a republic? The United States is a republic, yet most people refer to it as a democracy. A good informative speech would not only explain why this is the case but also point out the specific attributes that distinguish a republic from a democracy.

In selecting a topic for a speech that explains a process or a concept, keep in mind that the topic should be relevant to the audience, something they are capable of understanding, and something you can explain in the time allotted. Although the theory of relativity is highly relevant, explaining it in a 5- to 10-minute speech is a tall order.

The message attribute of accessibility is particularly important in speeches that explain. Recall that one way to reduce complexity for an audience is to use an analogy. Consider the use of analogy in this excerpt from a speech by Jonathan Studebaker explaining his disease:

> Like I said, I'm a nice person. I'm cheerful, I'm energetic. Okay, so I have a disability. I was born with osteogenesis imperfecta, a disease which causes my bones to be fragile. Have you ever accidentally dropped a glass on the floor? What happens? It breaks. Well, my bones kinda break like glass, which is why I tell people, when you carry me, treat me like your best crystal.[7]

The use of a simple analogy of bones to glass helps the audience understand a disease most of us cannot even pronounce. For Jonathan's purposes, which are to introduce himself and explain his disability, that is the extent of the technical information his audience needs to know.

A second factor that is important in speeches that explain a process or a concept is to make it observable with visuals. They can make an abstract concept concrete and thus easier to understand.

During your college career, you will undoubtedly be called on to explain something to an audience, if not in your public speaking class, then in another setting. Similarly, in the professional world, it is common for people to be called on to explain everything from a new product idea to why the last quarter's sales were so bad. Using the principle of accessibility can help you enhance your explanations.

Speeches That Instruct

Informative speaking can also be used to instruct an audience. The key to instruction is to provide new information the audience can put to use, or a new perspective on old information. Modern educational theory emphasizes observable behavioral objectives; that is, after receiving instruction, students should be able to show that they have mastered the subject, either by answering questions or by engaging in some activity.

Involving the speech audience is important to speeches that provide instruction. Unless the information in a speech presents new information or a *fresh perspective* to our audience, all we have done is bore them with what they already know. For example, speeches on how to ride a bike or how to pack a suitcase are unlikely to provide anything new to an audience. However, even new topics can be perceived as irrelevant by large portions of an audience. For example, a speech on how to wax your skis is old news to experienced skiers but irrelevant to nonskiers in the class.

So, the key to speeches that instruct is to provide new, yet relevant information to your audience, or at least a new perspective on such information. That means using the novelty of your topic to involve people while pointing out how learning the information can be life enriching.

Certainly Arin Larson's speech on sex preselection was probably a novel topic for most of her classmates. You can read the outline in the box, "In Their Own Words: Choosing Your Baby: The Methods of Sex Preselection" (pages 378–379).

OLC www.mhhe.com/brydon6

To gain a clearer understanding of an informative speech to instruct, click on the Speech Coach link on our Online Learning Center Web site, and go to Segment 13.2 to view Arin Larson's speech on sex preselection.

Speeches That Demonstrate How to Do Something

Speeches with a demonstration are closely related to those that provide instruction, but the speaker actually shows the audience how to do something. Further, a good demonstration allows the audience to try out what is being demonstrated, if not during the speech itself, then later on their own.

A good example of speeches that demonstrate can be found on the Food Network channel. As Rachel Ray explains one of her 30-minute meals and Bobby Flay talks about the thrill of the grill, they simultaneously demonstrate what the audience needs to re-create at home.

A demonstration speaker needs to provide audience members with enough information to do the activity on their own or with information on where to

In Their Own Words

Sample Informative Speech Outline

BEES AND BEEKEEPING
by Trevor Morgan

Specific Purpose: To discuss a different side of bees and beekeeping that is less well-known to most people.

Trevor Morgan

Introduction

Notice how the speaker both gains attention and connects with the audience.

I. **Open with Impact/Connect with Audience:** A show of hands: How many people do not like or are even scared of bees?
II. **Thesis Statement:** Due to the majority of people being unfamiliar with bees, bees tend to get a bad reputation that I hope to change.
III. **Preview:** I am going to discuss types of bees, species, and pollination.

The three-point organization is clearly previewed and easy to follow.

Body

I. **Main Point:** There are three main types of bees: queen bee, drone bee, and the worker bee.

The speaker provided notations to himself about using visual aids.

   A. Queen bee:
      1. Head of all bees in a colony. (Visual Aid)
      2. Colony would not function properly without her.
      3. Longer body than the worker bee.
      4. Main job in hive is to lay eggs—up to 3,000 eggs a day.
      5. Only stings other queen bees—not people; multiple stings.
   B. Drone bee:
      1. The only male bee—doesn't have a stinger.
      2. Only takes about twenty-five flights in its life.
      3. Specially designed for mating only with the queens.
      4. Very lazy. When the mating process is over, the worker bees kill the drone because it is no longer productive.
   C. Worker bee:
      1. The powerhouse of the hive.
      2. Does all the work and carries out all the functions in the hive.
      3. Undeveloped female that is unable to lay eggs.
      4. They have pollen baskets used for pollination (Morse, 1975).
      5. They do not act as individuals—they work together.

The speaker not only cites his source, he held up the book at this point.

(**Transition:** Now that you know the three main types, I'll discuss some species.)

The speaker uses clear transitional statements.

II. Main Point: There are hundreds of different species of bees.

A. There are African, Italian, Irish, Yugoslavian, etc., but I'll discuss two main types of bees.

B. The African Bee:

1. Originated in Africa and smuggled into the United States.
2. Very aggressive and attacks in large numbers. (Visual Aid)
3. Africanized bees cannot survive Northern California winters.

C. The Italian Bee:

1. Most common around this area.
2. Very gentle bee compared to the African bee. (Visual Aid)

At this point, the speaker held up a box with about 5,000 bees in it.

(**Transition:** Now that you know two different types of species, I'm going to discuss the important topic of pollination.)

III. Main Point: Pollination by bees is very important.

A. The honeybee is the most important insect in pollination of agricultural crops.

B. Without a doubt, the honeybee is far more important and valuable to mankind as a pollinator than as a honey producer.

C. Approximately one-third of our food supply is either directly or indirectly dependent on bee-pollinated plants (Root, 1983).

D. Two main types of flower pollination:

1. Nectar pollination.
2. The transfer of stamen (male) pollen to the pistil (female).

The significance of this topic to our lives is stressed and a source is cited. He refers to the book as the bible of beekeeping.

Conclusion

I. Summarize: Now you know:

A. Types of Bees

B. Species

C. Pollination

II. Close with Impact: So the next time you see a bee flying around your dorm room or your car, instead of squishing it, just remember how important bees are and let it go.

Closing statement directly connects to the audience.

References

Africanized honeybee range in U.S. (picture). (n.d.). Retrieved May 5, 2005, from http://www.stingshield.com

Morse, R. (1975). *Bees and beekeeping.* New York: Cornell University Press.

Root, A. (1983). *The abc and xyz of bee culture.* Ohio: A. I. Root Company.

obtain further instruction so that they can try out the activity. For example, although no one can master karate from just listening to a single speech, or even a series of speeches, a demonstration of karate moves can spur an audience member to seek out individual instruction in the martial arts. In fact, many martial arts studios make a practice of giving demonstrations in schools and at public events as a way of recruiting new students.

Topics for speeches that demonstrate need to be chosen with care. A complex, difficult task cannot be adequately demonstrated in a few minutes. There can even be the danger of making people think they know how to do something based on a speech when in fact they do not. Few of us could do CPR, for example, based on simply watching a speaker demonstrate the activity. We need the opportunity to try it out (perhaps on a life-size doll) before we can know if we can do it. On the other hand, another lifesaving technique, the Heimlich maneuver, is often the subject of demonstration and can be learned in a reasonably short time.

The key to making a demonstration effective is careful planning. For example, if you have ever watched syndicated reruns of the show *Home Improvement,* you know that Tim "The Tool Man" Taylor rarely has practiced what he

Failure to properly prepare for a demonstration is the hallmark of Tim Allen's comedy on *Home Improvement,* but it can lead to disaster in an informative speech.

is demonstrating. If you plan to demonstrate a process in your speech, rehearse it carefully. Also, it is sometimes useful to prepare various steps of the process in advance. Watch any cooking show demonstration on TV. The onions are already chopped, the flour is already sifted and measured, and an example of the finished product is near at hand. We don't want the audience drifting off as we measure ingredients or sift the flour. Providing a written recipe in a handout or as a visual will save a lot of time and let the audience focus on watching the demonstration. In short, a demonstration requires extra preparation.

In addition, we should be sure that the demonstration is an accurate re-creation. If we misinform an audience, we have done more harm than good. Depending on what we are demonstrating, we might even be inviting injury to the audience members or someone else. We must make certain, therefore, that we can accurately demonstrate the process in the time allowed.

Finally, we should make sure the demonstration is visible to the audience. A demonstration speech on making sushi, or small origami paper figures, may initially seem like a good idea. Unless there is a way to magnify the demonstration so that all the audience can see what the speaker is doing, making sushi or origami figures isn't a very good idea.

Speeches That Describe

Another function of informative speeches is description. Using visuals can enhance a descriptive speech. Not only can visuals be useful; you may also want to provide a word picture of the subject. Consider the following description of a familiar character, Mickey Mouse, provided by student speaker Jennie Rees:

> They designed him using a circle for his head and oblong circles for his nose and snout. They also drew circles for his ears and drew them in such a way that they appeared to look the same any way Mickey turned his head. They gave him a pear-shaped body with pipe-stem legs, and stuffed them in big, oversized shoes, making him look like a little kid wearing his father's shoes.[8]

Can't you almost picture Mickey from that description? Visual language is key to effective description.

Examples of speech topics for each type of informative speech are offered in Exhibit 14.2 on page 380

Tips and Tactics

Informative Speaking

When putting an informative speech together, we need to do the following:

- Use words that appeal to the different learning styles of audience members.
- Use techniques that make the speech involving, appropriate, accessible, and potentially life enriching.
- Establish whether the speech purpose is to explain a concept or a process, instruct, demonstrate, or describe.
- Maximize observability through the use of appropriate visual aids.

In Their Own Words

Sample Informative Speech Outline

CHOOSING YOUR BABY: THE METHODS OF SEX PRESELECTION
by Arin Larson

Arin Larson

Specific Purpose: To inform the audience of the methods of sex selection and the pros and cons of each.

Introduction

Speaker begins with an analogy her classmates can relate to.

I. **Open with Impact:** Imagine you have decided to add a pet to your family.
   A. Some may prefer to get a cat, some a dog, and some both but would choose one before the other.
   B. Some people also have a preference of which sex of child they would like to add to their family.
   C. Sex selection is the way to do just that.

II. **Thesis Statement:** Sex selection has two methods; the method used depends on the individual.

She clearly states the benefit for audience members of learning this information.

III. **Connect With the Audience:** Sex selection can benefit you in many ways.
   A. It allows families to choose the birth order/sex of their children.
   B. It allows families with multiple same sex children to conceive a child of the opposite sex.
   C. It allows people to select against sex-linked defects and disease.

IV. **Preview:** Today, I will explain the two types of sex selection methods: MicroSort and the Shettles method, as well as the foundational facts that make it possible.

Body

The science behind sex preselection is explained in an accessible manner.

I. **Main Point:** Sex selection is based on the fundamental understanding that there are two types of sperm.
   A. When cells become reproductive cells, they divide their chromosomes—including the 23rd pair that codes for sex.
   B. Since males all carry an "XY" chromosomal pair, half of the haploid or sperm cells have an "X" and half have a "Y."
   C. Since females are "XX" all eggs are "X" after division. Sex of the baby depends on whether an "X"-bearing sperm or a "Y"-bearing sperm reached it first.

(**Transition:** Now that you know how the sex of the baby is determined, I will explain the first method for selecting for a certain sex.)

II. **Main Point:** This method is called MicroSort and is used in conjunction with in vitro fertilization.
   A. The man produces a sperm sample.
   B. The sperm DNA is stained with fluorescent dye.
      1. A laser is shined on them.
         a. Sperm is sifted using a cell sorter.
         b. Each cell's DNA is measured.
      2. This process takes a full day to sort one sperm sample.
   C. The desired sperm are then implanted in the woman's uterus to join with her egg.

(**Transition:** Now that you know the laboratory method, I will explain the method you can do right at home.)

III. **Main Point:** This method was developed by Dr. Landrum B. Shettles, M.D., who has been researching this subject since the late 1960s.
   A. Dr. Shettles's method is based on a similar scientific principle as MicroSort.
      1. Since the "Y" sperm are lacking that extra bit to make it an "X," "Y" sperm are smaller and faster than "X" sperm.
         a. This means they outswim the "X" sperm and get to the egg first.
         b. They also die faster and are easier to kill with acid than the "X" sperm.
      2. The "X" sperm are larger and slower than the "Y" sperm and take longer to reach the egg.
         a. They, in favorable conditions, will get beaten to the egg.
         b. However, they survive longer and are harder to kill. So by manipulating when and where they are introduced, they can outlast the "Y" sperm and reach the egg first.
   B. The woman through a series of practice cycles determines her ovulation point.
      1. She can use the CM, or cervical mucus, method.
         a. She checks her CM daily and records on a chart where her CM indicates ovulation.
         b. After a few months of doing this, she is reasonably certain of when she ovulates.
      2. She can use the BBT, or basal body temperature, method.
         a. She takes her temperature every morning.
         b. She plots on a chart when her temperature drops each month, indicating ovulation.
   C. She has sex with her partner at a time determined by which sex of child they are trying to conceive.
      1. For a boy, abstain for 4–5 days or as close to ovulation day, as possible; then have sex.
         a. Use rear, or deep, penetration.
         b. The woman should orgasm just before the man.
      2. For a girl, have sex everyday until between 4 and 2 days before ovulation, and then stop.
         a. Use missionary, or shallow, penetration.
         b. No female orgasm.

The source of the method of preselection is explained.

Again, the science is explained in an accessible way.

Although the topic might be delicate for some, she uses clinical language and treats it respectfully, not in a distasteful manner.

Conclusion

I. **Summarize:** To conclude, I have explained to you that sex selection is a fairly simple and successful procedure once you know the fundamentals.
   A. Sperm come in two types, "X" and "Y," and they are different.
   B. The MicroSort method involves manually screening out the undesired sperm to ensure conception of the desired sex.
   C. Shettles method involves making conditions more favorable for one or the other—giving the desired sperm the advantage.

II. **Close with Impact:** Now that you know how to conceive a boy or a girl, you can use this procedure to get the one you want. Until then, though, there's no harm in practicing!

Her close definitely is memorable with a touch of humor.

References

Associated Press. *Researchers Report Success with Sex Selection Method* (1998). Retrieved September 21, 2004, from http://www.cnn.com/HEALTH/9809/09/babysex/

Refined Techniques of FEMcide: Fetal sex determination and sex preselection/technical aspects. (n.d.) Retrieved September 21, 2004, from http://www.hsph.harvard.edu/organizations/healthnet/reprorights/sexpapers.html

Shettles, L.B. (1997). *How to Choose the Sex of Your Baby.* New York: Broadway Books.

Exhibit 14.2
Possible Speech Topics for Informative Speeches

Explaining a process such as . . .	Explaining a concept such as . . .
• Global warming • How hydrogen can power cars • How solar panels convert sunlight into electricity • How West Nile Virus is transmitted • How exposure to UV rays causes skin cancer	• Credit card fees and how they can accumulate • A type of art; for example, impressionism • The nature of a disease; for example, muscular dystrophy • Compound interest and how a small amount invested over time can grow • Musical harmony
Demonstrating how to . . .	**Describing . . .**
• Grow your own herbs • Fill out the EZ1040 income tax form • Fly fish • Give CPR • Prepare your favorite food • Properly protect yourself from injury while skiing	• A visit to Rio de Janeiro • The most unforgettable person you ever met • The weaknesses in airport security allowing hijackers to take over planes • The beauty of Yosemite National Park • The judging of an Olympic sport such as gymnastics

One Final Word

If a word could be used to summarize the difference between an outstanding and less successful informative speech it would have to be *enthusiasm*. There is simply no substitute for your enthusiasm with your topic and the pleasure your audience senses that you receive from talking about it. Enthusiasm is contagious. When you are enthused, it is hard for your audience to avoid sharing your enthusiasm. Obviously, this fact reminds us of an additional one: Your success with informative speaking depends upon a carefully selected and researched topic you care about!

Summary

www.mhhe.com/brydon6

To evaluate your understanding of this chapter, visit our Online Learning Center Web site for quizzes and other chapter study aids.

Informative speaking is the process by which an audience gains new information or a new perspective on old information from a speaker.

- Learning is frequently the goal of informative speaking.
- Informative and persuasive speaking are two opposite ends of a continuum.
- It's important that the individual learning styles of audience members be reflected in the verbal and nonverbal content of informative speeches.

- Informative speeches are common in the classroom, the workplace, and the community.
- Successful informative speeches are audience involving, audience appropriate, audience accessible, and potentially life enriching.
- Informative speeches can be used to explain, instruct, demonstrate, or describe processes, concepts, and skills.

Check Your Understanding: Exercises and Activities

1. Develop an outline for a brief speech in which you inform an audience about a topic with which you are personally familiar. Then show how you would adapt the speech to each of the following learnings styles: Auditory linguistic, visual linguistic, auditory numerical, visual numerical, and audio-visual-kinesthetic combination.
2. Come up with at least two possible topics each for speeches that explain, instruct, demonstrate, and describe. Do some topics seem to fall naturally into one category? Are there other topics that might be used for more than one type of speech?
3. What is your preferred learning style? To find out, go to http://www.engr.ncsu.edu/learningstyles/ilsweb.html and take the "Index of Learning Styles Questionnaire" developed by Barbara A. Solomon and Richard A. Felder of North Carolina State.

Notes

1. Jay Mathews, *Escalante: The Best Teacher in America* (New York: Henry Holt, 1988), 191.
2. *Stand and Deliver,* director Tom Menendez, with Edward James Olmos, Lou Diamond Phillips, Rosana De Soto, and Andy Garcia, An American Playhouse Theatrical Film, A Menendez/Musca & Olmos Production, Warner Bros., 1988.
3. P. Friedman and R. Alley, "Learning/Teaching Styles: Applying the Principles," *Theory Into Practice,* 23 (1984): 77–81. Based on R. Dunn and K. Dunn, *Teaching Students Through Their Individual Learning Styles: A Practical Approach* (Reston, VA: Reston Publishing, 1978).
4. Michael D. Scott and Scott Elliot, "Innovation in the Classroom: Toward a Reconceptualization of Instructional Communication" (paper presented at the annual meeting of the International Communication Association, Dallas, Texas, 1983).
5. "Reagan Calls for Increased Stem Cell Research," *CNN.Com Inside Politics,* 28 July 2004. [Retrieved from http://www.cnn.com/2004/ALLPOLITICS/07/27/dems.reagan/, 11 August 2004.]
6. Everett M. Rogers, *Diffusion of Innovations* (New York: Free Press, 1983).
7. Jonathan Studebaker, "Speech of Self-Introduction: Who Am I?" The full text appears in Chapter 3.
8. Jennie Rees, "Informative Speech: Mickey: A Changing Image," California State University, Chico, 1992.

In subtle and not so subtle ways, we are faced with persuasive messages every day.

Persuasive Communication

Burt Pryor and Jim Katt

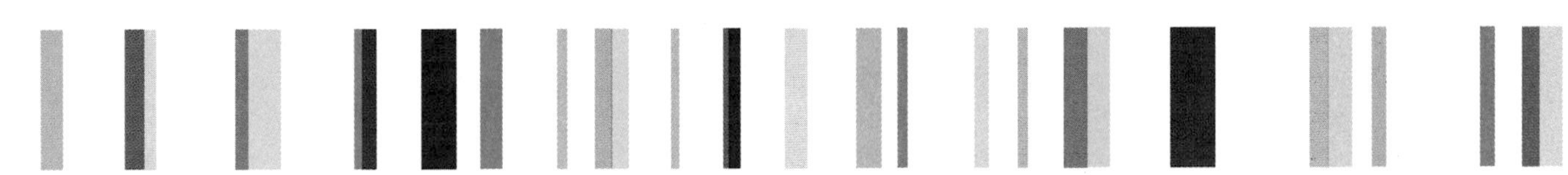

Objectives

After reading and discussing this chapter, you should be able to:

- Define the concept of persuasion
- Discuss the influence of the Elaboration Likelihood Model
- Discuss how the central and peripheral routes allow persuasion to occur
- Understand the effect of source, message, channel, and receiver on an audience's likelihood to elaborate
- Define the three types of persuasive effects
- Explain how one-sided versus two-sided messages, inoculation theory, use of statistical and story evidence, and fear appeals can make messages more persuasive.
- Understand how speaker characteristics, message-related peripheral cues, and compliance-gaining strategies influence persuasion

Key Concepts

Elaboration Likelihood Model

Peripheral route processing

Central route processing

Wear-out point

Selective exposure

One-sided messages

Two-sided nonrefutational messages

Two-sided refutational messages

> “I would rather try to persuade a man to go along, because once I have persuaded him he will stick. If I scare him, he will stay just as long as he is scared, and then he is gone.”
>
> – DWIGHT D. EISENHOWER

Persuasion is so much a routine part of our lives that most of us are probably not aware of its pervasiveness unless it is called to our attention. Literally everyone is in the business of persuasion. If you were to keep a log of every persuasion attempt that you encountered in a given day as a persuader, receiver, or observer, you would soon realize the necessity of having that log available wherever you went. Think of those who practice persuasion professionally: advertisers, attorneys, politicians, educators (including the authors of the message you are reading right now), clergy, salespeople (including telemarketers), media consultants, managers, coaches–even engineers. The list is practically endless. We receive direct mail ads on a daily basis, the so-called "junk mail." Pratkanis & Aronson (2001) reported that adults are exposed to an average of 750 television ads per week. We are also bombarded with advertising through other media, including newspapers, magazines, radio and the Internet. When we are driving in our cars, the persuasive messages on the radio, billboards, and bumper stickers permeate our consciousness. Even our clothing carries persuasive messages. Hats and T-shirts display the logos and slogans of manufacturers, and our casual clothing is commonly decorated with designer labels. Add to this the daily interpersonal influences involving parents, couples, children, friends, and relatives, and one begins to see that we humans are constant participants in this process we call persuasion. Because of its central role in our daily lives, it is an understatement to say it makes sense to study persuasion. The potential benefits of a better understanding of the persuasion process, from the perspectives of both the persuader and the ones being persuaded, go well beyond the speech classroom.

Defining the Concept of Persuasion

Persuasion is the process by which attitudes or behaviors are influenced as a result of receiving a message (Anderson & Pryor, 1992). However, definitions of persuasion vary according to whether they recognize *unintentional influence* as persuasion. For example, let's assume you plan an "informative" speech about recycling programs, including their costs and benefits. Though your purpose may only be to inform, it is quite plausible that your discussion about the long-term benefits of recycling on the environment may influence your classmates' attitudes and even their behaviors involving recycling. So, your "informative speech" might also persuade the receivers. A broad definition of persuasion might include this type of unintentional persuasion.

Narrower definitions of persuasion typically limit what we call persuasion to situations that include an intentional persuader. It should be noted that those who espouse the "intentional" model of persuasion do not argue that people's minds and behaviors are never changed without an intentional persuader. They just believe that attitude or behavior change without an intentional persuader should not be classified as persuasion. Most of the research on persuasion works from this narrower definition of persuasion.

It is also important to distinguish between coercion, which is based on reward and punishment power and receivers' lack of perceived choice, and persuasion, which is based on information power. The statement, "Give me your money, or I will shoot you" allows the receiver little choice in light of the punishment for refusing to give up the money. The lack of perceived choice is what separates persuasion from coercion. So, if you are thinking that a gun threat is pretty persuasive, it isn't. It is, however, pretty coercive.

This chapter focuses on strategies that speakers can implement to increase the persuasiveness of their messages. The strategies are derived from systematic research conducted by social scientists over the past few decades that has led to better understanding of cause-effect relationships in persuasion. A large body of research has led to the development of theories and guidelines that persuaders can use to increase their odds of success. This chapter offers an overview of the areas of persuasion research that are most applicable to public speaking situations. We will begin with a more extensive examination of the Elaboration Likelihood Model, explore the two main routes to persuasion that the model offers, and then look at tools you as a speaker can use to build a strong message.

The Elaboration Likelihood Model

The persuasion strategies relating to source, message, channel, and receiver factors will be discussed within the framework of the most comprehensive theory yet developed in the field of persuasion, the Elaboration Likelihood Model, also known as the ELM (Petty & Cacioppo, 1986). The ELM was introduced in Chapter 2, now we will delve more deeply into the ELM research and discuss what that research can tell us about becoming more effective when attempting to be persuasive.

As suggested by its name, the Elaboration Likelihood Model predicts the likelihood that receivers will "elaborate" (process, think about) a message under various circumstances. The ELM suggests that people want to make "correct" decisions about how to respond to persuasive messages, but cannot possibly scrutinize every persuasive message that comes their way. Sometimes we engage in effortful, elaborative processing; other times, we may choose not to mentally elaborate on the message. According to the ELM and its research findings, the two major determinants of whether or not receivers engage in message elaboration are their motivation and ability to process the message. Those who are motivated (they really want to process a message) and are able (they can process a message) tend to engage in elaborative message processing. Those who lack motivation or ability tend to process the message superficially.

Two Routes to Persuasion: Central and Peripheral

That the ELM identifies two main routes to persuasion–the **central route** and the **peripheral route**. Essentially, the central route involves persuasion achieved by the quality of the arguments in the message, while peripheral route persuasion occurs when receivers are influenced by factors other than argument quality (e.g., speaker expertise or attractiveness). The ELM holds that receivers will focus on the message arguments to the extent that they are both motivated and able to process the message. Central route persuasion, then, relies on high message elaboration.

On the other hand, to the extent that receivers are lacking in either the motivation or ability to process the message, persuasion, if it happens at all, will be based on factors outside the message. These are called peripheral cues. As demonstrated earlier, we are inundated with persuasive messages on a continual basis. We simply

central route processing
Persuasion achieved by the quality of the arguments in a message.

peripheral route processing
Influence based upon factors outside of the quality of the message.

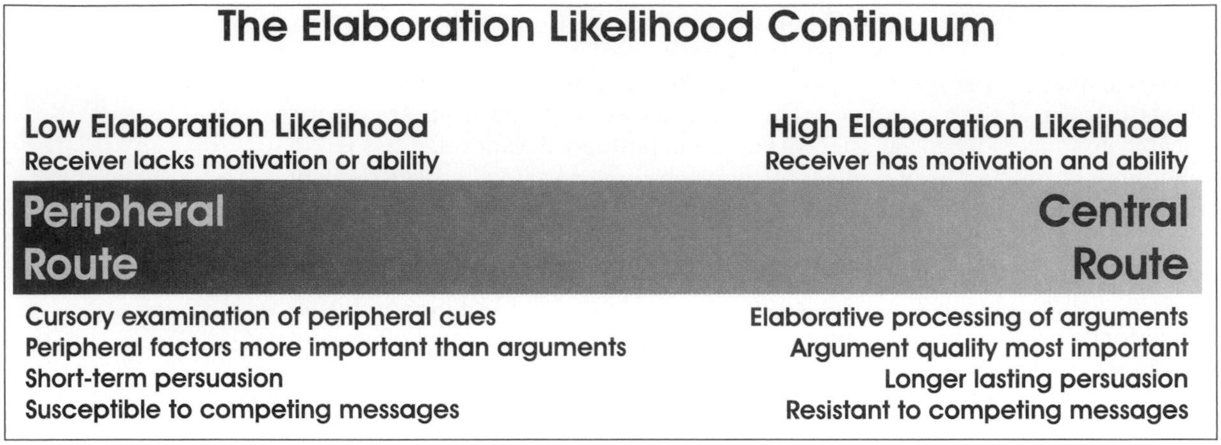

The Elaboration Likelihood Continuum

Low Elaboration Likelihood	High Elaboration Likelihood
Receiver lacks motivation or ability	Receiver has motivation and ability
Peripheral Route	Central Route
Cursory examination of peripheral cues	Elaborative processing of arguments
Peripheral factors more important than arguments	Argument quality most important
Short-term persuasion	Longer lasting persuasion
Susceptible to competing messages	Resistant to competing messages

The central/peripheral routes to persuasion are not an either/or relationship. Instead they represent a continuum.

do not have the time or energy to thoroughly process every message that comes our way, lest we pull our cars to side of the road to make sure we carefully consider every billboard. Think of it as literally "paying" attention: it costs us time and energy to process a message. Consequently, we use decision rules, or mental shortcuts, in response to many persuasive messages, particularly those we perceive as low in relevance or consequence for our daily lives. We often quickly accept or reject persuasive appeals, from advertisements to issues of national scope, on the basis of peripheral cues–such as whether or not we like the speaker, or how expert we perceive the speaker to be–without even examining the arguments the speaker presents.

It is important to note, though, that the central-peripheral distinction represents a continuum, not an "either /or" relationship. It is not a matter of using one route or the other exclusively, but of relying more on the central route than the peripheral route in some situations, and more on the peripheral route than the central route in others.

What ELM Research Offers Persuaders

The ELM has spawned a body of research about how numerous factors affect the likelihood of message elaboration. The research has shown two main advantages of central route over peripheral route persuasion. Because it is more grounded in substantive attitude and belief modification than persuasion achieved through the peripheral route, central route persuasion is (1) longer lasting, and (2) more resistant to subsequent competing messages (Petty & Cacioppo, 1986). Since listeners will process the message more thoroughly when they are using the central route, it makes sense that a speaker should use high quality arguments to be successful. Consider a speech where receivers are highly motivated and able to scrutinize the message, but the message contains weak arguments. For example, "We should raise the drinking age to 23 because several prominent politicians think it is a good idea and some think it will curb alcohol sales." In this situation, the persuader would be better off if receivers processed the message less thoroughly because thorough processing of weak arguments only accentuates receivers' negative responses to the message. The critical point here is that strategically increasing receivers' attention to a set of arguments is not always a good thing. It's a good idea only if the receivers perceive the arguments to be strong.

Central Route Factors: Things that make elaboration more likely

We have already stated that receivers engage in effortful information processing (elaboration) of a message when they are both motivated and able. This section introduces some of the factors that have been shown to make elaboration more likely. These include characteristics of the speaker, elements of the message, the use of multiple channels, and the attitudes and perceptions of the receivers. Once we've examined the research, we will explore some practical applications you can use as a speaker.

Speaker Characteristics

Speaker expertise

Speaker expertise refers to receivers' perceptions of the speaker's knowledge, qualifications, and competence. Although speaker expertise has its most direct impact on persuasion as a peripheral cue (discussed in detail later in this chapter), it can affect receivers' motivation and thus be a factor in determining how much elaboration receivers will engage in. Speaker expertise has little effect on information processing of highly relevant messages because receivers are already motivated to process the message; however, some studies (e.g., Petty & Cacioppo, 1984) have shown that expert sources increase receivers' motivation to process messages when issue relevance is moderate or ambiguous. Petty & Cacioppo (1986) explain that when receivers are not sure whether a message merits their attention, "characteristics of the message source can help a person decide if the message is worth thinking about" (p. 206).

Number of Sources and Arguments

Harkins and Petty (1981) examined the effects of multiple sources/multiple arguments on receivers' message processing and attitude change. Participants listened to messages from one speaker or from three speakers that utilized one argument or three different arguments. The combination of three speakers, each with a different strong argument, produced more positive thoughts about the issue and more persuasion than any of the other conditions. Harkins and Petty concluded that each time the participants heard the voice of a new speaker (changing stimulus) they were re-stimulated to process the message. Since the arguments were strong, this increased attention to the message resulted in more favorable thoughts and more persuasion. Had the arguments been weak, the ELM would predict the increased processing brought by multiple sources and multiple arguments would only increase receivers' negative thoughts, decreasing persuasion in comparison to the other conditions.

The relationship between attention and stimulus variety has been well documented in social science research. Vernon (1962, p. 183) concluded from early research that "normal consciousness, perception, and thought can be maintained only in a constantly changing environment." It has been said that variety is the "spice of life." This research suggests that adding a little of that spice to your presentation might help motivate your audience to more thoughtfully process your message.

Message Characteristics

ELM research has identified several message characteristics that affect receivers' motivation and ability to process information. Two that can be applied to public speaking are forewarning of persuasive intent and message repetition.

Forewarning and Resistance to Persuasion

You have probably heard someone say that "forewarned is forearmed." In other words, if we know something is coming, a hurricane, cutback in work hours, or the need to make repairs on a declining old car, we will be more likely to prepare for it. In the case of persuasive messages, this statement should be amended to say that forewarned is forearmed, but only if (1) the issue is personally relevant to the receiver, (2) the message is intended to change attitudes (not create or reinforce attitudes), and (3), the receivers have at least a few minutes to arm themselves. Sometimes we receive warnings that we are soon to be the target of a persuasion attempt. A friend may warn you that a mutual acquaintance plans to talk to you about joining a pyramid business scheme; your mother may alert you that she and Dad want to sit down with you to discuss your progress toward graduation; a company may alert you that a salesperson will be "in your area" next week. The ELM research shows that these warnings can render you more, or less, susceptible to influence, depending on the three factors listed above.

Participants in research by Petty and Cacioppo (1977) listened to a live class presentation in which a speaker, identified as psychologist from the testing center, presented strong arguments for initiating comprehensive exams as a graduation requirement. Since a previous survey had shown that students were against this policy change, the message constituted an attempt to change attitudes. In various classes, the students were either informed (warned) about the persuasive intent of the impending presentation five minutes prior to the speaker's arrival, told of the intent as the speaker was introduced, or not warned at all.

Only the group that received the five-minute warning resisted being persuaded. The data showed that they had spent the time following the warning thinking of counterarguments to the anticipated presentation. The forewarning had motivated them to do so. For this group, forewarned was forearmed. Since the participants who were warned immediately prior to the presentation had no time to develop their defenses, they were persuaded, along with the unwarned group, by the strong arguments.

Forewarning and Increased Persuasion

At other times, forewarning can lead to increased persuasion. For example, when issue relevance is low, receivers are less motivated to devote efforts to building ammunition to defend against the anticipated message. This is particularly true in interpersonal situations where friendship and harmony may take priority over rejecting someone's influence attempt on a topic of low importance (see Cialdini, Levy, Herman, Kozlowski, & Petty, 1976). Another situation where warning may heighten susceptibility to persuasion is when issue relevance is high, but the position taken is consistent with the receiver's attitude. Under such circumstances, the ELM would predict that the warning would cause receivers to experience mostly positive thoughts in anticipation of the message, leading to increased susceptibility to attitude reinforcement.

Message Repetition

Persuaders often use repetition for purposes of clarifying, reminding, or reinforcing message effects. This tactic is most common in advertising, where the same commercial airs repeatedly until it reaches the **wear-out point** for its audience. Virtually all persuaders–such as the clergy, attorneys, parents, teachers and students–employ message repetition in their efforts to influence listeners. ELM research, including its applied studies in advertising, has yielded consistent results on the effects of message repetition on information processing and persuasion. With messages that initially produce positive responses to a set of strong arguments, or to a novel, clever commercial, the repetition effects follow an inverted U-shaped pattern. That is, positive thoughts and persuasion increase up to a wear-out point, then decrease as receivers begin to tire of the message. Wear-out points vary, largely as a function of the complexity and novelty of messages, but the pattern does not. At some point, even the cleverest commercial begins to lose its appeal.

wear-out point
The point at which a repeated persuasive message loses its effectiveness.

In an experiment by Cacioppo and Petty (1979), participants listened to strong arguments that advocated increasing tuition to facilitate hiring more faculty, offering more classes, and other student-oriented improvements. Each participant listened to the message one, three, or five times. Participants who heard the message once generated mostly positive thoughts and were influenced by the strong

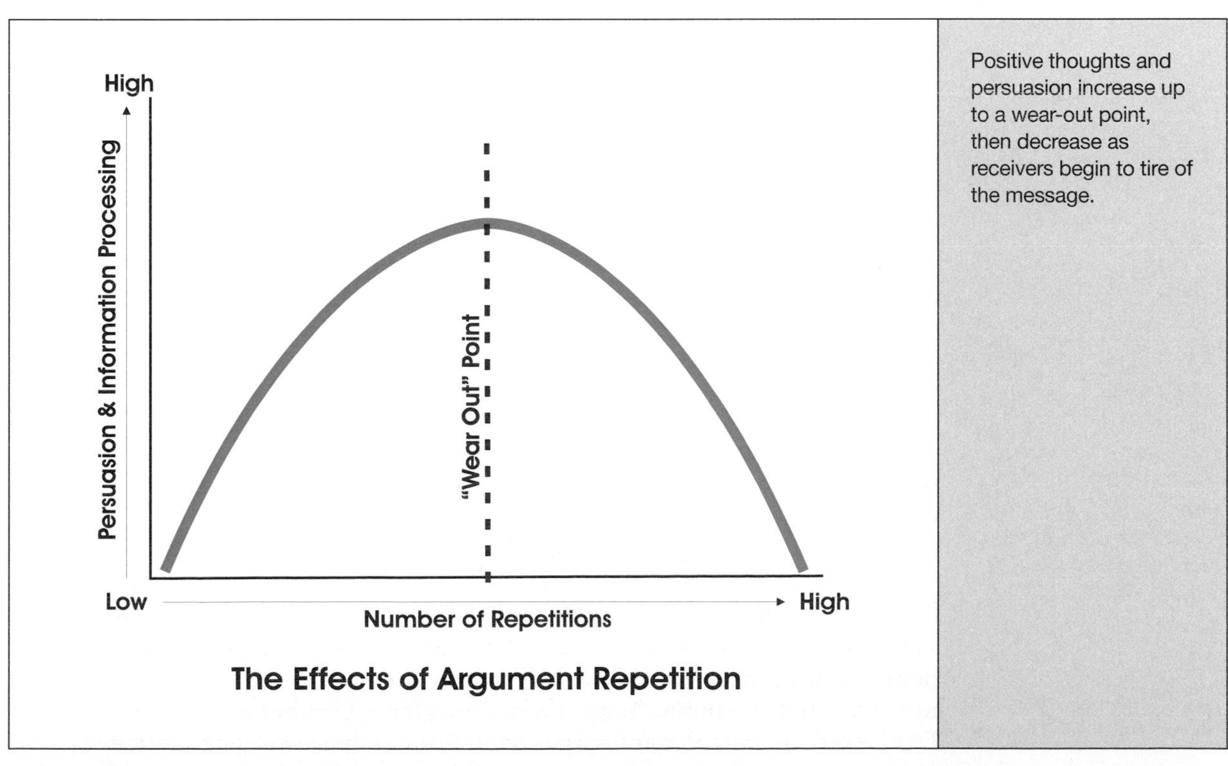

Positive thoughts and persuasion increase up to a wear-out point, then decrease as receivers begin to tire of the message.

arguments. Attitude change and the number of positive thoughts increased in the three-repetition condition, but decreased with five repetitions. Petty and Cacioppo reasoned that repeating the message three times increased receivers' ability to think about the strong argument, but five repetitions was too much, causing feelings of boredom and tedium.

A subsequent study by Petty and Cacioppo (1985) showed that three repetitions of weak arguments increased receivers' negative thoughts and reduced attitude change. Repetition of the weak arguments gave participants more opportunity to recognize just how weak the arguments were.

Channel Options

Information processing is also affected by whether the message is transmitted through written or spoken channels. Research (e.g., Chaiken & Eagly, 1976) indicates that when messages are complex, written versions are more persuasive than spoken versions. This finding has been attributed to greater comprehension of complex or difficult material when receivers can process (read) the message at their own pace. In ELM terms, the written channel increases receivers' ability to process the message; however, one does not have the opportunity to slow down or revisit material when they are listening to a speaker. Since the receivers' re-reading of material is actually a form of message repetition, one could infer from this research that, when dealing with complex oral messages, using an alternate channel to provide some form of repetition might increase the audience's ability to elaborate on the message.

Receiver Characteristics and Information Processing

Receiver's Initial Position

The receiver's initial position on a topic determines which of three types of persuasive effects are possible. The three main types of persuasive effects are (1) creating a new attitude, (2) reinforcing an existing attitude or behavior, and (3) changing an attitude and/or behavior.

The three types of persuasive effects are
- create a new attitude
- reinforce an existing attitude
- change an attitude or behavior

When the receiver has had no previous exposure to a topic, the effects of a persuasive message are to **create a new attitude**. The new attitude may also lead to new behavior. Examples of this type of persuasion include consumers seeing an advertisement for a new product, jurors hearing initial evidence in a court case, or employers interviewing a job candidate or seeing a candidate's resume for the first time. The new attitudes toward the product, defendant, and job candidate will likely affect the receiver's behaviors when making a decision about purchasing the product, voting for guilt or innocence, or hiring the applicant.

The majority of persuasive messages that we pay attention to involve the second type of persuasive effect: **reinforcement of an existing attitude**. This is because people tend to place themselves in environments where others' viewpoints and messages coincide with their own attitudes. Republicans would usually rather listen to Republican candidates for office; Democrats prefer listening to Democrats; we attend to messages that reinforce our own religious views; we'd rather watch our favorite team play while surrounded by supporters of that team.

People attend church, political rallies, and fundraisers for a favored charity, knowing that the persuasive messages they will hear will be reinforcing, consistent with their own views. Social scientists refer to our tendency to place ourselves in "like-minded" situations as **selective exposure**. This may be seen as a defense mechanism that helps us avoid the psychological discomfort of listening to messages that conflict with our views.

selective exposure
The tendency to place ourselves in environments with others who think as we do.

The third type of persuasive effect involves **attitude or behavior change**. Despite our preference for information that supports our views, we often come into contact with competing views. You might hate minivans, but you will have a difficult time avoiding every minivan commercial. You might disagree with a television host's position on a political candidate, but you watch the show because you do like the featured guest's views. And, you will undoubtedly have speakers in your class who argue positions that you do not support. Though receivers are exposed to competing views in these situations, they sometimes engage in selective attention as a defense. In other words, receivers can still avoid the message by not paying attention to it. Speakers who present material that is counter to their listeners' attitudes must overcome the selective attention barrier. As you will see in the following sections, there are numerous strategies that can be used to motivate receivers to actively process a message.

Receiver's Involvement (Relevance)

Perhaps the most important determinant of the amount of effort audience members will expend to process (comprehend and evaluate) a message is their involvement in the issue. When receivers perceive that a message is personally relevant and that the information being presented has useful or important implications for their lives, they tend to pay close attention, processing the information carefully and discerning the strengths and weaknesses of the arguments. This has been shown in numerous experiments. Let's examine one experiment by ELM researchers Petty and Cacioppo.

Petty and Cacioppo (1979) developed persuasive messages of high quality and low quality that argued for instituting required senior comprehensive exams. The high quality message contained eight strong arguments. The low quality message contained eight weak arguments. The participants in the experiment were asked to listen to either the high or low quality message and then complete a questionnaire on which they recorded their attitudes toward the issue. They were also tested to determine how much effort they had put into processing the messages.

Half of the participants (in both the high and low quality conditions) were told the exams were being considered for their university (high involvement). The other half were told the exams were being considered for a different, far-away university (low involvement). Participants who were led to believe they would be the ones taking the exams evaluated the messages more carefully. Because the message was personally relevant, they were motivated to pay close attention. Accordingly, they were very aware of the weaknesses in the low quality message, but also very aware of the strong points in the high quality message. Responses to the questionnaire showed that these highly involved participants responded more positively to the strong message, and were more persuaded than participants who thought the exams were intended for students at another university. But, the highly involved participants listed a greater number of negative thoughts and were *less persuaded* than the participants with low involvement when the arguments were of low quality.

It is important to note that it is the audience's perception of relevance, not the "actual" relevance of the message that counts when it comes to providing motivation to elaborate. In the examples cited above, it is unlikely that perceptions differed from reality; comprehensive tests being considered for *your* university are relevant to you and you would be unlikely to perceive otherwise. Conversely, comprehensive tests being considered for some other university would have nothing to do with you and you would be unlikely to perceive the topic as relevant.

APPLYING WHAT THE RESEARCH TELLS US ABOUT THE EFFECTS OF SOURCE, MESSAGE, CHANNEL, AND RECEIVER FACTORS ON THE LIKELIHOOD TO ELABORATE

- You will certainly want your audience to view you as a knowledgeable and expert source on each speech topic you present.
- Audience perceptions of your expertise will directly enhance speech effects mostly when issue relevance is *low*.
- An important indirect effect of source expertise occurs when issue relevance is *moderate*. Under these conditions, your demonstrated **speaker expertise** will motivate listeners to process the message more actively. By this point, you know what that means for the impact of argument quality. Anything that increases receivers' active processing of the message also increases the importance of argument quality. The perceived relevance of most issues is likely to vary among your classmates. A speech on the value of mastering a second language may be highly relevant to some audience members, but moderately or minimally relevant to others. It seems reasonable to suggest that many issues will not be particularly high or low for many class members, but will fall into the moderate relevance range. Your demonstrated expertise will help motivate audience members to process your message in those situations.
- Presenting the actual arguments of **multiple sources**, rather than relying on just one source, not only varies the stimulus, but also has the potential to increase message credibility by showing the audience that several different sources have independently arrived at a similar position or conclusion. So, make sure you have several different, high quality sources to reinforce your argument.
- You would not want your audience to have prior knowledge of your intent if you were planning to try to change their attitudes on an issue important to them. Whether it takes the form of telling audience members about your topic or even inadvertently displaying your PowerPoint slides while setting up for your presentation, **forewarning** could provide the chance for your audience to build defenses in the form of thoughts that are negative to your purpose. On the other hand, it is probably best to reveal your intent in advance of a speech that will coincide with most audience members' attitudes.
- Organizing speeches to provide moderate **repetition** of strong arguments is an effective strategy. One way to apply this strategy is to introduce or preview strong arguments in an introduction, develop them in the body of the speech, and then include them in a summary. Although there is no formula for calculating the best use of repetition, it is likely that the wear-out point will be higher for messages that are complex or novel, while commonly used phrases, like "reduce, reuse, recycle" have probably outlived their effectiveness.
- Use **alternate channels** to provide repetition. While you will rely primarily on the spoken channel in your speeches, repetition can be accomplished by reinforcing your message with presentational aids, such as PowerPoint or other means of displaying key points in written form. Assuming your message is of high quality, such repetition should produce an increase in receivers' positive thoughts and persuasion. Of course, too much repetition can bore or annoy your audience, so be careful not to overdo it.
- Conducting an audience analysis prior to planning your speech will help you determine your audience's **initial position** on your topic. Will you be attempting to create a new attitude, reinforce an existing attitude, or change an existing attitude? Note that the same message has the potential to produce all three effects, depending on the controversial level of the issue and the receivers' initial positions.
- Your audience's perception of the **relevance** of your speech may be the most important factor in determining their motivation to elaborate on your message. Either choose a topic that your audience already perceives to be important to them, or explain to your audience why your topic is important to them. Perceptions of relevance will increase your listeners' motivation to process the message, but be sure your message contains high quality arguments. Speakers who pique listeners' interests, but then provide weak arguments that cause listeners to rehearse negative thoughts in their minds, are likely to succeed only in increasing opposition to their position.

But what about all of the topics that are potentially relevant to your audience, but not necessarily perceived to be relevant? For example, it may be true that global warming *should* be relevant to everyone, but many do not perceive it to be relevant. Almost every speech textbook encourages speakers to remind their audiences why their messages are relevant. Although the research is still evolving in this area, Katt (2004) found that for some topics even a single statement explaining why a topic is relevant can increase receivers' perceptions of relevance, and based on previous ELM research, we would expect increased perceptions of relevance to be accompanied by increased elaborative message processing.

Argument Quality: How to Plan a Strong Message

Our discussion of the persuasion research has so far centered on characteristics of source, channel, receiver, and message that affect the likelihood receivers will actively process the message. The ELM research shows that if you increase receivers' processing by employing one or more of these characteristics, the receivers will be persuaded based primarily on the quality of your arguments. Increased processing leads to more persuasion when the arguments are strong, but decreased persuasion if the arguments are weak. The arguments used in the ELM research were all pretested to validate that the strong arguments elicited mostly positive thoughts from receivers and the weak arguments produced mostly negative thoughts. But what was it about the "strong" messages that made them stronger than the "weak" messages? We must look at research outside the ELM for answers to this question.

Research on one-sided versus two-sided messages, inoculation theory, use of statistical and story evidence, and fear appeals has identified message strategies for how to make a message more persuasive. While the research in these areas has not been conducted within the ELM framework, the ELM would suggest that effective message strategies would have their greatest impact when motivation and ability (and thus the likelihood for central route processing) are high.

One-sided versus Two-sided Messages

Suppose you were planning a speech to persuade your class to support a proposed tuition increase. In terms of the "**message-sidedness**" research, you could elect to use one of three strategies. These include the **one-sided, two-sided nonrefutational,** and **two-sided refutational approaches**. One-sided messages provide only the arguments that support one's position, never acknowledging competing views. If you were to adopt the one-sided strategy, you would cite all the benefits the tuition hike would provide to students, e.g., more summer classes, more parking facilities, availability of more sections of required classes at varied times of day.

> **message-sideness**
> **One-sided messages** provide only the arguments that support your message; **two-sided nonrefutational messages** provide a counterargument but do not refute that argument; **two-side refutational messages** provide and refute counter arguments.

You would go one step further if you chose to use the two-sided nonrefutational approach. Here, you would present the reasons why some students are against the proposal, but continue to emphasize the benefits of the increase. You might say, for example, "Some students feel the increase is too much, but let's look again at what you get for your money." Notice that the opposing view (counterargument) that the increase is too much was not directly refuted. The two-sided nonrefutional strategy identifies opposing views, then tries to overcome them with additional one-sided arguments. Research has generally shown two-sided nonrefutational strategies to be less persuasive than one-sided messages. One possible explanation for this is that identifying competing arguments but failing to show they can be refuted lends additional credence to those competing views.

The two-sided refutational approach has been shown to be the most effective of the message-sidedness strategies (see Allen, 1991; O'Keefe, 1999). Were you to select this message strategy for your tuition increase speech, you would not only identify specific competing arguments, you would also attempt to directly refute them. For example, after acknowledging that some students feel the proposed increase is too much, you might compare the increase with rising costs of products and services, the cost of living index, or higher tuition rates at other schools.

Inoculation Theory: Resistance to Persuasion

As the heading states, this section deals with resistance to persuasion, not persuasion. Much of the work on resistance to persuasion has been conducted within a theory known as Inoculation Theory (McGuire, 1964; see Szabo & Pfau, 2002 for a review and analysis of research on this theory). This research is closely related to the message-sidedness research, as it deals with the effectiveness of one-sided versus two-sided refutational messages in conferring resistance to subsequent counter-persuasion. Going back to your persuasive speech on the tuition increase, let's assume that you used the one-sided strategy, giving only the arguments in support of your position. Let's assume further that in the days following your speech, your audience members were exposed to competing views from other sources. Even if you had been successful in persuading many of your audience members, you would not have prepared them to resist the "counterattacks." Would your audience members have been better able to resist the counter-persuasion had you identified and refuted the arguments they subsequently heard? The research tells us that they would.

Two-sided refutational messages "inoculate" receivers, making them better able to resist counter-persuasion similar to the way that a biological inoculation helps us to better resist certain diseases. The research findings show that receivers who are first given a two-sided refutational message rate subsequent, opposing arguments as less credible than receivers who are first exposed to a one-sided message (see Pryor & Steinfatt, 1978, for further explanation).

Evidence: Statistics versus Stories

As you might expect, the research has shown clearly that citing evidence to support one's claims increases persuasiveness (Maurin, 2000). The two main types of evidence are statistical and story evidence. Statistical evidence is usually based on averages or percentages from a sample of many, while story evidence is based on a single case. For example, if you were trying to persuade your audience about the need for organ donations, you could support your contention by providing statistics showing the national shortage of available organs, or you could develop a story about a person who went through a long and life-threatening wait for an organ transplant. While statistical evidence may be seen as more valid than a single story, receivers may be more attentive to an interesting story that supports a point. The question of whether statistical or story evidence is most effective has been extensively researched. Some studies have concluded that statistical evidence is superior (e.g., Hoeken, 1999), some show an advantage for story evidence (e.g., Koballa, 1986), while still others (e.g., Krupat, Smith, Leach, & Jackson, 1997) report no difference. At this point, the best conclusion is that both types of evidence are more effective than no evidence, but there is no consistent advantage to one over the other.

Fear Appeals

The use of fear appeals as a persuasive strategy is a common practice. Advertisers suggest that if we fail to buy the their brand of tires, we are risking the safety of our families, anti-cigarette ads depict the dire consequences of nicotine addiction, and public service ads ("Click it or ticket") threaten that the police will be ticketing us if we are caught not wearing our seatbelts. Parents, managers, and relationship partners sometimes resort to threats in their efforts to persuade. Do fear appeals work? The answer is not a simple yes or no, but the research does provide guidelines about how best to use fear as a persuasion tactic.

Though researchers have been interested in fear appeals for decades, the most consistent and useful findings have grown out of a theory developed by Witte (1992) known as the Extended Parallel Process Model (EPPM). The EPPM holds that the persuasiveness of a fear appeal hinges on receivers' parallel processing about the threat and the solution offered in the message. According to the EPPM, receivers assess the threat in two ways, including (1) the severity of the consequences of not following the source's recommendations and (2) the likelihood that they, personally, would fall prey to those consequences. Receivers are also said to consider the solution in two ways, including assessments about (1) whether the recommended solution would work, and (2) whether they are capable of following the recommendation. Research has been supportive of the theory (see, for example, Regan, 2001; Witte, Cameron & McKeon, 1998).

An example will help clarify the EPPM terminology. Assume you have decided to use a fear appeal strategy in a speech about seatbelts. Following the EPPM guidelines you would try to demonstrate both the likelihood and severity of the threat. You could use statistical evidence to show your listeners (1) the likelihood that each of them will be involved in a car crash at some point in their lives, and (2) the possible increased severity of the consequences of being in a crash while not wearing a seatbelt. The severity issue could be demonstrated with story and statistical evidence, and perhaps some photos. If you are successful in convincing your audience of the severity and likelihood of the threat, your success as a persuader will depend on convincing your listeners that (1) seatbelts do work to reduce injury, and (2) they are capable of wearing a seatbelt every time they travel by car. You may have to deal with misconceptions ("I'll be trapped in my seatbelt in a bad crash") and concerns ("Seatbelts wrinkle my clothes") by using two-sided refutational arguments.

APPLYING WHAT THE RESEARCH TELLS US ABOUT THE CREATION OF STRONG ARGUMENTS

- Should you use a **one-sided** or **two-sided** message? The research evidence is clear. You are best advised to use the two-sided refutational strategy in a persuasive speech. You may need to do some research to identify the potential counterarguments and how best to refute them, but your efforts should enhance the persuasiveness of your speech.
- **Inoculation theory** suggests that knowing both sides of an argument makes one less susceptible to being "un-persuaded." Speakers can benefit from the use of two-sided refutational messages, not only in terms of increased persuasiveness, but also from the perspective of inducing resistance to counter-persuasion. One-sided messages do not prepare receivers to resist counter-persuasion.
- Though the research has focused primarily on whether **statistical** or **story evidence** is more persuasive, the best approach might be to use both. This would take advantage of both the interest value of story evidence, and the validity value of statistical evidence. In any case, you will be more persuasive if your claims are supported by evidence.
- Notice the next time you hear **fear appeals** whether the Extended Parallel Process Model (EPPM) guidelines seem to be met. This will help you understand and apply the EPPM. If you are planning to use fear in a persuasive speech, make sure that you carefully consider each of the four steps in the model. It is essential that you provide a high quality solution, meaning that receivers are convinced both that the solution will work, and that they are capable of applying the solution. Research has also shown that when fear is aroused without a high quality solution, receivers may defensively avoid thinking about the message (see Regan, 2001). There is psychological discomfort in being shown a problem for which no good solution is given. Consider a physician who uses a fear message in an effort to motivate obese patients to follow a certain diet. If the patients believe that though the diet is good, but they, personally, could not stick to it, the fear message could cause the patients to avoid dealing with the problem.

Peripheral Route Persuasion Cues

To reiterate our earlier explanation, when we lack either motivation or ability to engage in effortful processing, we rely more on simple decision rules, called peripheral cues, to determine responses to persuasive messages. Use of these cues provides us with decision shortcuts made necessary by our increasingly busy lives. In most public speaking situations, we would probably choose to make the case that our topic is relevant and then back up our position with strong arguments, hoping our audience would take the trouble to engage in elaborative processing and rely primarily on the central route to react to our message. But even our best efforts cannot guarantee that each audience member will focus on our arguments. At least part of their attention will fall on peripheral cues, so it is also important make those elements of our presentation as persuasive as possible. The peripheral cues that will be covered in this section include characteristics of the speaker, message-related peripheral cues, and compliance-gaining strategies that place the receiver in a position of reliance on decision rules.

Speaker Characteristics

Credibility

speaker credibility
The image held of a communicator by a receiver at a given time.

Speaker credibility has been defined as "the image held of a communicator at a given time" (Andersen & Clevenger, 1963, p. 59). This definition captures two important characteristics of the concept. First, any source of information will hold varying levels of credibility for different receivers, depending on how those receivers evaluate the expertise and character of the source. While one receiver may believe that a certain presidential candidate is extremely competent and of high moral character, others may question that candidate's competence, character, or both. The words "image held" in this definition mean that the receiver assigns source credibility. The second important feature of the definition is contained in the words "at a given time." This phrase makes the point that a speaker's credibility can fluctuate over time even in the eyes of the same receiver. If a star athlete or politician behaves in a way that you feel shows bad character, your assessment of that person's character may be lowered. If a physician misdiagnoses your illness, you may revise you evaluation of that physician's expertise. Research has identified expertise (competence) and character (trustworthiness) as the two main components of speaker credibility (see, for example, McCroskey, 1966). From these examples you can see that speaker credibility, including both the expertise and character components, is a dynamic variable, with the potential for favorable and unfavorable fluctuations.

Both the competence and character dimensions of speaker credibility have been shown to affect persuasion (for a review of this research, see O'Keefe, 2002). Petty, Cacioppo, and Goldman (1981) demonstrated that source effects have their greatest impact when issue relevance is low. Consistent with ELM predictions, when participants in the experiment thought the issue advocated in the message *would not* affect them (low relevance) they were more influenced by speaker expertise, the peripheral persuasion cue, than by the argument quality. Because the listeners thought they would be unaffected by the issue, they put less effort into processing the message. As a result, they were not as tuned in to the strengths and weaknesses of the arguments. Instead, the participants with low involvement used speaker expertise as a shortcut to determine their responses to the message. As you should now be able to predict, the listeners who thought the issue would affect them (high relevance) were motivated to carefully process the message and were more influenced by the quality of the arguments than by speaker expertise. Because they engaged in effortful processing, they noticed the quality of the argument and were more persuaded by strong arguments than weak arguments.

How to Build Your Credibility

How can you build your credibility as a speaker in this class? Strategies for developing the audiences' perceptions of speakers' expertise and character may be classified as message factors or delivery factors.

Building Credibility through Message Factors

Use of strategies outlined in the previous section on argument quality will serve to demonstrate your expertise about your speech topics. For example, use of evidence and two-sided messages show that you have made efforts to research your topic, and that you are speaking from a position of knowledge and understanding regarding your topic. It lets your audience know that if you are not an expert on your topic, then you are relying on those who are. Telling the audience of your own topic-relevant experience is another effective message strategy for enhancing your expertise. For example, if you were attempting to convince your listeners that yoga is an excellent workout option, your expertise would be judged higher if you were a yoga instructor, or had been practicing yoga over a period of time, than if you had limited experience with yoga.

Regarding character ratings, research has also shown that when the position you take appears to be self serving, receivers may question your sincerity. One of your authors witnessed a student speech that compared the virtues of various vacuum cleaners. The speaker consistently portrayed one of the brands as superior to the others. When questioned by the class following the speech, it was revealed that the speaker currently held a sales job with that company. Research on "vested interest" has shown that speakers are viewed as more trustworthy when they appear to speak from unbiased positions (see, for example, Peters, Covello, & McCallum, 1997).

Building Credibility through Delivery Factors

Certain delivery characteristics also affect ratings of speakers' expertise. Monotone speech (Addington, 1968), and nonfluent speech, including vocalized pauses, such as "um," "uh," and "you know," word repetitions, and pronunciation corrections (Bledsoe, 1984), appear to damage ratings of speakers' expertise. Studies have shown that maintaining eye contact with the audience throughout most of the speech has a favorable impact on expertise ratings (see, for example, Wagner, 1999).

Research also shows that certain delivery characteristics are related to ratings of a speaker's trustworthiness. Pearce and Conklin (1971) reported that a conversational delivery style produced higher ratings of honesty and trustworthiness than a highly dynamic style. The authors speculated that extreme levels of dynamism, marked by wide variations in pitch and loudness, might lead to perceptions of affectation and manipulative intent. Late-night infomercials are filled with examples of this. Accordingly, the more moderate levels of dynamism that define the conversational style evoke more favorable ratings of a speaker's genuineness and trustworthiness. Too little dynamism, as exhibited in monotone speech, lowers ratings of a speaker's trustworthiness (Addington, 1968). As was the case with expertise, research shows that nonfluencies and lack of eye contact are detrimental to ratings of trustworthiness.

Speaker Attractiveness

Research indicates that physical attractiveness correlates positively with persuasiveness. For example, Chaiken (1979) measured the effectiveness of 68 college student speakers in persuading their peers to support a new policy regarding the university's food plan. Judges rated the attractiveness of each speaker, based on photographs and videotaped speeches. Chaiken reported that the 34 most attractive speakers were significantly more persuasive than the 34 least attractive speakers, regardless of whether the receivers were male or female. This result is consistent with other research on the topic (see Knapp & Hall, 2002). Research has also shown that attractive people tend to be more liked (see O'Keefe, 2002). The increased liking is one explanation for why attractive people are more persuasive than less attractive people.

Clothing also contributes to perceptions of attractiveness. Since dress has been shown to affect ratings of both competence and character, it follows that dress can serve as a peripheral persuasion cue. Mills and Aronson (1965) used clothing and makeup to make a female speaker appear attractive (fashionable clothing and make-up), or unattractive (poorly fitted clothing, no make-up). Though the speaker and speech were the same in each case, the attractive condition obtained greater persuasion. Similar findings have been reached in other studies (see Knapp & Hall, 2002).

A neat, clean appearance with appropriate dress will contribute to your credibility and persuasiveness.

Speaker Similarity

Speaker similarity is another important source-related peripheral cue. Research has consistently demonstrated that similarity breeds liking (see O'Keefe, 2002). For example, Byrne (1961) asked participants to complete a questionnaire about their beliefs on various issues, and then evaluate another participant on the basis of their responses to the questions. The evaluators' responses showed a distinct preference for others who displayed beliefs that were highly similar to their own. Concluding from research on the connection between similarity and liking, Cialdini (2001) stated "those who want us to like them so that we will comply with them can accomplish that purpose by appearing similar to us in a wide variety of ways" (p. 150). Like all peripheral cues, we would expect attractiveness and similarity to be less important when the receivers are engaged in elaborative processing, but because central and peripheral routes are not mutually exclusive, we would do well to pay attention to any factors that may affect our persuasiveness.

APPLYING WHAT THE RESEARCH TELLS US ABOUT THE EFFECTS OF PERIPHERAL SPEAKER CHARACTERISTICS ON PERSUASION

- If your message is perceived to be relevant and understandable, your audience will be more likely to focus more on your message (central route) than on peripheral factors such as your appearance, your credibility, or their perceptions of you being likeable or similar to them. But, even in high relevance situations, they will pay *some* attention to the peripheral elements, so we would do well to take them into consideration.
- You can build your **credibility** in the eyes of your audience with high quality messages and good delivery. Conscientious preparation of the message content and practice are necessary. Practice your speech until you can deliver it fluently, while maintaining eye contact with the audience throughout most of the presentation.
- In cases where your audience does not perceive your message as relevant, they may use your **appearance** as a peripheral cue. Either way, as a speaker, it is in your best interest to present an attractive appearance. As the research tells us, a neat, clean appearance with appropriate dress will contribute to your credibility and persuasiveness.
- Speakers can take advantage of the peripheral cue effects of **similarity** and **liking** by demonstrating what they and the audience have in common. Similarities in dress, demographics, experiences, and interests have all been shown to contribute to liking (Cialdini, 2001). However, be cautious in utilizing attire that may be perfectly appropriate for everyday wear, but inappropriate for a public speaking context.

Message-Related Factors as Peripheral Persuasion Cues

Conformity Effect

Asch (1951) published a series of experiments on what he called the conformity effect. In Asch's experiments, participants were asked to look at several straight lines projected on a screen. Each participant was asked to pick out which lines were the same length. When performing this task alone, everyone correctly identified which lines were the same length. In another treatment however, participants were asked the same question after they witnessed others (who were secretly in collusion with Asch) give a wrong answer. Nearly all participants who witnessed one or two others give the wrong answer still answered correctly themselves, but an amazing thing happened when the number of people giving the same wrong answer reached three. At that point, one-third of the subjects "conformed" by giving the same wrong answer. Subjects no longer trusted their ability to judge line lengths when their perceptions were threatened by the judgments of three others. No additional conformity effects were observed as the number of confederates was further increased. Summing up this and other research on the conformity effect, Cialdini (2001, p. 100) concluded: "Whether the question is what to do with the empty popcorn box in a movie theater, how fast to drive on a certain stretch of the highway, or how to eat the chicken at a dinner party, the actions of those around us will be important guides in defining the answer."

Compliance-Gaining Strategies as Peripheral Cues

Compliance-gaining strategies are persuasion techniques that rely on decision rules, not quality arguments, for their success. Persuasion practitioners employ these techniques when the main goal is to elicit desired behaviors (compliance) rather than to change attitudes. An understanding of three compliance techniques is valuable for persuaders and potential persuadees.

Foot-in-the-Door Strategy (FID)

The FID strategy is so labeled because its practitioner first tries to get a "foot-in-the-door" by getting the receiver to comply with a simple, small request. Once that is accomplished, the persuader attempts to capitalize on the initial commitment by getting the receiver to agree to a second, larger request. The first request is a tactic to increase the chances of getting compliance with the real behavior that the persuader wants. The effectiveness of this strategy has been documented in numerous experiments (see, Cialdini, 2001). For example, Freedman and Fraser (1966) showed that California homeowners were more likely to agree to place a 4' by 6' "Be a Safe Driver" sign on their front lawns to support Safe Driver Week if they had previously agreed to sign a petition or display a window sticker in support of the cause. The FID strategy is predicated on the premium people place on remaining consistent with their commitments, a principle most of us learn from our parents early in life. If we make a commitment to do something, we are taught, it is our responsibility to keep it. Persuasion practitioners take advantage of this belief with the FID strategy. In one application of this strategy, Sherman (1980) reported a 700% increase in American Cancer Society collection volunteers by individuals who, a few days earlier, had answered yes to a survey question that asked them to predict what they would say if asked to donate three hours of their time to this organization.

Door-in-the-Face (DIF)

The DIF strategy employs the opposite sequence of requests. Practitioners first ask for a large "favor" that they know will be refused. The goal is to then get the receiver to compromise by agreeing to a smaller request. Research has shown DIF to be an effective technique. For example, Cialdini and Ascani (1976) reported that college students who had previously been asked to donate blood regularly for two years were more likely to agree to donate blood once than students who were simply asked to donate once. Various explanations have been offered for the effectiveness of DIF, including perceptual contrast (the second request seems smaller when you are first exposed to the large request), guilt about refusing the first request, or compromise. The effects are probably best explained by a combination of these factors.

Low-Ball

Another compliance strategy that relies on the power of commitment is called the low-ball technique. In this strategy, the persuader tries to elicit a commitment from the receiver before revealing all of the "costs." For example, after inducing a customer to commit to a deal at a certain price, a car salesperson might add on a dealer fee of several hundred dollars. Or, you might agree to assume an office with a school organization, only to find out afterwards that the job requires far more time than you thought. The research indicates that your initial commitment makes it less likely that you will reverse your decision. For example, Cialdini, Cacioppo, Bassett, and Miller (1978) obtained greater compliance from students asked to participate in a 7:00 A.M. experiment when they obtained a commitment to participate before informing the students of the time than when students were told "up front' of the early starting time.

APPLYING WHAT THE RESEARCH TELLS US ABOUT OTHER PERIPHERAL ROUTE FACTORS

- Even when you do everything you can to increase your audience's motivation and ability to engage in elaborative processing of your message, there may be some audience members who are unwilling to expend the mental effort and are looking for a shortcut to help them decide whether or not to accept your position. Available research suggests several elements that might serve as mental shortcuts for those audience members.
- People have a tendency to go along with the crowd. You may be able to employ the **conformity effect** by citing evidence that a majority of others who are similar to your audience support your contention. For example, in a speech favoring a tuition hike, you may be able to cite statistics that a majority of students support a proposed tuition hike for improved parking facilities and for more summer classes.
- We have all experienced each of these **compliance strategies**, as both persuaders and as the ones being persuaded. Your agreement to complete a brief telephone survey may have led to your compliance with a request for an "obligation-free" trial of a product or service (FID); your refusal to loan a friend $50 may have resulted in a $20 loan (DIF); and you have probably agreed to help out on a project that later required a much larger commitment than you were initially led to expect (low-ball). You may be able to design ways to apply one or more of these techniques in your speeches. For example, you might ask audience members to promise themselves they will take certain actions (private commitment), or you might ask for a public commitment, such as signing a petition. In any case, you must keep ethical considerations in mind when using these compliance strategies. The same strategy (FID, for example) can be used for ethical purposes—persuading your out-of-shape friend to visit the fitness center just once, or unethical purposes—the drug dealer who convinces your nephew to try cocaine "just one time."

Summary

The results of a large body of research help us understand the process of persuasion and provide strategies for increasing our effectiveness as persuasive communicators. The Elaboration Likelihood Model helps us understand that people who have sufficient motivation and ability tend to engage in effortful processing of messages. This message scrutiny results in their reacting positively to strong arguments and negatively to weak arguments. So, when attempting to persuade an audience, we must first create relevant and understandable messages, to increase the likelihood for elaboration. Then we must proffer the strongest possible arguments, to increase the possibility for persuasion.

The likelihood for elaboration can also be influenced by speaker factors (expertise and use of outside sources), channel factors (the use of the visual channel to enhance the audience's ability to process the message), message factors (forewarning and repetition), and audience factors (their initial position or their level of involvement with the topic). Of these, audience involvement–their perception of the relevance of the message–may be the most important determinant of likelihood for elaboration.

Receivers who engage in elaborative processing are persuaded mainly by strong arguments, so we also discussed strategies for making messages strong, including the appropriate use of one and two-sided messages, the use of statistical or anecdotal evidence, and the use of fear appeals.

Because the central/peripheral distinction is not an either-or proposition, and we cannot be sure that all members of our audience will feel motivated and able, we should also pay attention to peripheral cues. Credibility, attractiveness, and similarity are some of the source characteristics that may serve as peripheral cues. The message can also contain elements that may serve as peripheral cues, such as appeals to our audience's need for conformity, and the use of compliance gaining strategies.

Speaking of . . .

Six Principles of Influence

Robert Cialdini is not just a highly respected scholar; he is also an in-demand public speaker who frequently presents his message to gatherings of CEOs, Wall Street traders, international diplomats, and fellow academics. He speaks about what he knows best—the how and why of influence. His advice is grounded in theory and research but also is easy to grasp and put into practice.

Cialdini suggests that people have been conditioned over thousands of years of civilized life to respond positively to six simple principles embedded in the concepts of reciprocity, liking, authority, social support, scarcity, and commitment.

Reciprocity

The saying "You scratch my back, and I'll scratch yours" illustrates reciprocity A reciprocity-based appeal can work in one of two ways in a persuasive speech. Candidates for political office often promise to give something in return for a person's vote. They may promise to reciprocate by proposing legislation, supporting a specific bill, or voicing a concern of their constituency.

Another common way reciprocity is used in a persuasive speech is when the speaker calls on the audience to reciprocate. During homecoming week, as a case in point, the school president may appeal to alumni for financial support. The appeal is usually couched in terms of "giving something back to the institution that gave you so much."

Reciprocity appeals are effective because people are conditioned from an early age to return favors, gifts, and services. Reciprocity is a norm. Thus, when people receive a promise or are asked to return something received, the conditioned response is to reciprocate in kind.

Liking

Appeals based on liking are commonly used in persuasive campaigns. Politicians, for instance, enlist stars from film and music to speak persuasively on their behalf. The assumption is that if a star is well liked, the feeling may be generalized to the candidate endorsed by the star. Liking is a staple of advertisers, who employ well-known people as spokespersons for a product. It's not that the celebrities are experts on the product, but they are well liked by the public. Thus, if well-liked figures Tiger Woods and LeBron James wear Nikes, the hope is that the public will also like the product.

Authority

Research shows that some people are predisposed to comply with the requests of individuals and institutions perceived as authoritative. Examples of these authoritative sources range from members of law enforcement and the clergy to federal agencies such as the military. Thus, a speaker attempting to encourage a group of conservative Catholics to voice their opposition to stem cell research might use the words of the Pope as an appeal. Similarly, a politician speaking to veterans might rely on an endorsement received from a military hero to win the audience's vote in the election.

Social Support

An appeal based on social support is nothing more than an appeal based on numbers. There's a tendency among people to think that if enough folks say something is so, then it must be so. Thus, product advertisers tout their product as "the number-one seller in its class" in an effort to convince consumers that their product must be the best. Research shows that when people are confronted with an appeal supported by large numbers, they are much more likely to be persuaded by the appeal–to jump on the bandwagon, so to speak. In a sense, they accept social support as a form of grounds for the argument.

Scarcity

The appeal to scarcity is based on the law of supply and demand. It is a maxim in economics that when demand exceeds supply, the value of the commodity increases. Thus, an appeal based on scarcity is also one based on relative value. As is the case with reciprocity, authority, and social support, people are conditioned to believe that something that is scarce is valuable enough to demand their attention. Persuasive speeches about the environment frequently use scarcity as the basis of appeal. For instance, the ecological benefit of the rain forests is made even more valuable when the speaker tells the audience that the world's rain forests are disappearing at an alarming rate.

Celebrities such as Tiger Woods are effective in promoting products because they are well liked by the public.

Commitment

One of the most powerful methods of persuasion is the appeal to commitment. In the aftermath of September 11, 2001, millions of Americans made the commitment to donate blood. Even when the blood banks were overwhelmed with more donors than they could take, people were encouraged to pledge that they would come back at a later date when blood supplies needed replenishment. When people make even small commitments as a result of a persuasive message, the principle of psychological consistency comes into play. This principle tells us that we all feel pressure to keep our attitudes, beliefs, and values consistent with our commitments. If an appeal to commitment leads a person to write a letter, to volunteer, or to sign a petition, it increases the chances that the person's attitudes, beliefs, and values will reflect the commitment. In some cases, action may actually precede changes in attitude, reversing the normal order of persuasive goals.

To reiterate, the appeals you make in your persuasive message should reflect your goal and your audience. Not all audiences jump aboard the bandwagon after hearing an appeal based on social support. There are those who steadfastly refuse to get on a bandwagon, no matter how many other people have already done so. Choosing the right appeals to flesh out your persuasive message, therefore, is part science and part art.

References

Addington, D. (1968). The relationship of selected vocal characteristics to personality perception. *Speech Monographs*, 35, 492-503.

Allen, M. (1991). Meta-analysis comparing the persuasiveness of one-sided and two-sided messages. *Western Journal of Speech Communication*, 55, 390-404.

Andersen, K., & Clevenger, T., (1963). A summary of experimental research in ethos. *Speech Monographs*, 30, 59-78.

Andersen, S., & Pryor, B. (1992). *Speech fundamentals: A contemporary approach.* Needham Heights, MA: Ginn Press.

Asch, S. (1951). Effects of group pressure upon the modification of and distortion of judgment. In H. Guetzhow (Ed.), *Groups, leadership, and men.* Pittsburgh: Carnegie.

Bledsoe, D. (1984). *Nonfluencies and distraction theory: A proattitudinal approach.* Unpublished masters thesis, University of Central Florida.

Byrne, D. (1961). Interpersonal attraction and attitude similarity. *Journal of Abnormal and Social Psychology*, 62, 713-715.

Cacioppo, J. T. & Petty, R.E. (1979). Effects of message repetition and position on responses, recall, and persuasion. *Journal of Personality and Social Psychology*, 37, 97-109.

Cacioppo, J. T. & Petty, R.E. (1982). The need for cognition. *Journal of Personality and Social Psychology*, 42, 116-131.

Cacioppo, J. T. & Petty, R.E. (1984). The need for cognition: Relationship to attitudinal processes. In R. McGlynn, J. Maddux, C. Stoltenberg, and J. Harvey (Eds.), *Social perception in clinical and counseling psychology.* Lubbock: Texas Tech Press.

Cacioppo, J. T. & Petty, R. E. (1985). Central and peripheral routes to persuasion: The role of message repetition. In A. Mitchell & L. Alwitt (Eds.), *Psychological processes and advertising effects.* Hillsdale, NJ: Erlbaum.

Chaiken, S. (1979). Communicator physical attractiveness and persuasion. *Journal of Personality and Social Psychology*, 37, 1387-1397.

Chaiken, S. & Eagly, A.H. (1976). Communication modality as a determinant of message persuasiveness and message comprehensibility. *Journal of Personality and Social Psychology*, 39, 752-766.

Cialdini, R. (2001). *Influence: Science and practice.* Boston: Allyn and Bacon.

Cialdini, R., & Ascani, K. (1976). Test of a concession procedure for inducing verbal, behavioral, and further compliance with a request to give blood. *Journal of Applied Psychology*, 61, 295-300.

Cialdini, R. B., Levy, A., Herman, P., Koslowski, L & Petty, R.E. (1976). Elastic shifts of opinion: Determinants of direction and durability. *Journal of Personality and Social Psychology*, 34, 663-672.

Cialdini, R. B., Cacioppo, J. R., Bassett, R. & Miller, J. A. (1978). The low-ball procedure for producing compliance: Commitment then cost. *Journal of Personality and Social Psychology*, 36, 463-476.

Freedman, J., & Fraser, S. (1966). Compliance without pressure: The foot-in-the-door technique. *Journal of Personality and Social Psychology*, 4, 195-202.

Harkins, S. G. & Petty, R. E. (1981). The multiple source effect in persuasion: The effects of distraction. *Personality and Social Psychology Bulletin*, 7, 627-635.

Hoeken, H. (1999). The perceived and actual persuasiveness of different types of inductive arguments. In F. van Eemeren, R. Grootendorst, J. Blair, & C. Willard, (Eds.), *Proceedings of the fourth international conference of the International Society for the Study of Argumentation* (pp. 353-357). Amsterdam: Sic Sat.

Katt, J. (2004, November). *Influencing perceptions of relevance.* Paper presented at the annual conference of the National Communication Association, Chicago, IL.

Knapp, M., & Hall, J. (2002). Nonverbal communication in human interaction. Fort Worth: Harcourt Brace.

Koballa, T. (1986). Persuading teachers to reexamine the innovative elementary science programs of yesterday: The effect of anecdotal versus data-summary communications. *Journal of Research in Science Teaching*, 23, 437-449.

Krupat, E., Smith, R., Leach, C., & Jackson, M. (1997). Generalizing from atypical cases: How general a tendency? *Basic and Applied Psychology*, 19, 345-361.

Maurin, P. (2000). *The effects of statistical and story evidence on attitude change.* Unpublished masters thesis, University of Central Florida.

McCroskey, J. C. (1966). Scales for measurement of ethos. *Speech Monographs*, 33, 65-72.

McGuire, W. J. (1964). Inducing resistance to persuasion: Some contemporary approaches. In L. Berkowitz (Ed.), *Advances in experimental social psychology*, (Vol.1). New York: Academic Press.

Mills, J., & Aronson, E., (1965). Opinion change as a function of the communicator's attractiveness and desire to influence. *Journal of Personality and Social Psychology*, 1, 173-177.

O'Keefe, D. (1999). How to handle opposing arguments in persuasive messages. A meta-analytic review of the effects of one-sided and two-sided messages. *Communication Yearbook*, 22, 209-249.

O'Keefe, D. (2002). *Persuasion: Theory and research.* Thousand Oaks, CA: Sage.

Pearce, W. B. & Conklin, F, (1971). Nonverbal vocalic communication and perceptions of a speaker. *Speech Monographs*, 38, 235-241.

Peters, R., Covello, V., & McCallum, D. (1997). The determinants of trust and credibility in environmental risk communication: An empirical study. *Risk Analysis*, 17, 43-54.

Petty, R. E. & Cacioppo, J. T. (1977). Forewarning, cognitive responding, and resistance to persuasion. *Journal of Personality and Social Psychology*, 35, 645-655.

Petty, R. E. & Cacioppo, J. T. (1979). Issue involvement can increase or decrease persuasion by enhancing message-relevant cognitive responses. *Journal of Personality and Social Psychology*, 37, 1915-1926.

Petty, R. E. & Cacioppo, J. T. (1984). Source factors and the elaboration likelihood model of persuasion. *Advances in Consumer Research*, 11, 668-672.

Petty, R. E. & Cacioppo, J. T. (1984). The effects of involvement on responses to argument quality and quantity: Central and peripheral route to persuasion. *Journal of Personality and Social Psychology*, 46, 69-81.

Petty, R. E. & Cacioppo, J. T. (1986). *Communication and persuasion: Central and peripheral routes to attitude change.* New York: Springer-Verlag.

Petty, R. E., Cacioppo, J. T., & Goldman, R. (1981). Personal involvement as a determinant of argument-based persuasion. *Journal of Personality and Social Psychology*, 41, 847-855.

Pratkanis, A. & Aronson, E. (2002). *The age of propaganda: The everyday use and abuse of persuasion.* New York: W.H. Freeman & Co.

Pryor, B. & Steinfatt, T. M. (1978). The effects of initial belief level on inoculation theory and its proposed mechanism. *Human Communication Research*, 4, 217-230.

Regan, N., (2001). *Fear appeals and health communication: The effects of threat and efficacy on intentions to modify behavior.* Unpublished masters thesis, University of Central Florida.

Sereno, K. K. & Hawkins, G. J. (1967). The effects of variations in speakers' nonfluency upon audience ratings of attitude toward the speech topic and speakers' credibility. *Speech Monographs*, 34, 58-64.

Sherman, S. (1980). On the self-erasing nature of errors of prediction. *Journal of Personality and Social Psychology*, 39, 211-221.

Szabo, E., & Pfau, M. (2002). Nuances in inoculation: Theory and applications. In J. Dillard & M. Pfau (Eds.), *The persuasion handbook: Developments in theory and practice.* Thousand Oaks, CA: Sage.

Vernon, M. (1962). *The psychology of perception.* Baltimore: Penguin Books.

Wagner, T. (1999). *Effects of various levels of speakers' eye contact on receivers' assessments of the speaker and the speech*. Unpublished masters thesis, University of Central Florida.

Witte, K. (1992). Putting the fear back in fear appeals: The extended parallel process model. *Communication Monographs*, 59, 329-349.

Witte, K., Berkowitz, J., Cameron, K., & McKeon, J. (1998). Preventing the spread of genital warts: Using fear appeals to promote self-protective behaviors. *Health Education and Behavior*, 25, 571-585.

Al Gore hopes to provoke viewers to think critically about global warming in his film *An Inconvenient Truth.*

Thinking and Speaking Critically

Objectives

After reading this chapter and reviewing the online learning resources at www.mhhe.com/brydon6, you should be able to:

- Explain the difference between argumentativeness and verbal aggressiveness.
- Evaluate arguments using the Toulmin model of reasoning.
- Differentiate among patterns of reasoning.
- Identify and refute common fallacies of argument.

Key Concepts

ad hominem
arguing in a circle (begging the question)
argumentativeness
critical thinking
distorted evidence
fallacy
false analogy
false dilemma
halo effect
hasty generalization
hyperbole
ignoring the issue
inference
isolated examples
loaded language
mistaking correlation for cause
misused numerical data
non sequitur
post hoc, ergo propter hoc
pseudoreasoning
red herring (smoke screen)
slippery slope
stereotyping
straw person
unsupported assertion
verbal aggressiveness

"It is better to debate a question without settling it than to settle a question without debating it."

–JOSEPH JOUBERT

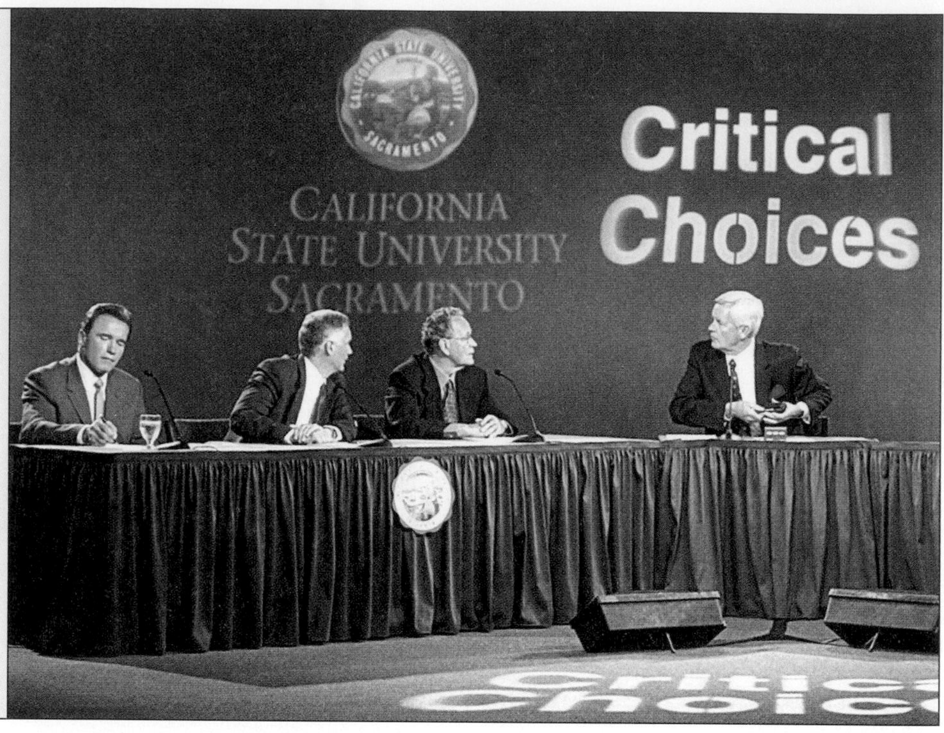

During the California Recall, voters had the chance to use their critical thinking skills while watching Arnold Schwarzenegger, Tom McClintock, and Peter Camejo in a debate moderated by Stan Statham.

What do you think? Is smoking marijuana any more harmful to your health than drinking alcohol? Does the recreational use of cocaine or ecstasy inevitably lead to a life of ruin? Should drug addicts be punished as criminals, or should they receive medical treatment for their addiction?

What do you believe about the drug education programs you experienced in middle school and high school? Do you think they have reduced drug use in our country–for example, kept drugs out of the workplace or minimized their use among young people? Or do you think that the billions of dollars committed by government to drug education could have been better spent elsewhere?

These kinds of questions are not easily answered. Illegal drugs and their widespread use continue to be topics of heated discussions in the halls of Congress, during the meetings of school boards, and over the dinner table in many homes. What's more, they have even been the centerpieces of blockbuster films such as *Traffic,* which won four Academy Awards and was nominated for best picture, and *Blow,* which starred Penélope Cruz and Johnny Depp.

To view a video of Mitch Bacci's speech, click on the Speech Coach link on our Online Learning Center Web site and go to Segment 15.1.

Most of our students have participated in drug education programs in their middle school and secondary school careers. One of them, Mitch Bacci, spoke about what he believed were the failings of the Drug Abuse Resistance Education program. A transcript of his speech is found in the box "In Their Own Words . . . D.A.R.E." on pages 412–413. As you read it, ask yourself if he engages in logical reasoning and if his arguments against the D.A.R.E. program are sound. You can also view the speech on our Online Learning Center Web site. We will refer back to the speech throughout the chapter as we discuss the process of how to reason soundly.

This chapter continues Chapter 9's discussion of the use of grounds and warrants to support the claims we make. We continue to employ the Toulmin model of reasoning to help you further develop your ability to think critically, both as a speaker and a listener. If we want our audience to experience an enduring attitude change or to inoculate them against counterpersuasion following our speech, then the central route to persuasion is best. As listeners, we should always be critical of the claims speakers make when deciding whether to accept them. Whether we are speaking or listening to a message that seeks to persuade us, critical thinking is important.

Critical Thinking and Public Speaking

Critical thinking is the process of making sound inferences based on accurate evidence and valid reasoning. Understanding how to think critically about arguments is the first step to constructing and communicating those arguments to an audience. Logical proof should be an ethical part of any persuasive message. To successfully persuade others of our side of a controversial issue, it is important to have well-constructed, sound arguments for our side. As the elaboration likelihood model introduced in the preceding chapter shows, we are more likely to induce a permanent change in attitude if we use sound evidence and reasoning.

critical thinking
The process of making sound inferences based on accurate evidence and valid reasoning.

Pseudoreasoning and Fallacies

As both a speaker and a listener, it is important to differentiate messages that are logical from those that are not. We need to be on our guard against arguments that sound good but are actually illogical. **Pseudoreasoning** is an argument that appears sound at first glance but contains within it a flaw in reasoning that renders it unsound. Such a flaw in reasoning is called a **fallacy,** defined by philosophers Brook Noel Moore and Richard Parker as "an argument in which the reasons advanced for a claim fail to warrant acceptance of the claim."[1] Therefore, our goal in this chapter is to enable you to identify fallacies that signal pseudoreasoning. As speakers, we want to offer our audience members good reasons to accept our claims, and as listeners, we want to be sure that we only accept those claims offered by speakers who base their speeches on sound logic.

pseudoreasoning
An argument that appears sound at first glance but contains a fallacy of reasoning that renders it unsound.

fallacy
An argument in which the reasons advanced for a claim fail to warrant acceptance of that claim.

Argumentativeness and Verbal Aggressiveness

When listeners detect fallacious reasoning, they are ethically obligated to bring it to light. Simply remaining silent allows the speaker to mislead those who are not well trained in critical thinking. However, there is an important distinction between being argumentative and being verbally aggressive. In his book *Arguing Constructively,* Dominic Infante makes the distinction between these two personality traits.[2] **Argumentativeness** is the trait of arguing for and against the *positions* taken on controversial claims. For example, an argumentative person might say, "Legalizing drugs could lead to more accidents on the job and on roads, endangering the lives of innocent bystanders." **Verbal aggressiveness,** on the other hand, is the trait of attacking the *self-concept* of those with whom a person disagrees about controversial claims. A verbally aggressive person might say, "Only a drug-crazed maniac would favor legalizing

argumentativeness
The trait of arguing for and against the positions taken on controversial claims.

verbal aggressiveness
The trait of attacking the self-concept of those with whom a person disagrees about controversial claims.

In Their Own Words

Sample Persuasive Message

D.A.R.E.

by Mitch Bacci

Mitch Bacci

Who can tell me what D.A.R.E. stands for? How many of you in this room are D.A.R.E. graduates?

When I was in middle school, my classmates and I were some of the millions of students subjected to the lies and scare tactics produced by the Drug Abuse Resistance Education program, also known as "D.A.R.E." For a while it was fun. We played little games, got cool T-shirts, and watched funny little cartoons. Especially, I remember the cartoon about the rabbit snorting cocaine and at that time it was the funniest thing we'd ever seen (to me and my friends). By the time I reached ninth grade, I noticed that many of the kids I grew up with weren't around anymore. They dropped out of school and became what the officers in the D.A.R.E. program called a "loser." Although I cannot simply attribute this all to D.A.R.E., I know that it did have some part in it, and through my research I realized that D.A.R.E. is actually counterproductive and encourages kids to experiment with drugs.

D.A.R.E. is ineffective, sometimes even counterproductive, and should be terminated from schools worldwide.

Today, I'm going to go over this history of D.A.R.E., some of the program's main flaws, and the effects that it's had on millions of students worldwide and also offer some simple alternatives.

But first I'd like to start by giving you a brief history of D.A.R.E.

According to their Web site, D.A.R.E. is an international education program for kindergarten through twelfth graders which seeks to discourage drug, gang, and violent activity. It was created in 1983 by Los Angeles Police Chief Daryl Gates. Students enrolled in D.A.R.E. sign a waiver stating that they will never do drugs, join gangs, and that they will attend a series of lectures put on by the local police department over a 17-week period of time. Over this 17-week period of time, students participate in sing-alongs, role-playing exercises, and watch cartoons (like the one I mentioned earlier). Kids are also given T-shirts and little pins and accessories that bear the program's slogans, "D.A.R.E. to keep off drugs" and "D.A.R.E. to say no." According to Dare.com, these activities are created in order to teach the students "resistance skills," which they believe the students can use in real-life situations to combat the effects of peer pressure. Experts at D.A.R.E. believe that peer pressure is one of the main factors contributing to drug use and experimentation in children. According to AlcoholFacts.org, in 2004 D.A.R.E. was being used in 80 percent of the school districts in the United States, 54 countries around the world, and was being taught to 36 million students a year. Since then, the [Tulsa] Oklahoma Tribune *has reported that D.A.R.E. has shown massive drops in circulation of its curriculum due to complaints and lack of funding. According to that same article, D.A.R.E. is now revising their program in a last-ditch effort to gain funding.*

D.A.R.E.'s goal, like that of any other drug education program, is a good one—to keep kids off drugs. It's just how they go about it that's deeply flawed.

D.A.R.E. glamorizes drugs by attracting students to the program with T-shirts and other goodies, which, according to scientists at Wesleyan University, creates a psychological bond between the two. From my experience I know that D.A.R.E. doesn't differentiate between different types of drugs—it just lumps them all into one big category as "risk-taking" behavior. This, in turn, causes students to believe that drugs don't differentiate in severity and leads to heavy experimentation. Students are taught harmful stereotypes such as,

"Anyone who tries drugs is a 'loser' and will become an addict." This makes them believe that once they've tried drugs, they will be shunned by their friends and family. This whole "loser" idea stems from the gateway drug concept. The gateway drug concept, simply stated, means that drugs like marijuana, cigarettes, and alcohol will lead to heavier drugs like cocaine and heroin. As a matter of fact, the "gateway drug" concept is nothing more than a false hypothesis. According to the American Journal of Public Health, *one out of 100 people that try marijuana move on to harder drugs. According to Marsha Rosenbaum, a well-known expert in the field of drug education, many students discover that what they've learned in the D.A.R.E. program is a lie and therefore become skeptical of any other drug information they hear in the future. D.A.R.E. graduates will then reject other drug education programs, and it leads to mistrust between students and the police officers because they're the ones delivering the information. Children consistently reject D.A.R.E. because rejection is the main lesson taught in the program—not how to make responsible decisions about drugs, just how to say "no" and be negative and intolerant. As I mentioned earlier, D.A.R.E. has not only shown to be ineffective but has been known to be counterproductive and has shown to cause an increase in drug use and abuse amongst graduates of its program. According to AlcoholFacts.org, when D.A.R.E. was at its peak in the last decade, it sucked up about 1 to 1.3 billion dollars a year. Now, according to the* Oklahoma Tribune, *this number has lowered to only 700 million dollars a year. Finally, D.A.R.E. has even been eliminated in Los Angeles—its city of birth.*

Now that I've talked about the qualities of a bad drug education program, I'll give some of the qualities of a good one.

As Dr. Brydon mentioned in one of his lectures, not all drug information is perfect for every age. D.A.R.E.'s "get 'em young" strategy is effective for younger children but is inappropriate and pointless for them to see. Older students will reject D.A.R.E. because they have learned to distrust authority figures like the police officers giving them the information. The real-life effects of drugs are harmful enough—they don't need to be twisted around or inflated to prove a point. According to Marsha Rosenbaum, inventor of one of D.A.R.E.'s most successful replacements (the Safety First program), it's also important to emphasize the legal consequences of drug use so kids truly understand what they're getting into. One of the main reasons why D.A.R.E. was so popular in the past few decades was because schools didn't have a lot of money to spend on drug education and the local police department put it on for free. Supporters of D.A.R.E. constantly bring this up as why it's so great (because schools didn't have to pay for it), but the people who were actually paying for it were the taxpayers. Finally, drug education doesn't have to be expensive. As part of my senior project, I brought some speakers from the local drug rehabilitation center to my middle school and had them talk to the kids about drugs and their experiences. I think it was really effective.

Tonight, I've talked to you about D.A.R.E.'s history, structural flaws, and I've gone over some simple alternatives which any school can take advantage of.

According to the editorial in the Oklahoma Tribune, *the only thing keeping D.A.R.E. alive now is a 700 million dollar grant which is due to run out sometime this month. This means politicians nationwide will be lobbied by D.A.R.E. for continued support. Therefore, I urge you all to go out, write your congressman (or whoever), and demand for D.A.R.E.'s termination because if we don't get rid of it now, our children could end up having the same ineffective and even counterproductive drug education that we did growing up. Thank you.*

Note: This was transcribed from a videotape of a speech given at California State University, Chico on December 1, 2006.

Representative Wally Herger is confronted by a verbally aggressive constituent.

drugs." Argumentativeness is not only socially beneficial, it is the only way to take the process of critical thinking into the public arena. Verbal aggressiveness, on the other hand, is a destructive and hostile trait that destroys personal relationships. Constructive argumentativeness is the best approach for the public speaker. Being able to disagree without being disagreeable fosters a positive communication transaction.

The authors have been witnesses to the possibility that people can disagree without being disagreeable. Mary Matalin, current adviser to Vice President Dick Cheney and former conservative talk show host, "debated" her husband, James Carville, who managed the 1992 presidential campaign of Bill Clinton and served as one of his chief defenders during the Lewinsky scandal. Despite their obvious political differences, they treated each other with good-humored respect. The audience, which was apparently deeply divided on partisan lines, nevertheless cheered both speakers and even gave them a standing ovation at the end of the evening. Learning to disagree about issues while respecting the other side's right to believe as they do, is the hallmark of civility in argument. You can be argumentative without being verbally aggressive.

The Toulmin Model of Argument

The Toulmin model of argument, depicted in Exhibit 16.1, was introduced in Chapter 9. All reasoning contains, at least implicitly, three things: *grounds,* to support the *claim* being made, and a *warrant* or linkage of the grounds and claim.[3] In Chapter 9 we introduced three types of claims (*fact, value,* and *policy*) and five types of warrants (*authority, generalization, comparison* or *analogy, causal,* and *sign*). Three other parts of the Toulmin model may be present but are not always needed. The *backing* provides support for a warrant that is either

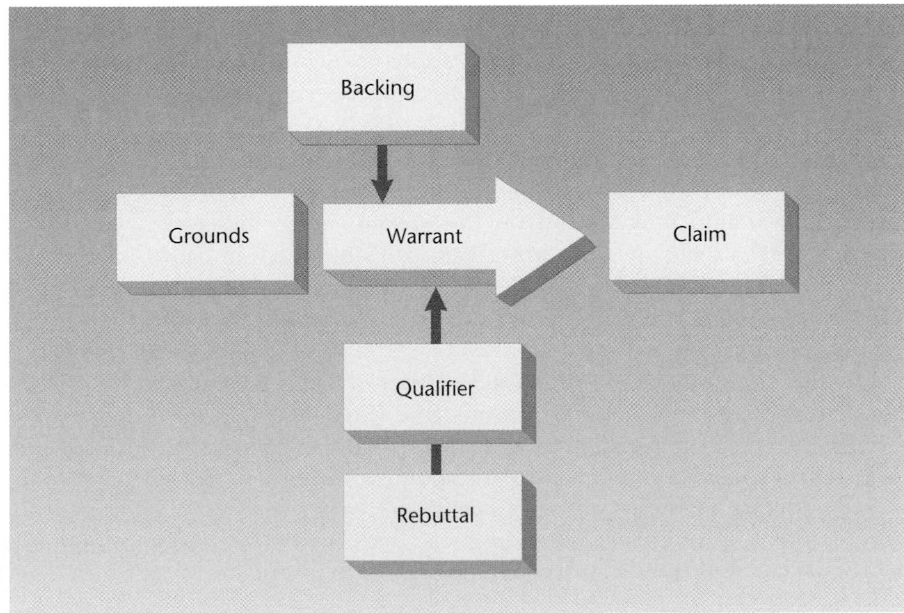

Exhibit 16.1
The Toulmin Model of Argument

Exhibit 16.2
Analysis of an Argument Using Toulmin's Model

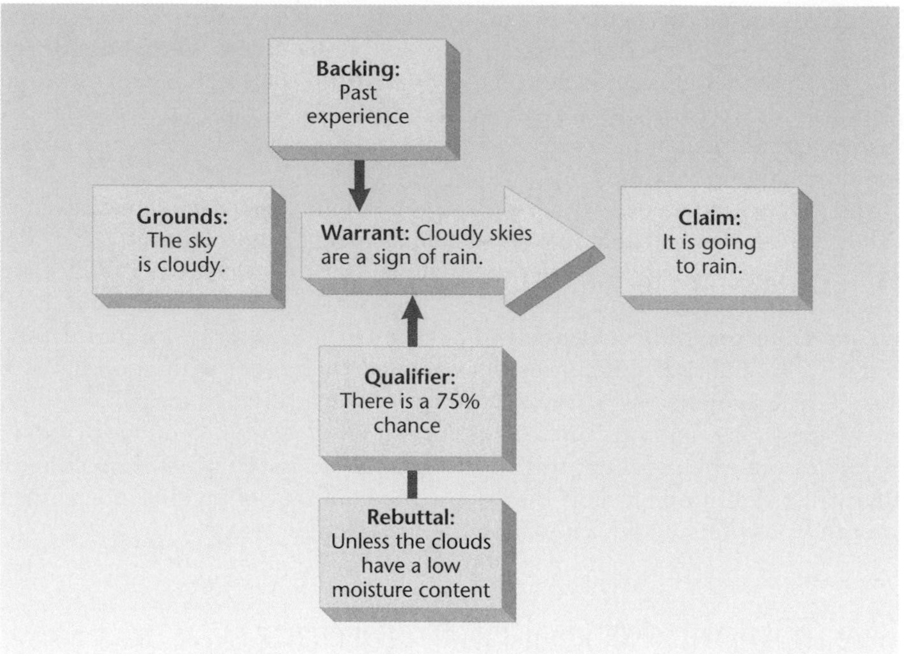

not accepted initially by an audience or that is challenged during the speech. A *rebuttal* is an exception or refutation to the argument. And a *qualifier* is an indicator of the degree of confidence we have in the claim we are making. Many of the fallacies we will discuss have to do with these three optional parts of the model. For example, claiming certainty for our reasoning, when there is actually only a chance that we are right, is fallacious. Ignoring legitimate rebuttals to our claims is also poor reasoning. Not backing up a disputable warrant is also a problem. Understanding the complete Toulmin model will help us construct better arguments as well as listen with a more critical ear to the arguments of others.

How does this model of argument apply in actual practice? Let's review the simple case we offered in Chapter 9. Suppose you glance out the window and the sky is filled with clouds. You think to yourself, "It's going to rain," and you grab your umbrella. Although you may not realize it, your reasoning can be analyzed as an argument using Toulmin's model. Exhibit 16.2 shows how this analysis would look. Based on the *grounds* of a cloudy sky, you reason using the *warrant,* cloudy skies are a sign of rain, which is based on the *backing* of your past experience, that there is a 75 percent chance (*qualifier*) of the truth of the *claim* that it is going to rain, unless (*rebuttal*) the clouds have a low moisture content.

Now that you understand this basic version of Toulmin's model, let's look at the relationships among claims, grounds, and warrants in more complicated situations. As the examples that follow will show, it is important for both speakers and listeners to test arguments for their soundness. Only in this way can speakers and audience members engage in constructive argumentation. Therefore, in the remainder of this chapter we introduce a number of the most common fallacies people use and show how they fit into Toulmin's model.

Fallacies Associated With Grounds

All arguments are built on the grounds, or evidence, which the arguer points to in supporting the claim. If the grounds are either absent or defective, then the argument cannot be sound. In Chapter 9, we discussed various types of supporting material that might form the grounds of an argument, including examples, facts, numerical data, expert opinion, explanations, descriptions, and narratives.

When you are examining the grounds of an argument, be sure that the examples are relevant, of sufficient quantity, and typical. Facts should come from a reliable source and be verifiable, recent, and consistent with other known facts. Numerical data should be taken from a reliable and unbiased source, based on fair questions, and accurately collected. You should be told how the sample was selected to ensure that it was random and representative. Any differences should be greater than the margin of error, and the base of any percentages should be stated. Expert opinion depends on the source's expertise, reliability, and lack of bias. Explanations should be clear and accurate. Descriptions should be accurate and vivid. Narratives must have probability (coherence) and fidelity to the real world.

Grounds that fail one or more of these tests are likely to constitute a fallacy. In particular, there are four fallacies associated with grounds: unsupported assertion, distorted evidence, isolated examples, and misused numerical data.

Unsupported Assertion

Unsupported assertions, the absence of any argument at all, can be found even in the best of speeches. For example, in his speech discussing alternatives to the D.A.R.E. program, Mitch Bacci talks about his senior project to discourage middle school children from using drugs. He says of the project, "I think it was really effective." Beyond that assertion, however, he offers no proof that his project discouraged anyone from using drugs. Unless a speaker is an expert on the topic, there's no reason to accept "I think . . ." claims as evidence of anything other than the speaker's personal opinion.

unsupported assertion
The absence of any argument at all.

Distorted Evidence

The **distorted evidence** fallacy occurs when speakers leave out or alter information to distort the true intent of their evidence. A good example of distorted evidence is found on the movie advertisement page of your local newspaper. Frequently, a movie will tout itself as "daring," "enthralling," or "thumbs up." Yet, a reading of the full review will reveal that these words were used in a different context. Perhaps the reviewers really said, "This movie was a daring attempt that missed the mark. The only thing that was enthralling about this movie was the credits that signaled it was ending. In deciding whether to rate this movie thumbs up, it took only about 10 minutes to see that this was thumbs way down!"

distorted evidence
Significant omissions or changes in the grounds of an argument that alter its original intent.

Isolated Examples

isolated examples
Nontypical or nonrepresentative examples that are used to prove a general claim.

Another problem with grounds can be the use of **isolated examples,** nontypical or nonrepresentative examples, to prove a general claim. Recall that to reason from examples requires that the instances be representative of the larger class–in a word, typical. It is almost always possible to find an isolated example to illustrate just about any claim. For example, we often hear about cases of welfare abuse. One radio commentator recently told the story of a man who reported to the police that his food stamps had been stolen from his car–a Mercedes. Of course, most people on welfare don't drive a Mercedes. Yet the image of welfare recipients living it up at the taxpayers' expense has been a staple of popular mythology for decades. The reality is that most people on welfare are children living in poverty. Isolated examples do not prove that everyone on welfare is lazy or abusing the system.

Misused Numerical Data

The most commonly misused numerical data are misleading statistics. Statistics are mathematical summaries of numerical data, for example averages and percentages. When using this type of data, beware of four common sources of **misused numerical data.**

misused numerical data
Statistics that involve errors such as poor sampling, lack of significant differences, misuse of average, or misuse of percentages.

Poor Sampling

Statistics based on self-selected or nonrandom samples are worse than useless–they're misleading. For instance, many television stations and newspapers now have call-in polls whereby we can express our opinion on the issues of the day by dialing one of two numbers, each representing one side of the issue. Of course, there is no guarantee that the station's audience represents the public at large or that members of the audience will call in proportion to their number in the general population. Also, the forced choice between only two options is a problem.

Lack of Significant Differences

Often the difference between two candidates in a preference poll is less than the poll's margin of error. Thus, if candidate A leads B by three points, but the poll has a five-point margin of error, there is no statistical significance to that difference, a fact often ignored by political pundits.

Misuse of "Average"

People frequently cite the "average," or mean, to support a claim. They say such things as, "The average salary for college graduates is X." The intent is for the audience to infer that most college graduates make the salary mentioned. However, the average (or mean) is only one of three numbers that can be used to describe a collection of numbers like the salaries paid to college graduates. The other two are the median and the mode. Further, the average is frequently misleading because it is so easily distorted by extreme numbers.

As an example, consider the differences between the mean, the median, and the mode of houses selling at a range of prices:

$250,000

$250,000

$300,000

$400,000

$2,000,000

Mean = $640,000

Median = $300,000

Mode = $250,000

The *mean* is simply the arithmetic average: Add all the selling prices, and divide the total by the number of houses sold. The *median* is the midpoint in a series of numbers. Half of the houses sold for more and half for less than the median. Finally, the *mode* is simply the most frequently occurring number or value. In most cases, the median is more accurate than the mean. Certainly that is the case here because the mean would lead you to believe that most houses in the area described are more expensive than they are in actuality. The single home selling for $2 million not only inflates the "average" but misleads your thinking in the process.

Misuse of Percentages

Percentages are meaningful only if you know the base on which they are computed. For example, suppose you are making $100,000 a year. You are told you must take a 10 percent pay cut because the company is in trouble. Reluctantly you agree. Now you are making only $90,000. The next year the company is doing better and says they will restore your pay by giving you a 10 percent increase. However, don't celebrate yet. The 10 percent is based on your current pay of $90,000, leading to a restored pay of only $99,000. Because the basis on which the percentage was figured changed, your 10 percent increase didn't really restore your pay cut. We need to be exceptionally careful in evaluating percentages to make sure apples are being compared to apples, not oranges. If you start out at a very low level, even large percentage increases may not be very large in real terms.

Mitch Bacci uses percentage figures in his speech to illustrate how D.A.R.E. has declined from being used in 80 percent of the school districts in the United States in 2004. However, he fails to mention the current percentage using the program, stating only that "the [Tulsa] *Oklahoma Tribune* has reported that D.A.R.E. has shown massive drops in circulation of its curriculum due to complaints and lack of funding." Without giving comparable statistics, the listener can't really judge if the decline is significant. What exactly is a "massive drop"?

Fallacies Associated With Claims

Sometimes fallacies are not so much in how we get to the claim, but in the nature of the claims themselves. The two fallacies discussed here have to do with the relevance of claims and whether the claims are being used to, in essence, prove themselves. We need to guard against these fallacies both in our speeches and as listeners to the speeches of others.

Red Herring

red herring (smoke screen)
An irrelevant issue introduced into a controversy to divert from the real controversy.

Sometimes called a *smoke screen,* a **red herring** is an irrelevant claim introduced into a controversy to divert attention from the real controversy. Debates over public issues are well known for the use of red herrings to divert attention from the issues that concern most people. For example, a letter to the editor in our local newspaper prior to the 2006 midterm elections urged voting against Democratic candidates. The writer suggested that if they won, organizations such as CODEPINK and MoveOn.org would become like Nazis and start gassing their enemies. Regardless of what you think of liberal groups like these, they have absolutely no connection to Nazi genocide. To introduce that issue into an argument to vote against liberals was clearly a red herring designed to divert the reader's attention from the fundamental issue.

Arguing in a Circle

arguing in a circle (begging the question)
An argument that proves nothing because the claim to be proved is used as the grounds or warrant for the argument.

Another common fallacy is the use of a claim to prove its own truth. **Arguing in a circle,** sometimes called *begging the question,* occurs when the argument actually proves nothing because the claim to be proved is used as the grounds or warrant for the argument. For example, consider the door-to-door evangelist who insists that you must believe in his or her version of the Bible. "Why?" you ask. The person immediately opens a Bible and quotes you scripture to support the claim. Basically the argument looks something like this:

Claim: My version of the Bible is the truth.

Grounds: Quotation from scripture.

Warrant: My version of the Bible is the truth.

In other words, the claim is also the warrant.

Of course, such clear-cut expressions of question-begging are rare. But many arguments, when distilled to their essence, do in fact beg the question.

Fallacies Associated With Warrants and Backing

Toulmin calls the connection between the grounds and the claim the warrant. The warrant is the license that authorizes an arguer to move from grounds to a claim. Thus, if you were to argue, as in our earlier example, that it's going to rain because it is cloudy, the observation about clouds only proves it will rain given the warrant that clouds are a sign of rain. The process of moving from grounds, via a warrant, to a claim is called an **inference.**

inference
The process of moving from grounds, via a warrant, to a claim.

Recall that Toulmin adds backing to his basic grounds-warrant-claim model. In some cases a warrant is readily believed by an audience. In others, the warrant needs additional backing in the form of evidence before the audience will believe it is true. For example, Al Gore's Oscar-winning movie, *An Inconvenient Truth,* is based on the warrant that global warming is caused by human activity. Although some of his critics, although they accept the grounds of his argument that the Earth's average temperatures are rising, they question the assumption that the cause is human activity. Instead, they point to the cyclical fluctuations of temperature throughout the planet's history. To back up his warrant, therefore, Gore cites numerous sources. At one point he claims that of 928 published studies, none denied the link between human activity and global warming. One could agree with everything else Gore says, but if the causal warrant is rejected, then all of his suggestions of how we can personally act to save the planet are irrelevant. Only if the backing for the warrant is convincing does it make sense to drive cars that emit fewer greenhouse gasses and take other actions to reduce these emissions. Backing is required, therefore, when a warrant either is not known to the audience or is contrary to what they already believe.

Different types of warrants provide different ways of moving from grounds to claim and are associated with different patterns of reasoning. In Chapter 9 we discussed the five most common types of warrants: authority, generalization, comparison, causal, and sign. In examining any argument, it is important to determine whether the warrant and its accompanying backing are sound. We look at each type of warrant and suggest some of the common fallacies peculiar to each type of argument.

Authority Warrants

When we use authority warrants, we are really saying that the reason the claim should be believed is because someone who is an expert says so. If our audience is not familiar with the source's qualifications, we need to provide backing for the warrant. For example, suppose I told you that Dr. John Doe said that the South Beach diet was the best way to lose weight. Why should you believe Dr. Doe? I would need more than just "Dr." preceding his name to back up my reasoning. Thus, as a listener, there are some important questions to ask about authority warrants.

Tips and Tactics

Evaluating Authority Warrants

- Is the authority an expert in the area under discussion?
- Has the speaker adequately backed the qualifications of the authority?
- Is the authority trustworthy and unbiased?
- Is the authority acting on reliable information?

Two common fallacies are associated with the misuse of authority warrants: halo effect and ad hominem.

Halo Effect

The **halo effect** fallacy is based on the presumption that because we like or respect certain people, we tend to believe them no matter what they say. This is commonly seen when movie stars and other celebrities endorse political causes. For example, although we enjoy Janine Garofalo's stand-up, that doesn't mean she's an expert on Iraq policy. Yet she is seen and heard discussing national security issues on cable TV and talk radio. We are not implying that her views are necessarily wrong. However, being a celebrity gives her no particular expertise or qualifications to discuss foreign policy. Unless she proves otherwise,

halo effect
The assumption that just because you like or respect a person, whatever he or she says must be true.

her opinion is just that–an opinion–and deserves no more weight than the opinion of any other citizen.

Ad Hominem

ad hominem
Attacking the person rather than the soundness of his or her argument.

In many ways, this is the reverse of the halo effect. **Ad hominem** means "against the person." This fallacy is based on attacking the person rather than the soundness of his or her argument. In many cases, this fallacy consists of simply substituting name-calling for reasoning. Numerous Web sites are devoted to trashing filmmaker Michael Moore. In fact, there's even a counterdocumentary called *Michael Moore Hates America*. Whether Michael Moore is a patriot or a traitor, his speeches, books, and films should be judged based on how well documented they are and whether their reasoning is sound, not on whether we like the author. As someone once said, even a broken clock is right twice a day. People we may dislike can be right as well as wrong. We deserve to give their views a hearing and then reach a conclusion based on the facts. As we pointed out in Chapter 5, civility is a virtue that's becoming increasingly rare in our public discourse. Ad hominem arguments and name-calling only denigrate the public dialogue.

Generalization Warrants

As we pointed out in Chapter 9, a generalization warrant is a statement that either establishes a general rule or principle or applies an established rule or principle to a specific case.

Establishing Generalizations

A warrant that establishes a generalization uses specific instances, as represented in examples, statistics, narratives, and the like, to reach general conclusions. For example, in his speech on D.A.R.E., Mitch Bacci mentions his own experience in the program. He states, "From my experience I know that D.A.R.E. doesn't differentiate between different types of drugs–it just lumps them all into one big category as 'risk-taking' behavior." If his experience is representative of the program, then that would support the generalization that D.A.R.E. doesn't differentiate among drugs. This generalization is essential to his later claim that students later perceive the program as "a lie." The question, of course, is whether or not the speaker's experience is in fact typical. Warrants establishing generalizations are subject to tests of relevance, quantity, typicality, precision, and negative example. These tests can be expressed in the questions listed in Tips and Tactics.

Tips and Tactics

Questions to Ask When Evaluating a Generalization

- Are the grounds relevant to the claim?
- Are there sufficient grounds to establish the claim?
- Are the grounds typical of the larger population?
- Is overgeneralization avoided?
- Are there significant negative examples?

Let's apply these tests to Mitch Bacci's speech. He generalizes that D.A.R.E. is ineffective and even counterproductive. Among the grounds he cites are his own experience, citations from authorities, and the fact that its use has declined, even to the point of being eliminated in the city of its birth, Los Angeles. Certainly these grounds are relevant to the claim that D.A.R.E. is ineffective. Are they sufficient? That is open to question. Regardless of his own experience with the program and the experts cited, he admits that the decline is also a result of funding cuts. That might be a sign that it is ineffective, but it is also the case that in an era of tight budgets, many good programs are sometimes canceled. Thus, we cannot be sure that he has not overgeneralized, especially since we are not provided with any counterexamples–situations where D.A.R.E. was successful. A two-sided presentation is generally more persuasive than a one-sided one. To really be persuasive, this speaker should have dealt with claims made by D.A.R.E.'s proponents that it was successful and shown that they did not refute his generalization.

Hasty Generalization. The most common fallacy associated with warrants that generalize from specific instances to a general conclusion is known as **hasty generalization.** This occurs when there are too few instances to support a generalization or the instances are unrepresentative of the generalization. The key here is to limit generalizations to the extent justified by the grounds. We live in a small college town. We often hear long-time citizens complain that college students are lazy, destructive, and irresponsible. These opinions are based on the misbehavior of a small fraction of the 16,000 students who attend our university. The tendency to generalize from a negative experience is a very human one and is part of our survival instinct. Our ancestors needed only one encounter with a saber-toothed tiger to know it was something to avoid. But this natural tendency to generalize from bad experiences can lead to very shoddy reasoning when those experiences are not really typical. This is also one of the reasons statisticians and quantitative researchers are so fond of the saying, "You can never generalize from a sample of one." Our individual experiences with the world may or may not be typical of others. Until the research is done, however, we cannot and should not be certain that they are.

hasty generalization
An argument that occurs when there are too few instances to support a generalization or the instances are unrepresentative of the generalization.

Occasionally, we are asked how a hasty generalization differs from an isolated example. The two fallacies are similar, but there is an important difference. The isolated example is a defect of *grounds* or evidence–the speaker doesn't have sufficient evidence to prove a general claim. On the other hand, the hasty generalization is a defect of *warrant.* The grounds are fine, but the speaker has generalized beyond what he or she can logically prove. For example, you meet one of the authors, Dr. Brydon, on the street. He's 5 feet, 8 inches. You conclude all the Brydons are shorter than 6 feet tall. Clearly, you haven't met enough of the family to reach any conclusions except about the one person. You've relied on an isolated (single) example.

On the other hand, the hasty generalization is a defect of warrant. Say you meet Brydon, his wife, and daughter–all of them are under 5 feet, 8 inches. You generalize, thinking you have met all the Brydons, that they are all shorter than 6 feet tall. Your defect here is in the warrant, thinking you have met all of them. But the problem is your warrant is defective because it didn't account for the fourth Brydon, the 6-foot-tall son. If there were only three Brydons, then the same evidence wouldn't be a hasty generalization because your warrant would be correct–you would have met the whole family.

Applying Generalizations

If we know a generalization is true, we can apply it to a specific instance and reach some valid conclusions about that specific instance. Warrants applying generalizations are subject to tests of applicability to all cases, exceptions, backing, and classification.

Tips and Tactics

Questions to Ask When Evaluating Applications of a Generalization

- Does the generalization apply to all possible cases?
- Are there exceptions to the generalization? If so, does the specific case fall within one of the exceptions?
- Is the generalization well backed?
- Does the specific instance fall clearly within the category specified by the generalization?

Exhibit 16.3 on page 425 illustrates an argument that applies a generalization. In this case, we know that the generalization *warrant,* all native-born Americans are citizens, is true because of the *backing* found in the U.S. laws and Constitution. Given the *grounds* that John is a native-born American, we can be almost certain (*qualifier*) that the *claim,* John is a U.S. citizen, is true. There is a possible *rebuttal,* however; the claim is true unless he has renounced his citizenship.

stereotyping
The assumption that what is considered to be true of a larger class is necessarily true of particular members of that class.

Stereotyping. The most common fallacy associated with warrants that apply established generalizations to specific instances is known as **stereotyping.** This fallacy assumes that what is considered to be true of a larger class is necessarily true of particular members of that class. We have known people with disabilities, for example, who are just as physically active as a person with no limitations. Jonathan Studebaker, who you learned about in Chapter 3, spent most of his adult life speaking to school-aged children about the importance of not stereotyping people just because they have a disability. In dealing with generalizations, there is always a danger of stereotyping the person, who is exceptional, based on the class of attributes that defines the group.

false dilemma
A generalization that implies there are only two choices when there are more than two.

False Dilemma. Another common fallacy associated with applying generalizations is the **false dilemma,** a generalization that implies there are only two choices when there are more than two. A true dilemma requires proof that there really are only two choices. Consider the following telephone call to a newspaper:

> *They should fight child abuse*
>
> I'd like to talk to the pro-lifers about abortion. They want to stop abortion so bad and they take their time to do it. Why don't they take the same painstaking time to help fight children being killed by dads and moms when they get a very light sentence?[4]

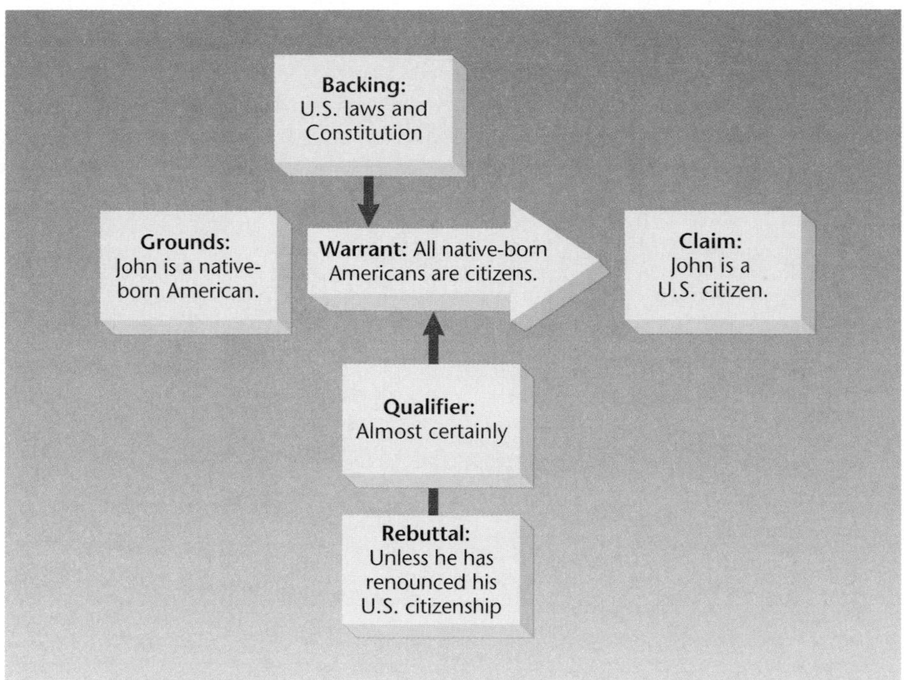

Exhibit 16.3
Argument Applying a Generalization

Of course, someone can be both pro-life (or anti-abortion) and against children being killed by their parents. The key to a real dilemma is that there are in fact only two choices and that they are mutually exclusive. In this case, someone could support both of these values without contradiction, and thus no real dilemma exists.

Comparison (Analogy) Warrants

As we explained in Chapter 9, reasoning based on a comparison (analogy) warrant claims that two cases that are similar in some known respects are also similar in some unknown respects. These arguments are called comparisons or, more commonly, analogies. The war on drugs is an analogy, but do the standards of a shooting war really apply to righting a social problem? Evaluate analogies by asking the following questions:

Tips and Tactics

Questions to Ask When Evaluating Comparisons or Analogies

- Are only literal analogies used for proof?
- Do the similarities outweigh the differences?
- Are the similarities more relevant than the differences to the claim being made?

Stereotypes about athletic skill among people with disabilities can be wrong as these athletes show.

False Analogy

false analogy
The comparison of two different things that are not really comparable.

The most common fallacy associated with comparison warrants is the **false analogy.** This occurs when two things that are not really comparable are compared as if they were essentially the same. For example, we recall a debate on our campus wherein a prominent administrator claimed that we should abolish our campus requirement for a public speaking course. "After all," he stated, "our students have been talking since they were two." Although talking and delivering a public speech might seem like a fair comparison to the uninformed, as you have presumably learned in this class, there's a lot more to giving a speech than just being able to talk. Fortunately, those in charge of general education at our university quickly recognized and rejected the false analogy.

Causal Warrants

As we pointed out in Chapter 9, reasoning based on a causal warrant claims that a cause will produce or has produced an effect. You can reason either from cause to effect or from effect to cause. Causal warrants are subject to tests of relatedness, other causes, other effects, and mistaking order in time for causality.

Tips and Tactics

Questions to Ask When Evaluating Causal Reasoning

- Is the cause related to the alleged effect?
- Are there other causes of the effect?
- Are there other effects from the same cause?
- Has the time sequence been mistaken for cause (post hoc fallacy)?

Causal arguments can be successfully and persuasively made. For example, there is considerable scientific evidence to support the effects of tobacco on health, and few independent scientists dispute the harmfulness of the product. A speaker relying on such experts and scientific studies would be on solid ground. Often a speaker is best advised to make causal arguments when they can be buttressed by expert testimony and scientific studies and clearly meet tests of relatedness, other causes and effects, and time sequence as outlined in this chapter.

Post Hoc

Warrants dealing with effect-to-cause reasoning frequently commit the fallacy of assuming that because one event preceded another, the first event must be the cause of the second event. Technically, this is known as the **post hoc, ergo propter hoc** fallacy ("after the fact, therefore because of the fact"). In a letter to the editor of a local newspaper heralding the end of a recent period of drought in California, the writer claimed that the drought had ended because of the prayers of the people of the small town of Paradise. The letter writer even referred to them as "God's chosen helpers." Far be it from us to denigrate anyone's faith, but clearly the drought was going to end some time (and it will return again). Just because this small community's prayers were followed by rain doesn't mean that's why the drought ended. Just because one event follows another doesn't prove they are cause and effect.

post hoc, ergo propter hoc
("after the fact, therefore because of the fact") The assumption that because one event preceded another, the first event must be the cause of the second event.

Slippery Slope

Warrants that reason from cause to effect are susceptible to the **slippery slope** fallacy. This fallacy involves assuming that just because one event occurs, it will automatically lead to a series of undesirable events, like a row of dominoes falling down automatically once you knock over the first one. In common language, this fallacy is sometimes expressed, "If you give them an inch, they'll take a mile."

slippery slope
The assumption that just because one event occurs, it will automatically lead to a series of undesirable events even though there is no relationship between the action and the projected events.

Mitch Bacci takes dead aim at a classic slippery slope fallacy in his speech when he attacks the concept of gateway drugs. It is, of course, well known that most hard drug abusers started with softer drugs, such as marijuana and alcohol. So, will using soft drugs be a gateway causing users to move up to hard drugs? Bacci addresses the issue directly:

> The gateway drug concept, simply stated, means that drugs like marijuana, cigarettes, and alcohol will lead to heavier drugs like cocaine and heroin. As a matter of fact, the "gateway drug" concept is nothing more than a false hypothesis. According to the *American Journal of Public Health,* one out of 100 people that try marijuana move on to harder drugs.

A one percent correlation is hardly proof of a causal relationship between soft and hard drugs. Just because someone uses marijuana or alcohol is no guarantee he or she will end up addicted to crack or heroin.

Nevertheless, it is not necessarily a slippery slope to argue that one action will follow another if the relationship can be clearly demonstrated. For example, it can be mathematically demonstrated that to continue to charge items on a credit card without paying any more than the minimum monthly payment will lead to deeper and deeper debt. And, of course, the judicial system relies heavily on the role of precedents in making decisions. Much of the debate surrounding the use of military tribunals to try suspected terrorists relied on the precedents set in the Civil War and World Wars I and II. So future effects are important, if they can be clearly shown by sound reasoning.

Sign Warrants

As we noted in Chapter 9, reasoning using a sign warrant infers the presence of an unobserved phenomenon from the presence of an observed one. Sign warrants are subject to tests of reliability and conflicting signs.

Tips and Tactics

Questions to Ask When Evaluating Sign Reasoning

- Are the signs reliable indicators of the claim?
- Are there conflicting signs?

In real life, reliable signs are hard to find. In testing sign reasoning, ask how reliable such signs have been in the past. For example, economists often make predictions about the future of the economy based on figures for unemployment, housing starts, and so on. A careful examination of their track record in making such predictions will suggest just how much confidence you should have in their reasoning.

The second test is to look for conflicting signs. Whereas one economist may point to decreased unemployment as a sign of economic upturn, another may conclude that there are fewer unemployed because the economy is so bad many workers have given up seeking jobs.

Unless a sign is infallible, most sign reasoning at best indicates the probability that a claim is true.

Mistaking Correlation for Cause

mistaking correlation for cause
The assumption that because one thing is the sign of another, they are causally related.

The most common fallacy associated with sign reasoning is **mistaking correlation for cause.** A correlation simply means two things occur in conjunction with each other, without regard to their cause. How often have you heard someone claim that one event caused another just because they occurred in tandem? Historically, when the stock market was on the rise, so were women's hemlines. Although one may be a "sign" of the other, it is ludicrous to assume the stock market caused the hemlines to go up or vice versa. Just because one event signifies another does not mean they are causally related. For example, a recent news report noted that there is a higher-than-normal incidence of heart disease among bald men. However, this does not prove that baldness causes heart disease or that a hair transplant will reduce the risk of heart attack. Although the two factors are correlated, the most likely explanation is that common underlying factors cause both baldness and heart disease.

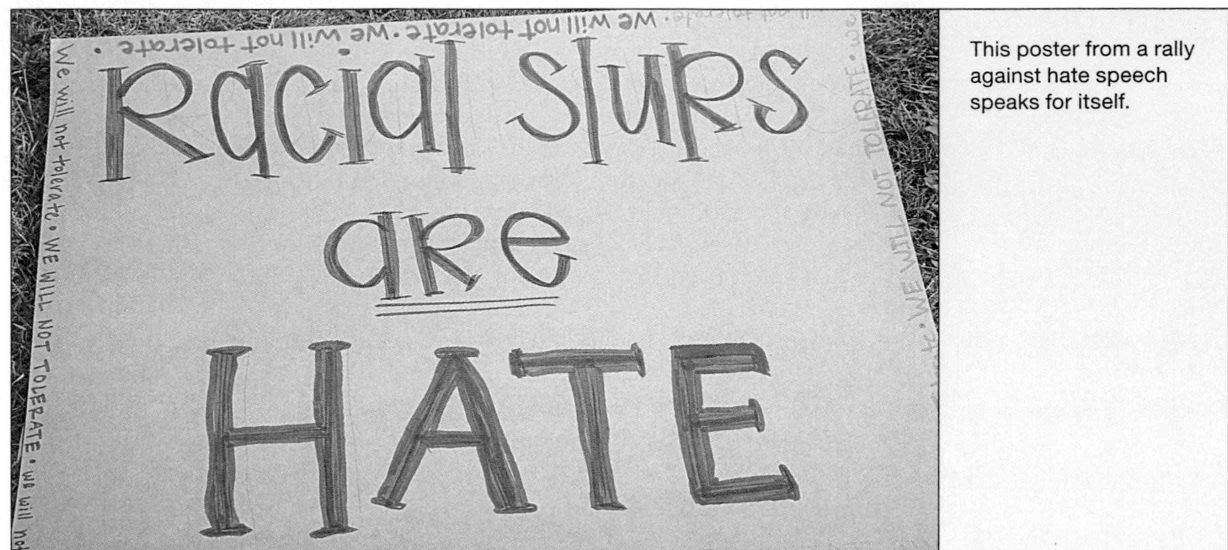

This poster from a rally against hate speech speaks for itself.

Fallacies Associated With Qualifiers

Toulmin believes that reasoners should qualify their claims. As we pointed out in Chapter 9, a qualifier is an indication of the level of probability of a claim. Some arguments are virtually certain to be true, whereas others have a much lower degree of certainty. Depending on the nature of the argument, a qualifier can make a big difference. For example, in a criminal trial, the claim that the defendant is guilty must be true "beyond a reasonable doubt," a phrase that acts as the qualifier of the argument for guilt. Thus, a very high degree of certainty is required before a jury can convict someone of a criminal offense. On the other hand, in a civil case, the standard is "a preponderance of evidence." That is, if it is more likely than not that the defendant wronged the plaintiff, the judgment should go to the plaintiff. Because of the difference in the level of proof required, someone found not guilty in a criminal trial can still be sued in civil court.

So, too, in our reasoning, we need to know what level of proof our audience will expect. As with virtually every other aspect of public speaking, the success of our reasoning depends on careful analysis of the audience. As listeners, we should also be clear about what level of proof we need before accepting a claim. Many of the fallacies of reasoning associated with qualifiers are a result of overstating or distorting the degree of certainty with which the arguer has supported his or her claim. Two such common fallacies are the use of loaded language and hyperbole.

Loaded Language

Language that triggers strong emotional and negative responses is termed **loaded language.** Depending on the specific characteristics of our audience, what we might consider neutral language may in fact carry strong emotional

loaded language
Language that triggers strong emotional and negative responses.

connotations. Recently our campus was the site of racist graffiti painted on dorm walls. In addition, white supremacist groups placed hate literature on front doorsteps throughout the county. The language used was both offensive and crude. Such loaded language elicits one of two responses. Some people respond in kind–leading to an ever-escalating spiral of hate. Others speak out against hate language itself. Many in our community chose the latter course–holding a rally against hate speech. Avoid loaded language when preparing a speech, and when such language is used in the speech of others, avoid the temptation to simply engage in a shouting match. A reasoned and forceful call for civility is the best answer.

Of course, effective persuasion often requires vivid, intense, and expressive language, as we discussed in Chapter 11. There is a fine but important line between language that is necessarily vivid and language that is so "loaded" that it distorts the reasoning being presented. There is no hard-and-fast rule that can be applied here. Speakers and listeners need to exercise their judgment in evaluating the use of language.

Hyperbole

hyperbole
An exaggeration of a claim.

Hyperbole is an exaggeration of a claim. Rather than properly qualifying or limiting the impact of a statement, the person engaged in hyperbole exaggerates the claim in question. When boxer Muhammad Ali declared himself to be "the greatest," it may have been an effective way to build interest in his fights, but it was certainly an exaggeration of his prowess, especially since he didn't limit his claim to the boxing ring. Other examples of hyperbole include the use of such terms as "superstar," "greatest ever," and "mega-hit." It often seems as if it is not enough anymore to be a star, to be great, or to have a mere hit. Hyperbole ends up cheapening the currency of language, inflating claims, and devaluing more moderate language.

Fallacies Associated With Rebuttals

The rebuttal to an argument is an exception to or refutation of an argument. It too can be flawed. Fallacies of rebuttal can occur when a speaker misanalyzes an opponent's argument or sidesteps the other side of the issue completely.

Straw Person

straw person
An argument made in refutation that misstates the argument being refuted. Rather than refuting the real argument, the other side constructs a person of straw, which is easy to knock down.

The **straw person** fallacy occurs when someone attempts to refute a claim by misstating the argument being refuted. Rather than refuting the real argument, the other side constructs a person of straw, which is easy to knock down.

An Associated Press article in 2006 pointed to the use of straw person arguments by politicians. For example, the article quotes President Bush as saying, "Some say if you're Muslim you can't be free." Of course, as the article points out, this is not a position taken by anyone in mainstream politics. As Wayne Fields of Washington University states, "It's such a phenomenal hole in the national debate that you can have arguments with nonexistent people. . . . All politicians try to get away with it to a certain extent."[5] We need to be sure that the rebuttal to an argument is actually refuting the argument that was presented, not some version that was concocted so that it would be easier to refute.

Ignoring the Issue

The fallacy of **igoring the issue** occurs when the claim made by one side in an argument is ignored by the other. For example, imagine that you are speaking before a group about the effects of the depletion of the ozone layer on the environment. Skin cancer death rates will increase, you argue. We need to change over to safer refrigerants in our cars' air conditioning systems. Suppose someone attempts to rebut your argument by saying that environmental extremists have killed loggers by spiking trees. This rebuttal is simply not responsive to the argument you have posed. In short, the issue you have presented has been ignored, and the rebuttalist has shifted ground to another issue entirely.

ignoring the issue
When a claim made by one side in an argument is ignored by the other side.

The Non Sequitur: An Argument That Does Not Follow

Until now, we've looked at each component of an argument as a separate source of fallacies. Of course, you also have to look at the argument as a whole. Even if the grounds are true, the warrant believable, and so on, an argument that doesn't hang together logically is still fallacious. Thus, the final fallacy of reasoning we examine is the non sequitur.

A **non sequitur** is an argument that does not follow from its premises. In Toulmin's terms, there is no logical connection between the claim, the grounds, and the warrant used to support the claim. Consider the example of a person who called in this opinion to a newspaper:

non sequitur
An argument that does not follow from its premises.

> *No wonder welfare is so popular*
>
> I'd like to thank the person who dropped the two little black lab-mix puppies off at the golf course some time in the week of Jan. 28. What irresponsible person caused others to try to find homes for these dogs? It's ama zing people don't take responsibility for their actions and cause other people to. No wonder everybody's on welfare.[6]

Aside from stereotyping people on welfare as irresponsible and hyperbolizing in claiming that "everybody's on welfare," this argument has absolutely no link between its grounds–the two dogs abandoned at the golf course–and its claim–that this irresponsibility is symptomatic of people on welfare.

We have discussed numerous fallacies in this chapter. To review them, see the box "Speaking of . . . Defects of Reasoning: The Fallacies."

Speaking of . . .

Defects of Reasoning: The Fallacies

Fallacies Associated With Grounds

unsupported assertion: The absence of any argument at all.

distorted evidence: Significant omissions or changes in the grounds of an argument that alter its original intent.

isolated examples: Nontypical or nonrepresentative examples that are used to prove a general claim.

misused numerical data: Statistics that involve errors such as poor sampling, lack of significant differences, misuse of average, or misuse of percentages.

Fallacies Associated With Claims

red herring (smoke screen): An irrelevant issue introduced into a controversy to divert attention from the real controversy.

arguing in a circle (begging the question): An argument that proves nothing because the claim to be proved is used as the grounds or warrant for the argument.

Fallacies Associated With Authority Warrants

halo effect: The assumption that just because you like or respect a person, whatever he or she says must be true.

ad hominem: Attacking the person rather than the soundness of his or her argument.

Fallacies Associated With Generalization Warrants

hasty generalization: An argument that occurs when there are too few instances to support a generalization or the instances are unrepresentative of the generalization.

stereotyping: The assumption that what is considered to be true of a larger class is necessarily true of particular members of that class.

false dilemma: A generalization that implies there are only two choices when there are more than two.

Fallacy Associated With Comparison (Analogy) Warrants

false analogy: The comparison of two different things that are not really comparable.

Fallacies Associated With Causal Warrants

post hoc, ergo propter hoc ("after the fact, therefore because of the fact"): The assumption that because one event preceded another, the first event must be the cause of the second event.

slippery slope: The assumption that just because one event occurs, it will automatically lead to a series of undesirable events even though there is no relationship between the action and the projected events.

Fallacy Associated With Sign Warrants

mistaking correlation for cause: The assumption that because one thing is the sign of another, they are causally related.

Fallacies Associated With Qualifiers

loaded language: Language that triggers strong emotional and negative responses.

hyperbole: An exaggeration of a claim.

Fallacies Associated With Rebuttals

straw person: An argument made in refutation that misstates the argument being refuted. Rather than refuting the real argument, the other side constructs a person of straw, which is easy to knock down.

ignoring the issue: An argument made in refutation that ignores the claim made by the other side.

Additional Fallacy

non sequitur: An argument that does not follow from its premises.

To evaluate your understanding of this chapter, visit our Online Learning Center Web site for quizzes and other chapter study aids.

Summary

Reasoning and critical thinking are important both in constructing good arguments and in listening to the arguments of others.

Argumentativeness is the trait of arguing for and against the positions taken on controversial claims.

Verbal aggressiveness is the trait of attacking the self-concept of those with whom a person disagrees about controversial claims.

Grounds for an argument consist of evidence supporting a claim.

Fallacies associated with defective grounds are:

- Unsupported assertions
- Distorted evidence
- Isolated examples
- Misused numerical data

Claims may contain the following fallacies:

- The red herring
- Arguing in a circle

Warrants link grounds and claims by means of:

- Authority
- Generalization
- Comparison
- Cause
- Sign

Backing is support for the warrant and is especially important in cases in which the audience is either unfamiliar with the warrant or unconvinced of its truth.

Fallacies associated with generalization warrants include:

- Hasty generalization
- Stereotyping
- False dilemmas

The one fallacy associated with comparison warrants is the false analogy.

Fallacies associated with causation warrants are:

- Post hoc, ergo propter hoc
- Slippery slope

The one fallacy associated with sign warrants is mistaking correlation for cause.

Fallacies associated with authority warrants are:

- The halo effect
- Ad hominem

Qualifiers are an indication of the level of probability of the claim. Fallacies associated with qualifiers are:

- Loaded language
- Hyperbole

A rebuttal is an exception to or refutation of an argument. Fallacies associated with rebuttals are:

- Straw person
- Ignoring the issue

The non sequitur is a fallacy that occurs when an argument does not follow from its premises.

Check Your Understanding: Exercises and Activities

1. Find a published argument, such as a letter to the editor, an advertisement, an editorial, or a political ad. Identify the claim being made and the grounds on which the claim is based. Is the warrant explicitly stated? If not, determine the implied warrant. What backing, if any, is offered for the warrant? Is the argument adequately qualified? Are there possible rebuttals to the argument? Are any fallacies present?
2. Find an example of each of the following types of arguments in a publication: cause to effect, effect to cause, sign, comparison, establishing a generalization, applying a generalization, authority. Which of these arguments is the strongest, logically, and which is the weakest? Explain your answer in terms of the tests of reasoning outlined in this chapter.
3. Pick an advertisement from any print medium–for example, magazines, newspapers, or direct mail. In a brief paper, identify at least three fallacies used in the advertisement. Define each fallacy in your own words. Cite the specific example of each fallacy from the ad, and explain why the example meets the definition. Finally, highlight the fallacies on a copy of the ad and attach the copy to your paper.
4. Analyze the arguments against D.A.R.E. presented by Mitch Bacci in this chapter. Do you detect any fallacies? Does the speaker identify any errors in the reasoning of those who support D.A.R.E.?

Notes

1. Brooke Noel Moore and Richard Parker, *Critical Thinking,* 5th ed. (Mountain View, Calif.: Mayfield, 1998), 476.
2. Dominic A. Infante, *Arguing Constructively* (Prospect Heights, Ill.: Waveland Press, 1988).
3. Stephen Toulmin, Richard Rieke, and Allan Janik, *An Introduction to Reasoning,* 2nd ed. (New York: Macmillan, 1984).
4. "Tell It to the ER," *Chico Enterprise Record,* 13 March 1992, 2A. Reprinted by permission.
5. Associated Press, "Bush uses straw-man arguments to attack opponents," *Chico Enterprise Record,* 19 March 2006, 9C.
6. "Tell It to the ER," *Chico Enterprise Record,* 16 February 1992, 2A. Reprinted by permission.

This class is just the beginning of your public speaking career.

"Real World" Speaking

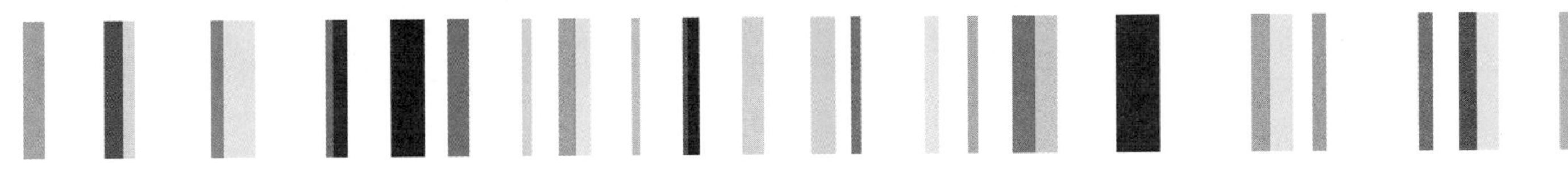

Objectives

After reading this chapter and reviewing the online learning resources at www.mhhe.com/brydon6, you should be able to:

- Present a speech of introduction.
- Present or accept an award.
- Make a speech of commemoration.
- Make a speech to entertain.
- Be interviewed on television.

Key Concepts

eulogy

reframing

speech of acceptance

speech of commemoration

speech of introduction

speech of recognition

speech to entertain

" You've been giving your attention to a turkey stuffed with sage; you are now about to consider a sage stuffed with turkey. "

–**WILLIAM MAXWELL EVARTS** (1818–1901)
American statesman, speaking after a Thanksgiving dinner[1]

When Russ Woody left our university to seek his fame and fortune in Hollywood, little did he know he would one day get a call to speak at his alma mater's commencement.

When Russ Woody graduated from Chico State University and moved to Hollywood to become a television writer, the last thing he expected was to one day get a call from his alma mater and be asked to deliver the university commencement address to 10,000 people. Yet that's exactly what happened to the Emmy Award-winning producer of such hit shows as *Becker* and *Murphy Brown*. As you can imagine, few audiences are as tough to please as a graduating class anxious to be handed their diplomas and begin celebrating in earnest. In the nearly 30 years' worth of commencement speeches the authors have witnessed, we've seen more speakers alienate or lose their audience than succeed.

Russ, we're pleased to say, was not one of them. Drawing on his own experience as a student at Chico and as a Hollywood insider, Russ shared the "lessons" he had learned and wished to pass on. Not only could everyone in his audience relate to his lessons, but they were also funny and self-effacing. As a result, Russ's speech made this particular commencement better–not just longer.

Although we may never be called on to speak at our alma mater's commencement ceremony, we will be called on to speak at occasions both ordinary and special over our life span. Public speaking is an essential part of many of our culture's most important rituals. It is expected in celebration of life's most significant events, for example, birthdays, weddings, and anniversaries. And it is expected in solemn tribute even at life's end.

This final chapter focuses on the predictable circumstances in which we will be required to speak, both in college and "the real world" that supposedly awaits you once you graduate. As we said at the very beginning of this book, public speaking is a skill people value and reward not just in the classroom but also in nearly every conceivable walk of life. The trick now is to skillfully apply what you've learned from our book and class to the rhetorical situations you *will* face in other classes, your civic life, and work. For some, public speaking may become the key to their life's work (see the box, "In Their Own Words: Speaking to Impact!" by Dr. Rick Rigsby). For most of us, it is an inevitable part of our personal and professional lives. Toward that end, we will focus on the most common examples of the different but predictable types of speeches you can expect to give in the near and distant future. These include saying thank you when you've

In Their Own Words

Speaking to Impact!

by Rick Rigsby, Ph.D.

Dr. Rick Rigsby is president and CEO of Rick Rigsby Communications and founder of Rick Rigsby Ministries. With over 200 engagements annually, Dr. Rigsby presents to diverse audiences ranging from Fortune 500 corporations to churches around the world. He is a featured speaker at the Promise Keepers national events and speaks at chapel services for numerous teams in the National Football League. A former award-winning communication professor at Texas A&M University, Dr. Rigsby continues to serve as chaplain for the Aggies football team. We asked him to discuss how his training and experience as a public speaker has impacted his life:

Dr. Rick Rigsby

The ability to speak passionately, powerfully, and persuasively will inspire people and offer you opportunities for a lifetime. My professional success is contingent on the ability to speak with precision, power, and authority. And so is yours!

As a motivational speaker, I must be my very best every time I take the stage. I cannot afford to be average or kind of good. I must be inspiring, motivating, provocative, knowledgeable, moving, and credible. In other words, I must make an IMPACT . . . and not just an impression.

I learned the value of rhetoric at an early age, realizing that through the use of language, tone, timing, and intent, I could summon the power to make people laugh, cry, or think. Moving from the streets of the San Francisco Bay Area to the college classroom, I learned formally about the rich tradition of rhetoric. I fell in love with the process of communication and the potential to influence lives through the power of the spoken word.

My education would serve me well—first during an exhilarating career as a television news reporter in Northern California. Eventually, I would attend graduate school earning a master's degree from my alma mater, California State University, Chico, followed by time at the University of Oregon where I earned a doctorate. I spent two decades teaching college students the power of communication and how the spoken word works to establish and maintain every contour of life.

As president of my own professional speaking organization, I use every communication lesson learned to insure that I am at the top of my game. With over two hundred engagements a year, and a stable of speakers that I am responsible for training, it is critical that I model the art of effective communication. Such an accomplishment would not be possible without my teachers—from Socrates, Plato, and Aristotle in Greece to Brydon and Scott at Chico State!

During a 30-year career built on the study and practice of oratory, I know how to use words to decrease my distance from my audience—thus creating a more intimate environment more conducive to listening and learning. I know how to be rhetorically bilingual—how to speak to both the head and the heart. Most of all I know how to engage audience members—whether 50 or 5000!

The art of persuasion is a learned behavior. If you are willing to learn, prepare your presentations, and practice your craft . . . you may find yourself one day standing in front of thousands and making millions! Are you ready? Well, what are you waiting for? Continue reading and discover how you can learn to move mountains . . . by making an impact with words!!!!

Storytelling never goes out of style.

been singled out for recognition, introducing someone who is being honored or who is the principal speaker of the occasion, or speaking to commemorate an occasion of celebration or solemnity. We begin by talking about reframing your perspective about speaking in situations both everyday and special.

Reframing: Speaking as Storytelling

The late Senator Robert F. Kennedy was fond of paraphrasing Irish playwright George Bernard Shaw by saying, "Some people see things as they are and say: why? I dream things that never were and say: why not?"[2] This familiar quotation eloquently alludes to the importance of perspective in analyzing and responding to circumstance. This kind of behavior can be thought of in terms of **reframing**–revising our view of a situation or an event. Recall that the degree to which we are anxious about a speaking transaction depends on how we view it. As we said early in this book, looking at a speech as a performance is likely to make us more anxious than looking at a speech as a natural but refined extension of our everyday communication skills.

reframing
Revising our view of a situation or an event, usually in a positive direction.

One effective way to reframe our point of view about the kind of speaking this chapter describes is to think of it as a form of storytelling. Although you probably gave few "speeches" prior to taking this class, chances are good that you told innumerable stories. Good stories share a similar organizational sequence with good speeches. An involving story hooks an audience with its introduction, builds to a climax either humorous or dramatic, and concludes with a memorable resolution to the climax.

Rhetorical scholar Walter R. Fisher argues that storytelling is not only an effective way to involve an audience but also an effective way to share a message.[3] Social psychologists such as Melanie Green echo what Fisher has said about storytelling, especially in terms of persuasion. There is a growing body of research in psychology, for example, that shows people are far more likely to relate and positively respond to persuasion in the form of a story than they are to more conventional forms of persuasion.[4] Thus, the lawyer who embeds arguments in a narrative is likely to be more persuasive with a jury than one who simply outlines the evidence that supports her arguments.

Storytelling needn't be long-winded nor overly complicated. To the contrary, many of the best stories are short and to the point. Effective stories or narratives share two common elements, as we first discussed in Chapter 9: *probability* and *fidelity*.

Probability

The property of storytelling termed probability is straightforward. Narrative probability is the internal coherence of the story. Coherence concerns the degree to which the structure of the story holds up in the eyes of an audience. Does the story make sense as told? Do the parts of the story hang together? Effective stories are logically consistent in structure, even if the content of the story requires that we suspend disbelief, as is the case with fairy tales and some science fiction. Did you know that Mark Twain, for example, was a gifted public speaker as well as writer? He could tell even the most improbable story in such a way that it seemed completely plausible. What's more, this was true whether he was talking about the exaggerated athleticism of a jumping frog in the gold fields of California or transporting a Connecticut man back into the time of King Arthur's court.

Fidelity

The second property of effective storytelling–fidelity–concerns truthfulness. We are predisposed to believe stories whose messages ring true with our own experience. Depending on the occasion, you probably share a lot in common with your audience, from being friends of the bride and groom at a wedding to sharing the sorrow of family members when giving a eulogy. You can draw on these commonalities to increase the narrative fidelity of your stories, whether they grow out of your individual experience or experiences with which most of your audience can relate.

Lest you think otherwise, even fictional persons, places, and things can be described by a speaker in such a way that the description rings true with our genuine experience. For example Garrison Keillor, the popular writer and host of the long-running National Public Radio series *A Prairie Home Companion,* tells his audience stories about a fictitious Minnesota town named Lake Wobegon. The stories are popular and succeed not because they are literally true but because the characters and situations Keillor describes remind us of people and situations in our own lives. Although Keillor's stories may not seem so initially, an analysis of them shows that they have much in common with effective public speeches.

It can be helpful to approach a speech task such as thanking people or making an introduction as a form of storytelling. Audiences relate well to recognition speeches and the like when they have a beginning, a middle, and a climactic end. Remember, though, that to be effective, our speech and the story it tells must meet the tests of probability and fidelity. This framework sets the stage for

Speaking of . . .

The Wedding Toast

Whereas 40 percent of people express fears about presenting a public speech, 97 percent report that they are fearful over the prospect of being asked to give a wedding toast. One potential consequence of this fact is that unrehearsed and poorly thought-out wedding toasts have become the rule rather than the exception. Wedding planner Deborah McCoy describes some of them in her book, *The World's Most Unforgettable Weddings.* They range from simply incoherent toasts by maids of honor to raunchy and obscenity-laced stories about the bachelor party by best men.

Simply put, there is no excuse for dishonoring a bride and groom with a terrible toast. And this is especially true of a best man or maid/matron of honor. The idea is to honor the couple—not get a laugh or worse at their expense.

Here are some tips for making an appropriately memorable wedding toast:

One of the most common speeches of tribute is the wedding toast.

1. Consult with the couple about what they expect from you.
2. Learn about who will be in attendance and take into account the diversity in age, education, and experience.
3. Talk to the wedding planner if it's an option.
4. Make it short, sweet, and memorable for the right reasons.
5. Prepare, including finding an appropriate story, anecdote, or quote that celebrates the event.
6. Rehearse.
7. Hold off on the champagne.
8. Speak clearly and loudly enough for all to hear.
9. Face the bride and groom, but don't turn your back on guests.
10. Ask the guests to join "with you" in your toast.

Source: J. Freedom du Lac, "Burnt Toasts: Bad Taste Seems To Be Rigueur At Many Weddings." *The Sacramento Bee.* June 17, 2003, E1–2.

preparing to meet head-on the predictable situations in which you will be expected to speak both now and in the future. One of the most common occasions most of us will face at some time is delivering a wedding toast. We offer some helpful tips in the box "Speaking of . . . The Wedding Toast."

Speaking on Special Occasions

Speaking on special occasions is likely during the course of our lives. At such times, our job is to emphasize the special nature of the occasion in thought, word, and deed. Most of the time we will be able to prepare and practice in advance of such situations. Other times we may be asked, in impromptu fashion, to "say a few words." The special occasions we can anticipate speaking at over the course of our lives include expressing thanks; introducing a speaker or an honored guest; speaking in recognition of a person, group, or organization; making a commemorative speech; and speaking to entertain people.

Speech of Acceptance

A **speech of acceptance** is a speech expressing thanks for an award or honor. In many cultures, calling attention to ourselves is considered to be in bad taste. Many of us have been taught this norm. Even so, there are times in our lives when we cannot help being the center of attention. One of them is when we are singled out publicly for some recognition or award. For some, this becomes a dilemma. On one hand, they know they need to accept the recognition or award in a fashion that recognizes and pays tribute to those responsible. On the other hand, they don't want to appear as if they expected the recognition or award and prepared their remarks well in advance of the event. All too often, therefore, they do not prepare or rehearse their response and end up appearing humble but tongue-tied. Believe us: Most audiences would prefer to hear someone accept recognition in a fashion that is both gracious and articulate. Being well spoken does not mean that we are self-absorbed or glib. The thank you also needn't be long.

speech of acceptance
A speech expressing thanks for an award or honor.

A good speech of acceptance should serve four functions. First, it should either be brief or within the time constraints imposed by the situation, as is the case when we are one of several people being recognized. Second, it should be genuine and heartfelt. Audience members can typically tell by the speaker's nonverbal behavior whether expressions of gratitude are sincere. Third, it should reciprocate the recognition by praising the people or group who have singled us out. Fourth, it should engender liking. People like people who like them. It's well worth the effort to make audience members feel liked and attractive.

Speech of Introduction

A **speech of introduction** briefly sets the stage for an upcoming speaker. Speeches of introduction are designed to meet two objectives. The first is to enlist the audience's attention and interest. The second objective is to reinforce or induce audience perceptions of credibility. Perhaps the most unusual speech of introduction we have heard was in 1998 when James Carville and Mary Matalin, a married couple who represent the liberal and conservative ends of the political spectrum, debated each other at our university. They were supposed to be introduced by political consultant Ed Rollins. However, he was unable to attend. So Carville, in what appeared to be an impromptu speech, introduced his own wife and adversary for the evening, praising her as "my best friend, and the best wife any man could have."[5] His introduction set the stage for a spirited and entertaining debate between the oddest of couples in contemporary American politics.

speech of introduction
A speech that briefly sets the stage for an upcoming speaker.

Although we may never introduce our own opponent in a debate, it is likely that at some time we will be called on to introduce a speaker to an audience. Usually, the audience is favorably disposed toward the speaker or they wouldn't be there. However, sometimes a speaker is not well known and needs a buildup of credibility before the speech. In any case, a good way to look at a speech of introduction is to remember the three basic principles of introducing any speech: Open with impact, connect with the audience, and focus on the upcoming presentation.

Open With Impact

Our first task as an introducer is to build enthusiasm for the main speaker. A lukewarm or trite introduction is worse than none at all. Thus, look for a way to capture the audience's attention immediately. Sometimes humor, a brief anecdote, or a moving story will fill the bill.

Connect With the Audience

Why should the audience listen to the speaker? What's in it for them? Just as we must connect with the audience in our own speeches, the same is true in a speech of introduction. What special qualifications does the speaker have? Why is the topic of special concern to the audience? We need to answer these questions in terms the audience can relate to if we want them to be motivated to listen. Focus on the speaker's competence and character. Even if a speaker's credibility is established, we should reinforce the perception by mentioning one or two examples that clearly emphasize competence and character. If the speaker's credibility has yet to be established, mention at least one thing that addresses the speaker's competence on the topic and one that addresses the speaker's good character.

Focus on the Upcoming Presentation

Finally, it is the introducer's task to focus the audience's attention on the upcoming presentation. Make sure you know the speaker's topic, and coordinate your introduction with his or her speech. Nothing is worse than preparing an audience to hear a speech on one topic only to have the speaker announce that the topic has been changed. There are also some general guidelines that you should follow for a speech of introduction.

Tips and Tactics

Guidelines for a Speech of Introduction

- *Be brief.* The audience came to hear the speaker, not the introducer. A one- or two-minute introduction is sufficient for most speech situations. For a particularly lengthy or formal speech situation, the introduction might be longer, but in no case should it exceed about 10 percent of the speaker's time (six minutes out of an hour, for example).
- *Don't steal the speaker's thunder.* Although you want to prepare the audience for what is to come by focusing their attention on the topic, you should not discuss the substance of the speech topic. Again, the audience wants to hear the speaker's views on the topic, not yours. Your job is to create an appetite for the upcoming main course, not fill up the audience with hors d'oeuvres.
- *Be prepared: Work with the speaker in advance.* It is best to talk to the speaker or a representative about your role as introducer. Are there specific points to be stressed? Is there anything the speaker wants to avoid? Some speakers may even want to preview your introductory remarks or may provide written suggestions for you.

Speech of Recognition

The elements of a good speech of introduction also apply to speeches of recognition. A **speech of recognition** is a speech presenting an award or honor to an individual. In such speeches we need to open by discussing the importance of the occasion, the award being made, or the special contribution made by the honoree. We also need to provide examples or testimony from those who know the honoree to illustrate his or her merit. Also, we should consider couching our speech in the form of a story about the person.

speech of recognition
A speech presenting an award or honor to an individual.

Connecting with our audience is equally important. We can give them a personal glimpse, either from our own experience or from testimony of those who know the honoree. It is important for our audience to feel that the award is, in a sense, coming from them.

Unless the name of the honoree is known in advance, it should be saved until the end of the recognition speech. Not only will this build suspense, audience members will start to guess at the honoree with each new bit of information we provide. As we conclude, we focus on the honoree by name. Usually a recognition speech ends something like this, "And so it is my great pleasure to announce the winner of the lifetime achievement award, our own Taylor Smith!"

Speech of Commemoration

A **speech of commemoration** calls attention to the stature of the person or people being honored, or emphasizes the significance of an occasion. There are several kinds of commemorative speeches. Some of these speeches focus on cause for celebration: for example, a national holiday or a 50th wedding anniversary. Remember, it is the occasion or people who have given cause for celebration that should be the focus of the speech.

speech of commemoration
A speech that calls attention to the stature of the person or people being honored, or emphasizes the significance of an occasion.

eulogy
A kind of commemorative speech about someone who has died that is usually given shortly after his or her death.

Another type of speech of commemoration is one given to memorialize a specific person (Martin Luther King Jr.) or the people we associate with a special and solemn occasion (members of the armed forces on Memorial Day). Finally, a **eulogy** is a kind of commemorative speech about someone who has died that is usually given shortly after his or her death. For example, when Earl Spencer eulogized his sister, Diana, Princess of Wales, he spoke lovingly of her as "the very essence of compassion, of duty, of style, of beauty. All over the world she was a symbol of selfless humanity, a standard-bearer for the rights of the downtrodden, a very British girl who transcended nationality, someone with a natural nobility who was classless, who proved in the last year that she needed no royal title to continue to generate her particular brand of magic."[6]

In many ways, a speech of commemoration is like an extended recognition speech. With the obvious exception of a eulogy, the honoree may even be present and be asked to say a few words after the commemoration. Sometimes these speeches take a humorous form, such as a "roast." Although jokes and embarrassing incidents are recited, they are done in good fun and ultimately the honoree is praised for his or her accomplishments.

A speech of commemoration should, like any other speech, open with impact. Begin by calling attention to the stature of the person being honored or the occasion that necessitates the memorial.

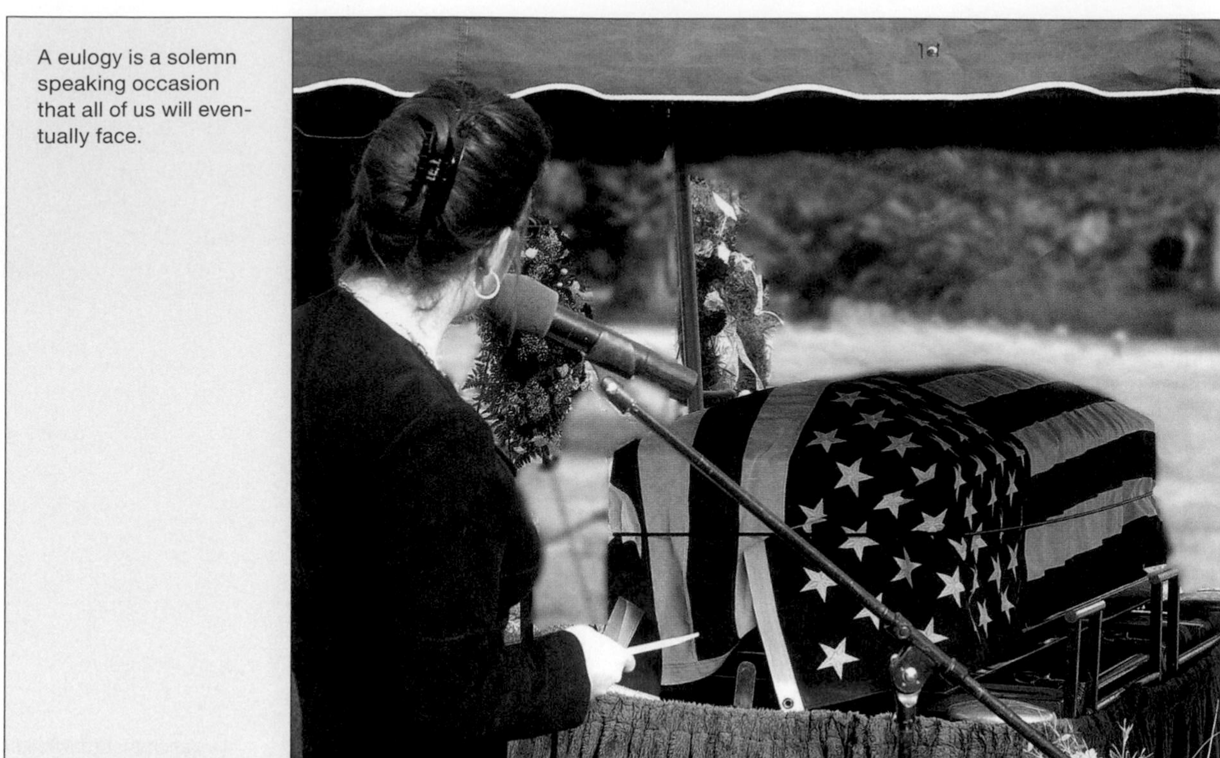

A eulogy is a solemn speaking occasion that all of us will eventually face.

As with any speech, it is important to connect with the audience. What ties the audience and the person, people, and occasion together? A eulogy often recounts the deceased's common ties to the audience. Family and friends are usually present, and recounting memorable events from the life of the deceased helps everyone cope with their loss.

For the honoree, focus on the best that person has accomplished. For a retiree, it might be his or her accomplishments in the workforce. For a public figure, it might be what he or she stood for. For a fallen hero, the deeds and cause that cost a life are a source of meaning.

The substance of a speech of commemoration is usually less structured than that of other speeches. Nevertheless, there should be a theme or an essential point that you want to share with the audience. For example, many extraordinary events that have taken place in recent history have been commemorated by people known only to those in their own community or by public figures known throughout the world. Examples range from commemorative speeches in honor of the soldiers who landed on the beaches of Normandy to begin the liberation of France from Nazi Germany to the victims of the horrific attacks on September 11, 2001. Themes in these speeches include honor and sacrifice, love of family, and living life to its fullest, to name but a few. Such themes have universal meaning and can serve to tie together even the most loosely organized narrative in a speech.

Finally, a speech of commemoration should close with impact, leaving a lasting impression. A verse of scripture might provide just the right note to close a eulogy. But so too could the right anecdote, if it illustrated something meaningful about the life of the deceased.

Speeches to Entertain[7]

Jon Stewart at the 2006 Academy Awards.

Sometimes known as after-dinner speaking because it's frequently given following a meal, a speech to entertain is more than just a string of jokes or a comedy monologue. A **speech to entertain** makes its point through the use of humor. Like all speeches, a speech to entertain should have a clear focus. Of course, many speeches contain humor as an element. What makes the speech to entertain different is that its primary purpose is to bring laughter to the audience, not to persuade or inform them, though that may occur along the way. A speech meant to entertain is ideally suited to the storytelling format of speaking. This type of speech is every bit as taxing as persuasive or informative speaking.

Selecting a Topic

speech to entertain
A speech that makes its point through the use of humor.

The first task is to select a topic. The best place to begin is with yourself. Have you had experiences that, at least looking back, were funny? A good topic needs to have the potential to develop into a full-blown speech, not just one or two good punch lines. It needs to be something your audience can relate to. Many of the funniest speeches are about the frustrations of everyday life. Avoid the temptation to adopt the latest routine from Chris Rock, Jon Stewart, or Stephen Colbert. Work from your own experiences and from experiences shared by those in your audience.

Consider your audience's expectations for the speech. You probably don't want to repeat stories you know your audience has heard before. If you are speaking to a group of lawyers, you probably can count on them having heard every lawyer joke known to humankind. Pick something that can connect you, assuming you are not a lawyer, to them. For example, there are few people today, including lawyers, who have not shared the frustrations of dealing with computers that seem to know just when to crash and make your life miserable.

You must, of course, be sensitive to an audience's diversity and state of mind in developing and delivering a speech to entertain. We live in an era in which a racial or ethnic joke that would have been accepted a few years ago can end a career or lead to the demise of a relationship. Remain mindful that what you say may find its way to an unintended audience too. Jokes of questionable taste about those not present may cause a minor firestorm, as Whoopi Goldberg has learned on more than one occasion.

In developing the content of your speech to entertain, brainstorming is a useful technique. Recall from Chapter 3 that brainstorming involves a group of people getting together and rapidly firing off ideas. Someone keeps a list. No criticism or evaluation of the ideas is permitted–that comes later. The key to brainstorming is to hitchhike one idea on another. The wilder and crazier the ideas, at this point, the better. You can always tone them down later.

Once you have a list of ideas, write each one on a card or slip of paper. The next step is to sort them out and organize them into a speech.

Organization

A speech to entertain should resemble any other good speech in organization: Open with impact, connect with your audience, and provide a clear thesis in your introduction. It is very important to capture your audience's attention almost immediately. Unless you are already a highly skilled and entertaining speaker, this is not the time for a three-minute story leading to one punch line. So, try to get a laugh in the first sentence or two. Sometimes just an outrageous statement will do this.

Russ Woody began his commencement speech by stating:

> Look . . . I write sitcoms for a living, so don't expect much. Which means . . . basically, I'm gonna tell a few jokes. Hit a few well-worn platitudes. And try to sell you a Dodge minivan.

Russ's helpful hints for writing humor are summarized in the box "Speaking of . . . Writing Humor?" on page 449.

Although it is important to focus the audience's attention on the topic of your speech, a preview of points is rare in a speech to entertain. Part of humor is surprise, and telegraphing your jokes in a preview will undermine the audience's surprise.

The body of the speech can be organized in a number of ways. A simple chronological or narrative form works well when telling a story or describing a series of events. A topical arrangement allows you to organize your speech around major topics.

In concluding a speech to entertain, you normally would not summarize your points. You would, however, want to close with impact or, as the old adage goes, "Leave 'em laughing."

Sources of Humor

What are some sources of humor? We hesitate to try to define what is funny. After all, everyone's sense of humor is different, and what is funny to one person will leave another completely stone-faced. Some people love Jon Stewart and hate Dennis Miller, others the reverse, and some people enjoy them both.

Nevertheless, a few traditional sources of humor deserve mention:

- *Exaggeration.* Exaggeration is a well-tested source of humor. Wits and comedians from Mark Twain to Will Ferrell have relied on exaggeration to make their point. Ferrell made his name playing an exaggerated version of then-presidential candidate George W. Bush, putting words such as "strategery" into the popular lexicon. No one who has seen it will ever forget his "more cowbell" skit on *Saturday Night Live.* He has gone on to play exaggerated characters, such as stock car racer Ricky Bobby, in a series of hit films.
- *Incongruity.* Something that doesn't fit in seems funny. Woody Allen once wore tennis shoes with a tuxedo (semiformal attire?). We frequently poke fun at politicians whose words and deeds don't match. When the state of California was sending out IOUs instead of checks, Jay Leno commented that the latest Southern California earthquake wasn't really an earthquake, just the governor bouncing more checks.

Speaking of . . .

Writing Humor? *by Russ Woody*

As a college student, Russ Woody excelled in an event called "Speech to Entertain." Not only was humor Russ's hobby, it became his profession. Russ began his writing career at MTM productions, where he wrote episodes for shows such as *Newhart, St. Elsewhere,* and *Hill Street Blues.* For two years he was a producer and writer for *Murphy Brown,* for which he received an Emmy in 1990. He received a Golden Globe as co-executive producer of *Cybill.* He has also served as a consulting producer for *Foxworthy* and was co-executive producer of *Becker.* We asked Russ to do the impossible: explain writing humor in 250 words or less. Here is the result.

Russ Woody

Writing Humor?

by Russ Woody

Two-hundred fifty words on how to write humor? Gee, can't I just whack myself in the forehead with a ball-peen hammer? Trying to explain humor is a little like trying to wrest a ripe banana from an immense and bitter gorilla. If not handled correctly, you can end up looking rather foolish.

With that in mind, "Hello, Mr. Gorilla . . ."

The fact of the matter is, humor is more difficult to write than drama. Because, while both humor and drama rely heavily on emotional content, humor is much more difficult to break down mechanically. Therefore it's more difficult to construct initially. It's relatively easy to figure out what makes a person sad or angry or uneasy or embarrassed or happy. Yet it is, for the most part, difficult to say why a person laughs.

So I guess the first thing you've got to do is figure out what type of humor appeals most to you. Monty Python, Andrew "Dice" Clay, The Naked Gun, Murphy Brown, Full House, Spy Magazine, Mad Magazine, Saturday Night Live. *Whichever it is, find it. Then—study it. Watch it, read it, take it apart, figure out how it's constructed, how it's set up, how it pays off—figure out the dynamics of humor. (Which will make it terribly unfunny when you do, but that's the perpetual hell comedy writers live in.)*

For instance—one of my favorite jokes of all time is in one of the Pink Panther *movies where Peter Sellers goes into a hotel and approaches a man at the desk who has a dog sitting beside him. Sellers says, "Does your dog bite?" The guy says no. So Sellers reaches over to pat the little pooch, and it tries to rip his arm off. Sellers then looks to the guy and says, "I thought you said your dog didn't bite?" The guy says, "It's not my dog."*

I love that joke because every element of it is real, and nobody involved thinks it's funny. The man was quite correct in his literal interpretation of Sellers's question. Sellers is more than a little annoyed at the man for misunderstanding what seemed to be a logical and straightforward question. And the dog is just pissed off. In a more general sense, one person becomes a victim because the other is a stickler for precise wording. It is extreme focus on one character's part and vulnerability on the other character's part. In a way, it's like the movie The In-Laws, *with Peter Falk and Alan Arkin. Falk is intensely focused on his job with the government, which, in turn makes Arkin's life a living hell. (If you've seen the movie, you know what I'm talking about—if you haven't, go see it, because I'm coming up on two-fifty pretty fast here, so I can't get into it.)*

When you've taken enough jokes and stories apart, you may start to get an idea of how to construct your own. That's when it gets really tough. Just be sure you always remember the one, underlying key to writing humor—oops, outta time.

- *Attacking authority*. The attack on authority has been a staple of humor since anyone can remember. Will Rogers made fun of Congress, Jay Leno makes fun of politicians, and Chris Rock makes fun of everybody, himself included!
- *Puns*. Use at your own risk!
- *Sarcasm*. Used with care, sarcasm can be a good source of humor (particularly when directed against sources of authority). But be careful you don't create sympathy for your victim. Sarcasm that is too edgy or biting can seem mean-spirited and bitter rather than funny. David Spade gets away with sarcasm because we know he is trying to be funny rather than deliberately hurtful.
- *Irony*. Sometimes a powerful source of humor, irony can also make a serious point. The fact that Microsoft founder and billionaire Bill Gates had his presentation of Windows 98 marred by a computer failure was a source of material for late-night comedians for several days.
- *The rule of three*. Milton Berle once claimed that he could make an audience laugh at anything if he preceded it with two funny jokes. Try it. Once you have people laughing, they often will continue to laugh even at a line that isn't funny.
- *Self-deprecating humor*. Often the safest humor is that directed at yourself. Not only do you avoid alienating anyone, you show that you are a regular person. When Hall-of-Fame quarterback Terry Bradshaw spoke at a "speechathon" along with such luminaries as former President Gerald Ford, former Congressman Jack Kemp, and former Senator Bill Bradley, he wondered out loud why he was there. Gazing out at an audience of prominent business leaders, he admitted, "I made my living, unlike you, by putting my hands under another man's butt."[8]
- *Delivery*. Humor depends on direct contact and immediacy with your audience. Thus, use of a manuscript or conspicuous notes will destroy the spontaneity of the experience. Even if you have memorized your speech, however, it is important that it sound fresh and spontaneous.

  Use a lively and animated manner in presenting your speech. Timing in comedy is everything. Knowing when to pause, what word to punch, and the right tone of voice to use are not things you can learn from reading a book. Only by trying out your speech with friends and experimenting with different ways of delivering the same line can you tell what delivery is best.

Not everyone is comfortable with speaking to entertain. But done well and tastefully, it can be an enjoyable experience for both the speaker and the audience.

Speaking on Television

At one time, appearing on TV was a rare event, reserved for newsmakers and icons in the popular culture. Today, appearing on TV is not just common; many people are required to appear on TV as a result of their job or their role in their

Speaking on television is becoming an important skill.

community. More than a few also aspire to be on TV, even if it means showing themselves in potentially embarrassing situations.

We think you should expect to be on TV at some point and prepare for the eventuality. If you become a business executive or a public servant, for example, the chances are good you will be interviewed on TV and peppered with questions not always friendly. Thus, you should be prepared to speak extemporaneously using the guidelines we have suggested in several chapters of this book. You want to appear organized, come across as firm rather than indecisive, and use powerful language. Speaking on TV also demands nonverbal immediacy behaviors, so you'll want to look back at Chapter 12 for a discussion of effective delivery tips.

One question that always arises when being interviewed on television is where to look. Do you look at the camera or at the interviewer or from one to the other? One suggestion comes from Dorothy Sarnoff, who provides communication training to corporate executives. She suggests: "Focus on the left eye of the interviewer, then the right eye—and back to the left. Not a windshield-wiper effect, but slowly so your own eyes don't look dead."[9] Some other suggestions for talking on television are included in the box "Speaking of . . . Chatting It Up on TV" on page 452.

In conclusion, the best advice we can give is to be prepared and stick to your theme. Interviews are frequently videotaped and then edited for a sound bite. You want to make sure that regardless of what is left on the cutting-room floor your essential message reaches the viewers.

Speaking of . . .

Chatting It Up on TV *by Paul Burnham Finney*

Many executives turn into TV regulars and routinely go out on cross-country tours to promote a new product or service. But few of the veterans take their camera assignments casually.

"Steal the show," says Mariana Field Hoppin, president of MFH Travel Marketing Ltd. and a longtime spokeswoman for Avis Europe. "When you walk into the studio, win over the camera crew and interviewer, and you've got them in the palm of your hands."

It's important to do that. "The public is taking the lazy way out—getting their information on the tube," as one corporate communications director puts it.

"Smart executives have to be prepared for surprises on the road," he goes on to say. When the Tylenol-tampering scare struck Johnson & Johnson, C.E.O. James E. Burke signed up for a crash course at the Executive Television Workshop [ETW] before facing the public.

Screen test: Among the tips ETW feeds its corporate students:

- Get a good fix on the questions you'll be asked by contacting the TV or radio station. (Ask around if the direct approach doesn't work.)
- Tell your story, or somebody else will—and not always correctly.
- Memorize the basic points you want to make, and keep them uppermost in your mind.
- Stick to solid colors in dress—no loud patterns allowed. And wear contacts rather than glasses, if possible.
- Women: don't show up in a short skirt that rides above the knees.
- Park yourself in the front third of the chair. You'll look more alert and interested that way.
- Glance at 3-by-5 card notes during commercials or station breaks—never when on camera.
- Say it all in 45 seconds when answering an interviewer. "Short, clear answers," as TV commentator David Brinkley advises.
- Use anecdotes and "sparklers" to brighten your delivery.
- Don't repeat a negative statement—it only lends credence to it.

Digestible bits: "We stress the importance of establishing a conversational tone," says Executive Television Workshop marketing director Carol Heimann. "Executives get very techy in the way they talk. A reporter is only a conduit to the public. Break your explanations into digestible bits. Try to act as though you're in a living room, chatting with someone."

Ultimately, the impression you leave with your audience counts more than your words. Some 90% of what they remember is your "voice" and "nonverbal communications," according to studies. In short, body language matters as much as your thoughts.

"One of your biggest assets," says Heimann, "is a smile. It can change a million opinions. You can disarm your audience. If you're relaxed, you'll relax the people who are watching."

Source: Article appeared first in *Newsweek*'s 1990 Special Ad Section, "Management Digest." Reprinted by permission.

A Parting Thought

Not long ago, we attended an event where distinguished alumni spoke to undergraduates at a career forum. They represented a wide spectrum of positions in business, civil service, education, engineering, entertainment, and science. Although we expected the few who had graduated with degrees in communication to talk about the role of public speaking in their success, we were most gratified by the fact that so many others echoed what they had to say. They were unanimous in letting students know that whatever their plans following graduation, they shouldn't pass on the opportunity to take a class in public speaking.

These alumni reinforced something we have learned from our experience. Sooner or later, successful college graduates move beyond the narrow confines of the professional path for which they were initially trained. The salesperson becomes the sales manager; the computer engineer becomes the CEO; the TV writer becomes an officer in the writers' guild; and the ecologist becomes a lobbyist. Chief among the responsibilities that both precede and follow such turning points is skill in the art and science of public speaking.

Summary

To evaluate your understanding of this chapter, visit our Online Learning Center Web site for quizzes and other chapter study aids.

Approach most special speaking occasions as storytelling. Good stories are:

- Organized
- Probable
- Have fidelity and ring true for the audience

Types of speeches that can benefit from storytelling include:

- Speeches of acceptance
- Speeches of introduction
- Speeches of recognition
- Speeches of commemoration, such as eulogies
- Speeches to entertain an audience

Advice for TV interviews includes:

- Be well prepared
- Look at the interviewer, not the camera
- Dress appropriately
- Keep answers brief
- Use anecdotes and sparklers
- Appear relaxed

Check Your Understanding: Exercises and Activities

1. Your best friend is getting married, and you will be asked to say a few words at the wedding. Prepare your toast. Do the same thing for a wedding anniversary, a baptism, and a bar or bat mitzvah.
2. Think of a special award for one of your classmates. Write a speech of recognition for presenting the award.

3. Track down several quotations and anecdotes that are general enough to be used as an opening or a closing for a speech of acceptance or a speech of recognition. Three sources to which you can turn are:

   Clifton Fadiman, ed., *The Little Brown Book of Anecdotes* (Boston: Little, Brown, 1985).

   Edmund Fuller, ed., 2,500 *Anecdotes for All Occasions* (New York: Avenel Books, 1980).

   James B. Simpson, ed., *Simpson's Contemporary Quotations: The Most Notable Quotes Since 1950* (Boston: Houghton Mifflin, 1988).

4. A speech of nomination can either make or break the nominee's chances for being elected to office. Speeches of nomination are more common than you may think. Social clubs such as fraternities and sororities, business and professional associations such as the Soroptimists, Rotary, or local Bar are all examples. On a separate sheet of paper, list and explain what you think are the essential characteristics of a speech of nomination. Then see if you can find a published example of a speech of nomination that conforms to your criteria. Note conforming examples on a copy of the speech with a highlighter and share your analysis with classmates.

Notes

1. Edmund Fuller, ed., *2,500 Anecdotes for All Occasions* (New York: Avenel Books, 1980), 135.
2. Theodore H. White, *The Making of the President 1968* (New York: Atheneum, 1969), 171. Shaw's original lines appear in his play *Back to Methuselah,* Part I, Act I. The Serpent in the Garden of Eden says to Eve, "You see things; and you say 'Why?' But I dream things that never were; and I say 'Why not?'" See George Bernard Shaw, *The Complete Plays of Bernard Shaw* (London: Odhams Press Limited, 1934), 857.
3. Walter R. Fisher, *Human Communication as Narration* (Columbia: University of South Carolina Press, 1987).
4. M. C. Green, J. J. Strange, and T. C. Brock, *Narrative Impact: Social and Cognitive Foundations* (Mahwah, NJ: Lawrence Erlbaum Associates, 2002).
5. Kevin Jeys, "Irreconcilable Differences," *Chico News and Review,* 8 October 1998, 29.
6. "I Stand Before You . . . ," *Newsweek,* 15 September 1997, 24.
7. Adapted from Jack Perella and Steven R. Brydon, "Speaking to Entertain," in *Intercollegiate Forensics: A Participant's Handbook,* ed. T. C. Winebrenner, 42–46. © 1992 Northern California Forensics Association.
8. Sam Stanton, "Clinton Remains Topic A at Cal Expo Speechathon," *Sacramento Bee,* 10 October 1998, A23.
9. Article appeared first in *Newsweek's* 1990 Special Ad Section, "Management Digest," Paul Burnham Finney, "The Business of Communicating," 16.

Appendix A

Guide to Source Citations

AMERICAN PSYCHOLOGICAL ASSOCIATION (APA) STYLE

For more information on citing sources in APA or MLA style, go to the Online Learning Center.

The following information is based on the *Publication Manual of the American Psychological Association,* Fifth Edition, 2001, and on their Web site, www.apastyle.org. Please note that there are several changes in APA style from the fourth edition. Hanging indents (not tabs) are to be used in the references list, titles should be *italicized* rather than underlined, and the citation of online sources has changed. It is important that you fully document the sources of information you use in preparing a speech outline. Cite the source in parentheses in the actual body of the outline by name and date. Include page numbers for quotations or specific facts, for example, (Jones, 2005, p. 1).

Include a list of "References" at the end of your outline. Always include the author, date, title, and facts of publication. Personal communications, such as letters, phone calls, e-mail, and interviews, are cited only in the text, not the reference list; for example, J. Q. Jones (personal communication, April 1, 2005). The format varies depending on the type of work referenced.

Here are some of the most common types of works you may use in a speech. Notice that APA style does not place quotation marks around the titles of articles or book chapters. Also, titles of books and articles are not capitalized, except for the first word, the first word following a colon, and proper names. Periodical titles are capitalized. Authors are listed by last name first, followed by first and sometimes middle initials.

Books

Single Author

Freeley, A. J. (1990). *Argumentation and debate: Critical thinking for reasoned decision making* (7th ed.). Belmont, CA: Wadsworth.

Multiple Authors

Germond, J. W., & Witcover, J. (1989). *Whose broad stripes and bright stars?* New York: Warner Books.

Corporate Author

American Psychological Association. (2001). *Publication manual of the American Psychological Association* (5th ed.). Washington, DC: Author.

Government Document

Department of Health and Human Services. (1989). *Smoking tobacco and health: A fact book.* (DHHS Publication No. CDC 87-8397). Washington, DC: U.S. Government Printing Office.

Chapter in a Book

Steeper, F. T. (1978). Public response to Gerald Ford's statements on Eastern Europe in the second debate. In G. F. Bishop, R. G. Meadow, & M. Jackson-Beeck (Eds.), *The presidential debates: Media, electoral, and policy perspectives* (pp. 81–101). New York: Praeger.

Periodicals

Weekly Magazine

Alter, J. (1988, September 26). The expectations game. *Newsweek, 112,* 16–18.

If the author is unknown, you would list the article as follows:

The expectations game. (1988, September 26). *Newsweek, 112,* 16–18.

Scholarly Journal Divided by Volume Numbers

Vancil, D. L., & Pendell, S. D. (1984). Winning presidential debates: An analysis of criteria influencing audience response. *Western Journal of Speech Communication, 48,* 63–74.

[This means the article was published in 1984, in volume 48, on pages 63–74.]

Newspaper

Rosentiel, T. H. (1988, October 14). Minus a Dukakis home run, Bush is called winner. *Los Angeles Times,* p. A25.

If the author is unknown, you would list the article as follows:

Minus a Dukakis home run, Bush is called winner. (1988, October 14). *Los Angeles Times,* p. A25.

Pamphlet (published by author)

American Diabetes Association. (1987). *Diabetes and you.* Alexandria, VA: Author.

Internet

As computer sources multiply, the citation format has been evolving. APA guidelines ask that you include the type of medium, the necessary electronic information to permit retrieval, and then the date you accessed the information. You should consult the APA Web site at www.apastyle.org for the most recent information on how to cite Internet resources. Here are examples based on the fifth edition of the APA *Publication Manual.*

Internet Articles Based on a Print Source Taken From a Library Subscription Database

Many databases provide assistance in how to cite sources. For example, if you click on the *help* link in the upper right corner of an EBSCOhost database citation, it will take you to a menu that includes a link to *styles of citation.* EBSCOhost provides examples for APA as well as numerous other citation styles.

Freeman, T., Sawyer, C. R., & Behnke, R. R. (1997). Behavioral inhibition and attribution of public speaking state anxiety. *Communication Education, 46,* 175–187. Retrieved September 3, 2004, from EBSCOhost Communication and Mass Media Complete database.

Article in an Internet-Only Journal

The date of retrieval and the URL are required in addition to normal publication information. Because a period can be confused with the dot (.) of a URL, there is no period at the end of the URL.

Guzley, R., Avanzino, S., and Bor, A. (2001, April). Simulated computer-mediated/video-interactive distance learning: A test of motivation, interaction satisfaction, delivery, learning & perceived effectiveness. *Journal of Commuter Mediated Communication, 6.* Retrieved September 3, 2004, from http://www.ascusc.org/jcmc/vol6/issue3/guzley.html

Internet Document, No Author Identified

Begin with the title of the article, followed by the date of last update and retrieval statement. You can find the date of many Web pages, even if they are not listed on the page itself, by going to the *File* menu and selecting *Properties* in Internet Explorer (PC version) or going to the *View* menu and selecting *Page info* in Netscape.

Overcoming stagefright. (2004, June 10). Retrieved September 3, 2004, from http://www.anxietycoach.com/social1.htm

If no date is available, use (n.d.) in place of the date. The date of retrieval is still required.

Overcoming stagefright. (n.d.). Retrieved September 3, 2004, from http://www.anxietycoach.com/social1.htm

All references are listed in alphabetical order by authors' last names, regardless of type, at the end of the speech outline. Works listed by title, where the author is not known, are placed alphabetically by title. For an example of a reference list using APA style, see the outline in Chapter 10 on pages 254–255.

MODERN LANGUAGE ASSOCIATION (MLA) STYLE

This section is based on Joseph Gibaldi, T*he MLA Handbook for Writers of Research Papers,* Sixth Edition, 2003. Also consult their Web site at www.mla.org/style_faq4. Although there are numerous similarities between APA and MLA style, there are also many differences. You may cite sources in parentheses in the actual body of the outline, as you do with APA, but you use only the author's name and the page number, not the date, for example, (Jones 1). Notice that in MLA style you do not separate the name and the page number by a comma, nor do you use the letter "p." MLA also allows you to incorporate the name of the author in your text and cite only the pages in parentheses. For example, John Jones tells us that "secondhand smoke is deadly" (1). Notice that the ending punctuation comes after the page number in this example.

Include a list of "Works Cited" at the end of your outline. Always include the author, title, facts of publication, and date. Personal communications are included in the Works Cited list, unlike in APA style. For example, an interview would be cited as follows: Jones, John Q. Personal interview. 1 Apr. 1992.

Here are some of the most common types of works you may use in a speech. Notice that MLA style does place quotation marks around the titles of articles or book chapters. Titles of books and periodicals may be underlined or *italicized,* although many instructors prefer underlining because it is easier to read. We have used underlining in the examples that follow. Also, titles of books, articles, and periodicals are capitalized. Authors are listed by last name first, followed by full first names and sometimes middle initials. Finally, the date comes at or near the end of the citation, not right after the author's name, as in APA style.

Books

Single Author

Freeley, Austin J. Argumentation and Debate: Critical Thinking for Reasoned Decision Making, 7th ed. Belmont, CA: Wadsworth, 1990.

Multiple Authors

Germond, Jack W., and Jules Witcover. Whose Broad Stripes and Bright Stars? New York: Warner Books, 1989.

Corporate Author

American Psychological Association. Publication Manual of the American Psychological Association, 5th ed. Washington, DC: American Psychological Association, 2001.

Government Document

United States. Dept. of Health and Human Services. Smoking Tobacco and Health: A Fact Book. Washington: GPO, 1989.

Chapter in a Book

Steeper, Frederick T. "Public Response to Gerald Ford's Statements on Eastern Europe in the Second Debate." The Presidential Debates: Media, Electoral, and Policy Perspectives. Eds. George F. Bishop, Robert G. Meadow, and Marilyn Jackson-Beeck. New York: Praeger, 1978. 81–101.

Periodicals

Weekly Magazine

Alter, Jonathan. "The Expectations Game." Newsweek 26 Sep. 1988: 16–18.

If the author is unknown, you would list the article as follows:

"The Expectations Game." Newsweek 26 Sept. 1988: 16–18.

Scholarly Journal Divided by Volume Numbers

Vancil, David L., and Susan D. Pendell. "Winning Presidential Debates: An Analysis of Criteria Influencing Audience Response." Western Journal of Speech Communication 48 (1984): 63–74.

[This means the article was published in 1984, in volume 48, on pages 63–74.]

Newspaper

Rosentiel, Tom H. "Minus a Dukakis Home Run, Bush Is Called Winner." Los Angeles Times 14 Oct. 1988: A25.

If the author is unknown, you would list the article as follows:

"Minus a Dukakis Home Run, Bush Is Called Winner." Los Angeles Times 14 Oct. 1988: A25.

Pamphlet (published by author)

American Diabetes Association. Diabetes and You. Alexandria, VA: ADA, 1987.

Internet

MLA has numerous differences from APA in citing Internet-based sources. Rather than a retrieval statement, the date of access is listed followed by the URL in angle brackets, for example: September 3, 2004 <http://www.urlname.com>. A period is placed after the last angle bracket, thus it cannot be confused with a dot (.) in a URL. The reader must infer that the date preceding the URL is the date of access. MLA requires that for printed documents, such as speech outlines, you turn off the autoformatting feature of your word processor. URLs are not underlined, they are enclosed in angle brackets. Here are some examples.

Internet Articles Based on a Print Source From a Library Subscription Database

Many databases provide assistance in how to cite sources. For example, if you click on the *help* link in the upper right corner of an EBSCOhost database citation, it will take you to a menu that includes a link to *styles of citation*. EBSCOhost provides examples for MLA as well as numerous other citation styles. In MLA both the name of the database (underlined) and the name of the subscribing library are required. Also, for the URL, if your database provides a persistent link to the article, use that as the URL. Otherwise use the URL of the service, such as <http://search.epnet.com>. In this example a persistent link is provided because it makes it easier for readers to find the article.

Freeman, Terri, Chris R. Sawyer, and Ralph R. Behnke. "Behavioral Inhibition and Attribution of Public Speaking State Anxiety." Communication Education, 46(1997), 175–187. Mass Media Complete. EBSCOhost. Meriam Library, California State University, Chico, CA. 3 Sep. 2004 <http://search.epnet.com/direct.asp?AuthType=cookie,ip,url,uid&db=ufh&an=9708011184>.

Article in an Internet-Only Journal

Ruth Guzley, Susan Avanzino, and Aaron Bor. "Simulated Computer-Mediated/Video-Interactive Distance Learning: A Test of Motivation, Interaction Satisfaction, Delivery, Learning & Perceived Effectiveness." Journal of Commuter Mediated Communication, 6 (2001, April). 3 Sep. 2004 <http://www.ascusc.org/jcmc/vol6/issue3/guzley.html>.

Internet Document, No Author Identified

Begin with the title of the article or the Web site, followed by the date the Web site was last updated. You can find the date of many Web pages, even if they are not listed on the page itself, by going to the *File* menu and selecting *Properties* in Internet Explorer (PC version) or going to the *View* menu and selecting *Page info* in Netscape. If there is a known date for the site, that date is listed first. If no date is known, then only the date of access is listed.

Overcoming Stagefright. 10 June 2004. 3 Sep. 2004 <http://www.anxietycoach.com/social1.htm>.

If there is no date for the article, only the date of retrieval is required.

Overcoming Stagefright. n. d. Sep. 2004 <http://www.anxietycoach.com/social1.htm>.

As with APA, a complete list of sources—called "Works Cited"—in alphabetical order by author (if none, use title) should follow the text. If more than one work by the same author is included, replace the author's name with three hyphens (---) in all listings after the first.

Appendix B
Public Speeches

REMARKS BEFORE THE 1992 REPUBLICAN NATIONAL CONVENTION,
by Mary Fisher[1]

This speech was delivered by Mary Fisher at the 1992 Republican National Convention in Houston, Texas, on Wednesday, August 19. As founder of the Family AIDS Network and a person who is HIV-positive, Fisher addressed a convention that was largely socially conservative about issues such as AIDS. As you read this speech, attempt to answer these questions:

- How well did Mary Fisher adapt to the situation she faced as a speaker at the Republican National Convention?
- To what audience or audiences was this speech addressed?
- What do you see as Fisher's purpose or purposes in presenting this speech?
- How do you feel about the issue of AIDS after reading this speech? Have you changed your beliefs, attitudes, values, or behaviors?

Thank you. Thank you.

Less than three months ago at Platform Hearings in Salt Lake City, I asked the Republican Party to lift the shroud of silence which has been draped over the issue of HIV and AIDS. I have come tonight to bring our silence to an end. I bear a message of challenge, not self-congratulation. I want your attention, not your applause.

I would never have asked to be HIV-positive, but I believe that in all things there is a purpose; and I stand before you and before this nation gladly. The reality of AIDS is brutally clear. Two hundred thousand Americans are dead or dying. A million more are infected. Worldwide, 40 million, 60 million, or 100 million infections will be counted in the coming few years. But despite science and research, White House meetings, and congressional hearings; despite good intentions and bold initiatives, campaign slogans, and hopeful promises, it is–despite it all–the epidemic which is winning tonight.

In the context of an election year, I ask you, here in this great hall, or listening in the quiet of your home, to recognize that the AIDS virus is not a political creature. It does not care whether you are Democratic or Republican; it does not ask whether you are black or white, male or female, gay or straight, young or

[1]This text is from the Official Report of the proceedings of the Thirty-Fifth Republican National Convention, published by the Republican National Committee.

old. Tonight, I represent an AIDS community whose members have been reluctantly drafted from every segment of American society.

Though I am white and a mother, I am one with a black infant struggling with tubes in a Philadelphia hospital.

Though I am female and contracted this disease in marriage and enjoy the warm support of my family, I am one with the lonely gay man sheltering a flickering candle from the cold wind of his family's rejection.

This is not a distant threat. It is a present danger. The rate of infection is increasing fastest among women and children. Largely unknown a decade ago, AIDS is the third leading killer of young adult Americans today. But it won't be third for long, because unlike other diseases, this one travels. Adolescents don't give each other cancer or heart disease because they believe they are in love, but HIV is different; and we have helped it along. We have killed each other with our ignorance, our prejudice, and our silence.

We may take refuge in our stereotypes, but we cannot hide there long, because HIV asks only one thing of those it attacks. Are you human? And this is the right question. Are you human? Because people with HIV have not entered some alien state of being. They are human. They have not earned cruelty, and they do not deserve meanness. They don't benefit from being isolated or treated as outcasts. Each of them is exactly what God made–a person, not evil, deserving of our judgment; not victims, longing for our pity–people, ready for support and worthy of compassion. (Applause.)

My call to you, my Party, is to take a public stand, no less compassionate than that of the President and Mrs. Bush. They have embraced me and my family in memorable ways. In the place of judgment, they have shown affection. In difficult moments, they have raised our spirits. In the darkest hours, I have seen them reaching out not only to me, but also to my parents, armed with that stunning grief and special grace that comes only to parents who have themselves leaned too long over the bedside of a dying child.

With the president's leadership, much good has been done. Much of the good has gone unheralded, and as the president has insisted, much remains to be done. But we do the president's cause no good if we praise the American family but ignore a virus that destroys it. (Applause.)

We must be consistent if we are to be believed. We cannot love justice and ignore prejudice, love our children and fear to teach them. Whatever our role as parent or policymaker, we must act as eloquently as we speak–else we have no integrity.

My call to the nation is a plea for awareness. If you believe you are safe, you are in danger. Because I was not hemophiliac, I was not at risk. Because I was not gay, I was not at risk. Because I did not inject drugs, I was not at risk.

My father has devoted much of his lifetime to guarding against another holocaust. He is part of the generation who heard Pastor Nemoeller come out of the Nazi death camps to say, "They came after the Jews and I was not a Jew, so, I did not protest. They came after the trade unionists, and I was not a trade unionist, so, I did not protest. Then they came after the Roman Catholics, and I was not a Roman Catholic, so, I did not protest. Then they came after me, and there was no one left to protest." (Applause.)

The lesson history teaches is this: If you believe you are safe, you are at risk. If you do not see this killer stalking your children, look again. There is no family or community, no race or religion, no place left in America that is safe. Until we genuinely embrace this message, we are a nation at risk. Tonight, HIV marches resolutely to AIDS in more than a million American homes. Littering its pathway with the bodies of the young men, young women, young parents, and young children. One of those families is mine. If it is true that HIV inevitably turns to AIDS, then my children will inevitably turn to orphans.

My family has been a rock of support. My 84-year-old father, who has pursued the healing of nations, will not accept the premise that he cannot heal his daughter. My mother refuses to be broken. She still calls at midnight to tell wonderful jokes that make me laugh. Sisters and friends, and my brother Phillip, whose birthday is today, all have helped carry me over the hardest places. I am blessed, richly and deeply blessed, to have such a family. (Applause.)

But not all of you have been so blessed. You are HIV-positive, but dare not say it. You have lost loved ones, but you dare not whisper the word AIDS–you weep silently. You grieve alone. I have a message for you. It is not you who should feel shame. It is we, we who tolerate ignorance and practice prejudice, we who have taught you to fear. We must lift our shroud of silence, making it safe for you to reach out for compassion. It is our task to seek safety for our children, not in quiet denial but in effective action.

Some day our children will be grown. My son Max, now 4, will take the measure of his mother; my son Zachary, now 2, will sort through his memories. I may not be here to hear their judgments, but I know already what I hope they are. I want my children to know that their mother was not a victim. She was a messenger. I do not want them to think, as I once did, that courage is the absence of fear. I want them to know that courage is the strength to act wisely when we are most afraid. I want them to have the courage to step forward when called by their nation or their party and give leadership, no matter what the personal cost. I ask no more of you than I ask of myself or my children. To the millions of you who are grieving, who are frightened, who have suffered the ravages of AIDS firsthand–have courage and you will find support. To the millions who are strong, I issue the plea–set aside prejudice and politics to make room for compassion and sound policy. (Applause.)

To my children, I make this pledge: "I will not give in, Zachary, because I draw my courage from you. Your silly giggle gives me hope; your gentle prayers give me strength; and you, my child, give me reason to say to America, 'You are at risk.' And I will not rest, Max, until I have done all I can to make your world safe. I will seek a place where intimacy is not the prelude to suffering. I will not hurry to leave you, my children, but when I go, I pray that you will not suffer shame on my account." To all within the sound of my voice, I appeal: "Learn with me the lessons of history and of grace, so my children will not be afraid to say the word AIDS when I am gone. Then, their children and yours may not need to whisper it at all." God bless the children, God bless us all, and good night.

REMARKS BEFORE THE 1996 DEMOCRATIC NATIONAL CONVENTION,

by Carolyn McCarthy[2]

This speech was delivered by Carolyn McCarthy at the 1996 Democratic National Convention in Chicago. As the wife and mother of two victims of the Long Island train massacre, McCarthy had become a spokesperson for the

[2]Reprinted by permission of the author.

victims of that crime and other violent crimes. When rebuffed by her Republican congressman, she registered as a Democrat and ran against him, defeating him and becoming a member of Congress herself. As you read this speech, ask yourself:

- How well did Carolyn McCarthy adapt to the situation she faced as a speaker at the Democratic National Convention?
- To what audience or audiences was this speech addressed?
- What do you see as McCarthy's purpose or purposes in presenting this speech?
- How do you feel about the issue of gun control after reading this speech? Have you changed your beliefs, attitudes, values, or behaviors?

December 7th, 1993–that was the day of the Long Island Railroad massacre. My life and the lives of many others changed forever. A man with a semiautomatic weapon boarded the train that my husband and my son took to work every day. He killed 6 people and wounded 19. My husband, Dennis, was one of those killed. My son, Kevin, was left partially paralyzed. Kevin has had a courageous recovery. He's back at work. But he still spends many hours a day with rehabilitation. It's every mother's dream to be able to stand up on national TV and say she's proud of her son. Kevin, I'm very proud of you.

On that day I started a journey, a journey against gun violence in this nation. Today I am here as a nurse, as a mother, as a person who isn't afraid to speak up on what is going on in this country.

Gun violence adds millions of dollars in hospital costs every year, and threatens families with a mountain of bills, and so much pain. Until our government listens to ordinary people speaking out against gun violence instead of listening to special interest groups like the NRA leadership, we are not going to have safety in our streets!

I was not planning on speaking here tonight, but this is where my journey has taken me–to the Democratic Party, the party that believes in including ordinary citizens. That's why I'm here. I am here as a woman with common sense and determination, and I am going to make a difference.

I will fight to keep the assault weapons ban the law of the land. I–Yeah, I will. I will work for the day when President Clinton's Victims Rights Amendment is in the Constitution. And those of us who are concerned about gun violence will not tolerate being ignored, as I was by my congressman, who voted to repeal the assault weapons bill.

We have all been ignored by the Gingrich congress. They have not listened to us on education, on the environment, or on making our streets safe. We will not be ignored. We will make them listen.

The journey I began in 1993 wasn't one that I had planned. Getting involved in politics wasn't anything I ever wanted to do. But this journey will make a difference when our neighborhoods pull together, when government listens to us again. When all of us, Democrats and Republicans, come together to solve our problems, not just fight about them. We have a responsibility to our children to speak up about what we know is right and to do what is right. I ask you to join me and my son, Kevin, on that journey. Thank you so very much.

ADDRESS TO THE NATION, JANUARY 10, 2007

by President George W. Bush[3]

On January 10, 2007, President George W. Bush addressed the nation from the Library in the White House to announce his plans for a new strategy in Iraq. Specifically, he acknowledged that the current strategy was not working and proposed to increase the level of American troops by over 20,000 to quell the violence then plaguing Iraq. As you read this speech, consider the following:

- Does President Bush make a convincing case for his plan for Iraq?
- Does the president deal effectively with arguments from those who oppose his plan?
- How effectively does the president use language in the speech?
- How effectively does the president use evidence in the speech?
- How effectively does the president appeal to emotions in the speech?
- What pattern of organization does the speech appear to follow?

THE PRESIDENT: Good evening. Tonight in Iraq, the Armed Forces of the United States are engaged in a struggle that will determine the direction of the global war on terror–and our safety here at home. The new strategy I outline tonight will change America's course in Iraq, and help us succeed in the fight against terror.

When I addressed you just over a year ago, nearly 12 million Iraqis had cast their ballots for a unified and democratic nation. The elections of 2005 were a stunning achievement. We thought that these elections would bring the Iraqis together, and that as we trained Iraqi security forces we could accomplish our mission with fewer American troops.

But in 2006, the opposite happened. The violence in Iraq–particularly in Baghdad–overwhelmed the political gains the Iraqis had made. Al Qaeda terrorists and Sunni insurgents recognized the mortal danger that Iraq's elections posed for their cause, and they responded with outrageous acts of murder aimed at innocent Iraqis. They blew up one of the holiest shrines in Shia Islam–the Golden Mosque of Samarra–in a calculated effort to provoke Iraq's Shia population to retaliate. Their strategy worked. Radical Shia elements, some supported by Iran, formed death squads. And the result was a vicious cycle of sectarian violence that continues today.

The situation in Iraq is unacceptable to the American people–and it is unacceptable to me. Our troops in Iraq have fought bravely. They have done everything we have asked them to do. Where mistakes have been made, the responsibility rests with me.

It is clear that we need to change our strategy in Iraq. So my national security team, military commanders, and diplomats conducted a comprehensive review. We consulted members of Congress from both parties, our allies abroad, and distinguished outside experts. We benefitted from the thoughtful recommendations of the Iraq Study Group, a bipartisan panel led by former Secretary of State James Baker and former Congressman Lee Hamilton. In our discussions, we all agreed that there is no magic formula for success in Iraq. And one

[3]George W. Bush, "President's Address to the Nation, January 10, 2007," The White House. 10 January 2007 <http://www.whitehouse.gov/news/releases/2007/01/print/20070110-7.html> 20 April 2007.

message came through loud and clear: Failure in Iraq would be a disaster for the United States.

The consequences of failure are clear: Radical Islamic extremists would grow in strength and gain new recruits. They would be in a better position to topple moderate governments, create chaos in the region, and use oil revenues to fund their ambitions. Iran would be emboldened in its pursuit of nuclear weapons. Our enemies would have a safe haven from which to plan and launch attacks on the American people. On September the 11th, 2001, we saw what a refuge for extremists on the other side of the world could bring to the streets of our own cities. For the safety of our people, America must succeed in Iraq.

The most urgent priority for success in Iraq is security, especially in Baghdad. Eighty percent of Iraq's sectarian violence occurs within 30 miles of the capital. This violence is splitting Baghdad into sectarian enclaves, and shaking the confidence of all Iraqis. Only Iraqis can end the sectarian violence and secure their people. And their government has put forward an aggressive plan to do it.

Our past efforts to secure Baghdad failed for two principal reasons: There were not enough Iraqi and American troops to secure neighborhoods that had been cleared of terrorists and insurgents. And there were too many restrictions on the troops we did have. Our military commanders reviewed the new Iraqi plan to ensure that it addressed these mistakes. They report that it does. They also report that this plan can work.

Now let me explain the main elements of this effort: The Iraqi government will appoint a military commander and two deputy commanders for their capital. The Iraqi government will deploy Iraqi Army and National Police brigades across Baghdad's nine districts. When these forces are fully deployed, there will be 18 Iraqi Army and National Police brigades committed to this effort, along with local police. These Iraqi forces will operate from local police stations—conducting patrols and setting up checkpoints, and going door-to-door to gain the trust of Baghdad residents.

This is a strong commitment. But for it to succeed, our commanders say the Iraqis will need our help. So America will change our strategy to help the Iraqis carry out their campaign to put down sectarian violence and bring security to the people of Baghdad. This will require increasing American force levels. So I've committed more than 20,000 additional American troops to Iraq. The vast majority of them—five brigades—will be deployed to Baghdad. These troops will work alongside Iraqi units and be embedded in their formations. Our troops will have a well-defined mission: to help Iraqis clear and secure neighborhoods, to help them protect the local population, and to help ensure that the Iraqi forces left behind are capable of providing the security that Baghdad needs.

Many listening tonight will ask why this effort will succeed when previous operations to secure Baghdad did not. Well, here are the differences: In earlier operations, Iraqi and American forces cleared many neighborhoods of terrorists and insurgents, but when our forces moved on to other targets, the killers returned. This time, we'll have the force levels we need to hold the areas that have been cleared. In earlier operations, political and sectarian interference prevented Iraqi and American forces from going into neighborhoods that are home to those fueling the sectarian violence. This time, Iraqi and American forces will have a green light to enter those neighborhoods—and Prime Minister Maliki has pledged that political or sectarian interference will not be tolerated.

I've made it clear to the Prime Minister and Iraq's other leaders that America's commitment is not open-ended. If the Iraqi government does not follow through on its promises, it will lose the support of the American people–and it will lose the support of the Iraqi people. Now is the time to act. The Prime Minister understands this. Here is what he told his people just last week: "The Baghdad security plan will not provide a safe haven for any outlaws, regardless of [their] sectarian or political affiliation."

This new strategy will not yield an immediate end to suicide bombings, assassinations, or IED attacks. Our enemies in Iraq will make every effort to ensure that our television screens are filled with images of death and suffering. Yet over time, we can expect to see Iraqi troops chasing down murderers, fewer brazen acts of terror, and growing trust and cooperation from Baghdad's residents. When this happens, daily life will improve, Iraqis will gain confidence in their leaders, and the government will have the breathing space it needs to make progress in other critical areas. Most of Iraq's Sunni and Shia want to live together in peace–and reducing the violence in Baghdad will help make reconciliation possible.

A successful strategy for Iraq goes beyond military operations. Ordinary Iraqi citizens must see that military operations are accompanied by visible improvements in their neighborhoods and communities. So America will hold the Iraqi government to the benchmarks it has announced.

To establish its authority, the Iraqi government plans to take responsibility for security in all of Iraq's provinces by November. To give every Iraqi citizen a stake in the country's economy, Iraq will pass legislation to share oil revenues among all Iraqis. To show that it is committed to delivering a better life, the Iraqi government will spend $10 billion of its own money on reconstruction and infrastructure projects that will create new jobs. To empower local leaders, Iraqis plan to hold provincial elections later this year. And to allow more Iraqis to re-enter their nation's political life, the government will reform de-Baathification laws, and establish a fair process of considering amendments to Iraq's constitution.

America will change our approach to help the Iraqi government as it works to meet these benchmarks. In keeping with the recommendations of the Iraq Study Group, we will increase the embedding of American advisers in Iraqi Army units, and partner a coalition brigade with every Iraqi Army division. We will help the Iraqis build a larger and better-equipped army, and we will accelerate the training of Iraqi forces, which remains the essential U.S. security mission in Iraq. We will give our commanders and civilians greater flexibility to spend funds for economic assistance. We will double the number of provincial reconstruction teams. These teams bring together military and civilian experts to help local Iraqi communities pursue reconciliation, strengthen the moderates, and speed the transition to Iraqi self-reliance. And Secretary Rice will soon appoint a reconstruction coordinator in Baghdad to ensure better results for economic assistance being spent in Iraq.

As we make these changes, we will continue to pursue al Qaeda and foreign fighters. Al Qaeda is still active in Iraq. Its home base is Anbar Province. Al Qaeda has helped make Anbar the most violent area of Iraq outside the capital. A captured al Qaeda document describes the terrorists' plan to infiltrate and seize control of the province. This would bring al Qaeda closer to its goals of taking down Iraq's democracy, building a radical Islamic empire, and launching new attacks on the United States at home and abroad.

Our military forces in Anbar are killing and capturing al Qaeda leaders, and they are protecting the local population. Recently, local tribal leaders have begun to show their willingness to take on al Qaeda. And as a result, our commanders believe we have an opportunity to deal a serious blow to the terrorists. So I have given orders to increase American forces in Anbar Province by 4,000 troops. These troops will work with Iraqi and tribal forces to keep up the pressure on the terrorists. America's men and women in uniform took away al Qaeda's safe haven in Afghanistan–and we will not allow them to re-establish it in Iraq.

Succeeding in Iraq also requires defending its territorial integrity and stabilizing the region in the face of extremist challenges. This begins with addressing Iran and Syria. These two regimes are allowing terrorists and insurgents to use their territory to move in and out of Iraq. Iran is providing material support for attacks on American troops. We will disrupt the attacks on our forces. We'll interrupt the flow of support from Iran and Syria. And we will seek out and destroy the networks providing advanced weaponry and training to our enemies in Iraq.

We're also taking other steps to bolster the security of Iraq and protect American interests in the Middle East. I recently ordered the deployment of an additional carrier strike group to the region. We will expand intelligence-sharing and deploy Patriot air defense systems to reassure our friends and allies. We will work with the governments of Turkey and Iraq to help them resolve problems along their border. And we will work with others to prevent Iran from gaining nuclear weapons and dominating the region.

We will use America's full diplomatic resources to rally support for Iraq from nations throughout the Middle East. Countries like Saudi Arabia, Egypt, Jordan, and the Gulf States need to understand that an American defeat in Iraq would create a new sanctuary for extremists and a strategic threat to their survival. These nations have a stake in a successful Iraq that is at peace with its neighbors, and they must step up their support for Iraq's unity government. We endorse the Iraqi government's call to finalize an International Compact that will bring new economic assistance in exchange for greater economic reform. And on Friday, Secretary Rice will leave for the region, to build support for Iraq and continue the urgent diplomacy required to help bring peace to the Middle East.

The challenge playing out across the broader Middle East is more than a military conflict. It is the decisive ideological struggle of our time. On one side are those who believe in freedom and moderation. On the other side are extremists who kill the innocent, and have declared their intention to destroy our way of life. In the long run, the most realistic way to protect the American people is to provide a hopeful alternative to the hateful ideology of the enemy, by advancing liberty across a troubled region. It is in the interests of the United States to stand with the brave men and women who are risking their lives to claim their freedom, and to help them as they work to raise up just and hopeful societies across the Middle East.

From Afghanistan to Lebanon to the Palestinian Territories, millions of ordinary people are sick of the violence, and want a future of peace and opportunity for their children. And they are looking at Iraq. They want to know: Will America withdraw and yield the future of that country to the extremists, or will we stand with the Iraqis who have made the choice for freedom?

The changes I have outlined tonight are aimed at ensuring the survival of a young democracy that is fighting for its life in a part of the world of enormous importance to American security. Let me be clear: The terrorists and insurgents in Iraq are without conscience, and they will make the year ahead bloody and violent. Even if our new strategy works exactly as planned, deadly acts of violence will continue–and we must expect more Iraqi and American casualties.

The question is whether our new strategy will bring us closer to success. I believe that it will.

Victory will not look like the ones our fathers and grandfathers achieved. There will be no surrender ceremony on the deck of a battleship. But victory in Iraq will bring something new in the Arab world–a functioning democracy that polices its territory, upholds the rule of law, respects fundamental human liberties, and answers to its people. A democratic Iraq will not be perfect. But it will be a country that fights terrorists instead of harboring them–and it will help bring a future of peace and security for our children and our grandchildren.

This new approach comes after consultations with Congress about the different courses we could take in Iraq. Many are concerned that the Iraqis are becoming too dependent on the United States, and therefore, our policy should focus on protecting Iraq's borders and hunting down al Qaeda. Their solution is to scale back America's efforts in Baghdad–or announce the phased withdrawal of our combat forces. We carefully considered these proposals. And we concluded that to step back now would force a collapse of the Iraqi goverment, tear the country apart, and result in mass killings on an unimaginable scale. Such a scenario would result in our troops being forced to stay in Iraq even longer, and confront an enemy that is even more lethal. If we increase our support at this crucial moment, and help the Iraqis break the current cycle of violence, we can hasten the day our troops begin coming home.

In the days ahead, my national security team will fully brief Congress on our new strategy. If members have improvements that can be made, we will make them. If circumstances change, we will adjust. Honorable people have different views, and they will voice their criticisms. It is fair to hold our views up to scrutiny. And all involved have a responsibility to explain how the path they propose would be more likely to succeed.

Acting on the good advice of Senator Joe Lieberman and other key members of Congress, we will form a new, bipartisan working group that will help us come together across party lines to win the war on terror. This group will meet regularly with me and my administration; it will help strengthen our relationship with Congress. We can begin by working together to increase the size of the active Army and Marine Corps, so that America has the Armed Forces we need for the 21st century. We also need to examine ways to mobilize talented American civilians to deploy overseas, where they can help build democratic institutions in communities and nations recovering from war and tyranny.

In these dangerous times, the United States is blessed to have extraordinary and selfless men and women willing to step forward and defend us. These young Americans understand that our cause in Iraq is noble and necessary–and that the advance of freedom is the calling of our time. They serve far from their families, who make the quiet sacrifices of lonely holidays and empty chairs at the dinner table. They have watched their comrades give their lives to ensure our liberty. We mourn the loss of every fallen American–and we owe it to them to build a future worthy of their sacrifice.

Fellow citizens: The year ahead will demand more patience, sacrifice, and resolve. It can be temping to think that America can put aside the burdens of freedom. Yet times of testing reveal the character of a nation. And throughout our history, Americans have always defied the pessimists and seen our faith in freedom redeemed. Now America is engaged in a new struggle that will set the course for a new century. We can, and we will, prevail.

We go forward with trust that the Author of Liberty will guide us through these trying hours. Thank you and good night.

PATRICK MURPHY SPEAKS ON HOUSE FLOOR TO OPPOSE PRESIDENT BUSH'S ESCALATION, FEBRUARY 13, 2007

by Representative Patrick Murphy[4]

On February 13, 2007, Representative Patrick Murphy (D-Pennsylvania), who was profiled in Chapter 7, spoke on the floor of the House of Representatives to oppose the troop increase in Iraq proposed by President Bush. Murphy was a Captain in the U.S. Army, served in both Bosnia and Iraq, and was the recipient of the bronze star. As you read this speech, ask yourself:

- Does Rep. Murphy make a convincing case against President Bush's plan?
- How does Rep. Murphy use his own experience in Iraq to make his case?
- How effectively does Rep. Murphy use language in the speech?
- How effectively does Rep. Murphy use evidence in the speech?
- How effectively does Rep. Murphy appeal to emotions in the speech?
- What pattern of organization does the speech appear to follow?

Thank you Mr. Speaker and thank you Mr. Chairman, I appreciate it.

I take the floor today not as a Democrat or Republican, but as an Iraq war veteran who was a Captain with the 82nd Airborne Division in Baghdad.

I speak with a heavy heart for my fellow paratrooper Specialist Chad Keith, Specialist James Lambert and 17 other brave men who I served with who never made it home.

I rise to give voice to hundreds of thousands of patriotic Pennsylvanians and veterans across the globe who are deeply troubled by the President's call to escalate the number of American troops in Iraq.

I served in Baghdad from June of 2003 to January of 2004. Walking in my own combat boots, I saw first hand this Administration's failed policy in Iraq.

I led convoys up and down "Ambush Alley" in a Humvee without doors–convoys that Americans still run today because too many Iraqis are still sitting on the sidelines.

I served in al-Rashid, Baghdad which, like Philadelphia, is home to 1.5 million people. While there are 7,000 Philadelphia police officers serving like my father in Philadelphia, protecting its citizens, there were only 3,500 of us in al-Rashid, Baghdad.

Mr. Speaker, the time for more troops was four years ago. But this President ignored military experts like General Shinseki & General Zinni, who in 2003, called for several hundred thousand troops to secure Iraq.

Now Mr. Speaker, our President again is ignoring military leaders. Patriots like General Colin Powell, like General Abizaid, and members of the bi-partisan Iraq Study Group who oppose this escalation.

[4]"Press Release: Patrick Murphy Speaks on House Floor to Oppose President Bush's Escalation," 13 February 2007. <http://www.house.gov/apps/list/press/pa08_murphy/021307IraqSpeech.html> 20 April 2007.

But most importantly, Mr. Speaker, Congresses in the past did not stand up to the President and his policies. But today I stand with my other military veterans some who were just elected–like Sergeant Major Tim Walz, Admiral Joe Sestak, and Commander Chris Carney. We stand together to tell this Administration that we are against this escalation and Congress will no longer give the President a blank check.

Mr. Speaker, close to my heart is a small park on the corner of 24th and Aspen Streets in Philadelphia. This is the Patrick Ward Memorial Park.

Patrick Ward was a door gunner in the U.S. Army during Vietnam. He was killed serving the country that he loved. He was the type of guy that neighborhoods devote street corners to and parents name their children after–including my parents, Marge and Jack Murphy.

Mr. Speaker, I ask you–how many more street-corner memorials are we going to have for *this* war?

This is what the President's proposal does–it sends more of our best and bravest to die refereeing a civil war.

Just a month ago Sgt. Jae Moon from my district in Levittown, Bucks County was killed in Iraq.

You know, a few blocks away from this great chamber, when you walk in the snow, is the Vietnam Memorial, where half of the soldiers listed on that wall died after America's leaders knew our strategy would not work.

It was immoral then and it would be immoral now to engage in the same delusion.

That's why Mr. Speaker, sending more troops into civil war is the wrong strategy. We need to win the War on Terror and reasonable people may disagree on what to do, but most will agree that it is immoral to send young Americans to fight and die in a conflict without a real strategy for success.

The President's current course is not resolute, it is reckless.

That is why I will vote to send a message to our President that staying the course is no longer an option.

Mr. Speaker, its time for a new direction in Iraq. From my time serving with the 82d Airborne Division in Iraq, it became clear that in order to succeed there, we must tell the Iraqis that we will not be there forever. Yet, three years now since I have been home, it's still Americans leading convoys up and down Ambush Alley and securing Iraqi street corners.

We must make Iraqis stand up for Iraq–and set a timeline to start bringing our heroes home.

That's why I am proud to be an original cosponsor–with Senator Barack Obama and fellow paratrooper, Congressman Mike Thompson–of the Iraq De-Escalation Act–a moderate and responsible plan to start bringing our troops home, mandating a surge in diplomacy, and refocusing our efforts on the War on Terror in Afghanistan.

Mr. Speaker, our country needs a real plan to get our troops out of Iraq, to protect our homeland and secure and refocus our efforts on capturing and killing Osama bin Laden and al Qaeda.

There are over 130,000 American servicemen and women serving bravely in Iraq. Unfortunately, thousands more are on the way.

Mr. Speaker, an open-ended strategy that ends in more faceless road-side bombs in Baghdad and more street-corner memorials in America, is *not* one that I will support.

I yield back the remainder of my time.

Glossary

A

abstract A summary of an article or a report.
ad hominem Attacking the person rather than the soundness of his or her argument.
adoption Consumers' decision to commit to a product, practice, or idea.
alphabetical pattern Main points are in alphabetical order or spell out a common word.
analogy An extended metaphor or simile. Suggesting that the rebuilding of Iraq is much like rebuilding Germany and Japan after WW II is an analogy.
antithesis The use of opposites, e.g., light–dark.
appreciative listening Listening that involves obtaining sensory stimulation or enjoyment from others.
arguing in a circle (begging the question) An argument that proves nothing because the claim to be proved is used as the grounds or warrant for the argument.
argumentativeness The trait of arguing for and against the positions taken on controversial claims.
attitude A learned predisposition to respond in a consistently favorable or unfavorable manner with respect to a given object.
audience The individuals who listen to a public speech.
audience accessible Content the audience is able to understand, regardless of its complexity.
audience appropriate Informative topic and speech that takes into account the occasion and audience members' belief systems.
audience diversity The cultural, demographic, and individual characteristics that vary among audience members.
audience involving Informative topic and speech that succeeds in gaining the audience's attention.
audio media Aural channels you can use to augment your speech, such as a recording of a famous speaker.
authority warrant Reasoning in which the claim is believed because of the authority of the source.

B

backing Support for a warrant.
bar chart A graphic used for comparing data side by side.
belief An assertion about the properties or characteristics of an object.
blog (short for Web log) A Web site that contains dated entries in reverse chronological order. They can range from serious commentary by experts to "ranting and raving" by people with no particular qualifications.
Boolean operators Terms, such as *and, or,* and *not,* used to narrow or broaden a computerized search of two or more related terms.
brainstorming A creative process used for generating a large number of ideas.
branding The process of creating a lasting impression about a name, company, or product.

C

canons of rhetoric The classical arts of invention, organization, style, memory, and delivery.
captive audience Listeners that have no choice about hearing a speech.
categorical imperative Immanuel Kant's ethical principle that we should act only in a way that we would will to be a universal law.
categorical pattern A pattern of organization based on natural divisions in the subject matter.
causal pattern A pattern of organization that moves from cause to effect or from effect to cause.
causal warrant A statement that a cause will produce or has produced an effect.
central beliefs Beliefs based directly or indirectly on authority.
change Substitute or modify attitudes, beliefs, and behaviors.
channel The physical medium through which communication occurs.
claim A conclusion that speakers want their audience to reach as a result of their speech.
communication apprehension Fear about communicating interpersonally and in groups, not just in public.
comparative advantage A pattern of organization based on the idea that things can be better even if they are not currently harmful.
comparison (analogy) warrant A statement that two cases that are similar in some known respects are also similar in some unknown respects.
connotation The secondary meaning of a word, often with a strong emotional, personal, and subjective component.
constraint A limitation on choices in a rhetorical situation.
constructive self-talk The use of positive coping statements instead of negative self-talk.
content (of messages) The essential meaning of what a speaker wants to convey.
context Information that surrounds an event and contributes to the meaning of that event.
coping skills Mental and physical techniques used to control arousal and anxiety in the course of speaking in public.
credibility The degree to which an audience trusts and believes in a speaker.
credibility-enhancing language Words that emphasize rather than undermine audience perceptions of a speaker's competence.
critical thinking The process of making sound inferences based on accurate evidence and valid reasoning.
cultural diversity Differences among people in terms of beliefs, customs, and values–in a sense, their worldview.
cultural relativism The notion that the criteria for ethical behavior in one culture should not necessarily be applied to other cultures.
culture A learned system of beliefs, customs, and values with which people identify.

D

decoding The process by which a code is translated back into ideas.

deep web (Proprietary Internet) Web sites accessible over the Internet only to authorized users and often at a cost.

deficiency needs Basic human needs, which must be satisfied before higher-order needs can be met. They include needs for food, water, air, physical safety, belongingness and love, and self-esteem and social esteem.

demographic diversity Variations among people in terms of such attributes as socioeconomic background and level of education.

demographics Basic and vital data regarding any population.

denotation The generally agreed upon meaning of a word, usually found in the dictionary.

distorted evidence Significant omissions or changes in the grounds of an argument that alter its original intent.

E

elaboration likelihood model A model of persuasion designed to explain why audience members will use an elaborated thinking process in some situations and not in others.

emblem A nonverbal symbol that can be substituted for a word.

empathic listening Listening for the purpose of understanding and relating to the origins of a speaker's thinking and feelings.

encoding The process by which ideas are translated into a code that can be understood by the receiver.

environment The physical surroundings as you speak and the physical distance separating you from your audience.

ethical relativism A philosophy based on the belief that there are no universal ethical principles.

ethics A system of principles of right and wrong that govern human conduct.

ethos The degree to which an audience perceives a speaker as credible.

eulogy A kind of commemorative speech about someone who has died that is usually given shortly after his or her death.

expert opinion A quotation from someone with special credentials in the subject matter.

extemporaneous delivery A mode of presentation that combines careful preparation with spontaneous speaking. The speaker generally uses brief notes rather than a full manuscript or an outline.

extended narrative A pattern of organization in which the entire body of the speech is the telling of a story.

F

fact Something that is verifiable as true.

fallacy An argument in which the reasons advanced for a claim fail to warrant acceptance of that claim.

false analogy The comparison of two different things that are not really comparable.

false dilemma A generalization that implies there are only two choices when there are more than two.

feedback Audience member responses, both verbal and nonverbal, to a speaker.

first-order data Evidence based on personal experience.

flip chart Large tablet used to preview the outline of a presentation or to record information generated by an audience.

flowchart A graphic designed to illustrate spatial relationships or the sequence of events in a process.

formal outline A detailed outline used in speech preparation, but not, in most cases, in the actual presentation.

G

ganas Spanish term that loosely translates as the desire to succeed.

general purpose The primary function of a speech. The three commonly agreed upon general purposes are to inform, to persuade, and to entertain.

generalization warrant A statement that either establishes a general rule or principle or applies an established rule or principle to a specific case.

good reasons Statements, based on moral principles, offered in support of propositions concerning what we should believe or how we should act.

goodwill The perception by the audience that a speaker cares about their needs and concerns.

grounds The evidence a speaker offers in support of a claim.

growth needs Higher-order human needs, which can be satisfied only after deficiency needs have been met. They include self-actualization (the process of fully realizing one's potential), knowledge and understanding, and aesthetic needs.

H

halo effect The assumption that just because you like or respect a person, whatever he or she says must be true.

hasty generalization An argument that occurs when there are too few instances to support a generalization or the instances are unrepresentative of the generalization.

hyperbole An exaggeration of a claim.

I

ignoring the issue When a claim made by one side in an argument is ignored by the other side.

illustrators Nonverbal symbols used to visualize what is being spoken.

immediate language Language that reduces the psychological distance that separates speakers and audience members and stresses that speech is a transaction.

impromptu delivery A spontaneous, unrehearsed mode of presenting a speech.

inclusive language Language that helps people believe that they not only have a stake in matters of societal importance but also have power in this regard.

index A listing of sources of information–usually in newspapers, journals, and magazines–alphabetically by topic.

individual diversity How individuals in an audience differ in terms of knowledge, beliefs, attitudes, values, motives, expectations, and needs.

inference The process of moving from grounds, via a warrant, to a claim.

informative speaking The process by which an audience gains new information or a new perspective on old information.

inoculation Techniques used to make people's belief systems resistant to counterpersuasion.

interdependence A relationship in which things have a reciprocal influence on each other.

invention The creative process by which the substance of a speech is generated.

isolated examples Nontypical or nonrepresentative examples that are used to prove a general claim.

K

key word A word in the abstract, title, subject heading, or text of an entry that can be used to search an electronic database.

L

language The rule-governed word system we use to verbally communicate.

language intensity The degree to which words and phrases deviate from neutral.

learning styles Differences in the way people think about and learn new information and skills.

line graph A graphic used to show points in time.

linguistic relativity hypothesis The idea that what people perceive is influenced by the language in which they think and speak.

listening The process of receiving, constructing meaning from, and responding to spoken and/or nonverbal messages.

loaded language Language that triggers strong emotional and negative responses.

logos The proof a speaker offers to an audience through the words of his or her message.

long-term goals Those ends that we can hope to achieve only over an extended period of time.

M

main points The key ideas that support the thesis statement of a speech.

manuscript delivery A mode of presentation that involves writing out a speech completely and reading it to the audience.

marginalizing language Language that diminishes people's importance and makes them appear to be less powerful, less significant, and less worthwhile than they are.

memorized delivery A mode of presentation in which a speech is written out and committed to memory before being presented to the audience without the use of notes.

message The meaning produced by communicators.

metaphor A figure of speech in which words and phrases that are primarily understood to mean one thing are used in place of another to suggest likeness or an analogy between them. Race car drivers, for example, may have to "wrestle with" a car that is difficult to control.

mindfulness The conscious awareness of the speech transaction including the people involved, their purpose for gathering, and the context in which they find themselves.

mistaking correlation for cause The assumption that because one thing is the sign of another, they are causally related.

misused numerical data Statistics that involve errors such as poor sampling, lack of significant differences, misuse of average, or misuse of percentages.

Monroe's motivated-sequence A five-step organizational scheme, developed by speech professor Alan Monroe, including (1) attention, (2) need, (3) satisfaction, (4) visualization, and (5) action.

N

narrative An extended story that is fully developed, with characters, scene, action, and plot.

narrative fidelity The degree to which a narrative rings true to real-life experience.

narrative probability The internal coherence or believability of a narrative.

negative self-talk A self-defeating pattern of intrapersonal communication, including self-criticizing, self-pressuring, and catastrophizing statements.

non sequitur An argument that does not follow from its premises.

nonverbal behavior A wordless system of communication.

O

online catalog A computerized database of library holdings.

opinion A judgment by someone that is subject to dispute.

organizational chart A graphic that illustrates hierarchical relationships.

overhead transparency A visual depiction that can be projected.

P

pathos The emotional states in an audience that a speaker can arouse and use to achieve persuasive goals.

perception The process by which we give meaning to our experiences.

peripheral beliefs The least central type of beliefs, the easiest to change.

persuasion The process by which a speaker influences what audience members think or do.

physical arousal The physical changes that occur when a person is aroused, such as increased pulse, greater alertness, and more energy.

pie chart A graphic often used to show proportions of a known quantity.

pinpoint concentration Listening that focuses on specific details rather than patterns in a message.

plagiarism Using the ideas of others and presenting them as your own.

podcast An audio broadcast that has been converted to a digital file such as MP3 for playback in a digital music player or computer.

post hoc, ergo propter hoc ("after the fact, therefore because of the fact") The assumption that because one event preceded another, the first event must be the cause of the second event.

presentational media Channels of communication that enhance the five basic senses: touch, sight, sound, taste, and smell.

preview A forecast of the main points of a speech.

primary sources Original sources of information.

primitive beliefs (also known as type A beliefs) Those beliefs learned by direct contact with the object of belief and reinforced by unanimous social consensus.

proactive delivery Taking the initiative, anticipating, and controlling variables that will affect speech delivery.

problem–solution pattern A pattern of organization that analyzes a problem in terms of (1) harm, (2) significance, and (3) cause, and proposes a solution that is (1) described, (2) feasible, and (3) advantageous.

pseudoreasoning An argument that appears sound at first glance but contains a fallacy of reasoning that renders it unsound.

Q

qualifier An indication of the level of probability of a claim.

R

rebuttal An exception to or a refutation of an argument.

receiver-centric A person's assumption that the meaning he or she gives to a word or a phrase is its exclusive meaning.

red herring (smoke screen) An irrelevant issue introduced into a controversy to divert from the real controversy.

reframing Revising our view of a situation or an event, usually in a positive direction.

refutational pattern A pattern of organization that involves (1) stating the argument to be refuted, (2) stating the objection to the argument, (3) proving the objection to the argument, and (4) presenting the impact of the refutation.

regulators Nonverbal behaviors that influence the speech transaction.

reinforcement Rewards given to strengthen attitudes, beliefs, values, and behaviors.

relational component (of messages) The combined impact of the verbal and nonverbal components of a message as it is conveyed.

research The process of finding and evaluating supporting materials.

rhetorical question A question that the audience isn't expected to answer out loud.

rhetorical situation A natural context of persons, events, objects, relations, and an exigence [goal] which strongly invites utterance.

RSS (Really Simple Syndication) A syndication format that aggregates updates from various news sites or blogs and transmits them to users.

S

secondary sources Information sources that rely on other (primary) sources rather than gathering information firsthand.

second-order data Evidence based on expert testimony.

selective attention Making a conscious choice to focus on some people and some messages, rather than others.

self-adapting behaviors Nonverbal behaviors used to cope with nervousness; for example, self-touching or grasping the sides of a lectern with hands.

self-talk Communicating silently with oneself (sometimes referred to as intrapersonal communication).

sexist language Language, such as *housewife* and *fireman,* that stereotypes gender roles.

short-term goals Those ends that we can reasonably expect to achieve in the near term.

sign warrant Reasoning in which the presence of an observed phenomenon is used to indicate the presence of an unobserved phenomenon.

signposts Transitional statements that bridge main points.

simile Invites the listener to make a direct comparison between two things or objects that are quite different, such as my roommate "lives like a pig in slop" or is "dumb as a rock."

situational ethics The philosophy that there are overriding ethical maxims, but that sometimes it is necessary to set them aside in particular situations to fulfill a higher law or principle.

slippery slope The assumption that just because one event occurs, it will automatically lead to a series of undesirable events even though there is no relationship between the action and the projected events.

socioeconomic status Social grouping and economic class to which people belong.

source credibility The audience's perception of the believability of the speaker.

spatial pattern A pattern of organization based on physical space or geography.

speaker's notes Brief notes with key words, usually written on cards, used by a speaker when presenting a speech.

specific purpose The goal or objective a speaker hopes to achieve in speaking to a particular audience.

speech anxiety The unpleasant thoughts and feelings aroused by the anticipation of a real or imagined speech in public.

speech of acceptance A speech expressing thanks for an award or honor.

speech of commemoration A speech that calls attention to the stature of the person or people being honored, or emphasizes the significance of an occasion.

speech of introduction A speech that briefly sets the stage for an upcoming speaker.

speech of recognition A speech presenting an award or honor to an individual.

speech to entertain A speech that makes its point through the use of humor.

spiral pattern A pattern of organization that employs repetition of points, with the points growing in intensity as the speech builds to its conclusion.

star pattern A pattern of organization in which all of the points are of equal importance and can be presented in any order to support the common theme.

stereotyping The assumption that what is considered to be true of a larger class is necessarily true of particular members of that class.

stock issues pattern A four-point pattern of organization that is based on (1) ill, (2) blame, (3) cure, and (4) cost.

straw person An argument made in refutation that misstates the argument being refuted. Rather than refuting the real argument, the other side constructs a person of straw, which is easy to knock down.

subject heading A standard word or phrase used by libraries to catalog books or other publications.

subpoint An idea that supports a main point.

supporting point An idea that supports a subpoint.

surface web (Open Internet) Web sites freely accessible to all users over the Internet.

symbol Something that stands for or suggests something else by reason of relationship or association.

system A collection of interdependent parts arranged so that a change in one produces corresponding changes in the remaining parts.

T

thesis statement A single declarative sentence that focuses the audience's attention on the central point of a speech.

third-order data Evidence based on facts and statistics.

time pattern A pattern of organization based on chronology or a sequence of events.

totalizing language Language that defines people exclusively on the basis of a single attribute, such as race, ethnicity, biological sex, or ability.

transaction An exchange of verbal and nonverbal messages between two or more people.

trustworthiness The perception by the audience that they can rely on a speaker's word.

U

universalism The philosophy that there are ethical standards that apply to all situations regardless of the individual, group, or culture.

unsupported assertion The absence of any argument at all.

URL Uniform Resource Locator–the address for Web sites, such as www.mhhe.com.

utilitarianism The philosophy based on the principle that the aim of any action should be to provide the greatest amount of happiness for the greatest number of people.

V

values Our most enduring beliefs about right and wrong.

verbal aggressiveness The trait of attacking the self-concept of those with whom a person disagrees about controversial claims.

verbal qualifiers Words and phrases that erode the impact of what a speaker says in a speech.

visual imagery The process of mentally seeing (imagining) oneself confidently and successfully performing an action or a series of actions.

visual aids Materials that an audience can see that help a speaker communicate a message, including posters, overhead transparencies, and computerized projections.

voluntary audience Listeners that choose to hear a speaker.

W

warrant The connection between grounds and claim.

wave pattern A pattern of organization in which the basic theme, often represented by a phrase, is repeated again and again, much like a wave cresting, receding, and then cresting again.

wide-band concentration Listening that focuses on patterns rather than details.

wiki The Hawaiian word for quick. A Web site that allows users to edit content easily and quickly, for example Wikipedia.

Z

zone of interaction Area of an audience in which speaker and audience members can make eye contact.

Index

Note: Italic page numbers indicate material in boxes, captions, and exhibits.